BIBLE BIBLIOGRAPHY
1967–1973
OLD TESTAMENT

BIBLE BIBLIOGRAPHY 1967–1973
OLD TESTAMENT

*The Book Lists of the
Society for Old Testament Study
1967–1973*

Edited by
Peter R. Ackroyd M.A., Ph.D., D.D.
*Samuel Davidson Professor of
Old Testament Studies
University of London, King's College*

BASIL BLACKWELL · OXFORD · 1974

ISBN 0 631 16071 1

Printed in Great Britain by
The Camelot Press Ltd, Southampton

Contents

Additional Notes on School Textbooks, etc.

Abbreviations

P.R.A.	= P. R. Ackroyd	R.L.	= R. Loewe
C.A.	= C. Alder	A.A.M.	= A. A. Macintosh
L.A.S.	= L. Alonso Schökel	W.D.McH.	= W. D. McHardy
G.W.A.	= G. W. Anderson	W.McK.	= W. McKane
D.R.Ap-T.	= D. R. Ap-Thomas	J.M.	= J. Mauchline
J.B.	= J. Barr	E.B.M.	= E. B. Mellor
J.R.B.	= J. R. Bartlett	A.R.M.	= A. R. Millard
J.M.T.B.	= J. M. T. Barton	R.M.	= R. Murray
M.B.	= M. Bič	E.W.N.	= E. W. Nicholson
M.Bl.	= M. Black	A.C.J.P.	= A. C. J. Phillips
I.B.	= I. Blythin	L.A.P.	= L. A. Poore
P.A.H.de B.	= P. A. H. de Boer	N.W.P.	= N. W. Porteous
S.P.B.	= S. P. Brock	J.R.P.	= J. R. Porter
L.H.B.	= L. H. Brockington	B.F.P.	= B. F. Price
F.F.B.	= F. F. Bruce	M.E.J.R.	= M. E. J. Richardson
E.G.C.	= E. G. Clarke	H.R.	= H. Ringgren
R.E.C.	= R. E. Clements	B.J.R.	= B. J. Roberts
R.J.C.	= R. J. Coggins	J.R.	= J. Robinson
R.D.	= R. Davidson	J.W.R.	= J. W. Rogerson
G.H.D	= G. H. Davies	E.I.J.R.	= E. I. J. Rosenthal
E.J.C.D.	= E. J. C. Davis	E.R.R.	= E. R. Rowlands
G.R.D.	= G. R. Driver	H.H.R.	= H. H. Rowley
J.H.E.	= J. H. Eaton	E.T.R.	= E. T. Ryder
J.A.E.	= J. A. Emerton	J.F.A.S.	= J. F. A. Sawyer
G.F.	= G. Farr	J.N.S.	= J. N. Schofield
R.S.F.	= R. S. Foster	U.E.S.	= U. E. Simon
W.J.F.	= W. J. Fuerst	W.W.S.	= W. W. Simpson
A.E.G.	= A. E. Goodman	J.S.	= J. Snaith
J.G.	= J. Gray	N.H.S.	= N. H. Snaith
O.R.G.	= O. R. Gurney	S.S.	= S. Stein
E.H.	= E. Hammershaimb	J.V.M.S.	= J. V. M. Sturdy
H.St.J.H.	= H. St. John Hart	D.W.T.	= D. W. Thomas
A.S.H.	= A. S. Herbert	M.E.T.	= M. E. Thrall
C.J.A.H.	= C. J. A. Hickling	E.J.T.	= E. J. Tinsley
S.H.H.	= S. H. Hooke	E.U.	= E. Ullendorff
M.D.H.	= M. D. Hooker	G.V.	= G. Vermes
A.R.J.	= A. R. Johnson	M.W.	= M. Wallenstein
D.R.J.	= D. R. Jones	J.W.	= J. Weingreen
M.A.K.	= M. A. Knibb	M.P.W.	= M. P. Weitzman
G.A.F.K.	= G. A. F. Knight	D.J.W.	= D. J. Wiseman
H.K.	= H. Kosmala	R.N.W.	= R. N. Whybray
W.G.L.	= W. G. Lambert	G.G.Y.	= G. G. Yates
A.R.C.L.	= A. R. C. Leaney		

Editor's Preface

This volume contains the seven *Book Lists* (1967–73) of the British Society for Old Testament Study which I edited on its behalf. Previous volumes—*Eleven Years of Bible Bibliography*, edited by the late Professor H. H. Rowley (The Falcon's Wing Press, 1957) and *A Decade of Bible Bibliography*, edited by Professor G. W. Anderson (Blackwell, 1967)—have brought together the *Book Lists* for which previous editors were responsible; and it seemed good to the Society and to the publishers that the policy of reissuing the *Lists* in this convenient form should be continued.

The editor of such a bibliographical aid is dependent on many people for assistance. He is indebted in the first instance to publishers who send copies of books for review, either spontaneously because they recognize the usefulness of these *Book Lists* or in response to requests from the editor. The list of reviewers (p. viii) provides an indication of the extent to which the editor depends on a large number of willing collaborators both here and abroad, and to this must be added the fact that reviewers and scholars abroad have given much help in drawing attention to books which might otherwise be missed. The editor has also been assisted by his colleagues and library staff in London, by those who have provided the essential secretarial support—and often considerable assistance in checking points of detail—and to the staff of B. H. Blackwell's bookshop in Oxford for bibliographical information.

In the preparation of this volume from the separate *Book Lists*, I must express my thanks to the publishers for their advice and help and to Miss Gillian Griffin in the preparation of the comprehensive index of authors and in other matters of detail.

The *Book List* of the Society for Old Testament Study continues to appear, now under the editorship of the Rev'd Dr.

R. N. Whybray of the University of Hull. Copies of the *Lists* from 1974 onwards may be obtained from the Society by non-members.

PETER R. ACKROYD

UNIVERSITY OF LONDON
KING'S COLLEGE

NOTE. It may be convenient for users of this volume outside Great Britain to be reminded that in 1971 decimal currency was introduced here. Prices therefore appear in 1967–70 in the old currency (£. s. d.), and in 1971–73 in the new (£. p.).

Book List 1967

GENERAL

ALBRIGHT, W. F.: *New Horizons in Biblical Research.* 1966. Pp. ix + 51 (Oxford University Press, London. Price: 10s. 6d.).

This work, which reproduces the three Whidden Lectures delivered at McMaster University in 1961, gives a survey of some of the ways in which our understanding of the Bible has been enriched by recent studies of the ancient Near East. The first lecture considers the bearing of archaeological discoveries on the first few chapters of Genesis, on the patriarchal stories, on the early poetry of Israel, and on the work of Moses. The second discusses 'The Ancient Israelite Mind in its Environmental Context', and maintains that 'the structure of a language does *not* determine the logic of the people speaking that language' (p. 22); the Old Testament is then considered according to the categories of 'proto-logical' and 'empirico-logical', as distinct from 'formal logical', thinking. Thirdly, there is an examination of the light thrown on the New Testament by the documents found at Qumran and Chenoboskion. As was to be expected, the book shows an extraordinarily wide range of knowledge and contains a forceful, and often controversial, attempt to synthesize the results of study in various disciplines. Although not every reader will be convinced that all the opinions confidently expressed by Professor Albright are justified by the evidence, it will be generally agreed that he has written an interesting and stimulating book.   J.A.E.

ALT, A.: *Essays on Old Testament History and Religion* (translated by R. A. Wilson). 1966. Pp. x + 274. (Basil Blackwell, Oxford. Price: 42s.).

The late Professor Alt exercised a profound influence on modern O.T. studies, and the three volumes of his *Kleine Schriften* (see the *Book List*, 1954, pp. 22 f., 1960, pp. 11 f., *Eleven Years*, pp. 559 f.) are among those writings on the subject to which reference is most frequently made. English-speaking students of the Bible will therefore warmly welcome this translation of five of his most important essays: on the God of the Fathers, the origins of Israelite law, the settlement of the Israelites in Palestine, the formation of the Israelite state, and the monarchy in Israel and Judah. There are full indexes.

J.A.E.

ALTMANN, A. (ed. by): *Biblical Motifs: Origins and Transformations.* (Brandeis University Studies and Texts, Vol. III). 1966. Pp. 252. (Harvard University Press, Cambridge, Mass; O.U.P. London. Price: $7.50; 60s.).

This volume contains nine essays read as papers at the Lown Institute Research Colloquia at Brandeis University. Cyrus Gordon writes on the source of the myth of Leviathan, while F. M. Cross, who writes on the Divine Warrior, criticizes the 'Myth and Ritual' school and the 'Heilsgeschichte' school, but declares them to be complementary. S. Talmon deals with the desert motif in the Old Testament, challenging the view of the idealization of the desert which

3

has long been common. M. C. Astour has an important article on Gen. 14, arguing on the basis of the Spartoli tablets that the four kings were not contemporaries but four attackers of Babylon, transferred to Palestine and synchronised by a Deuteronomist writer. D. Neiman maintains that the cursing of Canaan in Gen. 9 dates from *c.* 1180 B.C., when he dates the battle of Taanach, and thinks it reflects the *de facto* alliance between the Greeks attacking Troy and the Israelites attacking the Canaanites in Palestine. J. Goldin writes on the end of Ecclesiastes, maintaining that the opening saying of Pirqe Aboth is a corrupt comment on it, dating from the end of the third century B.C. R. J. Loewe finds in the Targum to the Song of Songs apologetic motifs aimed at Christian exegesis and Jewish esotericism. N. N. Glatzer writes on Jewish interpretations of the book of Job. Finally E. R. Goodenough writes on Greek garments on Jewish heroes in the Dura Synagogue, arguing that the robe was taken over as a symbol of holiness, but with the reinterpretation of its pagan symbolism. It will be seen that there are valuable and challenging articles, though not all the challenges will be readily approved.

                                                                      H.H.R.

DE BOER, P. A. H. (ed. by): *Volume du congrès international pour l'étude de l'ancien Testament, Genève 1965.* (Supplements to *Vetus Testamentum* XV). 1966. Pp. VIII + 326. (E. J. Brill, Leiden. Price: 72 guilders).

This volume follows in the line of those which have provided the texts of papers read at earlier congresses of the International Organisation for the Study of the Old Testament. It does not in fact contain all the papers read at the Geneva meeting, nor the public lectures delivered by Y. Yadin and W. Vischer; but it contains most of the main papers. There are too many to list in full, but the following brief resumé may help the reader. O. Eissfeldt reviews 60 years of Old Testament study; Deuteronomy studies are represented by three essays (C. Brekelmans, H. Cazelles, J. Dus); Job by two (M. Bič, S. Terrien). Narrative themes include the wilderness tradition (C. Barth), the substitute king (M. A. Beek), themes and motifs in J and the Succession history (J. Blenkinsopp). Prophecy is represented by Amos (A. S. Kapelrud), Isaiah (B. D. Napier), and the new Mari material (A. Malamat); so too are Canaanite religion (J. Gray), the judges (K.-D. Schunck), and the royalty of Yahweh (J. de Fraine). Specific studies of sections are on Ps. 74: 15 (J. A. Emerton), Goliath's armour (K. Galling), and Josh. 3–6 (J. A. Soggin). Qumran studies appear in a discussion of Melchisedek (R. Meyer) and Daniel as a pesher (A. Szörényi); Septuagint studies in a consideration of nepheš-psyche (N. P. Bratsiotis); and lastly biblical names (F. Zimmermann). The range is immense and the volume serves as a reminder to those who were present and as a stimulus to those who were not.   P.R.A.

Die O. T. Werkgemeenskap in Suid-Afrika: Studies on the Books of Hosea and Amos. Papers read at the 7th and 8th Meetings 1964–1965. 1966. Pp. 169. (Pro Rege-Pers Beperk, Potchefstroom. Price: R 1.50).

This, sixth, in the series of Collected Papers issued in English translation contains eight papers on the book of Hosea and seven on the book of Amos. It is therefore impossible to do more than list titles and authors. Professor van Zyl writes the short preface and then we have: The matrimonial life of H. (I. H. Eybers), The covenant-idea in the b. of H. (F. C. Fensham), Some semantic complexities in the b. of H. (J. J. Glück), The similes in the b. of H. (C. J. Labuschagne), Married life in Israel according to the b. of H. (L. M. Muntingh), Hosea and Canticles (A. van Selms), Echoes from the teaching of Hosea in Isaiah 40–55 (B. J. van der Merwe), The Southern Kingdom in Hosea (A. van Selms). On Amos we have: Three notes on the b. of A. (J. J. Glück), Amos' conception of God and the popular theology of his time (C. J. Labuschagne), Political and international relations of Israel's neighbouring peoples according to the oracles of A. (L. M. Muntingh), A few remarks on the religious terminology in Amos and Hosea (B. J. van der Merwe), Amos 3: 11 — a communication (H. S. Pelser), Isaac in Amos (A. van Selms), Amos' geographic horizon (A. van Selms). These annotated studies will repay attention and we congratulate the Society on keeping up their academic standards so successfully.   D.R.Ap-T.

EISSFELDT, O.: *Kleine Schriften*, herausgegeben von R. Sellheim und F. Maas. Dritter Band. 1966. Pp. VIII + 530 + 19 text ills.+ XII plates containing 34 ills. (J. C. B. Mohr, Tübingen. Price: paper, DM. 65; cloth, DM. 70).

The previous volumes in this series were noticed in *Book Lists* 1962, pp. 5 f., and 1964, pp. 7 f. It was originally intended that the present volume should be the last; but the available material was so abundant that a fourth volume is now planned to cover the years 1961–65. The collection now under review consists of 62 articles from the years 1945–60, beginning with Eissfeldt's contribution to the T. H. Robinson *Festschrift* and ending with his essay, 'Lade und Gesetzestafeln' in the Eichrodt *Festschrift*. Alike in his own independent studies and in his detailed discussions of the work of others, Eissfeldt displays his characteristic breadth of interest, precision and range of knowledge, and sureness of judgement. Taken together, the volumes provide not only a record of his own work but an invaluable chronicle of the development of Old Testament studies since 1914.   G.W.A.

ELLIGER, K.: *Kleine Schriften zum Alten Testament*. Theologische Bücherei 32. Neudrucke und Berichte aus dem 20. Jahrhundert. 1966. Pp. 276. (Chr. Kaiser Verlag, München. Price: DM. 19.50).

Eight studies published between 1934 and 1955 provide a representative collection of the writings of K. Elliger, and a bibliography sets them in the context of the whole of his work. Appropriately three are concerned with prophecy: 'Die Heimat des Propheten Micha' (1934); 'Prophet und Politik' (1935); 'Der Begriff "Geschichte" bei Deuterojesaja' (1953). Other aspects of Old Testament study are represented by a hermeneutical discussion on 'Der Jakobskampf am Jabbok' (1951); theology by 'Ich bin der Herr — euer Gott' (1954). In addition there are: 'Die dreissig Helden Davids' (1935); 'Sinn und Ursprung der priesterlichen Geschichtserzählung' (1952), and 'Das Gesetz Leviticus 18' (1955). Indexes of biblical references and place names are welcome in such a useful collection.   P.R.A.

FRIEDRICH, G. (ed. by): *Theologisches Wörterbuch zum Neuen Testament* (begun by G. Kittel). Band VIII, Lief. 3 and 4. 1966. Pp. 64; 64. (Kohlhammer, Stuttgart. Price: DM. 5.80 each Lief.).

Lieferung 3 continues the article by Rengstorf on *teras*. Balz writes on *tessares* and *tesserakonta* and their cognates and discusses the special significance which the letters 4 and 40 sometimes have. In the treatment of *tereo* by Riesenfeld there is a brief reference to the corresponding Hebrew verbs. Similarly in the article on *tithemi* by Maurer. Joh. Schneider in the article on *timē* has a section on the word-group 'honour' in Hellenistic Judaism.

Lieferung 4 begins with a thorough treatment of *maqom* both in the Old Testament and, more briefly, in later Jewish usage, in the article by Köster on *topos*. Goppelt deals with *trapeza*. Delling discusses *treis*, another number which has a special significance. In his article on *trecho* Bauernfeind discusses the word *ruṣ* in the Old Testament and Qumran. Attention should be drawn to the article on *Typos* by Goppelt which begins in this Lieferung. The subject dealt with is of importance in Old Testament Theology and it should be remembered that Goppelt has also written a book entitled *Typos: die typologische Deutung des Alten Testaments im Neuen Testament* which is frequently referred to in this connection.   N.W.P.

Hebrew Union College Annual XXXVI (ed. by Elias L. Epstein). 1965. Pp. 279 + 15 (in Hebrew). (Hebrew Union College, Cincinnati. Price: $6.00).

J. Morgenstern argues that the various literary units that make up Isa. xlix–lv belong to about 520 B.C. and a century or so later; they are thus closely linked with Trito-Isaiah. M. Tsevat, continuing his studies in the books of Samuel, suggests that the meaning of Yahweh Ṣeba'oth is 'Yahweh (Is) Armies'. The principles of institutional behaviour are applied by M. A. Cohen to the role of the Shilonite priesthood under the united monarchy. A. Cronbach considers a large number of O.T. passages which have been frequently used to convey meanings far different from anything that their authors had in mind, and discusses some of the reasons, for example, latitude in translation, which have given rise to such meanings. S. Cohen deals with the political background of the book of Amos in the light of the presence of many nations round about Israel, some of them active, others potential, enemies. R. A. Rosenberg believes that in Jerusalem Ṣedeq came to be identified with Yahweh's right hand or arm, an idea which may have been promulgated at the time of Josiah. M. Haran discusses the Tabernacle in the Priestly Writing — its form, furniture, the priestly vestments, and the taboo areas. H. M. Orlinsky examines in detail examples of Kethib and Qere in the book of Job in relation to the Septuagint. Abrabanel on prophecy is treated by A. J. Reines; Hazkarath Neshamoth by S. B. Freehof; some additional Genizah fragments of *She'eloth Attiqoth* by A. Scheiber; and more Eibenschütziana by B. Brilling. I. S. Emmanuel presents the Hebrew text, with three plates, of some seventeenth and eighteenth century documents of Sephardi Rabbanim in Amsterdam.   D.W.T.

HYATT, J. P. (ed. by): *The Bible in Modern Scholarship*. Papers read at the 100th Meeting of the Society of Biblical Literature. December 28–30, 1964. 1965. Pp. 400. (Abingdon Press, Nashville, Tennessee. Price: $7.50).

The Editor and the Society must be congratulated on this stimulating volume, even though it is weighted on the N.T. side. Almost all the essays are of a high standard and some are very good. 26 contributors are grouped in ten chapters. In five of these a major paper is presented followed by one or two 'Responses'. Of these major five, the two O.T. essays are entitled 'Method in the Study of Early Hebrew History' (R. de Vaux); 'The Role of the Cult in old Israel' (A. S. Kapelrud), the other three being mainly N.T. Four further chapters present two main essays each. The O.T. chapter, 'Prophecy and Apocalyptic', comprising 'The "office" of the Prophet in Ancient Israel' (J. Muilenburg); 'Apocalyptic and History' (S. B. Frost). 'Archaeology and the Future of Biblical Studies' is a separate chapter comprising studies on 'The Biblical Languages' (D. N. Freedman), and 'Culture and History' (J. B. Pritchard). The tenth chapter comprises 3 essays on N.T. textual criticism.
The volume affords interesting insights into contemporary Biblical Studies in the U.S.A.

G.H.D.

KOSMALA, H. (ed. by): *Annual of the Swedish Theological Institute*. Volume IV. 1965. Pp. 192. (E. J. Brill, Leiden. Price: Fl. 32).

Pride of place in this collection of ten articles goes to the editor's story of letters and talks with Martin Buber, which throws an interesting sidelight on this Sage, who surely was amongst the most-loved of Biblical scholars. Other papers consist of discussions on Genesis (M. Haran, The Religion of the Patriarchs), Isaiah (J. Lindblom, The oracle against Tyre, Is. XXIII), Psalms (A. Kapelrud, Scandinavian research in the Psalms after Mowinckel), Qumran (H. Kosmala, The Three Nets of Belial: terminology of Qumran and M.T.), Matthew (H. Kosmala, The conclusion of Matthew), Mark (H. Waetjen, The ending of Mark and the Gospel's shift in eschatology), Josephus (F. F. Bruce, Josephus and Daniel; A. Schalit, An Aramac Source in the Antiquities) and, finally, Targum Isaiah (J. van Zijl, Errata in Sperber's edition of Targum Isaiah). The last page gives a list of errata to Vol. III.

B.J.R.

KRAUS, H. J. (ed. by): *Zur Wissenschaft vom Alten Testament*. (*Verkündigung und Forschung*, Beihefte zu *Evangelische Theologie*, xi.l). 1966. Pp. 100. (Chr. Kaiser Verlag, München. Price: DM. 6).

This issue admirably fulfils its purpose as a guide to some recent German and Scandinavian studies in the field of the Old Testament. It offers a neat exposition by M. Metzger of the collected articles by M. Noth (*Book List* 1961, p. 10), G. von Rad (*Book List* 1960, p. 6), and W. Zimmerli (*Book List* 1964, p. 16), all presented from the standpoint of related themes; a brief survey by H. J. Kraus of recent monographs and other works too numerous to record here but including the second edition of J. Hempel's *Das Ethos des Alten Testaments* (*Book List* 1965, p. 46); a challenging review of the same scholar's *Geschichten und Geschichte im Alten Testament bis zur persischen Zeit* (*Book List* 1965, p. 34) by K. Schwarwäller; and an excellent survey by A. S. Kapelrud of Scandinavian work on the Psalter with pride of place inevitably given to that of S. Mowinckel.

A.R.J.

Leeds University Oriental Society, The Annual of: ed. by John Macdonald. Vol. V, 1963–1965, with Index to Vols. I–V. 1966. Pp. 140, Pl. II. (E. J. Brill, Leiden. Price: Fl. 36).

Members will appreciate the tribute paid by F. F. Bruce to the late Professor Alfred Guillaume, President of the Leeds Oriental Society from its inception. The rest of this volume covers a wide range of subjects in its seven papers. F. F. Bruce traces the career of Herod Antipas, while J. C. L. Gibson shows an interest in the same period with an important paper on the growth and dispersion of the Aramaic-speaking Church *From Qumran to Edessa*. J. S. Harris' article on *The Stones of the High Priest's Breastplate* has the advantage of being written by a gemmologist, and has an interesting Appended Note by the Editor on the Samaritan equivalents. J. Macdonald also sets down his *New Thoughts on a Biliteral Origin for the Semitic Verb*, and in complete contrast D. Patterson considers *Epistolary Elements in the Hebrew Novels of the Period of the Enlightenment*. N. H. Snaith gives his new thoughts on *The Advent of Monotheism in Israel*, identifying it with the acceptance of Yahweh as High and Low God together. G. E. Weil closes the contributions with a typical paper entitled, *Fragment d'une Massorah Alphabétique du Targ. Bab. du Pentateuque* with photographs of the Westminster College Ms. A volume well up to standard but forbiddingly expensive.

D.R.Ap-T.

McKENZIE, J. L.: *Dictionary of the Bible*. 1965. Pp. xviii + 954 + 15 maps. (Geoffrey Chapman, London — Dublin. Price: 100s.).

This one-volume Bible dictionary, over 800,000 words in length, is a remarkable achievement of modern Biblical scholarship by an American Jesuit who has now joined the staff of the Divinity School at the University of Chicago. It is a rather larger dictionary than Harper's (*anglice* Black's) which it resembles in format and appearance, and less detailed and technical than Hastings', and in larger print than these other one-volume dictionaries. The O.T. receives full treatment, a descriptive analysis of each book being included and due attention paid to biblical themes and concepts. The book is attractively produced with over 200 skilfully chosen illustrations. There are no separate bibliographies, but an introductory list of general works. This is a valuable and reliable work of reference which bears throughout the impress of a single mind.   L.A.P.

MILLARD, A. R. (ed. by): *Tyndale Bulletin*, 17. 1966. Pp. 120. (Tyndale Press, London. Price: 25s.).

Five of the seven articles in this issue of the *Tyndale Bulletin* deal with O.T. Subjects. In the first article, D. A. Hubbard traces the links between the Wisdom Literature and Israel's covenant faith.

K. A. Kitchen offers some criticism of the two fascicles which Eissfeldt has contributed to the new CAH I/II, especially the material dealing with the Patriarchs, the Exodus, and the period of the settlement. A number of scholars will agree with the arguments presented here. The other O.T. articles are rather short. In his treatment of Gen. ii. 5, 6, D. Kinder offers some interesting suggestions, but his approach stems from a desire to undermine the belief in the existence of two accounts of the creation. The phrase 'For he is good' is considered by A. R. Millard, and he suggests that the Hebrew term for 'good' can be added to the covenant vocabulary. In dealing with the 'thirtieth year' of Ezek. i. 1, S. G. Taylor sees stylistic affinity between this passage and Gen. viii. 13, and so produces another argument in favour of the traditional view that this is a reference to the age of the prophet. The remaining two articles deal with N.T. subjects, and are worthy of consideration. S. G. Smalley writes on 'New light on the Fourth Gospel', and R. A. Ward on 'The semantics of sacramental language'.

E.R.R.

NAAMANI, I. T., RUDAVSKY, D., EHLE, C. F. (ed. by): *Dōrōn: Hebraic Studies.* 1965. Pp. xiv + 236. (The Round Home Printers, Great Barrington, Mass. Price: $4.50).

This volume in honour of Professor I. Katsh, Director of the Institute of Hebrew Studies at New York University, contains a dedicatory preface, an introduction, and ten articles. The first four are concerned with the fields of education and methodology, the next five with what are broadly linguistic problems, and the last, a reprint of an article by Professor Katsh, with Hebraic foundations of American democracy. While this last, and the essays on Hebrew studies in American colleges and universities (D. Rudavsky), and on the teaching of Hebrew in Egyptian schools of the Alliance Israélite Universelle (J. Landau) and in secondary schools in Israel (R. Nir), have their interest for students of the O.T., those which will hold chief interest for them are the discussion of the application of the methods and perspectives of Statistical Linguistics to the study of the Hebrew vocabulary (C. T. Fritsch and R. D. Winter); the study of the phrase *'eben gelâl* (Ezra v. 8, vi. 4) and the suggestion that it means simply 'stone' without further specification (R. A. Bowman); the consideration of the location of Kedesh-naphtali in Lower Galilee and the reconstruction of the battle of Deborah (M. Kochavi); the survey of recent literature on the book of Ezekiel (W. A. Irwin); the treatment of consecutive constructions in the sectarian scrolls (S. J. Devries) — they reveal a lesser degree of decay in this respect than does ISA; and the survey of literature dealing with Christian exegesis of the O.T. (J. L. Mihelic). The essays, which are suitably documented, are generally of a high quality, and together they make up a volume of varied interest. A photograph of Professor Katsh is supplied.

D.W.T.

NOTH, M.: *The Laws in the Pentateuch and Other Essays*, trans. by D. R. Ap-Thomas. 1966. Pp. xiv + 289. (Oliver and Boyd, Edinburgh and London. Price: 55s.).

This collection of essays — commended in a preface by N. W. Porteous — needs no introducing to Old Testament scholars, who already know the original texts. We may simply welcome their appearance and note that the collection includes the long 'Laws in the Pentateuch' (pp. 1–107), and a whole group of short studies, mainly concerned with historical problems, including the important 'God, King, and Nation in the Old Testament' and 'History and Word of God in the Old Testament'. The volume includes a general index and one of Hebrew and Aramaic terms. We are much indebted to the translator.

P.R.A.

RIESENFELD, H. (ed. by): *Svensk exegetisk årsbok*, XXX (1965). 1966. Pp. 134. (C. W. K. Gleerup, Lund. Price: Sw.Kr. 15).

Of the articles in this issue, only one bears directly on the Old Testament, viz., a discussion (in Swedish) by J. B. Pritchard of the place of archaeology in the study of the Old Testament. Attention is focussed on Palestinian archaeology. After a brief recognition of factors which detract from the authority of archaeological evidence, the author proceeds to consider the contribution of archaeology to an evaluation of the Old Testament traditions about Israel's history and religion, and, in particular, those relating to the 'conquest' under Joshua. The negative results from Jericho, Ai, Eglon, Debir, Lachish, Beth-Shemesh, and Gibeon are noted, and it is emphasized that the evidence at Hazor of occupation before and after the conquest is not accompanied by indications of a break in cultural development. Other articles deal with New Testament themes and there are also reviews of recent literature.

G.W.A.

Studia theologica cura ordinum theologorum Scandinavicorum edita. Vol. 19, Fasc. 1–2 (1965). 1965. Pp. 268 + portrait. (Aarhus University, Aarhus. Price: D.Kr. 45).

This volume is dedicated to the memory of Professor Johannes Munck, formerly editor of the annual, and contains a brief outline of his life and an admirably full bibliography of his writings. Appropriately, the majority of the contributions to the volume are related to New Testament and patristic subjects. The only one which has a direct bearing on the Old Testament is a discussion, by the late Professor Sigmund Mowinckel, of the word *'uššarna'* (Ezra v. 3, 9), arguing, with particular reference to I Esdras vi. 4 and the occurrence of the word in the Elephantine Papyri, that the meaning is 'roof and other equipment'. Some of the essays on New Testament subjects incorporate Old Testament and Rabbinic material; e.g., 'L'apôtre Saint-Jean grand-prêtre' (J. Vikjaer Andersen), 'The Message to the Gentiles' (R. Bring), 'The Demand for a Sign from Heaven' (O. Linton), 'Zum Problem der vaticinia ex eventu' (S. Pedersen), 'Body and Soul in the New Testament' (B. Reicke).

G.W.A.

TALMON, S. (ed. by): *Textus: Annual of the Hebrew University Bible Project*, Vol. V. 1966. Pp. 156. (Magnes Press, Jerusalem and Oxford University Press, London. Price: 43s.).

This volume maintains the standard of the previous volumes and contains articles of great importance. There are twelve articles, of which eleven are in English and one in French, and there are Hebrew abstracts of all the articles at the end. The most important article is by Y. Yadin, who publishes the text, with facsimiles, of a Psalms fragment which he purchased from an undisclosed American citizen, and which he offers conclusive reasons for believing to have belonged to the Psalms Scroll from Cave 11, published by J. A. Sanders. This fragment contains parts of Pss. 118, 104, 147, 105 — in that order. M. H. Goshen-Gottstein has an article on the problem of the Canon and Text posed by the Psalms Scroll, and argues that it does not provide evidence of a variant Canon, but was a liturgical selection of passages. The same author has another contribution on some photographs published by J. Segall in 1910 and reissued in Plates here, which provide some columns from the lost portion of the Aleppo Codex. S. Iwry writes on the reading *whnmṣ'* in IQIs[a] (Is. 37: 31), and argues that here and in some other O.T. passages the word means 'survivor', 'captive', 'refugee'. C. Rabin examines the word *nōṣᵉrîm* in some O.T. passages and argues that it means 'crowd' or 'community', and finds here the explanation of the use of the word to denote Christians. Other articles are by H. S. Gehman, dealing with the meaning of some Septuagint terms, which literally render Hebrew idioms or which give a Hebrew meaning to a Greek word; J. Shunary, who deals with the avoidance of anthropomorphisms in the Targum of Psalms; S. Talmon, who writes on Pisqah Be'emṣa' Pasuq and llQPs[a]; S. Esh, who examines variant readings in Rashbam; Y. Ratzabi, who lists variations in a Babylonian-Yemenite MS of the Megilloth; Z. Zinger, who writes on Bible quotations in the Pesikta de Rav Kahana; and B. Keller, who writes in French on a fragment of a treatise on Massoretic exegesis, now in the Cambridge University Library, accompanied by three Plates.   H.H.R.

ARCHAEOLOGY AND EPIGRAPHY

*BARNETT, R. D.: *Illustrations of Old Testament History*. 1966. Pp. 91. (British Museum, London. Price: 10s. 6d.).

A very useful book for schools, delightfully printed with 54 excellent illustrations and a minimum amount of non-technical text in 23 short chapters. The illustrations cover the history from the Babylonian Flood tablets to the ossuary of Nicanor and there is a good bibliography. But as a popular work it should have kept to accurate facts. Did Amenhotep IV 'dream his dreams of religious reform' (12)? Are the Carthaginian child cemeteries called 'Topheth' and were the children sacrificed for fertility or, sometimes, to pay vows? (37). Was Amos the contemporary of Ahab? (42). And did the two cherubim span the approach to the Holy of Holies in Solomon's temple? (44).   J.N.S.

EPSTEIN, C.: *Palestinian Bichrome Ware*. (Documenta et Monumenta Orientis Antiqui, Vol. XII). 1966. Pp. 194 + 20 plates. (E. J. Brill, Leiden. Price: £9 9s. 6d.).

This handsome volume presents a careful analysis of the forms and decorative motive of bichrome pottery most familiar from the excavations of the late Sir Flinders Petrie at Tell el-Ajjul at the mouth of the Wadi Ghazzeh; hence the name 'Ajjul ware', which gave rise to the theory that the ware was the production of a school of potters or even an individual artist at Tell el-Ajjul. The author explodes this theory, by citing the wide distribution of the pottery to North Syria and Cyprus and the use of the decor on shapes which were certainly of North Syrian and Cypriot rather than Palestinian form. Affinities with Mitannian decoration in North Mesopotamia are claimed, and it is proposed that the diffusion of the ware southwards through Palestine was related to the expansion of the Hurrians in the same direction in the sixteenth century. This subject is discussed with particular evidence of the settlement of Hurrians and their association with the horse and war-chariot at archaeological stations in Syria and Palestine and in texts in chapter v, which Old Testament students will find most valuable in this excellent publication.   J.G.

KENYON, K. M.: *Amorites and Canaanites*. (The Schweich Lectures of the British Academy, 1963.) 1966. Pp. xvi + 80 (including 40 text-figures) + XXX plates. (Published for the British Academy by the Oxford University Press, London. Price: 30s.).

The title evokes terms familiar to every reader of the Old Testament, promises a presentation of the subject which will fill out or modify the popular impression of Canaanites and Amorites, for which the material remains evaluated by the authoress, texts from Egypt, Mesopotamia, Syria and Palestine, palaces, temples and their furniture, sculpture with or without inscriptions, figurines of gods, amulets etc. are now so abundant. The book, however, is rather for specialists, who will be grateful for the assembly and analysis of material evidence in the critical phases of the history of Syria and Palestine on which the writer has focussed her attention, particularly the period and extent of the settlement of 'Amorite' tribesmen *c.* 2300–1900, where she presents her well-known evidence from the tombs of the period at Jericho, now related by her to evidence of the same nature from elsewhere in Palestine and Syria, and a detailed discussion of the Hyksos glacis of Middle Bronze Age II (*c.* 1750–1600) and its distribution from Ras Shamra to Tell el-Yehudiyeh in the Delta.   J.G.

MAZAR, B., DOTHAN, T., DUNAYEVSKY, I.: *En-gedi Excavations in* 1961–1962 (*'atiqot* V). 1966. Pp. 100 and 37 full page plates. (Department of Antiquities and Museums, Israel Exploration Society, Jerusalem. Price: $5.00).

The book contains a History of the Oasis of En-gedi and its agriculture, an account of the excavations there of Tel Goren (Tell el-Jurn) in 1961–2 and of the remains found in the five strata covering the sixth centuries B.C.E. to the fifth century C.E.; a discussion of the coins by L. T. Rahmani, of the pottery and of the glass aryballos by D. Baraq. There are plans, maps, and many pages of line drawings of pottery.   J.N.S.

MUEHSAM, A.: *Coin & Temple, A Study of the Architectural Representation on Ancient Jewish Coins.* (Leeds University Oriental Society, Near Eastern Researches, 1). Pp. ix + 70, with eleven plates. (Leeds, 1966. Price: £3 15s.).

This is a very learned, well-documented, and excellently illustrated study, principally of the series of Jewish silver coins (*Hill*, Plate XXXII) with a tetrastyle façade on the obverse, usually called 'tetradrachms' and attributed *en bloc* to the time of Bar Kokhba. Dr. Muehsam finds that this obverse type represents the view from the Mount of Olives seen by the priest when sacrificing the *Red Heifer.* The colonnade below is Solomon's porch on the Eastern wall of the Temple Mount. The priest 'gazes in a straight line, at right angles to Solomon's Porch, above the Corinthian (Nicanor) Gate to the Great Gate which he sees in its full extent. In its center he perceives the *entrance* to the Temple itself, and the Holy of Holies is symbolized on the coin by the Ark of the Covenant' (p. 32). This interpretation is maintained with great skill, learning, and determination. It appears convincing. But Dr. Muehsam is left with a problem of dates. She does not feel it essential to her thesis that the Ark should still have been in existence at the time of the first creation of the coin-type, but she will have it that the Temple itself must still have been standing. Dr. Muehsam therefore proceeds with a very detailed examination of dies, die-links, and later use of earlier dies (ingeniously, and not therefore unconvincingly, accounting for overstrikes) — an examination of great value for its exhibition of the evidence. She finds that 'the coins of Year One and Year Two were apparently issued in the initial years' of the First Revolt 'i.e. A.D. 66–68, and the undated coins at a later time by Bar Kokhba' (p. 66). We must await the judgement of the numismatists on this part of her thesis. *Adhuc sub iudice lis est* — as we may hope Dr. Muehsam might perhaps say. But we shall all have much to learn from her book, even though she believes that her dating of these 'tetradrachms' automatically assigns the 'thick shekels' again to the Maccabees, 'which appears conformable to all circumstances' (p. 49, note 31). The Maccabaean dating of the 'thick shekels' does not seem any longer tenable (*pace* Wirgin; see e.g. A. Reifenberg, *Ancient Jewish Coins,*[2] 1947, pp. 30, 31; and now Yigael Yadin, *Masada,* London 1966, p. 108). But perhaps Dr. Muehsam's thesis about the 'tetradrachms' does not automatically put the 'thick shekels' back with the Maccabees.

H.St.J.H.

*VARDAMAN, J.: *Archaeology and the Living Word.* 1965. Pp. 128. (Broadman Press, Nashville, Tennessee. Price: $1.50).

This is a popular account of biblical archaeology written in easy, non-technical language. As such, it answers very well the layman who asks, 'What has archaeology discovered?' and evens tells him briefly how it was done. After two preliminary chapters, four are given to the Old Testament and five to the New, including two for the Greek Text and the Dead Sea Scrolls. A useful appetizer.

D.R.Ap-T.

VERGER, A.: *Ricerche Giuridiche sui Papri Aramaici di Elefantina*. 1965. Pp. 225. (Centro di Studi Semitici. Istituto di Studi del Vicino Oriente. Università, Roma).

This interesting and well-documented study of the juridical aspects of the Elephantine papyri recalls a work already extant in English, namely, R. Yaron's *Introduction to the Law of the Aramaic Papyri* (Clarendon Press, 1961. Cf. *B.L.* 1962, p. 57). It differs from the earlier monograph in that there is a long chapter (II) on Egypt in the fifth century B.C., which may be said to correspond on a smaller scale to E. G. Kraeling's historical introduction to his edition of the *Brooklyn Museum Aramaic Papyri*. Both Yaron and Verger devote many pages to the subject of marriage and divorce, but in regard to slavery Verger gives nearly forty pages to a topic which Yaron deals with in five. Conversely, Yaron's chapter on the law of property is far more thorough than Verger's. The latter, as was to be expected, does not agree at all points with earlier writers on this difficult and controversial aspect of the papyri, but is careful to quote his opponents fully and fairly where he dissents from their interpretations. An appendix contains a very thorough bibliography, which lists no fewer than three hundred and twenty-four books and articles bearing on the subject. A reader of both these monographs will find himself reasonably well informed on the main issues involved.

J.M.T.B.

HISTORY AND GEOGRAPHY

The Cambridge Ancient History: Revised Edition of Volumes I and II. Cyprus in the Neolithic and Bronze Age Periods: by H. W. Catling. Fasc. 43. Pp. 78. (Price: 8s. 6d.).

Anatolia: c. 1600–1380 B.C.: by O. R. Gurney. Fasc. 44. Pp. 30. (Price: 3s. 6d.).

The Amarna Letters from Palestine. Syria, the Philistines and Phoenicia: by W. F. Albright. Fasc. 51. Pp. 58. (Price: 6s.).

The first of these fascicles deals with Cyprus in its Neolithic and Bronze Age Periods. This is a particularly interesting fascicle. In addition to a full account of the results of recent archaeological work in Cyprus, Dr. Catling has discussed with assured mastery the long-standing problem of the identity of Cyprus with the Alashiya of the Amarna Letters, and has shown how formidable are the objections to the identification now accepted by many scholars. He has also discussed the extent to which archaeology supports the Greek foundation legends concerning Paphos, Tegea, Salamis and other sites.

In the second fascicle Professor Gurney continues his account of the founding and rise of the Hittite Empire which he began in fascicle 11. In this fascicle Professor Gurney unravels the complicated dynastic struggles which characterized the rise of the Hittite power to the point where the genius of Shuppiluliumash I 'raised the kingdom in one generation to a status of equality with the leading nations of the Near Eastern world'.

In the third fascicle the doyen of American archaeologists and Old Testament scholars, Professor Emeritus W. F. Albright, deals with material of great importance to students of the Old Testament. In the first section he gives a full account of the Amarna Letters from Palestine, in the light of much new material which has been discovered since the first discovery of the Letters in 1887. In the second section he deals with all the intricate problems raised by the movements of population at the end of the 2nd millennium B.C. In the discussion of the Amarna Letters Professor Albright throws much new light on the ancient problem of the Hapiru, and especially on the curious career of Labaya. Readers may be amused to observe that in the valuable bibliographies attached to the three fascicles, Dr. Catling only lists three of his own publications, Professor Gurney only two, while Professor Albright gives us a profusion of 32 items!

S.H.H.

The Cambridge Ancient History: Revised Edition of Volumes I and II.
Palestine during the Neolithic and Chalcolithic Periods: by R. de Vaux. Fasc. 47. Pp. 48. (Price: 6s.).
Palestine in the Early Bronze Age: by R. de Vaux. Fasc. 46. Pp. 33. (Price: 6s.).
Egypt: from the inception of the Nineteenth Dynasty to the death of Ramesses III: by R. O. Faulkner. Fasc. 52. Pp. 42. (Price: 6s.).

These three fascicles are all of special interest to students of the Old Testament. Père de Vaux has established his reputation, not only as one of the foremost of modern archaeologists, but also as an authority on the institutions of Israel. In the first of the two fascicles for which he is responsible he has thrown welcome light on the Neolithic and Chalcolithic periods in Palestine. He has placed Miss Kenyon's epoch-making work at Jericho in its perspective in relation to other excavated sites of the same period in Palestine, and has thrown new light on the problem of the discontinuity of habitation in many sites. In the second fascicle he has demonstrated the existence of four phases of the Early Bronze period in Palestine, and has given good grounds for his statement that the 'Canaanites' may be regarded as the founders of the Early Bronze Age.

The third fascicle, by Dr. R. O. Faulkner, deals with a period of Egyptian history which is generally regarded as covering the sojourn of Israel in Egypt and the Exodus, as well as the coming of the Sea-Peoples. But as Professor Eissfeldt has dealt with this part of the history in fascicles 31 and 32 (see *B.L.* 1966, p. 16), Dr. Faulkner has only touched lightly on it in relation to the stele of Merneptah, and has avoided the question whether Ramesses II was the Pharaoh of the oppression. But he has given a lucid account of the long drawn out struggle for the hegemony of Palestine between Egypt and the Hittite power, and much new light on the civilization of Egypt during the Nineteenth Dynasty.

S.H.H.

The Cambridge Ancient History: Revised Edition of Volumes I and II.
Palestine in the Middle Bronze Age: by Kathleen M. Kenyon. Fasc. 48. Pp. 43. (Price: 6s.).
The Earliest Populations of Man in Europe, W. Asia and N. Africa: by D. R. Hughes and D. R. Brothwell. Fasc. 50. Pp. 19. (Price: 3s. 6d.).
The Evidence of Language: by W. F. Albright and T. O. Lambdin. Fasc. 54. Pp. 40. (Price: 6s.).

These three fascicles are of great interest and importance. The one which will be of special interest to students of the Old Testament is

Miss Kenyon's masterly summing up of what archaeology has
revealed of populations and cultures in Palestine during the Middle
Bronze Age. No one can speak with greater authority than Miss
Kenyon on the period with which this fascicle deals. In her recently
published Schweich lectures, *Amorites and Canaanites* (see p. 12 of
this *Book List*), she has dealt more fully with one of the subjects
treated in the present fascicle, the advent of the Amorites in Palestine,
and the character of early Canaanite culture. An important feature
of her discussion of this period is her demonstration, if that is not
too strong a word to use, that the new type of rampart defence
revealed in her excavation of Jericho, and shown to exist in many
other Palestinian sites, is material evidence of the Hyksos period in
Palestine, and of the presence of an alien aristocracy, superimposed
upon the pre-existing population. She also suggests that the new
method of defence was probably the response to a new (or improved)
method of attack, the battering ram.

The second of these fascicles is short, but very important. It deals with
the earliest populations of man in those widely scattered areas which
he inhabited as he emerged from his pithecoid ancestry. Some of the
older theories of the causes of dispersion, such as Ellsworth Hunting-
ton's, are firmly dealt with and disposed of. The chapter shows what
immense advances and discoveries have been made in this field since
the first publication of the *C.A.H.*

The third fascicle deals with the immensely important subject of
the relation between language and history. It represents the ripe
experience of American scholarship in this field. The discussion
opens with the interesting suggestion that the types and degrees of
relationships existing among languages of a given family may be
studied under four ideal situations, or models. These are, (*a*) the
simple *linear* relationship, (*b*) the situation of *divergence in isolation*,
(*c*) the *dialect continuum*, causing the formation of linguistic sub-
communities, and (*d*) *interference*, to which a language community
can be subjected in a wide variety of ways. The problem of the
historical relation between the Sumerian and Semitic languages
receives a careful discussion, and it is interesting to note that the
authors come down firmly on the side of the superior antiquity of
Sumerian in relation to Egyptian. It may come as a surprise to learn
that the name Egypt, from the Greek *Aiguptos*, is a corruption of
one of the Egyptian names of Memphis, *Ḥekuptaḥ* (Temple of Ptah),
in Ugaritic *ḥkpt*.   S.H.H.

*The Cambridge Ancient History: Revised Edition of Volumes I and II.
Assyrian Military Power:* 1300–1200 B.C.: by J. M. Munn-Rankin. Fasc.
   49. Pp. 38. (Price: 6s.).
Assyria: c. 2600–1816 B.C.: by Hildegard Lewy. Fasc. 53. Pp. 50.
   (Price: 6s.).
Phrygia and the Peoples of Anatolia in the Iron Age: by R. D. Barnett.
   Fasc. 56. Pp. 32. (Price: 3s. 6d.).

Each of these fascicles bears witness to the immense increase of
knowledge about the ancient Near East which has accumulated
since the original volumes of this great work appeared in 1924.
Looking through the titles of the 60 fascicles which have already
appeared or are in the press, one is struck by the enormous increase

of specialization. An area of the field which, in the original volumes, was covered by a single author, is now divided up and dealt with by a number of authors who are each specialists in one particular aspect of that field. Another noticeable change is the increased international character of the contributors; America, France, Germany, Belgium, Canada, and Turkey are represented by distinguished scholars, while many new British names appear on the list. In the original volumes Professor Breasted of Chicago was the only American contributor, and there were no continental contributors.

With regard to the three fascicles named above, it may be said that each is the work of a specialist, and each maintains the same high standard of scholarship shown in the fascicles which have already appeared. The two which deal with Assyria will be of special interest to Old Testament students; they throw new light on the Subartu problem, and on the reasons for the meteoric rise and sudden collapse of the first Assyrian empire. It is surprising to find no mention of Professor Sidney Smith's valuable book *The Early History of Assyria* in the bibliography of Dr. Lewy's fascicle; the more so since Miss Munn-Rankin has included it in her bibliography. It is a book which is far from being out of date. Dr. Barnett's chapter on Phrygia gathers up the results of many years of research into the extraordinary variety of cultures and languages found in that bewildering area.

S.H.H.

CHAMBERLAYNE, J. H.: *Man in Society: the Old Testament Doctrine.* 1966. Pp. 255. (Epworth Press, London. Price: 35s.).

This book contains the Fernley Hartley Lecture 1966, and is mainly devoted to a study of the various social structures that are manifested in the course of Israel's history. It recognizes the tribal, nomadic, agricultural and urban factors and the effects of the instition of the monarchy. Its aim is 'to recognize fully the sociological, cultural and political factors in the life of the people of Israel' in order to find an adequate faith for a democratic order in the twentieth century. The Old Testament material which occupies most of the book is indebted especially to recent anthropological studies, notably those of J. Pedersen and W. Eichrodt. Some of the details of the book need checking: thus we are told that the *horim* are referred to in Jer. 26: 11, 12, 16, 23 and 2 Kgs 23: 6, and *lāmas* appears on p. 59 to be treated as a noun meaning hired workmen. Quotations are said to be from RSV but a number of instances occur which are not. The book will have its value particularly in circles where the wealth of Old Testament material is relatively unknown.

A.S.H.

HARRISON, R. H.: *Healing Herbs of the Bible.* 1966. Pp. 58. (E. J. Brill, Leiden. Price: Fl. 8.00).

Not only healing, but also culinary, poisonous and perfumery herbs are discussed in this reprint from Janus 50, 1961. The rendering of the Hebrew words corresponds closely to those found in Koehler-Baumgartner's Lexicon or in Hastings' Dictionary of the Bible (2nd edition) under RSV renderings. Some notes are added on extra-biblical uses and present-day (mainly oriental) practice.

A.S.H.

*KAPELRUD, A. S.: *Israel. From the Earliest Times to the Birth of Christ.*
Translated by J. M. Moe. 1966. Pp. viii + 152; 2 line maps;
14 ill. on VIII Pl. (Blackwell, Oxford. Price: 15s.).

Professor Kapelrud's previous studies have helped him to write this
concise historical sketch with a sure as well as light touch. A few
slips need to be corrected: Haran lies on the Bialikh, not up the
Tigris (p. 12); Gebal is not in Asia *Minor* (p. 15); and Antiochus IV
did not seize the throne in 164 and in 175 (p. 121). The translation
reads very smoothly and idiomatically but one or two names occur
in slightly unfamiliar form. This paperback may be warmly commended for those who wish to see the shape of the wood before
concentrating on individual, knotty, trees. Some good photographs,
a chronological table and an index add to its value.   D.R.Ap-T.

*MORIARTY, F.: *Introducing the Old Testament.* 1966. Pp. xiv + 253 + 2
maps. (Burns and Oates, London. Price: 15s.).

This paperback edition of a book first published in 1960 is addressed
to the general reader, and is a workmanlike introduction (in the
popular not technical sense of the word) to the O.T. history, which is
clearly etched in fifteen short biographical studies, ranging from
Abraham to Daniel. The narrative embodies the conclusions of
modern scholarship, is compact, easy to read and not overloaded
with detail. Written primarily for Roman Catholics, it should appeal
to a much wider circle of readers.   L.A.P.

SMITH, G. A.: *The Historical Geography of the Holy Land.* 1966. Pp. 512.
(Fontana Library of Theology and Philosophy; Collins, London.
Price: 21s.).

Professor Rowley provides a short introduction to this reprint of
a famous book. This is a paperback reproduction of the 1931
edition, i.e. the 25th edition which was revised throughout. No
changes have been made except that the original coloured maps have
been reproduced in black and white — this on the score of expense;
and the transliteration of Hebrew and Arabic place-names has been
standardized. The latest views can be found in modern atlases and
in various well-known books; but this remains as it was in the hope
that it will inspire another generation as it inspired some of us
fifty-odd years ago.   N.H.S.

TEXT AND VERSIONS

GINSBURG, C. D.: *Introduction to the Massoretico-Critical Edition of the
Hebrew Bible. With a Prolegomenon by Harry M. Orlinsky. The
Masoretic Text: a Critical Evaluation.* 1966. Pp. li + 1028 + 2 Tables.
(Ktav Publishing House, Inc., New York. Price: $22.50).

There are, of course, two items to be noted. Firstly, the re-issue of
Ginsburg's classic work, first published in 1897, which has been
needed for years. Despite changes in interpretation, it provides a

better source of information than any other lengthy work on the Massoretic text. Secondly, Dr. Orlinsky's Prolegomenon is one of the most fascinating treatments of the subject. To say that the author denies the existence of the Massoretic Text and even 'the Massoretic tradition' is simply to headline an article which is full of daring, as well as plausible argument, and useful bibliographical references. The whole publication is well worth the money.

B.J.R.

HANHART, R. (ed. by): *Septuaginta Vetus Testamentum Graecum auctoritate Societatis Litterarum Gottingensis editum.* Vol. VIII, fasc. 3: *Esther.* 1966. Pp. 208. (Vandenhoeck & Ruprecht, Göttingen. Price: paper, DM. 39.00; cloth, 43.00).

This is an important addition to the hand-book material available for the study of the Septuagint. The introduction (pp. 1–130) contains a full discussion of the characteristics of the manuscripts on which the text is based together with a study of the grammatical features. A most valuable part of this introduction is the discussion of the 'L-text' of MSS 19, 93 (108, 319) which, in spite of the normal grouping of these MSS with those that have a 'Lucianic' text, is shown not to be Lucianic but to be an independent version of the Septuagint text. This text has significant variations from LXX and is much shorter; it was probably produced some time before the Hexapla. To avoid confusion the term 'L-text' has been retained in this edition.

In printing the text (pp. 131–208) two forms are given, each with its *apparatus criticus*, that of the LXX at the top of the page and that of the L-text at the foot.

L.H.B.

EXEGESIS AND MODERN TRANSLATIONS

AUGÉ, R., FIGUERAS, A. M. and TRAGAN, P. M.: *La Biblia, versió dels textos originals i comentari.* XI. *Proverbis, Eclesiastès, Càntic dels Càntics.* 1966. Pp. 409. (Monastery of Montserrat: Price: 250 ptas.).

Here is another volume of the splendidly printed Montserrat commentary, which, as usual, provides concise introductions, the Vulgate text with a Catalan translation, and abundant exegetical matter. As always, there is a good deal of Hebrew type in the various parts of the work, the bibliographies are adequate, and the numerous schools of thought (more particularly on the controversial issues in Ecclesiastes and the Song of Songs) are fully represented. None of the three authors gives much sign of contributing original matter to his study of a book, but it is a great thing to have a fair appraisement of the standard authorities. No list of volumes already published or destined to appear in the future is provided.

J.M.T.B.

BREIT, H. and WESTERMANN, C. (ed. by): *Calwer Predigt-Hilfen*, Vol. 5. *Ausgewählte Alttestamentliche Texte.* 1966. Pp. 392. (Calwer Verlag, Stuttgart. Price: DM. 18.00).

This volume is intended to stimulate continuous exposition of sections of the Old Testament, based on the scholarly study of the text. There are four sections: the Joseph story, by C. Westermann; selected Psalms, by W. Rupprecht; passages from Jeremiah, by H. Breit; and passages from Amos, by W. Warth. To each section there is an introduction, followed by a good bibliography, and each of the passages selected is introduced by grammatical notes on Hebrew words it contains, notes on the structure of the passage, and an exposition. It would seem that in Germany as elsewhere there is need for expository preaching and for serious teaching on the original and the contemporary message of the Bible. It is good that preachers are encouraged to base their exposition on a study of the Hebrew text.   H.H.R.

CALVIN, J. *Commentaires sur l'Ancien Testament*. Tome Premier: *Le Livre de la Genèse*. 1961. Pp. 686. (Labor et Fides, Genève. Price: Sw.Fr. 52.00).

This massive volume is the first of a new French edition of Calvin's Bible Commentaries which is being published as a joint effort of *Labor et Fides* and La Société Calviniste de France. It is not clear how soon other volumes may be expected. To all those, however, who realize the importance of studying the history of biblical exegesis this effort to make more easily accessible the work of the great reformer will be most welcome. If one allows for the obvious fact that Calvin wrote his commentaries before the tremendous modern advances in biblical studies, what strikes one forcibly as one reads his expositions is the sobriety of his judgement, a quality which, after all necessary reservations have been made, ensures his enduring relevance to the concerns of the modern expositor.   N.W.P.

DEISSLER, A.: *Die Psalmen*. 3 Vols.: 1–41; 42–89; 90–150. (Die Welt der Bibel, Kleinkommentare, I–III). 1963–5. Pp. 169; 186; 227. (Patmos Verlag, Düsseldorf. Price: DM. 25.00 each).

The Roman Catholic paperback series, Die Welt der Bibel, is now to include a number of *Kleinkommentare* on individual books of the Bible. The first of these to appear, and the only one as yet concerned with the Old Testament, is this three-volume introduction to the Psalms. A brief introduction deals with the problems of the headings of the Psalms, and the history of Psalmody; and then gives an account of the form-critical method of analysing the different *Gattungen* of the Psalms.
The commentary itself consists of a translation of each Psalm, with short text-critical notes, an account of its *Sitz-im-Leben*, and then exegesis, first in Old Testament, then in New Testament terms. Not all will find the typology of this last section entirely convincing, but these three volumes certainly provide a good concise introduction to modern approaches to the Psalter.   R.J.C.

EICHRODT, W.: *Der Prophet Hesekiel: Kap. 19–48, übersetzt und erklärt*. (Das Alte Testament Deutsch 22/2). 1966. Pp. 159–421 + 37*. (Vandenhoeck & Ruprecht, Göttingen. Price: DM. 14.80).

The earlier part of this commentary was reviewed in *Book List* 1960, p. 19. The 37 pages appendix provides the Introduction and deals with the following subjects: the prophet in the history of his time (594–571 B.C.), a brief discussion of some alternative views, the form of the prophet's proclamation, the formation of the book, and the person and message of Ezekiel. The translation is accompanied by textual and exegetical notes. Words, phrases and sentences regarded as later additions are omitted from the text, but included among the footnotes. A re-arrangement of verses occurs in a number of chapters, e.g. 20: 1–14, 17, 15–16, 18–22, 28–29, 23–27, 30–44, with verses 12, 20, 29, 24, and a number of shorter phrases, omitted. The section on Gog is treated as a product of an Ezekiel school and shows the influence of post-exilic prophecy. One hardly needs to say that this is an important contribution to an understanding of this book, and of the prophet-priest whose words are recorded here.

A.S.H.

ELLIGER, K.: *Leviticus*. (Handbuch zum Alten Testament, 4). 1966. Pp. 402. (J. C. B. Mohr (Paul Siebeck), Tübingen. Price: paper, DM. 50; cloth, DM. 54).

There is a Foreword, 19 pages of Introduction, and the rest is Commentary. The pattern of the commentary is: translation, textual note, literary analysis, exegesis, and all this section by section. The learned author assumes different layers of P, and of the Holiness Code (chs. 17–26). The discussions of the sacrifices, their content and meaning, are found at the appropriate places in the commentary, and so also for the rules concerning uncleanness, and the constitution of the priesthood and the temple personnel. A thoroughly competent, comprehensive and efficient piece of work.

N.H.S.

HERBERT, A. S.: *Genesis* 12–50: *Abraham and his Heirs*. (Torch Bible Paperbacks). 1966. Pp. 160. (S.C.M. Press, London. Price: 8s. 6d.).

Professor Herbert's commentary of 1962 is here reprinted without change (see *Book List* 1963, p. 23).

M.A.K.

The Holy Bible. Revised Standard Version. Containing the Old and New Testaments. Catholic Edition. Prepared by the Catholic Biblical Association of Great Britain. With a Foreword by H.E. John Cardinal Heenan, Archbishop of Westminster. 1966. Pp. xii + 1017 + ii + 259. (Thomas Nelson, London. Price: 25s.).

There is not a great deal of difference between this Catholic edition and the one reviewed in the *Book List* for 1966, p. 25. Professor Rowley's introduction to the Apocrypha is omitted, and there are two sets of notes, one for the Old Testament (pp. 996–1007) and the other for the New Testament (pp. 239–250). The latter section includes a list of changes made for the Catholic edition, most of which are not of much importance. The long ending to St. Mark's Gospel, recently discussed by Professor B. M. Metzger in his *Text of the New Testament*, 1964, pp. 227–28, is inserted into the text after xvi, 8, and the *pericope de adultera* (Jn. vii, 52–viii, 11) is treated similarly. The *Comma Johanneum* (I Jo. v, 7–8) is omitted, as is now usual in recent Catholic editions, from text and notes, though a reference is made to it in the Introduction at p. vii.

J.M.T.B.

JACOB, E., KELLER, C. A., AMSLER, S.: *Osée, Joël, Amos, Abdias, Jonas.*
(Commentaire de l'Ancien Testament xi a). 1965. Pp. 296. (Delachaux & Niestlé, Neuchâtel. Price: Sw.Fr. 38.00).

This further volume in this new series of Old Testament commentaries
maintains the excellent standard with which it has begun. The
presentation consists of a short introduction to each book, a fresh
translation of the text with brief textual notes, and an exposition.
A basic modern bibliography is given without being exhaustive.
E. Jacob comments on Hosea, and accepts that chapters i–iii form a
unity in which chapter iii describes a later circumstance of the marriage described in chapter i. Gomer is regarded as a cult-prostitute.
C. A. Keller writes on Joel, which he dates *c.* 630–600 B.C. on the
evidence of iv. 1–8, and on Obadiah, where he accepts 1b–15 as
deriving from a single prophet *c.* 587 B.C.   He also contributes the
commentary on Jonah which he regards as a prophetic tale designed
to show that the justification of the prophetic message resides in the
faith of his hearers.
S. Amsler comments on Amos, and provides a cautious and balanced
exposition in which he refuses to cast Amos in a cult-prophetic mould.
He interprets 'Israel' as referring to the ten tribes of the North,
regards the doxologies as hymn fragments quoted by Amos, and
denies to the prophet's authorship ix, 11ff. This is an admirable
volume which combines sound scholarship with clarity, and avoids
speculative novelties.   R.E.C.

The Jerusalem Bible (ed. by A. Jones). 1966. Pp. xvi + 1547 + 498.
(Darton, Longman & Todd, London. Price: 84s.).

This finely printed and distinguished work has been long in the
making, and its conception may be said to date from the issue in
1956 of the one-volume edition of the *Bible de Jérusalem*, of which,
as the editor notes in his foreword, this is the English equivalent. It
differs from the generality of Bibles in having a large quantity of
introductory matter and notes, all of these having been usually
taken from the French original. The translation itself is not a version
of the French, though the first drafts of some books were based on
the French, and then were carefully compared with the Hebrew or
Aramaic originals. The majority of the books, however, were, from
the start, translations of the original tongues, which were later studied
in the light of what might be called the parent work. Throughout the
object was to produce 'an entirely faithful version of the ancient
texts', and the result is a courageous attempt to render the Bible into
contemporary English, and not into 'a kind of hieratic language'
judged by some to be specially biblical, or even into the 'timeless
English' envisaged by the late Mgr. Knox.
A lengthy review of this version has already appeared from the pen
of Fr. Robert Murray, S.J. in the December *Clergy Review*, and with
this I am in general agreement. Like Fr. Murray I consider the
Psalter quite the poorest section of the work, as being in many
passages so far removed from the poetic. The procedures adopted
by the editors of the *Revised Psalter* of 1964 might well have been
followed here, and the superb rhythm of the Vulgate Latin and of
the Prayer Book Version retained. In Ps. 122 an unfortunate omission
in verse 6 produces the line: 'Pay for peace in Jerusalem.' It appears
that many of the editors were not, in any accepted sense, biblical
scholars.   J.M.T.B.

KRAELING, E. G.: *Commentary on the Prophets. Vol. I Isaiah–Ezekiel; Vol. II Daniel–Malachi.* 1966. Pp. 543; 345. (Thomas Nelson and Son, Camden N.J. Price: $7.50 each volume).

These commentaries, based on the RSV, are intended for the general reader and are designed to give briefly the results of modern study: they include some more technical discussions, and adequate bibliographies for those who wish to go further. Each biblical book is provided with a short introduction and the text is then set out with the notes at the bottom of the page. Within the limits imposed, this is useful and clear.

P.R.A.

LEWIS, J. D. V.: *Llyfr y Salmau.* 1967. Pp. 117. (Ty John Penry, Swansea. Price: 10s. 6d.).

The author has been a member of the Society for almost forty-five years and his study of the Psalter goes back still further. In this volume he gives us the results of his lifetime labours in an entirely new translation of *Psalms i–xli* into 'timeless Welsh', with notes on difficult passages of the text. As is fitting, the depth of scholarship lying behind the translation never obtrudes, though one is conscious of its presence, but still more of the extent to which the translator has entered into the Psalmist's feelings. Scholar and ordinary reader will gain much from this excellent rendering.

D.R.Ap-T.

LINDBLOM, J.: *Boken om Job och hans lidande.* Second edition. 1966. Pp. 248. (Gleerups Förlag, Lund. Price: Sw.Kr. 9.75).

This book first appeared in 1940 and was reviewed by Professor Pedersen in *Book List* 1946, p. 26 (*Eleven Years*, p. 26). It is now reissued as a paper back. In structure and substance it remains the same; but some revision of the text has been carried out (e.g., reference is made to the 'Prayer of Nabonidus') and some references added to more recent literature. In clear and elegant Swedish the author presents a sensitive interpretation of the book of Job in its Israelite setting and in its relations with other literature.

G.W.A.

LOHFINK, N.: *Höre, Israel!* (Die Welt der Bibel, 18). 1965. Pp. 123. (Patmos-Verlag, Düsseldorf. Price: DM. 5.80).

This addition to the paperback series, Die Welt der Bibel, is concerned with Deuteronomy. The introductory chapter puts the book as a whole in its context, both in the Pentateuch and as introduction to the Deuteronomic history-work; and then considers the relation of D to the 622 law-book and the exile. The four main chapters of the book then give fuller exposition of four selected sections: Deut. 10, 12–11, 17; 6, 4–25; 8, 1–20; 4, 1–40. Each section has a large number of cross-references to other passages of similar historical or formal background. The whole makes a valuable introduction to recent insights into the place and purpose of the Deuteronomic literature.

R.J.C.

LÜTHI, W.: *L'Ecclésiaste a vécu la vie*. Un commentaire pour la communauté chrétienne. Traduction de Daniel Hatt. 1960. Pp. 131. (Éditions Labor et Fides, Genève. Price: Sw.Fr. 12.70).

Each chapter in turn of Ecclesiastes is printed in full and then receives expository treatment in this series of twelve sermons preached between 1951 and 1952 in the Cathedral at Berne and subsequently published under the title of *Der Prediger Salomo lebt das Leben*. The present translation has been undertaken with great sensitivity in order to convey as much as is possible of the distinctive style and appeal of the author. Considerable skill is apparent in the exposition of salient points of the chapters. Old and New Testaments have been drawn upon to interpret Ecclesiastes as one of robust faith who lived life to the full yet reckoned squarely with its inevitabilities of suffering and woe. His contribution therefore within the progressive development of Biblical thought must be considered as of positive value. There is much to stimulate and inspire in the quality and fine discernment of the preaching here offered, presented as it is with a directness and ruggedness in which humour is not lacking, and backed up by many a choice allusion.   E.T.R.

MAILLOT, A. and LELIÈVRE, A.: *Les Psaumes*. Commentaire—Première partie, Psaumes 1 à 50. 1961. Pp. 314. (Éditions Labor et Fides, Genève. Price: paper, Sw.Fr. 18.50; cloth, Sw.Fr. 22.50).

After a short introduction to the Psalms, the book proceeds to deal with Psalms 1–50. Each Psalm is translated, and where an amended text is followed, it is discussed in a short *apparatus criticus* which follows the translation. The content of the psalm is then analysed and its interpretation examined. Attention is called to the connection between the Psalms and the cult, and a particular emphasis is placed on the psalms as prayers. The authors do mention some of the important commentaries which have been used, but a fuller bibliography would add to the usefulness of this commentary.   E.R.R.

MAUCHLINE, J.: *Isaiah 1–39: Confidence in God*. (Torch Bible Paperbacks). 1966. Pp. 238. (S.C.M. Press, London. Price: 10s. 6d.).

This is an unchanged reprint in paperback form of the commentary published in 1962 (see *Book List* 1963, p. 25).   M.A.K.

NOTH, M.: *Das vierte Buch Mose. Numeri*. (Das Alte Testament Deutsch 7). 1966. Pp. 222. (Vandenhoeck und Ruprecht, Göttingen).

This volume completes the group Exodus to Numbers in this series for which Professor Noth is responsible, and since commentaries on these books are all too rare, it is very useful to have this available. The pattern is as in other volumes of the series: first a brief discussion of the book and its literary structure, together with an assessment of its place in the corpus to which it belongs, leading up to the conquest of the land, the tribes being shown as organized and ready for the settlement. An English translation of this volume, like its predecessors, is planned for the not too distant future.   P.R.A.

DE PURY, R.: *Job ou l'homme révolté*. (Les Cahiers du Renouveau 12). 3e édition. 1958. Pp. 60. (Éditions Labor et Fides, Genève. Price: Sw.Fr. 2.80).

Six short chapters here present a homiletical interpretation of the book of Job, the main sections of which with the exception of the Elihu speeches (Job xxxii–xxxvii) are successively considered. A conclusion entitled *Qui est Job?* draws attention to c.xxix.12ff. as in effect portraying the ministry of Jesus, in connection with which further parallels in the book are noted, and in whom the suffering and vindication of the Servant of God are seen to be fulfilled.

E.T.R.

VON RAD, G.: *Deuteronomy*, trans. by Dorothea Barton. 1966. Pp. 211. (Old Testament Library, S.C.M. Press, London. Price: 35s.).

This is a translation of *Das fünfte Buch Mose: Deuteronium*, no. 8 in *Das Alte Testament Deutsch*, and published in 1964 (see *Book List* 1965, p. 30). The biblical text followed is that of RSV, except where the author's own translation is retained, as indicated in a note. We have here von Rad's developed thought about Deuteronomy; covenant pattern with its credo and its spoken law. The reader is doubly in debt: to von Rad for his excellent expositions, and to the publisher for giving the English reader access to von Rad's work. There is easier German to read than von Rad's.

N.H.S.

RUDOLPH, W.: *Hosea* (Kommentar zum Alten Testament, Band XIII/1). 1966. Pp. 282. (Gütersloher Verlagshaus Gerd Mohn, Gütersloh. Price: DM. 42).

This stimulating and interesting commentary, which forms the latest addition to the new *Kommentar zum Alten Testament*, follows the pattern observed in the volumes of this series that have already appeared. The author's translation of the individual units is followed by detailed textual notes and then by a very full exegesis of the text, in the course of which the problems that are involved in the interpretation of the book are discussed at length. The work is prefaced by a quite short introduction and a bibliography, and is rounded off by an equally short summary of Hosea's preaching. A Chronological Table, compiled by Alfred Jepsen, is appended to the work, and this presumably will be added to all future volumes of the series. Rudolph argues that Gomer was not a prostitute, and that Hosea's marriage to her was entirely normal. Hosea's marriage relationship was not a symbol for him of Yahweh's relationship with Israel; rather the point of c.1 lies entirely in the significance of the names given to the children. The false description of Gomer as a prostitute is to be attributed to the work of the redactor of cc.1–3, who mistakenly saw behind the words of Yahweh's reproaches of Israel in 2.4ff. reminiscences of Hosea's reproach of his wife. C.3 is an account of a prophetic symbolic action; there is no question of marriage here, and the woman is not Gomer.

M.A.K.

DE SAUSSURE, J.: *Le Cantique de l'Église*. 1957. Pp. 73. (Éditions Labor et Fides, Genève. Price: Sw.Fr. 3.65).

In this short devotional study of *The Song of Songs* the author arranges his material successively around the three figures of the Shulammite as representing 'The Distress and Beauty of the Church', of Solomon as representing 'The Tempters of the Church', and of the Beloved as representing 'The Bridegroom of the Church'. An introductory chapter considers literal, allegorical, and 'significant' interpretation. The list of Scripture references in the last three pages is related in turn to this chapter and to the three already mentioned.

                                                                    E.T.R.

TE STROETE, G.: *Exodus uit de grondtekst vertaald en uitgelegd.* (De Boeken van het Oude Testament, Deel I, Boek II). 1966. Pp. 248. (Romen & Zonen, Roermond en Maaseik. Price: Fl. 15.50).

Like the other contributions to this excellent series, the volume on Exodus contains an introduction, a new translation into Dutch, exegetical commentary and an appendix indicating emendations adopted in the text. In the present volume this appendix is brief; there are some twenty-seven minor emendations, most of which follow the apparatus of BHK[3]. The introduction and commentary take full account of recent work on Exodus; accordingly, while the work is not itself an original contribution to scholarship (and indeed is not designed as such), it is a most useful handbook for the student. The introduction includes a careful examination of von Rad's thesis that the Hexateuch is in essence an elaboration of the cultic credo of Deut. xxvi and that the Sinai tradition was independent of the Exodus-Settlement tradition until the Yahwist brought them together; various arguments are adduced to show that there was from the first a closer connexion between the two traditions than von Rad allows, one of these arguments being based on the dominant part played by Moses in both traditions. Another section of the introduction presents a helpful summary of the place of the Exodus pattern in later Israelite and Christian tradition.   F.F.B.

TYCIAK, J.: *Prophetische Profile.* (Die Welt der Bibel, 19). 1965. Pp. 112. (Patmos-Verlag, Düsseldorf. Price: DM. 5.80).

Eleven of the twelve minor prophets are here presented (the exception being Haggai), each under a title aimed to bring out a dominant theme; thus Joel is the prophet of the spirit; Nahum of the triumph of God. An unexpected feature is the prominence given to Obadiah, who is treated in the first and one of the longest chapters, as Apocalyptist and Prophet. Any introductory treatment of this kind is bound to be selective, but this kind of approach is more satisfactory for the very short books than for a prophet like Hosea.   R.J.C.

VELLAS, B. M.: *Daniel. Eisagōgē — Metaphrasis ek tou Ebraïkou kai Aramaïkou — Keimenon Theodotiōnos — Ermēneia.* (Ermēneia Palaias Diathekes 7). 1966. Pp. 182. (Athens).

In a brief introduction Professor Vellas discusses (1) the traditions about Daniel, (2) the structure and composition of the book, (3) date of composition and authorship, (4) text and versions, (5) the teaching and character of the book. The several sections of the commentary proper contain (1) a translation of the Hebrew and Aramaic text, (2) the version of Theodotion, (3) exegesis. There is a useful, up-to-date bibliography; and account is taken throughout of the many-sided debate about the problems raised by the book. Vellas maintains that neither the difference in character between the two parts of Daniel nor the bilingual character of the book provide adequate arguments against its unity. He holds that the material in i–vi is pre-Maccabaean, and may well go back to the Persian and Babylonian periods; and while he admits that there is a change of emphasis and a sharper sense of crisis in vii–xii, he does not admit the need to bring the date of this material down to the time of the Antiochian persecution (citing Josephus, Ant. xi. 337 in support of his view), though he admits the presence in it of late additions, notably xi. The reviewer is not convinced that Professor Vellas has presented a coherent and cogent case against those from whom he differs; but the commentary is to be welcomed because of its freshness and independence, and not least because of its irenic spirit. G.W.A.

VISCHER, W.: *Le Prophète Habaquq*. Traduction française d'Albert Cavin. 1959. Pp. 61. (Éditions Labor et Fides, Genève. Price: Sw. Fr. 3.80).

A brief postscript informs the reader that this interpretation of Habakkuk was delivered in 1957 to pastors and elders of the Reformed Church of Yugoslavia. After a discussion of the significance of the prophet's name his message is expounded uncritically on the basis of all three chapters of the book. E.T.R.

VISCHER, W.: *Valeur de l'Ancien Testament*. Commentaire des livres de Job, Esther, l'Ecclésiaste, le second Esaie, précédés d'une introduction. 1965. Pp. 189. (Éditions Labor et Fides, Genève).

This is a finely produced and attractive paper-back with on its cover a good reproduction of a photograph of Michelangelo's Isaiah from the Sistine Chapel. The introductory essay is entitled 'La Signification de l'Ancien Testament pour la Vie Chrétienne', and provides a christological interpretation of the Old Testament which is pursued further in the sections on the four books studied. The commentary is, as might be expected in a book of this size, far from complete, but many passages from the books are used to support the argument. There is no index and no formal bibliography.

It may well be noted that, except as regards the assembling of the matter in a single volume, this is by no means a new work. The introduction was in the first place a conference given to what is styled a 'Congrès calviniste' in Edinburgh in 1938; the section on Job is a revised edition of some addresses given in Germany in 1931 and 1932; Esther was the subject of a conference in Germany in 1933 and 1934; Ecclesiastes was read in Italian to a Waldensian congress in Rome in 1953; and Isaiah supplied the matter for a course delivered to the Theologische Arbeitsgemeinschaft of Bethel, near Bielefeld, in 1929. All the component parts have already been in print in one of three languages (English, Italian or German). Ecclesiastes was written in French by the author himself; the remaining parts are the work of translators. J.M.T.B.

WEISER, A.: *Das Buch Jeremia.* (Das Alte Testament Deutsch, 20/21). 5th ed. 1966. Pp. xliv + 452. (Vandenhoeck und Ruprecht, Göttingen. Price: DM. 18.00).

The fifth edition of this valuable commentary (see *Book List* 1953, p. 41; 1955, p. 40) has been brought up to date with account taken of recent work, and its use facilitated by the addition of a subject index.   P.R.A.

WEISER, A.: *Die Psalmen.* (Das Alte Testament Deutsch, 14/15). 7th revised ed. 1966. Pp. 612. (Vandenhoeck und Ruprecht, Göttingen. Price: DM. 22.50).

The first edition of this valuable commentary appeared in 1950 (see *B.L.* 1951, p. 44, *Eleven Years*, p. 339). It has since gone through several editions (see *B.L.* 1956, p. 34, *Eleven Years*, p. 741) and an English translation appeared in 1962 made from the 5th edition (see *B.L.* 1963, p. 31). This latest edition has again been revised, and the useful additions have been made of indexes of biblical references and subjects.   P.R.A.

WESTERMANN, C.: *Das Buch Jesaja: Kap. 40–66, übersetzt und erklärt.* (Das Alte Testament Deutsch, 19). 1966. Pp. 342. (Vandenhoeck & Ruprecht, Göttingen. Price: paper, DM. 14.00; cloth, DM. 17.00).

In this book chs. 40–55 and 56–66 are treated separately by Westermann. He considers the whole of chs. 40–55 in its essentials to come from Deutero–Isaiah, the shorter pieces in chs. 40–45 being preserved in oral tradition, larger passages in written documents. Of the four Servant passages, he attributes the first three to Deutero–Isaiah.

Westermann regards Trito–Isaiah as a disciple of Deutero–Isaiah, who had at least a share in the preservation and editing of the records of the teachings of his master and in bringing them in due course to Judah. He exercised his ministry in Judah *c.* 530 B.C., trying to revive the faith of a small group of disappointed Jewish repatriates from Babylon. To each of the sections, 40–55 and 56–66, later additions were made, mostly to the latter.

The introduction to each section gives a discerning statement of the message of the prophet, pin-pointing his distinctive emphases, his debt to pre-exilic prophets, and the relevance of his message for the time in which he functioned. In addition, the literary affinities in the rest of the Old Testament of various passages in chs. 40–66 are discussed. In this commentary philological notes are given succinctly, and the contribution of each passage to the message of the prophet is carefully expounded. It can be said without hesitation that this volume constitutes an excellent addition to the series of commentaries in which it now takes its place.   J.M.

WILDBERGER, H.: *Jesaja.* (Biblischer Kommentar, Altes Testament, X, Lieferung 2). 1966. Pp. 81–160. (Verlag der Buchhandlung des Erziehungsvereins, Neukirchen-Vluyn. Price: 12s. 6d. approx.).

The second fascicle (for the first see the *Book List* 1966, p. 30) of this very detailed commentary on Isaiah deals with the text from ii. 1 to iv. 6. It may be noted that ii. 6–22 is thought to be, not a single poem with a recurring refrain, but a collection of fragments, and that the clapping of hands in ii. 6 is explained as a rite to ward off demonic powers. The high standard that Professor Wildberger set himself in the first fascicle is here successfully maintained.   J.A.E.

ZENKER, S.: *Prophetengebetbuch.* 1965. Pp. 212. (Kösel-Verlag, München. Price: DM. 7.80).

This little book is aimed at helping Roman Catholics in intelligent Bible reading. It consists of extracts mainly from the latter prophets, divided thematically into three main sections and seven sub-sections. In the last part, on the prophetic expectation of a new covenant, a number of New Testament extracts are set out as fulfilments of the prophetic promise. There are appended a small number of explanatory notes and a brief expository epilogue.   R.J.C.

LITERARY CRITICISM AND INTRODUCTION

(including History of Interpretation, Canon, and Special Studies)

BARTH, C. F.: Introduction to the Psalms, trans. by R. A. Wilson. 1966. Pp. 87. (Blackwell, Oxford. Price: 12s. 6d.).

This volume is translated from *Einführung in die Psalmen,* published in 1961 by Neukirchener Verlag. (See *Book List* 1962, p. 36). It is for the general reader rather than for the specialist, but is useful for the student as a good and trustworthy account of the modern attitude to the Psalms. The emphasis is on Gunkel's classification, and the 'enthronement' theories are treated as less important for the New Year Feast than the idea of the Covenant.   N.H.S.

EISSFELDT, O. (ed. by): *Franz Delitzsch und Wolf Graf Baudissin. Dokumente über die Anfänge ihrer Freundschaft aus dem Erlanger Wintersemester 1866/67.* (Sitzungsberichte der Sächsischen Akademie der Wissenschaften zu Leipzig. Phil.-hist. Klasse. Band 112, Heft 2). 1966. Pp. 28 + 21 Plates. (Akademie-Verlag, Berlin. Price: MDN. 4.80).

The editor of this monograph published in *Das Evangelische Deutschland* 7 (1930), pp. 444–6 = *Kl. Schr.* I (1962), pp. 234–8 a short note on the relationship between these two great scholars, with reference to the exercise book here reproduced and described. This reveals the teacher and pupil at work, engaged in Hebrew compositions which are in part a correspondence. A supplementary document shows Delitzsch planning the further studies of the younger man whom he wished to see develop into a scholar. We are given an interesting sidelight on methods of teaching Hebrew and on the scholarship of the nineteenth century, more leisurely days than ours.   P.R.A.

EISSFELDT, O.: *Die Komposition der Sinai-Erzählung Exodus 19–34.* (Sitzungsberichte der Sächsischen Akademie der Wissenschaften zu Leipzig, Phil.-hist. Klasse. Band 113, Heft 1). Pp. 31. 1966. (Akademie-Verlag, Berlin. Price: MDN. 2.30).

This monograph offers a renewed analysis of the material of this section of the Pentateuchal narrative. After the distinguishing of later additions, the four narrative strands P, E, J and L are set out — the whole text being given except for P — and the relationship to the Deuteronomic tradition is discussed. Attention is drawn to an examination of the problems of the decalogues by Goethe — an interesting comment on his qualities as a polymath and a contrast with the specialization of our own times. Professor Eissfeldt in his eightieth year offers yet another careful and detailed contribution to this most involved realm of Old Testament literary criticism.

P.R.A.

HAMMERSHAIMB, E.: *Some Aspects of Old Testament Prophecy from Isaiah to Malachi.* (Teologiske Skrifter; Série de Théologie, 4). 1966. Pp. 116. (Rosenkilde og Bagger, Copenhagen. D.Kr. 30).

This book contains five articles, four of which have been already published; 'The Immanuel Sign' in *Studia Theologica* (1949), pp. 124–142; 'Some Leading Ideas in the Book of Micah' in *Studia Theologica* (1961), pp. 11–34; 'Ezekiel's View of the Monarchy' in the Festskrift for Johannes Pedersen (*Studia Orientalia Johanni Pedersen dicata*, Copenhagen 1953), pp. 130–140; and 'On the Ethics of the Prophets' in S.V.T. VII (Oxford Congress, 1959); the fifth article, 'The Change in Prophecy during the Exile' has not appeared in print before.

This hitherto unprinted article begins with a survey of the pre-exilic prophets, in order that contrasts between them and later prophets may be indicated. According to Hammershaimb, these pre-exilic prophets addressed a society which represented a development of the tribe and its leaders, and they often prophesied national punishment for religious unfaithfulness and social vices. They were not in close association with the cult, but in varying degrees were bearers of tradition.

After the exile the situation in Judah was very different from what it had been before. Emphasis was now on the rebuilding of the temple, and that was advocated by prophet not less than by priest. Those parts of Zechariah 1–8 which make demands for social righteousness and justice in the same way as the pre-exilic prophets, Hammershaimb regards as intrusive pieces of moralizing. The doctrine of the remnant now gave occasion for a new interpretation. Prophets were addressing a situation in which sacral kingship vanished and national independence neither existed nor was hoped for. The individual thus came to a position of greater prominence, and a dogmatic view of history developed.

It is very helpful to have these five articles of Hammershaimb's brought within this one volume.

J.M.

HAURET, C.: *Initiation à l'Écriture Sainte.* 1966. Pp. 218 + 3 maps. (Beauchesne, Paris. Price: Fr. 9.90).

This is a short but brilliantly written and masterly introduction to the literature of the Bible addressed to educated Frenchmen by the Dean of the Faculty of Catholic Theology of the University of Strasbourg. The author traces the growth of the books of the Bible as a process of the *aggiornamento* of a living tradition, and deftly sketches the character of the Biblical salvation history, the emphasis throughout being on the writings of the O.T. The text is followed by a chronological table and a table of synchronisms.

L.A.P.

HERMANN, R.: *Gotteswort und Menschenwort in der Bibel.* (Eine Untersuchung zu theologischen Grundfragen der Hermeneutik). 1956.
Pp. 70. (Evangelische Verlagsanstalt, Berlin. Price: MDN. 2.00).

Biblical interpretation must always reckon with the fact that the Bible
is God's Word mediated through the lips and pens of men and it is
neither possible nor right to distinguish the boundaries. The Bible
is that which constantly brings to mind the Word of God. Exegesis
requires the self-commitment of the interpreter and must be controlled by an understanding of God who has given himself personally
in history until his self-offering in Christ.   A.S.H.

KAPELRUD, A. S.: *Profetene i det gamle Israel og Juda.* 1966. Pp. 138.
(Universitetsforlaget, Oslo. Price: N.Kr. 19.80).

In a number of earlier publications Professor Kapelrud has demonstrated his skill in popular presentation. This is yet another successful
venture in the same style, an exposition of Old Testament prophecy
written to meet the needs of the student and the general reader. After
brief discussions of seers and *nebi'im*, and of the 9th century prophets,
the canonical prophets are dealt with in chronological sequence. A
concluding chapter is devoted to the book of Daniel. The emphasis
is on the religious teaching of the prophets; but space is found for
descriptions of the successive historical situations. At some points
(e.g. the section on Joel) the author presents hypotheses for which he
has argued in his more technical works; but he gives fair notice of
what he is doing. This is an excellent introduction in which the
reader may hear 'the sound of running history'.   G.W.A.

KAPELRUD, A. S.: *Forelesninger over Exodus* 19–20. *Høstsemestret* 1963.
1966. Pp. 102 (mimeographed typescript). (Universitetsforlaget,
Oslo. Price: N.Kr. 12.00).

As the title indicates, this publication contains lectures on Exod. xix,
xx, delivered (presumably at the University of Oslo) during the
autumn of 1963. The material is not arranged in the form of separate
lectures, but consists simply of introduction and commentary. In
the introduction the author discusses the place of Exodus in the
Pentateuch and of these chapters in Exodus, surveys general critical
questions, and gives a discerning account of modern contributions
to the study of the form and *Sitz im Leben* of the laws. Like Beyerlin,
he does not accept the theory of an original sharp distinction between
the Exodus and Sinai traditions, and, following both Beyerlin and
Mowinckel, regards Kadesh as the *locus* of the covenant. The bulk
of the book consists of a running commentary on the text, mainly
exegetical in character, in which more detailed consideration is given
to the problems raised by these chapters, and particularly to the form
and content of the Decalogue. The entire study is lucid, readable,
fair in the presentation of the views of other scholars, and discerning
and balanced in judgement.   G.W.A.

KAYATZ, C.: *Studien zu Proverbien 1–9. Eine form- und motivgeschichtliche Untersuchung unter Einbeziehung ägyptischen Vergleichsmaterials.* (Wissenschaftliche Monographien zum alten und neuen Testament, 22). 1966. Pp. 147. (Neukirchener Verlag des Erziehungsvereins, Neukirchen-Vluyn. Price: paper, DM. 18.80; cloth, DM. 21.80).

This study, which had its origin in a dissertation submitted to the Evangelisch-Theologischen Fakultät at Heidelberg, consists of a careful comparison of Proverbs 1–9 with similar Egyptian material. After a survey of the relevant Egyptian writings the authoress gives an analysis of the form-types and of the themes in her Hebrew and Egyptian sources, and her general conclusion is that there is evidence for a connection between the two literatures, with the Egyptian supplying both forms and motifs for the Hebrew. Perhaps most interesting is the discussion of the origin of the Hebrew Wisdom in its various aspects in the Egyptian Maat. Unfortunately, Dr. Kayatz does not seem to have had access to R. N. Whybray's *Wisdom in Proverbs* (1965), which must be read along with the book under review.

W.D.McH.

LAGRANGE, M.-J.: *La Méthode Historique: La critique biblique et l'Église.* (Foi Vivante 31). 1966. Pp. 191. (Les Éditions du Cerf, Paris).

This book was originally published in 1903, and at that time could hardly do other than arouse controversy. The passage of time, and in particular the decree of Vatican II on Revelation has demonstrated the worth of the insights expressed in these pages. The chapter headings will indicate the course of the discussion. I. Critical Exegesis and the Church's Dogma. II. The Evolution of Dogma, especially in the Old Testament. III. The Concept of Revelation according to the biblical facts. IV. The Historical Method, even in matters of knowledge. V. The historical character of the civil legislation of the Hebrews. VI. The primitive history. An introduction has been provided by R. de Vaux, which briefly states the present position of Old Testament scholarship, and relates it to various official statements of the Church.

A.S.H.

LESCOW, T.: *Micha 6, 6–8. Studien zu Sprache, Form und Auslegung.* (Arbeiten zur Theologie, Reihe I, Heft 25). 1966. Pp. 72. (Calwer Verlag, Stuttgart. Price: DM. 7.80).

In this detailed study of Micah vi. 6–8 Lescow pays particular attention to the form of this prophecy, and denies that it is directly derived from the cultic entrance liturgies. He regards Mic. vi. 1–5 as a broken fragment of a lawsuit oracle, and sees in vv. 6–8 a prophetic transformation of the old cultic institution of inquiring of God through the sacred oracle. The cultic form, however, has been completely detached from its original setting, and now makes use of non-cultic language to affirm the prophetic demand for righteousness over against the assurances of the cult. No consideration is given to questions of date and authorship, but a concluding chapter examines Luther's translation of the verses.

R.E.C.

MICHAELI, F.: *39 livres en un seul.* 1962. Pp. 182. (Éditions Labor et Fides, Genève. Price: Sw.Fr. 7.50).

This is a simple, straightforward introduction to the books of the Old Testament. The author has decided to deal with the books in the order in which they occur in the Greek Bible (but omitting the books of the Apocrypha). Their content is analysed, and usually there is a brief statement and discussion of the critical problem which is peculiar to each book. It also discusses the message of the books, and whenever possible relates this to the modern situation. The book ends with a short chapter on the Apocrypha. The bibliography which is given in the Introduction and at the end of each chapter is limited, and is confined to French authors.   E.R.R.

MOWINCKEL, S.: *Studien zu dem Buche Ezra-Nehemia, III: Die Ezra-geschichte und das Gesetz Moses.* (Skrifter utgitt av Det Norske Videnskaps-Akademi i Oslo. II. Hist.-Filos. Klasse. Ny Serie, No. 7). 1965. Pp. 186. (Oslo University Press. Price: 19s. approx.).

The first two parts of this important study were reviewed in the *Book List* 1965, pp. 37f. It is impossible here to do more than indicate some of the positions Mowinckel adopts in this third part, after close examination in the light of the arguments advanced by many other scholars. He rejects the view that Neh. 8 originally followed Ezr. 8 in favour of the view that it followed Ezr. 10. He rejects the view that the Chronicler was the author of the Ezra story — and consequently Albright's view that Ezra was the Chronicler. He carefully analyses the Ezra story and considers its literary characteristics and rejects the fiasco hypothesis of Ezra's mission. The alternation between the first person singular and the third person he holds to be original and offers some other examples of this. He argues that the Chronicler supplemented but did not rewrite his sources. He rejects the view that Ezra was the author of the Ezra story or that it was an official report of his mission, but holds that it was written by a younger contemporary. On the question of the date of Ezra, he maintains that his work fell after Nehemiah's, but rejects the view that places it late in the reign of Artaxerxes I in favour of the view that it lay in the reign of Artaxerxes II. He believes that the author of the Ezra story knew the account of the work of Nehemiah. He accepts the substantial genuineness of the Rescript in Ezr. 7, and holds that Ezra's law-book included Deuteronomy, the Holiness Code and the Priestly Code. For the study of all of these questions Mowinckel's work will long be indispensable.   H.H.R.

RABINOWITZ, I.: *Towards a Valid Theory of Biblical Hebrew Literature.* (Reprinted from *The Classical Tradition: Literary and Historical Studies in Honor of Harry Caplan*). 1966. Pp. 315–328. (Cornell University Press, Ithaca, New York).

The main purpose of this article is to show that 'the editors, writers and readers of Ancient Israel held a broader concept than modern readers of the properties and potentialities of *words*'. The author's views are not entirely original and he himself quotes a number of recent authorities in the field of O.T. scholarship, foremost amongst them J. Lindblom, who have contributed to this branch of study. Yet there are a number of relevant observations, systematically classified, which throw new light on the meaning of *dabhar* in biblical Hebrew. It is shown to be effective not only as a means of communication, but of action and of the power to determine reality now and at a given time in the future. Sometimes words are conceived as quasi-concrete objects which can be eaten and do harm or good, as for instance in *Jeremiah* xv, 16; xxiii, 15; or *Ezekiel* ii, 8; iii, 3. A prophet can even slay by the word of his mouth (*Hosea* vi, 5). The wide range of the meanings of *dabhar* is not restricted to the writings of the prophets, but can also be found in the Pentateuch, the historical books of the O.T., in Wisdom, Apocryphal, Targumic and N.T. literature. To express it differently, man shares with God the ability to create or destroy by the Word. On a number of occasions prophetic *debharim* are addressed to people, often in the second person, who could obviously neither hear nor read them. Ezekiel, for instance, is in Babylonia when asked to address himself to Pharoah, then far away in Egypt (xxix, 1–3). In such cases a personal communication transcends into a message whose addressee is the world. The article, though brief, is definitely thought-provoking and will help many a reader to understand the O.T. on its own terms.

S.S.

RICHTER, W.: *Recht und Ethos. Versuch einer Ortung des weisheitlichen Mahnspruches.* (Studien zum Alten und Neuen Testament XV). 1966. Pp. 217. (Kösel Verlag, München. Price: DM. 38.00).

A thoroughgoing and most welcome examination of the sapiential Admonitory Proverb is undertaken in this *Habilitationsschrift*. Proverbs xxii. 17–xxiv. 22 and *The Instruction of Amen-em-ope* are first of all in this connection compared from the standpoint of literary and form criticism. The investigation is then in the second chapter continued through the O.T. so as to take in the remaining sections of Proverbs, other Wisdom writing, the Narratives, the Psalms, the Prophets, and the Law collections. In the third and fourth chapters detailed consideration is given to the relation of the Admonitory Proverb to the Apodictic Law and to the Prohibition. This includes analyses of the uses of the negatives *'al* with the jussive (*Der Vetitiv*) and *lō'* with the imperfect (*Der Prohibitiv*), and in this respect a further examination of the relevant literature. A final chapter is devoted in its concluding part to the light which the Admonitory Proverb thus studied sheds upon the contribution of the Wisdom School as a formative influence in the life and thought of ancient Israel. It is however with the basic ethical tendency of this type of proverb rather than with its actual form that the writer of this monograph is most concerned. He maintains that the School selected and adapted Wisdom material consonant with its practical needs in the training of the young for public service, developing an *Ethos* of its own. This may have been a contributory factor in the composition of the Book of the Covenant, Deuteronomy, and the Code of Holiness, and its impress is seen in the consciousness within the O.T. of a distinction between Law and *Ethos*.

E.T.R.

RIETZSCHEL, C.: *Das Problem der Urrolle. Ein Beitrag zur Redaktions-geschichte des Jeremiabuches.* 1966. Pp. 142. (Gütersloher Verlagshaus Gerd Mohn, Gütersloh. Price: DM. 12.80).

Rietzschel offers a new thesis regarding the composition of the book of Jeremiah. He accepts the basic principles of classification of the literary material on the grounds of form and style as developed by Duhm, Mowinckel and Rudolph, but denies that these can provide a sufficient indication of the way in which the book was composed. In particular he denies that we can assume that poetic and prose material was handed on separately, although he regards the Deutero-nomic prose material as undoubtedly of later origin. Following E. Janssen he links this material with the homiletical speeches in the Deuteronomistic Historical Work.

Rietzschel then offers a new theory regarding the primary collections from which the present book has been compiled. He distinguishes four main blocks of tradition: (1) chs. i-xxiv; (2) chs. xxvi-xxxv; (3) chs. xxxvi-xliv; (4) chs. xxv, xlvi-li. The suggestion is then made that Baruch's roll is to be found in chs. i-vi (not i-xvi as is wrongly stated on the dust-jacket), and that some of this material is to be dated not long before 605 B.C. This is an interesting and valuable thesis which rightly deserves a place alongside earlier attempts to solve the problems of the composition of the book of Jeremiah.

R.E.C.

SABOURIN, L.: *Un Classement Littéraire des Psaumes.* 1964. Pp. 38. (Desclée de Brouwer, Bruges. Price: Fr.B. 35.00 or N.F. 3.50).

This slight study, reprinted from *Sciences Ecclésiastiques* 16 (1964), pp. 23–58, is devoted to a form-critical classification of the psalms. The author does not profess to add anything new on this subject, but rather to provide a semi-popular survey for the use of French-speaking students.

M.A.K.

SCHMIDT, W. H.: *Königtum Gottes in Ugarit und Israel: Zur Herkunft der Königsprädikation Jahwes.* (B.Z.A.W. 80). 2nd ed. 1966. Pp. 106. (Verlag Alfred Töpelmann, Berlin. Price: DM. 28.00).

The first edition of this book was reviewed in *Book List* 1962, p. 55, and it is a measure of its success and usefulness that a second edition has been called for. The author has been able to revise the material taking account of new material and subsequent discussion. But it is odd that A. R. Johnson's *Sacral Kingship* does not appear in the bibliography.

P.R.A.

SEEBASS, H.: *Der Erzvater Israel und die Einführung der Jahweverehrung in Kanaan.* (Beihefte zur Zeitschrift für die alttestamentliche Wissen-schaft, 98). 1966. Pp. x + 112. (Verlag Alfred Töpelmann, Berlin. Price: DM. 30.00).

This study is divided into two parts. In the first Seebass examines the patriarchal traditions which concern Shechem and Bethel, and concludes that the particular ancestor of the Shechem tradition was

Israel. Jacob belonged more directly to Bethel, but the two traditions were united so that the two patriarchs became identified with each other, and the cult of Bethel was legitimized by the El-Elohe-Israel of Shechem. Seebass then re-examines the evidence for the nature of the patriarchal religion, and concludes that this originally took the form of the worship of anonymous deities known as 'the God of My Father', who were subsequently identified with the El deities of Shechem, Bethel and Beersheba. The second part deals with the introduction of Yahweh worship in Israel, and is centred upon the tradition of Shechem. Yahweh was originally the God of Sinai, and was associated with Moses, the Exodus, and the conclusion of a covenant there. Seebass argues that Joshua xxiv derives from the event in which the older El-Elohe-Israel of Shechem was replaced by Yahweh who thus became the God of Israel.

There is much that is interesting in this work, and not a little that is provocative, although the evidence for a southern tradition of Yahwism at Hebron under the Calebites is too hastily dismissed, and too much confidence is placed in the minutiae of literary criticism. The tendency is to build up a cumulative series of hypotheses. However it well repays careful study.

R.E.C.

SELLIN, E. and FOHRER, G.: *Einleitung in das Alte Testament*. 10th edition. 1965. Pp. 576. (Quelle & Meyer, Heidelberg. Price: DM. 36.00).

The first predecessor of this book was written by Sellin and published in 1910. The tenth edition, by Professor Fohrer, is more than a revision of the ninth (which was prepared by Professor Rost): it is considerably longer and is virtually a new work. It is characterized by massive learning and by extensive bibliographical references (though it is not as full as Eissfeldt's *Einleitung*), and yet it is never a mere catalogue of different opinions but presents the author's own point of view, which not infrequently disagrees with current fashions in scholarship. This substantial work is a most valuable addition to the number of introductions to the Old Testament. There are indexes of references to the Bible and other ancient texts and of subjects, but not of modern authors' names.

J.A.E.

THIELE, E. R.: *The Mysterious Numbers of the Hebrew Kings*. A Reconstruction of the Chronology of the Kingdoms of Israel and Judah. 2nd ed. 1966. Pp. xxiv + 232. (The Paternoster Press, Devon. Price: 30s.).

The first edition of this book was published in 1951 (see *Book List* 1952, p. 45; *Eleven Years*, p. 416): in this new edition the author indicates that no major change has been made in his approach, though new evidence enables precise fixing of some dates earlier uncertain. The argument has been elaborated especially in chapters 6 and 9.

P.R.A.

DE VAUX, R.: *Jerusalem and the Prophets*. The Goldenson Lecture, 1965. 1966. Pp. 26. (The Hebrew Union College Press, Cincinnati. Price: 60 cents).

This lecture surveys the place of Jerusalem in the religious tradition, tracing the attitude of the prophets to it as a holy place. It makes illuminating comments, of necessity briefly, on many points of interest — the relation to Shiloh, the ark, the tradition of inviolability especially in relation to Isaiah. There is a wealth of material, characteristically skilfully handled by Père de Vaux, in this valuable short study.   P.R.A.

VOGT, H. C. M.: *Studie zur Nachexilischen Gemeinde in Esra-Nehemia.* 1966. Pp. xix + 162. (Dietrich-Coelde-Verlag, Werl. Price: DM. 32).

In this interesting book the author examines the books of Ezra and Nehemiah for their picture of the post-exilic community. First of all he surveys some of the literature which deals with this subject, and then discusses the sources, and the questions of authorship and date. The thesis of the book is presented in three main chapters, and the method adopted is to conduct a lexical-historical examination of the various terms which refer to the returned community. Terms like captivity, remnant, Israel, Judah, people, nations, people of the land *etc.* are examined in their context in Ezra-Nehemiah. The three chapters deal with (*a*) the community as a whole, (*b*) groups within the community, and (*c*) the enemies of the community. Scholars who are interested in the post-exilic period, while they may not fully agree with all the suggestions made, yet will welcome this approach, and will find in it a great deal of useful material for their study.

E.R.R.

WATTS, J. D. W.: *Studying the Book of Amos.* 1966. Pp. 93. (Broadman Press, Nashville, Tennessee. Price: $1.50).

This book was planned as a study guide for the general reader. A brief introduction outlines the historical background of 8th century Israel, and the social and political situation in which Amos exercised his ministry. The major part of the book is devoted to the visions of Amos (including 9.1–6). These experiences, it is claimed, occasioned turning-points in the prophet's ministry. Each communicated new insights, and may have been quoted by the prophet to authenticate the message which he subsequently gave. Correlatively, the author quotes certain passages within chs. 1–6 as associated with each of the visions. Whether this correlation was made in his teaching by Amos himself or not, cannot be determined; but its use in this book will help the general reader to understand the teaching of the prophet more coherently. The book as a whole is written in a way to serve its professed purpose admirably.   J.M.

WEISER, A.: *Einleitung in das Alte Testament.* 6th ed., revised. 1966. Pp. 440. (Vandenhoeck and Ruprecht, Göttingen. Price: DM. 22.00).

The revision since the issue of the fifth edition (see *Book List* 1964, p. 53) consists of slight modifications of the text here and there and the bringing of the bibliographies up to date by the inclusion of work which has recently appeared. Altogether the volume is extended by nineteen pages. Its wide usefulness is proved by the call for so many successive editions.   H.H.R.

*Wood, J.: *Job and the Human Situation*. 1966. Pp. 158. (Geoffrey Bles, London. Price: 15s.).

Mature study and reflection have gone into the writing of this book. Its author, feeling that the book of Job has for too long remained almost entirely the preserve of the classroom, here seeks in good contemporary idiom to make it come alive to the ordinary man. In the arrangement of his chapters he follows the normal divisions of the book of Job, and often with fine insight shows that the questions raised are questions of vital concern in the human situation. The Elihu speeches (Job xxxii-xxxvii) are treated as of greater significance than is generally held, and c. xxviii is dealt with separately in one of two appendices, the second of which comprises an extended note on c. xix. 25–27 where it is argued that the *gō'ēl* envisaged may well be human. For the kind of reader intended, however, the rendering, apparently without explanation, of Satan for *hassāṭān* is open to misunderstanding.

                                                                    E.T.R.

LAW, RELIGION AND THEOLOGY

Barth, K.: *Hiob*. Edited by H. Gollwitzer. (Biblische Studien 49). 1966. Pp. 114. (Neukirchener Verlag des Erziehungsvereins, Neu-kirchen-Vluyn. Price: DM. 6.20).

In gratitude to Karl Barth on the occasion of his eightieth birthday the editor of this volume has brought together from the *Kirchliche Dogmatik* IV. 3, but under his own headings, three excerpts (pp. 444–448, 459–470, and 486–499) and an appendix (pp. 522–531) which deal with Barth's examination of the book of Job in relation to the doctrine of reconciliation. An introduction outlines the structure of Barth's exposition and there are short introductory notes also to the second and third sections as well as to the appendix.

                                                                    E.T.R.

Eichrodt, W.: *Theology of the Old Testament*. Vol. II, trans. by J. A. Baker. 1967. Pp. 573. (S.C.M. Press, London. Price: £2 15s.).

The publication of the second volume of the English translation of Eichrodt's important *Theology of the Old Testament*, providing, as it does, for those who do not read German the opportunity to compare at last Eichrodt's complete presentation of the Old Testament material with the very different, and equally important, presentation of von Rad, is a very welcome event indeed. The translation of the second volume, which contains parts 2 and 3 of the work, 'God and the World' and 'God and Man', has been made from the fifth German edition of 1964 (cf. the review of the fourth edition in *Book List* 1962, p. 44) and is of the same high standard as that of the first volume (see *Book List* 1962, pp. 43 f).

                                                                    M.A.K.

Ellison, H. L.: *Men Spake From God. Studies in the Hebrew Prophets*. 1966. Pp. 160. (Paternoster Press, Exeter. Price: 5s.).

This is a paperback edition of a work first published in 1952 (see *Book List* 1952, p. 53; *Eleven Years*, p. 424); it represents a careful revision 'in which as many necessary changes as were consistent with the publisher's needs have been made'. It might have been advisable to replace the page of bibliography near the end by a completely new one. The work remains a helpful introduction to the prophets for the non-specialist Bible student; its standpoint is conservative, but not rigidly so (e.g. Zech. ix-xi, xii-xiv and Malachi are recognized to be distinct and anonymous collections appended to the *Nebi'im*). For good measure the author gives us chapters on Daniel and Lamentations.

F.F.B.

GERSTENBERGER, E.: *Wesen und Herkunft des 'Apodiktischen Rechts'*. (Wissenschaftliche Monographien zum Alten und Neuen Testament, 20). 1965. Pp. VIII + 162. (Neukirchener Verlag des Erziehungsvereins, Neukirchen-Vluyn. Price: paper, DM. 15.80; cloth, DM. 18.80).

In this book the author maintains that the characteristics of the Old Testament apodictic laws, as set out by Alt, are not found consistently and comprehensively in these laws. In addition, many of the apodictic laws of participial or relative clause type are related to others of the casuistic type. Again, he finds that the authoritative quality attributed to apodictic laws is not peculiar to them, but is found expressed also in the apodosis of casuistic laws. These and other observations provide the starting point of this study. It deals not only with the form of apodictic laws but with the questions of their source and their authority. The former question gives occasion for a search for similar types in Near Eastern legal codes; the latter is considered in the relation to the covenant and the cult in Israel. The matter of the connection between the apodictic laws and the warnings and admonitions of O.T. wisdom literature is also raised. The book finishes with some relevant and interesting comments on the theological extension of the work of the Old Testament exegete, substantially on the basis that covenant which expresses itself in demand also implies and offers aid. This is a book which deserves close attention.

J.M.

GRELOT, P.: *Bible et Théologie* (Le Mystère Chrétien: Théologie Dogmatique). 1965. Pp. xvi + 207. (Desclée, Tournai. Price: B.Fr. 120).

The author explains in an *avertissement* that this is in the nature of an abridgement of two earlier works, one of these being entitled *Sens chrétien de l'Ancien Testament* (1962), and the other *La Bible, Parole de Dieu* (1965, noticed in the *Book List* 1966, p. 36). The first part of the present work has as title 'L'Ancien Alliance' (pp. 1–70 and is a treatise *De priore Testamento* of the sort that, centuries ago, figured as part of the course of dogmatic theology. In its present form it is not only shorter than the 1962 volume; it is also intended to be more elementary in treatment with a reduced bibliography that normally mentions only works in Latin and French. The author tells us that he has with some repugnance presented the matter in the form of theses (of which there are five in all for this Old Testament section). The work is not intended as controversial, and the theses do no more than clarify and condense the information given. The titles of the theses are the place of the Old Testament in the scheme of salvation; the presence of Christ in the Old Testament; laws and

institutions; the history of God's people; and the prophetic announcement of the New Testament.

Like all Grelot's works this is clear and methodical, and as in the
earlier books, is a vast improvement on the manuals published in
the first decades of this century.   J.M.T.B.

HAAG, H.: *Biblische Schöpfungslehre und kirchliche Erbsündenlehre.*
(Stuttgarter Bibel-Studien, 10). 1966. Pp. 76. (Verlag Katholisches
Bibelwerk, Stuttgart. Price: DM. 4.80).

This lucid volume is divided into three parts. The first part (pp. 13–
40) discusses the dogmatic and catechetical teaching of the Roman
Church concerning original sin. The second part (41–59) expounds
the break-in of sin and its universal spread among men in Gen. I–XI
according to P and J, and is concerned to emphasize that biblical
and ecclesiastical thought stress these features of sin rather than the
historicity of the details of the Eden stories. The exegesis is not
always convincing. The third part deals with the Pauline parallel
between Adam and Christ (Rom. 5: 12–21), and the consequences of
these two parts for certain Councils of the Church.   G.H.D.

HESSE, F.: *Das Alte Testament als Buch der Kirche.* 1966. Pp. 158.
(Gütersloher Verlagshaus Gerd Mohn, Gütersloh. Price: DM. 12.80).

The theme of this important little book is the problem of the validity
of the Old Testament in the Christian Church. In actual Church
practice the Old Testament tends to be misused or even neglected in
spite of the fact that it is right in the centre of theological discussion.
In this discussion two approaches can be distinguished, the *heilsgeschichtlich* and the existential. Both seem to have their validity
and the problem is how they are to be combined. In spite of their
differences this is a concern of both von Rad and Baumgärtel. Von
Rad lays the emphasis on the on-going movement of a history which
is always open towards the future and is marked by successive reinter-
pretations of tradition based on new acts of God. Baumgärtel, like
Bultmann, though he lays more stress than the latter does on the
Heilsgeschichte, is impressed by what is for him the radical break
between the Old Testament and the New Testament. The key word
for him is promise. The basic promise involved in Israel's Election
was understood by Israel in limited ways which do not concern us.
In Christ it was confirmed and re-interpreted and we are pointed
foward to the final consummation. Hesse, while paying tribute to
von Rad's achievement, inclines to Baumgärtel's view. He criticizes
von Rad for what he regards as his neglect of actual history, in, with
and under which he sees God's action. The Old Testament is relevant
to the Christian positively as witnessing to God's enduring promise
and negatively as warning him in the light of the Gospel of the ways in
which the promise has been and still can be misinterpreted.

N.W.P.

VAN IMSCHOOT, P.: *Theology of the Old Testament*. Vol. I. *God*. (Translated from the French by Sullivan and Buck). 1965. Pp. xvi + 300. (Desclée Company, New York, Tournai, Paris, Rome. Price: 40s. 6d.).

The appearance of an English translation of Volume I of this important Roman Catholic Theology of the Old Testament may be heartily welcomed. The book was reviewed at some length in the *Book List* for 1955, pp. 50–51. One may express regret that the learned author has not used the occasion of this translation to take some account of the extended debate which has been in progress during these past years regarding the true nature of biblical theology. N.W.P.

KRAUS, H.-J.: *Worship in Israel: A Cultic History of the Old Testament*. 1966. Pp. xii + 246. (Blackwell, Oxford. Price: 37s. 6d.).

This is a translation of the author's *Gottesdienst in Israel* (*Book List* 1963, pp. 51 f.), by G. Buswell. Footnotes have been expanded to include publications since 1962 and especially to English translations of German contributions. A translation was obviously necessary. Perhaps the most valuable part of this study is that concerned with Cultic Calendars and Regulations. That concerned with the central sanctuaries of Israel and their cultic traditions and the cultic traditions of Jerusalem is stimulating but will be read with caution. It is unfortunate that the book contains a number of misprints especially of words in Hebrew, but also of some biblical references.

A.S.H.

LABUSCHAGNE, C. J.: *The Incomparability of Yahweh in the Old Testament*. (Pretoria Oriental Series V). 1966. Pp. xii + 164. (E. J. Brill, Leiden. Price: 26 guilders).

This interesting study, based on a doctoral thesis, deals with a subject which appears not to have been treated in a separate work before. It begins with a careful survey of the expressions by which incomparability may be expressed in Hebrew — both religious and secular; and adduces detailed evidence for the important comparable statements in Assyro–Babylonian religion, and the smaller amount of evidence from Egypt. No evidence is found in the Ras Shamra texts. This last point is viewed cautiously as evidence against too easily accepting that Israel adopted such expressions of incomparability from elsewhere. The book continues with an analysis of important Old Testament passages — much here is of great interest, though not always convincing — concentrating on the Exodus and Creation themes in relation to statements about God. Consequences are drawn concerning the origins of the ideas and the relevance of these points especially for Israel's understanding of the knowledge of God, of what is meant by monotheism, and of Israel's own special position. If at times too much stress seems to be laid on Israel's originality as a protest against borrowing, there is much value in the interpretation of the Old Testament from itself. This is a useful and stimulating contribution to Old Testament theology. P.R.A.

RINGGREN, H.: *Israelite Religion*. Trans. by David Green. 1966. Pp. xvi + 392. (S.P.C.K., London. Price: 42s.).

The German original from which this book is translated was published in 1963 and reviewed then (see *B.L.* 1964, p. 64). The author has corrected some errors which were pointed out to him and has added somewhat to the text and notes. Its strèngth is evident, in an orderly and informed discussion of the earlier period and particularly that of the monarchy. Its weakness remains, namely that it covers the whole exilic and post-exilic period in fifty pages. But it is rightly a history of the religion and not a theology, and such a synthesis is particularly welcome in English. The translation reads smoothly; the present reviewer has not attempted to check its accuracy.

P.R.A.

SCHELKLE, K. H.: *Wort und Schrift: Beiträge zur Auslegung und Auslegungsgeschichte des Neuen Testamentes*. 1966. Pp. 322. (Patmos-Verlag, Düsseldorf. Price: DM. 34.00).

This is a Roman Catholic work on the hermeneutics and history of hermeneutics of the New Testament. The book is of some relevance to the special interests of Old Testament scholars in that account is taken of the method of handling the Old Testament by the various New Testament writers. Attention may in particular be drawn to the section entitled 'Hermeneutische Regeln im Neuen Testament', pp. 31–44, which traces the development of exegetical methods within the New Testament itself.

N.W.P.

SCHOFIELD, J. N.: *Introducing Old Testament Theology*. (S.C.M. Cheap Edition). 1966. Pp. 126. (S.C.M. Press, London. Price: 6s. 6d.).

This is a paperback re-issue of Mr. Schofield's useful survey which was first published in 1964 (see *Book List* 1965, pp. 52f.).

M.A.K.

SCHREINER, J.: *Die Zehn Gebote im Leben des Gottesvolkes*. 1966. Pp. 122. (Kösel-Verlag, München. Price: DM. 15.80).

Professor Schreiner of Munster treats of the concept of the Decalogue, its relation to preaching and in the context of the ethical teaching of the O.T. He emphasizes the close 'Zusammengehörigkeits-verhältnis' (p. 28) of Covenant and Decalogue as expressing the divine 'Ausschliesslichkeitsanspruch', and discusses the meaning, role, educational and election values of law in the O.T. Other chapters expound commandments 5–10 and the first and great commandment. A useful and often stimulating survey of the originality of the Decalogue.

G.H.D.

WANKE, G.: *Die Zionstheologie der Korachiten in ihrem traditionsgeschichtlichen Zusammenhang*. (Beihefte zur Zeitschrift für die alttestamentliche Wissenschaft, 97). 1966. Pp. VIII + 120 (Verlag Alfred Töpelmann, Berlin. Price: DM. 28.00).

Wanke examines Pss. xlii/xliii, xlvi, xlviii, lxxxiv, lxxxvii and finds in them a Zion theology which he assigns to the Korahites, who belonged to the post-exilic era. These were not merely collectors of psalms, but the authors of many that are now ascribed to them, and particularly of these Zion psalms. Thus this Zion-theology is a late construction, built up from a variety of themes and motifs at a time when Jewish life was centred upon Jerusalem. Much of the study consists of an attempt to show that older features contained in these psalms show evidence of a late adaptation to the post-exilic situation, and a dependence on the eschatological (post-exilic) prophets. Wanke rejects the theory of a distinctive pre-exilic cult tradition in Jerusalem, influenced from the earlier El-'Elyon cult, and regards the Zion-theology as a pastiche of different motifs, rather than the product of a single local tradition. The arguments used to affirm late dates for material that most recent commentators have regarded as early are tortuous and strained, and very little at all is left as evidence for the worship of Jerusalem before the exile.

R.E.C.

THE LIFE AND THOUGHT OF THE SURROUNDING PEOPLES

KITCHEN, K. A.: *Alter Orient und Altes Testament: Probleme und ihre Lösungen. Aufklärung und Erläuterung.* 1965. Pp. 117. (R. Brockhaus Verlag, Wuppertal. Price: DM. 7.20).

KITCHEN, K. A.: *Ancient Orient and Old Testament.* 1966. Pp. 191. (The Tyndale Press, London. Price: 18s. 6d.).

This work had its origin in two lectures which the author delivered in 1962 during the International Student Conference held under the auspices of the Vereinigte Bibelgruppen von Schweiz at Casa Moscia. His aim is to show how research into the world of the ancient Near East can contribute to the solution of problems raised by O.T. research. The topics he has selected relate to some of the major problems in O.T. study, and if his treatment of them tends to be sketchy, due allowance must be made for the limited time at his disposal. He has, with commendable clarity, provided some useful guide lines for students, with plentiful illustrative material, frequently from Egyptian sources. Valuable supplementation is supplied by the voluminous notes, which reveal the author's acquaintance with a wide range of literature. Though he leans to a conservative stand-point, he is very far from advocating a return to pre-critical days. There is an index of biblical passages, as well as a chronological table and two maps. The translation from English into German was made by Frau Ilse Fuhr. The book in English is a revised version of the original English text.

D.W.T.

LAMBERT, W. G., PARKER, S. B.: *Enuma Eliš, the Babylonian Epic of Creation, The Cuneiform Text.* 1966. Pp. 47. (Clarendon Press, Oxford. Price: 12s. 6d.).

Mr. Lambert here establishes a composite and up-to-date text from all available sources. He thus provides a useful aid for all who teach or learn Akkadian since some of the original texts from which he draws are not otherwise readily available. We must, however, await the promised critical edition of all Babylonian creation myths for the transliterations and translations, as for the variants, commentaries and sources, which will enable the reader to relate this text to his other Semitic studies. Mr. Parker's manuscript of the text is usually clear if not elegant. It is intended for the beginner who may be acquainted only with the Neo-Assyrian sign forms into which the texts of all periods have been transposed.　　　　D.J.W.

MALLOWAN, M. E. L.: *Nimrud and its Remains*. 1966. Vol. I, pp. 1–358; Vol. II, pp. 359–680. Pl. in colour IX; line and half-tone, 594. Maps, plans and sections: in text, 19; separately bound, 8. (Collins, London. Price: £16 16s.).

This work records the 1949–1963 'centenary' excavations at Old Testament Calah, first excavated by Sir Henry Layard. His mode of presentation is consciously followed (*mutatis mutandis!*) in this sumptuously produced publication; and this will add greatly to the number who will read it with pleasure and profit. The un-romantic archaeologist on the search for a specific unadorned fact may complain at the time he must spend in locating his requirements — not always helped by a rather meagre index — but he will have to do it, at least until such time as the more specialized monographs mentioned in the Preface shall have appeared. This is, and will remain, *the* book on Nimrud, a pleasure to handle and a delight to read. Will 'someone' please soon produce a condensed version, keeping a reasonable number of the beautiful plates, at a price nearer to the pocket of those who can only look in envy at a borrowed copy of this one!　　　　D.R.Ap-T.

MORGENSTERN, J.: *Rites of Birth, Marriage, Death and Kindred Occasions among the Semites*. 1966. Pp. 320. (Hebrew Union College Press, Cincinnati and Quadrangle Books, Chicago. Price: $8.95).

Professor Morgenstern has presented material from the publications of the foremost field observers in the Arab East and in old Jewish communities there which he has assembled and studied with intention of publication for over forty-five years. He adds his own contribution from his critical studies in the Old Testament, notably the Pentateuch, and the result is a valuable synthesis of evidence. The main thesis is that the prophylactic rites associated with the transitional periods such as birth, marriage and death were imposed by apprehension of the influence of dead ancestors, apprehended as especially active at such a time. The author relates the active belief in such influences to an early stage in communal life, when *beena*-marriage was prevalent. With the development of *ba'al*-marriage and larger communities the religions familiar in the literary period developed, the rites associated with transitional periods surviving as vestiges of a more primitive animism. The thesis is well sustained in notes and appendices, the latter being particularly valuable from a writer of the acknowledged authority of Professor Morgenstern, and a full bibliography will stimulate further study.　　　　J.G.

QUMRAN STUDIES

BLACK, M.: *The Dead Sea Scrolls and Christian Doctrine*. (The Ethel M. Wood Lecture. 1966). 1966. Pp. 24. (University of London, The Athlone Press. Price: 5s.).

This lecture offers useful comments on three main themes: sacerdotal messianism, the doctrine of the atonement, eschatology; an appendix treats briefly of salvation. Though the relationship of Christian and Qumran thought is the main concern, there is much of interest for the better understanding of the Scrolls.　　　　　　　　　　　　　　P.R.A.

FITZMYER, J. A.: *The Genesis Apocryphon of Qumran Cave I.* (Biblica et Orientalia, No. 18). 1966. Pp. xvi + 232. (Pontifical Biblical Institute, Rome. Price: Lire 3000 or $5.00).

The Scroll now known as the Genesis Apocryphon — previously thought to be the lost Book of Lamech — was published in part by Avigad and Yadin in 1956 (see *B.L.* 1957, pp. 63f.). It has proved particularly difficult to unroll and to decipher, and many columns have still not been published. Of the columns published there have been several studies, especially of the language. Now we are given the first edition with complete commentary. The excellent introduction deals with all the major questions raised by the Scroll — its name, its literary *genre*, its palaeography, the date of the manuscript and of the composition of the work, its language, its text, and its relation to the Targums. There is a good bibliography, an edition of the text in printed Hebrew with English translation on opposite pages, followed by a full and careful commentary. Father Fitzmyer doubts the appropriateness of the title now given to the work, and dates the Qumran copy between 50 B.C. and A.D. 70, and thinks it may be the author's autograph or a very early copy. There are valuable appendices on related literature, on Qumran Aramaic, and a glossary. This edition is indispensable for all further study, and will be particularly valuable when the Job Targum becomes available.　　　　　　H.H.R.

HAAG, H.: *Die Handschriftenfunde in der Wüste Juda*. (Stuttgarter Bibelstudien, 6). 1965. Pp. 73. (Verlag Katholisches Bibelwerk, Stuttgart. Price: DM. 5.80).

The booklet outlines the story of the Qumran discoveries and the main contributions and problems to which they have given rise. It first appeared in 1958, but some account is taken of publications and discussions since that time. The text of the book is clear and, in general, provides an adequate survey of the usual topics; the annotations contain useful aids to further reading. But there are instances of serious over-simplification and omission in both text and notes.

　　　　　　　　　　　　　　　　　　　　　　　　　　　　　B.J.R.

LEANEY, A. R. C.: *The Rule of Qumran and its Meaning. Introduction, translation and commentary*. 1966. Pp. 310. (S.C.M. Press, London. Price: 50s.).

The fact that this distinguished addition to literature on Qumran appears as a volume in the publishers' New Testament Library is probably a token of tacit recognition that, apart from the biblical texts, the Qumran documents are more relevant to New Testament than to Old Testament studies. To show this relevance, indeed, is one of the author's stated aims; others are to show how the *Rule* fits into its historical setting, to demonstrate how far back into the past we must press in order to discover the ultimate sources of Qumran thinking, to bring out the characteristics of that thinking as it is revealed in the *Rule*, and 'to contribute towards the ultimate healing of the tragic breach between Judaism and Christianity'. It is to be hoped that he will be as successful in this last aim as he manifestly is in all the others.

The first chapter, 'Man and the Universe', deals mainly with astronomy and the calendar — not congenial subjects to non-mathematically-minded biblical scholars, but essential for appreciating the Qumran outlook. The history and teaching of the community are then set forth. The author, like E. F. Sutcliffe, takes the twelve men and three priests in 1QS viii.1 to be the original nucleus of the community. He envisages an original 'founder' of the community twenty years before the Teacher of Righteousness appeared; a more natural inference from CD i. 8–12 is that the godly remnant which wandered aimlessly for twenty years before the Teacher was raised up had no leader until he appeared. The promise in 1QS iv. 20 ff. that God will make manifest (or purify) *kol ma'ase geber* is interpreted in reference to mankind as a whole and not messianically; it is curious that J. A. T. Robinson's study of this passage receives no mention. The Qumran community is envisaged as a special form of an order or movement which existed in various branches in the towns and villages of Palestine; Josephus' description of the Essene rules of admission refers to this order as a whole whereas in 1QS vi. 13–23 we have the entrance rules of the sect which derived from it.

F.F.B.

RABIN, C. and YADIN, Y. (ed. by): *Aspects of the Dead Sea Scrolls*. (Scripta Hierosolymitana, IV). 2nd ed. 1966. Pp. x + 282. (Magnes Press. Oxford University Press, London. Price: £2 3s.).

This collection of studies, originally published in 1958 (see *B.L.* 1959, p. 39), has now been re-issued after being out of print for some time.

M.A.K.

ROTH, C.: *The Dead Sea Scrolls: A New Historical Approach*. 1965. Pp. xx + 99. (W. W. Norton, New York. Price: $1.25).

This is a paperback edition of the book, issued unchanged (see *B.L.* 1966, p. 60; cf. also *B.L.* 1959, p. 40 for the review of the original book).

P.R.A.

APOCRYPHA AND POST-BIBLICAL STUDIES

AL-ḌĀHRĪ, ZACHARIĀ: *Sefer Hammusar*, ed. by Y. Ratzaby. 1965. Pp. 500. (Published by The Ben-Zvi Institute, Jerusalem, Israel. Price: $11.00).

This book, also known by the name of *Sepher Hamaḥbereth*, is the most important of *belles-lettres* ever produced by the Jews in the

Yemen. Its author, who lived in the sixteenth century, tells in the *meqana* fashion about his travels in the Middle East and beyond. The Biblical scholar will find interest in the author's language, made up as it is throughout of fragments of Biblical passages. These, arranged in their respective rhyming groups, are skilfully strung together to form the material with which to clothe the narrative. The editor, a Yemenite scholar, has done his work well, and both he and The Ben-Zvi Institute are to be congratulated on this fine publication.   M.W.

DUBARLE, A. M.: *Judith: Formes et Sens des Diverses Traditions.* Tome I: Études. Tome II: Textes. (Analecta Biblica, 24). 1966. Pp. 192 and 204. (Institut Biblique Pontifical, Rome. Price: £3; $5.00).

A Hebrew MS of Judith in the Bodleian Library, said to belong to the 12th century, and here edited for the first time, is made the opportunity for a reappraisal of the text of the book. Vol. I contains a description of the extant texts, Hebrew, Greek and Latin and of witnesses to the story in ancient Jewish (Midrashic) and Christian tradition. In face of this wealth of tradition the author claims that there is a kernel of truth in the story, namely that a woman, at some time in the Persian period, saved the people of a town (Bethulia or Jerusalem?) in time of siege. This minimal fact was embroidered in the book with details reminiscent of stories in the Old Testament with which the author of *Judith* was throughly familiar. The Greek translator is shown to have had a predilection for Septuagintal phrases and may not therefore represent the Semitic original faithfully.

Vol. II contains a critical edition of the Bodleian MS together with two other forms of a Hebrew text: the texts are printed in columns with the text of the Vulgate for comparison. Dubarle regards the Hebrew text as an original form and not a translation. This volume also contains the text of the ancient witnesses to the story with a French translation.   L.H.B.

FALK, Z. W.: *Jewish Matrimonial Law in the Middle Ages.* (Scripta Judaica VI). 1966. Pp. xvi + 154. (Oxford University Press. Price: 40s.).

The book under review falls into five main sections: Monogamy, Matrimony, The Matrimonial Match, Divorce and a very short chapter on the Status of Woman. Apart from the Hebrew Bible, the Elephantine Papyri, the Zadokite Documents, Philo, the New Testament and Josephus, the sources collected comprise post-biblical Hebrew or Aramaic writings such as Mishnah, Gemara, the Codes, Responsa and Customaries, as well as Egyptian, Graeco-Roman and Franco–German secular legal literature. They also include a competent and cautious assessment of the influence of Islamic and Canon Law on the various eastern and western centres of the Jewish Diaspora. In addition, there is an almost complete list of works relevant to and used for the analysis of the differences and affinities which evolved between the different civilizations.

Alttestamentler will mainly be interested in the author's observations on biblical law: it clearly pre-supposes polygamy. Tendencies towards monogamy, however, are said to appear in the writings of some of the prophets of the Babylonian captivity and in the Book of Proverbs. The reviewer would point out that they all stand in a context which objects to adultery with foreign or idolatrous women rather than to polygamy. It is rightly stressed that marriage arrangements between the parties concerned depended on contract and not on law. This is illustrated by *Genesis* XXXI, 50 and by the Aramaic *Kethubbah* from Elephantine, dating from the time of Nehemiah (Kraeling, No. 7), but it seems far-fetched to connect the text of the latter with that of a Genizah fragment of the 12th Century. A clear objection to polygamy is to be found for the first time in the Zadokite documents, but it took more than a millennium before such an attitude, though supported by different reasons, gained a foothold in normative Judaism. The book is well written and will for a long time be indispensable for scholars in this field of study.   S.S.

GLATZER, N. N.: *Anfänge des Judentums. Eine Einführung.* 1966. Pp. 104. (Gütersloher Verlagshaus Gerd Mohn, Gütersloh. Price: DM. 16.80).

After a very brief sketch of the historical background of the period from the Exile to the fifth Christian century, and an equally brief sketch of Hellenistic Judaism, the author devotes the central, and largest, section of this short work to a discussion of six important themes in Rabbinic Judaism (God; Man; Torah; Synagogue and Prayer; Attitude to Prophecy; Messianic Beliefs). There follows an account of the Qumran and the Ebionite communities, while in the last part of the work the significance of four representative figures (Hillel; Josephus; Johanan ben Zakkai; Johanan of Tiberias) is examined. There is a short bibliography and a name- and subject-index. The work is intended merely as an introduction, and as such this quite lively account should prove useful.   M.A.K.

HARTMAN, L.: *Prophecy Interpreted: The Formation of some Jewish Apocalyptic Texts and of the Eschatological Discourse Mark 13 par.* (Coniectanea Biblica, N.T. Series I). 1966. Pp. 299. (Gleerup, Lund. Price: Sw.Kr. 40).

As the sub-title indicates this study is devoted mainly to the intertestamental literature and certain New Testament passages, in the light of their Old Testament background. In the first part the author notes some elements of the raw material of Jewish Apocalyptic texts, material which is far from evenly distributed among the texts examined, and then outlines two patterns of thought, in one of which the Messiah does not figure and in the other of which he does, and examines passages in which an earthquake motif figures and one in which the assault of the heathen figures, and then considers the composition of four specific passages. The author defends this atomistic approach, partly on the ground that it is common to find that the apocalyptic works are composite. Turning to the New Testament, he examines the eschatological discourse in the Gospels and in Paul's Epistles to the Thessalonians and traces the history from a midrash on passages from Daniel, into which sayings of Jesus were woven, to which Paul had access at a stage earlier than that represented in Mark.   H.H.R.

LISOWSKY, G.: *Uḳṣim* (Stiele). (Die Mischna, Text, Übersetzung u. . . . Erklärung . . . herausgegeben von K. H. Rengstorf u. L. Rost, VI. Seder: *Ṭoharot*. 12. Traktat: *Uḳṣim*). 1967. Pp. vi + 62. (Alfred Töpelmann, Berlin. Price: DM. 21.00).

The venerable, yet regenerated Giessen Mishnah is now creaking its way towards its terminus, though the appearance of the ultimate tractate leaves a lot of stations to be visited. Readers shaky on 'stalks [, potential uncleanness of]', may take comfort in that R. Simeon b. Gamaliel was also weak on the tractate (T.B. *Horayoth* 13b). Even if its subject-matter may be less significant for the rabbinic law of evidence through its (apparent) link with R. Yohanan b. Zakkai (*Sanhedrin* 5, 2) and with *Susannah* 54 and 58, than is sometimes claimed, it is important in its own right — not least botanically. The translator takes full advantage here in his notes of the work of I. Löw and of Dalman, and in a brief introduction he explains both the main institutions handled and the categories which it presupposes (referring, without repitition, to what he has put into his editions of tractates *Ṭebul Yom* and *Yadayim*), and also the relationship of this Mishnah to its parallel *Tosefta*. The editor has missed — or chosen to pass over — a connection between Islam and the edificatory epilogue in which R. Joshua b. Levi promised the righteous 310 [future] 'worlds', 310 being the numerical value of *yesh* in *Prov*. 8, 20: in the Arab world these '*olamoth* were to be transformed into '*alamoth*.   R.L.

LOEWE, R.: *The Position of Women in Judaism*. 1966. Pp. 63. (S.P.C.K. in conjunction with the Hillel Foundation, London. Price: 12s. 6d.).

In this informative sketch, the material for which is derived mainly from the Bible, Mishnah, Talmud and Maimonides, the attitude of traditional Judaism is presented. With certain mitigations, the subordination of women is plain, but in her role as home-maker she finds fulfilment. In relation to the current debate on the ordination of women, it is suggested that for those Churches which set a positive value on the family, marriage might be an essential precondition. The author frankly acknowledges that this orthodox Jewish attitude is in conflict with contemporary Western life and with certain aspects of Israeli life.   A.S.H.

LOEWE, R. (ed. by): *Studies in Rationalism, Judaism and Universalism, in memory of Leon Roth*. 1966. Pp. xiv + 358. (Routledge & Kegan Paul, London. Price: 50s.).

The volume contains 15 essays, a brief memoir and a bibliography. The essays are intended to echo Roth's main interests and bear the following titles: Moses Mendelssohn on Leibniz and Spinoza (Alt-mann), Israel and the *Oikoumenē* (Bergman), Paul a Hellenistic Schoolmaster? (Daube), 'Knowest Thou . . .?' Notes on the Book of Job (Glatzer), The Doctrine of the 'Divine Spark' in Man in Jewish Sources (Jacobs), Potentialities and Limitations of Universalism in the *Halakhah* (Loewe), Jew, Christian and Muslim in the Secular Age (Maybaum), Rabbinic Adumbrations of Non-violence: Israel and Canaan (Neher), Rationalism in Hobbes' Political Philosophy

(Raphael), Torah and *Nomos* in Medieval Jewish Philosophy (Rosenthal), Ethics and Education (Rotenstreich), Herbert Samuel's Moral Philosophy (Schmidt), Thought Categories in the Hebrew Bible (Ullendorff), The Idea of Humanity in Judaism (Wilhelm), Maimonides on Modes and Universals (Wolfson). Those by Glatzer and Ullendorff are of more interest to O.T. scholars.

L.H.B.

MEYER, R.: *Tradition und Neuschöpfung im Antiken Judentum, dargestellt an der Geschichte des Pharisäismus.*

WEISS, H.-F.: *Der Pharisäismus im Lichte der Überlieferung des Neuen Testaments.* 1965. Pp. 132. (Akademie-Verlag, Berlin. Price: MDN. 8.30).

These are complementary studies. The first, that of R. Meyer, makes a fresh appraisal of the nature and development of Pharisaism, with special reference to the texts from Qumran and Murabba'at, and shows that Pharisaism did not really come into its own, nor, indeed, was it clearly defined, until after the fall of Jerusalem. The second shows how the anti-Pharisaism of the Gospels reflects the mood of the early church and the tension between Christians, Jewish Christians and Jews. In the nature of the case, if Meyer is right, there was only an incipient Pharisaism at the time of Jesus.

L.H.B.

SCOBIE, C. H. H.: *John the Baptist.* (1964). This ed. 1966. Pp. 224. (S.C.M. Press, Ltd., London. Price: paperback, 12s. 6d.; cloth, 22s. 6d.).

The author describes this book as a 'new quest of the historical John'. It is a quest which can now be conducted, not only in the light of modern critical evaluations of the Gospel material, but against the rich background of our increasing knowledge of contemporary Judaism and in particular the Qumran scrolls.
Dr. Scobie makes full and competent use of the new discoveries and finds behind the Gospel reports an even more remarkable figure than the Gospels themselves seem to allow. The group around John, practising a 'baptism of repentance for the remission of sins', took its origins out of the widespread 'non-conformist' Baptist movement of the period although John himself did not belong to any single sectarian group. The movement initiated by John was not entirely swallowed up in Christianity, for the Baptist retained a certain following even after his death.
This is a thoroughly competent piece of scholarship by the Professor of New Testament at Presbyterian College, Montreal, Canada.

M.Bl.

YADIN, Y.: *Masada: Herod's Fortress and the Zealots' Last Stand.* 1966. Pp. 272. (Weidenfeld and Nicolson, London. Price: 63s.).

This fascinating and superbly illustrated preliminary account of the brilliant excavation of Masada directed by Professor Yadin is of considerable importance to Biblical students. It describes the remarkable complex of buildings which were found within the fortress and the confirmation of many of the details of the description given by Josephus, which had been doubted by many scholars. The material finds were often as surprising as they were welcome, and of particular importance were the finds of Scrolls which must have lain where they were found since A.D. 73, and which therefore must be earlier than this. These comprised fragments of Biblical texts of Psalms, Leviticus and Ezekiel, and of Ecclesiasticus and Jubilees, together with a fragment of one of the texts of the Qumran sectaries, hitherto known only from the Qumran finds. Dr. Yadin describes the difficulties of the operation and gives credit to the various members of his team for their individual share, with touches of humour, and movingly tells of the evidence of the tragic sacrifice of the heroic defenders.

H.H.R.

PHILOLOGY AND GRAMMAR

ALBRIGHT, W. F.: *The Proto-Sinaitic Inscriptions and their Decipherment*. (Harvard Theological Series XXII). 1966. Pp. iv + 45 with 10 figures on 8 plates. (Harvard University Press. Oxford University Press, London. Price: 16s.).

After a brief sketch of previous attempts to decipher these fragmentary texts (pp. 1–9) and an even briefer sketch of their historical background and the inferences that may be drawn from them (pp. 10–15), Prof. Albright transliterates and translates the texts, using photographic reproductions of drawings made from Fr. Butin's squeezes and two direct photographs of texts. This interpretation starts from Cowley's *l-b'lt* 'for Baalat', which is still the only inscription of which the interpretation remains undisputed; for those of Prof. Albright, however ingenious, yield in many if not in most cases but dubious sense: why, for example, should a hero who has saved the donor from two lionesses be asked to give an oracle and be bidden to swear to offer a cow to an unnamed deity? And what does 'O Serpent Lady, (his) two lords, bring a sacrifice' mean? The language, described as 'vulgar Canaanite' in 1948 but as 'good Canaanite' in 1949, has now become 'a kind of Canaanite *koinē* (*lingua vulgaris*)', as it is called on p. 37; what it really may have been no one knows! However this may be, the little book is a useful *corpus* of these obscure inscriptions (what a pity the learned author has not heard of the admirable copies given by Sir Alan Gardiner to the Ashmolean Museum!) and will be of use to future decipherers; but not much can be expected in the few, chiefly damaged, inscriptions as yet available for study.

G.R.D.

LEVENSTON, E. A., SIVAN, R.: *The Megiddo Modern Dictionary. Hebrew-English; English-Hebrew*. 1965; 1966. Pp. xiv + 711; xvi + 1267. (Megiddo Publishing Co. Ltd., Tel-Aviv. Price: £7).

This twin-dictionary embodies some essential features lacking in the crop of dictionaries which has appeared in Palestine and later in Israel in the last few decades. The more pronounced amongst them are to be found (*a*) in the *choice* of vocabulary; (*b*) in orthography. As to (*a*), one can observe both a distinct elimination of dead wood, accumulated in the course of time, which kept on appearing in pre-

vious dictionaries and a distinct addition of *very fresh* coinages drawn
from literary and non-literary sources. As to (*b*), words are given in
full plena as laid down by the Hebrew Language Academy (— a
plena which generally prevails in unpointed texts in Israel), pointing
them at the same time in the manner the Masoretes pointed similar
full plena in the Bible (see, e.g. II Ch. viii. 18; Ex. xxv. 31; Ez. xx. 18).
Both dictionaries are well produced and Hebrew scholars will greatly
benefit by consulting them.   M.W.

MACUCH, R.: *Handbook of Classical and Modern Mandaic.* 1965. Pp.
lxviii + 649. (Walter de Gruyter, Berlin. Price: £18 6s.).

Professor Macuch's *Handbook* is an exhaustive study of the Mandaic
dialect both as enshrined in the almost exclusively religious literature
of the Mandaeans and as spoken in the dwindling communities that
still use it. He deals at length with the script and pronunciation
(pp. 1–26), phonetics (pp. 29–148), morphology (pp. 151–380) and
syntax (pp. 383–463); he also includes a bibliography (pp. 467–477),
appendices containing a classical text transliterated, with notes on
the pronunciation, and translated, and samples of the vernacular
speech with an English–Mandaic vocabulary (which, so far as the
reviewer knows, is a unique contribution to the subject), as well as
additions to the Mandaic Dictionary published in 1963 by Lady
Drower and himself (pp. 478–546) and complete indices (pp. 549–649).
This new work does not entirely replace Nöldeke's *Mandäische
Grammatik* (1875), if only because that uses the Hebrew script
whereas this is entirely in transliteration (except for a sample of the
script); but it has two great advantages, that the author has been
able to use many literary texts not available to Nöldeke and that he
includes the modern language, which he has studied at first hand. A
reviewer hardly knows which is most praiseworthy: his industry, his
massive learning yet lucid arrangement of a vast collection of matter,
or the general accuracy of the work (in spite of a small sprinkling of
misprints which are scarcely avoidable in such a work and a few
solecisms in his English idiom); the book is and will long remain
indispensable to Mandaic (and indeed to all Semitic) students.

                                                          G.R.D.

SPERBER, A.: *A Historical Grammar of Biblical Hebrew. A Presentation of
problems with suggestions to their solution.* 1966. Pp. xiv + 705.
(E. J. Brill, Leiden. Price: 175 guilders).

This *indigesta moles* of miscellaneous information, arguments and
conclusions, contains eight monographs published since 1934,
inflated with additional matter. Much that is collected here is hardly
apposite to 'grammar' in the strict sense and much is over-argued,
while the inflation has increased the obscurity, so that the reader has
the greatest difficulty in following the arguments and discovering
what bearing, if any, they have on the conclusions which they are
supposed to prove. Further, not a little of the proof consists in
denunciation of other scholars (including the reviewer, whose explanation of the Hebrew verbal system as here 'potted' is hopelessly
garbled). The main conclusions seem to be the following: (1) Biblical

Hebrew is the result of the 'confluence' of two ancient Hebrew dialects, Israelitish and Judaean; (2) the Samaritan Pentateuch is not a heretic version but an alternative recension of the Pentateuch; (3) Origen did not use a Hebrew Bible; (4) his *Hexapla* was based on two sources representing two Hebrew Bibles; (5) there was no uniform pronunciation of Hebrew in his time; (6) LXX A and B go back to different sources, A representing the Massoretic Pentateuch, the parallel passages of the historical books in *Chronicles* and the *qěrê*-readings of the M.T., and B representing the Samaritan Pentateuch, the parallel passages in Samuel and Kings and the *kětîb*-readings; (7) the Massoretic notes are not a 'unity'; (8) the Tiberian vocalization is composite, reflecting two distinct dialects with different Hebrew pronunciations. Some of these points have long been recognized; others, however suggestive, require strict proof such as the arguments here accumulated hardly provide. The author's arguments are often obscured by the fact that he seems to be thinking in one language and writing in another and by the German-American jargon which he uses, as for example in 'the *daghesh forte* to substitute is based for such a consonant'. Indeed, errors of every sort abound, e.g. 'sybillants', 'genetive', 'particle' for preposition and 'preposition' for conjunction, the description of *daghesh forte* and *lene* as 'composite vowels', 'cheatful', 'noisome' for 'noisy', the solecistic *sub alia exemplaria* (accus. for abl. case), 'Gindzburg' for Ginsberg (Editor of the Hebrew Bible), and so on. Many statements will startle the reader, e.g. that 'both perfect and imperfect are interchangeably used to indicate present, past or future'; if this were so, intelligible negotiations between man and man would be impossible! The writer has failed to observe that the forms are sometimes distinguished by vocalization (for example *yāqûm* 'he will arise' but *-yáqom* 'he arose') and commonly by the accent, although the Massoretes obscured or lost many of the distinguishing marks. Equally strange is the observation that the accent was the cause of cantillation, not cantillation the cause of the accent. Nor is the Greek evidence properly used, for example in the use of ε for final guttural sounds and in the failure to see that consecutive *wa-* (with *a*) is recognized only twice in Greek transliterations. Briefly, the work is marred by failure to recognize the unscientific nature of Greek and Latin transliterations of Hebrew words, to establish what 'Hebrew' (whether the language of David or of Zerubbabel, of Origen's and Jerome's advisors or of the Massoretes) means, to distinguish the spoken from the written language, and to take the corresponding forms in the cognate languages into consideration; this neglect of comparative philology is fatal to the author's entire work. None the less, the compilation of information is useful, even though it must be used with caution.   G.R.D.

WAGNER, M.: *Die lexikalischen und grammatikalischen Aramaismen im alttestamentlichen Hebräisch.* (Beihefte zur Zeitschrift für die alttestamentliche Wissenschaft, 96). 1966. Pp. x + 176. (Verlag Alfred Töpelmann, Berlin. Price: DM. 46.00).

The introductory part of this monograph sketches the history of the Aramaic and Hebrew languages, summarizes previous scholarly studies of Aramaisms in Biblical Hebrew, and describes the methods used by Dr. Wagner himself. The central part lists and comments on first the lexical and then the grammatical Aramaisms in the Old

Testament. Dr. Wagner concludes his study by an evaluation of his findings. Finally, there are lists of abbreviations with an extensive (though not complete) bibliography. This collection of material and discussion of its significance is a valuable contribution to the study of a difficult subject.

                                                                    J.A.E.

WILENSKY, M.: *Sēfer hā-Riqmāh of R. Jonah ibn Janâḥ in the Hebrew translation of R. Judah ibn Tibbûn* prepared for publication by David Tene in consultation with Zvi Ben-Ḥayyîm. 1964. Vol. I. Pp. 12 + 1–398 with portrait; Vol. II. Pp. 12 + 399–735 with four plates. (Dvir Publishing Co., Tel-Aviv on behalf of the Academy to the Hebrew Language, The Hebrew University, Jerusalem. Price: £10 approx.).

The late Dr. A. Neubauer's edition of ibn Janâḥ's 'Book of Roots' (that is, his Hebrew–Arabic lexicon of the language of the Old Testament), published in 1875 at Oxford, has long been a valued companion to the Hebrew philologist; and the publication of the same Jewish scholar's Arabic *Sēfer hā-Riqmāh* in the Hebrew translation of ibn Tibbûn (c. A.D. 1120–1190) is a welcome event, even though the translator's Hebrew (as he himself admits) is not perfect; for ibn Janâḥ, following the two eminent Jewish grammarians Menahem ben Saruq and Dunash ben Labrat, completed the process of laying firm scientific foundations for the study of Hebrew grammar. The present edition, carefully prepared for the press by the two editors, contains in Vol. I the complete Hebrew text with brief notes on the text itself and, where necessary, on its interpretation, biblical references and so on, as well as a photograph of Wilensky, and in Vol. II introductory matter and additional notes from Wilensky's *Nachlass*, a list of technical terms with their meanings, additions and corrections and indices, together with four photographs of sheets of the MSS. The work seems to be very well done and indeed leaves little that can be said in elucidation of the text unsaid, and the printing is singularly free from misprints (for example a *nûn* upside down on p. 6, 1.22), although much of it is very small, with the consequent result that the lines, especially of the notes, are unduly long; as the whole work, text and notes, is in Hebrew fount, reading is apt to be tiring, at any rate to readers well advanced in years.

                                                                    G.R.D.

Book List 1968

GENERAL

ANDERSON, G. W. (ed.): *A Decade of Bible Bibliography*. 1967. Pp. 706. (Basil Blackwell, Oxford. Price: 84s.)

The reprinting of the ten years of the Book Lists for 1957–66 makes these available in more permanent form, and provides a valuable successor to the *Eleven Years of Bible Bibliography* (1957) which covered the period 1946–56. A complete index is provided.

P.R.A.

AVIGAD, N., and others (ed.): *E. L. Sukenik Memorial Volume* (*Erets-Israel*, vol. VIII). 1967. Pp. xi + 79 in English and other European languages; pp. xxvii + 328 in Hebrew. Plates. (Jerusalem, Israel Exploration Society)

This sumptuous and scholarly work in memory of E. L. Sukenik cannot be summarized in a few words. Fifty scholars, renowned in the fields of Bible and archaeology, have contributed to this volume, and it would be invidious to single out individual articles. Y. Yadin, Sukenik's son, contributes a note in English, a substantial article (in Hebrew) on the Ben Sira Scroll from Masada, as well as a biography of his father. The book also contains a bibliography of Sukenik's writings running to 200 items.

The width of interest is indicated by studies ranging from the origin and early evolution of the alphabet (F. M. Cross) to Nabataean symbols of immortality (N. Glueck), from the early relations between Canaan and Egypt (S. Yeivin) to the masterly decipherment of the exceptionally difficult Greek documents from the family archive of Babatha (H. J. Polotsky). C. Rabin writes on Og and A. Malamat on prophetic revelations in new documents from Mari. Altogether a rich fare of fresh material and ingenious interpretation.

E.U.

*BARKER, W. P.: *Everyone in the Bible*. 1967. Pp. 350. (Oliphants, London. Price: 37s. 6d.)

Contains short accounts of the biblical information about the persons mentioned in the Bible, excluding the Apocrypha. Its claim to completeness is not quite accurate. The reviewer has noted thirty-one omissions, including Chedorlaomer and Lois. The reader is promised that entries are normally in R.S.V. form, except in the case of names commonly known in the forms given in earlier translations. In fact A.V. is frequently followed, against R.V. and R.S.V., in quite uncommon names, and in some A.V., R.V. and R.S.V. are all set aside for such forms as Adar, Jechiliah, Meriah, while Aridal and Tertellus are plain errors. Despite these blemishes, this will often prove a useful tool for students and teachers.

H.H.R.

BIČ, M. and SOUČEK, J. B. (ed. by): *Biblická Konkordance*, Part 31. 1967. Pp. 60. (Edice Kalich, Prague. Price: Kčs. 10.50)

This part completes the great Concordance to the Czech Bible, showing Hebrew and Greek equivalents in the Old Testament and Greek equivalents in the New Testament. This great enterprise has

taken many years to bring to its completion, and the editors have
rendered a signal service to Czech readers, who will be envied by
readers in other countries in having so much information gathered
in a single volume. Previous parts have been noted in the Book List
(see *B.L.*, 1966, p. 3; *Decade*, p. 623), with the exception of parts
28–30, which have not been received. The whole work comprises
three volumes and a total of 2442 pages.   M.B./H.H.R.

BOWMAN, J. (ed.): *Abr-Nahrain* V., 1966. Pp. 89. (Brill, Leiden. Price:
  Fl. 32)

The current volume of *Abr-Nahrain* is devoted to three articles. The
first by D. Leslie, is on 'The Chinese-Hebrew Memorial Book of the
Jewish Community of K'aifeng', with lists of clans and family
genealogies from between the 10th and 13th centuries to the 17th
century. This is to be continued. The second article is a very soundly
informed and sober assessment of the affinity between Canaanite
and Homeric literary tradition, in which the author, Father A. F.
Campbell finds insufficient evidence to justify the theses of C. H.
Gordon. S. Coleman presents a midrashic interpretation of the book
of Habakkuk, which goes back reputedly to Rabbinic authority in
the 4th and 5th centuries.   J.G.

COENEN, L., BEYREUTHER, E., BIETENHARD, H. (ed.): *Theologisches-
  Begriffslexicon zum Neuen Testament* Vol. I. 1967. (In five fascicles,
  each of 112 pp. + xxxii — Abraham–Glaube.) (R. Brockhaus Verlag.
  Wuppertal. Price: DM. 16.90 each fascicle)

These fascicles, forming the first volume of a new lexicon which is in
process of appearing, give a good indication of its range and use. A
preface sets out the purpose — the bridging of the gap between
adequate understanding of the biblical material and the translation
of that understanding into modern terms. The arrangement is in
alphabetical order of German terms, but this enables all the significant
New Testament words to be handled, singly or in groups. Thus there
are similarities to *T.W.N.T.* (of which the fascicles are reviewed in
this Book List) but an article is likely to cover more than one Greek
word, and avoids a merely lexical division. Indexes to each fascicle
and to the first volume, paving the way for a full index, give an oversight to the compass of the work.
Although primarily hermeneutical in purpose, the lexicon includes
careful and scholarly discussion of the Old Testament background,
together with LXX, Qumran and rabbinic material. Thus for major
figures such as Abraham — with which the lexicon begins — an
analysis of Old Testament references is provided and an assessment
of the place of such names in Old Testament theological statement.
'Babylon' is given historical as well as ideological background. The
article on 'feasts' (*Feste*) offers a very capable short survey of the
ancient background, with sound analysis of the evidence. The articles
contain brief outlines of linguistic information, background material,
biblical usage, and in most cases a final section on 'preaching',
often revealing sensitivity to the problems of words whose meaning
has changed. Much of the work is written by pastors, and its primary
aim is practical, but its scholarship is sound (H. Seebass is largely
responsible for the editing of Old Testament matter), and it contains a
wealth of information.   P.R.A.

FOHRER, GEORG: *Studien zur Alttestamentlichen Prophetie* (1949–65). (Beiheft zur Zeitschrift für die alttestamentliche Wissenschaft 99.) 1967. Pp. xii + 303. (Verlag Alfred Töpelmann, Berlin. Price: DM. 60)

This volume contains a group of articles already published but now presented in revised form, lengthened or shortened as required in each case; taking into account the recent writing on the various subjects, the author now gives his mature reflections on them. Some of the articles deal with particular subjects, no fewer than five of them being related to the Book of Isaiah (Origin, Composition and Transmission of Isaiah 1–39, Isaiah 1 as a summary of the prophet's message, Isaiah 7:14 in the context of 7:10–22, the text of 41:8–13, and the structure of the apocalypse of chs 24–7). Others tackle wide-ranging subjects such as prophecy and history, prophecy and magic and the structure of Old Testament eschatology; there is one on new developments in Old Testament studies; and there is a small group concerned with literary analysis and *formgeschichtliche* study, including one on the short verse, another on the type of record which is given of the use of symbolic action by the prophets and a third on the glosses in the Book of Ezekiel. It is convenient to have these excellent articles within one volume and it is good to know that another is to follow, dealing with Old Testament history and theology. J.M.

FRIEDRICH, G. (ed. by): *Theologisches Wörterbuch zum Neuen Testament* (begun by G. Kittel). Band VIII. Lief. 5 and 6. 1966 and 1967. Pp. 64; 64. (Kohlhammer, Stuttgart. Price: DM. 5.80 each Lief.)

Lieferung 5 contains Goppelt's article on *typos*. This is followed by a short article on *typtō* by Stählin and a long one on *typhlos, typhloō* by Schrage which has a section devoted to these words and their equivalents in Judaism and in particular in Philo. An article by G. Bertram on *hybris* and its cognates discusses various Old Testament words from roots like *g'h, zyd* which convey a similar idea and there is a section on the occurrence of the idea in Judaism. After a short article on *hygies* by Luck, a long treatment of *hydor* by Goppelt begins and is continued into Lieferung 6. The rest of Lieferung 6 is taken up with an elaborate treatment of *hyios, hyiohesia* by a number of scholars. Fohrer is responsible for the Old Testament section and Schweizer and Lohse for the sections dealing with Hellenistic and Palestinian Judaism respectively. This whole article (not yet complete) is obviously of great theological importance. N.W.P.

Hebrew Union College Annual XXXVII (ed. by E. L. Epstein). 1966. Pp. 222 + 90 (in Hebrew). (Hebrew Union College, Cincinnati.)

This volume, dedicated to the memory of Leon J. Liebreich, comprises nine articles in English and four in Hebrew. Of direct interest to the biblical scholar are the following: 'Further Light from the Book of Isaiah upon the Catastrophe of 485 B.C.' (J. Morgenstern); 'The Origin of the "Day of the Lord" Reconsidered' (M. Weiss); 'The Meaning of the Book of Job' (M. Tsevat). Of indirect interest 'Abrabanel on Prophecy in the *Moreh Nebhukhim* (Chapter v)' (A. J. Reines) and '*Merosh Miqqadhmay 'Erez Nesukhah*' — a *zulath* on the demise of Moses by Yehoseph Ha'ezobhi (L. J. Weinberger). The concluding line of each stanza of this *piyyuṭ* is made up of a biblical passage. M.W.

Internationale Zeitschriftenschau für Bibelwissenschaft und Grenzgebiete.
Vol. 13. 1966/67. 1967. Pp. xiv + 334 (Patmos-Verlag, Düsseldorf.
Price: DM. 68.00; $17.00)

The latest volume of this most valuable index of articles in periodicals
and in composite volumes, which includes also some monographs
published in series and a small number of books, provides an indispensable tool for biblical research. The pattern of arrangement shown
at the end in a table of contents, is as in previous volumes. A comprehensive list shows which volumes or issues of each periodical are
covered; for the most part these are the issues of 1964–5. To this is
added a list of series and composite volumes. Most of the entries are
supplied with a summary, though in some cases only sub-headings
are given and in a relatively small number of cases no information
other than the titles and references is available. Full lists of abbreviations, of authors and of collaborators are included. Some previous
volumes have been noted in the book lists (see *B.L.*, 1961, p. 9;
Decade, p. 247).   P.R.A.

MAASS, F. (ed.): *Das Ferne und Nahe Wort. Festschrift Leonhard Rost zur
Vollendung seines 70. Lebensjahres am 30. November 1966 gewidmet*
(Beiheft zur Zeitschrift für die alttestamentliche Wissenschaft, 105).
1967. Pp. (8) + 275. One plate. (Verlag Alfred Töpelmann, Berlin.
Price: DM. 62)

The range of contributions by L. Rost to Old Testament studies and
to related fields is great; so too is that of this volume dedicated to
him. Its title is designed to emphasize the connection between the
study of the ancient world and the importance of discussing its
contemporary meaning. Twenty-seven contributions cover a wide
range. There is a bibliography of Rost's writings, but unfortunately
no index of biblical references.
A brief indication may be given of the main contents. Literary
critical questions are discussed by O. Eissfeldt (1 Kings 16:29–2 Kings
13:25), E. Würthwein (1 Kings 22:1–28); H. J. Stoebe deals with hero
saga in the books of Samuel, and L. Delekat with the David–Solomon
narrative; the Temple of Solomon is discussed by A. Kuschke, that of
Ezekiel by W. Eichrodt, while R. de Vaux discusses the 'place which
YHWH has chosen . . .'. Prophecy is represented by F. Maass on
the question of Trito-Isaiah, W. Rudolph on the date of Joel, G. Wallis
on Malachi, G. Fohrer on Micah 1, H. Bardtke on prophetic elements
in Job. Messianic psalms are discussed by F. Baumgärtel, Ps. 131
by G. Quell, LXX Ps. 151 by R. Meyer. K. Elliger criticizes H. Kosmala's poetic theory; G. Sauer writes on Zerubbabel; W. Zimmerli
on Abraham and Melchizedek; B. Reicke on 'knowledge' in the
Servant material; C. Westermann on ideas of creation; S. Herrmann
on cultic functions in Israel and Egypt; E. Kutsch on pre-Deuteronomic use of *bᵉrit*; and A. Jepsen on words meaning 'Why?' In addition there are two New Testament articles and one on hermeneutical
history dealing with Eichhorn and Kant (O. Kaiser). This is a rich
collection, but one may regret that no attempt was made to produce a
volume which had a real unity.   P.R.A.

NOBER, P.: *Elenchus Bibliographicus Biblicus*, Vol. XLVII. 1966. Pp. xii + 390. (Pontificio Istituto Biblico, Rome)

This is the bibliographical section of the four issues of *Biblica* for the year, containing a classified bibliography including 4383 items of articles, books and reviews of books, on biblical subjects, together with an author index. The sections on History, Archaeology, and Geography, and on Judaism, are not included, but will be included in the 1968 volume, when the *Elenchus* will be separated from *Biblica* and will be an independent publication, price $7.50. This *Elenchus* is an indispensable tool for research in the biblical field. H.H.R.

Die Ou-Testamentiese Werkgemeenskap in Suid-Afrika: Biblical Essays (Proceedings of the Ninth Meeting), with *Die Nuwe-Testamentiese Werkgemeenskap van Suid-Afrika* (Proceedings of the Second Meeting). 1966. Pp. 264 + Pl. II. (Pro Rege-Pers, S. Africa. Price: R. 2.90)

In its centenary year the University of Stellenbosch invited both Societies to hold their congresses there, and the Rector H. B. Thom has contributed a message of greeting to this volume of papers then read. Space forbids any more than a listing of the O.T. contributors, four foreign scholars and eleven others, together with the titles of their papers. They are: J. Bright ('The prophetic reminiscence: its place and function in the book of Jeremiah'), G. Fohrer ('Action of God and decision of man in the O.T.'), A. Malamat ('The ban in Mari and in the Bible'), T. C. Vriezen ('Ruach Yahweh (Elohim) in the O.T.'); A. H. van Zyl (editorial, and 'Psalm 19'), S. du Toit ('Exegesis and Philosophy'), I. H. Eybers ('Relations between Jews and Samaritans in the Persian Period'), F. C. Fensham ('A possible origin of the concept of the Day of the Lord') J. J. Glück ('The conquest of Jerusalem in the account of II Sam. 5:6–8a'), L. M. Muntingh ('Some aspects of West-Semitic kingship in the period of the Hebrew patriarchs'), H. S. Pelser ('The origin of the Syrian Asceticism or Monasticism'), A. van Selms ('How do books of the Bible commence?'), P. J. van Zyl (' *'tb'l* in the Phoenician and Biblical Literature'), P. A. Verhoef ('Some notes on Mal. 1:11'), E. J. Smit ('Death- and burial-formulas in Kings and Chronicles relating to the kings of Judah'). D.R.Ap-T.

PORTEOUS, N. W.: *Living the Mystery. Collected Essays*. 1968. Pp. xii + 188. (Basil Blackwell, Oxford. Price: 35s.)

The twelve essays which make up this volume extend over a period of about twenty years and, together with some others noted at the end of the book, provide a picture of the movement of the author's mind in the pursuit of that elusive subject 'Old Testament Theology'.
Here are essays on the nature of Old Testament Theology, on ethics and prophecy, on Royal Wisdom and on Zion, on the nature of continuity and actualization, and on the relevance of the Old Testament to life and to thought. While we wait for the fuller treatment which has been promised, there is here an ample attestation of his richness of thought concerning some of the themes which the subject raises, not least in his criticisms of a conception of Old Testament

Theology primarily in terms of description and in his search for a standpoint from which the subject can be appraised. Indexes of biblical references and of authors' names are provided.   P.R.A.

REICKE, B. and ROST, L. (ed. by): *Biblisch-historisches Handwörterbuch. Landeskunde, Geschichte, Religion, Kultur, Literatur*. Band III, P-Z. 1966. Pp. 1 + xvi + cols 1361–2256 + 1 coloured plate. 20 black and white plates and 130 drawings. (Vandenhoeck & Ruprecht, Göttingen. Price: DM. 74)

This is the third volume of this useful biblical dictionary, the first two of which were reviewed in *B.L.* 1965, p. 10; *Decade*, p. 562. It completes the coverage of main articles, but is still to be supplemented by an index volume. The standard of illustration is excellent, and the entries are scholarly, up-to-date and concise, with useful bibliographies. It provides a very convenient guide to modern biblical studies in most of their varied aspects. C. Westermann's article on the prophets may be especially commended.   R.E.C.

*RICHARDS, H. J.: *A.B.C. of the Bible*. 1967. Pp. 216. (Geoffrey Chapman, London. Price: 21s.)

This Bible Dictionary, by the Principal of Corpus Christi College, London, has nearly 400 articles, varying in length from a few lines to 24 pages (Bible, including the Apocrypha). The material is up-to-date and the style is popular yet scholarly, but with a minimum of technical detail.   G.F.

RIENECKER, F., SEEWALD, G., COENEN, L. (ed. by): *Lexikon zur Bibel*, 6th edn, 1967. Pp. xii + 867 (text in double columns), Pl. 100 (many with two photographs per plate), numerous line drawings in text. (R. Brockhaus Verlag, Wuppertal. Price: DM. 90)

This is a very well produced, conservatively orientated, but not obscurantist or polemical, Bible Dictionary written mainly by qualified pastors for those desiring knowledge of biblical *Realien*. It has excellent illustrations and is still reasonably up-to-date (being a reprint, apparently, of the 3rd edn, 1961; 1st edn, 1960), even in archaeology.

The chronological chart commences with Abraham, for whom alternative datings are given, depending on whether the exodus is to be dated in 1445 or in 1270. There are four maps in colour (plates 97–100): O.T. Palestine (with a transparent overlay showing early 1967 state boundaries), N.T. Palestine, a Vegetation map, and a noteworthy double-page reproduction of the Madeba map based on Aharoni and with translations and restorations on a transparent overlay. The *Lexikon* ends with the chronological chart mentioned, a Gospel harmony, classified bibliography, classified directory of all illustrations, an index to non-biblical toponyms, and a glossary to help users of other German versions find the keywords which are taken from Luther's translation. This must be among the best one-volume dictionaries for the German reading laity.   D.R.Ap-T.

RIESENFELD, H. (ed. by): *Svensk exegetisk årsbok*. XXXI. 1966. Pp. 138 + 46 (*Symbolae Biblicae Upsalienses* 17) + 42 (*Symbolae Biblicae Upsalienses* 18). XXXII. 1967. Pp. 162 + 18 (*Symbolae Biblicae Upsalienses* 19). (C. W. K. Gleerup, Lund. Price: Sw.Kr. 11 and 15 respectively)

In XXXI R. Rendtorff contributes a discussion (in Swedish) of literary criticism and tradition history which is in some sort an eirenic comparison of the methods adopted by German and Scandinavian scholars. E. M. Good presents a careful and detailed study (in English) of the composition of Hosea. B. Noack writes (in Danish) on the background of the Sibylline oracles. In the New Testament field, but with considerable reference to the Jewish background, B. Gerhardsson examines in detail (in Swedish) the interpretation of the four kinds of soil in the Gospel parable of the sower. An unusual new feature in the review section is an account (in Swedish) by R. A. Carlson of his own work: *David, the Chosen King*. The two supplements are an introduction to and translation into Swedish of the Gospel of Philip, by B. Frid (*SBU* 17), and a catalogue of illustrations in Swedish Bibles (16th century to 1963) and devotional works (16th century to mid-19th century), by G. Olingdahl.

In XXXII all the articles except one are in Swedish. B. Albrektson writes on Luther's attitude to the allegorical interpretation of the Old Testament. Notes on the Hebrew text of Hosea which have survived from I. Engnell's advanced seminar are now printed: for the latter part of the book they provide a new translation. A. Haldar discusses the origins of the belief in resurrection. A. Negoitsa writes (in English) on the use of the Psalter in the Orthodox Church. J. Barr argues for a positive theological evaluation of post-biblical Judaism. B. Gerhardsson's lengthy study of the Passion narrative in Matthew has much of interest for the student of the Old Testament and of Judaism. There are articles in other fields by J. B. Skemp and H. Ljungvik. In the review section, L. Hartmann gives an account of his own work: *Prophecy Interpreted*. The supplement (*SBU* 19) is an introduction to and translation into Swedish of the Coptic text *De Resurrectione* from Nag-Hammadi. G.W.A.

Studia Theologica. Scandinavian Journal of Theology. Vol. 20, No. 1 (1966) and No. 2 (1967). 1966. Pp. 1–94, 95–157. (Universitetsforlaget, Oslo. Subscription price: N.Kr. 48, $8, £2 8s., or DM. 28 each volume)

This volume of *Studia Theologica*, which is now edited by Professors A. S. Kapelrud and J. Jervell of Oslo, contains two Old Testament articles, both in the second fascicle. The Peshiṭta of the book of Malachi is discussed by L. Kruse-Blinkenberg, who considers its relation to the LXX and to the Targum as well as to the Massoretic Text. J. Strange examines 'The Inheritance of Dan' in Joshua 19: 40–8 and argues that it is based on a list compiled in the reign of Josiah. J.A.E.

VAN UNNIK, W. C. and VAN DER WOUDE, A. S. (ed.): *Studia Biblica et Semitica Theodoro Christiano Vriezen Dedicata*. 1966. Pp. 406. (H. Veenman & Zonen N. V., Wageningen. Price: Fl. 36, bound Fl. 39.50)

This *Festschrift* for T. C. Vriezen commemorates his 25 years as Professor of Theology, and after a greeting in Dutch and a bibliography of his main writings, contains 35 contributions. Merely to list them would occupy too much space and convey little; a selection may serve to indicate the rich variety of this impressive volume. Old Testament theology is represented by contributions from N. W. Porteous, G. von Rad, ('Das Werk Jahwes'), and G. E. Wright, though theological emphasis is to be found repeatedly in other contributions. Studies on prophecy include Obadiah (G. Fohrer), Hosea's language (W. Rudolph), Elijah at Horeb (J.-J. Stamm), Isa. 48 (C. Westermann). The patriarchal and early traditions are discussed in relation to Joseph as successor to Jacob and its subsequent repercussions (B. J. van der Merwe), and in O. Eissfeldt's endeavour to distinguish ancient historical elements in leader narratives. Psalm study is represented by articles on Pss 51 (N. H. Ridderbos) and 139 (J. L. Koole), by a review of approaches to *Gattungsforschung* (J. P. M. van der Ploeg), and by a study of stylistic features in the Psalm of Exod. 15 (J. Muilenburg). More technical linguistic studies deal with the particles '*al-ken* (R. Frankena) and *gam* (C. J. Labuschagne), important recognitions of the weight which often rests upon the correct definition of their meaning in context. These and others, including some which overlap into New Testament and Rabbinic and Jewish studies, though inevitably creating a somewhat varied picture, nevertheless not inappropriately pay tribute to the breadth of interest which is to be seen in the writings of the scholar they are designed to honour.

P.R.A.

DE VAUX, R.: *Bible et Orient*. (Cogitatio Fidei 24.) 1967. Pp. 542 + x Pl. (Les Éditions du Cerf, Paris. Price: Fr. 48)

The value and importance of the work of Père de Vaux in every branch of Old Testament study is too well known to need any comment. It is a pleasure to welcome the appearance of this collection in which twenty-eight of his shorter studies, published in various places between 1933 and 1967, have been reproduced, unchanged except for the correction of misprints. There are too many articles for them to be listed in full, but some indication of the scope of the collection is given by the titles of the five sections into which the work is divided: Théologie et Critique Littéraire; Histoire d'Israel; Institutions de l'Ancien Testament; Les Manuscrits de la Mer Morte; Bible, Archéologie et Histoire des Religions. There is a biblical index and a short name and subject index.

M.A.K.

ARCHAEOLOGY AND EPIGRAPHY

AMADASI, M. G.: *L'Iconografia del Carro da Guerra in Siria e Palestina*. 1965. Pp. 192; 29 figs. (Centro di Studi Semitici, Istituto di Studi del Vicino Oriente, University of Rome, Rome. Price: Lire 4.000; $7.00)

This is an archaeological study of the light two-wheeled war-chariot, the appearance of which in Syria the author associates with the horse just before the Hyksos period, particularly associated with the Hittites and Mitanni. In her penetrating analysis of material and iconographic evidence to determine the origin of the chariot and its various features and their particular development from the middle of the 2nd millennium to the beginning of the 6th century B.C., when the chariot was replaced by mounted cavalry, the author concludes that there is no evidence of a single place of origin, but that diversity of features characterizes the earliest evidence. She notes two main variations, the Egyptian and the Mesopotamian. The former influenced Palestine and coastal Syria; the latter inland Syria and Anatolia. Mycenaean modifications in Cyprus, Palestine and coastal Syria are also noted, with specifically Mitannian features in the interior of Syria, a distinctive Assyrian type developing after c. 800 B.C.

J.G.

JAMES, E. O.: *The Tree of Life.* (Supplements to *Numen*, XI) 1966. Pp. 293. (Brill, Leiden. Price: Fl. 45)

The author, who is well known for his studies in comparative religion, has assembled a great deal of material bearing upon the sacred tree as a medium of revival and rejuvenation, both in literature and art. The persistence and development of the motif is traced into Jewish and Christian eschatology. The work, however, is decidedly discursive and the field so wide as to permit vagueness and irrelevance. There are many digressions and lengthy repetitions, as for instance in the case of the general references to the fertility-cult in Palestine, where the scriptural references will be felt to be overpressed. Those most familiar with the material and textual matter from the Near East will notice the derivative character of the work at this point, where too much is assumed uncritically where authorities themselves are in doubt. The book, if read in sections, into which it is conveniently divided, will be found full of interest and information, but a stronger impression of the significance of the tree of life would have been left had the evidence from the various regions been coordinated and more concisely presented.

J.G.

KAPELRUD, A. S.: *Med spade i bibeljord.* 1967. Pp. 108 + 1 map + 8 plates. (Universitetsforlaget, Oslo. Price: N.Kr. 10.60)

This popular presentation of the importance of Near Eastern archaeology for Old Testament study lays special emphasis on Palestinian discoveries and on recent developments, but indicates the place of the former within the wider geographical context and of the latter within the general progress of archaeological research. Particular attention is devoted to the work at Masada; but Mari, Nuzi, Jerusalem, Jericho, Gibeon, and Ugarit are all referred to. The bearing of the various discoveries on the biblical text is indicated; and there are useful discussions of the historicity of the patriarchal narratives, the composition of the Pentateuch, and the background of Jewish eschatology.

G.W.A.

KELSO, J.: *Archaeology and our Old Testament contemporaries.* 1966. Pp. 192. (Zondervan Publishing House, Grand Rapids, Michigan. Price: $4.95)

Lavishly illustrated, this book shows by its chapter headings its attempt to popularize Old Testament studies: Abraham, International Business Genius and Christian Saint; Moses, History's Most Unique

Statesman; The Statesmen, David and Churchill; Solomon, The King with many a Ph.D. The author is a staunch conservative whose archaeological reputation is guaranteed by the Foreword by W. F. Albright, but many sweeping statements would be difficult to prove. It is interesting and sometimes amusing. J.N.S.

LAPP, P. W.: *The Dhahr Mirzbâneh Tombs.* (*Three Intermediate Bronze Age Cemeteries in Jordan*) (A.S.O.R. — Publications of the Jerusalem School of Archaeology. IV). 1966. Pp. x + 117, 44 figs, XV Plates. (American Schools of Oriental Research, New Haven. Price: $8.00)

The present Director of the American School of Oriental Research in Jerusalem presents interesting evidence in pottery and a limited quantity of bronze-work from two cemeteries of shaft burials from the period *c.* 2100 to 1800, which he designates Intermediate Bronze I and II, which supplement the burials of various types in shaft-graves at Jericho, Lachish, Tell el-Ajjul, el-Jib and Megiddo. This he uses, together with archaeological evidence of the period in Syria, to give an appraisal of the current views of experts on the historical and ethnic situation in Palestine in the period of urban and cultural recession prior to the urban revival of the Middle Bronze Age proper, *c.* 1800. He considers that the evidence points to a more complicated situation than settlement by Amorite tribesmen and their eventual sedentarization, as proposed by de Vaux and Albright, and he develops Dr Kenyon's thesis which recognizes another non-Semitic element from further afield than the North Arabian Steppes, which was associated with the development of metallurgy, which is most marked in the urban revival in Syria. It is proposed that these people came by way of Anatolia and the Syrian coast, possibly in certain cases reaching S. Palestine by sea. An ultimate provenance from Bokara is suggested by Dr Lapp by archaeological evidence from that region considered by him to relate to some of the material evidence from the IB shaft-graves in Palestine. Since this is dated by Russian archaeologists between the 5th century B.C. and the 6th century A.D., Dr Lapp's claims are sensational, and it will be interesting to see the reaction of western archaeologists to the new Russian evidence and of the Russian archaeologists to the evidence from Palestine and Syria of which Dr Lapp's study will apprise them.

J.G.

PARROT, A.: *Mission archéologique de Mari*, vol. III. *Les Temples d'Ishtarat et de Ninni-zaza.* 1967. Pp. 354 + 84 black and 5 coloured plates, with 348 illustrations in the text. (Geuthner, Paris. Price: Fr. 120)

This third volume of the definitive report on the excavations at Mari, which were interrupted by the war in 1939 and resumed from 1951 to 1955 and then from 1960 on, deals with two contiguous pre-Sargonic temples, which were without communication with one another. These were the temples of Ishtarat, a Semitic goddess, and of Ninni-zaza, a Sumerian Goddess. Preliminary reports have been published in *Syria* and elsewhere. Here there are careful descriptions of the temples and of all the objects found in them, including some fine statuary and various objects in stone, mother-of-pearl, metal and pottery. The whole volume is superbly and lavishly illustrated. A few inscriptions on the objects found are edited by G. Dossin, and the author has also had the assistance of L. Laroche in the preparation of the volume.   H.H.R.

PFEIFFER, C. F. (ed.): *The Biblical World. A Dictionary of Biblical Archaeology.* 1966. Pp. 612 inc. 273 ills. (Baker Book House, Grand Rapids, Michigan. Price: $8.95)

This dictionary of Biblical archaeology, the first of its kind, is the work of over forty American scholars. It contains general articles, e.g. Agriculture, Archaeologists and their work (over 200 names are listed), Law, Medicine, Pottery; articles on ancient cities and excavated sites; and articles on the major texts and literature discovered by archaeologists. Comprehensive as the work is, the editor has had to be selective; there is no article on Sacrifice, and no reference to it in the article on Religion, though there is an entry on Altars; there is an article on Marriage, but none on Slavery. The presentation is popular and non-technical, though many entries have short bibliographies. The articles are readable and informative; the many illustrations are well chosen. This is a welcome addition to the reference books now available to the Bible student.   L.A.P.

THOMAS, D. WINTON (ed. by): *Archaeology and Old Testament Study.* 1967. Pp. xxxii + 492. (Clarendon Press, Oxford. Price: 75s.)

This splendid volume, issued to mark the Jubilee of S.O.T.S., increases the already great debt owed by the Society and Old Testament scholarship in general to the editor, who himself contributes a most balanced Introduction on the value and limitations of archaeology for the study of the Old Testament. In contrast to other books with somewhat similar titles, this work consists of a series of essays by different scholars, carefully describing the main archaeological discoveries from a particular site or area and then assessing what evidence they provide for the elucidation of the biblical literature. This is not the place to discuss the individual contributions: suffice it to say that they are all thoroughly up-to-date and display sound and cautious scholarship in their judgements. It is particularly useful to have in a single book so many surveys covering the extensive archaeological work now being done on sites in Palestine itself. Inevitably some of the essays seem more directly related to the Bible than others, and, if one were to venture a small criticism, it would be to point to the comparative neglect of the post-exilic Old Testament period — there is virtually nothing, for example, on Elephantine or the Persian Empire.   J.R.P.

*WILLIAMS, WALTER G.: *Archaeology in Biblical Research.* 1966. Pp. 223; line drawings and maps 8; Pll. xxviii. (Lutterworth Press, London. Price: 35s.)

This convenient handbook for the non-specialist was first published in the U.S.A. by Abingdon Press and still bears some marks of its first home. The 15 chapters are divided into three Parts, the first of which is devoted to a mainly historical survey. The second part deals with aspects of field work, and the last seeks to garner up the fruits according to their kinds, e.g. 'The Location of Bible Sites', 'Biblical and Extra-Biblical Mss'. The emphasis throughout is on the Old Testament, and the information given is sound and interestingly imparted, though occasionally (pp. 16, 17, cf. p. 162) the careless reader may be misled into believing that on some points archaeology has proved more than the facts bear out.

The illustrations are clear and meaningful and the indexes are ample. The longish bibliography lists many 'popular' articles by scholars and names the main journals of importance for biblical archaeologists.

D.R.Ap-T.

HISTORY AND GEOGRAPHY

AHARONI, Y.: *The Land of the Bible: A Historical Geography*, translated from the Hebrew by A. F. Rainey. 1967. Pp. 409 + xiv + 34 maps. (Burns & Oates, London. Price: 63s.)

This well-produced book contains two parts: an introductory survey of the geography of Palestine and the historical sources of our information (117 pp.) and a history of the land through the ages from the Canaanite period to the end of the monarchy with 10 pages on the Exile and the restoration (240 pp.). The author shows his intimate knowledge of the land, and good maps illustrate the divisions at various periods. There is a useful chronological table, a list of site identifications and indexes of biblical references and of geographical names.   J.N.S.

*AVI-YONAH, M.: *The Holy Land, from the Persian to the Arab conquests (536 B.C. to A.D. 640). A Historical Geography*. 1966. Pp. 232. 24 maps in the text. (Baker Book House, Grand Rapids, Mich. Price: $5.95)

This book is the result of many years of work on historical and geographical problems, and it is particularly useful that it covers in its first part that historical period which is at many points less well-known because of the problems of the biblical sources. It reveals how much can be gleaned about the history and geography of the post-exilic period from the apparently meagre information available. Part two deals with city territories from the end of the 3rd century A.D.; part three with the Roman road system and with questions concerning economy and population. It is a book rich in up-to-date information.

P.R.A.

BAR-DEROMA, H.: *A series of studies on the Bible and the land of the Bible* (Gernham's Library). I. '*Ye mountains of Gilboa*' (pp. ix, 49 with 9 illustrations and map; 1966). II. '*The River of Egypt*' (pp. v, 52 with 15 illustrations and map; 1966). III. '*Kadesh Barnea*' (pp. x, 68 with 11 illustrations and 2 maps; 1967). IV. '*Even that Sinai*' (pp. iv, 53 with 12 illustrations; 1967). (B.E.R. Publishing Co., Jerusalem)

These four guides, bound in black cloth, slim volumes of uniform size and intended to go easily into the pocket, are a new venture intended for visitors to famous sites in Israel, written in lucid modern Hebrew which English biblical scholars will not find too difficult, especially as the Hebrew type is unusually clear, even in the notes. They provide brief summaries of the biblical history of each site, with adequate references to the Old Testament and discussions (where necessary) of disputed locations, and in the case of Sinai some account of the Christian tradition. The illustrations, some photographs and others drawings, are well chosen and generally well reproduced. The first three volumes have loose folding maps at the end; but the Hebrew names on them are not always very easy to read, and the maps themselves are unfortunately not attached to the volume but loose, so that they may easily be lost.   G.R.D.

The Cambridge Ancient History: Revised Edition of Volumes I and II. The Development of Cities, from Al-'Ubaid to the End of Uruk 5: by M. E. L. Mallowan. Fasc. 58, Parts 1 and 2. Pp. 83 and 60. (Price: 10s. 6d. and 6s.)

Immigrants from the North: by R. A. Crossland. Fasc. 60. Pp. 61. (Price: 6s.)

With these two fascicles the complicated project of issuing a new edition of the first two volumes of the *Cambridge Ancient History* is nearing completion.

Professor Mallowan gives us a masterly survey of the numerous excavated sites of his period (Al-'Ubaid to Uruk 5) from the coast of Syria in the west to the central Persian desert in the east, and from the Caspian Sea to Susiana in the south. Part 1 describes the central area of Babylonia and Mesopotamia, and Assyria. Part 2 contains the sections on the two peripheral regions of Syria and Iran. Each site is separately described and its archaeological characteristics summarized. The period is a prehistoric one and the purely archaeological approach is perhaps inevitable. One could wish, however, that after the presentation of so much detail the chapter might have ended with some attempt at a general historical interpretation of the phenomena such as is implied in the title.

Professor Crossland, an Indo-European philologist and an authority on Hittite and the Anatolian languages, writes on the earliest Indo-European immigrants into the Middle East, India and the Mediterranean. After announcing the basic principles governing the use of the available evidence, he first surveys the recorded languages and dialects, then the archaeological facts, and concludes with two sections in which he draws the necessary deductions regarding the original home of the Indo-Europeans and describes the impact of these northerners on the societies into which they moved. European prehistory is treated only in summary form, being outside the scope of the chapter.   O.R.G.

MOWINCKEL, S.: *Israels opphav og eldste historie.* (Scandinavian University Books.) 1967. Pp. xvi + 378 + 20 plates + map on endpapers. (Universitetsforlaget, Oslo. Price: N.Kr. 38)

This posthumously published work contains the material presented by Professor Mowinckel in two series of lectures which he delivered in the University of Oslo after his retirement. He discusses the patriarchal narratives and the problems which they raise, the life and religion of the Israelite tribes during the sojourn in Egypt and the wilderness wandering, the process of settlement on both sides of the Jordan, and the culture, organization and religious life of Israel in Canaan in the early period. Mowinckel combines in a remarkable way a survey of recent discussion of the many complex problems raised with the presentation of his own independent conclusions. The volume is well documented; and there is an excellent bibliography. An English translation is in course of preparation.   G.W.A.

ORLINSKY, H. M.: *L'antico Israele*. Pp. 196. (L. Cappelli, Rocca San Casciano. Price: L. 500)

This is an Italian translation of a work originally written in English, and published under the title of *Ancient Israel* in 1954. It was noted in *B.L.* 1954, p. 23; *Eleven Years*, p. 560.   J.M.T.B.

PATTEN, D. W.: *The Biblical Flood and the Ice Epoch. A Study in Scientific History*. 2nd edition, 1967. Pp. 336. (Pacific Meridian Publishing Co., Seattle. Price: $7.50)

This is a book that will convince the scientific humanist that those who believe in the authority of the Bible need not be taken seriously. It is doubtful, however, whether any biblical scholar would find this 'scientific history' convincing. The main thesis is that there was a great Ice Age and universal Flood in *c*. 2800 B.C. caused by the irruption of an astral visitor (probably Mercury) into the solar system which dumped its ice on the earth in passing. There were two subsequent catastrophes in the 15th century (Jos. 10:12–14) and the 8th century (Isa. 38:8, etc.) caused by interaction with Mars and Venus. To all this the Bible and legends all over the world bear witness. The book is a fine example of dazzling with scientific terminology.   A.S.H.

PFEIFFER, C. F.: *The Divided Kingdom*. 1967. Pp. 117 inc. 1 map and 30 ills. (Baker Book House, Grand Rapids, Michigan. Price: $2.95)

A feature of this history of Israel from the death of Solomon to the fall of Jerusalem in 586 B.C. is the emphasis on Israel's relations with the surrounding nations and on archaeological discovery. The author's standpoint is conservative and there is no evaluation of the sources. The subject matter is so arranged that there is a good deal of repetition. The illustrations are well chosen and add to the interest of the book.   L.A.P.

*ROWLEY, H. H. (ed.): *Atlas zur Bibel*. 1965. Pp. 48. (R. Brockhaus Verlag, Wuppertal. Price: DM. 9.80)

This German translation and adaptation of the *Student's Bible Atlas* (London, Lutterworth Press, 1965) which does not appear to have been noted in the *Book List*, provides chronological tables, maps covering not only biblical times but also Church history to the present day, charts showing the spread of the Church (with special reference to German aspects), and an index. The title is thus strictly too limited for the book. The maps are very clear, and a particularly useful device is that of having a transparency with modern names to cover the map of Israel in Canaan.   P.R.A.

*RUSSELL, D. S.: *The Jews from Alexander to Herod.* (The New Clarendon Bible. Old Testament, Volume v.) 1967. Pp. xvi + 330 (with 21 illustrations in the text and a chronological table). (Oxford University Press, London. Price: 25s.)

Dr Russell is well known for his contributions to the study of the intertestamental period. He here provides a worthwhile and valuable successor to Box's *Judaism in the Greek Period* (1932), which formed volume v of the original Clarendon Bible. The work falls into three parts: an account of Jewish history from Alexander to Herod, a sketch of the religious background and a discussion of some of the literary products of Judaism, canonical and extra-canonical, with notes on selected passages. The work has been well written and attractively produced, and the volume will certainly prove of considerable value for use in schools. But its general utility would have been enhanced if, instead of merely extending the scope of the work from 63 to 4 B.C., the opportunity had been taken to carry the narrative down to A.D. 70, which would seem to form a more obvious stopping-place. Two points of detail: it seems curious that in referring to the Qumran fragments of *Sir.* the author does not mention *11QPs^a* (nor indeed the Masada material), and is it quite true to state that the Hodayot 'have no divisions between them, and so it is difficult to say where one hymn begins and another ends' (p. 294)?

                                                                M.A.K.

SKROBUCHA, H.: *Sinai.* 1966. Pp. viii + 120. Photographs by George W. Allan; translated by Geoffrey Hunt. (Oxford University Press. Price: 70s.)

This splendidly produced volume was first published in German in 1959. It is the story of the Sinai peninsula in general and of Mount Sinai in particular, from earliest times to the present-day. It includes the story of the hermits and monks, of Moslem occupation, and of the Monastery of St Katherine and its treasures. The production and format is excellent. It contains 56 illustrations, many of them full-page and 21 of them superbly coloured. A book for bibliophiles.

                                                                N.H.S.

TEXT AND VERSIONS

DUNAND, F.: *Papyrus grecs bibliques* (*Papyrus F. Inv. 266*): *Volumina de la Genèse et du Deutéronome.* (Recherches d'Archéologie, de Philologie et d'Histoire, XXVII.) 1966. Pp. 64. (Institut français d'archéologie orientale, Cairo. Price: £1 4s.)

P. Fuad 266 consists of 115 fragments, three of Genesis, the remainder from the second half of Deuteronomy, one of which was published by Waddell in 1944–5 in *J.T.S.* Further fragments were later made known by Baars (not mentioned by Dunand) and Vaccari. This introductory volume (the text itself is to appear in *Études de Papyrologie*, IX, pp. 81–150) deals with the reconstruction of the columns of the Deuteronomy fragments, the dating (probably mid-1st century B.C.), and the textual affinities. The last three chapters then discuss the problem of the origin of the LXX (the author shows herself a follower of Kahle), and the rendering of the Tetragrammaton.

S.P.B.

MCNAMARA, M.: *The New Testament and the Palestinian Targum to the Pentateuch*. (Analecta Biblica, 27.) 1966. Pp. xxiv + 285. (Pontifical Biblical Institute, Rome. Price: L. 5.700 = $9.50)

This comprehensive and valuable work is divided into two parts. The first is introductory and ranges from an historical outline of various Targums and Targumic Studies to a detailed examination of relevant topics in the New Testament. They include 'Traditions relating to Moses, Jannes and Jambres', 'The Divine Name and the "Second Death" in the Apocalypse', treatment of specified passages in the Gospels. The second part contains a closer study of topics, all of which are interesting and some very important. They include 2 Cor. 3:7–4:6, and a number of passages in Rev. which have relationships with Targum Pseudo-Jonathan in particular. Messianic themes provide the topic for yet another chapter, and the whole is rounded off with a survey of 'conclusions'. Most New Testament scholars will feel that they knew much of what is to be found here, but it is doubtful whether so much relevant material has been elsewhere assembled in one convenient volume and presented in such a fascinating manner. The book has a good bibliography and indexes.

B.J.R.

(*Peshiṭta*): *The Old Testament in Syriac according to the Peshiṭta Version*, edited on behalf of the International Organization for the study of the Old Testament by the Peshiṭta Institute of the University of Leiden. Sample edition: Song of Songs — Tobit — 4 Ezra. 1966. Pp. xxii + xxii + 24 + xii + 56 + ii + 54. (E. J. Brill, Leiden. Price: Fl. 30)

This volume bears the first-fruits of the Peshiṭta Institute's long preparatory work towards the production of a critical edition of the Peshiṭta O.T. It follows upon their *List of Old Testament Peshiṭta Manuscripts* published in 1961 (see *B.L.* 1962, p. 23; *Decade*, p. 333), to which the reader needs to refer, and is under the editorship of Professor P. A. H. de Boer in collaboration with W. Baars (co-editor). The editors state that the object of their undertaking is to present as clearly as possible within reasonable limits of space the evidence from a more or less representative array of MSS such as will illustrate the tradition of the Peshiṭta text. They draw attention to the fact that this is a *sample* edition, and that they hope to learn from its evaluation by those who make use of it. The General Preface sets out in detail the 'Rules' which are to govern the editing of the Peshiṭta as a whole. The basic text is to be that of 'Milan Ambrosian Library, MS. B.21. Inferiore', other MSS being selected where this codex is wanting. Details are given of sigla to be adopted, of the upper

critical apparatus which forms together with the basic text a dip-
lomatic reproduction of that text, of the lower critical apparatus
containing variants in other MSS chosen for the edition, and notes
on the latter, and of an *index orthographicus* to be included with each
of the books edited. The main part of the volume consists of critical
editions of Song of Songs by J. A. Emerton, Tobit by J. C. H. Lebram, and 4 Ezra by R. J. Bidawid. In these the detailed plan set out in
the Preface is seen in action. The result in each case is a clear, concise
and objective delineation of the Syriac text and its variants, and the
authors, as well as the general editors, are to be congratulated on
what has so far been achieved. Once the system of the sigla has been
grasped, one can readily follow the many complexities inherent in this
important project.   A.E.G.

RAEDER, S.: *Die Benutzung des masoretischen Texts bei Luther in der Zeit
zwischen der ersten und zweiten Psalmenvorlesung* (1515–1518). (Beiträge
zur historischen Theologie, 38.) 1967. Pp. viii + 117. (J. C. B. Mohr
(Paul Siebeck), Tübingen. Price: DM. 26.00)

Following on his masterly treatment of Luther's use of the Hebrew
Old Testament (*Das Hebräische bei Luther untersucht bis zum Ende
der ersten Psalmenvorlesung*, 1961) Dr Raeder now gives a detailed
study of the early phases. By means of a close scrutiny of the Peni-
tential Psalms, together with a few other passages, he demonstrates
Luther's familiarity with Hebrew even in the *Dictata super Psalterium*
(1513–1515); it is in subsequent works, however, that great significance
is attached to it. The texts available to him were the Basel Psalter
(1516), Quadruplex — an edition attached to Erasmus' works of
Jerome (1516), and, in view of Luther's treatment of Hebrew outside
the Psalms, it is also likely that he used the Brescia Bible of 1494.

                                                                         B.J.R.

REIDER, J. and TURNER, N.: *An Index to Aquila* (Supplements to Vetus
Testamentum, Vol. XII). 1966. Pp. xii + 331. (E. J. Brill, Leiden.
Price: Fl. 75)

The manuscript of the Index compiled by Reider in 1913 and deposited
in the Library of Dropsie College has been completed, extended and
thoroughly revised by Nigel Turner. The main part of the work is the
Greek–Hebrew index (pp. 1–261), each word being followed by its
Hebrew equivalent and the biblical references. The index includes
words found in the Syriac, Latin and Armenian sources; they are
given in a Greek rendering, are underlined and their source indicated
by either syr., lat. or arm. The book also contains a Hebrew–Greek
index (pp. 262–318) and a Latin–Hebrew index (pp. 324–31) of words
taken from Latin, Armenian or Syriac sources. On pages 318–23
there is a Hebrew–Greek index of proper names.
The appearance of this index, anticipated more than fifty years ago,
will be welcomed by Septuagint and Old Testament scholars alike,
and will be of inestimable value in the study of the pre-Massoretic
Hebrew text.   L.H.B.

WAHL, O.: *Die Prophetenzitate der Sacra Parallela in ihrem Verhältnis zur Septuaginta-Textüberlieferung.* (Studien zum Alten und Neuen Testament. Bd. XIII.) 1965. 2 vols. Pp. xiii + 717, ix + 718–1162. (Kösel-Verlag. Munich. Price: DM. 120 the set)

This amazingly long work consists of a doctoral thesis, and carries both the merits and weakness generally found in such publications. The merits lie in the extremely thorough and workmanl'ke performance, the weakness in that both are paraded in the published form. The last page consists of one paragraph, in double-spaced lettering (the whole book is typed) and simply says that the nett result of the enquiry is that the text examined here supports the Lucianic recension of the LXX.

But the work is an important one. By dealing with an apposite text from the *Florilegia*, the *Sacra Parallela* of John of Damascus, the author has opened out a field of study hitherto largely ignored — and not only by textualists — except in a very general way. Secondly, by demonstrating the relevance of the history of the transmission in this particular text, the author, by implication, draws attention to the hazards of referring to a textual form whose *bona fides* have not been tested. Thirdly — a point explicitly discussed by the author — the measure of interplay of recensional and other activities in 'secondary texts' (such as the *Florilegia*) is a study in itself, and gives rise to its own peculiar problems which are more complicated even than those faced by an editor of the Septuagint itself. The meagre 'nett result', therefore, is not altogether a fair reflexion on the quality of the book. Nevertheless, a book of one tenth the size would have been ample.

B.J.R.

EXEGESIS AND MODERN TRANSLATIONS

CRAMPON, A.: *La Bible.* (1960). New edition. Pp. lviii + 1164 + 362 + 12 maps. (Desclée et Cie., Tournai. Price: Fr.B. 140; Can. $3.50)

This pocket bible, of which the Old Testament part has been revised by J. Bonsirven, S.J., offers not only the complete text in French, but also short introductions to all the books, chronological tables, maps, and a short dictionary to the New Testament. The text is accompanied by brief notes commenting on the interpretation, on the content and on many points of detail. Cross references are provided in a middle column to the text.

P.R.A.

CUNDALL, A. E.: *Judges.* MORRIS, L.: *Ruth.* (Tyndale Old Testament Commentaries.) 1968. Pp. 318. (The Tyndale Press, London. Price: 15s. 6d.)

While both these commentaries are conservative in their approach they are not excessively so. Both make use of the techniques of literary and textual criticism.

The difficulties of equating Judges 1 with Joshua are recognized and it is suggested that 'Joshua may occasionally be given credit for action carried out by individual tribes'. At Judges 5 a useful though brief note is given on the forms of Hebrew poetry, and the poem 'has undoubtedly suffered in transmission'. In 5:5 *zeh* does not appear to have been recognized as a relative. Some further comment is needed on the name Jerubbaal, and the note on 'Levite' at 17:7 is hardly adequate. Worth noting is the comment that the exploits of Samson 'read like the actions of an uncontrollable juvenile delinquent'. Elsewhere it is noted that 'composition and editorship are as much the province of inspiration as actual authorship'.

Ruth is dated as probably from the early monarchy period. After noting various views as to the purpose of the book, Canon Morris concludes that it was to show the sovereignty of God, with 2:12 as the key to the book. On pages 282 f. there is a useful note on *g'l*.

A.S.H.

DAVIES, G. HENTON: *Exodus: Introduction and Commentary* (Torch Bible Commentaries). 1967. Pp. 253. (S.C.M. Press, London. Price: 22s. 6d.)

Principal Henton Davies affirms that the persistent theme of the Book of Exodus is the presence of Yahweh. The record as it stands in the book reflects prophet and priest, has undergone expansion, and has become part of the P complex of tradition, Genesis to Numbers. In answer to the question of how much in the record is historical, it is said that the basic facts (or bare facts) 'shine through whatever of prophetical, liturgical or social expansions have taken place'. If these bare facts have undergone, in many cases, cultic glorification, this distinction 'loses much of its validity when the bare facts are seen to be facts of worship and cult'. In reading this book one has often the impression of problems of literary criticism and of interpretation to be tackled, and a lack of sufficient space for the purpose. It is admitted, for example, that the infliction of plagues on the Egyptians and the hardening of Pharaoh's heart to effect the release of the Israelites offend our theological sense; but then the words, 'These stories are intended to teach the efficacy of intercession' are quoted, apparently with approbation. The author has, on the whole, made good use of the space available to him, and where he has not been able to develop a subject as he would have liked, has referred the reader to other works for further study.

J.M.

DHORME, E.: *A Commentary on the Book of Job*. Translated by H. Knight. 1967. Pp. ccxxiv + 675. (Thomas Nelson, London. Price: £10 10s.)

It is unusual for a book, still less a commentary, to be translated forty years after its original publication (*Le livre de Job*, Paris, 1926). But the reputation enjoyed by this commentary and the fact that the original has for long been difficult of access, certainly justify the labour involved in producing this English edition, to which H. H. Rowley contributes a prefatory note and in which he has given assistance at many points. The substantial introduction (pp. vii–ccxxiv) covers questions both of composition and of content; the commentary provides a wealth of detailed information, especially concerning the versions. The material is set out with great clarity and the translation reads smoothly.

The problems of producing an adequate commentary on the book of Job are enormous. Of course, as a result of advances in Hebrew philology, there are matters here which are out of date; as a result of the development of literary and form-critical study, there are new approaches which this commentary does not touch. But the method adopted here enables the problems of text and interpretation to be approached clearly, and a sound foundation is laid on to which newer information can be built. The insights of the author are a continuous gain.

The price is heavy, presumably because only a limited edition has been printed. Certainly every theological library must acquire it, and every scholar and student who is working on the text of Job, at whatever level, will find it an indispensable tool.　　P.R.A.

EATON, J. H.: *Psalms: Introduction and Commentary.* (Torch Bible Commentaries.) 1967. Pp. 318. (S.C.M. Press, London. Price: 25s.)

Mr Eaton is to be congratulated on the skill with which he has used the space available to him. The subjects selected for inclusion in his brief introduction prepare the reader for what he will find in the commentary: an interpretation of the psalms which is, in general, based on Gunkel's literary classification, Mowinckel's cult functional approach, A. R. Johnson's exposition of sacral kingship, and Birkeland's theory of the identity of the 'I' and the enemies. RSV has been adopted as the basis of the commentary but not slavishly followed. The discussion of each psalm ends with a paragraph relating it to Christian theology and devotion. Here the emphasis is strongly Christological.　　G.W.A.

EICHRODT, W.: *Der Herr der Geschichte:* Jesaja 13–23, 28–39 übersetzt und ausgelegt. (Die Botschaft des Alten Testaments 17, II.) 1967. Pp. 282. (Calwer Verlag, Stuttgart. Price: DM. 18.00)

The first part of Eichrodt's exposition of Isaiah 1–39 was noticed in *B.L.* 1961, p. 30 (*Decade*, p. 268). It was there stated that the introduction was reserved for the second volume. But there is no introduction, no doubt because it is considered unnecessary for this kind of expository commentary. A retrospective review of the preaching of Isaiah is given in the last ten pages. The theological exegesis forms the main character and strength of the commentary, and this is often penetrating. Otherwise the critical positions are conservative, sometimes startlingly so, as in the first volume. Much that is normally attributed to later prophets is firmly attributed to Isaiah of Jerusalem, and little use is made of recent form-critical contributions. On the other hand chapters 24–7 are dated in the beginning of the 3rd century and are left to be dealt with by Werner Kessler in the volume on Isaiah 56–66. New Testament fulfilment is kept in mind.　　D.R.J.

ELLISON, H. L.: *Ezekiel: The Man and His Message.* (Mount Radford Reprints.) 1967. Pp. 144. (The Paternoster Press, Exeter. Price: 6s.)

This is an unaltered paperback reprint of a work originally published in 1956. (See *B.L.* 1957, p. 31; *Decade*, p. 31.)　　G.W.A.

ELLISON, H. L.: *From Tragedy to Triumph: The Message of the Book of Job*. (Mount Radford Reprints.) 1967. Pp. 128. (The Paternoster Press, Exeter. Price: 5s.)

This is an unaltered paperback reprint of a work originally published in 1958. (See *B.L.* 1959, p. 17; *Decade*, p. 153.)   G.W.A.

FOHRER, G.: *Das Buch Jesaja*. 1. Band, Kapitel 1–23; 2. Band, Kapitel 24–39. (Zürcher Bibelkommentare.) 2nd revised ed. 1966; 1967. Pp. VIII + 264; VIII + 204. (Zwingli Verlag, Zürich and Stuttgart. Price: Sw.Fr. 17.40; 13:40)

This is a revised and enlarged edition of Fohrer's very useful commentary on First Isaiah. Volume I was originally published in 1960, volume II in 1962 (see *B.L.* 1961, p. 31 and 1963, p. 22; *Decade*, pp. 269, 416.)   M.A.K.

GOLLWITZER, H., JÄNICKE, T., MARQUARDT, F.-W.: *Unser Vater Abraham*. (Alttestamentliche Predigten 8.) 1967. Pp. 110. (Neukirchener Verlag des Erziehungsvereins. Price: DM. 8.80)

For some years now the pastor of the Jesus-Christ Church in Berlin-Dahlem, Theodor Jänicke, and Helmut Gollwitzer and Friedrich-Wilhelm Marquardt of the Free University of Berlin, have preached a course of sermons on a series of Old Testament subjects during a University semester. This volume which contains the sermons preached by them in the summer semester of 1966 is the third series of such sermons to be published. The passages chosen are from Genesis 11–23 and most of them are concerned with Abraham. The sermons are scriptural, exegetical and related with freshness, directness and percipience to the modern world, so that what might be regarded as stories of a bygone day are given contemporary relevance and become charged with urgent demand. And this is done in the basic belief that the community of Israel and the Christian community belong together in the faith, so that the men of the old covenant can speak to the men of the new. This book shows that they can.   J.M.

GONZÁLEZ, A.: *El libro de los Salmos: Introducción, versión y comentario*. (Biblioteca Herder, Sección de Sagrada Escritura 73.) 1966. Pp. 730. (Editorial Herder, S. A., Barcelona. Price: 480 ptas.)

This is one of the volumes of Herder's Biblioteca that was from the start written in Castilian, whereas many of the earlier volumes are translations from English, French and German. It is a finely produced work with excellent indices and every proof that Dr Angel Gonzalez has made a thorough examination of the psalter and has his own point of view in such matters. The verse translations of the psalms appear to be musical and clearly expressed.   J.M.T.B.

GRAY, J.: *Joshua, Judges and Ruth*. (The Century Bible: new edition.) 1967. Pp. xii + 435. (Thomas Nelson and Sons, London. Price: 50s.)

It is so long since any major commentaries on these books appeared in English that there can be no hesitation in saying that this volume must now rank as the standard work in that language. In addition to Gray's own insights, among which may particularly be noted the frequent citation of Ugaritic parallels, the work reflects at every point the important contributions of recent foreign scholarship. As far as Joshua is concerned, Gray basically adopts the standpoint of Noth's famous commentary, but he also gives full weight to the importance of cultic materials, such as have been emphasized by H.-J. Kraus. At the same time, archaeological and topographical evidence is fully utilized and an interesting attempt made to reconstruct the actual events on which the traditions rest: certainly this work illustrates how false is the dichotomy so often drawn between a recognition of the great significance of aetiological and cultic factors and the genuine historicity of the material. In the treatment of Judges, of particular interest is Gray's working out of Beyerlin's view that much of the so-called editorial matter is pre-Deuteronomic and indicates an earlier collection of local and tribal traditions, presented in language drawn from the liturgy of the Covenant cult. Rather surprisingly, Gray does not give as much weight as he might have done to the evidence for the hero cycles having originally come into existence as collections at particular sanctuaries. The purpose of Ruth remains a problem and Gray's solution is not wholly satisfactory. He sees the book as addressed to the situation of returning exiles and the problem of their integration into the society of those who had remained in Palestine. But if this is so, one can hardly avoid wondering why a *Moabite* woman is the central figure of the story. The style of the whole commentary could sometimes be improved. Too often the author's language is so opaque that it is almost impossible to grasp his exact meaning and the same information tends to be repeated unnecessarily — e.g. virtually the same comment on the expression 'the Lord God of Israel' recurs on pages 86, 87, 95, and 192.

J.R.P.

The Holy Psalter: The Psalms of David from the Septuagint. 1966. Pp. xxv + 184. (The Diocesan Press, Madras)

This translation of the Psalter from the Greek has been made primarily for use in the services of the Orthodox Church. Each psalm is provided with a descriptive title — not infrequently embodying a Christological interpretation — in addition to the title found in the Septuagint. In general the translation reads well enough, but there are inelegances, e.g. 'So they ate and were thoroughly stuffed', Ps 77:29. The introduction and notes draw largely upon the New Testament and the Church Fathers, and are mainly of a devotional nature, e.g. 'The earth has yielded her fruit', Ps 66:7, evokes the comment 'Mary has borne Jesus'. The name of the translator is not given, but any communication in connection with the translation may be addressed to Fr Lazarus, c/o The Diocesan Press, Post Box 455, Madras 7, South India.

D.W.T.

KELLEY, P. H.: *The Book of Amos. A Study Manual.* 1966. Pp. 98. (Baker Book House, Grand Rapids, Michigan. Price: $1.50)

This study outline, consisting of an introduction and commentary, is reliable and based on sound scholarship. It is intended for pastors and Church groups as well as College students; hence no doubt the occasional pointing of the moral with modern instances and a tendency to exhortation.

L.A.P.

KIDNER, D.: *Genesis. An Introduction and a Commentary.* (Tyndale Old Testament Commentaries.) 1967. Pp. 224. (Tyndale Press, London. Price: 11s. 6d.)

This is a further volume of this series (cf. *B.L.* 1965, p. 26; *Decade*, p. 578), intended to supply the student with handy, up-to-date commentaries, with the primary emphasis on exegesis. The editor is at pains to rebut the conventional Pentateuchal criticism, leaves the Mosaic authorship of Genesis an open question, excludes the category of myth and accepts the historicity of the Fall, regards the abnormal patriarchal life-span as a special providence, and incidentally attributes the authorship of Psalm 110 to David. Allowing for this literalism the exegesis is careful and often illuminating. L.A.P.

KRAVITZ, N.: *Genesis. A New Interpretation of the First Three Chapters.* Pp. 83. (Philosophical Library, New York. Price: $3.95)

While one would wish to acknowledge the evident piety and devotion of the author, one may question whether his 'interpretation' owes much to Genesis 1–3. We may agree that the Genesis stories are reflective, products of reason and imagination and serve as background material for a faith in the Unity of God, of the world under God, and of Man. But we would not be convinced by this kind of eisegesis. The biblical text has to be fitted into the author's philosophy, e.g. 'without form and void' will not suit, so the Hebrew words are no more than an interjection of astonishment. The treatment of the Tetragrammaton seems to ignore all philological probability: the consonants represent the five primary long vowels which are not represented and which thus lead to the idea of God as invisible and primal. A.S.H.

LACOCQUE, A.: *Le devenir de Dieu. Commentaire biblique.* (Encyclopédie universitaire.) 1967. Pp. 192. (Éditions universitaires, Paris. Price: Fr. 38.60)

Professor Lacocque offers a detailed verse by verse commentary upon Exodus 1–4. Matters of grammatical, religious and historical interest are investigated in the light of modern research, although the main tendency is a conservative and apologetic one. Source criticism is given little attention, but extensive reference is made to relevant literature, both ancient and modern, and a careful translation is provided. R.E.C.

MCKANE, W.: *I & II Samuel: The Way to the Throne.* (Torch Bible Paperbacks.) 1967. Pp. 304. (S.C.M. Press, London. Price: 13s. 6d.)

Professor McKane's commentary of 1963 (see *B.L.* 1964, p. 37; *Decade*, p. 505) forms the latest addition to this series of paperback reprints. M.A.K.

MICHAELI, F.: *Les Livres des Chroniques, d'Esdras et de Néhémie* (Commentaire de l'ancien Testament xvi). 1967. Pp. 370. (Delachaux & Niestlé. Price: Sw.Fr. 35.00; bound 38.00)

It is good to see in this further volume in this series the policy of having the commentary on the whole of the Chronicler's work done as a unity, and not subdivided. The result is a valuable overall presentation in which the commentator sees the unity of the work lying in its understanding of Jerusalem (see pp. 33 ff.), and accordingly he divides the whole work into sections, showing in each the relationship to this underlying idea. Useful *excursuses* deal, e.g. with the relative dating of Ezra and Nehemiah — Michaeli comes down firmly for the later date for Ezra in the time of Artaxerxes II; with the work and person of Ezra, and of Nehemiah. There is good appraisal of the theology of the author who is dated to the Greek period. The variety of views on different questions is clearly set out and the commentator's preferences carefully indicated. There is no general discussion of textual questions, though the notes to the translation comment on points of detail; this omission is intelligible in a commentary of this kind, but some account does need to be taken of the nature of the relationship between the text of Chronicles and Samuel/Kings in view of the Qumran evidence; this is not simply a textual but also a literary problem, and it affects judgements on the nature of the Chronicler's presentation of his source material.

P.R.A.

NOTH, M.: *Könige*. (Biblischer Kommentar, Altes Testament, ix/3.) 1967. Pp. 161–240. (Neukirchener Verlag des Erziehungsvereins, Neukirchen-Vluyn. Price: DM. 7.75)

Readers will use this fascicle like the earlier ones (see *B.L.* 1965, p. 29; *Decade*, p. 581 for No. 1) with a growing appreciation for the quality of this masterly commentary, which now reaches the close of Solomon's reign. It continues the plan of providing a new translation in sections, with detailed notes on the text, literary form and origin, and exegesis; concluding each section with a summing-up on its aim. There is no doubt of the importance of this work for scholars.

D.R.Ap-T.

RENNES, J.: *Le Deutéronome*. 1967. Pp. 262. (Éditions Labor et Fides. Geneva. Price: Sw.Fr. 18.90; bound 24.00)

This is a combination of study guide and commentary to the book of Deuteronomy. A translation is given, largely following that of E. Dhorme, followed by notes on the literary character of the book and a general survey of its main theological ideas. Apart from a short bibliography no detailed reference is made to recent study, and the work is designed for the general reader rather than the scholar.

R.E.C.

*SARNA, N. M.: *Understanding Genesis*. (The Heritage of Biblical Israel, Vol. i of the Melton Research Center Series.) 1966. Pp. xxx + 267. (The Jewish Theological Seminary of America, New York; McGraw-Hill Book Company, New York. Price: $6.95)

There is a freshness and originality about this book, especially in its treatment of Gen. 1–11, which is greatly to be welcomed. It is frankly recognized that the contents of these chapters cannot be equated with the findings of modern science, and that use has been made of the myths of the Ancient Near East. But it is the use that matters, and the author has finely presented the aims of the book of Genesis in the proclamation of the faith. There may be occasional over-statement (as in the comment on the Cain and Abel story), and sometimes a too hasty application of archaeological findings (as in Gen. 14), but the treatment as a whole is scholarly and animated by a deep devotion to the faith.

The first three chapters are devoted to Creation, the Flood and the Tower of Babel, the remaining ten to the Patriarchal narratives. The book may be commended to the thoughtful layman, to divinity specialists in Colleges of Education and to all who in the modern climate of thought, find Genesis a difficult book. The book contains a full bibliography. A.S.H.

SCAMMON, J. H.: *Living with the Psalms*. 1967. Pp. 157. (The Judson Press, Valley Forge, Pa. Price: $3.95)

Dr Scammon, following J. E. McFadyen's *Ten Studies in the Psalms* (1907), offers studies in ten psalms to illustrate mainly Gunkel's types. Seven homilies including renderings of the Psalms from recent translations, etc., are devoted to each Psalm and quotations from commentators old and new abound. The book reflects the kindly spirit of this devout teacher of the O.T. G.H.D.

SCOFIELD, C. I.: *The New Scofield Reference Bible*. 1967. Pp. 1392 + 192 + 9 maps. (Oxford University Press, New York, London, Toronto. Price: 50s.)

Those who have used the earlier editions of this annotated Bible (1909, 1917) will welcome this new edition, revised by a committee of American scholars under the chairmanship of Dr E. Schuyler English. The text is substantially that of AV, but many archaic and obsolete words have been modernized and proper names in the NT have been accommodated to their OT form. Some notes refer to recent archaeological discoveries (but nothing about Ai). The attitude is of course conservative: Moses was the author of the Pentateuch; Isaiah of the book by that name. In the chronological order of the Prophets, Joel is given as 9th or 8th century, Hosea, 760–710 B.C., Micah 740, Jonah *c.* 800, Daniel 604–535. The notes, though not always convincing, are usually sober and restrained, but few would be satisfied with the statement that the Mosaic, Davidic and New Covenants chiefly add detail or development to the four in Genesis. This is a finely-printed edition and remarkable for its low price. A.S.H.

VAN SELMS, A., and VAN DER WOUDE, A. S. (ed.): *De Prediking van het Oude Testament*. 1967. *Genesis*, by A. van Selms, Deel I. Pp. 269. Deel II. Pp. 319. *I Koningen*, by H. A. Brongers. Pp. 235. (G. F. Callenbach, Nijkerk, Holland. Price: Fl. 19.50; 22.50; 19.50 resp.)

These are the first three volumes in a new series on the message of the Old Testament, uniform with a similar series on the New Testament already being issued by the same publishers. The aim of these volumes

is to bring out the permanent message of each Old Testament book
which they treat, and of each division of the several books. But before
this message is extracted and expounded, due account is taken of
questions of introduction and exegesis, so that each passage may be
understood in its historical and literary setting. The preacher on
Gen. 2:4–4:26, for example, must first be told something about the
relation between the two creation narratives, non-Israelite parallels
to the Paradise and Fall stories, and the cultural implications of
Tubal-cain's double name; then he is equipped to learn and teach the
abiding lesson of these chapters. What we have, in fact, in these
volumes is a sort of Dutch counterpart to *The Interpreter's Bible* —
with a number of differences, the chief of which is that the exposition
is more directly controlled by the introduction and exegesis than in
the American work. In churches, like those of Holland, where the
tradition of solid expository preaching still flourishes — and long
may it do so! — a series such as this is bound to prove very helpful.

                                                                      F.F.B.

SMART, J. D.: *History and Theology in Second Isaiah.* 1967. Pp. 304.
(Epworth Press, London. Price: 35s.)

Professor Smart has in previous works indicated his dissatisfaction
with the usual critical view of Deutero-Isaiah; and here he sets out his
own position. The work (first published in the U.S.A. in 1965)
consists of a commentary on Isaiah 40–66, together with *c*. 35 (all
of which he takes as the work of one prophet); this is preceded by an
introduction which outlines first the recent history of criticism and
then Smart's own approach; there are excursuses on the Babylon–
Chaldea passages and on the references to Cyrus; and an appendix
on the New Testament context. The main contentions of the book are
that the prophet lived in Palestine; that the setting in the context of a
return from exile in Babylon is secondary; and that the message of
the prophet must essentially be understood in eschatological terms.
On the other hand little attention is paid to recent studies in the literary
forms of Deutero-Isaiah — or indeed to any other work on the
prophet save the commentaries of Duhm, Volz, Torrey and Muilenburg. Within these self-imposed limitations, Smart makes many
valuable points, and his views will certainly have to be taken into
account by future commentators, but I doubt if those who adhere to
the more generally held position will be convinced.
The attempt to combine a scholarly and a popular approach is not
entirely satisfactory; in particular the lack of an index and the almost
complete absence of footnotes is tiresome in a work of this kind.

                                                                      R.J.C.

SNAITH, N. H.: *Leviticus and Numbers.* (The Century Bible, New Edition.)
1967. Pp. xii + 352. (Nelson, London. Price: 50s.)

Professor Snaith's interest in the festivals and the altar sacrifices of
ancient Israel is well known, and this volume gives him an opportunity to exercise it; this he does, much to the profit of the reader.
He writes a combined introduction to the two books on which he
offers a commentary. Some of the topics which he surveys briefly in
the introduction, e.g. the sources of the books, the history of the
priesthood, the temple sacrifices and the wilderness itinerary, take

him inevitably beyond the range of these two books. Therefore, he has often to make summary statements and to refer his readers to other books for more detailed treatment. He says acquiescently that Zadok is 'generally thought to belong to the ancient Jebusite priesthood of Jerusalem'. He believes that he can detect in the Holiness Code responses which point to its use in the cult. He shows an aptitude to quote from rabbinic sources to illumine regulations and practices and he always seeks to answer the questions which readers are most likely to ask. His philological and lexicographical notes will be found to be very useful. J.M.

WARD, J. M.: *Hosea: a Theological Commentary*. 1966. Pp. xxi + 264. (Harper & Row, New York. Price: $5.00)

The aim of this work is to elucidate the theology (here defined as 'deliberate discourse about God and the world') of Hosea rather than to deal primarily with historical or personal allusions. But since, clearly, in a difficult book like Hosea, no theology is possible until a number of textual matters have been cleared up, each section consists of a translation of a portion of the book, followed by textual notes and then the theological exposition. There are additional notes appended on the designations of Hosea's audience, his possible dependence on the Decalogue, and the references to Judah. Professor Ward takes into account the developments of understanding of the prophetic tradition which have taken place in the last generation, and, though there are no startling new viewpoints, the whole is a well-written and perceptive study of a difficult theme, which should be widely welcomed. The book is generally well-produced, except for a number of points at which the Hebrew is printed upside-down.

R.J.C.

WEISER, A.: *Das Buch Hiob*. (Das Alte Testament Deutsch 13) 5th ed. 1968. Pp. 272. (Vandenhoeck und Ruprecht, Göttingen)

This well-known commentary of which the first edition appeared in 1951 (*B.L.* 1952, p. 37; *Eleven Years*, p. 408) has been revised for this fifth edition. A few pages have been added to its length — nearly a page at the beginning on textual matters — and the bibliography has been considerably extended. The continued reissue of the volumes in this series shows what a success they have been. P.R.A.

WESTERMANN, C.: *Genesis*. (Biblischer Kommentar, Altes Testament, I, 1.) 1966. Pp. 80. (Neukirchener Verlag des Erziehungsvereins, Neukirchen-Vluyn. Price: DM. 7.75)

This *Lieferung* is part of an Introduction to the book of Genesis; the last page ends in the middle of a sentence. It draws attention to the importance of Gen. 1–11, not only for the book of Genesis, but as a preparation for the Exodus event and for the Bible as it finds its climax in the coming of the Saviour of the world. The J and P genealogies are examined and seen as having theological significance. The closing section discusses the narrative elements in these chapters and compares and contrasts them with similar material in the myths of Mesopotamia, Ugarit and Egypt. This fascicle alone will indicate the importance of the complete commentary. A.S.H.

WILDBERGER, H.: *Jesaja*. (Biblischer Kommentar, Altes Testament, x, 3.) 1968. Pp. 161–240. (Verlag der Buchhandlung des Erziehungsvereins, Neukirchen-Vluyn. Price: DM. 7.75)

The third fascicle (see *B.L.* 1967, p. 28) of this excellent commentary on Isaiah completes the discussion of 4:2–6, and goes on to deal with the following passages: (*a*) 5:1–7; (*b*) 5:8–24; 10:1–4 (a fresh attempt is made to solve the famous crux in verse 4); (*c*) 9:7–20; 5:25–30; (*d*) 6.

J.A.E.

WOLFF, H. W.: *Dodekapropheton: Amos*. (Biblischer Kommentar, Altes Testament, xiv, 6.) 1967. Pp. 80. (Neukirchener Verlag. Price: DM. 7.75)

This fascicle provides the introduction to the Book of Amos and the commentary on 1 : 1–2 : 16. The introduction deals with such questions as when, where and for how long the prophet exercised his ministry and what were the main emphases in the message which he gave to his hearers. But the main part of it is concerned with an analysis of the various literary forms and modes which are to be found in the book. The words of Amos in chs 3–6 go back in their essence to the prophet, and the same is true of the *Zyklenniederschrift* in chs 1–2, 7–9; but elements of deuteronomic redaction are to be discerned in it and of post-exilic *Heilseschatologie*.

The commentary on Amos 1:1–2:16 is in two parts. There is first a verse by verse textual and philological section which is admirably done. That is followed by the second part whose interests are literary and historical, but not notably theological. This is an excellent addition to an excellent series.

J.M.

YOUNG, E. J.: *Genesis 3. A devotional and expository study*. 1966. Pp. 165. (Banner of Truth Trust, London. Price: 5s.)

This verse-by-verse exposition of Genesis 3 will appeal to those who share the author's critical and theological assumptions. He attributes the chapter to Moses and regards Adam and Eve and the story of the Fall as completely historical; a real snake really spoke to Eve, being an instrument of the devil.

L.A.P.

ZIMMERLI, W.: *1. Mose 1–11. Die Urgeschichte*. (Zürcher Bibelkommentare.) 3rd ed. 1967. Pp. 436. (Zwingli Verlag, Zürich and Stuttgart. Price: Sw.Fr. 22.40)

The first edition of this commentary appeared in 1944 (see *B.L.* 1946, p. 35; *Eleven Years*, p. 35), the second in 1957. It appears now for the first time in the series *Zürcher Bibelkommentare*, but it retains its original character. It is intended for the laity and lacks the technical apparatus of scholarly publications, but it assumes that its readers are intelligent and serious and offers a detailed exposition in which, while other matters are not neglected, the emphasis falls on the theological significance of the text. The author's comments are helpful and illuminating, and the result is a work of considerable value and interest, which is a model of its kind.

M.A.K.

LITERARY CRITICISM AND INTRODUCTION
(including History of Interpretation, Canon, and Special Studies)

*ANDERSON, B. W.: *The Living World of the Old Testament*. 1967. Second Edition. Pp. xxi + 586. (Longmans, London. Price: 45s.)

The original American title of this book was *Understanding the Old Testament*, and the first edition was highly praised in the *Book List* (1958, p. 25; *Decade*, p. 101). It appeared in an English edition under its present title in 1958, and since then has proved to be outstanding among works of its kind in introducing students to the Old Testament. The need for a second edition has now enabled the author to make a number of changes which should still further enhance its value. There is a new chapter on the Psalms, as well as numerous minor changes in the text; a number of new illustrations including eight in colour; a considerable increase in footnote references; and an improved bibliography which has been numbered and brought up-to-date. The only criticism I would make is that, though produced by an English publisher, this is still very much an American book; the divergent spelling is a very minor matter, but it is a pity that bibliographical references are regularly to American and not to English editions.   R.J.C.

*ANDERSON, G. W.: *Prophetic Contemporaries: A Study of Jeremiah and Ezekiel*. (Manuals of Fellowship IV, 5.) 1967. Pp. 31. (Epworth Press, London. Price: 2s. 6d.)

A brief account of the contemporary situation is followed by four short chapters, two on Jeremiah and two on Ezekiel. Questions for discussion make this booklet appropriate for use in study groups and schools.   P.R.A.

BARTH, C. F.: *Introduction to the Psalms*, trans. by R. A. Wilson. 1966. Pp. 87. (Blackwell, Oxford. Price: 12s. 6d.)

This volume is translated from *Einführung in die Psalmen*, published in 1961 by Neukirchener Verlag. (See *B.L.* 1962, p. 36; *Decade*, p. 346.) It is for the general reader rather than for the specialist, but is useful for the student as a good and trustworthy account of the modern attitude to the Psalms. The emphasis is on Gunkel's classification, and the 'enthronement' theories are treated as less important for the New Year Feast than the idea of the Covenant.   N.H.S.

BARUZI, J.: *Luis de León, interprete du Livre de Job*. 1966. Pp. 76. (Presses Universitaires de France, Paris. Price: Fr. 5)

Baruzi (1881–1953) completed this short work on one of Luis de León's masterpieces shortly before his death. Luis de León, best known for his work *De los Nombres de Cristo*, prepared a translation and a commentary on Job, but the work did not appear until nearly two centuries after its author's death. Luis is regarded as a great poet, a remarkable exegete, and a splendid Hebraist, and the many extracts from the translation given by Baruzi seem fully to maintain their author's reputation. Perhaps one of the best chapters is No. VII, which is concerned with Job 28.   J.M.T.B.

BECKER, J.: *Israel deutet seine Psalmen: Urform und Neuinterpretation in den Psalmen* (Stuttgarter Bibelstudien 18). 1966, ²1967. Pp. 94. (Verlag Katholisches Bibelwerk, Stuttgart. Price: DM. 5.80)

This study examines in an illuminating manner the problem of reinterpretation of psalm-material, primarily as this may be traced within the Old Testament itself. The first part discusses the nature of such reinterpretation, with some comments on the meaning of inspiration, and with useful observations on the emphasis on 'origins' which often dominates in Old Testament study. The remainder of the book discusses particular psalms as illustrations of the process of reinterpretation. The study thus stresses the important point that however much the original text of a passage — whether psalm or ' prophecy or other kind of writing — may be recovered, our concern must still be with the text as it is eventually formulated.   P.R.A.

CHARBEL, A.: *Il Sacrificio pacifico nei suoi riti e nel suo significato religioso e figurativo*. 1967. Pp. xi + 108. (Privately published for the author by Commercial Press, Jerusalem)

The subject of *zébaḥ šᵉlâmîm* does not always receive much attention in the works on Semitic sacrifices. Charbel, who is a pupil of Vaccari, here presents a reasonably full treatment of the peace-offering, beginning with a short introduction on the various types of Jewish sacrifice, and continuing with chapters on the exact meaning of the peace-offering and its various types (impetrative, votive and the rest), on the details of the rite (laying on of hands, immolation of the victim, and destruction by fire), on the etymological and real significance of the rite, and on the meanings of the blood-shedding in sacrifices in general, and in the *šᵉlâmîm* in particular. A final chapter considers the religious and figurative significance of the rite. If there is nothing here that is very new, the subject is well-treated with ample reference to earlier writers. It is curious that de Vaux's *Institutions* does not appear in the bibliography.   J.M.T.B.

CHILDS, BREVARD S.: *Isaiah and the Assyrian Crisis*. (Studies in Biblical Theology, Second Series, 3.) 1967. Pp. 114. (S.C.M. Press, London. Price: 13s. 6d.)

The aim of this book is to examine afresh the biblical sources for the Assyrian invasion of 701 B.C. The method is to study form-critically all the passages bearing on it: (a) in Isaiah, 'invective-threats', oracles against the nations and oracles of promise; (b) 2 Kings 18–19 which is divided into 18:13–16 (A), 18:17–19a, 36–7 (B¹) and 19:9b–35 (B²). 2 Chron. 32 and Isaiah 33 (regarded as late) are also analysed. The result is clarification of the nature of the sources, but also reservations about using them for the recovery of the sequence of historical events. The author thinks that nothing short of the discovery of new extra-biblical evidence will help here. In an excursus a new form-critical category is proposed. This is named the 'summary-appraisal', a form which is claimed to be traditional in the Wisdom schools and used by Isaiah. There seems to be something in this, though perhaps a less clumsy term could be invented!   D.R.J.

CLEMENTS, R. E.: *Abraham and David. Genesis 15 and its Meaning for Israelite Tradition*. (S.C.M. Studies in Biblical Theology, Second Series, 5.) 1967. Pp. 96. (S.C.M. Press, London. Price: 10s. 6d.)

The basic form of the Abrahamic covenant in Gen. 15.1–6 is traced in terms of tradition history to a cult aetiological legend giving the approval of El, probably El Shaddai, to Abrahamic settlement at Mamre; El being replaced by Yahweh in southern tribal tradition. Through David's early association with Hebron, this tradition in its promissory character influenced the Davidic covenant tradition which, in turn, has shaped the form in which Gen. 15 now exists. Lack of references to the Abraham tradition in the pre-exilic prophets is partly explained by the fact that this tradition is subsumed under the Davidic tradition to re-emerge when the future of the Davidic dynasty is in jeopardy in the exilic period. Both D and P are attempts to harmonize this tradition with Sinai-Horeb, D by stressing the Horeb tradition with Abrahamic promise as its prophetic anticipation, P by subordinating the Sinai tradition to the Abrahamic covenant. There is much critical and theological stimulus to be gained from this finely-argued thesis, which includes, *inter alia*, a radical critique of A. Alt's thesis concerning the nomadic origins of patriarchal religion.   R.D.

*CLEMENTS, R. E.: *The Conscience of the Nation. A Study of Early Israelite Prophecy*. 1967. Pp. 119. (Oxford University Press, London. Price: 9s. 6d.)

This volume of the 'Approaching the Bible' series, intended for the non-specialist reader, surveys the background and content of the prophecies of Amos, Hosea and Isaiah ben Amoz. There follows an interesting chapter on Prophecy and History and a useful appendix of notes for the teacher by the late Miss Violet Wilkinson.

L.A.P.

CLEMENTS, R. E.: *God's Chosen People. A Theological Interpretation of the Book of Deuteronomy*. 1968. Pp. 126. (S.C.M. Press Ltd., London. Price: 9s. 6d.)

Deuteronomy is regarded as a key to understanding the religious meaning of the Old Testament. It is not merely an account of Israel's religion but an interpretation whereby Israel should come to a clearer understanding of God and its unique relationship with him. It is a theological interpretation of tradition and cult. It reckons with a state and a state religion; it is a last great attempt to call for national reform but requires a response from the individual. Some passages in this treatment require further explication. Is the concept of Israel as the chosen nation first found in Deuteronomy? Did Deuteronomy wish to avoid the idea that God himself was present in the sanctuary or really present with the worshipper? This book contains much that is interesting and stimulating.   A.S.H.

GÖRG, M.: *Das Zelt der Begegnung*. (Bonner Biblische Beiträge No. 27.) 1967. Pp. 174. (Peter Hanstein, Bonn. Price: DM. 36.00)

Dr Görg first surveys the history of the study of his subject over the last 160 years. He then considers the literary and form criticism of

the passages dealing with the multi-formed and many layered picture
of the tent sanctuary in the priestly tradition (Ex. 26, 25, 35, etc.),
and analyses the functions of the sacred tent and its door. His second
part deals with the tent of the dynastic tradition (mainly 2 Sam.
7:1–7), including nearly 30 pages on the meaning of the root *škn*, and
with the Gibeon traditions in this connection. The third section is
concerned with the E tent (Num. 11, 12; Deut. 31 and Ex. 33:7–11).
This work is an important and detailed study of the scripture passages concerning the tent of meeting.   G.H.D.

*GRELOT, P.: *Introduction to the Bible*. Translated by G. P. Campbell.
1967. Pp. 436 + 12 maps. (Burns and Oates, London; Herder and
Herder, New York. Price: 50s.)

The original French edition, *Introduction aux Livres Saints,* was
reviewed in *B.L.* 1954, p. 36: *Eleven Years,* p. 743. The present
translation represents a revision of the second French edition, with
an increase in the number of extra-biblical texts cited — these, with
the exception of the Egyptian texts, have been checked by the author
with the original languages. The bibliographies, criticized in the
earlier review for being too narrowly conceived, now include a wide
range of literature both Roman Catholic and Protestant. The method
of citing Old Testament references by numerals which refer to an
index of important passages is perhaps a little clumsy, but this index
provides a good selective reading list of biblical passages which may
usefully be followed at the level at which this kind of study is being
undertaken. The book provides a good and reliable general introduction at a simple and non-technical level.   P.R.A.

GROSS, H.: *Kleine Bibelkunde zum Alten Testament*. 1967. Pp. 131.
(Kosel-Verlag, Munich. Price: DM. 8.50)

This short, simple and informative guide to the O.T. consists of a
survey of the Vulgate O.T. book by book with a brief introduction
and an epilogue, the emphasis throughout being on biblical theology.
                                                                   L.A.P.

GUTHRIE, H. H.: *Israel's Sacred Songs. A Study of Dominant Themes.*
1966. Pp. 242. (The Seabury Press, New York. Price: $5.95)

Recent scholarship on the Psalms is presented here in a convenient
and judicial survey. The form-critical method and cultic approach
is firmly advocated, and the views of Mowinckel, Weiser, Johnson
and Kraus are set out in a readable and constructive way. Each of
the chapters tends to deal largely with the work and views of one of
these scholars, and inconsistencies are not always avoided. The book
is scholarly and well abreast of modern scholarship, although it
does not offer anything significantly new.   R.E.C.

GUTHRIE, H. H.: *Wisdom and Canon: Meanings of the Law and the
Prophets*. (Winslow Lecture 1966.) 1966. Pp. 37. (Seabury-Western
Theological Seminary, Evanston, Ill.)

This short study offers an often illuminating presentation of the
development in understanding of the biblical material. The author

seeks to show the ways in which the earlier traditions come to be reinterpreted in the context of the post-exilic community, and sees the place of wisdom concepts in this. He ends by suggesting the relevance of this to New Testament thinking. If at times the material seems to be rather forced into a pattern, the line of thought is nevertheless one which evokes considerable interest in relation to the problems of canonical authority.

P.R.A.

*JACOB, E.: *L'Ancien Testament* ('Que sais-je?' Le Point des Connaissances Actuelles. No. 1280.) 1967. Pp. 128. (Presses Universitaires de France, Paris. Price: Fr. 3)

This attractively written little introduction to the Old Testament provides in a minimum of space a great deal of up-to-date information — on the language and text, on each of the books and groups of books, on the formation of the literature, and of the canon. It combines elegance and readability with sound content.

P.R.A.

JONES, G. H.: *Arweiniad i'r Hen Destament*. 1966. Pp. 410. (University of Wales Press, Cardiff. Price: 22s.)

An Introduction to the Books of the Old Testament, to gather up the results of international scholarship over the past decades, has for some time been needed by those pursuing advanced courses in Biblical Studies through the medium of Welsh. This book very adequately meets the need, whether in Theological College, University or College of Education. From a moderate critical standpoint it treats clearly and succinctly of Canon, Text, Versions and Literary Patterns before dealing with the individual books. Finally there is an appendix on the Old Testament as Christian Literature, a chronological chart, and a useful bibliography and index. This will be the standard book on the subject in Welsh for some time.

D.R.Ap-T.

KELLERMANN, U.: *Nehemia: Quellen Überlieferung und Geschichte* (Beiheft zur Zeitschrift für die Alttestamentliche Wissenschaft, 102). 1967. Pp. xii + 227. (Verlag A. Töpelmann, Berlin. Price: DM. 50)

In many respects the most interesting part of this very comprehensive study is its third chapter in which the tradition concerning Nehemiah is traced from the basic material in the narratives in the book of Nehemiah through the subsequent redactional activity, through Ben Sira and 2 Macc. and on into the apocryphal writings to Josephus. This is prefaced by an analysis of the book of Nehemiah, and by a careful investigation of the Nehemiah source, particularly in regard to its form. Kellermann traces this to the 'Gebet des Angeklagten' but shows how it is modified in this presentation. A useful note here on the problem of using this material as a historical source points forward beyond the study of the tradition to a closer investigation of the historical problems, an analysis of the position occupied by Nehemiah, described in terms of his relation to the tensions between a conception of the community which is 'Zionist' and one which is 'theocratic'. Not least illuminating here is an attempt at investigating the underlying reasons for the actions of Sanballat and the other opponents of Nehemiah. A final short chapter attempts a reasoned historical reconstruction.

If this study sometimes errs in trying to be too precise in delineating reasons for the modifying of the tradition or of the material, and offers some interpretations which may be questioned, it is nevertheless both an important contribution to the obscure period of Nehemiah and also a valuable corrective to oversimple use of the Nehemiah narratives.

P.R.A.

KILIAN, R.: *Die vorpriesterlichen Abrahamsüberlieferungen literarkritisch und traditionsgeschichtlich untersucht.* (Bonner biblische Beiträge 24.) 1966. Pp. 320. (Peter Hanstein Verlag, Bonn. Price: DM. 56)

Professor Kilian examines in very great detail the material between Genesis 12–26 which is usually ascribed to JE. Each chapter is subjected to a thorough analysis and the basis for the JE division is reconsidered and largely re-affirmed. Beyond this, however, the author attempts an identification of the oldest strata within each section, endeavouring to reach a nucleus around which the tradition has been built up. The whole is carried through with great care and patience, and is invaluable for further work in this area. A weakness appears in the failure to consider the earliest strata of the separate chapters in relation to each other, since their identification is arrived at independently and only subsequently are they considered together. Thus the oral stage of transmission is treated almost identically with the literary stage. Nevertheless this is an important contribution towards an understanding of the religious and historical significance of the patriarchs.

R.E.C.

KRENTZ, E.: *Biblical Studies Today: A Guide to Current Issues and Trends.* (Concordia Biblical Monographs.) 1966. Pp. 80. (Concordia Publishing House, St. Louis Mo. and London. Price: $1.75)

This short survey is more concentrated on New Testament problems, but it illustrates the values of the various types of approach to biblical material of the last half-century with useful references also to problems of Old Testament interpretation. In particular it examines the significance of R. Bultmann's work, and includes useful bibliographies.

P.R.A.

KUTSCH, E.: *Sein Leiden und Tod — unser Heil. Eine auslegung von Jesaja* 52, 13–53, 12. (Biblische Studien 52.) 1967. Pp. 46. (Neukirchener Verlag des Erziehungsvereins. Price: DM. 3.90)

A brief but interesting study of the fourth servant song containing a careful exegesis of the text and a discussion of its theological significance. The author inclines to the view that the servant of the Songs is Deutero-Isaiah. His main concern is to show that in Isaiah 53 there is a meeting of two Old Testament streams of thought, that represented by Genesis 18 and Jeremiah 5 which suggest the vicarious efficacy of the righteous to avert the punishment of the wicked and that represented, e.g. by Ezekiel 14 and Zephaniah 2 which insist on the punishment of the guilty. Punishment falls indeed, but on one who is innocent. He suffers death but is promised a glorious future.

N.W.P.

LIPINSKI, E.: *Le Poème royal du Psaume lxxxix, 1–5.20–38.* (Cahiers de la Revue Biblique 6.) 1967. Pp. 110. (J. Gabalda, Paris. Price: Fr. 37)

The author of this monograph has already subjected Pss 93, 97, and 99 to an exhaustive treatment (cf. *B.L.* 1966, p. 50; *Decade*, p. 670), and he now offers an equally detailed study of Ps. 89:1–5, 20–38, which cannot but arouse admiration for his industry. He argues in keeping with the title to the psalm that these sections were composed by Eytan the Ezraḥite, an Edomite at the royal court in Jerusalem, as a piece of royal propaganda which may date from as far back as the end of the 10th century B.C. Verses 39–52 are summarily dismissed as a lamentation which was 'undoubtedly' composed after the death of Josiah at the battle of Megiddo in 609 B.C., while verses 6–19, which are treated as a cosmic hymn that was inserted into the supposed original work, cannot have been written by Eytan because it refers to Tabor and Hermon and must, therefore, have been composed in the north! The author leans heavily upon the text of verses 20–3, 26–8, and 31, as preserved in 4QPs. 89, and in many other ways he has again drawn liberally upon comparative data offered by archeological discovery, some of which are of real value; but when, for example, almost ten pages are spent on trying to show that the reference to Yahweh as 'Father' reflects the wording of treaties between vassals and their suzerains in the ancient Near East, one's fears are renewed that we are in grave danger of over-emphasizing the value of such data for our understanding of the covenant ideas in the Old Testament. A.R.J.

LOERSCH, S.: *Das Deuteronomium und seine Deutungen. Ein forschungsgeschichtliche Überblick.* (Stuttgarter Bibelstudien 22.) 1967. Pp. 116. (Verlag Katholisches Bibelwerk, Stuttgart. Price: DM. 6.80)

This is an excellent survey of the criticism of Deuteronomy since the work of De Wette. The basic methods of research in history of religion, literary criticism, form criticism and tradition-history are well set out by describing the work of representative scholars in each field. The recent Catholic researches of Cazelles, McCarthy and Lohfink are particularly noted. The volume makes a good introduction to an important and extensive area of study. R.E.C.

LYS, DANIEL: *La chair dans l'Ancien Testament.* '*Bâsâr*'. (Encyclopédie universitaire.) 1967. Pp. 176. (Éditions Universitaires, Paris. Price: Fr. 24.70)

This study consists of a detailed analysis and statistical survey of the use of the noun *basar* in the Old Testament. The material is arranged in the probable chronological order of the literature, and an overall Hebrew concept of 'flesh' is sought as part of a comprehensive biblical doctrine of man. Thus the study is intended to be related to the author's earlier researches into *nephesh* and *ruaḥ* as an attempt to show a distinct revelatory content in Israel's anthropology.

R.E.C.

McCarthy, D. J.: *Der Gottesbund im Alten Testament*. (Stuttgarter
Bibelstudien 13.) 1966. Pp. 96. (Verlag Katholisches Bibelwerk,
Stuttgart. Price: DM. 5.80)

Professor McCarthy's earlier study of the covenant form in the Old
Testament has received wide acclaim, and this essay is an expansion
of an article 'Covenant in the Old Testament. The Present State of
Enquiry' which appeared in *C.B.Q.* 27 (1965), pages 217–40. It is a
bibliographical review of the past decade of research into the subject
of the form and nature of Israel's covenants, with special regard to the
arguments for a dependence on the form of political vassal treaties
It is a most useful guide for students and scholars alike.   R.E.C.

Mayer, R.: *Einleitung in das Alte Testament. 1 Teil. Allgemeine Einleitung*. 1965. Pp. 168. (Max Hueber Verlag, Munich. Price: DM.
11.80)

The book contains the kind of material generally placed at the
beginning or at the end of O.T. Introductions, and tells of the major
book divisions, the history of the canon, the biblical languages,
writing and the Masoretic Text. Then come the versions and the
practice of textual criticism. Another major section is concerned with
background — the ancient empires, the immediate neighbours, and
the later empires of Persia and Greece.
Such an ordinary-sounding outline, however, should not be allowed
to prejudice the potential buyer: the book is well-written and goes
over well-trodden paths in a lively manner. Sometimes, however, one
has the impression that not all aspects of a problem have been squarely
faced by the author.   B.J.R.

Nicholson, E. W.: *Deuteronomy and Tradition*. 1967. Pp. xii + 145.
(Basil Blackwell, Oxford. Price: 25s.)

This useful study of the origins of the book of Deuteronomy takes
cognizance of the standard works on the subject and shows the
influence of Alt, von Rad and M. Noth. Nicholson however, is not
afraid to criticize and to take an independent line. The basis for
Deuteronomy is found in the Mosaic traditions clustering around
the ancient covenant renewal festival celebrated annually, probably in
the autumn, at the amphictyonic central shrine — originally Shechem,
later Shiloh. After 721 B.C. prophetic circles carried the traditions
south, where they were codified and adapted, and played a part in
Josiah's reformation. More stress is laid on the Sinai covenant at
the expense of the Davidic one, and the latter's vocabulary of election
is appropriated for Jerusalem as the seat of Yahweh's Name.
The work has a bibliography and the usual indexes; it is well produced
and may be recommended.   D.R.Ap-T.

Orlinsky, H. M. and Snaith, N. H.: *Studies on the Second Part of the
Book of Isaiah*. (Supplements to Vetus Testamentum, Vol. xiv.)
1967. Pp. 264. (E. J. Brill, Leiden. Price: Fl. 60)

Two veteran scholars present here extended versions of lectures
given on different occasions. Whereas Orlinsky refers to earlier work

by Snaith, as evidenced by the index, Snaith does not cite Orlinsky and also lacks a full index. Both studies, though unrelated, pursue similar, but by no means identical, aims. They continue the polemics of past and present generations. Orlinsky seeks to bring down the 'Ebed YHWH from his isolated and exalted position which only post-biblical eisegesis invented for him by coining a technical term. The 'Ebed songs do not exist independently in the Isaiah corpus, vicarious suffering is never hinted at, and the prophet himself is the central personage in a realistic political struggle which excluded an international vocation. Snaith also attacks unrealistic estimates of the prophetic enterprise; all the great themes in chs 40–66 are subservient to the return and the tasks of the nation. Yet the 'Ebed obtains a separate identity, first in the exiles of 597, later in all the 'good figs' in Babylon. The innocent victim leads all exiles back in triumph: the suffering Servant is really the triumphant conqueror. Jesus, himself a nationalist, deliberately modelled his ministry on this concept of the Servant. For Orlinsky, Miss Hooker is nearly right in her estimate of the Servant in the Gospel tradition, but does not go nearly far enough in seeing the complete irrelevance; for Snaith she is on the right scent but goes too far in the wrong direction, for the 'Ebed pattern governs the mind of Jesus and the Gospels. Both essays are readable, odd bed-fellows though they are. Neither seems to allow for a form-critical estimate of the tradition behind these chapters. They leave the field open to future ex- and eisegesis, which would be unwise to ignore these far-reaching claims.   U.E.S.

OTWELL, J. H.: *A New Approach to the Old Testament.* 1967. Pp. 196. (S.C.M. Press Ltd, London. Price: 15s.)

Professor Otwell gives a general popular introduction to the Old Testament based on the results of modern scholarship. He briefly outlines basic methods of study, and then proceeds through the main sections of literature, with broad surveys of content, literary structure and religious interest. Particular stress is laid upon the work of M. Noth and G. von Rad, whose main positions are presented in outline. There is some over-simplification, but the style is very fluent and persuasive.   R.E.C.

PLÖGER, J. G.: *Literarkritische, Formgeschichtliche und Stilkritische Untersuchungen zum Deuteronomium.* (Bonner Biblische Beiträge, Band 26.) 1967. Pp. xxvii + 225. (Peter Hanstein Verlag, Bonn. Price: DM. 48)

This work comprises three sections. The first (pp. 1–59) presents a detailed analysis of Deuteronomy 1:6–3:29. Here Plöger argues that the 'we' passages in these chapters (1:6–8, 19, 2:1, 8, 13b–15, 30, 32–36, 3:1, 3–8, 12, 29) constitute an originally independent account of the route followed by the Israelites in the wilderness and the military conflicts in which they were involved at that time. This account has been utilized by the Deuteronomists from whom the 'you' material with which it is now surcharged derived. The second section (pp. 60–129) offers a thorough investigation of the Deuteronomic statements concerning the Land and the various formulae employed are carefully discussed. The statements concerning Egypt,

Ammon, Edom, Heshbon, Bashan, Moab and Canaan are also examined. The third and final section (pp. 130–217) offers a thorough analysis of Deuteronomy 28 and a discussion of the *Sitz im Leben* of the blessing and curse formulae it contains. Each section contains copious textual and critical notes and the documentation is extensive. This is an important work and contributes significantly to the discussion of Deuteronomy.   E.W.N.

PORTER, J. R.: *The extended family in the Old Testament.* (Occasional Papers in Social and Economic Administration, No. 6.) 1967. Pp. 21. (Edutext Publications Ltd., 82 Fryent Way, London, N.W.9. Price: 6s. 6d.)

This significant sociological study is primarily concerned with showing, especially from Lev. 18, the evidence for the existence and nature of the extended family in the Old Testament. Incidentally it sheds light on other passages which are concerned with the maintenance of right family relationships, and suggests that Lev. 18 and 20 reflect different types of social organization and are concerned with different social problems.   P.R.A.

RENGSTORF, K. H.: *Die Delitzsch'sche Sache. Ein Kapitel preussischer Kirchen- und Fakultätspolitik im Vormärz.* (Arbeiten zur Geschichte und Theologie des Luthertums XIX.) 1967. Pp. 84. (Lutherisches Verlagshaus, Berlin. Price: DM. 12.80)

This study is entirely concerned with the religious and academic politics of the period in Germany preceding the revolution of 1848, but it provides interesting insights into the involvement in this situation of one of the greatest names in Old Testament scholarship, that of Franz Delitzsch, and the struggles in which he was involved before he was appointed to a professorship.   P.R.A.

SCHARBERT, J.: *Fleisch, Geist und Seele im Pentateuch: Ein Beitrag zur Anthropologie der Pentateuchquellen.* (Stuttgarter Bibelstudien 19.) 1966. Pp. 87. (Verlag Katholisches Bibelwerk, Stuttgart. Price: DM. 5.80)

A short introduction is followed by five sections in which the words *ruᵃch, nᵉšamah, nefeš, basar,* and *šᵉ'er* are examined as they occur in JEDP and in the ancient traditions preserved in Gen. 6:1–4; 14:49; and Exod. 15:21–23. A concluding summary accompanies each section, and a final summary conveniently brings together the main results of the enquiry. While there is much agreement in the use of these words in the Pentateuchal documents, there are distinct differences, and sometimes development in their use can be traced. This useful and well-presented study illustrates the value of a careful examination of the linguistic usage and range of meaning of individual terms in the Pentateuchal sources as a prelude to the attempt to formulate a synthesis of the religious ideas contained in them.

                                                                    D.W.T.

SCHMID, H. H.: *Wesen und Geschichte der Weisheit. Eine Untersuchung zur Altorientalischen und Israelitischen Weisheitsliteratur.* (Beiheft zur Zeitschrift für die alttestamentliche Wissenschaft, 101.) 1966. Pp. 250. (Verlag Alfred Töpelmann, Berlin. Price: DM. 52)

The three parts of the book deal in turn with Egyptian, Mesopotamian (Sumerian and Accadian treated separately) and Israelite wisdom and the intention of the third part is to set Israelite wisdom in the context of ancient oriental wisdom. The differing contents of Egyptian and Mesopotamian wisdom literatures are noted, the one dominated by the 'Instruction' and the other setting out from a cataloguing or inventory type of list and developing particularly in the direction of a proverbial literature which is almost entirely absent from Egyptian wisdom (it is found in *Onchsheshonqy*). The discussion is throughout anchored to the texts and the thesis that these can only be understood as historically conditioned writings is not so obvious or ordinary as might appear. The structural changes undergone by the wisdom literature in the course of this history are similar in Egypt, Mesopotamia and Israel and so the discussion in each part of the book can take the same shape.

The wisdom tradition in Egypt, Mesopotamia and Israel follows a course which, in important respects, is the same. At first the concept of Order which makes an intelligible and harmonious unity of all reality is compatible with a serious regard for actually existent political and social realities. Then there is the tendency towards a certain disengagement from experience, perhaps occasioned by its recalcitrance in relation to a concept of Order and the trend to make wisdom into an ideal structure which purports to dictate to experience but has lost touch with it and become unreal theorizing or dogma. It is this movement which produces the crisis of wisdom in connexion with which there is an interesting discussion of the 'Sumerian Job', *Ludlul bēl nēmeqi* and the 'Babylonian Theodicy' in part two and Job and Ecclesiastes in part three. Among the high points of the book are the treatment of *Maat*, the observations on the peculiar hermeneutical openness of the proverb and the evaluation of the antithesis of 'righteous' and 'wicked' in the book of Proverbs.

The book is to be valued for its insights into the exegetical problems associated with the wisdom literature. Doubt may, however, be expressed concerning the over-systematizing of the discussion. The same vocabulary does not mean the same in different situations and one can only ask about the meaning of the wisdom literature in relation to a given historical and discourse situation.   W.McK.

SCHOLDER, K.: *Ursprünge und Probleme der Bibelkritik im 17. Jahrhundert. Ein Beitrag zur Entstehung der historisch-kritischen Theologie.* (Forschungen zur Geschichte und Lehre des Protestantismus, 10te Reihe, Band XXXIII.) 1966. Pp. 195. (Chr. Kaiser Verlag, München. Price: DM. 18)

This book will be found extremely valuable by anyone who wishes to understand the development of biblical criticism in the period when reason was gradually winning the battle over tradition. The real struggle began when tradition was faced with the modern world view resulting from the Copernican revolution and the modern view of history which owed a great deal to geographical discoveries. The rearguard actions fought by tradition are carefully documented. Attempts at compromise are indicated, such as the use of the word 'hypothesis' to make revolutionary views acceptable. The significance of sundry individuals is made clear, e.g. La Peyrère with his pre-Adamite theory. The victory of Rationalism is identified with the breakthrough of the Cartesian philosophy. This is a book of genuine historical scholarship which repays the closest attention. It would be well worthwhile having it translated.   N.W.P.

SOISALON-SOININEN, I.: *Aabrahamista Joosofinn.* 1965. Pp. 196. (Kirjayhtymä, Helsinki.)

In this book, in Finnish, the title of which means *From Abraham to Joseph,* Prof. Soisalon-Soininen offers an investigation of the history of the patriarchal traditions in Genesis. He supplements the documentary hypothesis with a traditio-historical approach much in the way of contemporary German exegesis. His most valuable contribution seems to be the introduction of the concept of function instead of *Sitz im Leben,* which seems to open up new vistas for tradition history.   H.R.

STAMM, J. J., with ANDREW, M. E.: *The Ten Commandments in Recent Research.* (Studies in Biblical Theology, Second Series, 2.) 1967. Pp. 119. (S.C.M. Press, London. Price: 15s.)

The kernel of this book is based on the revised and enlarged (1962), second edition of Professor Stamm's book on the subject, with additions by Dr Andrew to bring the record of research up-to-date. The question of casuistic and apodictic laws is examined, and the view is presented that the use of the latter was not confined to Israel. As to the origin of apodictic laws in Israel, Dr Andrew takes the view that it was not in the cult, nor by derivation from Assyrian or Hittite treaty forms, but within the clan. He considers the time after the Israelite conquest of Palestine as the one most likely for the creation of the decalogue as a whole, although the origin of individual laws may go back to Moses. If that was so, such laws were preserved and handed down at one of the great festivals and/or through the agency of the priests, the minor judges, or a mediator of the covenant; but on these subjects assurance is not yet possible.
This is an excellent survey of recent research on the subject of the Ten Commandments.   J.M.

STECK, O. H.: *Israel und das gewaltsame Geschick der Propheten. Untersuchungen zur Überlieferung des deuteronomischen Geschichtsbildes im Alten Testament, Spätjudentum und Urchristentum.* (Wissenschaftliche Monographien zum Alten und Neuen Testament, 23.) 1967. Pp. 380. (Neukirchener Verlag, Neukirchen-Vluyn. Price: DM. 41.80, paper 39.80)

The tradition of the violent death of the prophets at the hands of the Jewish people to whom they preached repentance (Neh. 9:26, Luke 13:34, etc.) is shown to be a theological judgement on Israel rather than a historical fact about the fate of the prophets, individually or collectively. It came to be embedded in the Deuteronomic conception of history as a standing symbol of the obstinacy of Israel and of her rejection of the prophetic teaching and admonition. It is submitted here to careful and thorough examination from all angles, form-critical, traditional and historical, and shown to have been a long-lived and widely held tradition beginning in the Old Testament, continuing in post-biblical literature and going on into the New Testament — continuing and yet changing with the changing historical background. The book bears the marks of a definitive treatment.

L.H.B.

STENDAHL, K.: *The Bible and the Role of Women*. (Facet Books, Biblical Series 15.) 1966. Pp. 48. (Fortress Press, Philadelphia. Price: 85c.)

The current debate concerning the ordination of women to the ministry will need to take careful note of this little book. It is in two main sections, 'The Bible and the Ordination of Women' in which the important distinction between exegesis and hermeneutic is defined; 'The Biblical view of Male and Female' which leads up to a convincing treatment of Gal. 3:28. These lead to a brief statement on 'Emancipation and Ordination'. The pamphlet is mainly concerned with the New Testament, and originally directed to the Swedish situation. But the hermeneutics is of wide application.

A.S.H.

STENRING, K.: *The Enclosed Garden*. 1965. Pp. 101. (Almqvist and Wiksell, Stockholm. Price: Sw.Kr. 18)

An explanation is offered of all the chronological data from Creation to the time of Ezra. It is claimed that the author has discovered a 'uniform but deliberately concealed chronological system'. Taking the biblical data literally the author smooths out the well-known inconsistencies by combining lunar, Egyptian solar, and standard solar years. The details of the system are set out in an extensive table, together with 34 diagrams which are completely unintelligible. It is supposed that the alleged secret chronological system is an artificial creation of late editors who were more interested in 'magic' numbers than in strict chronology.

G.G.Y.

*STOCKS, M.: *Unread Best-seller, Reflections on the Old Testament*. 1967. Pp. 72. (B.B.C. Publications, London. Price: 5s. 6d.)

This is a collection of talks delivered by Baroness Stocks between 1957 and 1964 in the Programme *Lift Up Your Hearts*. It represents the thought of an unusually percipient layman who handles the Old Testament from an entirely contemporary point of view and without overmuch technical equipment. Rarely does she fall to the temptation of wresting lessons from unwilling material. More often than not she goes to the root of the matter. This is interesting evidence of what such a person finds significant and required reading for those engaged in *haute vulgarization*.

D.R.J.

*SWAIM, J. C.: *The Bible: Questions and Answers.* 1966. Pp. 441. (Collins, London. Price: 30s.)

This work consists of sections dealing with each book of the Bible including the Apocrypha, in the form of answers to questions concerning the contents and general introductory matter. A good deal of useful information is thus conveyed, though the manner of presentation is very artificial in that the questions are devised merely to provide an opportunity for the answers that the author wishes to give. The standpoint is what might be termed 'critical orthodoxy'. The factual information is reliable in all save a very few instances.

R.J.C.

WÄCHTER, L.: *Der Tod im Testament.* (Arbeiten zur Theologie, II, 8.) 1967. Pp. 234. (Calwer Verlag, Stuttgart. Price: DM. 34)

This book represents a thesis submitted in 1964, now printed with little change. Two-thirds of it is devoted to a detailed cataloguing and analysis of attitudes to death, most prominently that of fear — the various metaphors are described, and where appropriate, comparison made with the use of the same metaphors in Babylonian and Egyptian texts. There is recognition of a more positive attitude to death when it comes in fulness of old age, and a short section on suicide. The attitude of men to death as their common lot is also discussed. The remaining part of the book is devoted to the religious evaluation of death, and here the main concentration is on death as the divine punishment for communities. Particular cases of individual rescue from such judgement, or of individual punishment to save the community are noted, and cases of individual judgement are also examined. A brief excursus deals with the state of man after death and the final sections discuss whether mortality is in itself to be regarded as divine punishment — a useful consideration of Gen. 3 and the use of death as a warning. A mass of material is provided in this book and here lies its value. It is usefully indexed.   P.R.A.

WESTERMANN, C.: *Jeremia.* 1967. Pp. 94. (Calwer Verlag, Stuttgart. Price: DM. 8.50)

This popular introduction to the book of Jeremiah, in the same series as *Der Psalter* (next entry in this list), provides a good oversight of the period and activity of the prophet, with a brief account of the making of the book, summaries of the different aspects of his teaching, and an assessment of his person and his place in the Bible. There is much useful comment on individual sections, though it is unsatisfactory to find the major narrative section (most of chs 26–44) described, as is so commonly done, as 'Baruch's narrative of Jeremiah's passion'. This is a doubtful definition. The promise on the back cover of references to the most important literature for further study is hardly fulfilled by the scanty footnotes. A short reading list at the end such as is provided in *Der Psalter* is more serviceable.   P.R.A.

WESTERMANN, C.: *Der Psalter.* 1967. Pp. 106. (Calwer Verlag, Stuttgart. Price: DM. 8.50)

This is an attractively written introduction to the Psalms for the general reader. It outlines the structure of the Psalter, and traces the origin of such psalm compositions in worship. Special attention is given to the classification of types of psalms and examples are given showing their characteristics and structure. Special categories are then dealt with in a similar way. Throughout sound scholarship is combined with balanced judgement to provide a helpful work in brief compass, which will have a particular value for the student and beginner.   R.E.C.

WESTERMANN, C.: *Basic Forms of Prophetic Speech*. Translated by H. C. White. 1967. Pp. 222. (Lutterworth Press, London. Price: 30s.)

This book, originally published as *Grundformen prophetischer Rede* (1960, 2nd ed. 1964, Chr. Kaiser, Munich), now appears in an English translation. The original was not noted in the *Book List*. In his introductory survey Westermann shows how the form-critical approach to the prophetic writings was only gradually developed during the present century. He distils from these advances such positive gains as to present the reader with a convincing analysis of the forms of prophecy. He eschews ambiguous abstractions and asks the basic questions: 'Who speaks? To whom does the messenger (God) speak? What takes place in this speaking?' He distinguishes carefully between different groups of oracles and cites extra-biblical texts for comparison to clarify concepts such as revelation and message. These structural parallels provide evidence for the formal characteristics of the messenger's speech. Westermann investigates the place of the accusation and the announcement in the typical judgement proclamations with their considerable variations, and argues for the emergence of the corporate from the individual genre. The expansion of the form may be hailed as the creative climax by which legal formulae, for example, become integrated in the great classical oracles. The form dissolves at length after the Exile when the call to repentance and the promise of salvation use the basic structure with a new orientation. The light which this book throws upon prophetic speech genres will be welcomed by many grateful readers. But they will still wish to press on further to relate *Heils-* and *Unheils-*forms, if only because the author has put into their hands the tools which open new doors of perception.   U.E.S.

WESTERMANN, C.: *Handbook to the Old Testament*. 1967. Pp. xvi + 285. (Augsburg Publishing House, Minneapolis. Price: $5.95)

The Old Testament is expertly covered within the limits of one volume. No detailed commentary is possible, and, whilst matters of Introduction to the O.T. books are raised, the emphasis is on content, often presented diagrammatically. The individual books are divided into sections with appropriate titles, yet the unity of the basic themes of the O.T. comes out clearly. Its essential message is presented with frequent flashes of insight. This volume is a translation of the introduction and O.T. sections of *Abriss der Bibelkunde* (1962), but the translator, R. H. Boyd, has occasionally modified and expanded the original text with the author's approval.   G.F.

*WILKINSON, V.: *Israel's Praise. A Study of the Psalms.* 1967. Pp. 96. (Oxford University Press, London. Price: 9s. 6d.)

This volume is the work of a gifted teacher who was killed in a road accident after passing it for the press. It belongs to a series, 'Approaching the Bible', intended to popularize the achievement of modern scholarship for the general reader, and particularly non-specialist teachers of Religious Education. This book deals imaginatively with the background of the psalms, the different types of psalms, the Christian use of the Psalter and the use of the psalms in school. It deserves a wide welcome.   L.A.P.

WOOD, J.: *Wisdom Literature: An Introduction.* (Studies in Theology No. 64.) 1967. Pp. xii + 169. (Duckworth, London. Price: 15s.)

It is here contended that Wisdom thought has greater significance for biblical theology in general and for Christology in particular than has often been recognized. Attention accordingly is given not only to extra-Israelite Wisdom and to the material present in the Old Testament and in the Apocrypha and Pseudepigrapha, but also and in some detail to the development of Wisdom thought in the New Testament writings. Special interest attaches in this connection to the figure of Wisdom, and in the first appendix Wisdom is adjudged, for the later period at least, an hypostasis. In the second appendix on Wisdom and the Virgin Mary it is argued that Jesus Christ alone is the power and Wisdom of God.   E.T.R.

LAW, RELIGION AND THEOLOGY

ALBREKTSON, B.: *History and the Gods.* (Coniectanea Biblica. Old Testament Series 1.) 1967. Pp. 138. (C. W. K. Gleerup, Lund. Price: Sw.Kr. 26)

Professor Albrektson examines two widely-held views, that an Old Testament 'revelation of God in history' contrasts with a general ancient Near Eastern experience of God in nature, and that for the Old Testament revelation is classically through event, not word. Extensive quotations of Accadian, Assyrian and Hittite material suggest that here too Gods are seen as active in history. While the Old Testament speaks little of a single divine plan in history, a view of a purposeful divine control of history is also found throughout the ancient Near East. Revelation through word is strongly attested both here and in Israel. The author concludes that whatever is distinctive about Israelite thought on revelation and history, it must be expressed much more cautiously and subtly than is usual. This is an important and well-documented book, which seems to make its case, and has implications for systematic theology as well as for Old Testament study.   J.V.M.S.

ALONSO SCHÖKEL, L.: *The Inspired Word. Scripture in the Light of Language and Literature.* Translated by F. Martin. 1967. Pp. 418. (Burns and Oates, London; Herder and Herder, New York. Price: 63s.)

The original edition, *La Palabra Inspirada* (Editorial Herder S.A., Barcelona, 1966), was not noted in this *Book List*. It is concerned with

the theology of the Word of God, a study directed to the educated reader but not technical, and written in the context of recent discussion in the Roman Catholic Church of the place and significance of the Bible. It is an examination of the relationship between the human words of the Bible and that which they seek to express, and this is done by a discussion of the nature of the word, of the nature of inspiration, and in particular of the place of the author within the religious community, the relation between the spoken and the written word, and the problems posed by translation. Throughout, this is a deeply theological work, written by one who is not only a scholar of high repute but also a man to whom the words of the Bible clearly speak with great power. A wide range of literature is mentioned in footnotes and in the bibliographical comments at the end of each chapter.
P.R.A.

AUGSBURGER, M. S.: *Principles of Biblical Interpretation in Mennonite Theology.* 1967. Pp. 39. (Herald Press, Scottdale, Pa.)

This is a brief essay on hermeneutics in which the Bible is recognized as Revelation in deed and word. Formal contradictions and progress of doctrine are seen as necessary elements in man's growing perception of God. The revelation leads to Christ who is the Lord of the Scriptures and re-interprets 'sub-Christian' elements in the Old Testament. The Spirit is the necessary agent in understanding for the Bible can only be rightly understood by one who stands within the faith. Account is taken of the historical-literary perspectives and of development in the Bible. A great many issues are raised which need to be more fully developed.
A.S.H.

BARR, J.: *Alt und Neu in der biblischen Überlieferung, Eine Studie über die beiden Testamente,* trans. by E. Gerstenberger. 1967. Pp. 206. (Chr. Kaiser Verlag, München. Price: Paper, DM. 16.00; bound, DM. 19.00)

This is the German translation of *Old and New in Interpretation: A Study of the Two Testaments* (S.C.M., London, 1966), reviewed in *B.L.* 1966, p. 43; *Decade*, p. 663. It is good to see that this discussion of hermeneutical problems will be contributing to the continental debate on these issues, but odd that the bibliography has been omitted.
P.R.A.

BRIGHT, J.: *The Authority of the Old Testament.* (Lectures on The James A. Gray Fund of the Divinity School of Duke University, Durham, North Carolina.) 1967. Pp. 272. (Abingdon Press, Nashville and New York; and S.C.M. Press, London. Price: $5.50 and 40s.)

Professor Bright here discusses the place of the Old Testament in the Christian Canon of Scripture, the various ways in which the relationship of the Old Testament to the New has been understood, and the essential theological content of the Old Testament and of the Bible as a whole, and proceeds to show, both in general terms and by specific examples, how the Old Testament material may be used in Christian preaching. He insists on the duty of using all the available resources of scientific study. He also maintains that, though there is much in the Old Testament that is not directly normative, there is reflected in its varied contents a coherent 'structure of faith' which remains normative. The author's vigorous style and clear presentation of his arguments make this book an exhilarating one to read. The survey of recent discussions of biblical theology and hermeneutics displays an enviable skill in making turbid waters limpid; and the book as a whole makes a valuable contribution to these discussions.

G.W.A.

BUBER, M.: *Kingship of God.* Translated by Richard Scheimann. 1967. Pp. 222. (George Allen and Unwin, London. Price: 30s.)

This is a translation of the third and final edition of *Königtum Gottes* (*B.L.* 1957, p. 42; *Decade*, p. 42). The reviewer then welcomed the reissue of 'this challenging work', and one would like similarly to welcome its appearance now in English. Unhappily this is difficult to do in view of the extremely poor quality of the translation. The translator tells us that he originally intended to break up Buber's long sentences into small units, and this is a clear case of first thoughts being best, for his insistence on translating what he calls 'literally' very frequently produces a result which is not only clumsy but also profoundly obscure. His knowledge of German appears to be inadequate: to give one instance out of many, *wobei ein Nachbarstamm nach dem andern an die Reihe kommt* cannot possibly mean 'whereby one neighbouring tribe after another dies' (p. 66). The same must be said of his knowledge of Hebrew: otherwise he could not have so completely misunderstood the German of Buber's rendering of Ex. 20:23 (p. 166) or produced such forms as *ssara* and *missra* for *fsara* and *mifsra* (p. 168).

J.R.P.

CROATTO, J. S., C.M.: *Historia de la Salvación. La experiencia religiosa del Pueblo de Dios.* (Colección Orientaciones Bíblicas.) 2nd ed. 1966. Pp. vii + 389. (Ediciones Paulinas, Florida — Province of Bs. As., Argentina. Price: 700 Arg. pesos)

This competent history of the religion of Israel is developed over a broad compass of biblical literature. Less specialized than the author's fine study of covenant, *Alianza y Experiencia salvífica en la Biblia*, 1964, it is written for the public and for experts. The conceptual framework is typological. For example, the author relates Solomon's sin to the fall of Adam, speaks often of 'archetypes', 'archetypal acts', and 'predicting', and affirms the unity in the economy of salvation. Yet he is solidly rooted in the proposition of eventful revelation, critically and determinedly seeking to draw biblical events together with Christ at the centre. Ten chapters on Old Testament history are followed by a chapter each on Christ and the Church. The scope of intended readership may explain the unusual combination of critical awareness, some casually uncritical assumptions, and occasional defensiveness about inspiration. The text lacks footnotes, but appended to each chapter is a bibliography which indicates especially the literature available in Spanish.

The author is Professor of Sacred Scripture at the Jesuit seminary in San Miguel, province of Buenos Aires, and Professor of the History of Religions in the Facultad de Filosofía y Letras of the University of Buenos Aires. This important contribution to biblical literature in Argentina appeared in two editions in 1966. Its significance is underscored by the paucity of original biblical studies in Spanish, and its appearance dramatizes the growing energy and productivity of Latin American scholarship.   W.J.F.

ENGNELL, I.: *Studies in Divine Kingship in the Ancient Near East.* Second edition 1967. Pp. xxviii + 261. (Basil Blackwell, Oxford. Price: 50s.)

This first edition of this book, published in 1943 (see *B.L.* 1946, p. 44; *Eleven Years*, p. 44), has had such an influence in the study of ancient kingship that it is good to see a new and revised edition, incorporating the author's own revisions and with supplementary material, including a substantial additional bibliography supplied by G. W. Anderson. Engnell's intention to write a further volume dealing with the Old Testament material was never fulfilled. In this book the evidence from Egyptian, Mesopotamian, Hittite and West-Semitic (mainly Ugaritic) sources is displayed, with a great deal of detailed comment. The author's characteristic trenchancy of expression and his firm adherence to the position that 'divine kingship' is the justified term, remain unaltered. If at many points his work has been overtaken, it remains a vivid and exciting book, with the texts set out so that much more is here than the author's conclusions. G. W. Anderson contributes a preface and C. R. North an appreciation of Ivan Engnell. A list of the latter's published works is appended.

                                                        P.R.A.

GROSS, H., LOHFINK, N., SCHARBERT, J., SCHILLING, O. and SCHLIER, H.: *Die religiöse und theologische Bedeutung des Alten Testaments.* (Studien und Berichte der katholischen Akademie in Bayern. Heft 33.) n.d. Pp. 192. (Echter Verlag, Bayern. Price: DM. 8.80)

There are collected here six lectures given by distinguished younger Roman Catholic scholars to theological students. They survey recent work on such major themes as covenant, understanding of history, eschatology and messianism, seeking to present the main problems of interpretation and the lines of research. Basic bibliographical references are given, and the whole work is presented in a non-technical fashion. H. Schlier concludes with a study of the mystery of Israel seen from the New Testament viewpoint.   R.E.C.

HABEL, N. C.: *Yahweh versus Baal: A Conflict of Religious Cultures.* A Study in the Relevance of Ugaritic Materials for the Early Faith of Israel. (Graduate Studies Series of Concordia Seminary, St Louis, Missouri. No. VI.) 1964. Pp. 128. (Bookman Associates, New York. Price: $3.50)

It seems proper to include a brief note on this study, although it was published some years ago, since it has not become widely known as a result of its publication in a limited series. It is a vividly written short study of various aspects of Israel's faith — the covenant, the ancient traditions concerning Yahweh, his kingship, his self-revelation, his nature as life-giver — seen against the background of corresponding ideas in Canaanite religion, with particular stress laid upon the polemical element in the Old Testament presentation. It offers much that is penetrating and challenging in this portrayal of religious conflict, and deserves to be more widely known. The transliterated Hebrew occasionally needs correction.   P.R.A.

HERRMANN, S.: *Die prophetischen Heilserwartungen im Alten Testament. Ursprung und Gestaltwandel.* (Beiträge zur Wissenschaft vom Alten und Neuen Testament 85 = 5te Folge. Heft 5.) 1965. Pp. viii + 325. (W. Kohlhammer Verlag, Stuttgart. Price: DM. 36)

This is a substantial and significant contribution to the study of Hebrew prophecy dealing with the origin of the salvation oracles (promise associated with land, covenant and throne of David), the form they took in the 8th-century prophets, in particular in Isaiah (remnant, house of David, Zion) and the nature of the transformation the expectations of salvation underwent which is associated with Jeremiah, Ezekiel and Deutero-Isaiah. In an opening section prophetic phenomena in Egypt, Mesopotamia, Syria and Anatolia are discussed, in particular what may be learned from Egyptian sources to illustrate the formation of the prophetic books. The main contention of the work is that the books of Jeremiah and Ezekiel, while containing the prophetic legacy of these two prophets, represent the systemization of their thought brought about by the Deuterononomic renaissance of Hebrew religion and in the case of Ezekiel also by priestly interests. It is pointed out that it is in the prose 'sermons' in these books, which are labelled as Deuteronomic, that the coincidences of thought between these prophets occur. Both books are held to have received their present form in Palestine in contrast to Isaiah 40–55 which was edited in Babylon and is characterized by a universalizing of Israel's hopes and reveals a lessening of interest in the covenant and the Davidic house. The author does not deny the originality of the prophets but assigns a larger place than many could accept to the systematizing procedures which conserved and adapted the prophetic insights for the upbuilding of the post-exilic religious community.   N.W.P.

HERRMANN, S.: *Prophetie und Wirklichkeit in der Epoche des Babylonischen Exils.* (Arbeiten zur Theologie, I, 32.) 1967. Pp. 32. (Calwer Verlag, Stuttgart. Price: DM. 4.80)

This study, with which may be compared Herrmann's larger work noted above, provides a short survey of the situation and interpretation of the exilic age. It stresses the importance of recognizing the sensitivity of the prophets to their contemporary situation, and shows how the crisis of the 6th century necessitated a critique — offered in the Deuteronomic History as also in Ezekiel — of the *Heilsgeschichte*. It notes the variety and richness of presentations and interpretations of this complex situation. Though brief, the study contains much that is illuminating.   P.R.A.

HILLMANN, R.: *Wasser und Berg. Kosmische Verbindungslinien zwischen dem kanaanäischen Wettergott und Jahwe.* 1965. Pp. 200 + xxxiii + 35 pl. (photo-mechanic reproduction of doctoral dissertation. Halle (Saale))

Ugaritic specialists and serious students of the Old Testament will warmly welcome this doctoral thesis, which has been supervised by Professors Eissfeldt and Wallis. The writer studies the association of Baal locally with Mt Saphon, or Kasios, where Baal's conflict with the sea is located, and emphasizes the character of the god as a high-god, potent in the clouds and fertility, in which character his cult clashed with that of Yahweh in Israel, notably at the famous ordeal on Carmel, one of the coastal eminences to which the cult of Baal was disseminated from Mount Saphon. By this time the conception of Baal of the Heavens had developed towards monotheism, and in spite of conflict Yahwism assimilated much from this advanced conception of Baal. The imagery of the Canaanite conception of Baal is very thoroughly studied, with the implications of each detail, both in the Ras Shamra context and in its application in the Old Testament. The writer gives evidence of very great industry and discernment in his citation and analysis of an exceptional range of material, both literary and archaeological. The influence of Eissfeldt's theses is obvious throughout, but this is a worthy development of the thought of the master.   J.G.

L'HOUR, J.: *La morale de l'alliance.* (Cahiers de la Revue Biblique 5.) 1966. Pp. 126. (J. Gabalda & Cie, Paris. Price: Fr. 20)

The comparison of Old Testament covenant accounts with Near Eastern vassal treaties continues apace. L'Hour accepts a basic dependence of Israelite covenants upon this form, and shows the influence of such a covenant ideology upon Israelite ethics. Morality is a response to the divine grace, affirmed in the covenant and manifested in history. Israelite law obtains its distinctive character through its presentation as covenant stipulations, and the covenant blessings and curses provide an ethical basis for the interpretation of history. A final chapter discusses the social consequences of Israel's covenant ethic. The study is concise and scholarly, but places too much weight on the analogy with vassal treaties, and, from an ethical viewpoint, assumes too readily that a national morality can be transferred to a universal context.   R.E.C.

L'HOUR, J.: *Die Ethik des Bundestradition im Alten Testament.* (Stuttgarter Bibelstudien, 14. Aus dem französischen übersetzt von Margid Breithaupt.) 1967. Pp. 156. (Verlag Katholisches Bibelwerk, Stuttgart. Price: DM. 7.80)

See above on the French edition.

JOHNSON, A. R.: *Sacral Kingship in Ancient Israel.* 2nd edition. 1967. Pp. xiv + 167. (University of Wales Press, Cardiff. Price: 30s.)

This volume, originally published in 1955 (see *B.L.* 1956, p. 47, *Eleven Years*, p. 754) has now, like others of this author's monographs, been reissued with only minor revision of the text, but with considerable expansion of the footnotes. The revisions represent a response to more recent discussion, and in part a reply to misrepresentation of the author's views. The reappearance of this volume thus revised is much to be welcomed.   P.R.A.

KUITERT, H. M.: *Gott in Menschengestalt. Eine dogmatisch-hermeneutische Studie über die Anthropomorphismen der Bibel.* 1967. Pp. 252. (Chr. Kaiser Verlag, München. Price: DM. 24)

The theme of this important book is not to deal with the anthropomorphisms of the Bible phenomenologically but to proceed from them to a theological discussion of their significance. The author argues rightly that one must proceed from the biblical thought that man is made in the image of God, is theomorphic, and only then reverse the process and think of God as anthropomorphic, or better Hebraeomorphic. Man on the biblical view is God's partner and God is Israel's God who wills to be known, and that (according to the Hebrew view of knowledge) means to be loved, obeyed and served. This implies an intimate relationship between God and Israel which is described by the words 'covenant', 'election'. In opposition to Bultmann and the existentialists it is argued that we must not try to translate Israel's anthropomorphic language into timeless ideas. The God of Israel is not an unknown God. The proper task of theology is to understand the way in which God and man converse as partners. The problem of communication, of course, is how to translate the biblical language into 'profane' speech without losing its essential meaning.   N.W.P.

KUNTZ, J. K.: *The Self-revelation of God.* 1967. Pp. 254. (Westminster Press, Philadelphia. Price: $7)

A study of theophany in the Old Testament, expanded from a Union Theological Seminary dissertation dealing particularly with theophany in the Psalter, and independent of the work of Jörg Jeremias, which reached the author too late to be of use and which is referred to in the Preface, where he indicates the complete divergence of their approaches to the subject. The author defines theophany as 'a temporal, partial, and intentionally allusive self-disclosure initiated by the sovereign deity at a particular place, the reality of which evokes the convulsion of nature and the fear and dread of man, and whose unfolding emphasizes visual and audible aspects generally according to a recognized literary form'. He finds the clearest actualization of the *Gattung* in Gen. 26:23–5. From here he moves to the theophany at Sinai and then back to the study of the theophanies associated with the patriarchs. Next he examines the theophanies experienced by the prophets and theophany in the Psalter, and finally theophany as a cultic experience. A valuable study, which would have been more valuable if more concisely expressed.   H.H.R.

LAPOINTE, R.: *Les Trois Dimensions de l'herméneutique.* (Cahiers de la Revue Biblique, 8.) 1967. Pp. 151. (Gabalda, Paris. Price: Fr. 37)

This is probably one of the most ingenious, detailed and penetrating studies of what is sometimes regarded as the science of hermeneutics to appear in recent times. The author quite correctly asserts that many earlier writers consider the essential problems to be already solved. In his first chapter he surveys the whole domain of hermeneutics, and in the following chapter discusses some disputed topics, such as the relation between dogma and exegesis, the place of myth, and the application of interpretative principles to the Old Testament. The core of the work, however, is to be found in chapters III to VII, where he determines the three dimensions of hermeneutics (which he also styles the three parameters, so introducing a term borrowed from mathematics), which are the aesthetic, the ontological, and the existential. By way of illustration he selects a Venetian gondola, which may be regarded as a barque measuring 11 m. by 1.50 m., made of ten different types of wood, painted now in black (aesthetic parameter); of uncertain origin, possibly showing Egyptian influence (ontological parameter); and the delight of tourists (existential parameter). The arguments cannot be said to be easy, but the interest is maintained. A final chapter contrasts biblical hermeneutics with hermeneutics in general, and has something to say about scriptural inspiration.   J.M.T.B.

LINDBLOM, J.: *Israels religion i gammaltestamentlig tid.* 4th ed., 1967. Pp. 286. (Svenska Kyrkans Diakonistyrelses Bokförlag, Stockholm. Price: Paperback, Kr. 16; cloth, Kr. 21)

Earlier editions of this excellent manual of Old Testament religion were reviewed in *B.L.* 1953, p. 58: *Eleven Years*, p. 511, and *B.L.* 1965, p. 48: *Decade*, p. 600. The structure and substance of the book have not been altered, but account has been taken of recent literature, and a page of additional bibliographical references has been appended. We congratulate our esteemed honorary member on his continued literary activity and on the lasting usefulness of his earlier writings.

G.W.A.

MAERTENS, T.: *Bible Themes.* Vol. I. Pp. 502. Vol. II. Pp. 507. 1967. (Darton, Longman & Todd, London; Fides Publishers Inc., Indiana. Price: Paperback, 25s. each; hard binding, 37s. 6d.)

The main headings under which these themes are presented are God, Christ, the Church, the Holy Spirit and the Liturgy, the Holy Spirit in Human conduct, Realities of Human Life. Each main heading has a number of sub-headings ranging from forty-five to one hundred and five. Old Testament references are given to the Douai version. Some comments may need a second thought, e.g. I. p. 60 'Songs meant for human weddings were then incorporated into the Sacred Book in order to sing of the love of God and His Bride' which seems to confuse post hoc with propter hoc; or I. p. 195 '. . . David presented himself as a gentle king'. These volumes will be of great value to preachers, teachers and to all who use the Bible as a means of devotion. The original French edition was published in 1964.   A.S.H.

MILDENBERGER, F.: *Die halbe Wahrheit oder die ganze Schrift. Zum Streit zwischen Bibelglauben und historischer Kritik.* 1967. Pp. 99. (Chr. Kaiser Verlag, München. Price: DM. 9.80)

This little monograph is devoted to a study of the problem of reconciling biblical history with scientific history based on historical criticism. Whereas the Bible used to provide the framework for world history, the relationship is now reversed. Characteristic of biblical history is the word 'election' and this gives a particular quality to it which unfits it from being simply inserted in general history. This particularity tends to become equated with a subjective belief in a divine event which is reduced to general truths and in this way easily reconciled with religious experience. The particular, however, must not be lost sight of or explained away. The relation of 'God's time' to human time is discussed and a compromise suggested which seeks to make possible a critical approach without denying the claims of faith.   N.W.P.

MISKOTTE, K. H.: *When the Gods are Silent*. Trans. by John W. Dober-stein. 1967. Pp. xviii + 494. (Collins, London. Price: 65s.)

This translation incorporates the author's revisions and additions made for the German edition of the Dutch original. The German translation was reviewed in *B.L.* 1964, p. 61; *Decade*, p. 529. It is a work which has attracted considerable attention on the Continent and it is valuable to have it available now for a wider audience. Nothing could make Miskotte easy to read, but the translator has struggled manfully with the difficulties and obscurities of the original, in general with considerable success.   J.R.P.

VAN OYEN, H.: *Ethik des Alten Testaments*. (Geschichte der Ethik, Band 2.) 1967. Pp. 208. (Gütersloher Verlagshaus Gerd Mohn, Gütersloh. Price: DM. 25)

As the second of twelve volumes serially planned on the History of Ethics from antiquity to the present day this work outlines and assesses the Old Testament contribution in eight chapters, of which the first is introductory and the remaining seven deal respectively with the Theological foundations, the Human setting, the Law, the Prophets, Wisdom, Social and Political life. The characteristic features of Old Testament ethics are emphasized and the Decalogue is considered at some length. Thus it is shown that the Old Testament ethos is based on the Covenant and Israelite conduct inspired by the belief in Yahweh as the one true God. Although reference to some of the most recent literature is occasionally lacking, this survey is of value for its theological insight.   E.T.R.

VON RAD, G.: *Théologie de L'Ancien Testament*. II. Translated by A. Goy from the 4th German edition, 1965. n.d. (1967). Pp. 408. (Labor et Fides, Geneva. Price: Sw.Fr. 39; bound, 45)

The French translation of Vol. I was made in 1963; the English translations are noted in *B.L.* 1966, p.52; *Decade*, p. 672. The completion of the French translation of this influential work may be warmly welcomed.   P.R.A.

RENDTORFF, R.: *Väter, Könige, Propheten, Gestalten des Alten Testaments*. 1967. Pp. 214. (Kreuz-Verlag, Stuttgart. Price: DM. 14.80)

A short introductory chapter indicates the method of study by which an approach is made to presenting the nature of the tradition concerning certain persons and groups of persons in the Old Testament

— named figures such as Abraham and Moses, groups such as the kings of Israel and Judah and the Psalmists. It is a presentation of the life of Israel through these personalities — not as if their history could be constructed, but as they are revealed in the tradition. The studies are vividly written, clear and scholarly. An English edition is forthcoming.

P.R.A.

ROWLEY, H. H.: *Worship in Ancient Israel*. Its Forms and Meaning. 1967. Pp. xv + 307. (S.P.C.K., London. Price: 42s.)

In this work, which reproduces the Edward Cadbury Lectures given at Birmingham University in 1965, Professor Rowley sums up a lifetime's study of worship in the Old Testament. He first discusses worship in the patriarchal age, and then in the period from the exodus to the building of the temple; the remaining chapters examine in turn the temple, sacrifice, the attitude of the prophets to the cult, the Psalms, the synagogue, and finally 'The Forms and the Spirit'. Like all Dr Rowley's works, the book is clearly written and sound in judgement, and is very fully documented; there are indexes of subjects, authors, and biblical references. It will be used and valued both by advanced scholars and by elementary students.

J.A.E.

SCHWARZWÄLLER, K. *Theologie oder Phänomenologie. Erwägungen zur Methodik theologischen Verstehens*. (Beiträge zur evangelischen Theologie. Band 42.) 1966. Pp. 274. (Chr. Kaiser Verlag, München. Price: DM. 20)

This book cannot be recommended to anyone who is not familiar with the writings of the philosopher Heidegger (it is phenomenology in his use of the word which is discussed here), and with the obscure jargon which he employs. One has to fight one's way through a barbed-wire entanglement to reach discussions of the so-called Myth and Ritual School and the Scandinavians, of Westermann's treatment of the Psalms, of the theological views of Pannenberg, which are, of course, important for current hermeneutical discussions, and of Bultmann's attitude to the Old Testament. One cannot help wondering if all this obscurity is really necessary. It is a pity that presumably important contributions to thought should be made virtually inaccessible by their esoteric style.

N.W.P.

THOMAS, D. WINTON: *Understanding the Old Testament*. (Ethel M. Wood Lecture, 1967.) 1967. Pp. 22. (University of London, Athlone Press. Price: 5s.)

In this characteristically clear exposition, the author presents his approach to the problems of understanding what the Old Testament says, through research into its language, indicating the limitations of our knowledge and the avenues which are open. It is useful to have such a discussion of technical questions in a style which makes them plain to the non-specialist reader.

P.R.A.

VRIEZEN, TH. C.: *The Religion of Ancient Israel.* 1967. Pp. 328. (Lutterworth Press, London; Westminster Press, Philadelphia. Price: 45s.)

This is a welcome and smooth translation of *Das godsdienst van Israël* published in 1963 and reviewed in *B.L.* 1964, p. 67; *Decade* p. 535. Its strength lies in its clear delineation of the historical emergence and triumph of Yahwism; its weakness in its all too brief, 35 page, treatment of the exilic and post-exilic period. It forms an indispensible companion volume to the author's *An Outline of Old Testament Theology.*   R.D.

THE LIFE AND THOUGHT OF THE
SURROUNDING PEOPLES

BRANDON, S. G. F.: *The Judgment of the Dead.* 1967. Pp. xiv + 300. (Weidenfeld and Nicholson, London. Price: 50s.)

This historical and comparative study of a *post-mortem* judgement in the major religions is written for the general reader. Professor Brandon interprets the relevant texts and iconography to trace the development of a belief now in decline. Hebrew religion offers in this context less than most, especially if one isolates one strand of belief from the rest. The author accepts a convention in which eschatology as such emerges late. Certain gaps in the Yahweh tradition are seen to have given rise to the principle of divine vindication. In this respect Brandon concedes surprisingly little to the advocates of early eschatological strata in the O.T. nor does he seem to be impressed by formcritical considerations, e.g. the prophetic indictment and warning as such. His summary is perhaps too brief to plumb these complexities of the subject in this special field.   U.E.S.

BRESCIANI, E. and KAMIL, M.: *Le Lettere aramaiche de Hermopoli.* (Accademia Nazionale dei Lincei, Memorie, Classe di Scienze morali, storiche e filologiche, Serie VIII, Volume XII, Fascicolo 5.) 1966. Pp. 71 + x plates. (Accademia Nazionale dei Lincei, Rome. Price: £1 2s.)

These eight Aramaic papyri from Hermopolis West, which were discovered in 1945, consist of private letters (all but nos 6 and 8 are in an excellent state of preservation), dating from the mid-5th century B.C., and originating in a pagan milieu. Among the many features of interest for Old Testament studies may be noted the presence of Bethel and Malkath-Shamin in the pantheon, and the character of the Aramaic employed, with several differences from the contemporary Elephantine papyri (e.g. prevalence of *'af'el* over *haf'el*). The editors provide a short introduction, transcription, translation, and notes, followed by a full index verborum, and plates.   S.P.B.

CASTELLINO, G. R.: *Mitologia Sumerico-Accadica.* 1967. Pp. 214. (Società Editrice Internazionale di Torino. Price: Lire 2.500)

This is a delightfully produced and systematic study of Semitic and Accadian mythology, with a very full bibliography, which is well digested and critically treated. The author prefaces his work with an account of various views of the myths, their significance and relevance to the life of the Sumerians and Semites. In Part I he proceeds to an analysis of the Sumerian material, treating myths of origin, the creation of man and the world and the organization of nature, heaven and the underworld. In Part II he analyses Babylonian and Assyrian myths along similar lines. In Part III texts are cited in translation, with critical footnotes. Here the author's selection of less accessible material and less known texts will be welcomed by all interested in the subject. This is a masterly study, which will certainly take its place along with the sterling work of the masters in the field.

J.G.

GAMPER, A.: *Gott als Richter in Mesopotamien und im Alten Testament. Zum Verständnis einer Gebetsbitte.* 1966. Pp. viii + 256. (Universitätsverlag Wagner, Innsbruck. Price: Austr. Schill. 180)

The purpose of this dissertation is to examine the meaning and content of such prayers as 'plead my cause' and 'judge me' to see if they really mean 'do me justice' and even 'help me' and 'save me'; and, if so, how they have acquired such connotations and how they can then be explained if the suppliant is not an innocent person. The author examines in the first part what he calls *irdische Gerichtsbarkeit* and divine justice in Sumerian, Babylonian and Assyrian, literature and in the second legal procedure and *Gottesgericht* in the O.T. Mesopotamian law provides him with abundant material both in law-codes and in records of private law-suits; the fragmentary and composite legal parts of the O.T., however, are inadequate for his purpose, so that he is compelled to draw on the historical and other non-legal books, especially that of Proverbs. A fairly exhaustive collection of Mesopotamian texts are quoted in translation, while the original texts are given in transcription in the notes; these, he argues, show an 'astounding similarity' to those in the O.T. The conclusions which he reaches are that the whole *Rechtsordnung* derives from God, that God gives the law which is always *Gesetz Yahwehs* and that no one else, even the king, can make laws, and that the agents of the law (judges, elders, king) are but intermediaries under the covenant between God and man. God judges the nations, usually for punishment, and out of this activity salvation often comes to the Chosen People; but they too are subject to God's judgement as also the individual person is, and condemnation and punishment or help and salvation may result from such judgement. In this sense 'judge me' comes to connote 'do me justice' and even 'help me' or 'save me'.

The case is fully argued, though perhaps at excessive length; but the whole thesis is lucidly set out and the large collection of relevant texts is welcome, even though the interpretation of some of the excerpts may not accord with the latest results of modern scholarship. Slips and misprints are laudably few; but the reviewer notes that, while his own works on Babylonian and Assyrian Law are nowhere cited, two of his father's works are ascribed to him by way of compensation in the bibliography!

G.R.D.

MALAMAT, A.: *Prophecy in the Mari Documents and the Bible.* 1967. Pp. 28. (Israel Exploration Society, Jerusalem)

This booklet contains reprints of three articles in Hebrew which have appeared in *Eretz-Israel*; the English summaries which appeared originally are not included. The first, 'Prophecy in the Mari Documents' is from *EI* 4 (1956), pp. 74–84; the second, 'History and Prophetic Vision in a Mari Letter' from *EI* 5 (1958), pp. 67–73; the third, 'Prophetic Revelations in New Documents from Mari and the Bible' from *EI* 8 (1967), pp. 231–40. This last appeared in an English Version in *VTS* 15 (1966), pp. 207–27, *B.L.* 1967, p. 4. These are three useful discussions of texts and their relevance to the study of O.T. prophecy in its international setting.   P.R.A.

NOUGAYROL, J. and AYNARD, J.-M.: *La Mésopotamie* (Religions du Monde.) 1965. Pp. 120, 41 photo. ill. + 1 map + 1 plan + 2 drawings. (Bloud et Gay, Paris. Price: Fr. 9)

This authoritative paperback maintains the lead long established by French scholars in the study of Babylonian and Assyrian religion. In sharp contrast to the current notion that it is not possible to write a history of religion from such sources, the authors give succinct surveys of distinct aspects of religious life and thought, each introduced by extracts from the relevant texts. Thus introductions are provided to the pantheon, mythology, cult (including the New Year festival), divination and magic. One unusual feature is the analysis of recurring themes, travel by deities, feasting, fertility, fabulous plants (the tree and plant of life), paradise and creation. Sections are devoted also to the temples and clergy, death and the afterlife (there was no judgement of the dead), sin and suffering, hymns and prayers. While no direct comparison is made with Old Testament material sufficient detail is there for the intelligent reader to do this for himself.   D.J.W.

PETTINATO, G.: *Die Ölwahrsagung bei den Babyloniern.* (Studi Semitici 21, 22.) 1966. 2 Vols. 228 + 148 pp. (Istituto di studi del Vicino Oriente, Rome. Price: Lire 8.000; $14.00)

From the early second millennium B.C. or earlier the Babylonians practised lekanomancy and hydromancy using the services of a *barū-priest* ('seer') to observe the forms and colours of oil dropped on water or of water on oil. By this means interpretations were sought for the actions taken by the gods, and answers found to questions whether state or personal, concerning the outcome of projected actions be it the prospects of a military expedition or of a marriage, or the outcome of litigation or sickness. Brief mention is made of similar practices among the Hittites and Greeks. However, the author doubts whether Joseph's act of divining with a cup (Gen. 44:5, 15) was of this type. Yet this must be a possibility since lekanomancy played a distinct part in later Egyptian and Hebrew practice (see S. Daiches, *Babylonian oil magic in the Talmud and in later Jewish literature*, 1913) and would well be classed among the forms of divination denounced by the prophets from the monarchy onwards. Water and oil are used in many Babylonian rituals not covered by these volumes which aim to provide the specialist with reconstructed texts (totalling 251 lines) with translations and linguistic commentary.

                    D.J.W.

RINGGREN, H.: *Främre Orientens religioner i gammal tid.* (Scandinavian University Books.) 1967. Pp. 232, with many illustrations. (Svenska Bokförlaget/Bonniers, Stockholm)

This excellently produced text book is intended to serve the needs both of those who wish to begin the study of ancient Near Eastern religions for their own sake and also of students of the Old Testament who want background material. There are three main sections: I. Sumerian religion; II. Babylonian and Assyrian religion; III. West-Semitic religion. In each section a rounded and balanced presentation is given of religious belief and practice; and the entire treatment is illustrated not only pictorially but by appropriate citation of texts in translation. There is a useful select bibliography. Lucid, readable, authorative, and (notably in the Ugaritic field) up-to-date, this work will admirably serve its purpose.   G.W.A.

QUMRAN STUDIES

ALLEGRO, J. M.: *Sokroviŝĉa mĕdnogo svitka.* (*The Treasures of the Copper Scroll.*) 1967. Pp. 189 + 10 drawings of maps and plans. (Akademija nauk SSSR., Izdatěl'stvo 'Nauka', Moscow. Price: 35 kop.)

This book (see *B.L.* 1961, p. 58; *Decade,* p. 296) has now been translated into Russian by G. M. Bauer and provided with a detailed and well-informed introduction by J. D. Amussin. This introduction is a valuable complement to the author's otherwise too one-sided and subjective presentation. The text of the copper scroll is reproduced, drawn from the original, with a parallel transcription (in Roman letters) and translation (in Russian letters). The translation is supplemented by 323 notes which are gathered at the end of the book (pp. 137–85), together with indexes and maps and plans. The translation was made from the American edition (Doubleday, N.Y., 1960). The author has provided a short foreword to the Russian edition.

M.B.

HARRIS, J. G.: *The Qumran Commentary on Habakkuk.* (Contemporary Studies in Theology, 9.) 1966. Pp. vi + 66. (A. R. Mowbray & Co. Ltd, London. Price: 10s. 6d.)

This work is intended as a popular introduction for the general reader to certain aspects of the study of *IQpHab.* Although as a work of popularization this short study has some value, it seems curious that amongst the things the author has included there is very little discussion of the various historical allusions in the *Commentary,* and of the information which these give us about the Qumran community, and equally curious that there is a (somewhat unsatisfactory) discussion of the orthography of *IQpHab*; one wonders how many general readers know any Hebrew. It is also unfortunate that the work contains some simplifications which are misleading, while it is not clear to the reviewer why a paraphrase of the *Commentary* was thought to be of more use than a precise translation.   M.A.K.

SANDERS, J. A.: *The Dead Sea Psalms Scroll*. 1967. Pp. xii + 174 (with six illustrations and a map). (Cornell University Press, Ithaca, N.Y. Price: $10.00)

> To describe this as a popular edition of 11 QPsᵃ, originally edited by the same author in *Discoveries in the Judaean Desert* IV (1965) (see *B.L.* 1960, p. 60; *Decade*, p. 680) is both proper — since here the material is clearly set out and much valuable explanatory and comparative information is given — and inadequate — since this volume is more complete than the original edition, including as it does the Fragment E published by Y. Yadin in *Textus 5*, and it also provides a very broad-based discussion of many questions which arise from this important document. Its title is perhaps not sufficiently precise, since there are other 'Psalms Scrolls' though none as yet so full as this. The first part of the book gives a clear and interesting account of the finding, unrolling and contents of the scroll, noting the deviations of order and of reading. Part two provides a transliteration and translation of the text with brief notes. Part three deals in detail with the apocryphal compositions. Appendices cover the Syriac Psalms (IV and V) not included in this manuscript; a list of Pre-Masoretic texts from Qumran and elsewhere, with an index; and bibliography. A Postscript covers Fragment E and includes some discussion of the problems of the Psalter in the light of the new evidence provided by the various psalms manuscripts now gradually being published. This is a very well-produced and useful volume.   P.R.A.

YALON, H.: *Studies in the Dead Sea Scrolls. Philological Essays 1949–1952*. 1967. Pp. xi (English), 119, (Hebrew). (Shrine of the Book Fund, America–Israel Cultural Foundation and Kiryath Sepher Ltd, Jerusalem)

> These studies are based on E. L. Sukenik's two preliminary studies of the scrolls (Jerusalem 1948 and 1950) and articles reproduced from journals. They include technical discussion of such matters as the evidence of spelling and orthography for the date and contemporary pronunciation of the scrolls' vocabulary, finding influence of Aramaic and Samaritan, and above all affinity with Mishnaic Hebrew. The summary in English assists reference to some interesting discussion showing the considerable variety of forms (sometimes mistakenly taken as errors) used by the different scribes of the scrolls and by the same scribe.   A.R.C.L.

APOCRYPHA AND POST-BIBLICAL STUDIES

BARON, S. W.: *A Social and Religious History of the Jews*. Late Middle Ages and Era of European Expansion (1200–1650): Vol. XI, *Citizen or Alien Conjurer*. 2nd Edition. 1967. Pp. 422. (Price: 90s. 0d.) Vol. XII. *Economic Catalyst*. 2nd Edition. 1967. Pp. 359. (Price: 90s. 0d.) (Columbia University Press, New York and London.)

> These volumes maintain the high standard of their preceding companions*. They examine closely some outstanding Jewish facets of late Medieval political and economic history. We thus have here a fine elaboration of the more chronological and topographical description given in the earlier volumes. Scholars are awaiting with keen desire the appearance of the subsequent volumes.
> *For reviews of vols I–II; III–V; VI–VIII, see *B.L.* 1953, p. 24, *Eleven*

Years p. 477; 1958, p. 52; 1959, p. 41, *Decade* pp. 128, 177 respectively. A review of Index to vols I–VIII appeared in *B.L.* 1961, p. 63,
Decade p. 301. (Vols IX–X have not been reviewed in *B.L.*)   M.W.

BOUSSET, W. and GRESSMANN, H.: *Die Religion des Judentums im späthel-
lenistischen Zeitalter.* (Handbuch zum Neuen Testament 21.) 4th
edition. 1966. Pp. XVI + 576. (J. C. B. Mohr (Paul Siebeck), Tübingen.
Price: DM. 47)

This justly famous work, whose republication is most welcome, needs
no introduction. It is reprinted without change except for the addition
of a brief preface by E. Lohse, who gives a short appreciation of the
contributions of Bousset and Gressmann, discusses the significance
of some of the more recent developments in the study of Judaism
in the inter-testamental period and provides a bibliography of the
more important books on the subject that have been published since
the third edition appeared in 1926.   M.A.K.

BRANDON, S. G. F.: *Jesus and the Zealots: A Study of the Political Factor
in Primitive Christianity.* 1967. Pp. xvi + 413. (Manchester University
Press. Price: 55s.)

In his earlier book, *The Fall of Jerusalem and the Christian Church*,
Professor Brandon, in an attempt to assess the effect of the First
Jewish Revolt on the history of the early Church, revived the view of
Robert Eisler of a political involvement of Jesus of Nazareth which
precipitated the Trial and Crucifixion. This view is now argued afresh
in the light of an extensive and detailed study of the Zealot movement
in the 1st century. The new evidence from Qumran and Masada is
now added to our previous knowledge of the Zealots: a historical
survey covers the period from the incorporation of Judaea into the
Roman Empire in A.D. 6 to the last stand of the Zealots at Masada in
A.D. 73. The relation of the Jewish Christians to the Revolt is discussed, and, against this Jewish and Jewish Christian background,
Dr Brandon develops his theme that Mark presents a view of the
Crucifixion which not only plays down but even deliberately obscures
the political aspects of the movement of Jesus of Nazareth; Mark's
'apologetic' is then elaborated in Matthew and Luke into the concept
of the 'pacific Christ'.
Its central thesis apart — and its weakest link may still be felt to be
the interpretation of the Gospel evidence — the book is a valuable
contribution to our fuller understanding of that violent movement of
political fanaticism, led by the people called Zealots, which cul-
minated in the First Revolt.   M.Bl.

BÜCHLER, A.: *Studies in Sin and Atonement in the Rabbinic Literature of
the First Century.* Prolegomenon by F. C. Grant. (Library of Biblical
Studies, ed. by H. M. Orlinsky.) 1967. Pp. xl + 462. (Ktav Publishing
House, Inc., New York. Price: $12.50)

In a lively introduction to this reprint of Büchler's *Studies in Sin and
Atonement* (first published in 1928) Professor Grant outlines the
contents of the work, and then discusses the concept of sin and
atonement in general terms, and in the context of early Christianity.

                                                          M.A.K.

DELLING, G.: *Jüdische Lehre und Frömmigkeit in den Paralipomena Jeremiae*. (Beiheft zur Zeitschrift für die alttestamentliche Wissenschaft, 100.) 1967. Pp. 74. (Verlag Alfred Töpelmann, Berlin. Price: DM. 24)

The author accepts the 2nd century A.D. date for the Paralipomena of Jeremiah, the Jewish authorship of its main part, and the certainty that its original language was a Palestinian one. He takes four points for comparison with Pharisaic Judaism: personal piety, the divine attributes, the separateness of the people of God, and the expectation of a future life. In all these he shows by the examination of the Greek phrases used that for the most part they represent time-honoured Hebrew phrases and echo pretty closely the general pattern of Jewish belief.

L.H.B.

FINLEY, M. I. (ed.): *Josephus. The Jewish War and Other Selections from Flavius Josephus* translated by H. St J. Thackeray and R. Marcus. (The Great Histories.) 1966. Pp. xxxvi + 348. (The New English Library Limited, London. Price: 7s. 6d.)

This addition to the paperback series *The Great Histories* presents a collection of extracts from the *Loeb Classical Library* translation of the works of Josephus, which will undoubtedly prove extremely useful to students, especially now that G. A. Williamson's Penguin translation of the *War* is out of print. The bulk of the work (pp. 79–336) is, rightly, devoted to extensive excerpts from the *War*. Besides this the editor has included brief extracts from the *Life* and *Against Apion*, and three sections from the *Antiquities* (from Books I, II and X), which are intended to illustrate how Josephus retells the biblical stories. The work is prefaced by a very readable introduction which contains just enough about Josephus and his period to make what follows intelligible. There are two maps, reproduced from the Loeb edition, and an index.

M.A.K.

GOETTMANN, J.: *Tobie. Livre des fiancés et des pélerins.* 1966. Pp. 250. (Desclée de Brouwer, Bruges. Price: Fr. 16.50)

This is a devotional study of the Book of Tobit seeking to show how it holds within itself a two-fold pattern, that of the development of God's grace in the Old Testament from creation onwards, and that of the Gospel, especially as told by Luke. It is a book for the prayer-desk rather than the study table.

L.H.B.

HANHART, R.: *Drei Studien zum Judentum.* (Theologische Existenz Heute, No. 140.) 1967. Pp. 64. (Chr. Kaiser Verlag, München. Price: DM. 4.90)

The three studies are: Kriterien Geschichtlicher Wahrheit in der Makkabäerzeit; Zur Geistesgeschichtlichen Bestimmung des Judentums; Die Bedeutung der Septuaginta-Forschung für die Theologie.
The essays have in common that they touch upon the significance of Apocalyptic and of the changes in meaning consequent upon translation from Hebrew to Greek. The first essay discusses the criteria by

which we can derive historical truth from the changing interpretation of prophetic and apocalyptic words in subsequent generations. The second discusses the definition of Judaism and finds the significant factors to be the emergence of Apocalyptic after the loss of prophetic utterance (whether or not the words had been fulfilled), and the representation of the written revelation in a second language. The third essay, admitting the possibility of change of meaning in transmitting the Hebrew canon in a Greek form, argues that the rendering remains basically true to its Jewish background and that it is not right to speak of a 'Theology of the Septuagint'.　　　　L.H.B.

HASPECKER, J.: *Gottesfurcht bei Jesus Sirach. Ihre religiöse Struktur und ihre literarische und doktrinäre Bedeutung.* (Analecta Biblica, 30.) 1967. Pp. xxvi + 355. (Päpstliches Bibelinstitut, Rom. Price: Lire 5.700; $9.50)

This is a searching and thoroughgoing study of what ben Sira meant by 'the fear of God'. In the course of it the author first sketches other scholars' opinions about the depth of ben Sira's religious life, follows this with a detailed and critical study of the passages where ben Sira mentions the fear of God, and devotes the rest of the book to building up what he regards as the content, for ben Sira, of the phrase 'fear of God', namely, a sincere and whole-hearted devotion to God, a reverent quest for him, and a full trust in and love for him, in all humility.

References to the fear of God are scattered more or less evenly throughout Ecclesiasticus (with some exceptions, notably 42:15–50:26), although not always attested by all the ancient forms of the text (Greek, Hebrew and Syriac). It is often so placed within the section to which it belongs as to make it not only one element in a series of rules for behaviour but an organic and determining factor. It is shown to be explained by its context and is seen to have as its main element a vigorous trust and hope in God (e.g. 34:13–17) for its own sake and not for the reward it may bring.

Although somewhat long and repetitive in its arguments, the book does seem to demonstrate successfully that ben Sira was a deeply religious teacher.　　　　L.H.B.

LIFSHITZ, B.: *Donateurs et Fondateurs dans les Synagogues Juives. Répertoire des dédicaces grecques relatives à la construction et à la refection des synagogues.* (Cahiers de la Revue Biblique 7.) 1967. Pp. 94. (Gabalda, Paris. Price: Fr. 35)

This convenient *répertoire* brings together all known synagogal inscriptions in Greek of ancient date; they muster over 100, ranging geographically from Dura Europos through Palestine to Spain and chronologically from the 3rd century B.C.E. to the 6th century C.E. All have been previously published (bibliographies are given in each case), but some are very recent discoveries. For readers of this *Book List* the most useful item will probably be the excellent index to the Greek vocabulary of the inscriptions. They will note an interesting occurrence of the term *Ioudaismós* (no. 10, from Paeonia, late 3rd century C.E.), the sense of which has conceivably been misinterpreted

by the editor. They will also observe with interest that although post-
biblical Hebrew firmly restricts *moshia'* as a devine epithet, and
Christianity makes a *sōtēr* of its own Messiah, the Greek-speaking
Synagogue 'de-soteriologised' the abstract *sōtēria*. It figures frequently
in honorific contexts in these dedications (*hypèr sōtērías* before the
names of living persons, corresponding to donations *le-ḥayyē peloni*
in the modern Synagogue), and points forward to the restoration of a
feature in the Ostia synagogue labelled *pro salute Augusti*, and so
ultimately to the Portuguese *saude* retained in a similar formula by
the Sephardic synagogue at Amsterdam until today.   R.L.

MORGENSTERN, J.: *Some Significant Antecedents of Christianity*. 1966.
Pp. xii + 112. (E. J. Brill, Leiden. Price: Fl. 26)

This collection of occasional studies by a well-known *Alttestamentler*
seeks to discuss and illumine New Testament problems against the
background of the Old Testament. With two exceptions, 'The Passover in the Sypnotics and John' and 'Palm Sunday and Easter Sunday', the essays deal with christological themes, from a study of
'Jesus the Teacher' to the more controversial topics of 'Jesus as the
Suffering Servant', 'Jesus as the Son of Man', 'The Antecedents
of the Eucharist and of the Doctrines of the Virgin Birth
and the Trinity'. The collection ends with a chapter on General
Conclusions summarizing the previous discussion: Jesus and his
disciples, for instance, while not 'non-conformist' vis-à-vis official
Judaism, must have preserved and observed certain distinctive
traditions, e.g. calendrical, from an earlier age. In the christological
essays not every scholar will go so far as to be prepared to consider
the Suffering Servant as 'a supernatural being, perhaps even the
divine Son of the Father' (p. 48). (Dan. 7 is understood along similar
lines.)
These essays are the late gleanings of a rich harvest of Old Testament
study, written by one with a deep and intimate knowledge of the Old
Testament and more than a passing interest in the New.   M.Bl.

PFEIFER, G.: *Ursprung und Wesen der Hypostasenvorstellungen im Judentum.*
(Arbeiten zur Theologie I/31.) 1967. Pp. 110. (Calwer Verlag, Stuttgart. Price: DM. 12.50)

In the first part of this study — a thesis submitted to the Faculty
of Theology at Jena — the author systematically examines the entire
corpus of Jewish literature from *Trito-Isaiah* to the *Odes of Solomon*
(which are held to have a Jewish *Grundlage*) for possible occurrences of
hypostatic conceptions. On the basis of this survey he concludes that,
with the exception of the hypostasis Wisdom, and of Philo, such
conceptions are only relatively rarely to be found, and that they are
usually introduced quite incidentally. As in other religions hypostases
have for the most part developed as the culmination of a process
whereby divine attributes and functions become more and more
independent, but there are examples of the reverse process, the most
important being Wisdom, which in the earliest traditions (*Job* 28;
Prov. 8:22–31) is held to be completely independent of God at first,
and only subsequently to have been acquired by him. The second part
of the work is devoted to the question of origins, and the author

considers in turn the various influences — Israelite, Canaanite, Egyptian, Mesopotamian, Iranian, Hellenistic — which might conceivably have affected the development of hypostatic conceptions. Pfeifer argues that most of the hypostases which emerge in Judaism derive from concepts present already in Israelite religion, but that there is evidence of some Egyptian influence, and of strong Hellenistic influence in the later stages, particularly upon *Sap. Sal.* and Philo. There remain two hypostases which cannot be explained in either of these ways, namely Law and Wisdom. The author thinks that these represent original Jewish developments. He further suggests that the origin of hypostasized Wisdom is to be sought in a female deity (of the type represented by Anatjahu of Elephantine and the Queen of Heaven of *Jer.* 44:17) who was attached to Yahweh as consort — but this stage can no longer be traced directly in our texts.

M.A.K.

RAPPOPORT, A. S.: *Myth and Legend of Ancient Israel.* With an Introduction and Additional Notes by R. Patai. 3 Vols. 1966. Pp. iv + xviii + 264; viii + 400; viii + 296. (Ktav Publishing House Inc., New York. Price: 3 vols .$19.95)

This collection of myths and legends was originally published in 1928. It contains a vast amount of material, derived chiefly from Rabbinic, but also from non-Jewish sources, which is arranged by subject and embraces within its scope the characters and events of the biblical narrative from the Creation to Esther. For this new edition Patai has contributed a short introduction in which he attempts to assess the value of the work in the light of the advances made in the study of mythology and folklore in the past forty years. He has also provided a short memoir of Rappoport, and some additional notes which are intended to emphasize 'the *meaningful aspect of Hebrew mythology*' (p. xv). Patai argues that despite its limitations the work retains its value because of the nature and abundance of the material it presents. Fascinating as the work is, present day readers are likely to find the style and method of presentation less than satisfactory.

M.A.K.

RENGSTORF, K. H.: *Die Re-Investitur des Verlorenen Sohnes in der Gleichniserzählung Jesu Luk.* 15, 11–32. (Arbeitsgemeinschaft für Forschung des Landes Nordrhein-Westfalen, Heft 137.) 1967. Pp. 78 + XIII plates. (Westdeutscher Verlag, Köln und Opladen. Price: DM. 14.30)

A study of the parable of the Prodigal Son suggests that there lies in the background the legal custom of the *keṣāṣāh*, whereby a man who had offended against the interests of his family or tribe had his connection with them forcibly dissolved and lost his status. The parable is chiefly concerned, however, with the cancellation of the *keṣāṣāh*. This takes the form of a re-investiture. The returning son is given the garment which he had formerly worn as an emblem of his status, a ring which symbolizes the authority his father confers on him, and shoes which are a sign of his right of tenure. The legal symbolism of the ring in the pre-Christian era is substantiated by a series of archaeological illustrations, and that of the garment by reference to the accounts in I Maccabees and Josephus of the death of Antiochus Epiphanes. Evidence for the symbolism of the shoes is less direct and convincing. The author claims that the portrayal of the son's restoration as a legal act illustrates the theological principle of the *justificatio impii*.   M.E.T.

SCHLATTER, A.: *Synagoge und Kirche bis zum Barkochba-Aufstand. Vier Studien zur Geschichte des Rabbinats und der jüdischen Christenheit in den ersten zwei Jahrhunderten.* (Kleinere Schriften von Adolf Schlatter, neu herausgegeben von Th. Schlatter, Bd. 3.) 1966. Pp. 304. (Calwer Verlag, Stuttgart. Price: DM. 29.00)

The four studies which are here reprinted were all published originally in the series *Beiträge zur Förderung christlicher Theologie*. The titles are: 'Die Tage Trajans und Hadrians' (1897); 'Die Kirche Jerusalems vom Jahr 70 bis 130' (1898); 'Jochanan ben Zakkai, der Zeitgenosse der Apostel' (1899); 'Der Märtyrer in den Anfängen der Kirche' (1915). In a short preface Professor J. Jeremias pays tribute to the pioneering nature and abiding value of Schlatter's work in the fields represented by these studies, which it is good to have made generally available once more.   M.A.K.

SIMON, M.: *Jewish Sects at the Time of Jesus.* Translated by J. H. Farley. 1967. Pp. xii + 180. (Fortress Press, Philadelphia. Price: $2.95)

The author's purpose in this short paperback study, which has been translated from the French edition of 1960 (not noticed in *B.L.*), is to make clear how very varied were the different currents that combined to form Judaism in the time of Jesus. After a thought-provoking discussion of the significance of the term 'sect' in this context, there are chapters on Sadducees, Pharisees and Zealots, on the Essenes, on other, more marginal, Palestinian groups, on Philo and the Therapeutae, and, finally, on the relationship between the Jewish sects and Christianity. Although there are individual statements with which one would disagree, particularly in what is said about the Teacher of Righteousness, in general the author has provided us with a balanced and perceptive introduction to his subject. The reviewer has not attempted to check the accuracy of the translation, but errors were noticed on pages 21 and 82. It is a pity that there has been some dislocation of the type on page 102.   M.A.K.

URBACH, E. E.: *Class Status and Leadership in the World of the Palestinian Sages.* (Proceedings of the Israel Academy of Sciences and Humanities, II. 4. Trans. by I. Abrahams.) 1966. Pp. 37. (Central Press, Jerusalem. Price: $0.75)

Careful study of Talmudic sources has yielded the present essay on the vicissitudes in the social status and leadership of the Palestinian Sages, heirs of the Hasidim, during the period from the later years of the Second Temple to the compilation of the Mishna. As exponents and practitioners of the Torah the Sages, whether for the time

being prominent in the nation's affairs with the standing of a
privileged caste or temporarily in eclipse, and though on occasion
torn by faction and strife, were yet a formative and leavening influence
ever seeking to improve the system for which they regarded themselves as responsible.
                                                                    E.T.R.

PHILOLOGY AND GRAMMAR

BEN-MEIR, A.: *Initiation à l'hébreu vivant*. 1ᵉʳ fascicule. 1965. Pp.
xv + 162. (Librairie Rene Giard, Lille. Price: Fr. 20)

For Hebrew language-teachers this latest attempt to combine some
of the results of recent research into linguistics and language-teaching with the current boom in Israel's tourist trade, should be of considerable interest. 'Hébreu vivant', in this context, includes both
biblical and modern Israeli Hebrew, so that by the end of the first
fascicle the student is reading the first five verses of Genesis, on his
own or with an instructor, as well as a rich, wittily illustrated variety
of modern Israeli dialogues, adventures and songs (with music).
The method is meant to be as painless as possible: the division of
nouns into declensions is dropped; the construct state is described in
one lesson, construct forms in the next lesson; the past tense of the
verb is left for the second fascicle; the 600-word vocabulary is
introduced, carefully classified as *Racines verbales*, *Noms*, *Adjectifs*,
and *Particules* (which refers to everything from '*et* to *šum dabar*);
and about half of each lesson is composed of exercises. The relation
of this grammar to the traditional grammars, however, is slightly
uneasy, being at the same time revolutionary and reactionary. The
p'l-terminology for verbal paradigms is completely dropped: e.g.
Niphal is called '2ème forme', *piel* '3ème forme', and so on; '*Ayin waw*
verbs are described as monosyllabic verbs. But the vowels are still
given their Hebrew names, *pataḥ*, *ḳamaṣ*, etc. *Dagesh lene* and silent
shwa are no longer printed, but the *rapheh* is introduced to indicate
aspirated *bgdkpt*. A similar uneasiness is evident in the rather in-
accurate definition of '*ayin* (p. 2). Is this grammar intended for
serious students of the language who must know the traditional
jargon, in which case why drop the *p'l*-paradigm? Or if it is intended
for kibbutz-holidays, why the *rapheh* and the *pataḥ furtif*?
These criticisms may be answered in the second fascicle, where a
careful index and some verb tables will presumably also clarify the
author's method. Meanwhile, in spite of several misprints and the
inevitable blurring of the offset-printing process, this is a good start;
and as an indication of the progress towards bringing Hebrew
teaching into line with other 20th-century school and university
disciplines, it is significant that the alphabetical table of this predominantly modern Hebrew grammar actually includes, for reference
and general interest, the ancient Hebrew script, a thing which none of
our most widely used elementary grammars of the ancient language
have thought it useful to include.
                                                                    J.F.A.S.

BLACK, M.: *An Aramaic Approach to the Gospels and Acts*. 3rd ed. 1967.
Pp. viii + 359. (Clarendon Press, Oxford. Price: 60s.)

The first and second editions of this work were reviewed in the *B.L.*
1947, p. 38, and 1955, p. 70; *Eleven Years*, pp. 100, 703. The new

edition has been expanded chiefly by the addition of a chapter on
'Recent discoveries and developments in Palestinian Aramaic', and
by an appendix by Dr G. Vermes on the use of *bar nash(a')* in Jewish
Aramaic. The additions render this very useful book yet more
valuable.   J.A.E.

GORDON, C. H.: *Ugaritic Textbook.* Grammar, Texts in transliteration,
Cuneiform selections, Glossary, Indices (Analecta Orientalis 38).
(1965.) Reeditio photomechanica 1967 with supplement. Pp. xvi + 556.
(Pontificium Institutum Biblicum, Rome. Price: Ll. 17.400, $29.00)

This volume was reviewed in *B.L.* 1966, p. 65; *Decade*, p. 685. To
its 1965 form a supplement has been added by the author covering
pp. 549–56. He indicates additional texts, some of which have been
utilized here before their publication by C. Virolleaud in *Ugaritica
VA.* The remaining material consists of addenda to the glossary, and
a brief note on yet further information from the 1966 finds.

                                                                    P.R.A.

GUILLAUME, A.: *Hebrew and Arabic Lexicography, a comparative study.*
1965. Pp. 91. (Leiden, E. J. Brill. Price: Fl. 16)

This is a collection of four studies reprinted from vols I–IV (1959–65)
of *Abr-Nahrain.* Each one of the very many words and comparisons
discussed by the late Professor Guillaume would require detailed
comment in a review that aimed at doing justice to his long and
arduous labours. This, alas, is impossible in the present context.
It must, however, be averred — sadly — that the methods used cannot lead to satisfactory results. The table of interchanges of consonants (p. 4) must be condemned in the strongest terms; and since it has
been taken as the basis of this comparative study we can scarcely be
surprised at some of the conclusions that have been reached on such
evidence. The resources of the Arabic dictionary have certainly not
been exhausted for the elucidation of the Hebrew lexicon, but
offerings from Arabic dialects, from distinct linguistic layers, in terms
of chronology and social structure, have to be examined and sifted
before they can be applied to enhance our understanding of the Old
Testament. At best this monograph may serve as a random collection
of material upon which future scholars will bring to bear the full
rigour of modern methodology and sound judgement.   E.U.

JAMME, A.: *Sabaean and Ḥasaean Inscriptions from Saudi Arabia.* (Studi
Semitici, 23.) 1966. Pp. 107 with 18 figures comprising a map and
transcribed inscriptions and 21 photographic plates. (Istituto di Studi
del Vicino Oriente. Università di Roma, Rome. Price: Lire 4.000;
$7.00)

The present volume contains the texts of 26 Sabaean inscriptions from
Central Arabia and 20 in an Eastern Old-Arabic Dialect (here called
'Hasaean' from the District of Ḥasâ, collected by Fr Jamme and
others who have helped him in searching out and photographing
inscribed stones. One is an important historical text in 12 lines, dated

in the 6th century B.C., which deals with the military operations of the Jewish king of South Arabia, Gusup 'A'sar Yat'-ar (cf. Ryckmans 508); the rest are *graffiti* of the usual type, which are of interest only to specialists in South Arabian studies, chiefly as contributions to onomatology. The style of the editor's comments is such that the reader may not always easily see what he means; for example, what can he mean by 'the other handle . . . , not found, was stamped with the name of the eponym or dating authority' on p. 83? The jargon, too, in which they are expressed is sometimes deplorable, i.e. in using 'conjunction' for 'particle' on p. 42, 'who' for 'things' and 'which' for women and 'those' for 'these' on p. 31, in the remarkable '(a man) light, active' on p. 60, in the adjective 'clanic' on p. 79, and so on. Finally, can any purpose be served by publishing what can only be called 'non-inscriptions', i.e. stones from which the texts have been more or less completely erased? The persevering student, however, will find much that is of interest in this small volume.

G.R.D.

MARTINEZ, ERNEST R. (compiler): *Hebrew-Ugaritic Index to the writings of Mitchell J. Dahood.* 1967. Pp. 120. (Pontifical Biblical Institute, Rome. Price: Lire 1.500, $2.50)

This monograph offers a bibliography of Father M. J. Dahood's writings over the past fifteen years and lists 135 items. This is followed by indexes of Scriptural passages, of Hebrew and Ugaritic words, and of grammatical observations contributed by Father Dahood in those 135 items of his bibliography. The avowed purpose of this labour of love is to 'provide the biblical scholar . . . with a helpful guide for finding what Professor Dahood has written with reference to numerous Hebrew words and passages of Scripture, valuable work that might otherwise remain buried in scattered periodicals'.

Father Martinez's enterprise raises some points of principle. If this sort of thing were done by dutiful disciples for all scholars, we would witness the development of a wholly undesirable form of Parkinsonism in scholarly circles. Father Dahood is a man at the height of his powers; we may hope that to the 15 years of scientific output hitherto accomplished he will add at least another 30 or 40 years. The mind boggles at the man-hours required to index and cross-reference his future writings and those of his fellow-workers in Ugaritic and biblical studies!

E.U.

MAUCHLINE, J.: *An Introductory Hebrew Grammar.* (A. B. Davidson, 26th ed.) 1966. Pp. xii + 319. (T. and T. Clark, Edinburgh. Price: 35s.)

This edition of 'Davidson's' Grammar is substantially Professor Mauchline's revision, which appeared as the 25th edition in 1962 (see *B.L.* 1963, p. 71; *Decade*, p. 465). Most, though not all, of the misprints have been corrected. The paragraphs dealing with gutterals, the jussive, and the Pi'el have each been simplified to advantage and a summary of the early sections dealing with vocalization has been added to enable the student to get over this hurdle as quickly as possible. However, this summary has been added at the end of the book, out of order, and is not noted in the table of contents. It is too, condensed rather than simplified. What will the beginner make of 'preclitic element'? This edition is an improvement on the earlier one but is still likely to be criticized as formidably academic by some students and teachers.

J.R.

SPULER, B. (ed.): *Handbuch der Orientalistik*, vol. III, SEMITISTIK. 1964. Pp. 398. (E. J. Brill, Leiden. Price: Fl. 55)

This is a photographic reprint of a work which first appeared in 1953–4. Several of the contributions, despite the inclusion of some illustrious names, could not — even at that time — be considered to reflect the state of current knowledge. Four of the eight contributors have since died, and one feels sure that they would scarcely have approved of an unamended reprint. It is difficult to see what purpose a work of this type is to serve when its methodology — apart from some minor exceptions — is that of the 19th century and its bibliographical coverage sadly inadequate and out-of-date. The strictures voiced by the present reviewer (particularly upon the performance of the editor) in *Orientalia* 1958/1, p. 68, esp. note (2), apply *a fortiori* to this unexpurgated reissue. At a time when the photographic reprint industry has reached such vast dimensions some thought ought to be given to the fact that very few books can bear reprinting without taking account of work accomplished in the interval. This is certainly true of the present volume.

E.U.

WATTS, J. D. W.: *Lists of Words occurring frequently in the Hebrew Bible*. (Hebrew–English Edition. Seminary Edition.) 1967. Second Edition. Pp. 33. (E. J. Brill, Leiden. Price: Fl. 3)

This booklet was welcomed in its original edition (*Book List* 1960, p. 57; *Decade*, p. 237) and the demand for a new edition has enabled some useful changes to be made: an additional list, of particles, has been added; and some corrections have been made, both of the consonantal text and of the vocalization and accentuation. Certain anomalies in the presentation of the forms have also been ironed out. Unfortunately, a few new printing errors in the vocalization have crept in, and in one table the Hebrew is rather badly out of line; but these are minor blemishes in a work which will no doubt continue to serve a useful purpose.

R.J.C.

ADDITIONAL NOTES ON SCHOOL TEXTBOOKS, ETC.

*BROWN, J. G.: *The People of the Bible. The Lands of the Bible*. (Cornerstone Bible Series, Units One and Two.) 1967. Pp. 117, 121. (Holmes McDougall Ltd, Educational Books, Edinburgh. Price: 12s. 6d. each)

The aim of this new series of text-books for Secondary Schools is to make the Bible living, meaningful and exciting. The first volume describes in six chapters the life of the peoples of the Bible lands, their homes, their occupations, food and clothing, way of life and worship. The second volume deals similarly with the lands — the Middle East today, Palestine, biblical sites, Jerusalem, archaeology and its contribution. O.T. material abounds. The texts are informative and interesting, based on wide reading and sound scholarship. Each chapter has a supplement of Bible references, interesting facts, vocabulary and things to do. The illustrations are attractive and the book is well produced.

L.A.P.

*KLINK, J. L.: *Bible for Children*. Volume One: *The Old Testament with Songs and Plays*. 1967. Pp. 313. (Burke Publishing Co. Ltd, London. Price: 30s. 0d.)

This handsomely-produced book, translated from the Dutch, is an original and imaginative presentation of the O.T. story in simple, direct narrative accompanied by poems, songs (including Negro spirituals) and short plays, the text brilliantly illustrated by Piete Klaasse. It is regrettable that in such a generally attractive book no distinction is made between story and history, apart from the Creation narratives; even the stories of Balaam, Jonah and Daniel are presented as presumably historical.

L.A.P.

*MEADE, F. H. M. and ZIMMERMANN, A. W.: *The School Study Bible*. (Books 1–6 and book 7, Religions of the World.) 1960–6. (McDougall's Educational Co. Ltd, Edinburgh. Price: 7s. each)

The O.T. content of these text-books is arranged as follows: Book 1, The Garden of Eden and Joseph in Egypt; Book 2, The Flight from Egypt and Settlement in the Promised Land; Book 3, Early Kings of the O.T.; Book 4, The Prophets, the Exile and Return. A Chapter on Judaism appears in Book 7. Brief extracts from the text of the A.V. are followed by illustrations and brief explanatory notes. The method and presentation are rather old-fashioned and the notes are note always reliable.

L.A.P.

*SHAW, W. A.: *Living Bible*. Books 1 and 2. Pp. 95 each volume. 1966. (McDougall's Educational Co. Ltd, Edinburgh. Price: 9s. 6d. each)

These books, which belong to the post-Loukes era, represent a new and exciting development in R.K. text-books. They are adventurous and contemporary, intended to arouse the pupil's interest and make him think for himself. The first book includes sections on Abraham, Moses and the Exodus, David and Solomon, and the second book the Creation stories, Elijah on Mount Carmel and Job. Various modern translations are used for the Bible text and the illustrations are unusually vivid and imaginative.

L.A.P.

Book List 1969

GENERAL

ACKROYD, P. R. and LINDARS, B. (ed.): *Words and Meanings. Essays presented to David Winton Thomas on his retirement from the Regius Professorship of Hebrew in the University of Cambridge, 1968*. 1968. Pp. xiii, 239. One plate. (Cambridge University Press. Price: 45s.)

As will be clear from the title, the fifteen contributions to this volume are all concerned with that branch of O.T. study which, through a long and distinguished career, Professor D. W. Thomas has made peculiarly his own. Some of the essays are primarily philological in the narrower sense of the term, while others cover a broader area. Two contributions of a wide-ranging character are those by P. R. Ackroyd on 'Meaning and Exegesis' and G. Fohrer on 'Twofold Aspects of Hebrew Words'. Six of the authors are concerned with the Pentateuch: J. Weingreen discusses the possible existence of folk-tales about Abraham lying behind Gen. 15:7, J. A. Emerton writes on 'Some difficult words in Gen. 49', B. Albrektson criticizes the views of E. Schild and J. Lindblom on Ex. 3:14, J. Muilenberg has a characteristic discussion of 'The Intercession of the Covenant Mediator in Ex. 33', R. Loewe traces the treatment of Num. 13:34 in the Versions and Rabbinic commentators and B. Lindars deals with the new significance of the word *tōrāh* which he finds in Deut. Two essays are concerned with aspects of the prophetical books: G. R. Driver's 'Another little drink' offers a fresh translation and exegesis of Is. 28: 1–22, and A. Phillips discusses 'The ecstatics' father'. Other contributors write on subjects with which they have long been concerned, D. Diringer and S. P. Brock on early Hebrew inscriptions and B. J. Roberts on biblical exegesis in Qumran. The remaining essays are those of P. A. H. de Boer on Job. 39: 25, O. Eissfeldt on 'Renaming in the O.T.', and A. E. Goodman on *hesed* and *tōdāh* in the Hebrew psalter and the Versions.

It need hardly be said that all the articles are of a high order and the whole volume is a most worthy and appropriate tribute to the fine scholar whom it commemorates. The book includes a useful bibliography of Winton Thomas's writings and an index of references to the primary authorities.

J.R.P.

BOWMAN, J. (ed.): *Abr-Nahrain* VI (1965–66). 1967. Pp. 99. (E. J. Brill, Leiden. Price: Fl. 32)

In this issue D. D. Leslie concludes his erudite study of 'The Chinese-Hebrew Memorial Book of the Jewish Community of K'aifeng', S. Ahmed writes on 'Ashurbanipal and Shamash-Shum-Ukin during Esarhaddon's reign', and we have the first part of S. A. A. Rizvi's history of the Afghan sufi 'Rawshaniyya Movement'. There is also a longish review in which A. F. Cambell, S.J. deals fairly critically with M. C. Astour's *Hellenosemitica*. The high standard of previous volumes is fully maintained.

D.R.Ap-T.

BRUCE, F. F. and RUPP, E. G. (ed.): *Holy Book and Holy Tradition*. 1968. Pp. viii, 244. (Manchester University Press. Price: 42s.)

This volume contains twelve papers delivered at an international colloquium held in the Faculty of Theology of the University of Manchester in November 1966. They cover a very wide range, providing a broad setting for the consideration of the relationship between written scripture and the tradition of the community or church to which that scripture belongs. The issues raised are important for the theological and hermeneutical aspects of O.T. study. Only a limited number of the papers is of direct concern for Old Testament scholarship. J. Weingreen, 'Oral Torah and Written Records' continues his examination of an area in which he has already published a number of papers, discussing the extent to which there can be demonstrated a continuing tradition alongside the evolution of the written text. F. F. Bruce deals with 'Scripture and Tradition in the New Testament'. But the consideration of the problems of scripture and tradition in various areas of Christian theology, as well as in Islamic and other cultures, is a useful reminder of the inter-relationship of the problems of one area with those of another.   P.R.A.

COENEN, L., BEYREUTHER, E., BIETENHARD, H. (ed.): *Theologisches Begriffslexikon zum Neuen Testament*. Fasc. 6, 7. 1968. 112 pp. each. (Gleich-Himmel, Hindern-Kirche). (R. Brockhaus Verlag, Wuppertal. Price: DM. 16.90 each fascicle)

The first five fascicles of this lexicon were reviewed in *B.L.* 1968, p. 4, and a general description was given there of the intentions of the work. It is primarily hermeneutical in purpose, but these fascicles continue the careful and scholarly discussion, including here such important articles as those on *Gott, Heilig, Herr, Israel, Jesus Christus*. The usefulness of the work to German-speaking clergy and teachers is very evident.   P.R.A.

VAN DEURSEN, A.: *Illustrated Dictionary of Bible Manners and Customs*. 1967. Pp. 142. (Philosophical Library, Inc. N.Y. Price: $4.75)

The aim of this dictionary is to show how objects met with in the Bible really looked. It is a pity, therefore, that the drawings should be of such poor quality and all in black and white. Many are much too small and no scale is given (e.g. the hyrax or coney appears as large as the sheep, and the quail nearly three times as large as either, p. 95). A number of the drawings are hypothetical reconstructions but the source of such a reconstruction usually appears in the text. The author does not distinguish between modern drawings and reconstructions and those taken from ancient reliefs or paintings. It would have been useful to know where the latter could be seen. Often a photograph would have been better than a drawing but this would doubtless have made the price even higher. The objects listed in the text are well supplied with biblical references. There are just over two pages of bibliography.   C.A.

EISSFELDT, O.: *Kleine Schriften*, herausgegeben von R. Sellheim und F. Maas. Vierter Band. 1968. Pp. viii, 304. (J. C. B. Mohr, Tübingen. Price: paper, DM. 43.50; cloth, DM. 70)

The previous volumes in this series were noticed in *Book Lists* 1962, pp. 5 f. (*Decade*, pp. 315 f.), 1964, pp. 7 f. (*Decade*, pp. 475 f.) and 1967, p. 5. Like its predecessor, the present volume was to have been the last of the series; but since the task of compiling an analytical index to the entire collection will take a considerable time, it was decided to include in Volume 4 Professor Eissfeldt's publications from the years 1961-6, and to leave work from subsequent years to appear in Volume 5, together with comprehensive indexes, bibliography, etc. The present volume displays the same scholarly precision and variety of subject matter as its predecessors. The bulk of the material consists of rigorous critical analyses of O.T. passages and problems; but there are also illuminating obituary articles, e.g. of Kahle and Hempel. The author's continuing literary activity ensures an equally rich content for the promised final volume.   G.W.A.

EPSTEIN, E. L. (ed.): *Hebrew Union College Annual* XXXVIII. 1967. Pp. 295, 23 (in Hebrew), 4 tables, index to Vols I–XXXVII. (Hebrew Union College, Cincinnati)

Of the thirteen articles in English and one in Hebrew contained in this volume the following bear directly on the O.T.: 'The *ḤASĪDĪM* — Who Were They?' (J. Morgenstern); 'The Alas-Oracles of the Eighth Century Prophets' (J. G. Williams); 'The Structure and Theme of the Solomon Narrative (I Kings 3–11)' (B. Porten); and 'He set Ephraim before Manasseh' (E. C. Kingsbury). Others of less direct interest are: 'Offerings to the Temple Gates at Ur' (B. A. Levine); 'The End of the Jewish Sacrificial Cult' (A. Guttmann); 'Maimonides and Job: An Inquiry as to the Method of the *Moreh*' (L. S. Kravitz); 'Abrabanel on Prophecy in the *Moreh Nebhukhim* (Chapter VI)' (A. J. Reines); and 'Qabbalah as a Metonym for the Prophets and Hagiographa' (N. M. Bronznick).   E.T.R.

FRIEDRICH, G. (ed. by): *Theologisches Wörterbuch zum Neuen Testament* (begun by G. Kittel). Band VIII. Doppellieferung 7/8. 1967. Pp. 128. (Kohlhammer, Stuttgart. Price: DM. 14.40)

Doppellieferung 7/8 continues the treatment of *hyios, hyiothesia* by several scholars, viz. Schweizer, Schneemelcher and Wülfing v. Martitz. There comes next a long and elaborate article by Colpe on *ho hyios tou anthropou*, which is followed by one by Lohse on *hyios David*. Also of interest to O.T. scholars is Delling's article on *hymnos, hymneō, psallō* and *psalmos*.   N.W.P.

HAAG, H. (ed.): *Bibel-Lexikon*. 1968. Pp. xx + 1964 cols. (Benziger Verlag, Einsiedeln and Cologne. Price: DM./Sw.Fr. 158)

From 1951 to 1956 Haag's *Bibel-Lexikon* appeared in eight parts, which were all noted in the *Book List* as they were issued. Now a new edition, revised or rewritten and with many new entries, has appeared in a substantially enlarged volume. In the old edition signed articles were rare and the names of six Dutch scholars, who were responsible with Professor Haag for most of the articles, were given at the end. For the new edition a list of more than a hundred collaborators is given and the articles are signed. Most of the collaborators are German scholars, though there are very many others, the great majority being Catholic scholars. The quality of the scholarship is very high and there are valuable bibliographies at the ends of articles. The article which J. van der Ploeg contributed on the Dead Sea Scrolls has now been transferred to Qumran and brought up to date by the same scholar. There are some fine plates, and maps are on the end-papers with a number of others in the text. The whole constitutes an excellent work of reference.   H.H.R.

HARTMANN, B. *et al.* (ed. by): *Hebräische Wortforschung. Festschrift zum 80. Geburtstag von Walter Baumgartner.* (Supplements to *Vetus Testamentum,* XVI). 1967. Pp. x, 429. (E. J. Brill, Leiden. Price: Fl. 88)

About two thirds of the contributions in this *Festschrift* relate to its over-all theme whilst the remainder are concerned with textual and other aspects of O.T. study, the whole appropriately reflecting the continuing pre-occupation as well as the wide ranging interests of the very distinguished scholar in whose honour it has been published.

To the former category belong articles on *'algummim/'almuggīm* (J. C. Greenfield and, for the Sanskrit, M. Mayrhofer); *yāsad* (P. Humbert); *'ābad* (E. Jenni); *nōqēd* (S. Segert); *he'ᵉmīn* — twice (R. Smend and H. Wildberger); and *ra'ᵃnān* (D. Winton Thomas); on expressions relating to social psychology (C. Rabin); legal procedure (I. L. Seeligmann); and spoil and plunder (H. J. Stoebe); on Hebrew homonyms (G. R. Driver); women's names in Hebrew — a full length study (J. J. Stamm); and Aramaisms in Old Testament Hebrew (M. Wagner); with lexicographical notes (H. L. Ginsberg); and Joel notes (W. Rudolph); and contributions from the fields of Samaritan (Z. Ben-Ḥayyim); post-biblical Hebrew and Jewish Aramaic (E. Y. Kutscher); Ugaritic — two (B. Hartmann and W. von Soden); Akkadian (B. Landsberger); and Old South Arabic (M. Höfner).

In the latter category are 'Vocalization and the Analysis of Hebrew among the Ancient Translators' (J. Barr); a note on the Hebrew of Sir. 44:12a (P. A. H. de Boer); 'Deuteronomic Formulae of the Exodus Tradition' (B. S. Childs); 'Congruity of Metaphors' (M. Dahood); 'Bist du Elia, so bin ich Isebel' (O. Eissfeldt); 'Die Heiligen des Höchsten' (R. Hanhart); 'Das sogenannte Feueropfer' (J. Hoftijzer); 'Sichembund und Vätergötter' (V. Maag); 'Vers une traduction française oecuménique de la Bible' (P. Reymond); and 'Ezechieltempel und Salomostadt' (W. Zimmerli).

So many articles representative of the best in international O.T. and Semitic scholarship besides contributing greatly to the furtherance of *hebräische Wortforschung* also combine to make this volume outstanding in its series.   E.T.R.

KAPELRUD, A. S. and JERVELL, J. (ed.): *Studia Theologica.* Scandinavian Journal of Theology. Vol. 20, No. 2 (1967). 1967. Pp. 83–202. (Universitetsforlaget, Oslo. Subscription price: N.Kr. 48, $8.00, £2 8s., or DM. 28 each volume)

This issue contains four articles, only one of which has any direct relevance to O.T. study. This is 'Über den Begriff der Traditionsgebundenheit' by O. Castrén (pp. 182–202), primarily concerned with the interpretation of tradition in the church, but opening with some discussion of the biblical aspects of the problem and noting the variety and richness of the biblical tradition.   P.R.A.

KOSMALA, H. (ed. by): *Annual of the Swedish Theological Institute.* Vol. v. 1967. Pp. 132. (E. J. Brill, Leiden. Price: Fl. 24)]

This volume begins with a comprehensive and discerning survey of the contribution of Sigmund Mowinckel to O.T. study, contributed by A. S. Kapelrud. It is followed by two papers read to this Society: G. Henton Davies' Presidential Address, 'The Ark of the Covenant', and 'Old Testament Exegesis and the Problem of Ambiguity' by

D. F. Payne. H. Kosmala's examination of 'Form and Structure of Isaiah 58' is a sequel to the paper which he read to the Society in 1964. P. R. Ackroyd contributes notes on the phrase *māḳôm 'aḥēr* in Esther 4: 14 and *māḳôm 'eḥāḏ* in Eccles 6: 6. There are two articles on N.T. subjects: 'In My Name', by H. Kosmala, and 'The Conclusion of Matthew in a New Jewish-Christian Source', by D. Flusser. Another study by H. Kosmala, 'Warum isst man Karpas am Sederabend?' rounds off this interesting and valuable collection of articles. G.W.A.

LÉON-DUFOUR, X. (ed.): *Dictionary of Biblical Theology.* 1967. Pp. xxix, 618. (Geoffrey Chapman, London, Dublin, Melbourne. Price: 63s.)

This book was originally published in French in 1962, but not noted in the *Book List*. It represents the effort of a distinguished group of Roman Catholic scholars to provide a theological dictionary of the Bible. The authors proceed from the conviction that through all the variety of the biblical witness there is an essential unity. A dictionary is unavoidably analytic but by careful editing and a system of cross references the aim of the work is to provide 'a synthetic understanding of the unique Word of God in all its aspects'. An introduction discusses the nature of biblical language and imagery and there is a brief account of the formation of the Bible which recognizes the rights of historical criticism. It is out of the question in a brief notice to discuss the content of the articles. Suffice it to say that they are of a high quality, though it is frankly admitted that they are written from a definite dogmatic standpoint. It is obvious that this must lead in places to interpretations based on presuppositions which not every reader will accept. But even those who do not accept all the dogmatic presuppositions will agree that the volume provides in lucid and scholarly fashion what it sets out to purvey and deserves to be widely used. It is most handsomely produced. N.W.P.

MACLAURIN, E. C. B. (ed.): *Essays in Honour of G. W. Thatcher 1863–1950.* 1967. Pp. ix, 255. (Sydney University Press, and Methuen, London. Price: 48s. $6.00)

This memorial volume is of the kind which exhibits the diversity of interests of the one commemorated rather than maintaining a common theme. Thus there are essays on Australian aboriginal culture, the Greek of the New Testament, Islam, Monophysitism, Early Christian Art, and the Samaritan Burial Liturgy. Of direct relevance to the Old Testament are 'Two Notes on Isaiah' (41:3 and 2:22) by D. R. Ap-Thomas, and the suggestion by L. H. Brockington that the Hebrew verb *yāshabh* may sometimes be understood as describing a cultic act. Indirectly related to Old Testament studies are an essay by E. O. James on 'The Tree of Life' and a study by J. Macdonald of the Arabic Derived Verb. R.J.C.

MALAMAT, A. and REVIV, H.: *A Bibliography of the Biblical Period* (With Emphasis on Publications in Modern Hebrew). 1968. Pp. 50. (Academon, Hebrew University, Jerusalem. Price: £Isr. 1.75)

This bibliography, intended primarily for the use of students, provides a very valuable short survey of the literature relevant to the study of O.T. history and life, arranged to cover the Ancient Near East, the Sources, Archaeology etc., History, and works of reference. The considerable lists of works in Modern Hebrew, both articles and books, will be of particular use to scholars who wish to have a convenient survey of recent material. One error may be corrected: *The Old Testament Library* (S.C.M.) is not the English translation of *Das Alte Testament Deutsch* (p. 44) though a number of volumes do coincide.   P.R.A.

NIELSEN, E. and NOACK, B. (ed.): *Gads Danske Bibel Leksikon.* Vol. 1, A–K 1965, Vol. 2 L–Ö 1966. (Gad, Copenhagen. Price: D.Kr. 244 and D.Kr. 264)

A Bible dictionary for the layman, generally presenting a 'Scandinavian' approach, reminiscent of the *Svenskt Bibliskt Uppslagsverk* but on a smaller scale and at a more popular level.   J.V.M.S.

RINALDI, G.: *Studi sull'Oriente e la Bibbia offerti al P. Giovanni Rinaldi* 1967. Pp. 390. (Editrice Studio e Vita, Piazza della Maddelena, Genova. Price: Lire 4.000)

It may be churlish to say so, but the literary *genre* of the *Festschrift* is awkward from a bibliographical point of view and to be discouraged from scholarly concerns, for *ad hoc* productions or searches in one's drawers rarely measure up to the standards generally expected and often attained. P. Giovanni Rinaldi's 60th birthday is here celebrated by more than forty contributions to the fields of philology, history, religion, and exegesis.

Since it is impossible even to summarize, within the space allotted, the salient points of these contributions, the reviewer must limit himself to mentioning those studies which he has found to be of particular interest to him. H. Cazelles, 'Argob biblique, Ugarit et les mouvements hurrites'; S. Moscati, 'Il "tofet" '; K. Tsereteli, 'The Static Verb in Modern Aramaic Dialects'; S. Segert, 'Surviving of Canaanite Elements in Israelite Religion'; P. de Benedetti, 'Lo šôfár dalla Bibbia alla liturgia'; A. Díez Macho, 'Deux nouveaux fragments du Targum palestinien à New York'; F. Michelini Tocci, 'Qumranica'; Ch. Rabin, 'An Arabic Phrase in Isaiah'.

The bibliography of Father Rinaldi's writings has been compiled by F. Luciani.   E.U.

*ROWLEY, H. H.: *Dictionary of Bible Personal Names.* 1968. Pp. 168. (Nelson, London. Price: 25s.)

This dictionary, based on the R.S.V., of every person mentioned in the Bible (including the Apocrypha) from Aaron to Zurishaddai, is an invaluable reference-book. There are biographical notes and frequent cross-references, but etymologies are not included.

L.A.P.

*ROWLEY, H. H.: *Dictionary of Bible Themes.* 1968. Pp. 114. (Nelson, London. Price: 18s.)

Professor Rowley has accomplished a most difficult task in this masterpiece of compression, dealing with such themes as the Kingdom of God in about 150 words and Son of Man in some 200 words, with adequate biblical references. The dictionary is based on the R.S.V. and intended for the general reader; it will also prove a valuable aid to students in schools and colleges, and to their teachers.

L.A.P.

SEGAL, M. H.: *The Pentateuch. Its Composition and its Authorship and Other Biblical Studies.* 1967 (1968). Pp. 256. (The Magnes Press, The Hebrew University, Jerusalem. Price: 62s.)

Many of the studies collected here have already appeared in various journals in slightly different form, and are brought together in a single volume which appeared shortly after the author's death in January 1968. The major part is given over to a study of the Pentateuch in which Segal completely rejects the Documentary theory of its origin as over-complex and based on false assumptions. Instead he argues that the Pentateuch is essentially a single uniform work, of which Moses is the author, but which has been supplemented by later editors in the spirit of Moses. Two further studies deal with the origin and composition of the Books of Samuel and of the Song of Songs. The former is ascribed to a final compiler who lived in the 8th century before the fall of Samaria, and who used earlier histories of David. The Song of Songs is traced to a school of poets living in Solomon's age who celebrated the beauty of true human love and marriage. R.E.C.

SPEISER, E. A.: *Oriental and Biblical Studies. Collected Writings of E. A. Speiser,* ed. by J. J. FINKELSTEIN and M. GREENBERG. 1967. Pp. 616. 1 plate. (University of Pennsylvania Press, Philadelphia; Oxford University Press. Price: 95s.)

The collected essays in this volume are divided into four groups. 1. Biblical Studies (18), of which half are devoted to Genesis and almost all involve questions of the relationship between biblical and other ancient near eastern material; 2. Ancient Near Eastern History and Culture (8), primarily concerned with Mesopotamian questions; 3. Linguistic Studies (7), mainly general or Akkadian, but with considerable relevance to Hebrew; 4. Perspectives (4), where the essays range over wide topics, particularly concerned with the society of the ancient near east. To these is appended a bibliography of Speiser's writings and an appreciation by J. J. Finkelstein which stresses most the strongly humanist (in the best sense) tendency of Speiser's writings and interests. Most of all, these essays are concerned with the reality of human life in the biblical world which Speiser so rightly saw as illuminated by our increasing knowledge of the culture of the ancient near east. Though the essays are printed in their original form, Speiser himself in a number of cases had added a final note to indicate more recent developments or alternative interpretations. This is a very rich collection and provides much stimulus in the approach to many biblical passages. As so often in such volumes, one regrets the absence of an index of biblical references. P.R.A.

DE VRIES, S. J.: *Bible and Theology in the Netherlands.* 1968. Pp. 150. (Veenman en Zonen, Wageningen. Price: Fl. 13,50)

The major part of this work is devoted to a study of Dutch Old Testament scholarship from 1850 to the First World War. The author has read widely, in Dutch journals as well as in books, and he deals not only with well-known scholars, such as Kuenen, Kosters, Wildeboer, Eerdmans, and Aalders, but with a great many writers who are little known, especially because of the language barrier, but who sometimes adopted positions which are common today. The study is objective and fair, and it will be found very instructive. H.H.R.

ARCHAEOLOGY AND EPIGRAPHY

AVIRAM, J. (ed.): *Jerusalem through the Ages. The Twenty-fifth Archaeological Convention, October 1967.* 1968. Pp. xi, 68 (non-Hebrew); v, 264 (Hebrew). Pll. ix + xv and text figures. (Israel Exploration Society, Jerusalem. Price: £Isr. 12)

Four papers are in English, one in Italian, one in French — these have summaries in Hebrew; the 18 others are in Hebrew, with summaries in English. The list is: P. W. Lapp, 'Bab edh-Dhra', Perizzites and Emim'; W. G. Dever, 'Excavations at Gezer, 1964–1967'; M. Noth, 'Jerusalem and the Northern Kingdom'; S. Saller, 'The Tombs of Dominus Flevit'; V. C. Corbo, 'L'Herodion di Giabal Fureidis'; P. Benoit, 'Découvertes archéologiques autour de la piscine de Béthesda'. In Hebrew we have: B. Mazar, 'The City of David and Mount Zion'; S. Yeivin, 'Solomon's Temple'; A. Malamat, 'The Last Kings of Judah and the Destruction of Jerusalem'; N. Avigad, 'The Tombs around Jerusalem'; M. Avi-Yonah, 'The Walls of Jerusalem'; Y. Yadin, 'The Temple Scroll'; Y. Aharoni, 'From Shiloh to Jerusalem'; Y. Karmon, 'The Mountains round about Jerusalem'; H. S. Hirschberg, 'The Temple Mount in Jewish and Mohammedan Traditions'; J. Braslavi, 'Pilgrimages to the Mount of Olives in the Middle Ages'; A. Shachar, 'The Urban Geography of Unified Jerusalem'; E. E. Urbach, 'Heavenly and Earthly Jerusalem'; Z. J. Werblowsky, 'Jerusalem — the Metropolis of all Countries'; J. Prawer, 'Christianity between Heavenly and Earthly Jerusalem'; U. Heyd, 'Jerusalem under the Mamluks and Turks'; Z. Vilnay, 'The Jewish Quarter in Old Jerusalem and its Synagogues'; Y. Weitz, 'The Roads in the Hills of Jerusalem'; M. Gur, 'At the Gates of Jerusalem'. Some of the latter papers are of peripheral O.T. interest, but the list of titles and the standing of the authors show how important most of this volume is for the biblical archaeologist and historian.

D.R.Ap-T.

*Everyday Life in Bible Times. 1967. Pp. 448. (National Geographic Society, Washington, D.C. Price: $9.95)

This sumptuous volume (of which two thirds is devoted to the O.T.) is lavishly produced with 528 illustrations (412 in colour), and 13 maps, including an excellent map supplement in the back of the book. J. B. Pritchard was the editorial consultant, and the 130,000 words of the text include essays by leading O.T. scholars. This really exciting book, with lively and informative text and magnificent illustrations, represents popularization at its best. Would there were a copy in every School and College library!

L.A.P.

KENYON, M.: *Jerusalem. Excavating 3000 Years of History.* (New Aspects of Antiquity, ed. by Sir Mortimer Wheeler). 1967. Pp. 211, Pll. in colour xxi, mono. 92, line drawings 16. (Thames and Hudson, London. Price: 84s.)

Any book on Jerusalem lends itself to pictorial illustration. The plates and drawings in this work have been chosen for their archaeological relevance but can still hold their own pictorially. This however is a book in which the text is of paramount importance, because it contains the archaeological history of the city of Jerusalem as corrected, newly discovered and maybe still further complicated by the excavations of 1961–7. These excavations under the aegis of the

British School of Archaeology in Jerusalem were conducted by the author herself and so, though the text is written so that the layman may appreciate what has been discovered, the expert too will grate-fully use what is given here and await the definitive technical pub-lication with what patience he can muster. D.R.Ap-T.

MADDEN, F. W.: *History of Jewish Coinage and of Money in the Old and New Testament.* Prolegomenon by Michael Avi-Yonah, 254 Woodcuts and Plate of Alphabets by F. W. Fairholt (Library of Biblical Studies. Ed. by H. M. Orlinsky), 1967. Pp. xlvii, 350. (Ktav Publishing House, Inc., New York. Price: $14.95)

This book, originally published in 1846, now reappears in the Series 'Library of Biblical Studies'. Madden's presentation of the biblical means of payment and of the first appearance of coined money in Lydia remain basically valid; recent studies have merely amplified them. However, in the light of modern numismatic studies, his con-clusions about the origin of Jewish coinage and certain portions of his treatment of Maccabean and Revolt coinage are now defective and faulty. The informative Prolegomenon supplied by Avi-Yonah is meant to act as a supplement and a corrective. For example, Madden assigns the first Jewish coinage to Simon Maccabeus, whereas we now know that the YHD coins of the Persian period mark the beginning of Jewish coined money. Furthermore, Avi-Yonah points out that most contemporary numismatists hold that the first Hasmonean ruler to have struck coins was not Simon, but John Hyrcanus.
While acknowledging the quality and the wide range of Avi-Yonah's contribution, one wonders whether the sponsors of this Series were wise in reproducing a book which, admittedly a major contribution to the study of Jewish coins a century ago, is now out of date, even though its defects are rectified in the Prolegomenon. It would surely have been more useful, both for the student and the trained scholar, to have commissioned an entirely new book on the history of Jewish coinage, based on the latest numismatic studies. In such a book recognition of Madden's work could find due expression, either in the text or in footnotes. J.W.

NORTH, R. (S.J.): *Les Fouilles dans la région de Jéricho.* 1967. Pp. 156 + 9 sketchmaps. (Pontifical Biblical Institute, Rome. Price: Lire 900 or $1.50)

Externally very similar to *Archeo-biblical Egypt* (cf. p. 56), this volume is a very mixed bag of some 15 occasional papers, reviews and dictionary articles in English, French, Italian, Latin and Spanish, all archaeological but not all covered by the title. The author's list of the 'Cent principales fouilles bibliques', with concise annotation, will justify the moderate price of acquisition for many.

D.R.Ap-T.

HISTORY AND GEOGRAPHY

*AHARONI, Y. and AVI-YONAH, M.: *The Macmillan Bible Atlas.* 1968. Pp. 184. 264 Maps. Numerous figures and plans in the text. (Macmillan, New York, and Collier-Macmillan, London. Price: $14.95, 70s.)

There are now several good modern atlases of the Bible. This is one of the best, combined and adapted from two recent publications in

Hebrew from two recent publications in Hebrew by the respective authors. The period covered is 3000 B.C. to 200 A.D., and the narrative — in short paragraphs — is closely linked to the Bible (RSV) or other texts where relevant, and put alongside the related map. There is therefore a large number of maps on specific themes, rather than a few large, comprehensive ones — it is a pity that two of the latter were not put on the doublespread of the endpapers. The maps are indexed for the early and biblical and some later names, and there is a useful scripture index and a chronological chart.   D.R.Ap-T.

BAR-DEROMA, H.: *A series of studies on the Bible and the land of the Bible* (Yeruham's Library) v. *Nahal Aithan*. 1968. Pp. iv, 71. (B.E.R. Publishing Co., Jerusalem. Price: £Isr. 4)

The purpose of this booklet, produced in the same form as the author's previous Studies (see *B.L.* 1968, p. 14, where Yeruham should be read for Gernham), is to argue that *naḥal 'êtān* 'perennial stream' (Deut. 21:4; Amos 5:24), as translated since Schultens, is wrongly so rendered; for the epithet, which the ancient translators rendered 'rough, hard, rocky', really designates 'solid, hard material, rock, mountain, foundation'. He holds that Maimonides in the 12th century by paraphrasing 'powerful, strong' as 'strongly flowing, flooding' is responsible for the mistranslation, while Reider alone of modern scholars has preserved the true sense, rendering the expression by *'ēmeq qāšeh* 'rough valley'. The author points to passages where 'perennial' seems unsuitable (e.g. Gen. 49:24; Job 12:19). He rounds off his argument by introducing various philological considerations, notably by comparing several words which resemble *'êtān* (e.g. *'eden* 'base') and illustrating it by fifteen snapshots showing the rough rugged ground of typical wadies. These snapshots however prove nothing; the words compared have no conceivable connection with *'êtān*, the meaning suggested while conceivable in the first passage, is impossible in the second, and the possible range of meanings in the Arabic *watana* 'was firm, lasting, perennial; flowed continuously' is not considered. The old meaning, therefore, as thus revived, cannot be said to be proved. In conclusion, Chapters 5, 6 and 7 of the text are given as 6, 7 and 5 in the Table of Contents.   G.R.D.

BAR-DEROMA, H.: *A series of studies on the Bible and the land of the Bible*. (Yeruham's Library) VI. *Kibbush Yahid*. 1968. Pp. 74 with 1 map and 11 photographs. (B.E.R. Publishing Co., Jerusalem. Price: £Isr. 4)

This book (cf. the previous item) is devoted to discussing the precise force of *kibbush yahid*, that is the conquest of a country by an individual conqueror not expressly commanded by God and not involving the whole nation. The author's purpose is to examine the application of this expression to David's conquest of Aram Naharaim and Aram Zobah. Looking into the geographical import of these two terms, he finds that, while the location of the former is well established, the location and limits of the latter are far from clear, and on his map he shows it in two places; (1) in the country bounded by the Euphrates and the Murad Su and the head-waters of the Tigris and (2) to the east of the Tigris between the Upper and Lower Zab, marking both attributions with a query; in the body of the text he opts for a location just beyond the Euphrates (cp. 2 Samuel 10:16), in the position described above, although the position of the Assyrian province of Ṣubite in the region of Baalbek hardly agrees with such a location. This Aram Zobah was also the 'third province' of the Mishnah. He then argues that the Davidic conquest of these two districts was such a *kibbush yahid* because, while not contrary to the law, it was a mere conquest followed neither by the expulsion of the native inhabitants nor by a permanent occupation by the conquerors; this view is confirmed by the fact that the Law, as exemplified in the payment of tithes of corn to the priests and Levites, was never enforced in either region. The author argues his case well, adducing all the relevant evidence from the Old Testament, Mishnah and Talmud, and also from Rabbinical authorities; and, carefully examining their often contradictory notices, he reaches conclusions which seem eminently sensible.   G.R.D.

The Cambridge Ancient History: Revised Edition of Volumes I and II. Syria before 2200 B.C.: by M. S. Drower and J. Bottéro. Fasc. 55. 1968. Pp. 54. (Cambridge University Press. Price: 6s.)

The Early Dynastic Period in Mesopotamia: by M. E. L. Mallowan. Fasc. 62. 1968. Pp. 71. (Price: 8s. 6d.)

This study of early Syria covers that brilliant period of Akkadian expansion to the West under Naram-Sin and his successors. The appearance of strong city-states in the Euphrates-Khabur region (including Mari) and on the 'Phoenician coast' is important for a proper understanding of Palestine then (the subject of a separate fascicule) and in the later 'Patriarchal' period. Egyptian influence is traced at Byblos — the key to 'God's land' — as well as in Palestine and Syria in useful detail.

Sir Max Mallowan continues his comprehensive survey of the excavated sites throughout Mesopotamia (see *B.L.* 1968, p. 15). Here he covers the Sumerian Flood and the end of Early Dynastic I and the temple architecture in the Diyala and elsewhere which preceded the ziggurat. The descriptions are arranged according to site and that for Ur with its Royal Graves and unusual rituals is the best yet. Professor Mallowan shows that Sumerian influence was direct and widespread through upper Mesopotamia into Syria (and thus Palestine?) in this early era. His caution on the acceptance of carbon-14 dates in the 550 year span of the Early Dynastic period (*c.* 3000 B.C.) is timely.

                                                                                D.J.W.

The Cambridge Ancient History: Revised Edition of Volumes I and II. Palestine in the Time of the Nineteenth Dynasty: (b) Archaeological Evidence, by H. J. Franken. Fasc. 67. 1968. Pp. 11. (Cambridge University Press. Price: 3s. 6d.)

This concludes the chapter begun by O. Eissfeldt (Fasc. 31, see *B.L.* 1966, p. 16; *Decade*, p. 636). When the phrase 'evidence from archaeology' tends to be bandied about too airily, it is essential to have this down-to-earth assessment by a practising archaeologist. Only direct archaeological evidence for Hebrew settlement in Palestine is discussed, and that very succinctly. The conclusion is: 'archaeologists would be totally unaware of any important changes at the end of the Late Bronze Age were it not for the biblical traditions', but the hope is allowed that further fieldwork may produce more positive evidence of demonstrably Israelite incursion.   D.R.Ap-T.

GALLING, K. (with EDEL, E. and BORGER, R.): *Textbuch zur Geschichte Israels*. 2nd ed. 1968. Pp. xi, 109, four maps. (Mohr, Tübingen. Price: DM. 17.50)

The first edition of this useful collection of texts was reviewed in *B.L.* 1950, p. 25; *Eleven Years*, p. 242. The second edition has 56 texts, omitting some which appeared in the earlier volume, and adding some new ones, notably the Idrimi inscription, extracts from 'Chronicles of Chaldaean Kings', the Hebrew letter from the seventh century, and two of the Elephantine letters. One might have expected an extract from the fourth century Samaria Papyri since they fill a gap in our knowledge. Comparison with the English volume *Documents from Old Testament Times* is interesting; the shorter compass of the German volume precludes more than the briefest notes, whereas the English one gains by its annotating of the texts. But this is a useful collection, and most of the texts have been newly translated for this second edition.

P.R.A.

HEATON, E. W.: *The Hebrew Kingdoms*. (The New Clarendon Bible. Old Testament, Vol. 3). 1968. Pp. xx, 437 (with 29 illustrations in the text, a chronological table and two end maps). (Oxford University Press, London. Price: 25s.)

This book is the successor to T. H. Robinson's *Decline and Fall of the Hebrew Kingdoms* (1926). The treatment of the subject follows the pattern set in the old Clarendon, i.e. a general essay is followed by a selection of relevant passages from the O.T. with detailed comment, but the content differs from that of the earlier work. In this Heaton accurately reflects the great changes which have taken place in O.T. studies in the last forty years. Particularly notable is the inclusion of parts of the O.T. which were not considered to belong to this period forty years ago; e.g. some of the psalms and the book of Proverbs.

After an introduction which describes the international background against which the two kingdoms must be seen, their life is depicted under five heads, History, Worship, Wisdom, Law and Prophecy. Heaton makes judgements which some may dispute, particularly in the long section on prophecy, but this is but a reflection of the openness of current O.T. studies. His presentation of his subject is always fair, clear and notably attractive. This book is a worthy successor to its distinguished predecessor and deserves to be used as widely.

J.R.

KITTEL, R.: *Great Men and Movements in Israel*. (The Library of Biblical Studies. Ed. by H. M. Orlinsky.) 1968. Pp. lii, 465. (Ktav Publishing House, New York. Price: $10.00)

The 1929 translation of Kittel's work is here reproduced, with an extended prolegomenon by T. H. Gaster, which draws attention not only to the merits of the work but also to its extreme tendentiousness in its application of *Führerprinzip* to the O.T. Some indication is also given of the results of more recent research where they modify Kittel's views; and while the enormous number of misprints remains in the text, a list of the most glaring errors has been provided.

R.J.C.

*KOLLEK, T. and PEARLMAN, M.: *Jerusalem Sacred City of Mankind: a History of Forty Centuries.* 1968. Pp. 287. Ill. in colour 61, black and white 138. (Weidenfeld and Nicolson, London. Price: 63s.)

As a collection of often superb photographic illustrations on its theme anyone might be glad to have this volume at such a reasonable price. As a history its worth must be considered in relation to both its scale and the clearly, though not vituperatively, partisan standpoint of the joint authors — the current mayor of Jerusalem and a former assistant to the Israeli minister of defence respectively. Being a work of popularization, it is not intended for the archaeologist and historian as such, but its sketch of what happened in and to Jerusalem between the 2nd and 20th centuries will help bridge a gap often neglected.

D.R.Ap-T.

McKENZIE, J. L.: *The World of the Judges.* 1967. Pp. x, 182. (Geoffrey Chapman, London. Price: 25s.)

This is a further volume in the American Roman Catholic series 'Backgrounds to the Bible', the general purpose of which is described as being 'to assist the educated but non-specialized reader to understand what biblical study in the age of archaeology is all about'. Archaeology is certainly not neglected in the present book, but there is also an excellent discussion of the even more fundamental question of the nature and purpose of the literary sources in the books of Joshua and Judges. The mass of recent work on the period in question is apt to confuse the beginner, and he will be greatly helped by the author's presentation and discussion of the issues, which is clear and methodical, without being over-simplified. Perhaps the key chapter is the one on 'The Israelite Settlement in Canaan', which deals very well with such important concerns of contemporary O.T. scholarship as the amphictyony, the covenant and the holy war. The least satisfactory sections are those dealing with the book of Judges: the author's assessment and treatment of the stories there as 'simple popular narratives' is much too naive. However, no writer on this subject can expect to win universal agreement and on the whole the work is to be highly commended.   J.R.P.

MOWINCKEL, S.: *Palestina för Israel.* 1965. (Universitetsforlaget, Oslo. Price: N.Kr. 29.50)

This is one of the two posthumous larger works of Mowinckel in Norwegian, together with *Israels opphav og eldste historie* (*B.L.* 1968, p. 15). It deals with the prehistoric period, and is the less important of the two books, since Mowinckel has less room to be original here.

J.V.M.S.

STECKOLL, S.: *The Gates of Jerusalem.* 1968. Pp. 55. VI Plates, 25 photographs. (George Allen and Unwin, Hemel Hempstead. Price: 40s.)

This is a popular account, pleasantly illustrated, containing a miscellany of information, ancient and modern. It does not set out to be a serious contribution to the subject.   P.R.A.

*SWANSTON, H.: *The Kings and the Covenant.* 1968. Pp. xviii, 214. (Burns and Oates, London. Price: 25s.)

This account of the history and traditions of the monarchical period in Israel is intended for use in the senior forms of schools. Good use is made of modern scholarship, and despite some — perhaps inevitable — over-simplification, the book should serve its purpose well.

R.J.C.

TEXT AND VERSIONS

Biblia Hebraica Stuttgartensia. Editio funditus renovata. Ed. K. ELLIGER and W. RUDOLPH. Fasc. 7. *Liber Jesaiae.* 1968. Pp. xxii, 105. (Württembergische Bibelanstalt, Suttgart. Price: 12s. 6d.)

The first fascicle of the long awaited new edition of Biblia Hebraica (BHK), associated for so long with the name of R. Kittel, has now appeared, prepared by D. Winton Thomas. The editors invite the use of the abbreviation BHS to distinguish this new edition from its predecessors. The prolegomena, in German and in English, provide two statements. The first covers the methods adopted and various notes on technical matters concerning the production of the newly printed and edited text of L (the text collated by H. P. Rüger). The second, by G. E. Weil, who is wholly responsible for the Masora, describes what has been done in the preparation of the *Masora parva* in the margins and what is to appear as a separate volume entitled *Massorah Gedolah (Masora Magna) iuxta codicem Leningradensem B 19A*. Discussion of the Masora must therefore wait on the appearance, promised for 1969, of this volume. The text of L, here presented for Isaiah as it appears in the latest hand of the manuscript, is provided with one series only of footnotes. These are clearly set out, and indeed the new type produced for the edition appears to be very readable. Much less annotation appears than in the previous edition, and not surprisingly much less of conjectural emendation. Any selection of evidence is bound to evoke criticism, but if the purpose of the edition is seen as particularly directed to those who are beginning work on the Hebrew text and who therefore need help and guidance in the handling of a modicum of textual and versional evidence, this procedure is sensible and useful. The publishing is going to take a long time — two or three fascicles a year, and an additional one on Sirach. One might only wonder whether the long delay already in production, no doubt due in some measure to the complexity of the Masora, might not have been reduced if that material, which can hardly be handled in the earlier stages of the study of the text, had been dealt with as a totally separate work.

P.R.A.

FRENSDORFF, S.: *The Massorah Magna. Part One, Massoretic Dictionary or The Massorah in Alphabetical Order. Prolegomenon* by Gérard E. Weil. (The Library of Biblical Studies. Ed. by H. M. Orlinsky.) 1968. Pp. xxii, ii, 340, 20, x. (Ktav Publishing House Inc., New York. Price: $22.50)

GINSBURG, C. D.: *Jacob Ben Chajim Ibn Adonijah's Introduction to The Rabbinic Bible, Hebrew and English with Explanatory Notes by Christian D. Ginsburg, LL.D.* and the *Massoreth ha-Massoreth of Elias Levita, being an Exposition of the Massoretic Notes on the Hebrew Bible . . . in Hebrew with an English translation and Critical and Explanatory Notes by Christian D. Ginsburg, LL.D. Prolegomenon* by N. H. Snaith. (The Library of Biblical Studies.) Ed. by H. M. Orlinsky. 1968. Pp. xxxvi, 91, 307. (Ktav Publishing House Inc., New York. Price: $14.95)

It is difficult to overpraise this series of reprints, edited by Professor Orlinsky, which is now following a fixed pattern. The *Prolegomenon*

is provided by a specialist, who presents current views on the topics dealt with in the old classic. And in both the works noticed here it would be difficult indeed to choose better pairs. Professor Weil surveys the history of the Massorah and Massoretic works, leading up to Frensdorff's list, and comments on the later Ginsburg Massorah; and his outline, different from previous bare lists, shows how his projected Massorah, to be published alongside the new *Biblia Hebraica*, will put Massoretic works in a proper perspective. By means of this work, and Weil's own fuller *Initiation à la Massorah* (Leiden, 1964), even the average student of the Hebrew Bible will appreciate the relevance of Massoretic studies. Frensdorff's own work, from 1876, long since out of reach for most University libraries, will have its appropriate place as one of the basic books of reference. Similarly Dr Snaith's *Prolegomenon* provides the background to Ginsburg's translations of Ben Chajim's *Introduction to the Hebrew Bible* and Levita's *Massoreth ha-Massoreth*, both from 1867. The treatment is fascinating and clear, and though the effect of Snaith's own work on the Bible Society's recent issue of the Hebrew Bible is naturally present, it does not unduly obtrude. Indeed, he gives a well-balanced discussion of a topic that in the past has lent itself all too readily to a confusing array of partisan views. The two works which it accompanies are again indispensable for the textual historian. The timing of these publications could not be better judged because of the projected publication of the Hebrew University Bible and the new edition of *Biblia Hebraica*.
B.J.R.

JELLICOE, S.: *The Septuagint and Modern Study*. 1968. Pp. xix, 424. (Oxford University Press. Price: 65s.)

Dr Jellicoe has placed students of the O.T. considerably in his debt by gathering into one volume the fruits of recent research in the field of Septuagint studies which in the main have only been accessible in learned journals. This is not a handbook of the LXX as such, but a compendium of recent research in which the results are set forth with clarity, and where occasion demands, are weighed with a matching clarity of judgement. The author expects the student to have read Swete's 'Introduction', and constantly refers the reader to it for further study and discussion. The book consists of an introduction and two parts. The Introduction surveys the beginnings of modern study of the LXX from Holmes and Parsons onwards. Part One deals with the much debated question of Origins, and with the history of the translation from the Revisions to the Recensions. Part Two is concerned with recent study on the text and language, and closes with a chapter on the current problems in the field of study and with future prospects. The book is brought to a close by two appendices on Sigla and manuscripts used in the modern editions from Cambridge and Göttingen, and by an extensive and useful bibliography.
E.J.C.D.

SWETE, H. B.: *An Introduction to the Old Testament in Greek*, revised by R. R. Ottley, with an Appendix containing the Letter of Aristeas ed. by H. St. J. Thackeray. Reprint 1968. Pp. xiv, 626. (Ktav Publishing House, Inc., New York. Price: $12.50)

This is a welcome reissue of a standard work, the revised form of the Introduction originally published in 1902 and issued in the revised form in 1914. It would have been proper to include this latter date and not only the date of the original edition on the back of the title page. But the 1914 preface is printed, though it has curiously slipped out of order into the middle of the original preface. The publishers are performing an invaluable service in their reissuing of such works as this, a service particularly useful for the many new libraries and for younger scholars who can only with difficulty obtain copies of such books.   P.R.A.

TALMON, S. (ed.): *Textus: Annual of the Hebrew University Bible Project*, Vol. VI. 1968. Pp. vi, 134 + 10 in Hebrew. (Magnes Press, Jerusalem, and Oxford University Press, London. Price: 49s.)

In addition to a report on the Bible Project this volume contains seven articles and a short note. Two of the articles are in French and the rest in English, and there are Hebrew summaries of them all. C. Rabin has an illuminating article on the general problems of translation and the special problems facing the translators of the Greek O.T. and the way they met them. M. Delcor presents a careful study of Sir. 51:13–20 in 11QPs^a compared with LXX, Vulgate, and Syriac texts, and M. E. Stone considers some readings of an Erevan Armenian MS of 4 Ezra in relation to a number of other MSS to illustrate the need for further study of this daughter version of the lost Greek version. F. Díaz Esteban studies references to Ben Asher and Ben Naphtali in the Massorah Magna of the margins of MS Leningrad B 19A. G. Weil edits some hitherto unpublished fragments of the Babylonian Massorah Magna in the Cambridge Taylor-Schechter collection, while N. Allony publishes another fragment in the same collection containing an autograph of Se'id Ben Farjoi, from the ninth century, with a study of its script, which he holds to be important for determining the date of the Aleppo Codex. N. Fried contributes some notes on Haftaroth Scrolls. R. Weiss offers a new explanation of lQIs^a reading of Isa. 38:12 and finds the principle behind it to explain some variations between the Chronicler and his sources and the variation between Ps. 14:5 f. and Ps. 53:6. The short note is by W. Baars and is on a Munich fragment of Dan. 3:51 f. in Greek. There are four pages of excellent plates.   H.H.R.

WALLENSTEIN, M.: *Genizah Fragments in the Chetham's Library. Manchester.* (Reprinted from the *Bulletin of the John Rylands Library*, Vol. 50, No. 1, 1967). 1967. Pp. 18. (The John Rylands Library, Manchester 3. Price: 7s. 6d.)

In this small collection (six pieces) of Genizah material, four biblical fragments range from a tenth-century Babylonian text to another from the thirteenth, and their main interest lies in the irregularity of Metheg and maqqeph usages. The two non-biblical fragments consist of a fragment of a thirteenth century copy of two elegies from the eleventh century. These are translated and annotated.

                                                                                               B.J.R.

EXEGESIS AND MODERN TRANSLATIONS

ASENSIO, F. (S.J.): *El Levitico: El Hombre responde a su Dios.* 1966. Pp. 180. (Editorial 'Sal Terrae', Santander. Price: 8s. 3d.)

The author, who has written more important works and is professor of Scripture in the Gregorian University in Rome, has furnished a short but quite masterly summary of Leviticus, with a running commentary to a text not provided here, which is grouped under six chapters that consider in turn sacrifice as a dialogue between God and man, the Aaronic priesthood, the laws affecting purity, the Day of Atonement, the code of holiness, and the final test, i.e. generosity in the service of divine worship. While this modest venture cannot be compared with Noth's fine volume, it should be of service to those beginning the study of Israelite worship.

J.M.T.B.

AUZOU, G.: *La Danse devant l'Arche. Étude du livre de Samuel.* (Connaissance de la Bible, 6). 1968. Pp. 421. (Éditions de l'Orante, Paris. Price: 47s. 6d.)

An earlier volume by the same author, *La Force de l'Esprit* (1966; not noted in the *Book List*), provided an introduction and running commentary on the book of Judges. Now the same is done for the two books of Samuel, under a title which is indicative both of the element of popularization and of the attempt at seeing the whole in relation to its central theme, namely the place of David and the eventual development of messianic thought. To this theme, the longest chapter is devoted, with a review of many of the relevant biblical passages (pp. 297–343), appropriately in the context of commentary on 2 Sam. 7. The biblical text is not printed, except for the psalm passages in the books of Samuel and quotations from elsewhere. The chapters are treated in an order which follows that of the text for the most part in 1 Sam., but departs from it substantially in 2 Sam., grouping together those which deal with David 'in the glorious years' and David 'in the dark years'. The purpose is mainly that of persuading the reader to find how thrilling a biblical book can be, and the comments range widely. But the author is sensitive to the literary questions, and succeeds in reminding the reader that, with all the importance that this material has for history and for theology, the books do after all provide a very exciting story, perhaps not altogether ineptly indicated by the title given to the chapter covering 1 Sam. 21–7, 29–30: 'Western in the Judaean deserts'.

P.R.A.

BEUKEN, W. A. M.: *Haggai-Sacharja* 1–8, trans. into German by E. Huger. 1967. Pp. xvii, 350. (Van Gorcum, Assen. Price: Fl. 26.90)

The aim of this book is to build upon the findings of traditio-historical criticism so as to distinguish between the prophecies of Haggai and Zechariah and the work of the redactor who imposes his own aims upon the final form of the tradition. The first chapter contains a review of previous work on these prophets; the second and third a study of the final form of the two books; the fourth and fifth an analysis of the work of the prophets themselves. It is concluded that the redactor was motivated by strongly chronological considerations and so turned the material into a narrative of salvation-history relevant to the later Jewish community. A levitical interest is postulated together with a style related to that of the Chronicler who supplies the chronological framework. As to the prophets themselves, Haggai represented the landed population of Judah amongst whom the old Yahwistic traditions lived on. Zechariah belonged to the *gôlāh*, preoccupied with the problems set by the fall of Jerusalem and the exile. His own influence is detected in the compilation of his prophecies. This is a useful discussion of a fruitful theme, not perhaps the less interesting if the author has, in places, overplayed his hand.

D.R.J.

BROWN, R. E., FITZMYER, J. A. and MURPHY, R. E. (eds): *The Jerome Biblical Commentary*. 1968. 2 Vols. bound as one. Pp. xxxvi, 637, 889. (Geoffrey Chapman, London. Price: £10 10s.)

This is the English edition of a new one-volume biblical commentary, published in the same year in the United States by Prentice-Hall, Englewood Cliffs, N.J. The foreword by the late Cardinal Bea emphasises its connection with the encouragement to biblical study expressed, though not initiated, in the Second Vatican Council. The list of its editors and contributors is a roll-call of the outstanding English speaking Roman Catholic biblical scholars of our time. The first volume contains commentaries on all the books of the O.T., including the Deuterocanonical works, together with a small number of general articles, e.g. on the Pentateuch, Prophecy, Poetry, Wisdom, the Post-Exilic Period. The second volume contains the N.T. commentaries and relevant general articles, but these are followed by 15 further general articles on such subjects as Inspiration, Canonicity, Text, Hermeneutics, Geography, Archaeology, History, Institutions, Thought. There is a general index and a 'basic bibliography', though each section also has its own bibliography. Indexing is by section number and paragraph number, and these are clearly indicated at the top centre of each page. No one translation of the Bible has been prescribed, it being recognized by the editors that 'part of the serious study of the Bible is the recognition of the limitations inherent in all translations' (p. xix).

The presentation is clear; where bold type is used for biblical references, it is easy to pick out what is being discussed. In some cases bold type is not used. The pattern of use is intelligible but sometimes makes it a little more difficult to see at once where things are.

As in all one-volume works, there are considerable limitations imposed upon editors and authors. The detail of commentary compares closely with the New Peake. Statements of alternative views are given and references to the literature, but the commentary is not overloaded, and provides clear and straightforward indications of the interpretation offered. The books are arranged in a sort of chronological order — thus the prophets begin with Amos, Hosea and Isaiah 1–39, and Jonah is placed right at the end, after the wisdom books and the psalms, along with Tobit, Judith and Esther. Such an arrangement is helpful to the general reader, though it has the disadvantage of dividing the book of Isaiah, and of making the presence of later material in Isa. 1–39 less clear, though the point is made in the introduction to that section. There are two maps as endpapers and two between the volumes. This is a very valuable volume. Though the future trend may, we hope, be away from the publishing of specifically Protestant or Roman Catholic volumes and towards a still greater measure of co-operation, the reader has here a picture of the present state of the best biblical study of the Roman Catholic church.

                                                                                    P.R.A.

CASSUTO, U.: *A Commentary on the Book of Exodus*. Translated by I. Abrahams. 1968. Pp. 510. (The Magnes Press. The Hebrew University, Jerusalem, Oxford University Press. Price: $10; 72s.)

This English translation of a commentary which was first published in 1951 is essentially a literary commentary upon the Hebrew text. Its Jewish author rejects the accepted Documentary hypothesis and argues that the book is a unity which grew up around an ancient epic poem describing the major events of the Exodus, Sinai revelation and Wilderness Wandering. Use is made of modern archaeological research, and especially of insights from ancient epic texts, but no overall critical history of the period is given, nor is there any new treatment of problems of the Hebrew text. The comments are essentially of a literary nature, elucidating the meaning and style of the text, and their intention is more to help the general reader than to provide a new interpretation for the scholar. As a commentary it comes rather between the critical and more popular works.

R.E.C.

DARLOW, T. H. and MOULE, H. F.: *Historical Catalogue of Printed Editions of the English Bible*, revised by Herbert, A. S., 1968. Pp. xxxi, 549. (British and Foreign Bible Society, London; American Bible Society, New York. Price: 84s.; $10.00)

Professor Herbert has devoted a great deal of time to the revision of this classical work of bibliography, first published in 1903 as Volume I of the catalogue of the library of the British and Foreign Bible Society.

The revised work lists more than two thousand editions of the Bible or parts thereof, in English, published between 1525 (Tyndale's N.T.) and 1961 (the New English Bible N.T.). Their locations are given for all Bibles up to 1640. In addition to descriptions, detailed enough for the identification of any particular Bible, we find copious notes on the historical background of the most notable translations. The whole catalogue is arranged on a chronological basis. In an appendix are listed 'Commentaries Containing Newly Translated Versions'. A second appendix lists versions in English provincial dialects. There are full indexes. This volume will long remain an indispensable work of reference for future historians of the English Bible.

B.F.P.

DUHM, B.: *Das Buch Jesaia* (5th edition). 1968. Pp. 490. (Vandenhoeck and Ruprecht, Göttingen. Price: DM. 46)

The publication of the 5th edition of a commentary on the Book of Isaiah whose 4th edition appeared in 1922 and the original in 1892 is a notable event. Duhm's literary-critical approach to the prophetical literature of the O.T., his thesis that the prophets were poets, and his critical appraisal of their extant work in the light of that thesis, so that he characterized much of it as *unecht* and made textual emendations with sanguine subjectivity, made him a man of portent to many and occasioned his reluctant departure from Göttingen, his academic home, in the midst of his career, to find hospitality and an academic welcome in Basel. W. Baumgartner has written a perceptive and very helpful introduction for this 5th edition, in which he assesses the value of Duhm's published work and its place in the context of O.T. scholarship, and, in addition, depicts the man himself in all the richness and strength of his personality. He describes him as a genial individualist who is not to be followed blindly and who can be but half known through his books. His personal influence was tremendous, and in Basel today, forty years after his death, it is still very much alive.

J.M.

HOLM-NIELSEN, S., NOACK, B., and ACHEN, S. T. (eds): *Det Gamle Testamente:* Vol. I. *Skabelse og Vandringstid;* Vol. II. *Fra Moses til kong David.* 1968. Pp. 528, 480. (Politikens forlag, Copenhagen. Price: D.Kr. 33.75 each)

> These are the first two volumes to be published of a nine volume series *Bibelen i kulturhistorisk lys.* The first contains the first four Books of Moses. The text is the Danish authorized version of 1931, printed with indication of the chapters and their contents, but without numbering of the verses. Noack has written a general introduction to the Bible, Holm-Nielsen an introduction to the O.T., and E. Nielsen a general introduction to the four Books of Moses and besides that a special one to each of them. The work is supplied with a great number of maps as well as illustrations, taken partly from excavations or from the modern Near East, partly from the work of artists with motifs from the Bible.
> The second volume contains the writings from the fifth Book of Moses to the Books of Samuel. Holm-Nielsen has written about the historical literature as a whole, E. Nielsen has given the introduction to the fifth Book of Moses and dealt with the reform of Josiah. S. Biørn has written on the immigration into Canaan and the introduction to the Book of Joshua and the Book of Judges, and J. H. Grønbaek has written the introduction to the Book of Ruth and the Books of Samuel.
> Although the work is meant to be popular the quality of the contributors guarantees the scientific level.   E.H.

HULME, W. E.: *Dialogue in Despair. Pastoral Commentary on the Book of Job.* 1968. Pp. 157. (Abingdon Press, Nashville and New York. Price: $3.50)

> Job in need of help and the friends who seek to give it to him are in this book, which is intended for laymen and ministers, treated as providing a valuable object lesson in pastoral counselling.

E.T.R.

JONES, E.: *Proverbs and Ecclesiastes* (Torch Bible Paperbacks). 1968. Pp. 349. S.C.M. Press, London. Price: 16s.)

> This is a paperback reprint, unchanged save for a new subtitle *Words of the Wise,* of the work first published in 1961 (see *B.L.* 1962, pp. 28 f.; *Decade,* p. 338)   R.J.C.

JOSUTTIS, M.: *Predigten zur Geschichte Davids* (Alttestamentliche Predigten, 9). 1968. Pp. 144. (Neukirchener Verlag des Erziehungsvereins, Neukirchen-Vluyn. Price: DM. 10.40)

> This is the latest volume in a series of courses of sermons on the Old Testament, one of which has already been noted in the *Book List* (1968, p. 23). It consists of thirteen sermons on episodes from the life of David, based on passages from 1 and 2 Samuel and 1 Kings 1 and 2. All were preached in village churches in Germany in 1965 and 1967. In a short final chapter the author, who has published a book on homiletics, adds an interesting discussion on some of the problems of preaching from the O.T. He also discusses the more general problem of combining a policy of preaching fixed courses of sermons with one of preaching on current events. His own sermons

show that this problem remains unsolved: for example, when he attempts to relate the story of David's sparing the life of Saul (1 Sam. 24:1–23) to the question of military service, or the rebellion of Sheba (2 Sam. 20:1–22) to the fiftieth anniversary of the Russian revolution, one cannot avoid the impression that the connexion between text and sermon is extremely tenuous.   R.N.W.

KOOLE, J. L.: *Haggaï*. (Commentaar op het Oude Testament). 1967. Pp. 105. (J. H. Kok, Kampen. Price: Fl. 9.75)

This is a very careful and thorough commentary in Dutch on the book of Haggai, published in the series edited by W. H. Gispen and N. H. Ridderbos. A quarter of the book is devoted to introductory matters — the structure of the work, the prophet himself and the contemporary situation, and a very positive appraisal of the theology of Haggai. A substantial bibliography is supplemented by references in the text to a very wide range of literature. Dr Koole is very closely acquainted with all that is relevant to his study, and this is further evident in the care with which the commentary itself is undertaken. Full justice is done to the text in a commentary which is conservative in the proper sense of that word, being fully appreciative of the place that Haggai occupies in post-exilic theology and in particular in the development of the idea of the temple.   P.R.A.

LANGE, E.: *Die verbesserliche Welt* (*Möglichkeiten christlicher Rede erprobt an der Geschichte vom Propheten Jona*). 1968. Pp. 94. (Kreuz-Verlag, Stuttgart, Berlin. Price: DM. 5.80)

Four homiletic studies on the book of Jonah followed by one on Luke 2:25–32 are contained in this book. They are followed by a *Predigtbesprechung* by D. Rössler.   A.S.H.

LESLIE, E. A.: *The Psalms. Translated and Interpreted in the Light of Hebrew Life and Worship*. Paperback ed. 1968 (1949). Pp. 448. (Abingdon Press, Nashville, Tenn. Price: $2.75)

This is a reprint of the volume reviewed in *B.L.* 1949, p. 25: *Eleven Years* p. 188. Its arrangement of psalms in types and its use of the then available continental literature marked it out as a useful volume. Its present reissue would be much more valuable if account had been taken of, for example, the re-statement of his views by S. Mowinckel.

P.R.A.

NOTH, M.: *Könige* (Biblischer Kommentar, Altes Testament, IX, 4). 1968. Pp. 241–340. (Neukirchener Verlag des Erziehungsvereins, Neukirchen-Vluyn. Price: DM. 7.75; by subscription, DM. 6.50)

Fasc. 4 covers 1 Kings 11:1–14:8 and keeps the same high standard as before (*B.L.* 1968, p. 26). The sudden death of the distinguished author means that this commentary, for which he was so eminently prepared, cannot be completed by his hand. We are glad to learn that arrangements have been made for its continuation by Professor R. Smend, and also applaud the decision to keep Professor Noth's own work (i.e. down to the end of 1 Kings 16) as a separately indexed volume.   D.R.Ap-T.

NOTH, M.: *Numbers*, Trans. by J. D. Martin. (Old Testament Library).
1968. Pp. x, 258. (S.C.M. Press, London. Price: 50s.)

> This is a translation of Noth's very useful commentary in the *Altes
> Testament Deutsch* series (*B.L.* 1967, p. 24). The translation is careful
> not to be too literal, but sometimes unnecessarily loses nuances
> present in the German in consequence, and very occasionally is
> misleading, although never seriously.   J.V.M.S.

OIKONOMOU, E. B.: *To Biblion tes Esther*. 1967. Pp. xiii, 159. (Bibliotheke
tes en Athenais Philekpaideutikes Hetaireias, Athens)

> This *Habilitationsschrift* submitted to the University of Athens
> examines the book of Esther in the light of its philological, historical
> and theological problems. The deuterocanonical parts of the book
> supplement and explain the protocanonical core, which is a literary
> unity, the work of one author, who had exceptionally accurate
> knowledge of his subject-matter, either because he himself was an
> eyewitness or because he depended on eyewitness testimony — in all
> probability Mordecai's. The book contains a factual account of
> events that took place in the reign of Xerxes; its historicity is not put
> in question by the failure of other sources to mention Esther and
> Mordecai any more than that of the Pentateuch is put in question
> by the absence of any references to Joseph and Moses in Egyptian
> records. The canonicity of the book is certain, for all the theological
> doubts that it may raise; it reproduces the 'soteriological' pattern
> of an age much earlier than its own — that of the judges.
>
>   F.F.B.

The Oxford Illustrated Old Testament. I. *The Pentateuch*. 1968. Pp. 435.
(Oxford University Press, London. Price: 63s.)

> This is the first of five finely produced volumes, containing illustrations
> of the Old Testament by a number of distinguished contemporary
> British artists: nine artists are responsible for the Pentateuch. The
> text is that of the A.V., but with modern paragraphing and with
> poetical passages printed as verse. At the end of the book, there are
> brief statements by the illustrators about their own particular approach
> to the work, which help to explain the widely differing styles of the
> artists. So Edward Bawden feels himself strongly influenced by a stay
> in Iraq, where he finds 'the same impression of life as it was lived in
> the past', while, to represent Moses, Carol Annand draws on images
> from sources 'such as newspaper photographs, cloth catalogues,
> furniture advertisements'. As a result, not the least interesting thing
> about this book is the interaction it reveals between the diversity of
> modern artistic expression and the diversity of contemporary ap-
> proaches to the O.T. Certainly the some 140 illustrations are superbly
> reproduced and the publisher's claims for the beauty of the volume
> fully justified. On p. 434, the reference to the Nazarite's vow should
> be to the *second* paragraph of Num. 6, as the relevant illustration
> clearly shows.   J.R.P.

The Oxford Illustrated Old Testament. II. *The Historical Books*. 1968.
Pp. 544; III. *The Poetical Books*. 1968. Pp. 368; IV. *The Prophets*. 1969;
V. *The Apocrypha*. 1969. (Oxford University Press. Price: 63s. each)

von Rad, G.: *La Genèse*. Translated by E. de Peyer. 1968. Pp. 454. (Labor et Fides, Geneva. Price: Sw.Fr. 33 (paper); 39 (bound))

> The original German of this now standard commentary was noted in
> *B.L.* 1950, p. 40; 1952, p. 36; 1954, p. 41 (*Eleven Years*, pp. 257, 407,
> 578), and the English translation of 1961 in *B.L.* 1962, p. 31; *Decade*,
> p 341. It is good to be able to draw attention to its availability now in
> a French translation. P.R.A.

Renckens, H.: *Israel's Concept of the Beginning. The Theology of Genesis 1–3*. Translated by C. Napier. 1964. Pp. 320. (Herder and Herder, New York. Price: $5.95)

> The French translation of the original Dutch *Israels Visie op het
> Verleden* (1958) was reviewed in *B.L.* 1965, p. 39; *Decade*, p. 591. Its
> simultaneous appearance in English was not then noted. The book
> provides much useful and stimulating discussion, particularly in
> drawing out modern implications in the material. As part of a process
> by which modern Roman Catholic studies of the O.T. are becoming
> available in English, it is to be welcomed. Not all the translation is
> entirely happy, as witness the chapter heading: 'The Sexual Stuff
> under the Hammer'. P.R.A.

Reventlow, H. Graf.: *Opfere deinen Sohn: Eine Auslegung von Genesis 22*. (Biblische Studien, 53) 1968. Pp. 87. (Neukirchener Verlag des Erziehungsvereins, Neukirchen-Vluyn. Price: DM. 5.50)

> The narrative in Gen. 22 is examined in five stages. 1. Historical truth.
> 2. Literary sources. 3. The original form and aim. 4. The treatment
> by the literary editor (E). 5. The Offering of Isaac in the thinking of
> the Christian era. The original narrative is seen to be contained in
> vv. 1–14, omitting v. 5, the names Isaac and Moriah and some
> 'editorial' words. This is a valuable study in form-criticism and the
> work of Israel's compilers of ancient saga. A.S.H.

van Rossum, J.: *De Praedeuteronomistische Bestanddelen van het Boek der Richters en hun betekenis voor onze kennis van de geschiedenis van het volk Israel en zijn godsdienst*. 1966. Pp. 160. (J. M. van Amstel, Winterswijk. Price: Fl. 15)

> This doctoral thesis has as its first part an analysis of the book of
> Judges so as to differentiate between the pre-Deuteronomic sections
> and the Deuteronomic editing and post-Deuteronomic additions.
> The discussion, with reference to earlier analyses, follows the normal
> pattern of critical scholarship. The second and third parts examine the
> contribution of the pre-Deuteronomic material to our understanding
> of first the history and then the religion of Israel. The various judge
> narratives are investigated in groups for the first purpose, and in
> this such unity as is to be detected is seen as arising rather from
> threats to the life of the tribes than from any 'amphictyonic' unity.
> Religion, however, is seen as providing a further bond, though the
> third section is largely concentrated on extracting from the narratives
> such information as is available concerning beliefs and practices and
> religious objects. The thesis thus covers fairly familiar ground. A
> two page summary in French is included. The copy supplied for
> review contained a very large number of misprints, many of which
> had been corrected by hand; but the reviewer found others which had
> not been noted. P.R.A.

SCHARBERT, J.: *Die Propheten Israels um 600 v. Chr.* 1967. Pp. 514, 3 maps and time chart. (Verlag J. P. Bachem, Cologne. Price: 97s.)

In 1965, Scharbert published what may appropriately be described as volume I of a three volume series on the prophets, dealing with prophecy up to 700 B.C. (See *B.L.* 1966, p. 54; *Decade*, p. 674). The third volume is to deal with the prophets of the later period, together with a more systematic presentation of the nature and theology of prophecy. Each volume is independent, but cross-reference is also frequently made. In this volume, separate chapters deal at appropriate points with the historical background from Manasseh to the death of Josiah, and from that moment to the fall of Jerusalem. In between are chapters dealing with the prophets of the period, arranged in chronological order. In particular Jeremiah is divided up into four chapters covering separate periods, in addition to a general chapter on the book as a whole; Ezekiel is divided similarly into prophecy before and after the fall of Jerusalem. A final chapter utilises other material, including passages from Lamentations and Psalms, to illuminate the exilic age. Such chronological ordering is inevitably rather uncertain, and its danger also is that in trying to set passages of prophecy at particular points, their reinterpretation and re-application cannot be adequately handled. The book is a good general presentation, at times rather over-simplified, but readable and stimulating.   P.R.A.

Schriften der Bibel: literaturgeschichtlich geordnet. Band I, *Vom Thronfolgebuch bis zur Priesterscrift.* 1968. Pp. 351. (Calver Verlag, Stuttgart; Kösel Verlag, München. Price: DM. 18)

The purpose of this book is to arrange the O.T. literature belonging to the period defined in categories according to differences of presentation and mode of communication and of literary form, and to treat each historically so that development of moral sensitivity and of spiritual insight may be readily discerned and appreciated by the reader. There are four sections in the book. The first deals with the Succession Narrative which is described as the first narrative work of the O.T., and with the work of the Yahwist (assigned to the time of Solomon). The contrasting features of these two works are skilfully delineated. The second section deals with poetry at court and sanctuary, the third with the work of the prophets up to the second half of the 6th century, and the fourth with the deuteronomic interpretation of Israel's history and the Priestly Document. Each section has a succinct and effective introduction, which is followed by a group of passages selected from the relevant O.T. literature. These introductions have been written and the selection of passages made by H. Schwager. In such an anthology of a body of literature much has to be omitted; but what has been included illustrates the Israelite belief in God's governance of human history. This method of O.T. interpretation oversimplifies the record but it will aid the general reader to grasp the essential unity which underlies the O.T. documents. Their diversity he may learn about more fully later.   J.M.

STALKER, D. M. G.: *Ezekiel.* (The Torch Bible Commentaries). 1968. Pp. 319. (S.C.M. Press. Price: 30s.)

This volume is the more important by reason of the paucity of modern English commentaries on Ezekiel. Perhaps heavy going for a popular series, it should nevertheless prove widely useful. It registers the increasing agreement among recent scholars that the book of Ezekiel is largely a unity, that it is a collection of oracles originally uttered orally (though the form-critical implications are not pursued), that the process of transmission and redaction was similar to the handling of the Isaiah and Jeremiah tradition, and that the prophet's ministry was carried out entirely in Babylonia. Though the commentary lacks distinctive features and is heavily, even wearisomely laden with quotations from previous commentators, it has the merit of reflecting some distinguished German work, and it is competent and reliable. There are two diagrams of the Temple and a sketch map of the redistributed land.   D.R.J.

Starý Zákon/překlad s výkladem: I. První kniha Mojžíšova — Genesis. (The Old Testament/translation with commentary: I. The First Book of Moses — Genesis). 1968. Pp. 285. (Kalich, Prague. Price: Kčs. 30)

Since 1961 a group of theologians and linguists has been working under the leadership of Professor Miloš Bič of Prague at a new translation of the Old Testament in Czech. It is the first Protestant translation since the work of the Bohemian Brethren (*Unitas Fratrum*) in the sixteenth century. It is taking place with ecumenical co-opera-tion by members of the World Council of Churches. At a future date, the co-operation of the Roman Catholic Church is also expected.

The new translation is based on the Leningrad Codex printed in Kittel's *Biblia Hebraica*, but in a critical apparatus includes also the variations of other ancient texts, in particular the Septuagint and the Vulgate, together also with various interpretations found in other translations, including Catholic and Jewish alongside Protestant. Cross references are provided for individual verses. The text is divided according to the content, and is accompanied by a continuous explanation. This is the first commentary on the whole Old Testament to be undertaken within Czech Protestantism. Genesis has now appeared as the first volume. Within a few months, the fourteenth (final) volume will appear as the next in the series, containing the Twelve Prophets (Hosea to Malachi). Further volumes are ready for the printer and will follow. When the whole work is complete, the translation is to be adopted as the new liturgical text.   M.B.

WEBER, J. J.: *Le Psautier. Texte et commentaires.* Édition refondue 1968. Pp. lix, 639. (Desclée, Tournai, Belgium. Price: Fr. 360)

This is a new edition of a translation and commentary on the Psalms which has proved serviceable for general purposes among French-speaking Catholics over the past thirty years. The author, a former Archbishop of Strasbourg, offers an informed exposition set in the context of Christian tradition. The influence of Gunkel and of French commentators is more apparent than that of Mowinckel. This edition, which is generously and clearly laid out, will continue to be of practical value.   J.H.E.

WESTERMANN, C.: *Genesis.* (Biblischer Kommentar, Altes Testament, I, 2). 1967. Pp. 81–160. (Neukirchener Verlag des Erziehungsvereins, Neukirchen-Vluyn. Price: DM. 7.75; by subscription, DM. 6.50)

This fascicle continues that reviewed in *B.L.* 1968, p. 29, continuing the introduction and leading into the commentary as far as Gen. 1:6–8. A section is devoted to the theological significance of the

primeval history as told in Genesis, though this too must be seen
against similar accounts in extra-biblical material. Nine pages of
bibliography, three of which relate to Gen. 1:1–2:4a, precede the
commentary. A translation is followed by a detailed analysis of
grammar, syntax and form, followed by exegesis. Notice is taken of
earlier and contemporary studies to which Westermann makes his
own contribution.
                                                                A.S.H.

ZÁVADA, V. and SEGERT, S.: *Kniha Jóbova* (*The Book of Job*). 1968.
Pp. 134. (Klub přátel poezie, výběrová řada 53, Prague. Price: Kčs. 12)

In 1958, S. Segert, the well-known Prague Semitist, translated and
copiously annotated the 'Five Scrolls' (*Pět svátečnich svitků*). He has
now published a new translation of the book of Job. In collaboration
with the poet Zavada, he has produced a work which provides for
the Czech reader a clear picture of the nature of Hebrew poetry.
To a theologian, it is true, it may be a matter of regret that the
biblical message is distorted by much textual conjecture, but the notes
which are added concerning the book, the home and period of Job
and the Job tradition, together with notes on individual passages,
will be valued by every reader. It is evident that they come from one
who is an expert, well-informed on a wide range of subjects. Dr
Segert also deserves praise for the fact that his work makes the
biblical material accessible to the wider circles of those who have no
church connections.
                                                                M.B.

ZIMMERLI, W.: *Ezechiel* (Biblischer Kommentar, Altes Testament, XIII,
13–14, 15). 1967, 1968. Pp. 979–1138, 1139–218. (Neukirchener Verlag
des Erziehungsvereins, Neukirchen-Vluyn. Price per Lieferung:
DM. 7.75; by subscription, DM. 6.50)

The above sections of this commentary begin with the closing
paragraphs of the introductory survey of 40:1–48:35 and extend to
the commentary on 48:22 f. Thus the author has almost reached the
end of his formidable task of translating, analysing, and interpreting
the text; but the introduction still remains to be published. Since the
discussion of 40–8 is still incomplete, readers also still await
Zimmerli's summing up of his treatment of that complex section of
the book. In his analysis of its main components (40:1–42:20,
43:1–46:24, 47:1–48:35), he acknowledges his debt to the penetrating
treatment of these chapters by H. Gese. Of the innumerable points
of detail which would call for comment in a full review, it must
suffice here to mention the admirable discussion of the Temple and
its gateways, clearly illustrated in the light of recent archaeological
discoveries. The entire treatment is a model of painstaking
thoroughness.
                                                                G.W.A.

LITERARY CRITICISM AND INTRODUCTION
(including History of Interpretation, Canon, and Special Studies)

ACKROYD, P. R.: *Exile and Restoration. A Study of Hebrew Thought of
the Sixth Century B.C.* (Old Testament Library). 1968. Pp. ix, 286.
(S.C.M. Press, London. Price: 55s.)

This is a much expanded edition of the Hulsean Lectures delivered in
1962. It contains a study of the conditions of the Jews in the Exilic

Age both in Babylonia and in Judah, and of the thinkers and prophets who spoke to this situation or reflected on it. Chapters are devoted to Jeremiah, the Deuteronomic History, the Priestly Work, Ezekiel, Deutero-Isaiah, Haggai and Zechariah. The approach to Jeremiah, Ezekiel and Deutero-Isaiah is characterized by a welcome emphasis on the ongoing, re-interpreting and supplementing tradition associated with the work of the prophets, and is not therefore inhibited by pre-occupation with the recovery of *ipsissima verba*. Haggai and Zechariah 1–8 are interpreted in minute detail and virtually a commentary on these prophecies is contained in the chapters devoted to them. If the result is a certain imbalance in the book as a whole, the value of this learned analysis is indisputable. At every point, the discussion is linked, both in the text and copious footnotes, with recent books and monographs. Though the student may find it difficult sometimes to see the wood for the trees, this book will surely become an indispensable authority on the period.   D.R.J.

ANDERS-RICHARDS, D.: *The Drama of the Psalms*. 1968. Pp. 122. (Darton, Longman and Todd, London. Price: 12s. 6d.)

'The purpose of this book is to set out and account for remarkable developments in the field of psalm study' during the last half-century. To a considerable extent this aim is achieved: the book is written in clear, non-technical language, with extensive quotations both from the Psalms and from modern scholars. Unfortunately, it gives a one-sided impression in places, relying too heavily on S. Mowinckel and A. R. Johnson. Some indication should have been given that, on the role of the king in particular, great differences of opinion still exist. The author does not always seem to be familiar with other aspects of O.T. study, and a number of lapses appear in consequence.
                                                                              R.J.C.

*BECK, E. and MILLER, G.: *A Guide to Understanding the Bible*. Vol. 1. *From Genesis to 1 Samuel*. 1967. Pp. 378. (Geoffrey Chapman, London. Price: 50s.)

The first volume, *Biblische Unterweisung*, in the series Handbuch zur Auswahlbibel Reich Gottes (Kosel-Verlag KG, Munich, 1964) has been translated by Michael Barry. It is based on *The Coming of the Kingdom, A Short Bible arranged to present the Story of Salvation*. (Geoffrey Chapman, 1965), to whose paragraph numbering, rather than to the biblical book, chapter and verse, references are related. This limits its usefulness to those who normally use this Short Bible in school, although a Table of Biblical Passages is given at the end. Teachers, expecially in Roman Catholic schools, will find this book helpful as it expresses 'that new understanding of the Bible which has developed since Pius XII's encyclical Divino Afflante Spiritu'. Helpful exegetical comments are given (though not all classroom difficulties are fully faced, e.g. the Flood, the fate of Lot's wife, etc.) as well as guidance for development in class and prayers. Additional notes give extra-biblical material.   A.S.H.

BLANK, S. H.: *Prophetic Faith in Isaiah*. 1967. Pp. x, 241. (Wayne State University Press, Detroit. Price: $2.50)

This is an unchanged reprint in paperback form of the work first published in 1958 (see *B.L.* 1961, p. 43; *Decade*, p. 281).   R.J.C.

BOWDEN, J.: *What about the Old Testament?* (S.C.M. Centrebooks). 1969. Pp. 127. S.C.M. Press, London. Price: 8s. 6d.)

The editor of the S.C.M. Press puts his hand to the task of introducing the Old Testament to the non-expert. He analyses the problem and sketches the rise of modern critical study in two stimulating chapters. He then starts his examination of the Old Testament at the 'Succession narrative' accepting the theory of R. N. Whybray that this belongs to the 'world of the wise', moving back into the past and forward into the future from this standpoint. It is a question whether the theory will stand what has been built upon it; a question also whether this approach does not complicate as much as it clarifies. What is not in question is that the book is interesting, provocative, well-informed and fresh.   D.R.J.

CALDERONE, P. J.: *Dynastic Oracle and Suzerainty Treaty. 2 Sam. 7, 8–16.* (Logos 1) 1966, Pp. 80. (Ateneo University Publications, Manila. Price: $1.00)

Whilst recognizing that there are differences in form between ancient vassal treaties and the dynastic oracle of 2 Sam. 7, this interesting monograph argues that there are close similarities in purpose and ideology. They are both very much concerned with royal succession. The vassal treaties, especially those of Esarhaddon, are concerned with securing agreement to, and recognition of, the king's successor, and this is also the purport of Yahweh's promise to David through Nathan. Calderone argues that this similarity of content is sufficient to indicate a direct dependence of the Nathan oracle upon earlier vassal treaties. Calderone argues his case very cautiously, and even those who doubt his conclusion regarding a direct borrowing will find this a very stimulating treatment of the much discussed Nathan oracle.   R.E.C.

COATS, G. W.: *The Murmuring Motif in the Wilderness Traditions of the Old Testament — Rebellion in the Wilderness.* 1968. Pp. 288. (Abingdon Press, Nashville and New York. Price: $6.50)

The purpose of this book is to give a detailed critical analysis of those passages in the Pentateuch which speak about murmurings, complaints and rebellion by the Israelites in the wilderness. In a preliminary section Dr Coats considers these passages with reference to a *rib* as a legal process, and he concludes that the murmurings are not a *rib* in that sense but may be regarded as the pre-official stage of it — a somewhat hard-pressed conclusion. He then inquires whether, in each particular case, the murmuring or rebellion is the main element in the narrative or a subsidiary one, and whether it was occasioned by very serious hardships (e.g. famine, thirst) or had its basis in general disillusionment and loss of confidence in Moses and faith in God.

Dr Coats attempts where possible to distinguish early traditions from later ones. The view he arrives at is that in the wilderness narrative the murmuring motif characterizes a basic tradition of the Document J, that its *Sitz im Leben* in final form was Jerusalem, and that it expressed a polemic against the northern Israelite cult; but later, especially Deuteronomic, revision substituted a theological for this polemical intent.

The whole work is done with meticulous (sometimes possibly over-elaborate) care and with commendable judgement; and important non-narrative texts (e.g. Pss. 78, 106) are also brought under survey to advantage.   J.M.

CULLEY, R. C.: *Oral Formulaic Language in the Biblical Psalms*. (Near and Middle East Series, No. 4). 1967. Pp. x, 140. (University of Toronto Press, Toronto; Oxford University Press. Price: 62s.)

The purpose of this treatise is to apply to the biblical psalms the methods adopted in the study of oral literature in other contexts: e.g. Homeric and Anglo-Saxon epic, Serbo-Croatian oral narrative poetry, and Russian oral narrative and ceremonial poetry. The author surveys much of the work recently accomplished in these fields, offers a valuable constructive critique of the technical terms used (formula, formulaic system, theme), and discusses the origin and recording of orally composed texts. He then relates his findings to the biblical psalms. On the basis of a detailed examination of the texts he suggests that the stylistic features of oral poetry and other archaic elements have been carried over into the literary period. The formulaic language is prominent in a small number of psalms; these psalms are mainly individual laments, individual thanksgivings, and hymns; and the formulaic phrases are distributed fairly evenly among the constituent elements of the various types of psalm. Cautious conclusions are drawn about the relative place of oral composition, literary borrowing, and the conventional use of traditional language. This is a workmanlike study, which could with profit be supplemented by a similar investigation of the Qumran poetry.   G.W.A.

DEBUS, J.: *Die Sünde Jerobeams*. (Forschungen zur Religion und Literatur des Alten und Neuen Testaments, 93). 1967. Pp. vii, 122. (Vandenhoeck and Ruprecht, Göttingen. Price: DM. 15.80 (paper); 19.80 (cloth))

This book, a doctoral thesis accepted by the University of Marburg, is a study of the traditions relating to Jeroboam, the founder of the northern kingdom, in the books of Kings, particularly 1 Kings 11:26–14:20. The text of Codex B of the Septuagint 3 Kings 12:24a–z, which has no parallel in the Massoretic text, is also examined. Dr Debus' conclusions are that the traditions concerning Jeroboam are not based on historical narratives but on community tradition. The narratives in the Greek text of B witness to an original Hebrew which has not been edited by the Deuteronomists as the Massoretic text has. The portrayal of Jeroboam in Kings as the archsinner who set up illegitimate sanctuaries at Bethel and Dan and thereby ensured Yahweh's condemnation of the northern kingdom is the Deuteronomist's way of accounting for the destruction and disappearance of that kingdom. This is a stimulating study which merits attention from all serious students of the books of Kings.   J.R.

DELEKAT, L.: *Asylie und Schutzorakel am Zionheiligtum. Eine Untersuchung zu den privaten Feindpsalmen mit zwei Exkursen*. 1967. Pp. viii, 432. (E. J. Brill, Leiden. Price: Fl. 68)

Here is another substantial attempt to solve the problems of the 'Individual Laments'. Indeed, almost half the Psalter is drawn into the orbit of the proposed theory and treated in detail. There is some kinship with the work of H. Schmidt and the early Bentzen, but also much originality. The laments are explained as the prayers of impoverished individuals ('ānî) appealing for protection in the asylum of the Temple. They, and their enemies outside, are eagerly awaiting the indication of God's will through the official omens or oracles. The details of their situation are ingeniously reconstructed; mostly they are day-labourers beset by debts or accusation of various

crimes; in Ps. 65 a group of workers has come out on strike and into
asylum just before harvest. The 'happy ending' often found in these
psalms is said to have been added later in acknowledgement of the
favourable decision, which has enabled the fugitive to leave with a
'safe conduct' or to remain as a Temple servant. But neither the
laments nor the acknowledgements are understood as living utterances,
but only as the silent witness of inscriptions laid up in the sanctuary
on memorial stones or scrolls. Nearly half of the book consists of
various appendages, chiefly on asylum in the rest of the O.T. and on
divine titles in the Psalms.   J.H.E.

VAN DIJK, H. J.: *Ezekiel's prophecy on Tyre* (*Ez. 26, 1–28, 19*): *A new
approach.* (Biblica et Orientalia, 20). 1968. Pp. xii, 149. (Pontifical
Biblical Institute, Rome. Price: Lire 2.400)

The author's aim is to use 'the new material of both lexical and
syntactical nature uncovered by comparative Canaanite and Semitic
studies' in explanation of the Hebrew text of Ez. 26:1–28:19, which is
regarded as substantially reliable so far as the consonantal text is
concerned. Other O.T. passages are also considered where relevant,
and some linguistic parallels in Ugaritic and other north-western
Semitic dialects are discussed at some length. Some interesting
suggestions are made, but not infrequently the Hebrew text can be
satisfactorily interpreted without recourse to unusual meanings of
Hebrew words based upon a comparison with cognate languages.
The work, in which the influence of M. Dahood is evident throughout,
will, however, repay study. There are useful indexes and a serviceable
bibliography.   D.W.T.

FENSHAM, F. C.: *'n Ondersoek na die Geskiedenis van die Interpretasie
van die Hebreeuse Poesie.* (Annale Universiteit van Stellenbosch,
Volume 30, Serie B, No. 1 (1966)). 1966. Pp. 24. (University of
Stellenbosch. Price: Sent 40)

The author provides an admirably concise survey of the main theories
which have been held about the structure and scansion of Hebrew
poetry. He argues that pre-exilic poetry must be scanned according
to the system of Sievers, and later poetry according to the system
of Bickell, Hölscher, and Mowinckel. He discusses the problem of
the short verse and appraises the parallels drawn between early
Hebrew and Ugaritic poetry.   G.W.A.

FUSS, W.: *Die sogenannte Paradieserzählung: Aufbau, Herkunft und
theologische Bedeutung.* 1968. Pp. 134. (Verlagshaus Gerd Mohn,
Gütersloh. Price: DM. 19.80)

This study is intended as an essay in *Redaktionsgeschichte* (p. 9). This
seems in effect to mean a very detailed literary-critical analysis, but
with a shift of emphasis on to the redactor, who was responsible for
many details which were formerly wrongly attributed to the sources
used by him (cf. pp. 77 ff., 83 ff.). Behind Gen. 2–3 lie two different
old stories. One was concentrated upon the Land and Man ('*ᵃdāmāh*,
'*ādām*), the other was about a Garden, in which God made a woman
(no man!) called Hawwāh, later to become Mother of All (and so, for
example, to have her son Cain as husband, p. 75). The establishment
of these two source stories occupies the very detailed analysis of
pp. 25–70. The reader might be well advised to begin with the results

(pp. 70–82) and take them as a guide through the close analytic argument. There are also chapters which survey the previous literature on the subject and which discuss the problem of identifying the story-tellers, the history of the diverse traditions, and the picture of man entertained by them. The tendency implies a certain reaction against form criticism (cf. p. 84). At times the analysis reads like a fascinating exercise in detection; the question will be whether the result will carry conviction at a time when such exact division between sources has come to be seen as somewhat out of fashion. There is no index and cross-reference is not always easy. J.B.

GLUECK, N.: *Hesed in the Bible*, trans. by A. Gottschalk, with an introduction by G. A. Larue. Edited by E. L. Epstein. 1967. Pp. x, 108. (The Hebrew Union College Press, Cincinnati. Price: $5.00)

This is a translation of Dr Glueck's well-known work, first published in German in 1927, and republished in Germany in 1961. A feature of it is the translation of biblical texts from the German in order to preserve the author's innovations and shades of meaning. The introduction provides a useful summary of recent trends in studies on *hesed*, from which the reader may assess the extent of Dr Glueck's influence upon later writers on the subject. D.W.T.

GONZÁLEZ, A.: *La Oración en la Biblia* (Teología y Siglo xx, No. 9). 1968. Pp. 450. (Ediciones Cristiandad, Madrid. Price: 41s.)

In the first part of this study the author examines the nature of prayer and its expression in ancient religion and in the great monotheistic religions and then turns to a more detailed examination of the practice of prayer in the O.T. and in the N.T. This is followed by the text of 276 prayers of the Bible in Spanish translation and this in turn by a brief commentary on each passage. Prayers from the deuterocanonical books are included, but not those of the Psalter, though these are frequently referred to in the earlier discussion of the varieties of prayer in the O.T. The Psalter is excluded from the text and commentary part of the volume, since it requires a separate volume to itself (see *B.L.* 1968, p. 23). The commentary consists in each case of a short note on the occasion and the character of the prayer.

H.H.R.

GUNKEL, H.: *The Psalms* (Facet Books, Biblical Series, 19). 1967. Pp. xi, 52. (Fortress Press, Philadelphia, Price: 85c.)

Gunkel's article on the Psalms from the second edition (1927–31) of *Die Religion in Geschichte und Gegenwart* is here translated by T. M. Horner. An Introduction by J. Muilenberg describes Gunkel's work and its importance, and he rightly characterizes the essay here translated as 'a succinct and admirable synopsis of Gunkel's larger monumental work'. Differences between the first and second editions of *RGG* are indicated in footnotes, and there are bibliographies both of the work of Gunkel and of recent literature on the Psalms.

R.J.C.

GUTBROD, K.: *Ein Gang durch die biblische Urgeschichte*. 1968. Pp. 110. (Calwer Verlag, Stuttgart. Price: DM. 8.50)

This treatment of Genesis 1 – 9:9 is to be warmly recommended. It succeeds to a remarkable degree in uniting critical and theological interests. The component traditions here woven together are to be rightly understood only as *biblische Urgeschichte*. They presuppose much of the content of the divine self-revelation to Israel beginning with the call of Abraham. The essential theme of these chapters is clearly delineated as man in his complex relationship to God.

R.D.

HERMISSON, H.-J.: *Studien zur israelitischen Spruchweisheit* (Wissenschaftliche Monographien zum Alten und Neuen Testament, 28). 1968. Pp. 208. (Neukirchener Verlag des Erziehungsvereins, Neukirchen-Vluyn. Price: DM. 22.80 (paper); 24.80 (cloth))

In this investigation into the origin of the proverbial literature of ancient Israel, the author makes a detailed study of the older 'collections' in Prov. 10–29 (chs 10–15; 16:1–22:16; 25–7; 28–9) and challenges the findings of earlier studies, especially those of O. Eissfeldt, E. Gerstenberger and H.-W. Wolff. His own conclusion is that there is little trace in these chapters either of popular sayings, whether in their original form or in an adapted form, or of a specifically tribal or clan 'wisdom' (*Sippenweisheit*). The so-called 'collections' are to a large extent original compositions by individual authors belonging to the circles of the wisdom schools, although these authors have incorporated some traditional material current in those schools. The 'collections' came to be used as part of the educational syllabus; they were not, however, composed for this purpose, but for the edification and entertainment of an educated public. In the first section, after giving his own definition of the adage (*Sprichwort*), the author divides the material into three types: *Sprichwörter*, didactic proverbs and admonitions (*Mahnworte*). Only in the case of the *Sprichwörter* is a popular origin conceivable, and even here it is improbable: with very few exceptions, the themes are no less relevant to educated people than to peasants or artisans, while in many instances a popular origin is excluded both by the theme and by the complexity of the thought. In the second section the author argues convincingly that the existence of wisdom schools in Israel must be regarded as certain, despite the lack of direct evidence. In the third section he maintains that the grammatical structure of the non-didactic proverbs was deliberately chosen as a vehicle for the expression of a belief in a cosmic 'Order' which the wise men of Israel shared with their Egyptian counterparts. This is the least convincing part of a book which, taken as a whole, is an important and stimulating contribution to the present debate on the nature of Israelite wisdom literature.

R.N.W.

*JONES, E.: *Profiles of the Prophets*. 1968. Pp. 204. (The Religious Education Press, Ltd., Oxford. Price: 15s.)

This guide to all the canonical prophets of the O.T. emphasizes the men and their message, for their contemporaries and for us today, with minimal reference to critical problems. It could be used as a textbook in the upper forms of Secondary schools and by non-specialist students in Colleges of Education.

L.A.P.

KÄHLER, M.: *Aufsätze zur Bibelfrage*. 1967. Pp. 296. (Chr. Kaiser Verlag, München. Price: DM. 14.50)

One can only applaud the reissue of these writings on the Bible by a great theologian of two generations ago which, though they are clearly dated, still seem in many ways strangely contemporary and should not be dismissed as mere echoes of outdated controversies. The first section deals with the debate about the Bible which Kähler recognized as in his time dividing Protestants from Protestants, whereas originally Protestants were ranged against Rome. The second section lays down sixteen theses which are amplified and defended in what follows. Kähler insists that the Bible still offers more than research material for scholars; it is vital for the life of the Church, mediating God's revelation of himself in his relationship to men in history and finally in Christ whose work it continues. It guards the Church against unhistorical mysticism and 'enthusiasm', while biblical criticism protects her against a mechanical reliance on the letter of Scripture. Verbal inspiration is firmly rejected and that by a positive theologian for whom the Bible is essential as the medium of the Word of God and can be replaced by no other literature. In the third section Kähler attempts at considerable length a sketch of the history of the part played by the Bible throughout the history of the Church, not only at the great turning-points, e.g. at the time of the Reformation, but in quiet ways in maintaining and controlling the faith of simple Christians. The spread of Christianity has to be looked at with reference to the part played in it by the Scriptures. There is much detail here which deserves careful study.

N.W.P.

KOCH, K.: *Was ist Formgeschichte? Neue Wege der Bibelexegese*. 2nd fully revised edition. 1967. Pp. xiii, 287. (Neukirchener Verlag des Erziehungs-vereins, Neukirchen-Vluyn. Price: DM. 24.80 (bound); DM. 19.80 (paper)). (Published also 1968 as a Lizenzausgabe for the German Democratic Republic, by the Evangelische Verlagsanstalt, Berlin)

A mere two years after its first publication (see *B.L.* 1965, p. 35; *Decade*, p. 587), the author has been able to produce a revised edition of his outstanding textbook on form criticism. The main argument of the book remains unchanged, but the examples discussed have been in some places substantially modified, in particular in providing a fresh discussion of aspects of the beatitudes and of the decalogue. This second edition has also appeared in identical form as a students' edition for use in the German Democratic Republic and in this way comes to be generally available to scholars and theological students in the countries of the east European area. Those who live in that area and who have no access to so many of the works which are published in the west owe a debt of gratitude for this to both author and publishers.

M.B./P.R.A.

KOCH, K.: *The Book of Books: The Growth of the Bible*. 1968. Pp. 192. (S.C.M. Press, London. Price: 10s. 6d.)

This is a translation of *Das Buch der Bücher, Die Entstehungsgeschichte der Bibel*. Attractively written and felicitiously translated, it describes in chronological sequence the growth of biblical literature beginning with the Court History of David. The O.T. section is particularly well done, not least the poetic material 'The Poetry of Home and Sanctuary'. It is surprising that the chronological treatment is not applied with the same rigour to the N.T., the Synoptic Gospels and Acts coming before the Pauline corpus.

R.D.

Kosak, H.: *Wegweisung in das Alte Testament*. (Biblisches Seminar im Calwer Verlag). 1968. Pp. 234. (Calwer Verlag, Stuttgart. Price: DM. 14.50)

This is a general introduction to the O.T. intended for readers without specialized theological training. The author's aim is to communicate the religious and theological content of the O.T. in the light of recent scholarship (he is particularly indebted to Alt, Noth, and von Rad), and to indicate how it may be applied in preaching and teaching. The five main sections deal principally with (i) the ancient forms of historical confession in the O.T., (ii) the main collections of historical traditions, (iii) prophecy, (iv) cultic life and cultic writings (Psalms and Megilloth), and (v) hermeneutical questions (the Canon and the relation of the two Testaments, the modern debate about typology, etc., exegesis and exposition). Theological considerations predominate over literary analysis and historical background; but the results of both literary and form criticism are drawn upon. Arrangement and presentation are skilfully executed; and the book will doubtless stimulate interest and provide valuable help for those for whom it is intended.

G.W.A.

Long, B. O.: *The Problem of Etiological Narrative in the Old Testament*. (Beihefte zur Zeitschrift für die alttestamentliche Wissenschaft, 108). 1968. Pp. 94. (Alfred Töpelmann, Berlin. Price: DM. 24)

This Yale doctoral thesis seeks by means of a careful analysis of forms to evaluate the function of etiological elements in the formation of historical narratives. The first section deals with etymological etiologies, and follows J. Fichtner in isolating two basic formulations (Forms I and II). In neither case does the etymology provide a focal point for extensive traditions, so Long concludes that it is somewhat misleading to speak of etymological etiological narrative.

The second section concerns significative etiologies, and examines various formulations in the P narrative materials which relate the emergence of signs (*'ōtōt*) and the question and answer formulations which are used to explain cultic matters. Overall Long concludes that etiologies did not possess the power to create extensive narratives and belong rather to briefer anecdotal traditions. This is a thorough piece of work with much important detailed discussion of relevant passages.

R.E.C.

Lutz, H.-M.: *Jahwe, Jerusalem und die Völker. Zur Vorgeschichte von Sach. 12, 1–8 und 14, 1–5*. (Wissenschaftliche Monographien zum Alten und Neuen Testament, 27). 1968. Pp. 237. (Neukirchener Verlag des Erziehungsvereins. Price: DM. 29.80)

The problem tackled in this distinguished dissertation is the relationship between chapters 12 and 14 of Zechariah, in some respects close in thought and purpose, in others distinct and opposed. The answer is sought by means of a comprehensive traditio-historical investigation, which serves to discover three motifs in the various relevant passages in prophecy and psalms. The oldest is the conflict between the nations and the city of God, going back, it is argued, to the pre-Israelite Jerusalem cult. (In this respect it is a pity that the work of A. R. Johnson is ignored.) This motif is represented in various psalms and in Zech. 12. The other motifs, which in various ways were linked together, are the conflict of Yahweh with the nations, and the conflict of Yahweh with Israel, which is understood as a prophetic reversal of the tradition of the wars of Yahweh, wherein it finds its origin. There is a line of development from Isa. 29, through Ezek. 38–9 to Zech. 14. Thus these chapters are not variants of a single tradition, but expressions of controversial viewpoints in the post-exilic Jewish community. The conclusions are closely related to O. Plöger's *Theocracy and Eschatology* (see review on p. 49).

D.R.J.

MALY, E. H.: *Prophets of Salvation*. 1967. Pp. 191. (Burns and Oates, London; Herder and Herder, New York. Price: 42s.; $4.50)

This popular presentation of the prophets from Nathan to Malachi grew out of a series of articles to Hi-Time Magazine. The author, an American Roman Catholic scholar, is at home in the critical orthodoxies of twenty years ago, and repeatedly one dissents from the underlying critical assumptions. But the power of his narrative is undeniable. This must be as readable an introduction to the prophets for the ordinary reader as it is possible to find. Perhaps the author would consider, in a new edition, devoting his interpretative skill also to the explanation of the strange unit structure of the prophetic books. The personalities live but their books remain puzzling.

D.R.J.

NIELSEN, E.: *The Ten Commandments in New Perspective. A traditio-historical approach.* (Studies in Biblical Theology. Second Series, 7). 1968. Pp. x, 162. (S.C.M. Press Ltd., London. Price: 21s.)

The Danish original of this work and the German version were reviewed in the *Book List* 1966, p. 38 (*Decade*, p. 658). The English translation, made from the German by D. J. Bourke, is greatly to be welcomed. It has indexes of subjects, authors, and biblical references.

J.A.E.

VAN OEVEREN, B.: *De Vrijsteden in het Oude Testament*. 1968. Pp. 284. (J. H. Kok, Kampen. Price: Fl. 14.75)

This doctoral dissertation, presented at the Free University of Amsterdam, is a study of the cities of refuge and related ideas. After an investigation of similar institutions and ideas outside Israel, the relevant O.T. passages are discussed, and it is argued that the setting apart of the cities goes back to Moses and Joshua. Finally, the significance of the institution and its relation to the New Testament are examined. The book has a map, a German summary, a bibliography, and indexes of authors' names and of biblical references.

J.A.E.

OIKONOMOU, E. B.: *Peirasmoi en te Palaia Diatheke*. 1965. Pp. viii, 152. (Bibliotheke tes en Athenais Philekpaideutikes Hetaireias, Athens)

The author, a former pupil of B. Vellas and K. Elliger, tackles his chosen theme, 'Temptations in the O.T.', from three angles: first, by a study of the Hebrew and Greek (LXX) words used to express various forms of testing; second, by an exegetical examination of some outstanding O.T. narratives of testing; third, by subjecting these narratives to form-critical analysis. God's testing Abraham (Gen. 22), the Israelites' putting God to the test (Num. 14) and the trial of Job receive special attention. An appendix deals with N.T. echoes of O.T. 'temptations', especially in the accounts of the temptation of Jesus in the wilderness.

F.F.B.

POULSSEN, N.: *König und Tempel im Glaubenszeugnis des Alten Testaments.*
(Stuttgarter Biblische Monographien, 3). 1967. Pp. 220. (Verlag
Katholisches Bibelwerk, Stuttgart. Price: DM. 32)

Recent study of both Israel's kingship and its temple has stressed the
close connection between the two, especially in the early period. This
insight is here examined and interpreted in a very careful and balanced
study, which is made all the more useful by detailed annotation.
Poulssen sees four main groups of interpretation, of which the first
is the early court tradition in which the Davidic dynasty and the
Jerusalem temple were given a close ideological relationship. This
stood in tension with the early theocratic faith of the tribal league.
The Deuteronomic movement sought to alleviate this tension by
setting both the kingship and the temple within the Mosaic tradition.
The later priestly view, found in the Priestly Document, Ezekiel,
Haggai and Zechariah, re-asserted the pre-eminence of the priesthood
and temple at the expense of the kingship. Finally the Chronicler
attempted a further re-evaluation in terms of a theocracy in which
the Davidic-messianic kingship played a prominent part. There is
much careful exegesis, although the main conclusions offer little
that is new.   R.E.C.

POWER, J.: *Set My Exiles Free. Introducing the Old Testament.* (Logos
Books). 1967. Pp. 195. (Gill and Son, Dublin and Sydney. Price: 18s.)

Father Power shows in this book a sensitiveness to the needs of the
faithful as they begin to read the O.T. Its theme is that of Salvation
History, of which the O.T. is Stage 1. About one half of the book is
given to the story from Abraham to Josiah, very briefly after Solomon.
The second half contains chapters on the Prophets, the formation of
the O.T., the Exile, the Psalter and the last 400 years. Inevitably in a
book of this kind statements are made which one would question,
e.g. Moses had mathematical knowledge and skill in design and
architecture derived from an Egyptian education; the prophets wrote
their books; Isaiah was a Foreign Secretary to kings; the Psalter is
an expansion of a nucleus of ceremonial hymns that have David for
their author. A misprint on p. 110 refers to Deutero-Isaiah as
Chapters 40–5. But it is an attractive book and will encourage the
reading of the O.T.   A.S.H.

VON RAD, G.: *The Message of the Prophets.* Translated by D. M. G.
Stalker. 1968. Pp. 289. (S.C.M. Press. Price: 30s.)

In 1967 von Rad published as a separate paperback the easily
detachable section on Prophecy from his *Theologie des Alten
Testaments.* (See *B.L.* 1966, p. 52, *Decade*, p. 672 and *B.L.* 1961,
pp. 51 f., *Decade*, p. 289.) He took the opportunity to revise it here and
there, particularly to write a new, short chapter on Apocalyptic, to
remove learned footnotes and to simplify technical expressions. It is
this edition which has been attractively published in the translation
of D. M. G. Stalker, and in this form, an already well-known and
influential work should reach a new range of English readers.

                                                              D.R.J.

RAHTJEN, B. D.: *Biblical Truth and Modern Man*. 1968. Pp. 143. (Abingdon Press, Nashville and New York. Price: $1.75)

This is a helpful layman's guide to understanding the Bible in an age of science, popular in style and colloquial in language and dealing with problems of interpretation in relation to science, history and faith.   L.A.P.

RENDTORFF, R.: *Studien zur Geschichte des Opfers im Alten Israel*. (Wissenschaftliche Monographien zum Alten und Neuen Testament, 24). 1967. Pp. xii, 277. (Neukirchener Verlag, Neukirchen-Vluyn. Price: DM. 29.80, or bound 34.80)

The author of this very thorough study, which is dedicated to Professor von Rad, does not essay a complete examination of the Israelite cultus or the origins of the various types of sacrifice. He first offers a careful study of the priestly texts of the O.T. dealing with sacrifice, including the Priestly Code, the Holiness Code, and Ezek. 40–8, and then of the remaining Old Testament texts, including legal passages, Pentateuchal narratives, the Deuteronomic corpus, the Prophets, the Psalms and the Wisdom Literature, and the Chronicler's Work. He then turns to the separate study of the forms and meaning of the varieties of sacrifice: '*ôlāh*, *zebaḥ* and *šᵉlāmîm*, *minḥāh* and *nesek*, *ḥaṭṭā't* and '*āšām*. The whole constitutes an important and valuable monograph.   H.H.R.

*RHYMER, J.: *The Beginnings of a People. A Way through the Old Testament. The Pentateuch*. 1967. Pp. xix, 168. (Sheed and Ward, London; Pflaum Press, Dayton, Ohio. Price: 12s. 6d.; $4.75)

*RHYMER, J.: *The Covenant and the Kingdom. A Way through the Old Testament. 2. The Kingdom*. 1968. Pp. xii, 150. (Sheed and Ward, London. Price: 15s.)

*RHYMER, J.: *The Prophets and the Law*. 1964. Pp. x, 194. (Sheed and Ward, London. Price: 12s. 6d.)

These are the first three volumes of a five volume introduction to the reading of the O.T. addressed to the general reader rather than the student. This is a generally reliable work, non-technical, but based on a thorough study of the relevant literature; the narrative is simple and often vivid and the author has a gift of lucid exposition. The frequent quotations are from the R.S.V. in the first two volumes and from the Jerusalem Bible in the third.   L.A.P.

ROBERT, A. and FEUILLET, A. (ed.): *Introduction to the Old Testament*. Translated from the 2nd French edition by a panel of translators. 1968. Pp. 650, 3 maps. (Desclée, New York. Price: $9.95)

The original French edition of this work was published in 1957 (*B.L.* 1958, p. 29; *Decade*, p. 105) as the first volume of a two volume introduction to the whole Bible, and including in the first volume a large section of general introduction. The English version, representing the most recent French edition, with updated bibliography and particularly the addition of items of use to English readers, omits the general introduction which is to be published separately. It differs from most works of its kind by including (pp. 3–64) an outline of the historical framework (E. Cavaignac and P. Grelot). The main sections of the canon are covered in turn: Torah (H. Cazelles), Former Prophets (J. Delorme), Latter Prophets, arranged chronologically

(A. Gelin), Psalms (P. Auvray), the other Writings (H. Lusseau).
The book naturally includes also the Deuterocanonical Books
(A. Lefèvre), and concludes with a historical survey of the evolution
of the literature and the formation of the O.T. (P. Grelot). There is
much on content and interpretation; there are important and
illuminating quotations from Roman Catholic pronouncements on
biblical interpretation. Very useful bibliographies (and footnotes)
provide the reader with a wide selection of works, both Catholic and
non-Catholic. This is a very welcome addition to the literature
available for the English reader.   P.R.A.

DE ROBERT, P.: *Le Berger d'Israel.* Pp. 100. 1968. (Delachaux and
Niestlé, Paris. Price: Sw.Fr. 9.50)

The sub-title to this work is *Essai sur le thème pastoral dans l'Ancien
Testament*, the author being a young agriculturalist who spent two
years in Algeria devoted to afforestation, and is now a theological
student in the Paris Protestant faculty. In the six chapters of his
thesis the author discusses the figure of the shepherd in the Ancient
East, pastoral life in the Bible and the vocabulary pertaining to it,
and then the evidence to be discussed in Israel's earliest period,
during the period of the monarchy, in the exilic period, and during
the years after the return from exile. He notes that the image of the
shepherd is not prominent in the wisdom literature, the only noteworthy references being to Eccl. 12:11 and Sirach 18:13. The thesis
shows every sign of wide and careful reading.   J.M.T.B.

SCHMID, H.: *Mose. Überlieferung und Geschichte.* (Beihefte zur Zeitschrift
für die alttestamentliche Wissenschaft, 110). 1968. Pp. 114. (Verlag
Alfred Töpelmann, Berlin. Price: DM. 32)

Schmid seeks to reconstruct the historical achievement of Moses by
using traditio-historical method along the lines laid down by M.
Noth. The conclusions reached are that Moses was linked with the
volcanic Mount Sinai in Midianite territory in N.W. Arabia, although
he was, as his name shows, of part Egyptian origin. He encouraged
the flight of a group of Hebrew slaves from Egypt, and acted as their
leader at the deliverance of the Sea of Reeds. Subsequently this Moses
group united with a Levitical-Aaronid group at Kadesh, where Moses
fostered the penetration of the cult of Yahweh of Sinai to the larger
community, who may have become united to the original Moses
group by covenant. From here Moses led the community into the
territory of Kadesh where he died. The reconstruction is careful,
well-documented and worth scholarly consideration, although the
author readily admits that much is conjectural. With so much
uncertainty and disagreement about the historical basis of many
major events in the tradition it is clear that until these problems are
resolved any attempt to define the work of Moses must be highly
provisional.   R.E.C.

SCHMIDT, W.: *Bibel im Kreuzverhör. Geschichte und Bedeutung der
historisch-kritischen Forschung mit Textanalysen von Herbert Donner,
Hans-Joachim Birkner und Hans Grass.* 1968. Pp. 143. (Verlagshaus
Gerd Mohn, Gütersloh. Price: DM. 9.80)

The writers of three of the chapters of this book are concerned with
the fact that the modern historical-critical approach to biblical
interpretation is not being adequately conveyed to the general public
through media which reach them. Therefore, these three scholars,

H. Donner, H.-J. Birkner and H. Grass, tried to supply this need on radio in respect of the Creation narratives of the O.T. and the Christmas and Easter narratives of the N.T. These broadcast talks are now published in this book, and another scholar, W. Schmidt, has written an introduction whose subject serves as the title of the book. Only the chapters by Schmidt and Donner need be mentioned here. The latter in his chapter distinguishes the two creation narratives in respect of form, literary style, content, and theological ideas, and then examines each narrative in detail in itself and against its cultural background. The subject is dealt with in a manner eminently suitable for the purpose for which it was intended.

The Introduction, on the other hand, deals with biblical interpretation from the time of Luther onwards, to show that, when we have to acknowledge that the books of the Bible bear the marks of time and place as well as of inevitable human finitude, we cannot regard the Bible as a whole simply as a textbook for life and faith. Rather are we ourselves to some degree in the same situation as the early Christians before they had confessional statements, written documents and constituted episcopal authority. This introduction is well-written and deals succinctly with the important aspects of the subject in hand, but it will prove to be stiff reading for the ordinary layman and compressed meat for his digestion.   J.M.

SCHOFIELD, J. N.: *Law, Prophets, and Writings. The Religion of the Books of the Old Testament.* 1969. Pp. xiv, 386. (S.P.C.K., London. Price: 50s.)

By a happy coincidence this book was published on the day on which the author was installed as President of the S.O.T.S. In his exposition of O.T. religion, he discards the developmental, patternist, and *heilsgeschichtlich* approaches and regards historical reconstruction as necessarily hypothetical and systematic exposition as misleading because abstract. His chosen method is 'to take the final form of the Hebrew O.T. as the basis of our study, and consider the religion as it is presented by the final editors'. The three main parts of the Hebrew Canon are taken in turn and examined, book by book and passage by passage. Thus the book is a running commentary on the entire O.T., with special emphasis on its religious content and attempting to elucidate such unity as it in fact displays. It has the merit that it treats of the O.T. in the form in which it lies before the reader, yet at the same time draws on the results of scholarly study by which the books have been put into historical perspective. Its quality is such that we may hope that it will prove to be not only the harvest of Mr Schofield's long experience as a teacher but also the firstfruits of a continuing literary activity in his retirement.   G.W.A.

SCOTT, R. B. Y.: *The Relevance of the Prophets.* Revd. ed. 1968. Pp. viii, 248. (Macmillan, New York; Collier-Macmillan, London. Price: $2.45)

The original edition of this book (1944) was reviewed in *B.L.* 1946, p. 51; *Eleven Years*, p. 51. It has been revised and in part rewritten, with references given to more recent literature of a kind useful to the general readers to whom the book is directed. It is a straightforward, sensible account of the prophetic movement, not concerned with the detailed description of any one prophet, but rather with the nature and origin of prophecy, with theological and interpretative questions, and with the question of relevance. A useful book to put in the hands of the interested general reader.   P.R.A.

SELLIN, E. and FOHRER, G.: *Introduction to the Old Testament*. Trans. by David Green. 1968. Pp. 540. (Abingdon Press, Nashville and New York. Price: $9.50)

A careful translation, occasionally over-literal, of Fohrer's 1965 rewriting of Sellin's Introduction (see *B.L.* 1967, p. 36), with minor corrections by the author and additional Bibliographical notes up to 1967. It is much to be regretted that no English publisher has taken on this book.

J.V.M.S.

SNAITH, N. H.: *The Book of Job. Its Origin and Purpose*. (S.C.M. Studies in Biblical Theology, Second Series, 11). 1968. Pp. x, 116. (S.C.M. Press, London. Price: 21s.)

It is here argued that the book of Job was composed in three stages by a single author, whose primary concern was with the problem of the relation between the High God and man, which is discussed against the background of Job's sufferings. Accordingly the first edition told the traditional story of Job, and included prologue, epilogue, Job's soliloquy (3, 29–31), and the speeches of Yahweh with Job's replies. In the second edition the friends were introduced (2:11–13) and the cycles of debate (4–27) inserted in order to ask why Job suffered so much, the poem on wisdom being included as offering (28:28) the practical advice to fear God and depart from evil. This advice is reinforced (37:24) in the Elihu speeches which, appearing in the final edition, are considered to present some of the most original material to be found in the book (e.g. 33:19–30) as well as the now aged author's revolt against orthodoxy. Appendices respectively on proposed reconstructions of 24–7 and 29–31 and on the so-called Aramaisms discerned in the book add to the usefulness of this fresh and thought-provoking study.

E.T.R.

SOGGIN, J. A.: *Das Königtum in Israel: Ursprünge, Spannungen, Entwicklung*. (Beihefte zur Zeitschrift für die Alttestamentliche Wissenschaft, 104). 1967. Pp. x, 167. (Verlag Alfred Töpelmann, Berlin. Price: DM. 36)

A work on the Israelite monarchy, based on the evidence of the O.T. historical books — as opposed to that of the Psalter, which has so far held the predominant place in the discussion — and giving an overall picture of the vast number of studies on the subject, is long overdue. To that extent, this book is to be welcomed, not least for its extensive bibliographical references, although, like many Continental scholars, the author is not as well acquainted as he might be with material in English. However, this is not yet the definitive study for which we have been waiting. Partly, this is the result of the author's conception of the scope of his investigation. In his preface, he tells us that he is concerned only incidentally with the idea of 'sacral kingship' and the sub-title of the book is 'origins, tensions and development'. Yet the problem of sacral kingship is central to at least the two latter concerns, and in fact the author is forced to mention it frequently. But he never really comes to grips with it, and this leads to some serious omissions in his whole treatment. So, e.g. he says very little about the vital significance of Jerusalem in the polity of David's kingdom, and there is no mention at all of Zadok, which results in a very inadequate account of what was involved in the struggle for the throne at the end of David's life. Again, terms such as 'state', 'democracy' or 'bureaucracy' are regularly used without sufficient consideration of their true applicability to the conditions of pre-exilic Israel. Nevertheless, it must be recognized that this is in many ways a pioneer study and, as such, it contains many stimulating suggestions and marks a genuine advance in the continuing discussion of Israelite kingship.   J.R.P.

STECK, O. H.: *Überlieferung und Zeitgeschichte in den Elia-Erzählungen.* (Wissenschaftliche Monographien zum Alten und Neuen Testament, 26). 1968. Pp. 160. (Neukirchener Verlag des Erziehungsvereins. Neukirchen-Vluyn. Price: DM. 22.80 (cloth); 20.80 (paper))

The author provides a detailed traditio-historical study of the Elijah narratives, showing how the various elements of the tradition reflect contemporary historical events between Ahab's reign and the rebellion led by Jehu. Jezebel became queen-mother after the death of Ahab, and her presence in the Naboth narrative is a retrospective interpretation reflecting this later situation. Steck claims that in Ahab's reign she would have had little chance to interfere in public affairs. Similarly Elijah's killing of the prophets of Baal is Jehu's action ascribed to Elijah. The linking of Jehu's revolt with the prophecies of Elijah was pre-Deuteronomic in its origin, and represents the action of military circles who were responsible for II Kings 9 f. taking up the traditions of earlier prophetic circles, whose work is shown in I Kings 21. The argument succeeds in making good historical sense out of difficult materials, and is well documented, although, surprisingly, the full bibliography makes no mention of John Gray's commentary on the Books of Kings.   R.E.C.

STRUYS, T.: *Ziekte en Genezing in het Oude Testament.* 1968. Pp. 466. (J. H. Kok N.V., Kampen. Price: Fl. 28.25)

This doctoral dissertation at the Free University of Amsterdam is a systematic and detailed study of the O.T. passages concerned with sickness and healing, of the terms used in them, and of related subjects, such as the influence of psychical or spiritual experiences on the body, and the relationship of sickness to magic and demons in the thought of Israelites and other peoples of the ancient Near East; there are also discussions of the figurative use of such language, and of the place of sickness and healing in the relations between God and his people. The book has a bibliography of two pages, an index of biblical references, and an English summary. Dr Struys has performed a useful service by collecting and discussing material on the subject, although his work would have been more satisfactory if he had shown greater awareness of the contributions made by scholars in the present century to the understanding of Hebrew words in the light of other Semitic languages.   J.A.E.

VAN UCHELEN, N. A.: *Abraham de Hebreeër.* (Studia Semitica Neerlandica, 5). 1964. Pp. vi, 121. (Van Gorcum and Comp. N.V., Assen. Price: Fl. 18.80)

This monograph is a study of the word 'Hebrew' in Genesis 14:13 in the light of other verses in the O.T. and of extra-biblical references to the *Habiru* and '*pr.w.* It is argued that the word used of Abram is not a gentilic, and that it closely resembles the non-Israelite terms in being applied to someone who is a warrior. The book has a bibliography, and an English summary.   J.A.E.

WEIPPERT, M.: *Die Landnahme der israelitischen Stämme in der neueren wissenschaftlichen Diskussion.* (Forschungen zur Religion und Literatur des Alten und Neuen Testaments, 92). 1967. Pp. 163, 2 maps. (Vandenhoeck und Ruprecht, Göttingen. Price: DM. 19.80)

This important and extremely well-written monograph offers an illuminating discussion of the problem of the settlement which, from the wealth of literature devoted to it in recent years, has become more and more difficult to handle. Weippert handles the literature with great expertise; he gives a clear discussion of the various approaches — in particular those of Alt and Noth, of Albright and Bright, and of Mendenhall — offering very careful and penetrating analysis of the strength and weakness of each position. He then takes up the difficult problems of *'Apiru* and Hebrews and of the various indications of nomadic peoples in the second millennium. The evaluation of archaeological and biblical material which leads up to a conclusion generally favouring the Alt/Noth approach is again rich in content and sound in judgement. The book is to be very strongly recommended. An English translation is in preparation.

P.R.A.

WESTERMANN, C.: *Der Segen in der Bibel und im Handeln der Kirche.* 1968. Pp. 118. (Chr. Kaiser Verlag, Munich. Price: DM. 9.80)

As the title indicates, the main interest of this book is in the word 'blessing'. It is maintained that 'to bless' must be treated separately from 'to save' in order to appreciate its full meaning, and attention is drawn to the theological implication of the distinction between 'the God who saves' and 'the God who blesses'. In order to demonstrate the significance and use of 'blessing', the author then undertakes a careful and comprehensive examination of the term 'to bless' in both O.T. and N.T. The material which has been assembled is of interest to students of the N.T. as well as those whose primary interest is the O.T. and they will find the study stimulating and rewarding. Of special interest to the O.T. scholar is the review of the treatment of 'blessing' in the principal works on the theology of the O.T.

E.R.R.

WHYBRAY, R. N.: *The Succession Narrative: a Study of II Samuel 9–20 and I Kings 1 and 2.* (Studies in Biblical Theology, Second Series, 9). 1968. Pp. 116. (S.C.M. Press, London. Price: 16s.)

Dr Whybray's stimulating and well-written book emphasizes the artistic qualities of the Succession Narrative, the subtlety of its characterization, and its unity as a work of art. His general conclusions that the work is a product of scribal culture from the period of the 'Solomonic enlightenment' are, in all probability, correct. It was written by a 'wise man' belonging to the circle of the court and its purpose was to establish the legitimacy of Solomon's succession and to unfold the concept of a Davidic dynasty. In the chapter where he correlates the Succession Narrative with sentences in the book of Proverbs he would seem to be in danger of overworking his thesis and his arguments do not always carry conviction. Yet there is no doubt that in the Ahithophel story and elsewhere there are evidences in the narrative of the cast of mind and style of life of the wise men.

The constructive aspects of Whybray's book, his analysis of the aesthetic merits of the Succession Narrative, the influence of Wisdom discoverable in it, the lines of connexion which he has drawn with the Egyptian political novel, are separable from his sceptical historical conclusions. It would be difficult to disprove his assertion that the narrative is novel rather than history, that it derives from invention and imagination rather than from events and encounters at court. Nor, however, is he able to demonstrate that this is so. The 'secret' character of the interviews which are described in the work is not an insuperable difficulty. Reports of what goes on at private interviews which are politically significant still leak out in more sophisticated times and it should not be too readily assumed that a historian at court would be incapable of gathering sufficiently reliable reports of such matters. Nor does the selective character of the Succession Narrative show that it is novel rather than history. It is not so easy to differentiate between historical novel and historiography. History is not so beautifully objective and certainly historians are selective and impose on their material a structure and unity which the material itself does not supply. The highly literary character of the Succession Narrative and its aesthetic finesse are not necessarily indications that it is fiction rather than historiography.   W.McK.

*WINWARD, S.: *A Guide to the Prophets.* 1968. Pp. 255. (Hodder and Stoughton, London. Price: 30s.)

Much is here packed into small compass to give a useful summary of the general conclusions accepted by scholars for the prophetic books in the O.T. Questions of date, authorship and composition are briefly handled, but the main interest is in the religious message of the prophets both for their own and for the present day.   R.D.

WISEMAN, P. J.: *Die Entstehung der Genesis* (*Das 1. Buch der Bibel im Licht der archäologischen Forschung*). 2nd Edition. 1968. Pp. 150. (R. Brockhaus Verlag, Wuppertal. Price: DM. 9.80)

This is a translation by E. Rosenbauer of the author's *New Discoveries about Genesis* (Marshall, Morgan and Scott, 1936), with a foreword by his son Professor D. J. Wiseman. The distinctive thesis is that the phrase: 'This is the generation of . . . ' refers to clay tablets written by, or in the possession of, the named person, containing what precedes. This conclusion is based on similar formulae in cuneiform documents, and it is therefore supposed that Moses gathered the material derived in the main from contemporary witnesses.

A.S.H.

LAW, RELIGION AND THEOLOGY

ALBRIGHT, W. F.: *Yahweh and the Gods of Canaan.* (School of Oriental and African Studies, University of London. Jordan Lectures in Comparative Religion, VII). 1968. Pp. xiv, 250. (University of London, Athlone Press, London. Price: 50s.)

This book, which is based on the Jordan Lectures for 1965, not only examines, as its title suggests, Canaanite religion and Israelite faith in Yahweh and the conflict between them, but also discusses the patriarchal stories, and the place of verse and prose in early Israelite tradition. As in Professor Albright's other writings, a wealth of learning in oriental subjects, especially archaeology, is brought together, and many fresh suggestions are made about particular biblical passages and about O.T. traditions in general. The book makes interesting and instructive reading and, even when its suggestions are not convincing, they are always stimulating. There are indexes of subjects, authors, and biblical references.   J.A.E.

*BELL, G. F.: *Seven Old Testament Figures*. 1968. Pp. 125. (Geoffrey Bles, London. Price: 6s.)

This paperback, with a foreword by the Bishop of London, is focused upon the figures of Abraham, Jacob, Moses, David, Amos, Isaiah and the writer of the book of Jonah. There is one short chapter on each except Moses, who is allotted two. The author, formerly Headmaster of Highgate School, sketches in the historical background so that the book becomes a limited but reliable guide to important periods in the life of Israel. In the process O.T. narrative and teaching are freshly presented.   G.F.

CHESNUT, J. S.: *The Old Testament Understanding of God*. 1968. Pp. 192. (Westminster Press, Philadelphia. Price: $2.45)

Students in particular will be grateful for this brief, yet commendably comprehensive, discussion of Hebrew thinking about God as represented in the O.T. The approach is basically topical-chronological, beginning with 'God in Early Hebrew Thought', i.e. pre-Mosaic, and ending with 'God in Wisdom and Poetry'. A concluding chapter indicates the author's view of the covenant as the bridge linking the O.T. and the N.T. The chronological treatment sometimes leads to difficulties, particularly in the early section where the criteria used to distinguish the genuinely early from later overworking of the material are not always clear.   R.D.

DENTAN, R. C.: *The Knowledge of God in Ancient Israel*. 1968. Pp. xii, 278. (The Seabury Press, New York. Price: $7.50)

This is a book of fine quality, marked by depth of understanding and written with grace and clarity. It is in effect an O.T. theology, though the writer would disclaim the title for his work. He admits, however, that the O.T. doctrine of God with which it deals is the heart of the subject and he approaches it by a discussion of the meaning of the *da'ath 'Elōhîm*, making it clear that this implies a response to God which includes emotion and will, in addition to knowledge. He then goes on to a consideration of God's dealings with Israel in its classic past as mirrored in the Hexateuch and leading up to the establishment of the monarchy, of his dealings with Israel in the present as witnessed to by priest, prophet and wise man, and of his dealings with Israel in the future (eschatology). There are chapters on the being and character of God and digressions on God and the natural world and on the names of God. The author is appreciative of the great works on O.T. theology by Eichrodt and von Rad but joins issue with the former for the degree of emphasis he lays on the Covenant and with the latter for his scepticism on the possibility of a unified theology of the O.T. This is a book which will prove to be one of the best introductions to O.T. thought for beginners and will serve the needs of maturer students as well.   N.W.P.

FOHRER, G.: *Elia.* (Abhandlungen zur Theologie des Alten und Neuen Testaments, 53). 2nd ed. 1968. Pp. 104. (Zwingli Verlag, Zurich. Price: Sw.Fr. 16)

The first edition of this study was published in 1957 (*B.L.* 1958, p. 26; *Decade*, p. 102). This new and expanded edition maintains the pattern of the first but brings it up to date with new references. As an assessment of the historicity and significance of Elijah, it is a study of considerable importance and usefulness. P.R.A.

FOHRER, G.: *Die symbolischen Handlungen der Propheten.* (Abhandlungen zur Theologie des Alten und Neuen Testaments, 54). 2nd ed. 1968. Pp. 126. (Zwingli Verlag, Zurich. Price: Sw.Fr. 18)

The original edition of this study, published in 1953, was reviewed in *B.L.* 1954, p. 61; *Eleven Years*, p. 598. It has been revised and brought up to date, though essentially the same pattern is followed as in the original form. The final chapter, which touches on a variety of problems in the interpretation of prophecy, is particularly useful for the appreciation of the place of the prophets within a tradition, and of the creative part which they play. P.R.A.

GELIN, A. (ed.): *Son and Saviour, The Divinity of Jesus Christ in the Scriptures.* 1965. Pp. xiv, 159. (Chapman, London. Price: 15s.)

This is by no means a new work. It appeared in French in 1953, the English translation dates from 1960, and a revised edition is here reprinted from 1962. It is a simple and readable account of the evidence for Christ's divinity, and all the authors are well-known French scholars. The late Abbé A. Gelin writes the introduction and has an essay on 'The Expectation of God in the Old Testament' as his chief contribution. This is the only section directly concerned with the O.T., the remainder of the book being devoted to N.T. matters. An index, or at least a list of biblical passages discussed, would have much increased the usefulness of the book. J.M.T.B.

GELIN, A.: *The Concept of Man in the Bible.* Translated by David M. Murphy. 1968. Pp. 165. (Chapman, London. Price: 25s.)

This book of Fr. Gelin's was published originally in French in 1962 (Ligel, Paris, not noted in the *Book List*), two years after the writer's death. The subject is treated in a way which is descriptive and expository rather than critically analytical. The style of writing is clear and uninvolved and the plan of the book is well-chosen. Fr. Gelin examines first of all man's nature, then man in society, as in marriage, in covenant relationship and in human society in general. That leads to a consideration of man in a state of tension or protest, of man with a sense of vocation, holding a faith and bearing witness to it, upheld by prayer and yet aware of failure, and of the New Man by the grace of God.

As an outline of the essential elements of its subject, this book is good; but it does not have room for dealing with problems of interpretation such as the meaning of the Hebrew verb *qûm* in specific passages which Fr. Gelin quotes or, as when he says that 'God's call is adapted to an individual's psychological framework and makes allowance for it'. J.M.

JACOB. E.: *Théologie de l'Ancien Testament.* Second, revised ed. 1968. Pp. xiii, 287. (Delachaux et Niestlé, Neuchâtel. Price: Sw.Fr. 18)

The first edition of this valuable study was published in 1955 (*B.L.* 1956, p. 46; *Eleven Years*, p. 753) and translated into English in 1958 (*B.L.* 1959, p. 29; *Decade*, p. 165). This second edition is explained by the author in a short preface; it is the same work, justified in its original form by the consideration of the assumptions upon which it is built. In a short discussion of the criticisms offered of it, and with more extended reference to the theology of the O.T. as conceived by G. von Rad, Professor Jacob points to the essential bases in historical, literary and religious study, without which an adequate appraisal of the presence and action of God, as set out in the O.T., cannot be undertaken. The preface is annotated with brief reference to the major works which have appeared in the period since the first edition.

If one might have wished for a new work, granted the knowledge that Professor Jacob brings careful and imaginative scholarship to bear on every matter to which he devotes his attention, one may sympathise with his awareness that nothing less than a complete re-writing would then suffice. Perhaps one might have hoped that the bibliographical notes at the head of each section could have been amplified and updated.   P.R.A.

MAERTENS, T.: *A Feast in Honour of Yahweh.* Translated by K. Sullivan. 1967. Pp. 246. (Geoffrey Chapman Ltd., London. Price: 25s.)

The original French edition of this book was reviewed in *B.L.* 1962, p. 50; *Decade*, p. 360. Its gathering of information about the festivals of O.T. religion and its correlation of this with Christian developments in worship make it a very valuable and stimulating study which it is good to see in English.   P.R.A.

PATAI, R.: *Man and Temple in Ancient Jewish Myth and Ritual.* 2nd Edition. 1967. Pp. 248. (Ktav Publishing House, Inc., New York. Price: $5.95)

The first edition of this book appeared in 1947 (*B.L.* 1948, p. 47; *Eleven Years*, p. 157). There is a new introduction outlining the history of the author's research and a postscript giving further notes on the main thesis concerning the mythological significance of the Jerusalem temple and its rituals. The main text is substantially unaltered.   R.E.C.

PATAI, R.: *The Hebrew Goddess.* 1967. Pp. 349. (Ktav Publishing House, Inc., New York. Price: $8.95)

According to the blurb, Dr Patai's central thesis 'is nothing less than revolutionary: it propounds that Hebrew and Jewish religion, far from being a consistently monotheistic faith, was, in many periods and in its popular manifestation, tinged with polytheism, and, what is even more remarkable, centred on the veneration of a goddess'. Much of what Dr. Patai has to say is certainly not revolutionary; perhaps he exaggerates a little the importance of the goddess, but this failing is an almost inevitable concomitant of any attempt to establish a thesis by selecting some facts and neglecting other, less welcome, data.

He pursues his goddess — Asherah, Astarte, Anath — through the O.T., Canaanite sources (he does not appear to be at home in Ugaritic and does not mention Cassuto's *Goddess Anath* in his bibliography), Rabbinic and Kabbalistic literature — even down to the Falasha Sabbath. There is much of interest and importance in Dr Patai's book, and the reviewer has derived much instruction from it. But the wide sweeps and inter-culture comparisons almost inevitably produce their casualties in errors of more or less trivial facts and in a somewhat cavalier treatment of details: thus Dr R. D. Barnett is described (p. 13) as 'Keeper of the British Museum', Geez is said to be (p. 253) 'the old Falasha language', and the role of the Queen of Sheba is assessed without reference to the very relevant version in the *Targum Sheni* to Esther.   E.U.

PLÖGER, O.: *Theocracy and Eschatology*. Translated by S. Rudman. 1968. Pp. viii, 123. (Basil Blackwell, Oxford. Price: 21s.)

This is a translation of the second edition (1962, virtually unaltered from the first, see *B.L.* 1964, p. 51; *Decade*, p. 519) of a work which originally appeared in 1959. It makes an important contribution to the understanding of the rise of apocalyptic eschatology in Israel. The reasons for Seleucid policy towards the Jews are carefully discussed and also the part played by the Ḥasidim both at the beginning of the Maccabaean revolt and after the victory of Judas. It is argued that the Book of Daniel is the work of someone connected with the Ḥasidim who had an eschatological outlook in tension with the more or less static theocratical views of the Jerusalem establishment. Incidentally it is suggested that it was men with this outlook who formed the prophetic Canon. An elaborate attempt is made to trace this eschatological development in earlier extant prophetical oracles, viz. the Isaiah Apocalypse, Isaiah 24–7, Zechariah 12–14 and Joel 3–4 — speculative but fascinating. Together with the author's commentary on the book of Daniel this volume represents an important contribution to Daniel research and does much to illuminate the obscure two centuries that followed the establishment of Judaism by Ezra and Nehemiah.   N.W.P.

PREUSS, H. D.: *Jahweglaube und Zukunftserwartung*. (Beiträge zur Wissenschaft vom Alten und Neuen Testament v:7 (87)). 1968. Pp. 256. (W. Kohlhammer Verlag, Stuttgart. Price: DM. 36)

Preuss attempts a thorough re-examination and re-evaluation of O.T. eschatology, and argues that it is a vital structural element in the whole O.T. faith in God. Eschatology arises when faith in Yahweh is applied to the future, so that this future is conceived in terms of a divine intervention in history. Preuss therefore carries Israel's future hope back to the earliest stage of its faith, and relates it to the exodus and Sinai traditions. The relationship between God and Israel has a historical perspective which looks to the future, and points to some kind of fulfilment of this relationship. Both the patriarchal and Davidic traditions also attest this future expectation, so that there is a groundwork of hope which permeates all O.T. faith. The prophets introduced into this hope a radical awareness of judgement, but they were the heirs rather than the creators of Israel's eschatology. Preuss sees a marked continuity of eschatological hope in the O.T., deriving from the events at the exodus and at Sinai and embracing both prophecy and apocalyptic. Although this emphasis upon the continuity of eschatological hope seems rather over-pressed, with too great a desire to present a uniform doctrinal development, the volume amply repays careful study, and deals competently with divergent views.

R.E.C.

RENCKENS, H.: *The Religion of Israel*. 1967. Pp. 369. (Sheed and Ward, London. Price: 37s. 6d.)

This survey of the religion of Israel was first published in 1962, *De Godsdienst van Israel* (not noted in the *Book List*). An introductory chapter 'The Mystery of Israel' discusses problems of methodology and indicates the chief concern of the book, the question of authenticity in Israel's religion and its relevance for present-day believers. The material is handled in successive historical phases, most emphasis being placed on the early seminal period. The Patriarchs receive longer treatment than post-exilic Judaism. There is much valuable material, notably in chapters on 'The God of Israel' and 'The Worship of Israel', but it is remarkable that in such a book no reference is made to Job or Ecclesiastes, and the Psalms receive only passing mention. An extensive bibliographical survey is of value up to the date of the Dutch original.

R.D.

RENDTORFF, R.: *Men of the Old Testament*. Translated by Frank Clarke. 1968. Pp. 156 inc. a chronological table. (S.C.M. Press, London. Price: 15s.)

This is the English translation of *Väter, Könige, Propheten: Gestalten des Alten Testaments* noted in *B.L.* 1968, p. 54. It approaches the history of Israel through the portraits of the great personalities of the Old Testament and sees these portraits as the product of community tradition. It is clearly and attractively written.

J.R.

RINGGREN, H.: *Israels Religion*. 1965. Pp. vii, 238. (Scandinavian University Books: Svenska Bokförlaget, Bonniers, Stockholm. Price: S.Kr. 25)

An abridgement in Swedish of the author's *Israelitische Religion* (cf. *B.L.* 1964, p. 64; *Decade*, p. 532; English translation *B.L.* 1967, p. 42), for the use of university students.

J.V.M.S.

SCHARBERT, J.: *Prolegomena eines Alttestamentlers zur Erbsündenlehre* (Quaestiones Disputatae, 37). 1968. Pp. 128. (Herder, Freiburg. Price: 30s.)

The common opinion that Gen. 3 says nothing about an 'inherited' sin is, according to Scharbert, superficial. Early Israelite thought was based on the clan and emphasized its solidarity; later this was replaced by a more national way of thinking; later again there was a revival of the older conception, illustrated by the interest in genealogies. In each of these stages the old traditions of the irruption of sin were valued and understood in different ways. The approach thus depends on a full use of Pentateuchal criticism and of *Redaktionsgeschichte*, and the Genesis texts are taken not only for what they themselves say but as expressions of the full experience of the various traditionists. Seen in this wider perspective, it is claimed, the texts do after all come close to the idea of inherited sin. Imaginative and in parts original, and with footnotes which bear witness to wide reading, this deserves to be known outside the circles of Roman Catholic theology for which it is primarily intended.

J.B.

SCHMID, H. H.: *Gerechtigkeit als Weltordnung*. (Beiträge zur historischen Theologie, 40). 1968. Pp. vii, 203. (J. C. B. Mohr (Paul Siebeck), Tübingen. Price: DM. 37.00 (cloth); DM. 32.00 (paper))

An interesting attempt to distinguish between the original Canaanite use of the terminology associated with √*ṣdk* and the modification which this appears to have undergone in Israelite thought. The study is carried out against the background furnished by the general notion of orderliness which the author finds in the literature of the ancient Near East. As a result the words in question are examined schematically in terms of justice, wisdom, nature, war, cult, and kingship; and, so far as the O.T. is concerned, the author's approach is governed by the commendable but inevitably somewhat hazardous aim of dealing with the material in chronological sequence. Throughout the work the reader is made aware of the problems attaching to the question of a root meaning *vis-à-vis* the diversity of significance which is revealed by the terminology under review; but, as commonly happens with semantic studies of this analytical kind, one is left with a renewed awareness of how difficult it is to make the words under discussion come alive as instruments of thought. Nevertheless the work may be recommended as a painstaking and, on the whole, well-documented contribution to the subject.   A.R.J.

SCHMIDT, W. H.: *Alttestamentlicher Glaube und seine Umwelt* (Neukirchener Studienbücher, 6). 1968. Pp. 252. (Neukirchenerverlag des Erziehungsvereins, Neukirchen-Vluyn. Price: DM. 14.80)

Books on the religion of Israel published recently by T. C. Vriezen and H. Ringgren and now this one by W. H. Schmidt provide evidence of a revived interest in this subject. In this book emphasis is put upon the relation of Israel's religious faith and practice to those of her neighbours, near at hand as in the case of the Canaanites, Syrians, etc., and distant as in the case of the Egyptians and the Mesopotamian peoples. The order of presentation is not topical but historical.

Israel did not live in cultural isolation; cultural influences had their effect on her modes of speech, her customs and ideas and her religion and ethics. This book asks such questions as these. Her conception of God as king, as living, as righteous, as holy, as self-revealing — how much of all this is derivative and how much original to Israel or at least distinctively domesticated? Myths of creation, of a primaeval struggle with the dragon of the deep, of a garden of paradise — how far have these been adapted in the O.T. from forms found in Israel's *Umwelt*? Theophany and covenant, altar and image, how far do we see in these both traditional form and revolt against tradition?

This book is well written, even if in parts it is inevitably brief. The available documents and the archaeological evidences are used with knowledge and discretion.   J.M.

SCHNACKENBURG, R.: *God's Rule and Kingdom*. 2nd enlarged edition. 1968. Pp. 400. (Burns and Oates, London; Herder, New York. Price: 50s.)

This book deals with the problem of God's present reign and future kingdom. This subtle relationship is reflected in the New Testament and later applied doctrinally to Christ and the Church. Schnackenburg uses the material of the O.T. and Judaism to introduce the subject. In this survey, which is only one tenth of the book, he relies mainly on

German-speaking scholars and follows Buber and Kraus in assessing the evidence. Kingship is not to be evaluated within a myth-ritual pattern but as a peculiar Israelite development. It found its expression at a royal festival of Zion and transmitted its force in post-exilic hopes. Davidic ideas fluctuated and eschatological expectations increased.   U.E.S.

SCHWEITZER, A.: *Reich Gottes und Christentum.* Herausgegeben und mit einem Vorwort versehen von U. Neuenschwander. 1967. Pp. viii, 212. (J. C. B. Mohr (Paul Siebeck), Tübingen. Price: DM. 16.50 (paper); DM. 21.00 (cloth))

SCHWEITZER, A.: *The Kingdom of God and Primitive Christianity.* Translated by L. A. Garrard. 1968. Pp. x, 193. (A. and C. Black, London. Price: 25s.)

As its title suggests, this last work of Schweitzer's, discovered only after his death, is mainly concerned with the N.T., but its first section deals with the view of the Kingdom of God in the Prophets and in late Judaism. In fact, this section is perhaps the most interesting, since in it Schweitzer sets out his conclusions about post-exilic Jewish teaching with regard to the Kingdom in a more systematic way than in any of his other writings, and thus provides the basis for his well-known claim that Jesus' view of the Kingdom is that of late Judaism. In general, the book is little more than a re-statement of the ideas found in *The Quest of the Historical Jesus* in a more popular and comprehensive form, and readers should be warned that Schweitzer's discussion of the O.T. and inter-testamental periods takes no account of recent developments in biblical scholarship or of new discoveries. Thus, the evidence he adduces for the apocalyptic beliefs of later Judaism is confined to the Apocalypses of Enoch, Baruch and Ezra and the Psalms of Solomon: he makes no reference at all to Qumran. The English translation is usually readable and accurate, but when a Hebrew phrase is reproduced it is invariably vilely mis-spelt.

J.R.P.

SMEND, R.: *Elemente alttestamentlichen Geschichtsdenkens.* (Theologische Studien, 95). 1968. Pp. 37. (EVZ-Verlag. Zürich. Price: Sw.Fr. 4.90)

A brief but penetrating and original essay on O.T. historical thought. After an introduction surveying the development from literary criticism of the documents to form criticism (in particular the epoch-making works of Alt, Noth and von Rad) the author gives an illuminating analysis of the way in which historical writing began in Israel with aetiology, then developed the characteristic of being exemplary and then finally passed on to the conception of order in events which resulted in the composition of extended histories. The process is then illustrated with reference to the narrative of Israel's occupation of Palestine. To understand its own existence Israel looked back behind the conquest to Moses, then to the Patriarchs and behind them to the primaeval history, which gave the aetiology of all the aetiologies of Israel, and forward from the conquest to the foundation of the monarchy and all that followed. Israel's tendency to historicize everything, however, had its dangers; the aetiologies and examples which the historian used for his narratives have something to say in their own right. Yet the attempt to control the present by precedents has also its dangers.   N.W.P.

Vos, C. J.: *Woman in Old Testament Worship*. 1968. Pp. x, 219. (Judels and Brinkman, Delft)

This dissertation presented to the Free University of Amsterdam by an American-born scholar argues that while in Israel as in the surrounding countries woman was socially subordinate to man, she was not regarded as spiritually inferior to him in the thought and legislation of the O.T. For functional and physical reasons she figured less than man in worship, but when she shared in it she was the equal of man in the eyes of God. That she was debarred from the priesthood may have been in part due to the place women had in the fertility cult. But she was free to approach God, and in some cases to fill the office of prophetess. The argument is sometimes laboured and not always convincing in detail, though the broad conclusions are sound enough. H.H.R.

WESTERMAN, C.: *Das Alte Testament und Jesus Christus*. 1968. Pp. 52. (Calwer Verlag, Stuttgart. Price: DM. 4.80)

This short study of the relation between the Testaments will furnish the reader with a number of fresh insights. In contrast to the traditional practice of linking individual texts taken out of their context, the author demonstrates the relevance to Christ of the main sections of the O.T., viz. the Historical Books (including the Pentateuch), the Prophets and the Writings. He argues that neither Testament can be summed up under the rubric 'Acts of God'. There is also the blessing which God bestows (see especially Genesis, Deuteronomy, an important aspect of the Davidic monarchy, many of the Psalms and aspects of the teaching of Jesus, especially in the Sermon on the Mount and in the Parables). The primaeval history and the promise to Abraham and various other parts of the O.T. correspond to the universalism of Christianity. The 'family' character of the patriarchal stories reveals Israel as a brotherhood before it was a people or a state and so points forward to a characteristic of Christianity with its emphasis on sacrifice on behalf of the brother. The psalms of the sufferer (e.g. Psalm 22) recognize God's identification of himself with his suffering people and point forward by way of the Servant Songs to the Incarnation. Second Isaiah is recognized as drawing together in a remarkable way the various strands of the O.T. and so high-lighting those insights which link it with the New Testament. Penetrating things are also said about the commands, the laws and the Law and the reader is warned against opposing the Old and New Testaments as Law and Gospel. This book has a value out of all proportion to its brevity. N.W.P.

WORDEN, T.: *The Psalms are Christian Prayers*. 1967. Pp. x, 219. (Geoffrey Chapman, Deacon Books, London. Price: 12s. 6d.)

This is an unchanged reprint, in paperback form, of the book first published in 1961 (see *B.L.* 1963, p. 57; *Decade*, p. 451). R.J.C.

ZIMMERLI, W.: *Der Mensch und seine Hoffnung im Alten Testament*. (Kleine Vandenhoeck-Reihe, 272). 1968. Pp. 190. (Vandenhoeck and Ruprecht, Göttingen. Price: DM. 7.80)

This book begins by contrasting the meaning of the word *elpis* in Greek literature with the use of it in the N.T., especially the Pauline epistles. In the latter the word means hope in God, related to human

condition and need. But the O.T. has no fixed terminology for
expressing hope; the words used mostly express a waiting for what is
not yet. But notably in LXX frequent use is made of the noun *elpis*
and of the related verb.

The old nomadic conception of life was not of an endless round, but
of here today and away tomorrow, nothing static but everything
on the move — nothing of hope but the groundwork of it. The
evidence of the books of the O.T. on hope is investigated systematically, a beginning being made with the Wisdom Literature in which
hope is often mentioned and is based on a belief in an established
order. Hope is not seen as an open human possibility, but as a gift
of God. But is it hope for Israel or for all men, for material prosperity
or for spiritual gifts, for the here and now or for life beyond death?
This book must have held the attention of the audience from all
faculties in Göttingen to which it was originally given in spoken
form; it deserves the wider public which it will reach now in print.

J.M.

THE LIFE AND THOUGHT OF THE
SURROUNDING PEOPLES

BERNHARDT, K.-H.: *Die Umwelt des Alten Testaments*. I. *Die Quellen und
ihre Erforschung*. 1967. Pp. xiv, 388. Pll. xvi in colour, xxxii black and
white. Sketchmaps 33, text figs 41. (Verlagshaus Gerd Mohn, Gütersloh.
Price: DM. 38)

This first volume of a planned trilogy is divided into six parts. The
first two give a brief review of what ancient writers and later travellers
have to say; the next two trace the development of classical and Near
Eastern archaeology, and summarize present-day techniques. Half
the volume is then devoted to excavations and their results in the
lands around Palestine; finally the last hundred pages discuss the
literary remains, and end with the necessary indexes. No one person
can be a specialist over such a wide field, nor can the treatment of
any one place or event included be more than brief, consequently the
constant though unevaluated documentation is most important and
underlines the assiduity of the author in collecting such a vast amount
of information and bringing it together in a controllable form. It
should prove a very useful reference work.   D.R.Ap-T.

GRÖNDAHL, F.: *Die Personennamen der Texte aus Ugarit* (Studia Pohl, 1).
1967. Pp. vii, 435. (Pontifical Biblical Institute, Rome. Price: Lire 3,000;
$5.00)

The volume here reviewed is the first of a collection dedicated to the
memory of the late Fr. Alfred Pohl, S.J., the well-known Assyriologist
of the Biblical Instutute at Rome; and the intention is to use it for
publishing, in phototypescript, specialist monographs on ancient
Middle Eastern philology and antiquities, which are often too
expensive for the ordinary means of publication. This is an excellent
scheme which, if the standard of the present work is maintained,
will be extremely valuable. The present volume is a catalogue of all
the personal names in both alphabetic and syllabic cuneiform scripts,
whether Semitic or not, found at Ugarit; it is therefore an indispensable companion to Aistleitner's *Wörterbuch der Ugaritischen Sprache*

(1967) and Huffmon's *Amorite Personal Names* (1968). Part I (pp. 10–202) deals with Semitic, Part II (pp. 203–67) with Hurrian, Part III (pp. 268–97) with Anatolian and Part IV (pp. 298–303) with Indo-Aryan and Egyptian names, while Part V (pp. 304–14) gives a list of names which cannot be explained; all this is followed by glossaries of all the names in both scripts (pp. 315–412), to which a list of additions is added (pp. 422–8). Each group begins with a section in which the forms of the names in it are analysed and their component elements listed and explained, while the concluding glossaries give references to the passages in which each name occurs in the published texts. So far as the reviewer can see, all these lists with the references to the texts are as exhaustive as they are accurate, while the typescript is beautifully reproduced. The work will therefore be an indispensable aid for the study of all the alphabetic and cuneiform texts from Ugarit as well as for early Semitic onomatology. G.R.D.

HERRMANN, W.: *Yariḫ und Nikkal und der Preis der Kuṭarāt-Göttinnen. Ein kultisch-magischer Text aus Ras Schamra.* (Beihefte zur Zeitschrift für die alttestamentliche Wissenschaft, 106). Pp. x, 48. (Verlag Alfred Töpelmann, Berlin. 1968. Price: DM. 18.00)

The poem concerning the moon-god *Yariḫ*, his spouse *Nikkal* and the *Kuṭarāt*-goddesses, which is still unparalleled in Semitic literature, is one of the most difficult of the texts recovered from Râs Shamrah (Ugarit), although it consists of only fifty lines of text. The editor of the present edition seems to have read all the relevant literature and made good use of it. He presents transliterated text and translation on opposite pages with concise but ample philological notes beneath it, together with a photograph of the tablet and another of Mlle. Herdner's transcription of the text in the original script. The concise but exhaustive philological notes set out almost every interpretation of each word and line with the editor's reasons for accepting or rejecting his predecessors' suggestions and, when he rejects them, his own interpretations with his reasons; in all this he has greatly advanced the study of the text beyond anything that has gone before. This part, occupying twenty-five pages, is followed by another twenty-two pages on the history of the interpretation of the poem, an analysis of it, its *Sitz im Leben*, and his own opinions on these questions. This, put briefly, is that it does not consist of two or three myths loosely strung together, but is a unity in praise of the *Kuṭarāt*-goddesses, who are invoked for the care of the newly born divine son of *Yariḫ* and *Nikkal* and for the match-making and payment of the bride-price and who are directly addressed in the closing lines, where the names of all seven of them are revealed. The editor's work throughout is careful as well as original and may be commended to all students of Ugaritic literature; and the hope may be expressed that he will undertake similar editions of the other Ugaritic poems. G.R.D.

LING, T.: *A History of Religion East and West: An Introduction and Interpretation.* 1968. Pp. xiv, 464. (Macmillan, London; St Martin's Press, New York. Price: 30s. (paper); 80s. (cloth))

In its conception and format this is an admirable book. Its aim is to provide a reliable and comprehensive Introduction to the ancient and living religions, ranging historically from the ancient context of the *deus otiosus* to the contemporary setting of the 'death of God' debate and comparatively exploring the inter-dependence of religions and their independent developments in given periods. It is a pity, therefore, that in his treatment of ancient Near Eastern religions the author leans heavily upon views which now have relevance for the history of interpretation only. This is notably true of the thesis of a common myth and ritual pattern (p. 7). Absent also is the clear influence of important research on the Hebrew Psalms in connection with the sacral role of the king and the possible early emergence of a universal eschatology in Israel.

But where Dr Ling's own specialist work is in evidence the book is of first rate value, and corrects and complements other similar books. This especially applies to his study of Buddhism and assessment of the aims and scope of Comparative Religion.   I.B.

MOSCATI, S.: *The World of the Phoenicians*, translated by A. Hamilton. 1968. Pp. xxii, 281. 53 photographs, 53 line drawings, 7 maps. (Weidenfeld and Nicolson, London. Price: 63s.)

This excellent work, translated from the Italian edition of 1966, summarizes what we have learnt, during the past decade or two, about the Phoenicians, in large measure thanks to the labours of Professor Moscati and his colleagues. The book deals with the Phoenicians in the East, in Africa, and on the Mediterranean islands and Spain. It provides an outline of the Phoenicians' and Carthaginians' history, religion, art, commercial activities, and language. This is a compendium which every Semitist, Old Testament scholar, and student of the Near East will frequently have to consult, and they may all do so with complete confidence in the information provided.

On p. 266 one misses a reference to N. Slouschz's *Thesaurus of Phoenician Inscriptions*; and C. H. Gordon's study of the alleged Phoenician text from Parahyba, Brazil, was probably too late to receive consideration here.

The Italian edition is more sumptuously provided with illustrations, especially in colour. The English translation inevitably shows traces of the original language, but it would be difficult to avoid this altogether without major recasting. Publishers ought to be disabused of the rather naïve notion that a book with footnotes will frighten off the 'general' reader; instead they make consultation by scholars as inconvenient as possible by assembling those notes at the end of the volume where they do *not* belong.   E.U.

NORTH, R. (S.J.): *Archeo-biblical Egypt*. 1967. Pp. 160. 3 sketchmaps. (Pontifical Biblical Institute, Rome. Price: Lire 900; $1.50)

These appear to be lithoprinted seminary notes, semi-popular but documented, on those antiquities of Egypt which the author deems of most importance for the Bible-oriented reader. Ch. 1 gives a rather superficial account of 'Monuments Attesting Immortality', but the next gives a fuller treatment of Tell el Amarna, the Letters and Akhenaten. Ch. 3 is devoted to 'Ramesses and Tanis', and the final essay treats 'New Testament (Coptic) Egypt'. It is helpful to have this contribution from a scholar with an up-to-date outlook and readable style.   D.R.Ap-T.

PARROT, A.: *Mission archéologique de Mari*, Vol. IV. *Le 'Trésor' d'Ur*. 1968. Pp. 68. 2 coloured and 22 monochrome plates and 42 illustrations in the text. (Geuthner, Paris. Price: Fr. 80)

In the 1965 excavations at Mari there was discovered in the pre-Sargonic palace a jar containing 52 items of treasure, which had been hidden, apparently in an hour of danger, and remained untouched until this discovery. The treasure includes a nude goddess, an ivory statuette of a nude woman, bracelets and pins, and cylinders depicting a variety of scenes. There was also a long, multi-faced object bearing an inscription stating that it was given by Mesannipadda, the founder of the first dynasty of Ur, to Gansud = Ansud, the founder of the dynasty of Mari, thus establishing the contemporaneity of these kings. Some of the other articles resemble finds at Ur, and it is possible that they also belonged to the gift from the monarch of Ur to the king of Mari. All the items suggest peace and culture rather than war, and Professor Parrot puts the date of the treasure at about 2600 B.C. and thinks it probable that the hiding of the jar took place in the time of Lugalzaggisi, king of Uruk, and that it has lain undisturbed for some 4500 years. There are fine plates of the items of treasure, together with full illustrations of these and other objects in the text, and a chapter by Professor G. Dossin deals with the text above-mentioned. H.H.R.

ULLENDORFF, E.: *Ethiopia and the Bible*. (The Schweich Lectures of the British Academy 1967). 1968. Pp. xiv, 174. III plates. (Published for the British Academy by Oxford University Press, London. Price: 42s.)

Drawing, in part, on the results of some of his earlier studies, Professor Ullendorff in three masterly chapters discusses Bible translations into Ethiopic, the impact of Hebraic and O.T. influences on the life of Ethiopia, and the legend of the Queen of Sheba. But this bare statement cannot make clear the wealth of information to be found in this volume, nor do justice to the many shrewd observations on both Ethiopia and the O.T. which it contains. Out of much that will be of considerable interest to O.T. scholars particular attention may perhaps be drawn to the section on the Gaʾəz Bible; Professor Ullendorff refers to the lack of prolegomena of serious dimensions in the field of Ethiopic Bible translations, but he offers us here a very valuable guide in an area in which few can claim competence, and indicates clearly the direction which future research should take. M.A.K.

QUMRAN STUDIES

ALLEGRO, J. M., with the collaboration of A. A. Anderson: *Discoveries in the Judaean Desert of Jordan*. V. *Qumrân Cave 4 I (4Q 158–4Q 186)*. 1968. Pp. 111, 31 plates. (Clarendon Press, Oxford University Press, London. Price: £4. 4s.)

It was the original intention of the editors that publication of the documents from Cave 4 should begin with the biblical manuscripts, but, owing to delays of one kind and another, it was thought advisable to publish first those texts which had been allotted to Mr Allegro for editing, and which were ready for press. Most of them have already been published in learned journals. In the present volume the pattern of previous volumes in this series is followed — the texts are transcribed, the non-biblical passages are translated where this serves some useful interpretative purpose, textual notes are supplied, there is an index of Hebrew words appearing in non-canonical texts, and there are thirty-one excellent facsimiles. The texts consist of twenty-nine Hebrew works — biblical paraphrases (Gen. Exod.), commentaries on Isa., Hos., Mic., Nah., Zeph., and Pss., collections of biblical quotations, exegetical treatments of O.T. passages, and other sectarian writings. Everyone interested in the scrolls will be grateful to the editor for his work, and also to Mr Anderson, to whose active collaboration the editor pays generous tribute. Between them they have produced a scholarly work which will be basic for further research on the scrolls. D.W.T.

KOFFMAHN, E.: *Die Doppelurkunden aus der Wüste Juda. Recht und Praxis der jüdischen Papyri des 1. und 2. Jahrhunderts n. Chr. samt Übertragung der Texte und deutscher Übersetzung.* (Studies on the Texts of the Desert of Judah, V.) 1968. Pp. viii, 208. (E. J. Brill, Leiden. Price: Fl. 54)

This interesting monograph is devoted to Hebrew, Aramaic and Greek legal papyri discovered in the Murabba'at caves and various other caches in the Judean Desert. Elisabeth Koffmahn first outlines the common features of 'twin deeds' (cf. Jer. 32: 10 ff.; mBB 10: 1–2; bBB 160b–161a), their method of dating, language and script, style and structure. She then translates and expounds in detail three types of documents: acknowledgements of debt, matrimonial deeds (*ketubbah* and *geṭ*) and contracts of sale of immovable property (dwelling house, vineyard, palm grove, etc.). In discussing their contents, she draws attention to significant links between these texts and Egyptian Hellenistic and demotic papyri and, at the same time, attempts also to relate them to rabbinic literature. In this last respect, scope is still left for the Jewish jurist. A select bibliography and several indices add to the intrinsic value of this study which will be welcomed by experts in Bible and Judaica as well as by students of legal institutions in the near-eastern provinces of the Roman empire.

G.V.

LARSON, M. A.: *The Essene Heritage.* 1967. Pp. xviii, 237. (Philosophical Library, New York. Price: $4.95)

Inspired by J. M. Allegro, the author attempts to explain Christianity as evolving directly from Essenism. In his view, the Essenes 'rejected Judaism *in toto*' and developed their ideology from Zoroastrianism and Greek mystery sources. Jesus and the early Church reproduced Essenism faithfully 'except for certain Buddhist accretions'. The resulting message was 'wholly unacceptable to the pagan world' so it was Hellenized under Stoic influence by Paul and the Fourth Gospel. Dr Larson's information is second-hand, when it is not third-hand, but the synthesis is largely his own. G.V.

MURPHY-O'CONNOR, J. (Ed.): *Paul and Qumran. Studies in New Testament Exegesis.* 1968. Pp. x, 254. (Geoffrey Chapman, London. Price: 30s.)

Nine valuable essays from writers of repute and moderation discuss parallels without forcing them between Pauline assumptions and doctrine and those of Qumran. The contributors are P. Benoit, O.P., J. A. Fitzmyer, S.J., J. Gnilka, M. Delcor, J. Murphy-O'Connor,

O.P., K. G. Kuhn, J. Coppens, F. Mussner, W. Grundmann. Subjects are angelology, 2 Cor. 6:14–7:1, church and sect courts, justification by faith, epistle to Ephesians (two essays), 'Mystery' and Truth. All the essays are of a high standard, include *inter alia* exploration of parallels in religious experience and adequate reference to previous work. Excellent full indexes.   A.R.C.L.

SANDERS, J. A.: *The Dead Sea Psalms Scroll.* 1967. Pp. xii, 174 (with six illustrations and a map). (Cornell University Press, Oxford University Press, London. Price: 95s.)

This is the English edition of the work reviewed in *B.L.* 1968, p. 60.
                                                                    M.A.K.

WAGNER, S. (ed.): *Bibel und Qumran. Beiträge zur Erforschung der Beziehungen zwischen Bibel- und Qumranwissenschaft.* 1969. Pp. 258. (Evangelische Haupt-Bibelgesellschaft zu Berlin. Price: DM. 28)

This collection of twenty-one papers was presented as a Festschrift to Professor Hans Bardtke of Leipzig on his 60th birthday in 1966, and it is appropriate that a scholar should be honoured who is one of the best-loved as well as being highly esteemed among Qumran specialists.

The writers are European, apart from O. Betz in Chicago; and with the exception of A. Strobel's account of Machaerus, the essays cover Qumran studies. There are one or two novelties; J. Irmscher surveys recent Greek contributions, and G. R. Driver has some comments on *gematria.* Two articles provide hitherto unpublished material — J. van der Ploeg gives Lev. 9.23–10.2 and A.S. van der Woude a Blessing (*11QBer*) which has affinities with *1QS^b*. Both are from the collection of Cave XI fragments acquired for publication by the Royal Netherlands Academy of Sciences.   B.J.R.

YIZHAR, M.: *Bibliography of Hebrew Publications on the Dead Sea Scrolls, 1948–1964.* (Harvard Theological Studies, XXIII.) 1967. Pp. vi, 48. (Harvard University Press, Camb., Mass., Oxford University Press, London. Price: 24s.)

There have been several bibliographies of books and articles dealing with the Scrolls, and these have included some Modern Hebrew entries, but nothing so comprehensive on Modern Hebrew work as this has previously appeared. The entries are classified as general works, works on the Qumran texts, or on finds from between the two Jewish revolts, or on the Masada excavations, or book reviews, or bibliographies. Altogether more than seven hundred items are included. It is intended to supplement this most useful bibliography from time to time by the issue of further lists.   H.H.R.

APOCRYPHA AND POST-BIBLICAL STUDIES

ARNALDEZ, R., MONDÉSERT, C. and POUILLOUX, J. (eds.): *Philon D'Alexandrie.* 1967. Pp. 382. (Centre National de la Recherche Scientifique, Paris. Price: Fr. 38)

The proceedings of the national conference on Philo held at Lyons, 11–15 September 1966. The papers, seventeen of them, are printed in full and a summary of the discussion follows each paper. It constitutes a fairly comprehensive study of Philo and includes papers on the place of the Alexandrian Jews in the Diaspora, Philo's allegorical interpretation, echoes of Greek mythology in his works, and of Greek cosmology, Philo and Gregory of Nyssa, to mention only a few.

L.H.B.

BOWMAN, J.: *Samaritanische Probleme*. 1967. Pp. 100. (Kohlhammer, Stuttgart. Price: DM. 18)

This work contains the Franz Delitzsch Lectures, 1959, on Samaritan history, with a useful section on the main Samaritan historical works; their religion, its characteristic features being expounded and special attention being given to sects within Samaritanism; the Samaritans and the Gospel, light being shed on the purpose of the Fourth Gospel and of Luke-Acts; and finally the Samaritans and Qumran, a number of striking parallels being noted. Many of the individual points made can already be found in various of Professor Bowman's many contributions to the periodical literature on the subject, but it is useful to have them brought together. One's main regret is the delay in publication since the lectures were originally delivered, as only footnote references to more recent literature are given.   R.J.C.

VAN DEN BORN, A.: *Wijsheid van Jesus Sirach (Ecclesiasticus)*. (De Boeken van Het Oude Testament, Deel VIII, Boek V.) 1968. Pp. 246. (J. J. Romen & Zonen. Roermond. Price: 94s. 6d.)

After a very brief introduction of ten pages, the book plunges into its translation and commentary. The translation, in single column, stands at the top of the page and the commentary, in double column, below. It is a straightforward piece of work designed for the ordinary (Dutch speaking) reader who is here provided with a devotional commentary with just enough critical notes to keep abreast of modern criticism. The critical notes are kept to a minimum in number and size, as for example those on the possible inclusion of Job in 49:9 and on the non-mention of Ezra, both on p. 235.   L.H.B.

BROCK, S. P. (ed.): *Testamentum Iobi*. PICARD, J.-C. (ed.): *Apocalypsi Baruchi Graece*. (Pseudepigrapha Veteris Testamenti Graece II.) 1967. Pp. 96. (Brill, Leiden. Price: Fl. 25)

The Testament of Job and the Greek Apocalypse of Baruch (i.e. III Baruch) are not perhaps as well known as some of the other pseudepigrapha, and for this reason, apart from any other, the publication of new editions of the Greek versions of these works is welcome, as serving to focus scholarly attention on them. Both texts were published by M. R. James in 1897, but the editors have collated the Greek manuscripts afresh, and correct the work of James in a fair number of places; Picard has also discovered the existence of a second Greek manuscript of Baruch. The editors have provided lucid and helpful introductions to their respective texts and the work forms a very useful addition to this new series.

(Note: Volume I of the series (not noticed in *B.L.*) contained *Testamenta XII Patriarchum*, ed. M. de Jonge, 1964).   M.A.K.

GUNDRY, R. H.: *The Use of the Old Testament in St Matthew's Gospel, with Special Reference to the Messianic Hope.* (*Supplements to Novum Testamentum*, Vol. 18.) 1967. Pp. xvi, 252. (E. J. Brill, Leiden. Price: Fl. 58.)

The author examines in detail the text-form of the Matthaean quotations from the O.T., including allusive as well as formal quotations. He finds that although the formal quotations common to Matthew and Mark adhere to the LXX, the remainder (like those in the other Synoptic traditions) have a mixed text. Dr Gundry is more convincing in this analytic work than in his ensuing discussion of the evangelist's methods. He attacks the view that the N.T. writers used scripture in an atomistic way: but his argument that Jesus is portrayed as fulfilling certain O.T. roles seems to beg the question. Finally he attempts to legitimatize this contextual use of the O.T. (which he traces to Jesus himself) by arguing that the messianic hope is much earlier than generally supposed, and that O.T. prophecies have a 'higher meaning' which is realized only in Jesus. M.D.H.

KUHN, P.: *Gottes Selbsterniedrigung in der Theologie der Rabbinen.* (Studien zum Alten und Neuen Testament, XVII.) 1968. Pp. 122. (Kösel Verlag, Munich. Price: DM. 22)

A little over half the book contains a selection of excerpts in translation from Rabbinic literature which reflect a belief in the self-abasement of God in his love and care for men and their welfare. Critical footnotes are given at the foot of each page. These are followed by a discussion of the meaning of the passages and their relation to the O.T. and to Christian thought. It is shown that the conception of God's self-abasement was well-established in Haggadic literature, that it was a natural growth from biblical ideas and that it had much in common with the corresponding conception in Christian thought. The uncertainty of the dates of the Rabbinic sources prevents any definite assessment of the possibility of the shaping of Christian ideas by the Jewish. L.H.B.

LEWIS, J. P.: *A Study of the Interpretation of Noah and the Flood in Jewish and Christian Literature.* 1968. Pp. x, 199. (E. J. Brill, Leiden. Price: Fl. 40)

The author devotes the largest part of his doctoral dissertation to the study of the Flood motive in Jewish writings, namely the Apocrypha and Pseudepigrapha, Philo, Pseudo-Philo and Josephus, the Greek and Aramaic versions of Genesis and rabbinic traditions relative to Noah. This is a varied collection of texts with no serious attempt at an historical assessment; nor are there any indices which might have made its consultation less onerous. G.V.

LINDBLOM, J.: *Gesichte und Offenbarungen. Vorstellungen von göttlichen Weisungen und übernatürlichen Erscheinungen im ältesten Christentum.* (Acta Reg. Societatis Humaniorum Litterarum Lundensis, LXV.) 1968. Pp. 272. (C. W. K. Gleerup, Lund. Price: Sw.Kr. 50)

This study, as its title indicates, is concerned with phenomena of revelation in early Christianity, but it is conceived as a continuation of much that Lindblom has written in his *Prophecy in Ancient Israel,* 1962 (*B.L.* 1962, p. 49; *Decade*, p. 359). The various sections, on dreams, visions, theophanies and the like, contain therefore numerous references to O.T. material. In so far as the analogy of N.T. evidence

is relevant to the interpretation of the O.T., the study may be seen to
contribute to the wider understanding of revelatory experience in
the O.T.
                                                                      P.R.A.

MARQUARDT, F.-W.: *Die Entdeckung des Judentums für die christliche
Theologie. Israel im Denken Karl Barths.* 1967. Pp. 369. (Chr. Kaiser
Verlag, München. Price: DM 27 (paper); 29.80 (cloth))

This substantial volume is the first of series of *Abhandlungen zum
christlich-jüdischen Dialog* edited by H. Gollwitzer. It is devoted
to an elaborate study of Barth's thought regarding the place of
Israel and Judaism in Christian theology, tracing its development
from as early as the first edition of the *Römerbrief* through the
political and religious struggles of the Thirties, when the Confessional
Church in Germany bravely condemned the persecution of the Jews,
and right on to the latest volumes of the *Kirchliche Dogmatik*. It is a
complicated story, made even more so by the unnecessarily difficult
style of the author. The book is, of course, not strictly a work of O.T.
scholarship, but it is of very real importance for those who are concerned about the question of Israel and who have been alerted to the
significance of contemporary thinking on the subject by such a book
as Vriezen's *Die Erwählung Israels nach dem Alten Testament*. The
author, in general agreement with Barth's plea, argues for the Christian Church's 'solidarity with Israel', that is to say, the Church and
Israel together before God rather than the Church with God against
Israel. Barth's view is essentially based on an exegesis of Romans
9–11 and he moves from an allegorizing of Israel as representative
of 'religious man' to a revolutionary view of the concrete phenomenon of Israel as the Church's partner under God's judgement
and grace.
                                                                      N.W.P.

MEEKS, W. A.: *The Prophet-King. Moses Traditions and the Johannine
Christology.* (Supplements to Novum Testamentum, XIV.) 1967. Pp. xv,
356. (E. J. Brill, Leiden. Price: Fl. 52)

This Yale dissertation is a characteristic example of the recent welcome tendency in New Testament scholarship to confront Gospel
concepts thoroughly with corresponding themes in early post-biblical
Jewish literature. The author compares the Johannine description of
Jesus as prophet and king with the portrait of Moses, also prophet
and ruler, in Philo, Josephus, the Apocrypha and Pseudepigrapha,
the Dead Sea Scrolls, the rabbinic haggadah as well as in Samaritan
and Mandaean writings. Existing English versions of the sources are
generally reproduced including, as in the case of Etheridge's rendering
of the Targums, certain of the mistranslations which they contain.
This promising work, which is stronger in analysis than in synthesis,
will be of considerable use to students of intertestamental and cognate
subjects.
                                                                      G.V.

MONTGOMERY, J. A.: *The Samaritans.* 1968. Pp. xxxiv, 358. 13 Pl., 13
illustrations, 2 maps. (Ktav Publishing House, New York. Price:
$12.50)

Despite much recent work on the Samaritans, Montgomery's survey
of their history, theology and literature, first published in 1907,
still in many ways provides the most complete picture available.
The present volume, an offset reprint of the original, is therefore to be
welcomed. The only new matter is a brief introduction by A. S.
Halkin.
                                                                      R.J.C.

PURVIS, J. D.: *The Samaritan Pentateuch and the Origin of the Samaritan Sect.* (Harvard Semitic Monographs, Vol. 2.) 1968. Pp. xiv, 147. (Harvard University Press, Oxford University Press. Price: 57s.)

This doctoral thesis falls into two main sections. The first considers the evidence afforded for the origin of the Samaritans in their recension of the Pentateuch by an examination of its script (illustrated by six palaeographic charts), orthography, and textual tradition. All of these are shown to point to the Hasmonean period as the most likely setting for the decisive break with Judaism. The second section suggests that the available historical evidence is best understood as pointing in the same direction. The author's article from *JNES* 24 on Ecclus. 50:25f. is included as an appendix, and there is an extensive bibliography.   R.J.C.

TETZNER, L.: *Megilla* (Die Mischna II Seder, 10 Traktat, ed. by K. H. Rengstorf and L. Rost.) 1968. Pp. vii, 154. (Verlag Alfred Töpelmann, Berlin. Price: DM. 50)

The well-known German edition of the Mishnah presents us here with the Hebrew text and a German translation of the tractate Megillah, together with a detailed running commentary and a text-critical appendix. The tractate deals with the time and the manner of the public reading of the book of Esther at the Feast of Purim. The greater part of the tractate, however, concerns itself with other questions which have nothing to do with the Esther Scroll, such as the difference between the various degrees of holiness and cleanness, certain ritual acts, the sale and purchase of sacred objects and synagogues, the public reading of the Torah and of portions from the other books of the Bible including their *targum*, and various regulations of the Synagogue service. Not all statements contained in the commentary are correct, but that is pardonable and probably inevitable, for *jüdische Wissenschaft* is a vast and intricate discipline and occasionally unmanageable — especially in a commentary on a single tractate which deals with all kinds of things. The author has done his best. One might have expected to hear a little more in the introduction about the importance of the book of Esther and the Purim Feast in Jewish life and thought as well as about the customs accompanying the reading of the Scroll.   H.K.

THACKERAY, H. ST J.: *Josephus. The Man and the Historian.* With a Preface by G. F. Moore and an Introduction by S. Sandmel. (The Hilda Stich Stroock Lectures for 1928.) 1967. Pp. xxii, 160. (Ktav Publishing House, Inc., New York. Price: $6.95)

This is a reissue of the volume published originally in 1929. In a new Introduction S. Sandmel pays tribute to Thackeray's work, and comments on the significance of Josephus in relation to other Jewish and Christian writings of the period.   M.A.K.

PHILOLOGY AND GRAMMAR

BARR, J.: *Comparative Philology and the Text of the Old Testament.* 1968. Pp. ix, 354. (Clarendon Press, Oxford. Price: 65s.)

Professor Barr has written a remarkable book, erudite in matter, up-to-date in method, and exceptionally competent in the mastery of linguistic problems. Its subject is the philological treatment of the Hebrew Bible in so far as it is concerned with the muster of the full resources of comparative Semitics for the elucidation of difficult or obscure Hebrew words and their meanings. He surveys the entire field both historically and by examining the methods currently employed, such as the use made of the lexical resources of other Semitic languages, problems of homonymy and their bearing on the efficiency of communication, samplings of real or alleged lexical overlaps, etc. There is no other work in existence which has dealt with these vital subjects so fully and so authoritatively.

This does not mean that one must necessarily assent to everything Professor Barr has said: the present reviewer is indicating some of the problems raised by this important book in a detailed review in *BSOAS* 1969/2. At times Professor Barr is, perhaps, inclined to concentrate on the criticism of present methods rather than on the elaboration of better ones; often there is nothing really wrong with some of the methods of comparative Semitic philology but rather with the competence of some individual practitioners. Every Semitist will profoundly agree with the author in deprecating searches in the dictionaries of other Semitic languages, for the purposes of comparative etymologies, without a profound and living acquaintance with the languages and literature which these dictionaries are intended to serve. The cavalier treatment of phonological correspondences, in particular, has proved to be the undoing of many an O.T. scholar.

E.U.

HILL, D.: *Greek Words and Hebrew Meanings: Studies in the Semantics of Soteriological Terms.* 1967. Pp. xv, 333. (Cambridge University Press. Price: 60s.)

Dr Hill's first and last chapters are largely devoted to an appraisal of Barr's strictures on the lexical approach to biblical theology: these are to some extent qualified, mainly on the basis of some contemporary studies in non-biblical semantics. On the whole, however, Barr's methodology is accepted, and five of the Kittel articles are in effect rewritten on the basis that 'the meaning of biblical language . . . can be grasped only by penetrating beyond the words and matters of usage to an understanding of the religious experience or perception of truth which they attempt to express' (p. 12). The words selected for this 'exercise in historical semantics' are *hilaskesthai, lutron, zoe* — these are short studies and only in the last case is much space given to the O.T. background — *dikaiosune* with its cognates, and *pneuma*: in these two cases the treatment is more full-scale (eighty and ninety-one pages respectively), and the O.T. Septuagintal, and inter-testamental connotations are investigated in some depth. There are interesting suggestions about, for example, the development of meaning in the *ṣedeq* group of words during the O.T. period, and about the interpretative nature of some of the Septuagint translations; and the following may be mentioned among the detailed conclusions offered: 'propitiation', not 'expiation', is the true meaning of *hilaskesthai*; 'mighty wind' is 'rather improbable' as a translation of *rûaḥ 'elōhîm* in Gen. 1; conformity to rule and custom as the basic connotation of *ṣedeq* indicates 'a forensic or judicial meaning' in the righteousness of Tamar (Gen. 38:26).   C.J.A.H.

JENNI, E.: *Das hebräische Pi'el. Syntaktisch-semasiologische Untersuchung einer Verbalform im Alten Testament.* 1968. Pp. 298. (EVZ-Verlag, Zürich. Price: Fr. 28)

Professor Jenni is dissatisfied with the interpretation of the *pi'el* as a primarily intensive theme, and here suggests a new understanding according to an explanation borrowed from Accadian grammar. He maintains that it has a factitive significance with verbs intransitive in the *qal*, and a resultative significance with transitive verbs; and he offers a detailed study of O.T. usage which makes plain what he means. The book has an appendix listing verbs used in the *pi'el* in the O.T., and indexes of Hebrew words and biblical references. Professor Jenni has not said the last word on the subject: some subtle shades of meaning that he finds in particular passages are questionable, and he himself recognizes the need to examine other themes in the biblical language, the *pi'el* in later Hebrew, and the corresponding II theme in Arabic, which has been understood by Arab grammarians to have an intensive meaning. Nevertheless, he has drawn attention to a real problem, and his solution deserves serious consideration.

J.A.E.

KOEHLER, L. and BAUMGARTNER, W.: *Hebräisches und Aramäisches Lexicon zum Alten Testament.* Dritte Auflage neu bearbeitet von W. Baumgartner unter Mitarbeit von B. Hartmann und E. Y. Kutscher. Lieferung 1 *'aleph-ṭebaḥ.* 1967. Pp. liv, 352. (E. J. Brill, Leiden. Price: Fl. 64)

The successive *Lieferungen* of the first edition of this lexicon (1953) were reviewed in earlier issues of the *B.L.* (1949, p. 54; 1950, p. 75; 1951, p. 73; 1952, p. 79; 1953, p. 82; 1954, p. 93; *Eleven Years*, pp. 217, 292, 368, 450, 535, 630). This first *Lieferung* of the revision of the 1953 edition exhibits many differences in detail. For example, the material in the *Supplement* (1958) has been worked into the revision; languages other than Hebrew and Greek are normally given in transcription; all English translation is omitted, a feature which will make the lexicon less useful to students; and grammatical references are more numerous. These changes, together with the inclusion of a great deal of new material — usefully described in the introduction — made it necessary to rewrite the lexicon and to print it afresh. Of particular interest and importance is the attention paid to Middle Hebrew and Jewish Aramaic material — the special contribution of E. Y. Kutscher — and to Samaritan. Sometimes antiquated meanings of words are perpetuated, and sometimes again relevant literature which merits a mention does not find a place. On the other hand, the revision offers much that is new with which the Hebraist will wish to acquaint himself. It is to be hoped that the next instalment will not be long delayed.

D.W.T.

ADDITIONAL NOTES ON SCHOOL TEXT-BOOKS, ETC.

BECK, E. and MILLER, G.: *Biblische Unterweisung. Handbuch zur Auswahlbibel Reich Gottes.* 2 volumes. 1964 and 1968. Pp. 322 and 375. (Kösel-Verlag, Munich. Price: DM. 30; DM. 40)

These two handsome volumes, written under the editorship of H. Fischer for the guidance of teachers in eight R.C. South German dioceses using the School Bible *Reich Gottes*, are a notable achievement. They are both scholarly and practical, presenting a running commentary on sections of the Bible text and a compendium of relevant information in the form of general introductions, excursuses on particular topics, annotations, and notes for the catechist, the aim being to enable teachers to acquire a thorough understanding of the O.T. text and its theological significance in the light of modern scholarship.

L.A.P.

*DICKSON, K. A.: *The History and Religion of Israel. From Samuel to the Fall of the Northern Kingdom.* 1968. Pp. 144 (including 3 maps). (Darton, Longman and Todd, London. Price: 7s.)

This school text-book, written for candidates for the 'O' level examination in Bible Knowledge of the West African Examinations Council, consists of a running commentary on selected passages (indicated in the margin) from 1 and 2 Samuel, 1 and 2 Kings, Amos and Hosea. It is a useful and competent book for its limited purpose.

L.A.P.

*HABEL, N. C.: *Are you joking, Jeremiah?* (Perspective Series, No. 4). 1967. Pp. 109. (Concordia Publishing House, St Louis, Missouri. Price: $1.25)

This booklet has a bright, modern format and an imaginative choice of good, strong illustrations. Aimed at teenagers, it is a dramatic commentary on the life of Jeremiah, inviting involvement in Jeremiah's revolution in the twentieth century. It is meant to jolt the performers and audience into a specifically Christian awareness of the current scene. That scene is American but this will in no way worry non-American teenagers. Rather it should stimulate them to compose their own comment and answer. It can be read without the Christian sections. This work will inevitably date because of the contemporary idiom used, but it is just the kind of serious throw-away material with punchy lines needed in schools and youth clubs today. Useful suggestions are given for use with folk guitarist, speech groups or normal liturgy.

C.A.

Book List 1970

GENERAL

BERGER, I.: *Analytical Subject Index to the Hebrew Union College Annual*, Vols. 1–37 (1924–66). 1969. Pp. (vi), 136. (Ktav Publishing House, Inc., New York. Price: $20.00)

The contributions to scholarship made through the pages of the *Hebrew Union College Annual* receive regular notice in this *Book List*. (The most recent issue is reviewed below on p. 14). This index contains 110 pages of subject headings with a fair number of cross-references, and in addition a complete author-title index to the 37 volumes covered. In the main list, additions have been made to the entries by means of asterisked references to volume and page numbers for articles in which a subject, though not the main topic of the article, receives brief treatment, and this enables the reader to discover a much wider range of information. It complements the concise Topical Index appended to Vol. 36.

The appearance of this comprehensive index coincides with the reissue of the complete set of 37 volumes at a price of $650.00, which will enable libraries (and individuals) to obtain this valuable collection of material on so wide a range of subjects.   P.R.A.

BLACK, M. and FOHRER, G. (ed.): *In Memoriam Paul Kahle* (Beihefte zur Zeitschrift für die alttestamentliche Wissenschaft, 103). 1968. Pp. 253. 20 plates. (Verlag Alfred Töpelmann, Berlin. Price: DM. 86)

This memorial volume to Paul Kahle has a preface from M. Black, whose essay here on the language of Jesus was also substantially his Presidential Address to the Society in January 1968. A brief memoir of Kahle is provided by H. S. Nyberg. The 27 essays represent something of the variety of Kahle's interests and of the scholarly heritage which he has left behind him. For Old Testament scholars the main interest will attach to the following: three essays on particular passages (G. R. Driver on Isa. 53, D. W. Thomas on Isa. 40:15, and W. D. McHardy on the horses in Zechariah — a suggestion dependent on the use of abbreviations by scribes); four on Targumic matters (A. Díez-Macho, M. C. Doubles, G. J. Kuiper, S. Lund); one on Hebrew MSS (P. A. H. de Boer); three on Massoretic matters (a note by R. Edelmann on the terms for scribes and punctuators, and articles on manuscripts by F. Pérez Castro with M. J. Azcárraga, and by G. E. Weil); two on Semitic philology more generally (J. Blau and A. Murtonen); three on more archaeological topics (O. Eissfeldt on the Phoenician Hermes, G. Levi Della Vida on the Siloam inscription — which he holds to be a quotation from a current literary chronicle — and A. v. R. Sauer on the pig in the cult). There are three on later Judaism: G. Vermes on the Minim ('liberal' Hellenistic Jews), A. Scheiber on the prayer-books of medieval proselytes, and G. Vajda on Qirqisānī. Fohrer's contribution is on a Samaritan subject. D. M. Dunlop provides evidence of early Arabic biblical translations, and W. B. Henning writes on a point in the Aramaic papyri. Two articles belong rather to the New Testament (G. D. Kilpatrick and J. Bowman), and others are of more general Oriental interest.

                                                                J.B.

DE BOER, P. A. H. (ed.): *Oudtestamentische Studiën XV. The Priestly Code and Seven Other Studies.* 1969. Pp. 250. (E. J. Brill, Leiden. Price: Fl. 72)

The main study, by J. G. Vink (English) covers pp. 1–144. It is concerned with the date and origin of the Priestly Code, representing a revised view of an earlier study by the same author in his commentary on Leviticus (Roermond, 1962; *B.L.*, 1963, p. 31; *Decade*, p. 425). It argues for a much later date for the Code than is normally suggested, and does this by means both of a study of the evidence for the Persian period and of detailed analysis of important passages. It is a study to be examined with close attention as a significant contribution. J. C. H. Lebram (German), starting from a painting of Rembrandt, investigates the presentation of the blessing of Jacob's sons as it appears in Gen. 48 and in Jewish and Christian (and Samaritan) tradition, an interesting study of exegesis. C. H. W. Brekelmans (English) comments usefully on 'Some translation problems' in Judg. 5:29, Ps. 120:7 and Jonah 4:9. H. A. Brongers (German) discusses the 'cup of wrath' and the possible origin of this symbol. J. Schoneveld (English) comments on Ezek. 14:1–8; N. A. van Uchelen (English) on '*anšê dāmîm* in the Psalms' examines the use of the phrase and supports the rendering 'bloodthirsty men'. N. H. Ridderbos (German) deals with 'The theophany in Ps. 50:1–6', pointing to its relationship to the Sinai traditions and suggesting a possible link with the reading of the law (Deut. 31). M. J. Mulder (French) discusses the work of the Dutch reformer Huibert Duifhuis in relation to the exegesis of Ps. 84:4. A valuable volume in the series.

P.R.A.

CAZELLES, H. (ed.): *De Mari à Qumran . . . Hommage à Mgr J. Coppens.* 1969. Pp. 158*, 370. (Lethielleux, Paris. Price: B.Fr. 800)

This is only one of three volumes designed as a *Festschrift* in honour of Mgr J. Coppens, who occupied the chair of Old Testament studies at Louvain from 1927 until 1967. The first part gives the text of the tributes paid to Mgr Coppens during the eighteenth series of *Journées Bibliques*, held at Louvain in August 1967. All these orations were delivered by Belgian bishops and professors, the latter group including the glowing personal tribute of Mgr G. Ryckmans (who has since died, in September 1969, in his eighty-third year) a close friend and colleague throughout the two professoriates. The larger part of the volume is given up to studies of the Old Testament milieu and writings, among which may be mentioned H. Cazelles, 'Positions actuelles dans l'exégèse du Pentateuch', D. Winton Thomas, 'A Consideration of Isaiah LIII in the Light of Recent Textual and Philological Study', and the late Professor H. H. Rowley's 'L'histoire de la Secte qumranienne'. An incomplete bibliography of Mgr Coppens' writings may be found on pp. 95*–132* in the present volume. It gives, at any rate, some indication of the wide range and depth of his study of the Old Testament and many cognate disciplines.

J.M.T.B.

COENEN, L., BEYREUTHER, E., BIETENHARD, H. (ed.): *Theologisches Begriffslexikon zum Neuen Testament*, Fasc. 8, 9. 1969. 112 pp. each

(Kirche-Liebe, Liebe-Priester). (R. Brockhaus Verlag, Wuppertal. Price: DM. 16.80 each fascicle)

Previous fascicles of this lexicon have been noted in *B.L.*, 1968, p. 4; 1969, p. 4; and a general description of its hermeneutical purpose has been given. These fascicles contain important and scholarly articles on, e.g. *Kraft, Lehre, Licht, Liebe, Mensch, Offenbarung, Priester*. With these, volume II.1 is now completed.   P.R.A.

---

*COLEMAN, E.: *The Bible in English Drama. An annotated list of plays including translations from other languages from the beginnings to 1931.* 1968 (1930–1). Pp. xiii, 212. (Ktav Publishing House, New York Public Library. Price: \$8.95)

This bibliography originally formed part of a larger work on the Jew in English drama. It is now prefaced by a survey of major recent plays (1931–68) by Isaiah Sheffer.

The works listed are based on themes from Old Testament, New Testament and Apocrypha and include plays for Jewish and Christian festivals. The annotations indicate contents but not merit. Especially useful on early English religious plays.   C.A.

Congress Volume, Rome, 1968 (Supplements to *Vetus Testamentum*, Vol. XVII). 1969. Pp. 244, 2 plates. (E. J. Brill, Leiden. Price: Fl. 44)

The papers read at the Rome congress cover a wide spread of Old Testament scholarship. The opening one, by Th. C. Vriezen, is on method in the study of the history of religions. Archaeology is represented by M. Dunand, who draws analogies between temple foundations of Achaemenid times in Jerusalem and elsewhere; and history by S. Herrmann, who considers autonomous developments in Judah and Israel and questions the centrality of the amphictyony idea. Particular passages occupy three contributions, those of G. W. Ahlström on Joel 2:23 and the 'teacher of justice', of J. de Savignac on Prov. 8:22–32 (connecting *'āmōn*, somewhat obscurely, with the game of draughts; does he have in mind the use of the hieroglyphic sign Gardiner Y 5 ?), and of W. Zimmerli on the pre-history of Isa. 53, with an emphasis on the phrase *naśa '^{a}won*. Articles on special subjects include E. Auerbach on Aaron and his connection with priestly genealogy, F. C. Fensham on the treaty-relations between Israel and Tyre, and H. Kosmala on *geber* (not merely a word for 'man' but one indicating certain ideals, developed particularly in Job and followed up at Qumran). On Job there are two articles: H. L. Ginsberg distinguishes the two strata of a patient Job and an impatient Job, and S. Terrien explores the idea that the book was connected with a partially cultic setting in the New Year festivities. D. Lys furnishes notes on some terms in the Song of Songs. J.-G. Heintz shows the presence at Mari at an ideology of Holy War, with relations to prophecy analogous to those found in Israel; he thinks the two words *ḥerem* ('ban' and 'net') have a common basis. H. J. Stoebe discusses the relation between standard forms and individual historical experience, with the story of David as the major illustration. Two articles are on linguistic matters, namely W. J. Martin's study of narratives in which events are reported out of their chronological

sequence, and·S. Segert's discussion of comparative Semitic lexicography, including a preliminary statement about a computerized
comparative dictionary now being produced in Prague. The one
article on text is by H. M. Orlinsky on the Greek Joshua.   J.B.

COPPENS, J.: *La carrière et l'oeuvre scientifique d'un maître louvaniste:
Hommage-Hulde J. Coppens 1927–1967* (Analecta Lovaniensia Biblica
et Orientalia, Ser. IV, Fasc. 49). 1969. Pp. 158. (Desclée de Brouwer,
Bruxelles–Paris)

On 25 August 1967, the closing day of the eighteenth Journées
Bibliques, tribute was paid to Monsignor Coppens on his becoming
emeritus after forty years' service as professor in the University of
Louvain. Belgian bishops, the Catholic University of Louvain, the
Faculty of Theology, the members of the Colloquium Biblicum
Lovaniense, as well as many colleagues and friends, participated in
the celebrations. In this volume are published the speeches, in French
and Dutch, which were delivered, together with a *tabula gratulatoria*,
a bibliography, nearly forty pages in length, of Monsignor Coppens'
writings, and two photographs of him. A pleasing memento of a
happy occasion.   D.W.T.

ELLIS, E. E. and WILCOX, M. (ed.): *Neotestamentica et Semitica. Studies in
honour of Matthew Black*. 1969. Pp. xxi, 297. (T. & T. Clark, Edinburgh.
Price: 55s.)

Four of these essays relate to the interpretation of the Old Testament
in the New. N. A. Dahl finds in Gal. 3 and Rom. 8:32 traces of a
Jewish–Christian midrash for which the Atonement was the promised
requital for the 'binding of Isaac'; E. E. Ellis argues that some of the
O.T. quotations were excerpted from Christian midrashim (this article
is particularly useful for its references); J. Jeremias sets the Hillelite
hermeneutical method in Paul beside other evidence confirming his
education in the school of Hillel; G. Vermes claims that manna
symbolizes Moses in a passage in Targum Neofiti which he compares
with texts from the Rabbinic sources, Josephus, and Philo, and
briefly also with John 6.
After listing the Danielic fragments at Qumran, F. F. Bruce shows
how closely the interpretation of contemporary events by the community continues that of the Book of Daniel, of which, it is suggested,
they were careful students. B. Reicke illustrates the variety of meanings attached in the intertestamental literature to *yd'* and (to a lesser
extent) *ginōskō* and their derivatives; R.McL. Wilson discusses
the significance of the allegedly Jewish 'Passion of Jesus' discovered
in 1966. In shorter essays, E. Stauffer sees in the Matthean genealogy
and elsewhere evidence of polemic against the Jewish slander on
Jesus' legitimacy; D. Daube comments on divorce in Deut. and in
Roman law; and O. Michel writes on the significance of miraculous
signs in Josephus. This valuable collection also includes a full bibliography of Principal Black's writings.   C.J.A.H.

FOHRER, G.: *Studien zur alttestamentlichen Theologie und Geschichte* *(1949–1966)*. (Beihefte zur Zeitschrift für die alttestamentliche Wissenschaft, 115). 1969. Pp. x, 372. (Alfred Töpelmann, Berlin. Price: DM. 74)

In this volume our distinguished new Honorary Member reissues 18 studies published in various periodicals and elsewhere during the period indicated. Appropriate modifications have been made both in content and in documentation. The studies are arranged in three sections: I. Religions- und Theologiegeschichte; II. Theologie; III. Geschichte. Special mention may be made of 'Tradition und Interpretation im Alten Testament', 'Altes Testament — "Amphiktyonie" und "Bund"?', and 'Das sogenannte apodiktisch formulierte Recht und der Dekalog' in the first section, of 'Zion-Jerusalem im Alten Testament', 'Die Weisheit im Alten Testament', and the article *sōzō* and related words in the O.T. in the second section, and in the third section of 'Israels Staatsordnung im Rahmen des Alten Orients' and 'Der Vertrag zwischen König und Volk in Israel'. But the whole volume is of interest and importance and provides ample evidence of the author's learning and industry.   G.W.A.

FRIEDRICH, G. (ed.): *Theologisches Wörterbuch zum Neuen Testament* (begun by G. Kittel). Band VIII. 1969. Pp. 619. (Kohlhammer, Stuttgart. Subskr. Price: DM. 80)
Band IX. Lieferung 1. 1969. Pp. 64. (Price: DM. 7.20)

The contents of Volume VIII have been noted in earlier issues of the *Book List*, all but the concluding part from p. 507 to the end. Perhaps the only articles which require special mention here are those on *hypnos* (H. Balz) and *hypokrinomai — hypokrites* (*in sensu malo* translated by *ḥanep*) (U. Wilckens).
Of particular interest in *Lieferung* 1 of Volume IX is the long article *Pharisaios* by K. Weiss.   N.W.P.

GRAHAM, E. C.: *Nothing is here for tears. A Memoir of S. H. Hooke.* 1969. Pp. vi, 121. (Blackwell, Oxford. Price: 25s.)

Members of the Society and Old Testament scholars throughout the world, as well as all those others who in one way or another have been touched by the influence of S. H. Hooke, stimulated by his scholarship, and warmed by his faith and friendship, will welcome the appearance of this memoir. It offers an illuminating and sensitive account of his life; a helpful and critical account of his writings; a delightful selection of his poems (and of poems written to him and about him); and a brief list of published works. It forms a fitting tribute to one who is remembered with very deep affection and whose work in the area of O.T. studies has been so widely influential.

P.R.A.

HALLO, W. W. (ed.): *Essays in memory of E. A. Speiser* (American Oriental Series, 53). 1968. Pp. viii, 201. 20 illustrations. (American Oriental Society, New Haven. Price: $4.00)

This important volume, full of worthy contributions, would have delighted the renowned Orientalist and biblical scholar (on whose

reprinted essays see *B.L.*, 1969, p. 9). For biblical studies special
mention must be made of A. Malamat's study of the O.T. genealogical
lists compared with their Old Babylonian counterparts; R. de Vaux on
'Le Pays de Canaan' finds idealism in Num. 34:3–12 and Ezek.
47:15–20 as does M. Greenberg in Num. 35:4–5 and Ezek. 48.
W. W. Hallo's 'Individual prayer in Sumerian' is essential for all
engaged in Psalter studies. S. N. Kramer gives a Sumerian parallel
to the 'Babel of tongues'. S. M. Paul seeks analogues in Deut.-Isa.
to the language, phraseology and ideology of the cuneiform royal
inscriptions and I. G. Gelb puts an end to 'East Canaanites' by
publishing texts listing good West Semitic names, designated
'Amorite', for both the Old Babylonian and earlier Ur III periods;
both represent the same ethnic group. A. L. Oppenheim finds the
'Eyes of the Lord' — a description of secret service officials acting in
extension of the royal presence — transferred on the spiritual level
to evil demons. E. Reiner on 'Thirty pieces of silver' shows that this
expression (as does 'thirty shekels') stands for a mere 'halfpenny-
worth'. M. Held discusses the root *zbl/sbl*.
D.J.W.

Interpreting the Prophetic Tradition. The Goldenson Lectures 1955–66.
Introduction by H. M. Orlinsky. (The Library of Biblical Studies. Ed. by
H. M. Orlinsky.) 1969. Pp. 343. (Ktav Publishing House, Inc., New
York. Price: $10.00)

This volume offers a reprint of this series of lectures, of which one,
'Jerusalem and the Prophets' by R. de Vaux, was noted in *B.L.*, 1967,
p. 36. In addition to this one, the following may be listed as of direct
concern to O.T. scholarship: S. H. Blank, ' "Of a truth the Lord hath
sent me": an inquiry into the source of the prophet's authority',
concerned almost entirely with the authority of Jeremiah; W. F.
Albright, 'Samuel and the beginnings of the prophetic movement', a
characteristic study which emphasizes, among many side issues, the
richness of the Samuel tradition; J. P. Hyatt, 'The prophetic criticism
of Israelite worship', maintaining the view that the prophets engaged
in a complete condemnation of worship; and H. M. Orlinsky, 'The
so-called "Suffering Servant" in Isaiah 53', a theme more fully set
out in V.T. Suppl. xiv (see *B.L.*, 1968, p. 38). The other lectures are
concerned rather with the interpretation of prophecy in the contemporary world.
P.R.A.

KAPELRUD, A. S. and JERVELL, J. (ed.): *Studia Theologica.* Scandinavian
Journal of Theology. Vol. 23, no. 1 (1969). 1968. Pp. 1–112. 2 tables.
(Universitetsforlaget, Oslo. Subscription price: N.Kr. 60.00 per volume)

Two of the three articles contained in this issue deal with O.T.
subjects. H. Sahlin ('Antiochus IV. Epiphanes und Judas Mackabäus',
pp. 41–68) argues that the main purpose of the book of Daniel in its
final form was to present Judas as the Messiah who would free
Israel from Antiochus and establish the Kingdom of God (thus, e.g.
the Son of Man was originally Judas), while K. T. Andersen ('Die
Chronologie der Könige von Israel und Judah', pp. 69–112 + 2
tables) essays a reconstruction of the chronology of the kings of
Israel and Judah.
M.A.K.

KAPELRUD, A. S. and JERVELL, J. (ed.): *Studia Theologica*. Scandinavian Journal of Theology. Vol. 23, no. 2. 1969. Pp. 115–40. (Universitets-forlaget, Oslo. Subscription price: N.Kr. 60)

This issue contains one study by M. Saebø, entitled 'Die deuterosa-charjanische Frage, Eine forschungsgeschichtliche Studie'.

Previous studies of the book of Zechariah are reviewed, the work of B. Stade providing the main point of reference. The thesis is maintained that investigators have narrowed their sights, so that they concentrated on part of the book rather than the whole, or on the question of date based on specific passages abstracted from the whole, or on exclusive questions of form or cultic background. Hence the medley of self-cancelling solutions. The many-sidedness and complexity of the texts are stressed. Perhaps this is not altogether fair to the best of the older scholars who presented their solutions as hypotheses to be tested and validated by their fitness to make sense of all the data. Although this survey is probably over schematic, it nevertheless provides a useful piece of mapwork. Its brevity means that wholesale judgements are made without supporting evidence, but the author will no doubt demonstrate the strength of his own solutions in the traditio-historical treatment of Zech. 9–14 which he promises.   D.R.J.

KOSMALA, H. (ed.): *Annual of the Swedish Theological Institute* (Vol. VI, 1967–8). 1968. Pp. 134. (E. J. Brill, Leiden. Price: Fl. 28)

Three contributions to this volume are of direct interest for O.T. study. G. W. Anderson writes a careful and illuminating survey of 'Johannes Lindblom's Contribution to Biblical Studies'; J. F. A. Sawyer's study of 'Spaciousness' considers the words and usages connected with both territorial and metaphorical concepts of space, particularly as these are linked with ideas of deliverance. R. J. Coggins' paper (delivered to the Society) on 'The Old Testament and Samaritan Origins' develops a careful critique of the evidence and problems and points to the importance of discerning the diverse elements within post-exilic Judaism. The remaining five articles have a primarily N.T. concern, but R. Leivestad's critical attack: 'Der Apokalyptische Menschensohn ein theologishes Phantom' has considerably wider implications, and A. Schalit sheds light on Davidic messianic ideas linked with the Herodian family.   P.R.A.

KRAUS, H.-J. (ed.): *Verkündigung und Forschung*. (Beihefte zu Evangelische Theologie, Heft 1). 1969. Pp. 86. (Chr. Kaiser Verlag, München. Price: DM. 7.00)

This volume contains reviews of recent and not so recent literature in Old Testament and related fields of study (creation myths, wisdom, apocalyptic and theophany). In so far as the works reviewed may be regarded as examples of new ways taken by *Religionsgeschichte* (that is, new attempts to define the relationship between Old Testa-ment or apocalyptic books and extra-Israelite material) the volume has unity of a kind and a connexion may be discerned between the opening general article on 'Alttestamentliche Religionsgeschichte' and those which follow it. The most interesting and incisive article

is that by H. E. von Waldow on 'Theophany'. The volume is not very
effective and the relation of its contents to the title of the publication
is not transparent, although there is a contribution by a Lutheran
pastor who discusses the use which he has made of the commentary
on the Psalms by H. J. Kraus.   W.McK.

NIELSEN, E. and SIMONSEN, H. (ed.): *Bibelen som helligskrift*. 1969. Pp. 216
(including 3 maps, 2 diagrams, and 1 chronological chart). 16 plates.
(Danmarks Radios grundbøger, Fremad)

This collection of essays is, in the best sense, a popular introduction
to Bible study, combining historical and literary presentation and
theological interpretation. It begins with a discussion (by E. Nielsen)
of the Bible and religion (including sections on Islam, Manicheism,
Zoroastrianism, and Buddhism). N. H. Gadegård contributes a
brief sketch of the O.T. as 'the first Bible', with an account of the
various literary types. B. Otzen writes on the prophets under the
rubric 'History and Revelation', S. Biørn on the Law (Judaism as a
book religion), and B. Salomonsen on later Judaism and the background of early Christianity. The N.T. is introduced by B. Wiberg.
H. Simonsen discusses the tradition about Jesus and the origins of the
Gospels. Paul and the gentile Christian congregations are the theme
of a comprehensive essay by S. Pedersen. J. Aagaard examines the
use of the Bible in the Church's mission, preaching, and teaching.
E. T. Pedersen's contribution combines a presentation of the biblical
Weltanschauung with a discussion of different approaches (e.g.
demythologizing) to the problem of communicating the biblical
message. E. Nielsen discusses the Bible and modern historical research.
H. Simonsen's concluding essay on 'the Bible and the Church'
takes up the central problems of the theological interpretation of
Scripture. Though 'popular', these essays are anything but superficial.
They provoke thought as well as imparting information. There is a
useful bibliography and a good index. The illustrations are attractive
and effective.   G.W.A.

NOBER, P.: *Elenchus Bibliographicus Biblicus*, Vol. 49. 1968. Pp. xix, 976.
(Biblical Institute Press, Rome. Subscription price: Lire 4,500)

This annual publication, now separated from *Biblica*, covers 8,879
entries of articles, books and reviews of books, on the whole biblical
field, classified under twenty-one headings, the first of which itself
covers bibliography. In addition, the volume is fully indexed, facilitating the discovery of a particular article or the studies of particular
Hebrew words. It is an indispensable tool, and the product of an
immense amount of work by its editor.   P.R.A.

NOTH, M.: *Gesammelte Studien zum Alten Testament II*. (Theologische
Bücherei 39.) 1969. Pp. 217. (Chr. Kaiser Verlag, Munich. Price:
DM. 16.80)

Here are reprinted nine further articles by our late Honorary Member
ranging in date from 1926 to 1968. H. W. Wolff writes a short Foreword, R. Smend appends an *In Memoriam*, and there is a bibliography
of the author's writings — including reviews — by H. Schult.

Everything Noth wrote is worthy of attention; it is therefore sufficient here to list the titles as printed: 'Zur Komposition d. Buches Daniel'; 'Die Historisierung d. Mythus im A.T.'; 'Zur Auslegung d. A.T.'; 'Von d. Knechtgestalt d. A.T. i.d. Verkündigung'; 'Die Bewährung v. Salomos "gottlicher Weisheit"'; 'Tendenzen theol. Forschung in Deutschland'; 'Jerusalem u.d. Nordreich'. Some have already appeared in more than one place, and some in English dress, but it is well worthwhile to have them brought together and well indexed. Two further volumes are to appear.

D.R.Ap-T.

RIESENFELD, H. (ed.): *Svensk exegetisk årsbok*, XXXIII. 1968. Pp. 198. (C. W. K. Gleerup, Lund. Price: Sw.Kr. 20)

Five of the main articles in this issue are of direct interest to the *Alttestamentler*. A. L. Merrill contributes an analysis and interpretation (in English) of the Keret Legend. In a lengthy article (in English), 'Historians and Prophets', P. R. Ackroyd examines the varying accounts of (a) the relationship between Isaiah and Ahaz in the Syro-Ephraimite crisis, and (b) Jeremiah and the fall of Jerusalem. The remaining contributions are all in Swedish. I. Soisalon-Soininen examines the concept of function in the study of O.T. traditions. H. Ringgren discusses *gā'al*, *gō'ēl*, and related terms with particular reference to the question how the study of 'concepts' may be satisfactorily carried out. S. Erlandsson re-examines the translation and interpretation of Amos 5:25-7. There are also five N.T. articles, and the volume also includes reviews and, in slightly revised form, the submissions made by Professor Ringgren and Riesenfeld in connection with the recent revision of the syllabus of religious studies in Swedish Universities. This is a volume of exceptional interest and importance.

G.W.A.

VAN SELMS, A., and VAN DER WOUDE, A. S. (ed.): *Adhuc Loquitur: Collected Essays of Dr B. Gemser*. (Pretoria Oriental Series, ed. A. Van Selms, Vol. VII.) 1968. Pp. 184. (E. J. Brill, Leiden. Price: Fl. 45)

This volume is a tribute to the memory of Prof. B. Gemser. The editors have selected eight essays which indicate the scope of his interests. The essays 'God in Genesis'; 'The Importance of the Motive Clause in Old Testament Law'; 'The *rîb* — or Controversy-Pattern in Hebrew mentality'; 'The Spiritual Structure of Biblical Aphoristic Wisdom', will already be known to most scholars as they have appeared in various journals. The other four essays have been translated from Dutch, and are 'Questions concerning the Religion of the Patriarchs'; 'Humilitas or Dignitas'; 'The Object of Moral Judgement in the Old Testament'; and 'Delayed Consciousness of Revelations'. The collecting together of these essays, and especially the inclusion of those translated from Dutch, will be welcomed by biblical scholars. The volume also contains a brief biographical sketch of Prof. B. Gemser, and a bibliography of his publications.

E.R.R.

SANDMEL, S. (ed.): *Old Testament Issues*. (S.C.M. Press Forum Books.) 1969. Pp. 266. (S.C.M. Press, London. Price: 25s.)

This is a collection of extracts on significant issues in Old Testament scholarship taken from books and articles written for the most part by well-known scholars. Thus extracts from the writings of F. M. Cross, M. Noth, E. Nielsen, J. Bright, and others are set out here. There is no single specific theme to the work, and the topics are largely chosen for their intrinsic interest. Surprisingly the editor shows considerable hostility to Wellhausen in particular, leading him to see recent scholarship as a disproving of this great scholar's work.

R.E.C.

THOMSEN, P.: *Die Palästina-Literatur. Eine internationale Bibliographie in systematischer Ordnung mit Autoren- und Sachregister*. Band VII. *Die Literatur der Jahre 1940–1945*. Lieferung 1 (pp. 1–176), 2 (pp. 177–320). Prepared for publication by O. Eissfeldt and L. Rost. 1969. Pp. xii, 320. (Akademie-Verlag, Berlin. Price: DM. 48.00 each fascicle)

The sixth volume of this bibliographical survey was published between 1954 and 1956 (see *B.L.*, 1954, p. 15; 1955, p. 13; 1957, p. 13; *Eleven Years*, pp. 552, 646; *Decade*, p. 13); this covered the period 1935–9, the earlier five volumes covering 1895–1934 having appeared between 1908 and 1938. In 1957–60 a supplementary Volume A was published (see *B.L.*, 1957, p. 14; 1959, p. 8; 1961, p. 14; *Decade*, pp. 14, 144, 252), covering the years 1878–94. Thomsen died in 1954, but among his papers were found the slips for this seventh volume, now being published with the assistance of a number of scholars who have thus provided a most valuable addition to the bibliographical aids available to biblical and other scholars. These two fascicles cover general bibliographical material, surveys, journals, *Festschrifts* and the like, and the major section on history; the remaining two fascicles will, as in the earlier volumes, cover the other areas of study, together with the indexes. Fascicles 3 and 4 are due to appear at the end of 1969 or the beginning of 1970 to complete the volume. It is much to be hoped that means will be found to continue this valuable work to cover the years since 1945.

P.R.A.

TSEVAT, M. (ed.): *Hebrew Union College Annual*, XXXIX. 1968. Pp. 230, 79 in Hebrew. Index to Vols I–XXXVIII. (Hebrew Union College, Cincinnati)

The first article in this volume, 'Old Assyrian Texts in the University Museum, Philadelphia, Pa.', gives the cuneiformist the opportunity of studying Prof. Hildegard Lewy's copies of the unpublished Kültepe tablets. Prof. S. N. Kramer has written a short introduction. Of the other twelve articles, one in German and two in Hebrew, two are of particular interest to the biblical scholar, 'On Faith and Revelation in the Bible' (H. C. Brichto), and 'Aspects of the Religion of the Book of Proverbs' (M. V. Fox). Though some of the remaining articles belong to the general field of Judaic studies, yet the biblical student will find plenty to interest him in 'Some Observations on Late Babylonian Texts and Rabbinic Literature' (D. B. Weisberg); '*Lag Ba'Omer* — Its origin and import' (J. Morgenstern); 'The Golden Calf Episode

In Post-biblical Literature' (L. Smolar and M. Aberbach); 'The Date of the Mekilta de-Rabbi Ishmael' (Ben Zion Wacholder); 'A Geniza Find of Saadya's Psalm-Preface and its Musical Aspects' (H. Avenary); 'Ein aus arabischer Gefangenschaft befreiter christlicher Proselyt in Jerusalem' (A. Scheiber); 'David Kimḥi and the Rationalist Tradition' (F. Talmage); 'Leviathan, Behemoth and Ziz: Jewish Messianic Symbols in Art' (J. Gutman).

E.R.R.

ARCHAEOLOGY AND EPIGRAPHY

BUHL, M.-L., and HOLM-NIELSEN, S.: *Shiloh. The Danish Excavations at Tall Sailun, Palestine, in 1926, 1929, 1932 and 1963. The Pre-Hellenistic Remains.* (Publications of the National Museum Archaeological-Historical Series I, Vol. XII.) 1969. Pp. 84. 14 photos and line-drawings in text, 286 photos of sherds and 286 line-drawn reconstructions of same, 1 large plan of tell and 11 of individual sites excavated. (National Museum of Denmark, Copenhagen. Price: D.Kr. 100)

At long last, thanks to patient efforts in face of daunting difficulties, the results of the first three Danish excavations at Shiloh are here presented in a worthy and usable form. The short fourth dig served not only to elucidate unclear points in the previous campaigns, but has also broken some new ground. Shiloh is now shown to have been occupied during the divided monarchy; so that Jeremiah's reference to its destruction must be an allusion to recent history and not — as so often repeated since the 1929 dig slipped up on chronology — to a hoary Philistine blitz. More might undoubtedly be learnt from this difficult site by further excavation, but the present authors and their architect seem to have salvaged all that is possible from the old records and, in doing so, have removed several anomalies from Palestinian pottery sequences, and laid us all in their debt.

D.R.Ap-T.

Eretz-Israel. Archaeological, Historical and Geographical Studies, Vol. IX, *W. F. Albright Volume.* 1969. Pp. xii, 176 (Hebrew), xii, 139 (non-Hebrew), 64 plates, and numerous drawings. (Israel Exploration Society, Jerusalem. Price: $18.00)

This work contains twenty-one articles in Hebrew (most of which are summarized in English), four in French, and fourteen in English, on linguistic, textual, and exegetical, as well as archaeological, historical, and geographical, subjects. There is a bibliography of Albright's writings published between the preparation of the earlier *Festschrift* (*B.L.*, 1962, p. 17; *Decade*, p. 327), a photograph of him, and a preface written in his honour by Y. Yadin. The S.O.T.S. welcomes this fitting tribute to one of its Honorary Members.

J.A.E.

FRANKEN, H. J.: *Van Aartsvaders tot Profeten. Een archaeologische verkenningstocht door het land van de Bijbel.* 1962. Pp. 263. (Strengholt, Amsterdam. Price: Fl. 12.50)

This well-illustrated work of *haute vulgarisation*, written by the Lecturer in Palestinian Archaeology in the University of Leiden, whose name is inseparably associated with the excavations at Deir Alla, is commended in a foreword by P. A. H. de Boer. Franken takes his readers first on a quick archaeological tour and then on a quick geographical tour of Palestine, before presenting an archaeological study of successive phases in its history, from the period of the Canaanites and the patriarchs to the Babylonian exile, which marked 'the end of Israel's proper Palestinian culture, *archaeologically speaking*'. The outstanding merit of this book is that, unlike so many popular books on biblical archaeology (even some which are written by experienced archaeologists), it shows the reader clearly the limits of the archaeological approach to the O.T. These limits must not be violated; when this is done, the road lies wide open to corruption, whether the intention is to establish or to undermine the truth of the Bible.

F.F.B.

FRANKEN, H. J.: *Excavations at Tell Deir 'Allâ. I. A Stratigraphical and Analytical Study of the Early Iron Age Pottery.* (Documenta et Monumenta Orientis Antiqui XVI.) 1969. Pp. xviii, 250. Figs. 82, Pls. xv. (E. J. Brill, Leiden. Price: Fl. 96)

This is a most important study of a crucial area and period. However much the author has still in hand to publish, it is to be hoped that further excavation on this site may some day be possible. The introductory chapter provides a good description of the practical details of setting up an archaeological dig, as well as justifying both the choice of this site and the excavator's refusal to accept the common identification of it with Succoth, in favour of Gilgal (1 Sam. 11:15) or the border shrine Ed (Josh. 22:11). But the marrow of the book, after the description of the two periods and twelve phases of occupation of this remarkable Early Settlement Period *haram*, is the analysis of the associated pottery. In connection with the latter, credit is given to J. Kalbeek, a practical potter and sculptor, who initiated some valuable new methods and lines of study — though spectrometry does not appear to have been used. Argument between ceramic experts will no doubt continue about some deductions, but the cultural break between the Late Bronze Age (Canaanites) and their Early Iron successors (presumably Israelites) seems to be proved, and is here dated to the beginning of the 12th century B.C. A simple sketchmap pinpointing the position of Deir 'Allâ would have been welcome.

D.R.Ap-T.

GILBERTSON, T.: *Uncovering Bible Times. A study in Biblical Archaeology.* 1969. Pp. 135, 20 illustrations. (Augsburg Publishing House, Minneapolis; Lutterworth Press, London. Price: 10s.)

This is a popular account of some archaeological finds chosen to show how they illustrate and confirm the accuracy of the Biblical narrative. Everything between Josiah and the New Testament is omitted. The archaeological material is used to illustrate the Bible with little respect for its integrity as a scientific study. This book is misleading and unworthy of its subject.

J.R.

KELSO, J. L.: *Archaeology and the Ancient Testament. The Christian's God of the Old Testament vs. the Canaanite religion.* 1968. Pp. 214. 57 illustrations. (Zondervan Publishing House, Grand Rapids, Michigan. Price: $4.95)

This is a brief, popular introduction to the Old Testament. The author's purpose is to illustrate from archaeology how superior Hebrew religion always was to the Canaanite religion that surrounded it. There is a good deal of homiletic material here which should interest and help those readers to whom the very prominent conservative evangelical presuppositions of the author are acceptable. Others will find the writing too subjective to be helpful.   J.R.

LAPP, P. W. (ed.): *The 1957 Excavations at Beth-Zur.* (Annual of the American Schools of Oriental Research, Vol. XXXVIII.) 1968. Pp. 87, 83 figures, plans and plates. (A.S.O.R., Cambridge, Mass)

This volume contains the account of the 1957 excavations at Beth-Zur conducted by O. R. Sellers, R. W. Funk, J. L. McKenzie, P. and N. Lapp, and has been well produced by orphan boys at the Schneller Press in Amman. Results of the first campaign at Khirbet et-Tubeiqa by O. R. Sellers and W. F. Albright were published in *B.A.S.O.R.*, 43 (1931). There is a history of the site from the Bronze Age to the Hellenistic period and an excellent account of the pottery, particularly the Hellenistic. Unfortunately it was not possible to revise the MS later than 1960.   J.N.S.

MAZAR, B.: *The Excavations in the Old City of Jerusalem. Preliminary Report of the First Season, 1968.* Also AVI-YONAH, M.: *The Latin Inscription from the Excavations in Jerusalem.* 1969. Pp. 24. 15 plates. (Israel Exploration Society, Jerusalem)

This booklet contains the English translation of one section of *Eretz-Israel*, Volume 9, reviewed on p. 15. It is almost entirely devoted to Mazar's account of the excavations recently undertaken at the south-western corner of the haram area, which brought to light important Omayyad and Herodian remains.   P.R.A.

PECKHAM, J. B.: *The Development of the late Phoenician Scripts* (Harvard Semitic Series, Vol. XX). 1968. Pp. 233 (including XVII Plates). (Harvard University Press, Cambridge, Mass. Price: 66s. 6d.)

This book, by a pupil of F. M. Cross, provides a much needed survey of Phoenician (including Punic) epigraphic scripts of the 8th to the 1st century B.C., at the same time giving a very useful inventory of the Phoenician inscriptional material for this period. There are numerous tables of alphabets.   S.P.B.

PFOHL, G. (ed.): *Das Alphabet: Entstehung und Entwicklung der griechischen Schrift.* (Wege der Forschung, LXXXVIII.) 1968. Pp. 40, 431. (Wissenschaftliche Buchgesellschaft, Darmstadt. Price: DM. 32.40)

The volume here reviewed consists of a long introduction by the editor, followed by twenty articles published between 1922 and 1963 from German, American or English (these last translated into German) sources; all are concerned primarily or exclusively with the origin and development of the Greek alphabet, some of them very technical and few likely to be of much interest to members of this Society. The introduction contains a mass of statistical and bibliographical matter, e.g. a list of scholars who have suggested dates ranging from 1400 B.C. to 700 B.C. for the transmission of the Phoenician alphabet to the Greeks and the half-dozen or so places through which this is supposed to have been effected. The first eight articles are devoted to these problems. Of the next two, both by O. Eissfeldt, the first discusses questions arising out of the relationship of the Ugaritic syllabary, the Phoenician and the Greek alphabets, to one another and the date of the transmission, which he puts at *c*. 1000 B.C. plus or minus 100 years; the second examines the order of the letters in the alphabet. The authors of the next eight articles go into the problems of the inner-Greek development of the alphabet, the local scripts and so on. The last two articles are reviews, for the most part highly favourable, of Miss L. Jeffrey's now well-known *Local Scripts of Archaic Greece* (Oxford, 1963). All the articles are of considerable interest, although some are from 50 to 30 years old. Numerous illustrations are scattered about the book, all printed and not all entirely legible (e.g. p. 309, no. 8 f., p. 359, no. 12; p. 365, no. 32). At the same time the prospective English reader may properly be warned that lucidity is not a characteristic mark of the German language, and that this warning is especially true of German 'translationese' and technical jargon.   G.R.D.

PRITCHARD, J. B.: *The Ancient Near East in Pictures Relating to the Old Testament*. 2nd ed. with supplement. 1969. Pp. xviii, 396. (Princeton University Press; Oxford University Press, London. Price: 120s.; $30.00)

This second edition of the volume noted in *B.L.*, 1955, p. 18 (*Eleven Years*, p. 651), contains a reprint of the material of the original edition, together with a supplement (pp. 341–84) and an index covering the whole volume. The supplement is arranged under the same headings as the original, the illustrations being numbered in sequence from 770 to 882. Among many notable and interesting additions there may be mentioned a useful series of weights, objects from the Jericho tombs, inscribed jar-handles including royal seal impressions, the tablet mentioning the capture of Jerusalem, the Meṣad-Hashavyahu letter and other documents. Particular attention has been given to the notable work done at Nimrud, Gibeon, Jericho, Hazor, Shechem and Arad, and a number of plans or panoramic photographs illustrate the work at some of these places.
The third edition of the *Ancient Near Eastern Texts* (1969. Pp. 758. Price: $30.00) has not yet been received. The two new volumes may be purchased together at a reduced price of $50.00. What is of particular interest to owners of the earlier editions is the publication, also not yet received, of a volume containing the supplementary material to both *ANET* and *ANEP*, including both indexes, and priced at $15.00. The author (and editor) is to be congratulated on thus making more up-to-date material readily available; and the publishers have performed a valuable service in making the new material available in its various forms.   P.R.A.

SWAUGER, J. L. (ed.): *The Excavation of Bethel, 1934–60.* (Annual of the American Schools of Oriental Research, Vol. XXXIX.) 1968. Pp. 128, 121 plates. (A.S.O.R., Cambridge, Mass.)

Excavations at Bethel in 1934 were directed by W. F. Albright, and in 1954, 1957, and 1960 by J. L. Kelso. This volume recounts the history of the site from the Chalcolithic to the Byzantine period, and catalogues and describes its flints and pottery. No trace was found of a temple built by Jeroboam I nor was it possible to fix more definitely than *c.* 553–30 the date of the 6th-century destruction, which is described as 'total'. Scholars may thus continue to speculate whether it was destroyed by Persians or rival Judaeans from Jerusalem. The importance of Bethel in the history, religion and literature of the Old Testament makes this excellent publication extremely valuable.

J.N.S.

HISTORY AND GEOGRAPHY

BERNHEIM, A. and MARAINI, F.: *Jerusalem, Rock of Ages.* 1969. Pp. 122. 12 plates in colour, 106 full-page monochrome gravure. (Hamish Hamilton, London; Chanticleer Press, New York. Price: 105s.)

This is not the place, nor is this reviewer competent, to assess the artistic merit of all these pictures, mainly of stonework in historic Jerusalem. Alfred Bernheim's gifts as an architectural photographer have been recognized by his government; here he is assisted by Ricarda Schwerin. The text, by an experienced travel writer, goes its own independent way and sketches, in a sympathetic and urbane manner, the history of Jerusalem from earliest times to the present. It has been culled from reliable sources and spiced with the author's personal views and experiences. The translation (with American spelling) by Judith Landry reads excellently. A book for the coffee table rather than the desk.

D.R.Ap-T.

*BRUCE, F. F.: *Israel and the Nations: from the Exodus to the Fall of the second Temple.* 1969. Pp. 254, 13 plates and 3 maps. (The Paternoster Press, London. Price: 25s.)

The first edition of this book was reviewed in *B.L.*, 1964, p. 24; *Decade*, p. 492. A new edition now appears with the original text, but with 36 excellent illustrations and 3 maps selected by Mr Alan Millard, which add to the attractiveness of a book that has proved its usefulness to many students and teachers.

L.A.P.

DONNER, H. and RÖLLIG, W.: *Kanaanäische und aramäische Inschriften, mit einem Beitrag von O. Rössler.* (Zweite Auflage.) Band I. 1966. Texte. Pp. XV, 54. Band II. 1968. Kommentar. Pp. XVI, 343. Band III. 1969. Pp. vii, 84, 34 plates. (Otto Harrassowitz, Wiesbaden.) Price: DM. 82)

The first edition of this extremely useful work was noticed in *B.L.*, 1964, p. 18 (Vol. I), and 1966, p. 12 (Vols. II and III) (*Decade*, pp. 486,

564). In this new edition three new texts are added (Pyrgi, Bahadïrlï, Kandahar), and six pages of additional notes, mostly of a bibliographical nature. The text itself remains unchanged, although most of the tiresome misprints of the first edition have been corrected.

S.P.B.

GALE, GENERAL SIR RICHARD: *Great Battles of Biblical History*. 1968. Pp. xii, 156. (Hutchinson, London. Price: 35s.)

This book spans the period from the Patriarchs to the capture of Masada by the Romans, but deals mostly with battles in O.T. times. The author, who has a good descriptive style, draws on his first-hand knowledge of the terrain of Palestine and also on his wide experience as a soldier. The student of the Bible will appreciate a fresh approach to these battles and also the application of the 'military and political lessons' to more modern situations. Unfortunately, the text is marred by many errors, such as 'Plain of Morah', 'Amalakites', 'Giliad', 'Issacher', and 'Waters of Morom'.   G.F.

*GILBERT, M.: *Jewish History Atlas*. 1969. (Pp. 146.) (Weidenfeld and Nicolson, London. Price: 35s.)

This atlas contains 112 maps, of which 11 relate to the O.T. period, illustrating the history, the sufferings, and the contribution to life and culture of the Jews from about 2000 B.C. to the present day. The maps are based on extensive research and introduce many unusual details. A useful bibliography is appended. This fascinating volume should be in every Secondary School and College library.   L.A.P.

*KRAMER, K. F.: *A Chronological Chart of Salvation History*. 1968. Pp. 32 with 5 full-colour, fold-out maps. (Burns and Oates, London, and Herder and Herder, New York. Price: 22s.)

This chronological chart of O.T. history, translated from the 4th German edition, records political and cultural events in Egypt, Canaan-Palestine and Western Asia from pre-historic times to A.D. 100. The maps are excellent and fully indexed. This is a useful reference book for all students of the O.T.   L.A.P.

*MALY, E. H.: *The World of David and Solomon* (Backgrounds to the Bible Series). 1966. Pp. x, 182. 2 maps. (Prentice-Hall, Englewood Cliffs. Price: 56s.)

This provides a general historical survey and a discussion of the relevant literature for each of the main periods of biblical history. The volume is attractively produced and is eminently readable. It provides a useful narrative presentation of the period from Samuel to Solomon, with a fair measure of comment on some of the main problems of the period. The volume suffers somewhat from a failure to

discuss really seriously the problem of historicity, being more dependent than the material warrants on the over-confident assumptions
of the direct historical worth of the narratives in the books of Samuel
and Kings which are particularly associated with the name of W. F.
Albright to whom appeal is often made. The result is a certain
unreality in considering the divergent estimates of such leading
figures as Samuel. But the author is very much aware that he is
handling material whose primary interest is theological rather than
historical, and he draws out the significance of the biblical narratives.
There is a curious unresolved overlap in two discussions of the
Ark on pp. 15 and 59, and the author also falls into the trap of
reading into 2 Sam. 24 information which is only to be found in the
writings of the Chronicler. (See also the note below on the volume
by J. M. Myers in the same series.)   P.R.A.

*MYERS, J. M.: *The World of the Restoration* (Backgrounds to the Bible
Series). 1968. Pp. 182. (Prentice-Hall Inc., Englewood Cliffs, N.J.;
Prentice-Hall International, Hemel Hempstead. Price: 56s.)

This volume sets out primarily to provide the setting of biblical
history, and its chapters are therefore arranged to cover the period of
Neo-Babylonian rule, of Cyrus and of his successors, with one chapter
devoted to Ezra. The biblical material is included, though inevitably
rather briefly and sometimes perhaps in rather too simple a manner.
There is much useful historical information. It is not always very clear
to what kind of reader the book is directed; the more technical
references appear to be somewhat out of place in a book which in
many respects is intended as a guide for students; in this it differs
markedly from the volume by E. H. Maly in the same series (see
above).   P.R.A.

NEGENMAN, J. H.: *Grosser Bildatlas zur Bibel*. German edition by
C. Rietzschel. 1969. Pp. 200. (Gütersloher Verlagshaus Gerd Mohn.
Price: DM. 48) (An English edition, edited by the late Professor H. H.
Rowley, has been published by Collins, London. Price: 105s.)

The original Dutch edition of this atlas (*De Bakermat van de Bijbel*,
1968. Elsevier, Amsterdam) was not noted in the *Book List*. It now
appears in magnificent form in German, with a wealth of illustrations
in colour and in black and white, and with a full series of maps,
mostly in colour. Like other biblical atlases of recent years, it is
much more than an atlas. It contains sections covering the main
historical periods from David to the end of the N.T. period. These
are preceded by three chapters of which the first two are unusual in a
volume of this kind; one covers the formation of the Bible, and the
second the development of writing well-documented and illustrated.
The third provides a fairly full account of the cultural and historical
environment of Israel's earliest history. The presentation is excellent.
The archaeological information is up-to-date. The illustrations are
carefully annotated and the maps are clear and do not attempt to
crowd too much into a limited space. This is the kind of book, which,

even if it does not provide new information, enables a better appreciation and appropriation of what is known, and certainly enriches biblical study. There is a full index and a list of biblical references.

P.R.A.

*REICKE, B.: *The New Testament Era. The World of the Bible from 500 B.C. to A.D. 100.* 1969. Pp. x, 336. 5 maps. (A. and C. Black, London. Price: 55s.)

This is a translation of *Neutestamentliche Zeitgeschichte* published in 1964. It is concentrated almost entirely on the latter part of the period, having only short and rather simplified opening chapters on the Persian period (pp. 5–33), the period of Greek rule (pp. 35–62) and the Hasmonean period (pp. 63–75). The account of the Roman period is much more detailed, and includes discussion both of the political issues and of the religious parties. The last chapters deal with Judaism and Christianity as they developed in the difficult years between A.D. 70 and 100. A lengthy bibliography is provided. This provides a useful background for the study of the later Old Testament, the Intertestamental, and New Testament periods.

P.R.A.

WEBER, M.: *Ancient Judaism.* 1967. Pp. xxvii, 484. (The Free Press, New York; Collier-Macmillan, London. Paperback. Price: 28s.)

The translation of this book, which the great sociologist wrote in 1917–19 and left unfinished at his death, was first published by Gerth and Martindale in 1952. This paperback edition now makes generally available a classic by a giant of the Marx–Freud era, who has bequeathed to us the widely accepted category of the 'charismatic', but has by no means exhausted his influence, particularly in presenting the events and ideas of the O.T. as responsible for the uniqueness of western civilization.

D.R.J.

WINN HASWELL, J. H.: *An Introduction to the Holy Land.* 1969. Pp. xii, 140, 57 illustrations. (Duckworth, London. Price: 42s.)

This is a popular pilgrim's guide written for the use of the contemporary traveller who wishes to visit the Holy Places and other sites mentioned in the Bible. It is attractively written out of deep knowledge and real love of its subject. The one limitation is that it deals only with those sites which are currently under the control of the state of Israel. There is no mention of Jerash or Petra.

J.R.

TEXT AND VERSIONS

BAARS, W.: *New Syro-Hexaplaric Texts, edited, commented upon and compared with the Septuagint.* 1968. Pp. vii, 157. (E. J. Brill, Leiden. Price: Fl. 43)

The first 40 pages of Dr Baars' work is devoted to an exhaustive list of all the books, parts of books and even mere quotations hitherto known of the Syrohexaplar Old Testament (i.e. Paul Bishop of Tella's Syriac version of the LXX, made *ca.* A.D. 613–17), together with full references to the various publications in which they appear. Pp. 41–131 contain the text of 24 pieces which have not yet been published (Gen. 1:1–19; 15:1–20; 19:1–14; 28:10–22; 32:12–21, 24–32; 49:1–7, 8–10, 19–28; Lev. 8:1–3; 23:33–41; Deut. 15:1–8; 32:1–43; Josh. 6:12–20; I Sam. 2:12–17, 22–4; 16:13; 20:27–33; II Sam. 6:1–6, 13–14; II Chron. 15:8–15; 17:3, 7–9; 18:31 + 19:1–3 + 25:5–12; 24:6–11; 36:11–13; Sir. 51:6–11) with the sources where the editor has found them, remarks on the method of translation and notes comparing the Syriac text with that of the Greek Septuagint. In pp. 132–45 is an appendix on Hexaplaric readings in Deut. 32:1–43. Finally, in pp. 146–9 the editor adds an Epilogue in which he briefly discusses how far his new texts preserve the original Syrohexaplaric text and their importance for the study of the LXX, to which he adds a list of *desiderata* for Hexaplaric study. Dr Baars' work can be praised without any reservation for its invaluable bibliographical matter, for the accuracy (so far as the reviewer can judge) of the new pieces, for their intrinsic importance, and lastly for the hints which he throws out for future lines of Hexaplaric study. G.R.D.

Biblia Hebraica Stuttgartensia. Editio funditus renovata ed. *K. Elliger et W. Rudolph.* Fasc. 11. *Liber Psalmorum,* praeparavit H. Bardtke. 1969. Pp. x, 140. (Württembergische Bibelanstalt, Stuttgart. Price: DM. 6.95)

The new *BHS* made its debut in 1968 (see *B.L.,* 1969, p. 15), and the present fascicle follows the pattern already set. The Prolegomena, however, are listed to *app. criticus, app. masorae,* and an index to the sigla and abbreviations of *masorae parvae.* In the first of these there are some legitimate divergences from those given in the Isaiah fascicle, though others of them are enigmatic. E.g. *Qumran Milḥama* is singled out for mention, and raises the question to what extent (if any) the non-biblical scrolls of Qumran should be included, especially before they have all been assessed for their validity as 'textual evidence' for the biblical text. Again since the Samaritan and the Targumic texts of the Pentateuch appear in fascicles containing Isaiah and Psalms, why is there no mention of *Sefer Abisha*' and of the *Neofiti MS.* although *TJ* and *TJii* have been listed? But, no doubt, these and other discrepancies will be ironed out in due course.

The textual notes on the Psalms seem to be more numerous than those in *BH*³ and also than those in the Isaiah fascicle. B.J.R.

BUTIN, R.: *The Ten Nequdoth of the Torah or The Meaning and Purpose of the Extraordinary Points of the Pentateuch. Prolegomenon* by S. Talmon. (The Library of Biblical Studies. Ed. by H. M. Orlinsky.) 1969. Pp. xxviii, 136. (First published 1906.) (Ktav Publishing House, New York. Price: $6.95)

EHRLICH, A. B.: *Mikrâ Ki-Pheshutô. The Bible according to its Literal Meaning. In Three Volumes. Prolegomenon* by H. M. Orlinsky. (*The Library of Biblical Studies.* Ed. by H. M. Orlinsky.) 1969. Pp. xxxiii, iv, 385; xi, 471; ii, 519. (First published: Vol. I, 1899; II, 1900; III, 1901.) (Ktav Publishing House, Inc., New York. Price: $25.00)

As in the previous *B.L.* (1969, pp. 16 f.), attention is drawn to two important issues of classical works by the Ktav Publishing House. The first by Butin, is well-known, but enriched by the workmanlike survey by S. Talmon in the *Prolegomenon*. He remarks that the *Neofiti 1* MS. of the Jerusalem Targum has a special contribution to make to the evidence of the Versions on the occurrences of the *puncta extraordinaria*, and he deals with ten specific cases. Again Qumran MSS suggest that the points have their origin in the early Hellenistic period, and throw further light on their functions.

The second is the massive three-volume work of A. B. Ehrlich. For most of us, his name conjures up the memory of his later work, *Randglossen*, but no one will cavil at the inclusion of the much larger work in this series, particularly after reading Orlinsky's masterpiece of an assessment in the *Prolegomenon*. As 'a master of the Hebrew language and a trained philologian', Ehrlich was admitted into a small circle of the learned of his own day, despite a native awkwardness which made him unpopular with the majority. Today, when we are seeking after a Hebraic *Sprachgefühl* as well as a scientific study of the text, we might well find his insights still more rewarding. The work is in Hebrew, the *Prolegomenon* in English.   B.J.R.

DIETRICH, M.: *Neue palästinisch punktierte Bibelfragmente, veröffentlicht und auf Text und Punktation hin untersucht* (Publications de l'Institut de Recherche et de l'Histoire des Textes, Section biblique et massorétique: Massorah, collection éditée par G. E. Weil, Série 11, Études, Premier Volume). 1968. Pp. xii, 135, 86 Hebrew text, two tables. (E. J. Brill, Leiden. Price: £9 14s.)

This volume contains a detailed study of some new biblical fragments with Palestinian vocalization which the author discovered in the Bodleian and in Cambridge University Library. An informative introduction is followed by a full description of the fragments, and by a careful discussion of the consonantal text, Massoretic notes, accentuation, vocalization, reading signs, and pronunciation. The Hebrew text of the fragments is provided, and the tables show the relative chronology of the manuscripts here published, and also of all known biblical fragments with Palestinian punctuation. There is a useful bibliography, which, however, stops short at 1960, after which date the author turned to other work. The whole is an important and admirably presented contribution to Geniza studies. Two interesting points are the absence of Tiberian influence in five of the newly-discovered fragments, and the scarcity of reading signs in genuine Palestinian manuscripts.   D.W.T.

DUNAND, F.: *Papyrus grecs bibliques (Papyrus F. Inv. 266). Volumina de la Genèse et du Deutéronome.* (Extrait des Études de Papyrologie, T. IX, pp. 81–150.) 1966. Pp. 70, xv Plates. (Institut français d'archéologie orientale, Cairo)

The prolegomena to this edition of P. Fuad, Inv. 266, were noticed in the *Book List*, 1967, pp. 17–18. The present volume gives the texts, a select apparatus, and plates.   S.P.B.

ETHERIDGE, J. W.: *The Targums of Onkelos and Jonathan ben Uzziel on the Pentateuch with the Fragments of the Jerusalem Targum from the Chaldee.* 1968. Pp. v, 580, and 688. (Ktav Publishing House, Inc., New York. Price: $19.95)

Etheridge's translation of the Pentateuch Targums, with an introduction, a 'Glossary of hieratic and legal terms', and a few addenda, was originally published in two volumes in 1862 (Genesis and Exodus) and 1865 (Leviticus–Deuteronomy), and has now been reprinted in a single volume (and it is to be hoped that the binding will be strong enough to hold together so large a number of pages). While Etheridge is not invariably a safe guide, and Targumic studies have made considerable progress since his day, readers will warmly welcome the reprint of this valuable tool.

J.A.E.

JOHNSON, B.: *Die armenische Bibelübersetzung als hexaplarischer Zeuge im l. Samuelbuch.* (Coniectanea Biblica, Old Testament Series 2.) 1968. Pp. 174. (C. W. K. Gleerup, Lund. Price: Sw.Kr. 35)

This study follows on the author's earlier work, *Die hexaplarische Rezension des I Samuelbuches der Septuaginta* (*B.L.*, 1964, p. 30; *Decade*, p. 498), and studies in detail the relationship between Arm. and the chief hexaplaric witnesses. Particularly useful is the information on early medieval Armenian manuscripts and their relationship to the printed text of Zohrab (1805): while attestation of the hexaplaric signs varies considerably in the manuscripts, the texts themselves provide few important variants from the printed one.

S.P.B.

MERCATI, I. CARD.: *Psalterii Hexapli Reliquiae. Pars prima: Codex rescriptus Bybliothecae Ambrosianae O.39.Sup.* (Vol. I) *Phototypice expressus et transcriptus.* Bybliotheca Vaticana, 1958. Pp. xxxix, 113; Pll. LVI. (Vol. II) *Osservazioni. Commento critico al testo dei frammenti esaplari.* (Bybliotheca Vaticana, 1965. Price: $86.40)

The existence of the Milan palimpsest containing the Hexapla of (and Catena to) LXX Psalms 17, 27–31, 34–5, 45, 48, 88, was made known as long ago as 1896, but for various reasons the definitive edition, magnificently produced, only appeared in 1958 (not noticed in the *Book List*). This first volume of Part I contains introductory remarks (with a novel theory about the position of Origen's revised LXX text) and the text (photographic reproduction and transcription), while the more recent second volume consists of detailed annotations on the text (often very hard to read). A second part is promised, which is to contain indirect hexaplaric material. The present two volumes, which have been seen through the press by G. R. Castellino, will in particular be an indispensable tool for all concerned with the Hebrew transcription of the second column.

S.P.B.

RYDER, N.: *Old Testament — New Church.* 1969. Pp. 28. (Privately printed by New Church College, Woodford Green, London. Price: 7s. 6d.)

This duplicated monograph contains the substance of a lecture delivered at the New Church (Swedenborgian) College in 1968.

The first part is devoted to a very short sketch of the transmission of the Massoretic Text; the second part is concerned with questions raised by textual uncertainties for the exegesis of the text by Swedenborg himself and his followers.

P.R.A.

SCHMITT, A.: *Stammt der sogenannte 'θ'-Text bei Daniel wirklich von Theodotion?* (Mitteilungen des Septuaginta-Unternehmens, IX). 1966. Pp. 114 (Vandenhoeck und Ruprecht, Göttingen. Price: DM. 17)

By means of a careful comparison of the vocabulary and syntax of the Greek version of Daniel attributed to Theodotion with genuine Theodotion material preserved elsewhere, Schmitt finds that Ziegler's doubts about the correctness of Jerome's attribution were amply justified. One claimant, at least, to be Ur-Theodotion can now be safely dismissed.

S.P.B.

SHENKEL, J. D.: *Chronology and Recensional Development in the Greek Text of Kings* (Harvard Semitic Monographs, Vol. I). 1968. Pp. 151. (Harvard University Press, Cambridge, Mass. Price: 62s.)

Those who are concerned with the chronology of the divided Kingdom tend either to dismiss the variant LXX data, or use it in a totally uncritical manner. Shenkel lucidly sorts out the several strata within the LXX tradition and shows that the chronology of the 'Old Greek' has a right to be considered side by side with that of MT, and indeed he makes out a good case that for the period Omri-Joram MT's system is definitely secondary.

S.P.B.

VATTIONI, F.: *Ecclesiastico. Texto ebraico con apparato critico e versioni greca, latina e siriaco.* (Pubblicazzioni del Seminario di Semitistica. Testi 1.) 1968. Pp. liv, 285. (Istituto Orientale di Napoli. Price: 120s. approx.)

Both the general editor, G. Garbini, and the particular editor, F. Vattioni, deserve the warmest congratulations of all students of the Semitic languages and of Hebrew literature for this new venture. The present work begins with an introduction dealing with the name and authorship, the date, the state of the text and an account of the (Greek, Latin, Syriac, Armenian, Arabic and other) versions, the arrangement of the chapters and historical notices of the book down to the Council of Carthage in 419; this is followed by an exhaustive bibliography of the literature dealing with it since the recovery of the Hebrew text, and a list of abbreviations. The text then follows, arranged with the Greek and Latin versions one above the other and the Hebrew and Syriac similarly arranged on the opposite page; under the Hebrew text is a full *apparatus criticus* with the variant Hebrew readings and the relevant quotations from the Talmud and so on. The Hebrew text contains all known fragments, arranged in their proper places and is invaluable for this alone. The Greek text is that of Ziegler, the Latin is that of the Benedictine edition prepared in the Abbey of San Girolamo in Rome (though without its multi-tudinous variant readings) and the Syriac that of Lagarde, photo-graphically reproduced. The work seems to have been done with the greatest care and will be invaluable to all students of this book on the score both of accuracy and of convenience.

G.R.D.

EXEGESIS AND MODERN TRANSLATIONS

*ABBOT, W. M.; GILBERT, A.; HUNT, R. L.; SWAIN, J. C. (ed.): *The Bible Reader. An Interfaith Interpretation.* 1969. Pp. 995. (Geoffrey Chapman Ltd., London; Bruce Books, New York. Price: 25s.; $3.95)

This Bible Reader, the outcome of dialogue and co-operation between a Rabbi, a Jesuit, and two Protestant editors, consists of selections from all the books of the O.T. and the N.T. and selected books of the Apocrypha 'with notes from Catholic, Protestant and Jewish Tradi-tions and references to Art, Literature, History and the Social Problems of Modern Man'. The text used is predominantly the R.S.V. but other Jewish and Christian versions are used occasionally. The Reader is intended for use in American public (State) schools, and the passages chosen those which the editors consider 'most important or current in our culture, those passages most associated with our respective religious observances and beliefs'. The annota-tions are generous in length, reflect the findings of modern scholar-ship and are likely to interest the intelligent pupil; they are written with American readers in mind. The book is very moderately priced.

L.A.P.

BARUCQ, A.: *Ecclésiaste* (Verbum Salutis, Ancien Testament 3). 1968. Pp. 214. (Beauchesne, Paris. Price: Fr. 16.50)

Much has been packed into brief compass in this excellent commen-tary. The standpoint throughout the introduction reveals a close acquaintanceship with modern studies on Ecclesiastes. The book is treated as a unity, only 1:1-2 and 12:9 f. being definitely attributed to editorial activity, although certain glosses are allowed for else-where. Ecclesiastes is seen as a voice of protest against some of the pretensions and over-simplifications in Israel's wisdom tradition. Extra-biblical texts expressive of the same mood as Ecclesiastes are cited, but wisely no dependence either way is claimed. The extent to which exegesis and translation are indissolubly linked is well illus-trated in the translation and accompanying commentary. Finally, an all too brief attempt is made to place Ecclesiastes in its setting in Jewish thinking and to indicate its relevance in the contemporary intellectual ferment.

R.D.

BIČ, M.: *Das Buch Amos.* 1969. Pp. 206. (Evangelische Verlagsanstalt, Berlin. Price: MDN. 9.80)

A short introduction indicates the main areas of debate, and a summarizing conclusion stresses particularly the position of Amos in the religious tradition. The commentary itself is detailed and contains a fuller development of views which Professor Bič has already expressed in earlier writings. Amos is a cult official, and this is argued both from the terms used and from the form-critical analysis of the material; it is a view which is difficult to resist, even if uncertainty in the interpretation of terms remains. The last verses of the book are regarded as belonging to that aspect of Amos' teaching which represents a total condemnation of the north. This is less easy to accept, especially since Bič stresses the oral transmission of the prophecies and clearly envisages some measure of adaptation of the prophet's message to later situations. A useful and stimulating study. The volume is uniform with Bič's earlier commentaries on Joel and Zechariah (*B.L.*, 1962, p. 24; 1965, p. 21; *Decade*, pp. 334, 573).

P.R.A.

BIČ, M.: *Trois prophètes dans un temps de ténèbres: Sophonie-Nahum-Habaquq.* (Lectio Divina, 48.) 1968. Pp. 135. (Les Éditions du Cerf, Paris)

The chief value of these brief commentaries lies in their clear presentation in summary form of the main alternative solutions which have been proposed to the problems of these three books. Although there is perhaps little here that is original, the author argues persuasively on behalf of those views which he himself prefers. Another valuable feature of the book is the sketch of the historical background which occupies most of the introductory chapter. The main conclusions are that Zephaniah prophesied about 630 B.C. and may have been one of the influences which led the young Josiah to initiate his reform; that Nahum was a temple prophet whose book is a liturgy of thanksgiving composed for the New Year Festival of 612, immediately after the fall of Nineveh; and that the book of Habakkuk, probably composed between 609 and 604, is also the work of a cult prophet, chapters 1 and 2 being a 'prophetic liturgy' or dialogue of the prophet with God.

R.N.W.

BRUNNER, R.: *Das Buch Ezechiel*, 2 vols. (Zürcher Bibelkommentare). 2nd ed. 1969. Pp. 268, 158. (Zwingli Verlag, Zürich and Stuttgart, Price: Sw.Fr. 15; bound, Sw.Fr. 21)

The first edition of this commentary appeared in the series *Prophezei: Schweizerisches Bibelwerk für die Gemeinde* and was reviewed in *B.L.*, 1946, p. 35 (*Eleven Years*, p. 35). The commentator's primary concern with theological exposition has made his work relatively immune from the changes in critical opinion. Accordingly the changes made are relatively unimportant, with one exception, which is to be regretted, viz. the omission of the useful indexes. But this eminently practical commentary should prolong its usefulness for many years to come.

G.W.A.

BUTTENWIESER, M.: *The Psalms, chronologically treated with a new translation. Prolegomenon* by N. M. Sarna. (The Library of Biblical Studies, ed. by H. M. Orlinsky.) 1969. Pp. xliv, 911. (Ktav Publishing House, Inc., New York. Price: $22.50)

Buttenwieser's commentary on the Psalms was published in 1937. As Sarna indicates in his prolegomenon, the commentary was in many respects representative of the by then outmoded view that psalms could be given precise historical settings. The confidence with which Buttenwieser assigned psalms to particular situations, and particularly to periods for which historical knowledge is sadly deficient — 29 psalms or part psalms to the period 520–359 B.C., 20 to the year 344 B.C. (a crisis better known to Buttenwieser from the psalms he assigned to it than from clear historical evidence) — makes this commentary a model of how not to date psalms. That there is much useful comment on points of detail is true. Sarna has provided a short and helpful survey of psalm criticism, and placed Buttenwieser within it. But it can hardly be held that he has shown that there was any particular justification for reprinting the commentary today. Its usefulness is very limited.   P.R.A.

CARTER, C. W., and OTHERS: *The Wesleyan Bible Commentary*, Vol. II, 1968. Pp. 660. (William B. Eerdmans Publishing Company, Grand Rapids, Michigan. Price: $8.95)

This is part of a six-volume commentary covering the whole Bible, intended to be 'evangelical, expositional, practical, homiletical, and devotional', and 'to maintain both the spiritual insight and sound biblical scholarship of John Wesley and Adam Clarke, but to express these characteristics in the context of contemporary life'. The text of the American Standard Version is printed; but account is taken of other versions. The general position of the contributors is conservative, but not extremely so. Given its aim and presuppositions, it is a competent and workmanlike volume. Although the expositions are fairly heavily dependent on the conservative exegesis of an earlier generation, more recent work representing other viewpoints is also cited. The contributors to this volume are: C. W. Carter (Job), W. R. Thompson (Psalms 1–72), G. H. Livingston (Psalms 73–150), G. Kufeldt (Proverbs), D. F. Kinlaw (Ecclesiastes and Song of Solomon).   G.W.A.

CHARY, T.: *Aggée-Zacharie Malachie*. (Sources Bibliques.) 1969. Pp. 282. (J. Gabalda et Cie, Paris. Price: Fr. 45)

This is an important work which fully maintains the quality of earlier volumes in the series *Sources Bibliques*. Translation, textual comments and exegesis are all carefully done, and full attention is paid to earlier work. In Haggai, the disputed passage 2:10–14 belongs to the beginning of Haggai's ministry and refers to the Jews, who are castigated for neglect of worship. Zech. 1–8 is composed of two groups of material with a number of somewhat later interpolations. In Zech. 9–14, which is the work of a single 'author-redactor' who worked between 332 and 300 B.C., a consistent plan may be recognized, but there were originally two separate collections of material, some of which is considerably older. In Malachi the theory of a literary presentation of actual prophetic 'disputations' is accepted. Among the most valuable features of the book are a detailed history of the exegesis of Zech. 9–14, a discussion of the textual problems of Zech. 9–14, and discussions of the message of Zech. 1–8, Zech. 9–14 and Malachi.   R.N.W.

COUROYER, B., O.P.: *L'Exode. La Sainte Bible. trad. en français à L'École Biblique de Jérusalem.* 1968. Pp. 42. (Les Editions du Cerf, Paris)

This is a third edition of an excellent annotated translation of the book of Exodus, of which the second edition was reviewed in *B.L.*, 1959, p. 19; *Decade*, p. 155. It is basically a reprint with a few minor additions and corrections.

R.E.C.

DAHOOD, M.: *Psalms II (51–100).* (The Anchor Bible, 17.) 1968. Pp. xxx, 399. (Doubleday & Company, Inc., Garden City, New York. Price: $6.00)

The first volume of this commentary on the Psalter was reviewed in *B.L.*, 1966, p. 22; *Decade*, p. 642. The second contains a list of abbreviations, a glossary of terms, a list of ancient Near Eastern texts, an introduction defending the first volume against some criticisms, a commentary on a further fifty psalms, and indexes of biblical passages, Hebrew words, and subjects. Dahood resolutely continues to work along the same lines as before, and the only substantial change made to the original plan is that a third volume is now thought necessary.

J.A.E.

EICHRODT, W.: *Ezekiel.* (Old Testament Library.) 1970. Pp. xiv, 594. (S.C.M. Press, London. Price: 110s.)

The two volumes of Eichrodt's commentary in Das Alte Testament Deutsch are here translated by C. Quin and afford the first major commentary on Ezekiel to appear in English for more than thirty years. The German originals were reviewed in *B.L.*, 1960, p. 19 (*Decade*, p. 199) and 1967, p. 20. This cannot have been an easy work to translate, and there is at times some lack of clarity, but in general the work has been well done and English-speaking students of Ezekiel will benefit greatly.

R.J.C.

EPPING, C. and NELIS, J. T.: *Job uit de grondtekst vertaald en uitgelegd* (De Boeken van het Oude Testament, ed. A. van den Born, W. Grossouw, J. van der Ploeg, VII A). 1968. Pp. 187. (J. J. Romen en Zonen, Roermond. Price: Fl. 19.15)

The death of Dr Epping in 1967 left a commentary up to 22:13 more or less in final shape, and preparatory material for the remaining chapters; none of the introduction had been prepared. Dr Nelis undertook to complete the work; he has made it his aim to preserve the character of Epping's approach, while undertaking some revision of the completed section. The result is a carefully argued, primarily exegetical, commentary not overloaded with textual notes, but well-informed and accurate. The introduction devotes substantial attention to the questions of integrity and of language, the latter section containing useful comment on the various hypotheses concerning the book's origin and on the nature of the vocabulary. The commentary is cautious and thorough. A select bibliography and a brief list of textual emendations is provided. The problem of the book is seen in broad terms, in the expounding of the mystery of the relationship between God and man, in which the more specific problems of suffering and finitude are subsumed. A sound contribution to a useful series (see *B.L.*, 1969, p. 60). P.R.A.

*Fuller, R. C., Johnson, L. and Kearns, C. (ed.): *A New Catholic Commentary on Holy Scripture*. 1969. Pp. 1377. (Thomas Nelson & Sons Ltd., London. Price: 168s.)

A *Catholic Commentary on Holy Scripture* first appeared in 1953 (see *B.L.*, 1953, p. 35; *Eleven Years*, p. 488). Successive reprintings proved its value. Although plan and format remain the same, this is in no sense another reprinting. Only one fifth of the material from the earlier volume remains. If the earlier volume was cautiously critical, this new commentary is marked by the increasing critical self-confidence among Roman Catholic scholars. Full cognizance is taken of recent studies even when they call in question traditional interpretations. The bibliographies and maps have been revised. Of particular theological interest is the essay by Cardinal Bea, 'The Bible in the Life of the Church' (§ 1-7) which analyses the Roman Catholic *Dei Verbum*. The whole volume shows critical scholarship creatively allied to the Catholic tradition of faith. R.D.

Gaide, G.: *Jérusalem voici ton roi* (*commentaire de Zacharie 9–14*). (Lectio Divina, 49.) 1968. Pp. 202. (Les Éditions du Cerf, Paris)

In this commentary the author, while admitting the value of earlier more analytic studies, uses a synthetic approach to Deutero-Zechariah in a new attempt to solve its problems. The book is the work of a single prophet, the earliest oracle being dated *c*. 332 B.C. and the latest a few years after 311. It consists of four 'cycles' of material (9:1–10; 9:11–10:12; 11:1–17; 12–14), each of which has its own theme and has been composed from shorter units with some degree of symmetry. The purpose of the book, the theological teaching of which is treated in a final section, was to encourage the prophet's contemporaries by the construction of a picture of the coming Messianic age on the basis of reminiscences of Israel's past experiences. Free use is made of earlier prophetical and historical biblical material. This is an interesting attempt to understand the book as a whole, which at the same time provides fairly detailed exegesis and a survey of earlier discussion. R.N.W.

*Gehrke, R. D.: *1–2 Samuel* (Concordia Commentary). 1968. Pp. 397. (Concordia Publishing House, St Louis and London. Price: $4.00)

*Habel, N. C.: *Jeremiah. Lamentations*. (Concordia Commentary.) 1968. Pp. 416. (Concordia Publishing House, St Louis and London. Price: $4.00)

These two volumes are the first in a new series designed to offer a running narrative interpretation of the RSV. The authors avoid technicalities in their exposition, but since they work from the original language they offer criticism as appropriate of the version printed. Each volume contains a general introduction, discussing the contents, origin and background of the book(s) under examination, and laying particular stress on the significance of the material. The commentaries are continuous, but contain many notes on points of detail. For the general reader, who wishes to see sections of a biblical book rather than be delayed continually by exegesis of individual verses, the method is a helpful one. The scholarship of the authors is evident but does not obtrude. For their purpose, these are useful volumes mediating sound understanding in an agreeable form.

P.R.A.

*GEYER, J.: *The Wisdom of Solomon.* (Torch Bible Paperbacks.) 1970. Pp. 128. (S.C.M. Press, London. Price: 9s.)

This commentary, reviewed in *B.L.*, 1964; *Decade*, p. 502, is reprinted as one of a series of paperback editions selected from the Torch Commentaries.   P.R.A.

HORST, F.: *Hiob* (Biblischer Kommentar, Altes Testament, XVI, 5). 1968. Pp. xii, 281–8. (Neukirchener Verlag, Neukirchen-Vluyn. Price: DM. 3.10; subscr. DM. 2.60. The complete volume: DM. 42; subscr. DM. 37.80)

Since Ernst Kutsch is for the present unable to complete this commentary (see *B.L.*, 1964, p. 36; *Decade*, p. 504), it has been decided to issue all that has appeared so far as the first volume of the work, and it is hoped that at some future time Kutsch's commentary on chs 19–42 will appear as the second volume. The article on Job which Professor Horst contributed to *Evangelisches Kirchenlexicon* is here reprinted as an introduction to the whole work. A photograph of him is included, and Rainer Kessler has prepared the general index, and the indexes of biblical passages and of Hebrew words.

D.W.T.

The Jerusalem Bible. The Psalms for Reading and Recitation. 1969. Pp. 357. (Darton, Longman and Todd, London. Price: 16s.; bound, 28s.)

It did not seem likely that the psalms of the Jerusalem Bible would be found suitable in worship. In this new version they have been considerably re-worded. 'The Lord' has mercifully replaced 'Yahweh' and he has dispensed with 'holocausts'. The editor-translator, Alan Neame, has been keen to improve the rhythm and has introduced many other preferences of his own. Certainly this is a stirring volume, all the better for lucid notes which show more insight than those of the original *Bible de Jérusalem*.   J.H.E.

LAMPARTER, H.: *Zum Wächter bestellt. Der Prophet Hesekiel übersetzt und ausgelegt.* (Die Botschaft des Alten Testaments, 21.) 1968. Pp. 318. (Calwer Verlag, Stuttgart. Price: DM. 18)

This volume conforms in general pattern and approach to the others in this well-known series. There is a short introduction, dealing with the prophet and his time, the book, and the superscription (1:3a). The exposition of the text follows a clearly presented pattern, which serves as an excellent guide to the reader. The aim is practical exposition; and discussion of critical questions is severely restricted. It is presupposed that, after uttering his prophecies, Ezekiel wrote them down, and that later editors arranged and added to them.

G.W.A.

LEUPOLD, H. C.: *Exposition of Isaiah* (Volume I, Chapters 1–39). 1968. Pp. 598. (Baker Book House Company, Grand Rapids, Michigan. Price: $7.95)

While the author accepts the view that Isaiah son of Amoz wrote the entire book, and chapters 1–35 in particular, he refers to scholars who hold other views. He makes cautious use of *formgeschichtliche* methods, especially as suggested by Westermann. He suggests a rearrangement of the last four chapters on chronological grounds — 38, 39, 36, 37. The text is newly translated, each section being followed by exposition and notes. The main purpose of the commentary is exegetical with a Christological *Tendenz*.

A.S.H.

MCKENZIE, J. L.: *Second Isaiah, Introduction, translation and notes.* (Anchor Bible, 20). 1968. Pp. lxxi, 226. (Doubleday & Co., New York. Price: $6.00)

A substantial and useful book on Isaiah 40–66. The long introduction discusses critical questions, historical background, literary form and structure, the Servant Songs, and the message of Second and Third Isaiah. There is a very short selected bibliography. The text includes as Scattered Poems Isaiah 34:1–17 and 35:1–10. Chapters 40–8 are called Deliverance from Babylon; 49–55 are Zion Poems; 56–66 is Third Isaiah. There are indices of biblical passages, Hebrew words, subjects, proper names and authors. Second Isaiah is regarded as a unity except for the Servant Songs and some passages against idolatry, and as having been written about 546 B.C.; Third Isaiah is a collection of poems and discourses from different periods and authors between 537 and 515 B.C. The Servant Songs are not related to their context nor to each other except by the 'response' that follows the first three songs.

J.N.S.

MAILLOT, A. et LELIÈVRE, A.: *Les Psaumes. Traduction nouvelle et commentaire.* Troisième partie. Psaumes 101 à 150 avec, en appendice, des Psaumes de Qumran. 1969. Pp. 286. (Editions Labor et Fides, Geneva. Price: Sw. Fr. 19.80; bound, 24.60)

Vol. I of this series was reviewed in the *B.L.*, 1967, p. 24. This last volume, dealing with Psalms 101 to 150, adopts the same pattern, providing brief textual notes and a general commentary. There is also a useful appendix dealing with the portions of the Psalms found among the Qumran discoveries.

E.R.R.

MAYS, J. L.: *Amos. A Commentary*. (The Old Testament Library.) 1969. Pp. viii, 168. (S.C.M. Press. Price: 40s.)

The Introduction to this book, which is succinct, discusses the historical setting of the authentic kernel of it, its later expansion and its composition in its present form, the literary forms of expression which are exemplified in it and the characteristics of Amos as a prophet and the dominant themes of his message. The claim that the term nōqēd (1:1) can be interpreted to mean that Amos was a sheep-breeder and, in consequence, a notable member of the community, may be disputed.

The commentary itself deals adequately with problems of text and interpretation and sometimes cites an earlier commentary for a statement of past scholarly discussion in a particular instance. But the author devotes more attention to the substance, the penetrating insight, the timely significance and the positive challenge of the preaching of Amos and analyses carefully its moral demand and theological importance. The whole is written with commendable clarity and shows a skill in correlating various parts of the book which will enable a reader to have a sense of the coherence of the book as a whole. This is an excellent addition to the series in which it has a place.

J.M.

MAYS, J. L.: *Hosea. A Commentary*. (The Old Testament Library.) 1969. Pp. x, 190. (S.C.M. Press. Price: 40s.)

Let it be said forthwith that this book affirms that Hosea's wife and children were historical persons and not merely symbolic figures, but maintains that their purpose is kerygmatic, not biographical; and claims that the symbolism and dramatic value of 3:1–5 are best served if the woman referred to there is regarded as Gomer. Hosea is described as the canonical prophet most versed in the traditions of his people; he portrays their twin apostasy, religious and political, as co-extensive with their residence in Palestine, and sees their only cure as the eradication of this corruption and the re-espousal of Yahweh and his people in the wilderness. Mays emphasizes Hosea's command of literary forms and his use of the resources of wisdom, and he deals with the many textual problems of the book with a fine discrimination. Throughout the commentary the fundamental teaching of Hosea is given prominence in such a way that it is never obscured by uncertainties in particular expressions of it. This is a satisfying and well-balanced book which refrains from claiming certitude of exegesis where the evidence does not provide sufficiently definite material for it.

J.M.

The New English Bible: Old Testament. Library edition. 1970. Pp. xxiv, 1366. (Oxford and Cambridge. Price: 50s. Also in standard edition: Bible with Apocrypha, 35s.; without Apocrypha, 30s.)

The publication of this new and long-awaited translation of the whole Old Testament is an event of outstanding importance for the mediation of new understandings of the biblical text, understandings to which Old Testament scholarship has been contributing steadily over the past generation and more. The influence of Professor Sir Godfrey

Driver is, as may be expected, very evident. The amount of scholarly information conveyed in the footnotes is considerable. Judgement of individual sections will be a matter for long-term reading and deliberation; but that much new light has been shed on the text for the benefit of the general reader is very clear. Scholars and others alike have good reason to be grateful for the work which has gone into this translation. (For the N.E.B. Apocrypha, see p. 78.)   P.R.A.

NOTH, M.: *Könige* (Biblischer Kommentar. Altes Testament, IX, 5). 1968. Pp. 321–66, title pages, Foreword, Contents List and portrait. (Neukirchener Verlag, Neukirchen-Vluyn. Price: DM. 6.20; subscr. DM. 5.20. The complete volume: DM. 47.80; subscr. DM. 43)

The present number of this magnificent commentary (see *Decade*, p. 581; *B.L.*, 1965, p. 29, 1968, p. 26) concludes with the exegetical analysis of 1 Kings 16 and brings us to the end of the material prepared by our late Honorary Member. The publishers therefore have wisely decided to make chs 1–16 a self-contained volume and, to that end, Jörg Jeremias has prepared for it the necessary indexes. We are glad to note that Rudolf Smend has undertaken the continuation of the commentary.   D.R.Ap-T.

OOSTERHUIS, H., VAN DER PLAS, M., DRIJVERS, P., RENCKENS, H., VAN BEECK, F. J., SMITH, D. and INGRAM, F.: *Fifty Psalms. An Attempt at a New Translation*. 1968. Pp. 156. (Burns and Oates, London. Price: 15s.)

A group of Dutch exegetes and poets worked experimentally to produce a translation published at Utrecht in 1967 as *Vijftig Psalmen, Proeve van een nieuwe vertaling*. This is here presented in English with the addition of an introduction and notes. The work is of considerable interest as a brave attempt to render into modern terms the total effect of passages, rather than the constituent elements.

J.H.E.

PELIKAN, J. (ed.): *Luther's Works*. Vol. 5. *Lectures on Genesis Chapters 26–30*. 1968. Pp. xii, 412. (Concordia Publishing House, Saint Louis. Price: $6.00)

Various translations of portions of Luther's voluminous works have appeared in the past both in this country and in America. The present volume, which provides a specimen of Luther's commentary on Genesis, belongs to a new edition which is planned to include fifty-five volumes, though even so Luther's works will not be presented in their entirety. With some slight modifications the translation is based on the Weimar Edition. The first thirty volumes will contain Luther's expository works.   N.W.P.

*ROBERTSON, E. H.: *Amos, Hosea, Micah, Isaiah 1–39*. (Mowbray's Mini-commentary, 8.) 1968. Pp. 70. (A. R. Mowbray and Co. Ltd., London. Price: 5s.)

*SIMPSON, W. W.: *The Pentateuch*. (Mowbray's Mini-commentary, 5.)
1969. Pp. 63. (A. R. Mowbray and Co. Ltd., London. Price: 5s.)

These paperbacks, based on the text of the Jerusalem Bible, appear in
a series of aptly styled 'mini-commentaries' under the general editorship of the Rev. Elsie Chamberlain. The scope of the series does not
allow any detailed expositions, but the notes, which are interesting
and informative, are intended to guide the general reader to a better
understanding of the biblical text.
                                                        L.A.P.

Starý Zákon / překlad s výkladem: 14. Dvanáct proroků. (The Old Testament / translation with commentary: 14. The Twelve Prophets —
Hosea to Malachi.) 1968. Pp. 311. (Kalich, Prague. Price: Kčs. 30)

As the second volume of the new Czech translation of the O.T. with
commentary there has now appeared the Book of the Twelve Prophets
(Hosea to Malachi). A description of the whole project was given in a
comment on the first volume (Genesis. See *B.L.*, 1969, p. 27). For
1970 the publication is planned of volumes 4 (Joshua–Judges–Ruth)
and 7 (Ezra–Nehemiah–Esther).
                                                        M.B.

STROBEL, A.: *Das Buch Prediger* (*Kohelet*). (Die Welt der Bibel: Kleinkommentare zur Heiligen Schrift. Band 9.) 1967. Pp. 191. (Patmos-
Verlag, Düsseldorf. Price: DM. 9.80)

This commentary on Ecclesiastes contains an Introduction dealing
with the place of the book in Israel's Wisdom literature and a consideration of the extra-biblical influences upon its author. The unity
of the book is defended and for his exegesis Strobel analyses it into
the following sections: 1:1–11; 1:12–2:26; 3:1–22; 4:1–16; 4:17–5:6;
5:7–6:12; 7:1–24; 7:25–9:16; 9:17–11:6;11:7–12:8; 12:9–14. The
exegesis of each pericope is accompanied in most instances by an
excursus dealing with theological issues which arise. There are
extensive references to other works on Ecclesiastes and at the end of
the volume there are seven pages of bibliography, all of which further
enhances the value of Strobel's work.
                                                        E.W.N.

TAYLOR, J. B.: *Ezekiel. An Introduction and Commentary*. (Tyndale Old
Testament Commentaries.) 1969. Pp. 285. (Tyndale Press, London.
Price: 15s. 6d.)

The aim of the Tyndale Old Testament Commentaries is to provide
a handy, up-to-date commentary on each book, with a primary
emphasis on exegesis. This aim has been kept in mind by the Vice-
Principal of Oak Hill College, London, in his writing of this commendable volume on the Book of Ezekiel. Its many textual problems
have been dealt with succinctly, clearly and with scholarly discrimination. The exegesis is concerned not only with the meaning of passages
as a whole but, where necessary, with individual verses, and with the
relation of particular aspects of Ezekiel's teaching to his message as a
whole. The introduction deals, *inter alia*, with Ezekiel the man,

especially with regard to his visionary experiences and so-called telepathic powers, in a way which avoids making him a bizarre personality and refuses to reduce him to the 'level of complete normalcy'. The point of view of the author is commonly conservative but that is not shown as a prevenient attitude but as a position which is arrived at after a careful scrutiny of proffered alternatives.

J.M.

WEISER, A.: *Das Buch des Propheten Jeremia.* (Das Alte Testament Deutsch, Teilband 20/21.). 6., verbesserte Auflage. 1969. Pp. 452. (Vandenhoeck und Ruprecht, Göttingen. Price: DM. 18)

The sixth edition of this valuable commentary is virtually a corrected reprint of the fifth edition (1966; cf. *B.L.*, 1967, p. 28) with some addition of references to more recent literature.

P.R.A.

WESTERMANN, C.: *Genesis.* (Biblischer Kommentar, Altes Testament, I, 3.) 1968. Pp. 80. (Neukirchener Verlag, Neukirchen-Vluyn. Price: DM. 7.75)

(For the previous fascicle see *B.L.*, 1969, p. 27.) This one covers Gen. 1:6–2:3. It contains a slip restoring the translation of Gen. 1:24 omitted from fascicle 2. Of special interest is the lengthy discussion of Gen. 1:26 f. It contains a summary of interpretation from Irenaeus to the present day. Westermann then proceeds to his own interpretation and emphasizes the fact that the text points not so much to an affirmation about man, but to the act of God. Man is created in order to rule over the rest of creation. The whole of humanity has God 'zu seinem Entsprechen'. The treatment of 2:1–3 will continue into the next fascicle.

A.S.H.

WESTERMANN, C.: *Isaiah 40–66*, trans. by D. M. G. Stalker (Old Testament Library). 1969. Pp. xvi, 429. (S.C.M. Press, London. 70s.)

A fluent translation of Das Alte Testament Deutsch 19, first published 1966 (see *B.L.*, 1967, p. 28). The book is in two parts: Deutero–Isaiah (40–55) and Trito–Isaiah (56–66) and each contains introduction, commentary, translation and sometimes a short bibliography. Deutero–Isaiah is regarded as living and working among the exiles in Babylon, 550–539 B.C.; Trito–Isaiah was a disciple living in Judaea about 530, having collected and brought back his master's oracles from Babylon. Some additions may have been made to 40–55, particularly the fourth Servant poem. The first three Servant poems may have been written by Deutero–Isaiah although they belong to a 'separate stream'. Trito–Isaiah is less a unity, its nucleus being the words of salvation in 57:14–20; 60–2; 65:16–25; 66:6–16. Short oracles in 40–5 are followed by longer literary units in 46–55, but all 40–55 is addressed to the whole of Israel. The author accepts the view that Deutero–Isaiah's characteristic literary form was the priestly oracle of salvation delivered in answer to a community lament, and that he had exceptional familiarity with the Psalter and was often verbally dependent on it. There are many interesting insights into the prophet's message.

J.N.S.

WILDBERGER, H.: *Jesaja.* (Biblischer Kommentar, Altes Testament, x, 4.) 1969. Pp. 241–320. (Neukirchener Verlag, Neukirchen-Vluyn. Price: DM. 7.75; subscr. DM. 6.50)

Professor Wildberger now continues to the end of 8:4 the commentary of which the earlier fascicles have been noted in *B.L.* (cf. 1968, p. 30 for the previous note). This fascicle includes a discussion of the Immanuel passage which, in Wildberger's opinion, refers to a future son of Ahaz and promises the continuance of the Davidic dynasty, but also warns of the disaster that will come upon the nation because of Ahaz's failure to respond to the prophet's message.

J.A.E.

WOLFF, H. W.: *Dodekapropheton: Amos* (Biblischer Kommentar, Altes Testament, xiv, 7). 1969. Pp. 185–264. (Neukirchener Verlag, Neukirchen-Vluyn. Price: DM. 7.75; subscr. DM. 6.50)

The first part of H. W. Wolff's commentary on the Book of Amos was reviewed in *B.L.*, 1968, p. 30. The good qualities which were noted in that part are continued in this one which covers the section 1:3–4:13. Little need be added now; but it may be said that such *cruces interpretum* as 3:12 and 4:2–3 receive a discriminating, well-balanced treatment and the significance of 3:2 for Israel's theological thought is carefully expounded. The bibliographical notes are excellent and it is clear that the commentary as a whole will take a prominent place among the studies of the Book of Amos which have appeared in recent years.

J.M.

WÜRTHWEIN, E., GALLING, K., PLÖGER, O.: *Die fünf Megilloth.* (Handbuch zum Alten Testament, Erste Reihe, 18.) 1969. Pp. 196. (J. C. B. Mohr (Paul Siebeck), Tübingen. Price: DM. 26.00; bound, 29.80)

This volume is not a reprinting of the commentary on *Die fünf Megilloth* which appeared in the Handbuch zum Alten Testament series in 1940, but is an entirely new work. E. Würthwein writes on *Ruth, Das Hohenlied,* and *Esther*; O. Plöger is responsible for *Das Klagelieder,* and K. Galling for *Der Prediger* (he was responsible for the same book in the 1940 issue). The introductions to the individual books, the *apparatus criticus,* and the general commentary have been thoroughly revised and rewritten. Also the bibliography has been brought up to date. At the same time the work follows the normal pattern adopted by this series. An indispensable commentary for all serious students of the *Five Megilloth.*

E.R.R.

ZIMMERLI, W.: *Ezechiel* (Biblischer Kommentar. Altes Testament, xiii, 16–17, 18). 1969. Pp. i-xvi, 1*–130*, 1219–86. (Neukirchener Verlag, Neukirchen-Vluyn. Price per Lieferung: DM. 7.75; subscr. DM. 6.50; Doppellieferung, DM. 12.40, 10.40.) [The whole work — ZIMMERLI, W.: *Ezechiel* (Biblischer Kommentar, xii/1, xiii/2). 1969. Pp. i-xvi, 1*–130*, 1–578, 579–1286. Price: DM. 165; subscr. 148.50]

Lieferung 18 is the sequel to 15. It contains the concluding comments on 47:22 f., the commentary on 48, a general discussion of the structural history of 40–8, and excursuses on the name of God in Ezekiel,

'Israel' in Ezekiel, and the use of the term *rûaḥ*. There are also indexes of scriptural and rabbinic passages, of names and subjects, and of Hebrew words, and three pages of corrections. The *Doppellieferung* 16–17 contains the introduction to the whole work, in which the author surveys all the main problems and provides an admirably full bibliography. Of particular note are the form-critical and traditio-historical sections and the examination of the relationships between Ezekiel and his prophetic predecessors and also the Deuteronomic, Holiness, and Priestly Codes. As might be expected from the commentary, the general position adopted in the introduction involves a rejection both of the extreme theories which were advanced in the period between the two World Wars and also of the view that the prophet himself was directly responsible for the literary composition of the book. Professor Zimmerli has dedicated his commentary to the Universities of Zürich and Göttingen, and to the S.B.L. and the S.O.T.S. In acknowledging this gracious gesture from our distinguished Honorary Member, we would offer him our congratulations on the completion of his monumental task. An English translation is in preparation.   G.W.A.

LITERARY CRITICISM AND INTRODUCTION
(including History of Interpretation, Canon, and Special Studies)

ALBREKTSON, B. and RINGGREN, H.: *En bok om Gamla testamentet*. 1969. Pp. 270. (C. W. K. Gleerup, Lund)

In the autumn term, 1969, a new basic course in religious studies was introduced in the Swedish universities. This excellent volume has been prepared as a textbook for the O.T. part of the course, which presupposes no knowledge of Hebrew. In the first part of the book, Professor Ringgren surveys the history and religion of Israel in three chapters devoted respectively to the early period, the monarchy, and the post-exilic period. These are followed by a section on the main themes of Old Testament theology. The second part of the book, for which Professor Albrektson is responsible, is an introduction to O.T. literature. After a preliminary account of the problems and methods of literary criticism, form criticism, and tradition history, there follow chapters on the narratives and legal collections, the poetic literature, Wisdom, prophetic literature, and Apocalyptic. Two further sections deal with the growth of the Canon and the history of the text. The book ends with a useful guide to further reading. This is a first-rate book: the material is effectively arranged and presented in such a way as to stimulate further reading and reflection.

G.W.A.

BAUER-KAYATZ, C.: *Einführung in die alttestamentliche Weisheit*. (Biblische Studien, 55.) Pp. 95. (Neukirchener Verlag, Neukirchen-Vluyn. Price: DM. 7.75)

The scope of this book is much narrower than the title suggests. Apart from a few pages of general introduction it is concerned exclusively with the book of Proverbs, and mainly with selected passages from Prov. 1–9. The first section offers a useful introduction to the types of proverb found in Prov. 10–31. In the second and longer section the author merely repeats the substance of her earlier work (C. Kayatz, *Studien zu Proverbien 1–9*: *B.L.*, 1967, p. 32), in which she argues for the influence of the Egyptian concept of *maat* on the personification of wisdom. There is insufficient reference to other views. The narrow scope of the book makes it unsuitable as a handbook for beginners, which it is presumably intended to be.

R.N.W.

BICKERMAN, E.: *Four Strange Books of the Bible. Jonah/Daniel/Koheleth/ Esther.* 1967. Pp. 240. (Schocken Books, New York. Price: $7.50)

The sub-title indicates which books are regarded as 'Strange Books', and the well-known classical scholar has shared with us his own ideas about these. The essays on Daniel and Esther are of particular value. As explained in the Preface, the main purpose is 'to understand Jonah, Daniel, Koheleth, and Esther as witnesses to the mentality of men' of the age of Greek intellectual dominance. Though one may disagree with some of the views expressed, yet one is fascinated by the range of the author's knowledge and interests, and the book is stimulating, at times even provocative.

E.R.R.

*BLENKINSOPP, J.: *The Men who spoke out. The Old Testament Prophets.* (Where We Stand series.) 1969. Pp. 121. (Darton, Longman & Todd. Price: 10s.)

This book is one of a series intended primarily for Colleges and Universities. As a quick introduction to prophecy in the Old Testament, it is admirable but, because of its brevity, it makes only a cursory reference to many questions which College students often ask. The plan of the book is good. First, the nature of prophecy, especially in its ecstatic and outré forms, is discussed and the compilation of the prophetical books. There follows a study of one prophet, Amos, which expounds his message and indicates its permanent qualities. The prophetic succession is then outlined, the most significant elements of the teaching of the various prophets being picked out and much inevitably being left out. The final part deals with the prophetic community and its witness, and refers as much to the New Testament as to the Old.

This is a commendable effort to provide *multum in parvo*.

J.M.

BOECKER, H. J.: *Die Beurteilung der Anfänge des Königtums in den deutero-nomistischen Abschnitten des 1 Samuelbuches. Ein Beitrag zum Problem des 'deuteronomistischen Geschichtswerks'.* (Wissenschaftliche Monographien zum alten und neuen Testament, 31.) 1969. Pp. 100. (Neukirchener Verlag, Neukirchen-Vluyn. Price: DM. 17.80; bound, 19.80)

This careful and detailed study investigates those passages in 1 Samuel which are normally described as hostile to the kingship; 1 Sam. 8; 10:17–27; 12, and which, by reason of their contrast with other passages, raise questions about the unity of the so-called Deuteronomic History. Boecker's examination of the passages leads him to the conclusion that they are not in fact hostile to the institution as such, but are critical both of any tendency to claim that the king replaces Yahweh as saviour and of certain aspects of royal behaviour (reflected also in the kingship law of Deut. 17) which fall under (prophetic) judgement. Excursuses deal with other related passages, and the whole sheds considerable light on the intentions and methods of the ultimate compilers of the work. If not every point convinces, it is clear that the exegesis of these passages must be very carefully reconsidered. Boecker has justified much more plainly the view that the whole work represents a critique of kingship rather than its rejection. An index of biblical references would have been a useful addition.   P.R.A.

BRONNER, LEAH: *The Stories of Elijah and Elisha as Polemics against Baal Worship.* (Pretoria Oriental Series, VI.) 1968. Pp. xix, 155. (E. J. Brill, Leiden. Price: Fl. 31)

This monograph is based on a doctoral thesis and cites many passages from Ugaritic literature which are taken by the author as showing the beliefs combatted by the author of *Kings* in his *heilsgeschichtlich* retelling of the Elijah-Elisha traditions. Bibliographical references and quotations are given in a rather idiosyncratic way and the proofs should have been better edited before printing, but the book brings out, often very successfully, the struggle between Baalist and Yahwist thought in monarchic Israel — whatever reservations there may be about the main thesis.   D.R.Ap-T.

BROWN, D.: *The Christian Scriptures.* (Christianity and Islam, 2.) 1968. Pp. xi, 67. (Sheldon Press, S.P.C.K., London. Price: 5s.)

As an elementary introduction to the Bible, which whilst in the first place designed for Muslim readers will doubtless be helpful to many Christians, this manual well fulfils its purpose. The story of the Bible, how and by whom it came to be written, and the variety of its literature together with the content of its books are all clearly set forth. Two concluding sections are concerned with the Scriptures and History and with the Scriptures and the Spirit of God.   E.T.R.

BRUEGGEMANN, W.: *Tradition for Crisis. A Study in Hosea.* 1968. Pp. 164. (John Knox Press, Richmond, Virginia. Price: $4.95)

This book performs a useful service in gathering together a number of recent insights into the nature of prophecy which are to be found in a variety of monographs and articles but which have up to now not received synthetic treatment. At the same time in illustrating his points from Hosea the author makes his own positive contribution to the study of that book. He regards the prophet as the authorized spokesman in a covenant liturgy, appealing to the covenant tradition but interpreting it creatively in face of the crisis of his own day. This re-interpretation can be seen in the use made of traditional forms as well as of content. Not all readers will agree with the definition of the cult in purely covenant terms; but the case for this view is well argued. The book concludes with some reflections on the prophetic office in the Church today.   R.N.W.

BRUNET, G.: *Les Lamentations contre Jérémie. Réinterprétation des quatre premières Lamentations.* (Bibliothèque de l'École des Hautes Études. Sciences Religieuses, Vol. LXXV.) 1968. Pp. viii, 200. (Presses Universitaires de France, Paris. Price: Fr. 65.00)

The author of this interesting monograph sets out to reverse the universal opinion that ascribes the Book of Lamentations to the prophet Jeremiah by showing them to have been directed against him, while leaving the fifth of the five poems to the traditional view. His main argument is that the 'foe (*ṣar*)' and the 'enemy ('*ôyēb*)' are not the same but distinct adversaries. The former refers to Nebuchadnezzar and the Chaldaeans while the latter designates Jewish collaborators, both within the city and outside with the Chaldaeans, in favour of submission; of these last Jeremiah was one. In discussing these diverse adversaries the author draws attention to the following points. The *ṣar* is a foreigner (1:10), the '*ôyēb* one who, though once a lover of Jerusalem, has now betrayed her (1:2); the nation has fallen into the hands of the *ṣar* (1:7), who has carried it into exile (1:5) and who has seized the national treasure (1:10); he is also in command of the invaders while the '*ôyēb* quietly prospers (1:5), sharing his triumph, which the poet finds hard to endure (1:9), especially as he is not the actual victor but has merely attached himself to the victorious invaders and so has made himself the stronger party in the nation (1:16); for the '*ôyēb*, though not the commander of the invaders, has succeeded in gaining possession of the principal buildings in the city (2:7) and rejoices in her defeat (2:17) and, though destitute of military power, has caused the ruin of her sons (2:22); he has also persecuted the poet with the support of the majority of the nation (3:52–3) and finally has entered the city by the gates with the victorious *ṣar* (4:12). The poet is a nationalist who, unlike the prophet, did not anticipate defeat but was surprised when it came (1:1, 2:1, 4:1); he was never pro-Chaldaean but was thrown into prison for his opinions by the dominant '*ôyēb* (3:52–3); he was faithful to the memory of Zedekiah (4:20), a respecter of the old order and an ardent Yahwist (3:40–1), a member of the minority who were largely responsible for the disaster (3:14, 34, 63). He was perhaps the high priest Serayah, although this identification cannot be proved (see pp. 140–5), and composed the four poems during the fatal 27 days of 587 B.C. (see p. 117, n. 1 and pp. 137–400). The picture thus drawn is that of a foreign invasion complicated by civil war, which differs considerably from that commonly found by combining what is said in the relevant chapters of Jeremiah with that revealed in these four poems; but it is supported by a number of points, acutely taken, which have hitherto been glossed over or explained away rather than explained, and future commentators will have to give it careful consideration whether they accept or reject it.   G.R.D.

BURTCHAELL, J. T.: *Catholic Theories of Biblical Inspiration since 1810.*
1969. Pp. 342. (Cambridge University Press. Price: 70s.)

The author, when setting out on his task of assessing the various
Catholic schools of thought on biblical inspiration since the first
decade of last century, rightly contends that the period is one that
has been 'Dashed over by several successive waves of theological
revival' (p. 3), and he begins his survey with the Catholic school of
Tübingen, in which Möhler and von Kuhn may be regarded as the
principal figures. His second chapter on 'Theories Dead and Buried'
seems, perhaps, to resurrect some of the burials, but there is an
exception in the case of Cardinal Newman, whose theories were given
a new lease of life by Jaak Seynaeve's *Cardinal Newman's Doctrine
on Holy Scripture*, published in 1953. After this there are assessments
of the work of Cardinal Franzelin, Père Lagrange and other writers.
The conclusion appears to be that 'The Benoit position rises as the
classic theory of the years immediately after *Divino Afflante Spiritu*'
(p. 245). The debate continues.   J.M.T.B.

BUSS, M. J.: *The Prophetic Word of Hosea. A Morphological Study.*
(Beihefte zur Zeitschrift für die alttestamentliche Wissenschaft, 111.)
1969. Pp. 142. (Alfred Töpelmann, Berlin. Price: DM. 46)

Buss concentrates on offering a detailed analytical examination of
the book of Hosea from the form-critical and stylistic point of view.
He provides a fresh translation, with textual annotation, and then
examines the structure of the work, and attempts to define the scope
and character of the individual oracles. This is broadened by an
examination of the traditions underlying the various motifs, concepts
and expressions used by the prophet. Buss's view of the historical
and religious significance of the prophecies appears rather incidentally to the main areas of examination, and is very cautiously presented.
Hos. 3 is interpreted as an unhistorical allegory, whilst Chapter 1 is
thought to be composed of two naming sermons of which the first
stands closest to the real life of the prophet. The detailed study of the
stylistic features of the prophet is very usefully pursued, though their
identification tends to dominate the exegesis to the exclusion of other
factors.   R.E.C.

CAZELLES, H. and BOUHOT, J. P.: *Il Pentateucho.* 1968. Pp. 342. (Paideia–
Brescia. Price: Lire 3,500)

In essentials this is not a new work. It is an Italian translation by
Tommaso Federici of the article 'Pentateuque' which appeared in
the *Supplément au Dictionnaire de la Bible*, Vol. VII, fascicles 38 and
39, in 1963 and 1964. It has been widely praised by many eminent
critics, and readers of this translation will have two advantages over
the readers of the French original. First and most important, the
authors assure us that the text has been thoroughly revised and
brought up to date. Secondly, this Italian version is printed in a
beautifully clear and large type, comforting to elderly eyes, and has an
index of chapters and sections that is easy to use.   J.M.T.B.

CLEMENTS, R. E.: *God's Chosen People*. 1969. Pp. 126. (S.C.M. Press, London. Price: 8s. 6d.)

This is an unchanged reprint, in paperback, of the work first published in 1968 (see *B.L.*, 1968, p. 33).
　　　　　　　　　　　　　　　　　　　　　　　　　　　　R.J.C.

COHN, G. H.: *Das Buch Jona im Lichte der biblischen Erzählkunst*. (Studia Semitica Neerlandica, 12.) 1969. Pp. 111. (Van Gorcum & Comp. N.V., Assen. Price: Fl. 17)

The author claims that this is the first attempt to apply to a biblical book a new method of literary criticism which he describes as 'a kind of structure-analysis'. He maintains that objective scientific and historical methods are incapable of penetrating to the real character of a literary work such as the Book of Jonah. This can only be done by the use of a sympathetic insight which seeks to understand the work as a whole from within. This necessitates close attention to such matters as literary structure, the use of language, keywords and symbolism.

In view of these claims it is disappointing to discover that the method when applied in detail reveals itself as far from the novelty it purports to be, and that the results in terms of a new understanding of the book are extremely meagre. The author does succeed in pointing to some stylistic and structural features which improve our understanding of it as a literary creation. But by adhering to the principle that such a work is essentially timeless, and that attempts to understand it in relation to a particular historical context are irrelevant, he reaches a conclusion which will seem to many readers to do less than justice to it, and which in any case could have been reached without much of the detailed analysis: its lesson is simply that man must realize that he cannot live by justice but only by grace, and that he must allow God to direct his life.
　　　　　　　　　　　　　　　　　　　　　　　　　　　　R.N.W.

COOLS, J. P. (ed.): *Geschichte und Religion des Alten Testaments*. (Das moderne Sachbuch, 77.) 1968. Pp. 352. (Walter- Verlag, Olten. Price: DM. 15)

This volume contains material selected from the larger *Die biblische Welt*, 1965 (Dutch original *De wereld van de bijbel*, 1964). It falls into three main sections: 1. The literature of the O.T. — the various textual traditions and a form-critical analysis of the literature. 2. History — the culture setting of the O.T. in the world of the Ancient Near East, Palestine, Syria, Arabia, Egypt and Mesopotamia, and a survey of O.T. history. 3. O.T. religion. The contributions, all by Roman Catholic scholars, are of a uniformly high standard. Good illustrations, clear maps, useful chronological tables and brief bibliographies enhance a very useful introduction to the study of the O.T.
　　　　　　　　　　　　　　　　　　　　　　　　　　　　R.D.

CRÜSEMANN, F.: *Studien zur Formgeschichte von Hymnus und Danklied in Israel*. (Wissenschaftliche Monographien zum Alten und Neuen

Testament, 32.) 1969. Pp. 350. (Neukirchener Verlag, Neukirchen-Vluyn. Price: DM. 54.80; bound 57.80)

Powered by an unsullied faith in form-criticism, this dissertation on the psalms steamrollers its way to the conclusion that the class 'Hymns' should include most of the so-called 'Thanksgivings of Israel' but not the 'Thanksgivings of the Individual'. This is a study which specialists must consult, though they may regret that the circles from which it emanates still show little appreciation for the insights of such as Mowinckel and Birkeland.   J.H.E.

DAVIS, J. J.: *Conquest and Crisis. Studies in Joshua, Judges and Ruth.* 1969. Pp. 176. (Baker Book House, Grand Rapids, Michigan. Price: $2.95)

In this book little attention is paid to literary criticism, relevant archaeological evidence is judiciously quoted and supernatural interventions determinative of critical human situations are accepted. It is the theological interest of the books which is given prominence and in this a conservative point of view is expressed. It is considered justifiable that the resident Canaanites were destroyed by the invading Israelites in order that the latter might be kept pure in faith and worship and that the former might be suitably punished for their neglect of the worship of Yahweh. But the compatibility of some of the theological ideas expressed is not worked out nor is the question of their relativity in respect of time and place adequately considered. The Book of Joshua is adjudged to be a literary unit, its author Joshua, although later additions to his work are admitted. The Book of Judges is attributed, in the main, to the early years of the United Monarchy, its author possibly Samuel, while the Book of Ruth is considered to have been written in the reign of king David because Solomon is not named in 4:22. The views of 'liberal criticism' are incidentally mentioned but they are seldom seriously assessed. But the author must have found the scanty space available to him very irksome.   J.M.

DOMMERSHAUSEN, W.: *Die Estherrolle.* (Stuttgarter Biblische Monographien, 6.) 1968. Pp. 174. (Verlag Katholisches Bibelwerk, Stuttgart. Price: DM. 20)

The book of Esther, regarded as a literary unity, is analysed into its smaller units, and the author claims that it is possible to detect the beginning and end of the units by noting the syntactic characteristics. Then each unit is classified according to type. And in addition each verse in each unit is examined in order to point out its literary features. This provides an excellent example of a study of the relation between literary style and the message of a book, and the claim is made that form is relevant to content and message. The book of Esther is said to have been composed about 250 B.C., and the purpose was to give a Jewish historical meaning to an originally Persian spring festival. It is a study which deserves serious consideration.   E.R.R.

ELLIS, P.: *The Yahwist. The Bible's First Theologian*. 1968. Pp. xii, 308 (English edition, 234). (Fides Publishers, Notre Dame, Indiana. Price: $8.95. Geoffrey Chapman, London. Price: 42s.)

The principal presuppositions of this work are that biblical theology is the crown of biblical study, that most of the biblical authors were primarily theologians, and that it is a grave error to read theology as if it were history. From this standpoint the author proceeds to examine the work of the Yahwist, surveying (1) the critical questions, (2) the background of the period in which he wrote (taken to be the reign of Soloman), (3) the Yahwist's sources (myths and sagas, but not the cultic credo), (4) his literary techniques, (5) the literary techniques which the Yahwist uses to bring out his theological message, and (6) the main themes of the Yahwist's theology: election; God's love; God's control of history; sin, punishment, and forgiveness; God as Lord of life and fertility; immortality; covenant theology; the monarchy; and universalism. Usefully, in the American edition, there is included the Jerusalem Bible version of the passages attributed to the Yahwist. While the reviewer would agree that the Yahwist displays both a theological purpose and theological insight, he finds it impossible to accept all that is here attributed to him, e.g. in relation to immortality and the monarchy. G.W.A.

ELLISON, H. L.: *The Message of the Old Testament*. 1969. Pp. 94. (The Paternoster Press, Exeter. Price: 6s.)

This introduction to the O.T. follows the order of the books in the Hebrew Bible. The Law, Prophets and Writings are covered in 30, 20 and 22 pages respectively. Within this compass, and as the title suggests, attention is focussed on the contents of the books rather than on their authorship and dates. The theological standpoint is moderately conservative with an occasional move towards the right or the left. The author rejects the allegorical interpretation in favour of restrained typology or careful analogy, but maintains that the whole of the O.T. cannot be interpreted Christologically. G.F.

ELLISON, H. L.: *The Prophets of Israel from Ahijah to Hosea*. 1969. Pp. 176. (The Paternoster Press, Exeter. Price: 21s.)

Prophets before Elijah are briefly referred to; Elisha receives more attention than does Elijah. There is a tendency to 'explain away' the religious difficulties in the Kings narratives. Jonah precedes Amos. The treatment of Hosea, especially in the closing chapter, may be regarded as the most satisfying in the book. A.S.H.

FOHRER, G.: *Das Alte Testament*, Erster Teil. 1969. Pp. 183. (Verlagshaus Gerd Mohn, Gütersloh. Price: DM. 16.80)

According to the distinction now being pressed in some quarters, this is *Einführing* rather than *Einleitung*. The basic structure is historical, and the O.T. period to the end of the monarchy is divided into four sections. Each section is approached from four standpoints;

the content of the literature, its origin and structure, the history of the period, and the religious thought of that period. The book has its origin in courses of lectures delivered to students, and its aim is to provide students, clergy and teachers with a basic textbook. The writing is uncompromising, as one would expect from the author, and no attempt is made to gild the gingerbread. The name of the author is itself a guarantee of reliability and soundness. A second volume, shortly to follow, will cover prophecy and the exilic and post-exilic period, treated in the same way. This is the kind of book which can achieve its purpose in the English-speaking world only in translation.

D.R.J.

FOHRER, G.: *Introduction to the Old Testament*. Trans. by D. Green. 1970. Pp. 540. (S.P.C.K., London. Price: 55s.)

This is the English edition of the work reviewed in *B.L.*, 1969, p. 42 (cf. *B.L.*, 1967, p. 36, for the German original).

M.A.K.

GUILLAUME, A.: *Studies in the Book of Job*. (Annual of Leeds University Oriental Society, Suppl. II.) 1968. Pp. xii, 150. (E. J. Brill, Leiden. Price: Fl. 25)

This work, a blindly partisan plea for an 'Arabic' approach to the background and language of Job, has three main sections. The first is a brief Introduction, giving some arguments in favour of the case advocated, and stressing particularly connections with the time of Nabonidus at Tema. The central section is an English translation of Job, and the third is a series of notes, most of which offer explanations on an Arabic basis. Guillaume must have been already in advanced years when this work was conceived, and at his death it was unfinished. The *pietas* of J. Macdonald has assembled the material left behind; but it might have been better for the memory of the author if it had been left unpublished.

The translation has, as a translation, little originality or merit; it is in fact a modified R.V., so far as one can tell (cf. remarks on pp. 1 f.). It looks as if Guillaume began by transcribing the R.V. with minor alterations, and then in the course of his work made further modifications to follow his notes. Long passages such as 7:1a–21, 19:1–23a, 40:25–32 (M.T. numbering), show little change in substance from R.V. This impression is strengthened in passages like chs 25–6, where there are no notes at all and where the translation is practically straight R.V.; and it is supported by the fact that the translation, in spite of Macdonald's efforts, often disagrees with the notes and even renders in a way explicitly rejected as wrong in the latter: e.g. 3:4, 15:22 (twice), 16:5, 19:27, 19:29, 20:25. At the end of ch. 40 the translation goes over to the English numbering (another symptom of its provenance) but the notes follow the Hebrew, and on eight verses affected by the overlap there are no notes at all. On p. 130 there is the curious misprint, 'Learus Major and Minor' (read 'Canis'), and 'trust' on p. 26 (7:18) should be 'test'. At 37:13 the *lešēbeṭ* of M.T. is taken to be *lešabbēṭ* (verb, piel) 'to bring heavy rain' (note on p. 128), but the translation misses it out altogether.

Little heed is paid to other scholars, and such distinguished interpreters of Job as N. H. Tur-Sinai, S. Terrien and even E. Dhorme
appear to be ignored. Some of the suggestions in the notes are worth
consideration, but the general effect will be to damage the Arabian
theory in the eyes of scholars.
                                                                    J.B.

HALL, W. G.: *The Genesis and the Genius of Man*. 1969. Pp. 104. (Regency
Press, London. Price: 21s.)

Unscientific linguistics and speculative exegesis make this study of
Gen. 1–9 worthless for the O.T. scholar and dangerous for others.
                                                                    R.D.

*HARGREAVES, J.: *A Guide to the Book of Genesis*. (Theological Education
Fund Study Guide, 3.) 1969. Pp. 180. (S.P.C.K., London. Price: 9s.)

This is the first Old Testament 'Guide' to appear in a series of which
two New Testament 'Guides' have appeared. It is written in response
to requests from teachers and students in Africa, Asia and the Pacific.
Each section consists of an outline of the biblical passage, interpretation, some exegetical notes, and suggestions for study, in the
last of which are some excellent pointers to the application of the
biblical passage to present-day situations. Included in the book are
some imaginatively chosen photographs relating the Genesis story
to the world of the readers. Finally, notes have been added on twenty
important words. The book is based on sound scholarship; it is
practical and reliable.
                                                                    A.S.H.

HARRISON, R. K.: *Introduction to the Old Testament*. 1970. Pp. 1216.
(Tyndale Press, London. Price: 60s.)

This massive (and surprisingly cheap) volume is almost an encyclopaedic account of O.T. study. It contains a brief survey of the history
of O.T. scholarship, a sketch of O.T. archaeology, a discussion of
ancient Near Eastern and O.T. chronology, an account of the O.T.
Text and Canon, a brief section on O.T. history (divided into
I. the study of O.T. history, and II. problems of O.T. history), two
considerably longer sections on O.T. religion and O.T. theology, and
eight further sections devoted to the main divisions of O.T. literature
(Pentateuch, Former Prophets, Major Latter Prophets, Minor Latter
Prophets, the books traditionally described as 'poetical', the Megilloth, and Daniel, Ezra–Nehemiah, and Chronicles. On any showing
this is considerable achievement, both in the formidable range of
subjects covered, and in the wealth of bibliographical documentation.
The author's concern at every point with problems of method is also
to be commended, since in the present situation these call for urgent
consideration in all the main fields of O.T. study. To criticize points
of detail in a short review would be unfair. But, looking at the volume
as a whole, one may legitimately ask whether the disposition of the
material is natural and logical. Should a discussion of Text and Canon
come between chronology and history and be so widely separated
from the sections devoted to special introduction? If so wide a range

of subjects is to be presented in one volume, surely they should be so arranged as to display their mutual relationship. The general approach of the writer may be described as that of a 'conservative' scholar (he holds, e.g. that there is a good case for ascribing much of the Pentateuchal material to Moses, and a very poor case for the Maccabean dating of Daniel) who is determined to take full account of all the available evidence.

G.W.A.

This *Introduction* was also published in 1969 by W. B. Eerdmans, Grand Rapids, Michigan (Pp. xvi, 1325. Price: $12.50). This form of the work also includes a section on the Apocrypha (pp. 1173–1276). The major part of this is devoted to introduction to each of the apocryphal books in turn; but it is prefaced by a general discussion. A survey of the history from Alexander to *c.* A.D. 100 is followed by a note on the books and their preparation and use, and by a short discussion of attitudes to the apocryphal books in the various Christian circles. An epilogue to the section comes down firmly against allowing any canonical authority to these books, whilst it recognizes their general usefulness. Such a statement depends, of course, on the general line of interpretation and authority of the biblical writings set out by Harrison in the main body of the book.

P.R.A.

KAISER, O.: *Einleitung in das Alte Testament. Eine Einführung in ihre Ergebnisse und Probleme.* 1969. Pp. 340. (Verlagshaus Gerd Mohn, Gütersloh. Price: DM. 24)

As the sub-title shows, this is not just another 'introduction'. It certainly contains a coverage of the questions normally included in such works, with a short discussion of the nature of the task, an indication of the geographical, historical and cultural presuppositions, and a consideration of the canon. (The history of the text is deliberately omitted.) The literature is divided into historical narrative, prophetic, and poetic, including wisdom. But each section, designed as is the book as a whole for the use of students, indicates the main course of critical investigation, the main conclusions and points of discussion, a keen awareness of the provisional nature of conclusions, and a pointer towards the lines of investigation which may usefully be pursued. It is therefore almost a programmatic work, and as such most stimulating and valuable. An index of authors' names would have added considerably to its usefulness.

P.R.A.

KEET, C. C.: *A Study of the Psalms of Ascents. A critical and exegetical commentary upon Psalms CXX to CXXXIV.* 1969. Pp. 192. (The Mitre Press, London. Price: 45s.)

The Vicar of S. Clement's, Cambridge, in what is clearly a labour of love, here offers an assortment of materials, including a commentary, on the Psalms of Ascents, which he thinks were originally associated with the presentation of the First Fruits. He vacillates between addressing the learned and the unlearned. The former will find here some points they have overlooked and many quotations from works now little used.

J.H.E.

KLATT, W.: *Hermann Gunkel. Zu seiner Theologie der Religionsgeschichte und zur Entstehung der formgeschichtlichen Methode.* (Forschungen zur Religion und Literatur des Alten und Neuen Testaments, 100.) 1969. Pp. 280. (Vandenhoeck und Ruprecht, Göttingen. Price: DM. 34)

It is difficult to imagine that there can be any serious student of the Old and indeed the New Testament who would fail to benefit from a reading of this critical survey of the life and work of Hermann Gunkel. The author's independent research and wide reading enable one to follow and to assess Gunkel's important contributions to biblical scholarship in a historical sequence which provides what may aptly be described as their own *Sitz im Leben*; and how valuable and inspiring this biographical approach proves to be! The creative impact of Gunkel's treatment of the different types of religious literature which are to be found in Genesis, the Psalms, and the Canonical Prophets is well-known; less familiar is the fact that he was deflected into this field of study by force of circumstance and was thus unable to pursue anything like so fully his primary interest in studying the Bible from the standpoint of its historical setting in the religious faith and worship of the ancient Near East, as illustrated by *Schöpfung und Chaos in Urzeit und Endzeit* (1895). It is much to be hoped that a fresh attempt may be made to carry through Gunkel's ambitious aims with an equal enthusiasm but, perhaps one should add, more balance and caution than appear to have been shown by this highly original scholar and some of his associates.   A.R.J.

KOCH, K.: *The Growth of the Biblical Tradition.* 1969. Pp. xv, 233. (A. & C. Black, London. Price: 42s.)

This translation by S. M. Cupitt of Koch's *Was ist Formgeschichte?* takes into account the second edition of the original (*B.L.* 1969, p. 35; for the first edition, see *B.L.*, 1965, p. 35; *Decade*, p. 587). The two main parts of the book deal respectively with the form-critic's methods, as applied to both Old and New Testaments, and with a number of selected examples from the Old Testament. Koch's definition of the scope of form-criticism is wider than is sometimes found, so that there is, for example, a useful section on Redaction History. This translation should enable the book to reach a wider audience, though 'students... who are beginning theological studies', for whom the book is aimed, will find it pretty demanding.

R.J.C.

KRAUS, H.-J.: *Geschichte der historisch-kritischen Erforschung des Alten Testaments von der Reformation bis zur Gegenwart.* 2. überarbeitete und erweiterte Auflage. 1969. Pp. viii, 549. (Neukirchener Verlag, Neukirchen-Vluyn. Price: DM. 48.00)

The first edition of this book was published in 1956 and reviewed in *B.L.*, 1957, p. 10; *Decade*, p. 19. This new edition is much larger than the original and a serious attempt has been made to supplement the first edition and to bring it up to date. The author gratefully acknowledges the service done to him by critics, especially by W. Baumgartner, whose lengthy and somewhat devastating review in *Theologische Rundschau* (N.F. 25 Jg. Heft 2, 1959) is in itself a valuable contribution to the subject of the book. One gets the impression that the author is not very well orientated in the British and American literature of his subject. He still completely ignores the important work of A. C. Welch on Deuteronomy and indeed never even mentions his name. There are new sections on the ideas of the *Aufklärung*, on Schleiermacher's criticism of the Old Testament, on Wellhausen's *Israelitische und jüdische Geschichte*, which he had previously overlooked, on Roman Catholic Old Testament scholarship, on the history of the biblical text and on textual criticism, and on Wisdom and Apocalyptic. He draws particular attention to R. Smend's work on de Wette and L. Perlitt's on Vatke and Wellhausen, which had involved a radical change of view on his part. One cannot expect perfection in a book of this kind. The ground to be covered is so vast. But Kraus has striven valiantly and his book will continue to be of great service, while we wait for the promised new edition of Diestel's classic work.   N.W.P.

G. W. H. LAMPE (ed.): *The Cambridge History of the Bible*, vol. 2: *The West from the Fathers to the Reformation*. 1959. Pp. ix, 566. 48 plates. (Cambridge University Press. Price: 70s.)

The first volume of this work was reviewed in *B.L.*, 1964, p. 9; *Decade*, p. 477. The present volume continues the story backwards, and the greater, and most valuable, part is concerned with the medieval period proper. R. Loewe contributes an excellent chapter on the Medieval History of the Latin Vulgate, various specialists cover the Exposition and Exegesis of Scripture during this long period and two chapters, by R. L. P. Milburn and F. Wormald, accompanied by well-chosen illustrations, deal with the Bible in the art of this time. Medieval Vernacular Scriptures are discussed by a number of experts and there is a concluding chapter on Erasmus by L. Bouyer. The first three chapters, which may be of even more direct interest to members, are perhaps less satisfactory. Their subject matter inevitably overlaps with the promised succeeding volume *From the Beginnings to Jerome*, and their aim, according to the editor, is to provide a useful summary for 'readers primarily concerned with the medieval period'. It is to be doubted whether the chapters by B. J. Roberts on the O.T. Manuscripts, Text and Versions and by C. S. C. Williams on the History of the Text and Canon of the N.T. to Jerome (for which, in spite of the editor's claim in the Preface, there is no bibliography) really succeed in doing this. On the one hand, they contain a great deal of information which the non-specialist will find hard to understand but which the specialist will inevitably find too brief. On the other, there is no real discussion of the growth of the O.T. canon, and, in particular, of the so-called 'Palestinian' and 'Alexandrian' canons, which is surely an essential preliminary to anyone wishing to understand the work of Jerome, described in a separate chapter by E. F. Sutcliffe.   J.R.P.

LANGLAMET, F.: *Gilgal et les Récits de la Traversée du Jourdain*. (JOS. III–IV.) (Cahiers de la Revue Biblique, 11.) 1969. Pp. 158. (J. Gabalda et Cie., Paris. Price: Fr. 56)

The basis of this book is a verse by verse study of Joshua 3–4 in respect of source material and text. The conclusion reached is that there are nine different types of literary material — primary and secondary, narratival, aetiological, catechetical, redactional and editorial, etc. In this literary analysis the author is in agreement mostly with Dus and de Vogt among modern scholars. He concludes that the narratives concerning the crossing of the Jordan and the conveyance of the ark to Gilgal gave such prestige to the sanctuary there and the aetiological stories about the memorial stones were so inseparable from it that it must be assumed that a festival commemorating the river crossing and the Israelite entry into Palestine was celebrated there, even when the ark became located elsewhere and the Jerusalem temple became prominent.

This is a very detailed study which raises the question of whether the author may not sometimes attribute to some particular features of the text, as it now stands, a value more precise than was ever intended or imagined by its authors or editors.   J.M.

LINDBLOM, J.: *Tio kapitel om bibelen.* 1969. Pp. 182. (C. W. K. Gleerup, Lund)

In these 'ten chapters about the Bible', Professor Lindblom gives lucid, readable, and informative accounts of 1. the growth of the canon of Scripture, 2. questions of language and text, 3. the literary forms contained in the Bible, 4. questions of authorship, 5. the translation and interpretation of Scripture, 6. the Bible as a historical and cultural document, 7. the relationship between the two Testaments, 8. the religious message of the Bible, 9. the use of the Bible in preaching, 10. the translation and dissemination of the Scriptures (with particular reference to the work of Bible Societies, and to the problems of making the Bible intelligible in cultural settings widely different from that in which it originated). The book ends with a useful classified bibliography and a glossary of technical terms. This is a little masterpiece of clarity and comprehensiveness.   G.W.A.

McKENZIE, J. L.: *Mastering the Meaning of the Bible.* 1969. Pp. 128. (Burns and Oates, London. Price: 18s.)

All the chapters in this book have appeared as articles in popular Roman Catholic periodicals. They range from 'How to read the Bible', through some of the major themes of biblical thought and the place of the Bible in the Roman Catholic church, to a perceptive essay on 'The Values of the O.T.' As always Father McKenzie reveals an enviable ability to communicate the perspectives of biblical scholarship to the layman in a stimulating way.   R.D.

MARTIN-ACHARD, R.: *Approche des Psaumes.* (Cahiers Théologiques, no. 60.) 1969. Pp. 107. (Delachaux et Niestlé, Neuchâtel. Price: Sw.Fr. 12)

This is a collection of introductory articles on the Psalms. Topics include Calvin's exegesis, the '*anawim*, sickness, death, and studies of Pss 8, 22 and 38. Footnotes give useful bibliography, especially French.   J.H.E.

LITERARY CRITICISM AND INTRODUCTION 243

VON DER OSTEN-SACKEN, P.: *Die Apokalyptik in ihrem Verhältnis zu Prophetie und Weisheit.* (Theologische Existenz heute, No. 157.) 1969. Pp. 64. (Chr. Kaiser Verlag, München. Price: DM. 6.80)

This short monograph is devoted to an examination of von Rad's thesis that apocalyptic is a product of wisdom. The author maintains that in considering this question attention ought to be concentrated on the oldest apocalypse (i.e. Daniel), and that, so far as the *origin* of apocalyptic is concerned, arguments based on features in the later apocalyptic writings may give rise to misleading conclusions. He examines the deterministic view of history reflected in Dan. 2 and finds its antecedents in prophecy, and more particularly in Second Isaiah. Prophetic influence is also held to be present in the more elaborate description of the events of the eschaton to be found in Dan. 7 and 8–12 which presuppose the same deterministic view of history as Dan. 2. This deterministic view of history is very different from the determinism of wisdom which is concerned with nature and with the life of the individual. But underlying the determinism of both wisdom and apocalyptic is the belief in God as Creator, and the absorption of wisdom elements into apocalyptic is perhaps to be attributed to the influence of this belief. But this belongs to a later stage in the development of apocalyptic, and marks a complete transformation of it.   M.A.K.

OTTOSSON, M.: *Gilead. Tradition and History.* (Coniectanea Biblica. Old Testament Series, 3.) 1969. Pp. 304 and map. (C. W. K. Gleerup, Lund)

This Uppsala doctoral thesis is a detailed examination of all the biblical material referring to Gilead, reviewing the historical information available, and looking for the ideology Israel had according to Ottoson of its right to the area as part of its *naḥalā*. Much of the book is a detailed examination of the relevant passages, with textual notes, with the literary treatment very dependent on the ideas of Engnell. The work is a little disappointing. It is not well arranged nor well balanced, the author has not really the mastery of his material, and the results are not very convincing.   J.V.M.S.

PACHE, R.: *Inspiration und Autorität der Bibel.* 1968. Pp. 332. (R. Brockhaus Verlag, Wuppertal. Price: DM. 14.80)

The original edition of this book appeared in French in 1967 under the title *L'Inspiration et l'Autorité de la Bible.* It contains an elaborate and sincere defence of the extreme right wing doctrine of the verbal inspiration of the Bible and the theory of biblical authority that goes with it. It will be useful to those who wish to understand the method of Scripture documentation which is characteristic of this school of interpretation. Biblical scholars quoted with approval include B. B. Warfield, R. D. Wilson and E. J. Young. On p. 161 the date of the Synod of Jamnia is given as about 90 B.C.   N.W.P.

Preus, J. S.: *From Shadow to Promise. Old Testament Interpretation from Augustine to the Young Luther*. 1969. Pp. xii, 301. (Harvard University Press; Oxford University Press, London. Price: $7.50; 72s.)

This book, which is described as an 'important breakthrough on the frontier between medieval and reformation studies' will be of absorbing interest to any student of the history of biblical hermeneutics. It demonstrates convincingly that in his lectures on the Psalms (1513–15) Luther can be seen struggling out of a medieval understanding of the Old Testament as to be interpreted Christologically and therefore as without theological significance in its own right to his characteristic interpretation of the Old Testament as promise, which became determinative for Reformation theology. The book is in two parts. Part I traces the history of medieval hermeneutics from Augustine to Faber Stapulensis, a contemporary of Luther, and demonstrates how ambiguous the expression *sensus literalis* could become. This is a study worthy to be put alongside Beryl Smalley's *The Study of the Bible in the Middle Ages*. Part II concentrates on the young Luther whose evolution out of his medieval heritage is exhaustively documented.   N.W.P.

Robert, A. and Feuillet, A. (ed.): *Interpreting the Scriptures*. Translated by P. W. Skehan, *et al*. 1969. Pp. xiv, 247. (Desclée, New York. Price: $6.75)

This volume provides the general introduction to accompany the *Introduction to the Old Testament* (*B.L.*, 1969, p. 39), produced under the same editors. It thus covers the material not in that volume which was included in the original French edition published in 1957 (*B.L.*, 1958, p. 29; *Decade*, p. 105) and revised in 1959. To this has been added a new appendix by W. Harrington and L. Walsh on 'The Dogmatic Constitution on Divine Revelation (*Dei Verbum*)' which includes both text and commentary of this important document of 1965. The main part of the book covers inspiration and canon (A. Barucq and H. Cazelles), criticism (H. Cazelles and P. Grelot), and Catholic interpretation (P. Grelot). There is a brief general bibliography and separate bibliographies for each section, these having been updated and made more suitable for the English reader, including very valuable references to important articles and books by both Catholic and other scholars. The book expounds Catholic views on these issues, so important for biblical interpretation; there is here a wealth of information and of discussion which faces the problems with clarity and honesty.   P.R.A.

Schmidt, J. M.: *Die jüdische Apokalyptik. Die Geschichte ihrer Erforschung von den Anfängen bis zu den Textfunden von Qumran*. 1969. Pp. xvi, 343. Neukirchener Verlag, Neukirchen-Vluyn. Price: DM. 44.80)

We have here a study of the way in which the two hundred years prior to 1947 had seen a deepening interest in the apocalyptic literature of post-exilic Judaism and the part which it played both in Judaism itself and in the emergence of Christianity. The survey is by

no means confined to German works, and it is carried out systematically with due reference to the literary character, historical factors,
and religious significance of these fantastic writings, so that the
book may be warmly welcomed as a useful introduction, in breadth
if not in depth, to the many problems involved.   A.R.J.

SCHÖKEL, L. ALONSO, S.J.: *Understanding Biblical Research*. Translated by
P. J. McCord, S.J. 1968 (1963). Pp. 130. (Burns & Oates/Herder &
Herder, London. Price: 16s.)

This volume, by a distinguished Spanish Jesuit scholar, is a well-
documented and beautifully written defence of the changes that have
occurred within Catholic biblical scholarship over the past half
century. The need for criticism, its relationship to religious understanding and the belief in divine inspiration are persuasively discussed and set alongside the contributions to research from literary,
textual and archaeological studies. The book is popular in method
and apologetic in intentions, but it is very well done, and has much to
say to Protestants as well as Catholics. It places Old Testament study
within a wide field of religious and cultural research.   R.E.C.

SCHOTTROFF, W.: *Der altisraelitische Fluchspruch*. (Wissenschaftliche
Monographien zum Alten und Neuen Testament, 30.) 1968. Pp. 280.
(Neukirchener Verlag, Neukirchen-Vluyn. Price: DM. 38; bound
DM. 40)

Old Testament curse formulae have been widely studied in connection
with the cult, and, more recently, the covenant institutions of Israel.
Schottroff here makes a further very detailed study of them, both in
their form and content, and argues that the connections both with
the cult and the covenant are secondary. Old Testament curses show a
distinctive form, when compared with other Near Eastern curse
material, and originated in early nomadic society as a formula for
expelling a wrongdoer, or other enemy, from the community. Often
this would be in a legal context when the particular wrongdoer was
unknown. In a secondary development such curses came to find a
place in Israel's cult, and then, at the hands of the Deuteronomists,
this cultic curse feature was related to the covenant. Any influence
from the curses of international vassal treaties was only peripheral,
and indeed the curses which such treaties contain were themselves
simply collections of earlier isolated curse formulations. With great
skill and thorough documentation Schottroff thus shows the weaknesses of two popular hypotheses, and in doing so provides a reappraisal with a great deal of positive value of its own.   R.E.C.

SCHREINER, J.: *Von Gottes Wort Gefordert: Aus der Verkündigung des
Propheten Jeremias*. (Die Welt der Bibel: Kleinkommentare zur Heiligen
Schrift. Band 20.) 1967. Pp. 127. (Patmos-Verlag, Düsseldorf. Price:
DM. 6.80)

This work presents a short commentary on selected passages from the
Book of Jeremiah (1:4–19; 7:1–15 and 26:1–6; 23:9–32; 11:18–
12:6; 31:1–6, 31–37; 15:10–21). The author regards the prose sermons

such as 7:1–15 as Jeremiah's own compositions and accepts the
widely held view that the narratives were composed by Baruch.
The critical questions to which each of the passages examined give
rise are briefly but comprehensively discussed. Whilst a serious
question mark may be placed against the acceptance of the prose
sermons and discourses among the passages discussed as Jeremiah's
own words, Schreiner's presentation of the prophet's mission and
message on the basis of these passages is a very helpful contribution
to the ongoing discussion of this important problem.   E.W.N.

SCHREINER, J. (ed.): *Wort und Botschaft. Eine theologische Einführung in
die Probleme des Alten Testaments.* 1967. Pp. 474. (Echter Verlag,
Würsburg. Price: DM. 34)

It would not be easy to disguise an introduction to the Old Testament
as something else, and this excellent manual, while aiming at simplicity and an untechnical approach, is like many other manuals of the
kind. No fewer than twenty-six contributors have assisted the editor.
They include Luis Alonso-Schökel, S.J., who introduces the work
with an essay on 'The Bible as man's word and as God's word'.
Other introductory essays study 'Faith and History in the Old
Testament as a reflection of its textual development and environment',
and 'Scholarly Endeavour towards the Understanding of the Old
Testament'. All four documents of the Hexateuch have a chapter
apiece to explain their origin and character. The two essays at the
end of the volume consider some examples of exegetical procedure
and give a synoptic table marking the occurrences of J, E and P.
The bibliography lists, in the main, German works, but includes some
English and French works in the original languages or in translations.

J.M.T.B.

SCHULZ, H.: *Das Todesrecht im Alten Testament. Studien zur Rechtsform
der Mot-Jumat-Sätze.* (Beihefte zur Zeitschrift für die alttestamentliche
Wissenschaft, 114.) 1969. Pp. 208. (Verlag Alfred Töpelmann, Berlin.
Price: DM. 42.00)

This book is about the *mōt yūmat* clause which according to Albrecht
Alt was a form of apodeictic law. Schulz expresses doubt as to the
usefulness of Alt's category of apodeictic law and builds on Gerstenberger's conclusion that all 'prohibitions' are to be traced to an
ultimate source in a clan or tribal ethic. The *mōt yūmat* clause is
then explained as a transformation of the prohibitive form which
arises in connexion with the moment when a community assumes the
responsibility of pronouncing a sentence of death on someone. In
view of the awful implications of shedding blood, the community
acts not merely as a local judiciary but in a sacral capacity for which
it uses a legal formulation which belongs to sacral law. The development of such a sacral function into a fully articulated cultic trans-
action, embracing a series of procedures which culminate in the
sentence of death, is to be found in Lev. 18–20, while the 'declaratory
formulae' of Ezekiel (14:1–20; 18:1–20; 22:1–16; 33:1–20) are
secondary literary phenomena which derive from this cultic basis.
The steps in this argument need careful scrutiny, not least the point

at which it depends on Gerstenberger's dubious conclusion that all the 'prohibitions' which occur in the Old Testament have a single source in clan or tribal ethics.   W.McK.

TROMP, N. J.: *Primitive conceptions of death and the nether world in the Old Testament*. (Biblica et Orientalia, N.21.) 1969. Pp. xxiv, 241. (Pontifical Biblical Institute, Rome.   Price: Lire 3.300; $5.50)

This work, which is a slightly revised doctoral dissertation, has as its aim a fresh examination of the allusions to death and the nether world in the O.T. — mostly in the poetical books, especially the Psalms — in the light of the language of the Ugaritic texts, and of the conceptions about these themes which are found in these texts. Part I deals with the local aspect of the names for the nether world, the relation to the dead implied by them, and the names suggesting a conception of death as a personal reality. In Part II the implications of these names and epithets are elaborated in other O.T. descriptions of life after death. The author's director was M. Dahood, whose influence inevitably pervades the book. If at times it seems that too much is claimed for the Ugaritic approach to the problems, the wealth of material which has been assembled, and the often interesting and novel interpretation of it, make the book deserving of careful study by all who are concerned with the subject. There are several useful indexes and a bibliography.   D.W.T.

UNGERN-STERNBERG, R. VON: *Redeweisen der Bibel*. (Biblische Studien, 54.) 1968. Pp. 96. (Neukirchener Verlag, Neukirchen-Vluyn. Price: DM. 7.75)

The author endeavours in this study to convey to the German reader the spirit of hebraic thought by a concentrated exploration of selected forms of speech. The divine accusations in the context of a trial do not exclude the style of lamentation. This specific understanding of judgement, as personal encounter and emotional involvement of God and people, creates the tension of 'old' and 'new'. The author rounds off the little book with an analysis of the concept 'fallen' and thoughts about the symbolical meaning of dress. These themes seem to have been chosen without any particular connection. Even the German laity may not easily respond to this mixture of form-critical expertise in unrelated areas and pietistic conclusions.

                                                                        U.E.S.

WALKENHORST, K.-H.: *Der Sinai im liturgischen Verständnis der Deuteronomistischen und Priesterlichen Traditions*. (Bonner Biblische Beiträge. Band 33.) 1969. Pp. xiv, 170. (Peter Hanstein Verlag, Bonn. Price: DM. 32)

After a brief Introduction, Walkenhorst presents a summary of the liturgical understanding of the Sinai tradition in modern scholarship, dealing with J. Wellhausen, S. Mowinckel, G. von Rad, M. Noth, F. Dumermuth, K. Koch, and H.-J. Kraus. In the second chapter he offers a literary analysis of the Priestly tradition of the institution

of the cult at Sinai with a detailed investigation of Exod. 29 and
Lev. 8–9, and in the third chapter he compares the liturgical understanding of Sinai in the older Priestly tradition with that of the
Deuteronomists. The book is prefaced with an extensive bibliography.
This work is marked by thoroughness and concern for detail and
constitutes an important contribution to the discussion of the central
issue in O.T. research with which it is concerned. 　　　　　E.W.N.

WARD, J. M.: *Amos and Isaiah. Prophets of the Word of God.* 1969. Pp. 287.
(Abingdon Press, Nashville, Tenn. Price: $6.50)

J. M. Ward's theological commentary on the book of Hosea (*B.L.*,
1968, p. 29) is now very usefully followed by a volume containing
studies of Amos and Isaiah, about half the book being devoted to
each. Although this is not commentary, the studies do in fact incorporate a great deal of direct exegesis of the text. The Amos studies
concentrate on questions of prophetic authority and of the nature of
righteousness, and include a very carefully argued chapter on the
relationship of Amos to the cult. The Isaiah section provides detailed
discussion of passages connected with the prophet's authority, the
relationship with Ahaz, the Zion theology, the remnant and
'messianic' ideas. There is much judicious and careful comment,
and useful discussion of some of the varieties of contemporary
interpretation. An excellent book for student use. 　　　　　P.R.A.

*WESTERMANN, C.: *Handbook to the Old Testament.* Translated and edited
by R. H. Boyd. 1969. Pp. xvi, 285. (S.P.C.K., London. Price: 30s.)

The American edition of this book (1967) was noted in *B.L.*, 1968,
p. 45. Its usefulness may again be stressed; its use of diagrammatic
presentation, even though inevitably this makes for some degree of
oversimplification, will make it of particular value as a reference
work for older school pupils. 　　　　　P.R.A.

WESTERMANN, C.: *Anfang und Ende in der Bibel.* (Calwer Hefte, 100.) 1969.
Pp. 47. (Calwer Verlag, Stuttgart. Price: DM. 2.50)

This useful discussion of the relationship between the beginning and
the end in the thought of the Bible, with special reference to Gen.
1–11 and the Book of Revelation, is tantalizingly brief and (no doubt
dictated by the limits of the popular series in which it appears),
undocumented. One wonders how far the biblical authors were
themselves aware of the decisive difference which Westermann
discovers between the mythologically expressed, universal framework
of the beginning and the end, and the historically conditioned story
of salvation wrought out in Israel and the Church. One also feels
that justice is not done to the eschatological dimension in Paul and
John, and that the brief incursions into Systematic Theology reveal
severe limitations. Nevertheless important issues are raised and
questions formulated in an illuminating way. The asterisks in the
diagram on p. 14 are unexplained and there is printing confusion on
p. 37. 　　　　　D.R.J.

WIJNGAARDS, J. N. M.: *The Dramatization of Salvific History in the Deuteronomic Schools.* (Oudtestamentische Studiën. Deel XVI.) 1969. Pp. vi, 132. (E.J. Brill, Leiden. Price: Fl. 55)

Briefly stated, the main thesis of this book is that the procession across the Jordan recorded in Josh. 3–4 was originally (1250–1050 B.C.) conducted, not from Shittim to Gilgal, but from Succoth to Shechem and that the Deuteronomic Law (Deut. 5:1–28:28) found its original setting in the covenantal instruction at Succoth as part of the preparation for the reaffirmation of the Land-giving at Shechem. The ceremony, which took place at the feast of Tabernacles during the Year of Release, later (929–722 B.C.) underwent certain developments: the crossing of the Jordan was seen as a re-enactment of the miracle at the Red Sea and the covenantal instruction was transferred to Shechem itself. It is then argued that the Deuteronomic historians (850–587 B.C.) took over the ceremony and traditions in question, including the Deuteronomic Law, and transferred them to their own cult centre at Gilgal.

This study certainly holds the attention of the reader, but in its main contentions, as well as in many of its details, it is very hypothetical.

E.W.N.

WILCH, J. R.: *Time and Event. An exegetical study of the use of* 'ēth *in the Old Testament in comparison to other temporal expressions in clarification of the concept of time.* Pp. 196. (E. J. Brill, Leiden. Price: Fl. 32.00)

Many studies on the Hebrew words for 'time' have appeared since Conrad von Orelli's *Die hebräischen Synonyma der Zeit und Ewigkeit* (1871), most of them concerned with the relationship of the Hebrew to the Greek words and importing therewith western philosophical concepts with which the ancient Hebrews are not likely to have had any acquaintance. The present work mercifully makes no such attempt, being confined to establishing the true import of '*ēt* 'time' within the Old Testament. The author begins with a concise survey of previous opinions, from von Orelli (1952) to Ebeling (1964). His conclusion, after a careful survey of all the passages in which '*ēt* occurs, is that it refers very rarely to a period or extension of time (e.g. Judges 11:6) but is concerned primarily with the relationship between occasions, pointing to the 'juncture of circumstances', i.e. to the specific occasion produced by this occasion; subsequently it comes to designate the particular occasion itself. In course of time, however, it loses its character of referring to a definite occasion and becomes merely a superfluous addition or conjunction. Further, it is often concerned not so much with the temporal aspect of the occasion as with the fact, content or concreteness, of the occasion. The plural form indicates not a sequence but only a plurality of occasions, such as the events experienced by David and so on. As to form, the author rejects the opinion that the word is derived from the √'*nh* and prefers to regard it as a primitive biliteral form. In conclusion, the author's opinion, based on a careful consideration of all the relevant passages, is very attractive and may well be right. What is not always right are occasional remarks about Hebrew expressions, e.g. his explanation of *kā'īt ḥayyāh* (pp. 23–5) and his condemnation of the syntax of *hadda*'t *ṭôb wā-rā'* (pp. 119–20), which is a construction found elsewhere in the Old Testament and in Arabic literature, and his transliteration of *hāmôn* as *chmwm* (p. 141) as well as a number of English solecisms, e.g. 'attributed with' (p. 138), 'abnormalcy' (p. 142), semantical (p. 163), and even 'comparison to' in the title. There are also no indices.

G.R.D.

WOLFF, H.-W.: *Die Stunde des Amos: Prophetie und Protest.* 1969. Pp. 216. (Chr. Kaiser Verlag, Münich. Price: DM. 14.50)

This is a book, not for specialists, but for everyman, especially for those who regard the Old Testament as without significance or meaning for the present generation and the modern world. Its main thesis is that Amos is the contemporary of any generation; his method of direct confrontation and searching challenge of both religious ideas and practices and the vices of human society may bring churchmen and revolutionary activists to the one table.

The author begins by analysing the work of Amos and the situation in which he prosecuted it. Then, using chs 3 and 4 of the Book of Amos, he gives illustrations of the method of serious biblical exegesis. This is followed by an analysis of the preaching values for today of various passages, and a translation of the whole book in which a reader may learn from the use of different printing types the parts which may be regarded as authentic and those which are later additions. This book has a vigorous thrust and a vivid style which will enable it to serve its purpose excellently.

J.M.

LAW, RELIGION AND THEOLOGY

ANDERSON, B. W.: *Creation Versus Chaos. The Reinterpretation of Mythical Symbolism in the Bible.* 1967. Pp. 192. (Association Press, New York. Price: $4.95)

The five chapters in this book (1. Creation and History; 2. Creation and Covenant; 3. Creation and Worship; 4. Creation and Consummation; 5. Creation and Conflict) were originally delivered as lectures in a theological seminary and at a theological conference. They present the mythical expression of the theme creation *v.* chaos in the ancient Near East, the use made of this in the O.T., and its relevance to the modern situation. Strong emphasis is laid on the importance for biblical thought of man's relation to the historical process. The work of Gunkel is the foundation of the whole argument; but, both implicitly and explicitly, account is taken of recent research and debate in the areas covered. The book is an excellent example of how the investigation of one theological theme in the Bible may illuminate much else. The quality of the subject matter is matched by the excellence of presentation.

G.W.A.

ANDERSON, B. W.: *The Old Testament and Christian Faith.* 1969. Pp. xii, 271. (Herder and Herder, New York; Burns and Oates, London. Price: $2.95; 27s.)

This volume is a paperback reprint of the original American edition which appeared in 1963. A British edition was published by the S.C.M. Press in 1964 and was reviewed in *B.L.*, 1965, p. 42; *Decade*, p. 594.

N.W.P.

BARR, J.: *Biblical Words for Time.* Revised Edition. (Studies in Biblical Theology. First Series 33.) 1969. Pp. 221. (S.C.M. Press, London. Price: 28s.)

Any new book by Professor Barr attracts immediate attention and so will this revised edition of a monograph originally published in 1962 and reviewed in *B.L.*, 1963, p. 43; *Decade*, p. 437. Few and only slight changes have been introduced in the text, but a most valuable and interesting 'Postscript and Retrospect (1969)' of over 30 pages has been added. The author claims that there has in these last years been 'a reduction of emphasis on "biblical theology" and on the "unity of the Bible" ', and so believes that people will stop talking about 'the biblical view of time' and that a more philosophical theology will prevail. The second section of the postscript gives an extremely useful detailed bibliography of recent discussions on time and incidentally gives an impressive glimpse into the thoroughness of Professor Barr's researches. Only a specialist can risk breaking a lance with him. A further section does the same for biblical semantics. After a short section on problems of translation, the author concludes with an illuminating apologia against the charges of philosophical heresy which have been brought against him, and this will reward careful study.   N.W.P.

BLENKINSOPP, J.: *A Sketchbook of Biblical Theology.* 1968. Pp. viii, 148. (Burns and Oates, London. Price: 25s.)

The title of this book might suggest that it is no more than a popular sketch of biblical theology. What it actually contains is a most interesting collection of essays on various biblical topics which illustrate vividly the new freedom which characterizes Roman Catholic theology since the Second Vatican Council. The book begins with essays on the nature of biblical theology, on the nature of revelation (its dialogue character affirmed), on biblical inspiration (emphasis on social aspect), on biblical inerrancy (claimed for final sense). Of particular interest are the essays on the Pentateuch, on the cursing psalms and on the impasse of death in the Old Testament.

                                                           N.W.P.

BRUCE, F. F.: *This is That. The New Testament Development of some Old Testament Themes.* 1968. Pp. 122. (The Paternoster Press, Exeter. Price: 18s.; W. B. Eerdmans, Grand Rapids. Price: $3.90)

The title, abbreviated from Acts 2: 16, well indicates the purpose of the book which is an extension of the Payton Lectures 1968 in Fuller Theological Seminary, California. Major themes in the Old Testament are presented briefly but clearly and their continuation into the New Testament, development and fulfilment is discussed. The author's name will give confidence for the scholarship, as also for felicity of expression and sobriety of judgement. The book may be commended to students in colleges and to those who are engaged in the Church's teaching ministry.   A.S.H.

CODY, A.: *A History of Old Testament Priesthood.* (Analecta Biblica, 35.) 1969. Pp. 216. (Pontifical Biblical Institute, Rome. Price: $4.50; Lire 2,700)

Cody here offers a first-rate study of the many problems connected with the history of priesthood in the Old Testament. He gives a brief survey of the Mesopotamian background of priesthood and considers the counterparts to the Israelite *kōhēn*, noting the primary role of the latter as a sanctuary attendant. He maintains that the Levites were at one time a secular tribe, which broke up for reasons which cannot now be traced, leaving the members as *gērîm* who came to specialize in priestly duties. Cody rejects any connection between these Levites and the *lw'* or *lw't* of the Dedan inscription. With Deuteronomy these Levites claimed that all their members were potentially priests, although at that time this neither was, nor ever had been, the case in Israel. The rise of the Aaronids during the exile is given a fresh and very plausible explanation which dissents from the widely held hypothesis of a connection with Bethel. Altogether this is a very competent and attractive work, which gives a clear presentation of familiar problems, and poses some interesting and well-argued solutions.   R.E.C.

COPPENS, J.: *Le messianisme royal. Ses origines. Son développement. Son accomplissement.* (Lectio Divina, 54.) 1968. Pp. 228. (Éditions du Cerf, Paris. Price: Fr. 21)

It may not always be meritorious to yield to student pressure; but we have reason to be thankful that Canon Coppens acceded to the request both of his former students and of his colleagues that he should publish a synthesis of his studies of messianism. For many years he has contributed to various learned journals discussions of various aspects of the subject and of recent literature on it. Now he has gathered together the fruits of his researches in this comprehensive volume. He traces the development of royal messianism from its origins, through the prophetic literature and through its decline and resurgence in the post-exilic period, and to its N.T. interpretation and fulfilment. This is not a work which one can easily summarize in a brief review. It must suffice to state briefly its great merits: clear and adequate presentation of the relevant texts, ample documentation and discussion of the complex scholarly debate, masterly presentation of the intricate ramifications of the main problems, and, not least, sound judgement. This is a work which every serious student of the Bible should have on his shelves. We note with satisfaction that our esteemed Honorary Member hopes to give us a further synthesis on the same subject.   G.W.A.

DAUBE, D.: *Studies in Biblical Law.* 1969. Pp. viii, 328. (Ktav Publishing House, New York. Price: $10)

This is a reprint of a work which was first published in 1947 (see *B.L.*, 1947, p. 26; *Eleven Years*, p. 88). The basic criticisms made then remain, namely that the author relies too much on Roman law to illuminate the workings of biblical law, and by and large ignores critical analysis of the O.T. text. But perhaps the real value of the work was not sufficiently stressed in the earlier notice. The author looks at O.T. law as *law*, that is as something which was actually practised and lived out in the community. In adopting this approach he implicitly challenges the isolation in which biblical scholars work, and indicates their need to draw on the technical insights of those trained in other disciplines.   A.C.J.P.

FOHRER, G.: *Geschichte der Israelitischen Religion.* 1969. Pp. 436. (Walter de Gruyter, Berlin. Price: DM. 32)

Written to supersede G. Hölscher's study in the Töpelmann series, Fohrer's work is a basic textbook on its subject of the historical development of Israel's religion. It succeeds very well in presenting a comprehensive survey of the complex movements involved, whilst remaining clear and readable. Especially noteworthy is the excellent way in which the author presents his own particular views on controversial points, whilst also giving a very fair presentation of alternative views. Thus his own very positive estimate of the contribution of Moses to Israel's religion, his scepticism regarding the amphictyonic organization of pre-monarchic Israel, and his reserve in regard to the influence of particular tradition motifs on the classical prophets, are set against the views of other scholars who differ from him. There are adequate footnotes indicating the most important literature on each subject so that the student is well directed for further study. An English translation is in hand, and there is no doubt that this will become a very widely read textbook on the religion of the O.T.

R.E.C.

LOHFINK, N.: *The Christian meaning of the Old Testament.* 1968. Pp. ix, 169. (Burns and Oates, London. Price: 35s.)

This book is the translation of *Das Siegeslied am Schilfmeer*, published in German in 1965 by Verlag Josef Knecht. Chapter IV, which treats of the song of victory at the Red Sea, is an argument for its original typological character and therefore for the legitimacy of extending the typological interpretation to Christian baptism. Chapter II on the inerrancy of Scripture presents an argument that inerrancy can only be claimed for the Bible as possessing organic unity and that we must accept the Christological intention with which Jesus and the New Testament writers read the Old Testament. One cannot help feeling that the word inerrancy is not given its natural meaning here. Particularly valuable are the discussions of 'the great commandment', of Israel's understanding of history and of the biblical attitude to death.   N.W.P.

McKENZIE, J. L., S.J.: *Vital Concepts of the Bible.* 1968. Pp. 126. (Burns and Oates, London. Price: 18s.)

The miscellany of articles published here all reveal the author's skill at relating biblical exegesis to important theological and spiritual problems of the contemporary scene. Among other subjects judgement, eschatology, vocation and demythologizing are discussed in a very clear way. They make a popular presentation of important issues of scholarship, and the author's considerable learning is deceptively hidden under the very readable style.   R.E.C.

MÜLLER, H.-P.: *Ursprünge und Strukturen alttestamentlicher Eschatologie.*
(Beihefte zur Zeitschrift für die alttestamentliche Wissenschaft, 109.)
1969. Pp. xii, 232. (Verlag Alfred Töpelmann, Berlin. Price: DM. 46)

The importance and difficulty of investigating the origins of eschatological ideas in the O.T. are matched by the distinction and thoroughness of this monograph. The author starts from von Rad's definition
of eschatology, and therefore first probes the finality of events
experienced within history and indeed in the present. There follows a
massive survey of every passage in which this experience of finality
may be sought, organized in three divisions, (a) the divine intervention in history, (b) the blessing, and (c) the covenant. The divine
intervention in history is sought first in Israel's 'descriptive praise',
and it is claimed that there is a breaking through to the idea of a
timeless eternity. (Boman is laid under contribution; Barr is ignored.)
But the finality is limited, and the disillusionment constitutes an
aporia. This *aporia* is present in the attempt to make a verbal actualization of past events, in all cultic actualization (as in the Sion psalms),
and in every presentation of the *Heilsgeschichte.* When the relativity
of the present intervention of God in history is recognized, and
finality is seen to lie only in the future, then eschatology begins to
exist. A new thing is to happen, freed from all that is preliminary and
relative, discontinuous with the past. The connection with past
events is by analogy. The beginnings of this true eschatological
thought are found in the concept of the Day of Yahweh, in the Sion
theology, and in the announcement of the new exodus by Deutero-
Isaiah. The prophetic oracles of doom against the nations are the
precursors of Apocalyptic, working out the Sion tradition in its
mythicized form. Thus biblical eschatology arises neither from
Mesopotamian myths, nor from the Israelite cult, but from the inner
dynamic of Israel's faith in God, and particularly where the War
of Yahweh traditions are freed from the clutches of the mythical-
cultic traditions. Myth and cultus provide no more than the raw
material of eschatological thought.
Those who find the abstract character of the discussion obscure will
yet find value in the clear presentation of fundamental research.

                                                                    D.R.J.

NÖTSCHER, F.: '*Das Angesicht Gottes schauen*' *nach biblischer und babylon-
ischer Auffassung.* First published 1924, 2nd edition, revised and corrected with the aid of Josef Scharbert; also VON BAUDISSIN, W. W. Graf:
'"Gott schauen" in der alttestamentlichen Religion', originally
published in *Archiv für Religionswissenschaft,* XVIII (1915). 1969. Pp. 261.
(Wissenschaftliche Buchgesellschaft, Darmstadt. Price: DM. 19)

The reviewer must confess that he has had this book on his reading-
list for many years, but, misled somewhat by the title, had failed to
realize what he was missing until this new edition appeared. The fact is
that this work offers far more than the title would lead one to suppose,
for it represents an exhaustive study of the use of the term *pānîm* as
perhaps the most intimate way of expressing Yahweh's personal
involvement in the life of mankind, the author's approach being
reinforced throughout by reference to comparative data available in
early Mesopotamian and occasionally Canaanite and Egyptian
sources. The familiar fact that the Hebrew expression behind the

title of the book could be used of visiting the sanctuary is thus but one small aspect of this semantic study which, despite its appearance nearly half a century ago, remains of basic importance and is indeed far-reaching in its implications. The publishers are to be thanked warmly for making this important monograph available once again and for including so usefully as an appendix the earlier suggestive and still valuable, if more limited, study by von Baudissin.

A.R.J.

RYDER SMITH, C.: *The Bible Doctrine of Salvation. A study of the Atonement.* (Finsbury Library.) (1941) 1969. Pp. 320 (Epworth Press, London. Price: 20s.)

The original publication of this book was noted in *B.L.*, 1946, p. 52; *Eleven Years*, p. 52. It is here reprinted without alteration. Like other volumes with comparable titles by the same author, it is a review of the biblical material, about half the book being devoted to O.T. and the intertestamental literature. If it is very largely a gathering of the passages which deal with ideas of salvation, the Messiah, suffering, sin and sacrifice, it nevertheless provides the raw material from which discussion of the meaning of atonement in biblical terms has to proceed. If, inevitably, it is dated, it is still useful to have the basic questions set out, and such an older study often stimulates new insights.

P.R.A.

WITTON DAVIES, T.: *Magic, Divination and Demonology among the Hebrews and their Neighbours; including an examination of Biblical references and of the Biblical terms.* 1969. Pp. 132. (Ktav Publishing House, New York. 1969. Price: $6.95)

This Leipzig Ph.D. dissertation, originally published in 1898, displays a pleasing undogmatic approach and a genuine insight into the subject. But in the time-scale of ancient Near Eastern scholarship, with its current wealth of archaeological data and firmer criteria of critical study, seven decades have petrified the work in another era. Of interest to Old Testament specialists will be the systematic examination of biblical passages and terms, but it is regrettable that the book lacks indexes. Nowadays it is the social and mystical dimensions of the subject which are being stressed, but there are indications also that there may be important connexions between this difficult subject and the group of strange and tantalizing phenomena known as ESP.

I.B.

THE LIFE AND THOUGHT OF THE
SURROUNDING PEOPLES

BUCCELLATI, G.: *Cities and Nations of Ancient Syria. An Essay on Political Institutions with Special Reference to the Israelite Kingdoms.* (Studi Semitici, 26.) 1967. Pp. 264. (Istituto di Studi del Vicino Oriente, University of Rome)

The relevance of this book for Old Testament studies is indicated by its sub-title. The first half is devoted to an analysis of the types of political state in Syria and Palestine (including Moab, Edom and

Ammon) in the second millennium and the first half of the first millennium B.C. A clear distinction is drawn between the territorial state, of which the city-state is one type, and the national state. In the second half of the book, which is devoted to the Israelite kingdoms, it is argued that these were national states based on a sense of kinship and coherence as a people and on the worship of a national god rather than on geographical factors, although during the course of their history they were influenced to some extent by the institutions of the city-state. The Old Testament evidence is fully discussed, and some of the conclusions reached challenge those of earlier scholars, especially those of Alt. By setting the Old Testament material against the background of political institutions in the area as a whole the author has succeeded in throwing new light on old problems, and his book is an important contribution to the subject.   R.N.W.

VAN DRIEL, G.: *The Cult of Aššur.* (Studia Semitica Neerlandica, 13.) 1969. Pp. 228, 3 plates, 1 chart. (Van Gorcum, Assen. Price: Fl. 49.90)

This thesis covers the archaeological and epigraphic evidence for the history and description of the temple of the god Ashur at the Assyrian capital. New texts give additional data for the cult calendar and ceremonies. A specialist Assyriological work of use to the biblical historian seeking comparative material on religious and ritual practice in ancient Mesopotamia.   D.J.W.

FITZMYER, J. A., S.J.: *The Aramaic Inscriptions of Sefire* (Biblica et Orientalia, N.19.) 1967. Pp. xiii, 207. 18 plates. (Pontifical Biblical Institute, Rome. Price: Lire 3000; $5.00)

The first of the three inscriptions here published was found about fifty years ago and was edited in 1930 by Fr S. Ronzevalle, who was misled into believing that it had been found at Sûjîn and named it after that place; the second and third, which were discovered more recently at Säfîräh, after which all three are now named, were excellently edited by Professor A. Dupont-Sommer and Fr J. Starcky with a fresh edition of the first inscription (1958–60). The village of Säfîräh lies about fifteen miles to the SE of Aleppo, and Sûjîn is about half-a-mile to the NE of Säfîräh. All three inscriptions seem to have been cut by the same engraver, and their language is very close to that of others dated in the middle of the 8th century B.C. (shortly after those of Kilamurva, Zakir and Panammuwa, but before those of Bar-Rekub and Azatiwadda). These three inscriptions preserve the text of treaties made by Matî'el son of 'Attarsamak king of Arpad with Bar-Ga'yah king of *Ktk*, a powerful Mesopotamian overlord whose vassal he was.

Fr Fitzmyer, whose work on other early Aramaic texts (notably his similar edition of the *Genesis Apocryphon* published in 1966, *B.L.*, 1967, p. 45) is well known for its high standard of scholarship, here lives up to his reputation. His present work, which is a revision of two articles which he wrote on these three inscriptions in 1954 (III) and 1961 (I and II), seems not only to have taken account of everything written on them in the meantime but also greatly to advance their interpretation with his own new insights.

He begins with a brief introduction on the discovery and decipherment of the three texts and their relation to one another and a full bibliography (pp. 1–8). Then each inscription is printed in beautifully clear Hebrew format and furnished with a translation on the opposite page; and each is followed by an exhaustive critical and philological commentary (pp. 9–120). This part is followed by short but informative essays on the relation of these inscriptions to those containing Hittite and Assyrian treaties and on the land of *Ktk*, of which the vocalization is not yet known (pp. 121–35). Then an invaluable appendix on the grammar and syntax of these texts (pp. 137–81), a complete glossary (pp. 182–92) and various indexes (pp. 193–207) bring this part of the work to a proper conclusion. They are followed by 18 plates which comprise a table of alphabets of the 9th and 8th centuries B.C., 12 hand-drawn copies and four photographs of the Aramaic texts, and a map of the relevant parts of the Middle East.

Nothing remains to be added to this catalogue of the contents of the book beyond the bare statement that it is fully worthy of these important and interesting texts; no student can dispense with Fr Fitzmyer's editions, and any future editor of them will have to take full account of everything said in it.

G.R.D.

HUNGER, H.: *Babylonische und assyrische Kolophone.* (Alter Orient und Altes Testament, 2.) 1968. Pp. viii, 189. (Butzon und Bercker, Kevelaer, Neukirchen-Vluyn. Price: DM. 39.60)

Cuneiform tablets of literary and other content that were handed down as library texts often end with a colophon giving details that the modern world places on title pages: about the text (e.g. its belonging to a series), about the scribe and owner and so forth. These notes are spread over some 1500 years and are of primary importance for the history of the transmission of cuneiform literature. This book is the first attempt to collect them systematically. They are given in transliteration and translation, carefully arranged, and with an Introduction summarizing their content. The work is competent but incomplete. There are some serious and surprising omissions.

W.G.L.

KAPELRUD, A. S.: *The Violent Goddess. Anat in the Ras Shamra Texts.* 1969. Pp. 126. (Universitetsforlaget, Oslo, for Scandinavian University Books. Price: N.Kr. 39)

This book, a sequel to the author's *Baal in the Ras Shamra Texts* (*B.L.*, 1952, p. 62; *Eleven Years*, p. 433), discusses other goddesses similar to Anat, the titles, family and entourage of Anat, and then translates and comments on the texts which refer directly to the goddess from Ugarit, bringing out her character as a goddess of war, violence, mourning, love and fertility. While there is little that is strictly new here, it is very useful to have all the material about Anat drawn together in this way.

J.V.M.S.

LAMBERT, W. G. and MILLARD, A. R.: *Atra-ḫasis; the Babylonian Story of the Flood.* 1969. Pp. xii, 198, 11 plates. (Clarendon Press, Oxford. Price: 70s.)

The introduction to this first edition of a Babylonian Epic (the text now two-thirds recovered) is written for non-cuneiformists. The account in one document of the creation of man following a strike by the gods, the subsequent population explosion and divine retribution by plague, famine and the flood, precedes the later *Epic of Gilgamesh* by some seven centuries. A revised translation of the Sumerian flood story (by M. Civil) now supersedes that offered in ANET², and implies that this was itself a translation from a Semitic original. Some aspects of the bearing of this new evidence on the O.T. are discussed, but the primary aim is to present a scholarly and reliable text, translation and philological notes on which all such future discussions must depend (cf. A. R. Millard, *Tyndale Bulletin*, 18 (1967), 3–18). Related texts from Ras Shamra (Akkadian) and Berossus are a useful addition.

D.J.W.

LORETZ, O.: *Texte aus Chagar Bazar und Tell Brak, Teil 1.* (Alter Orient und Altes Testament, 3.) 1969. Pp. 37. 40 plates. (Butzon & Bercker, Kevelaer, Neukirchen-Vluyn. Price: DM. 26)

This further volume in the new series Ancient Orient and Old Testament is a partial republication of some Akkadian texts from northern Mesopotamia. Being without translations it is useable only by Assyriologists and has no immediate application to O.T. studies.

D.J.W.

MOSCATI, S.: *Staré semitské civilizace.* (Ancient Semitic Civilizations.) Translated by Segert, S. 1969. Pp. 352. (Odeon, Prague. Price: Kčs. 20)

This is a Czech translation of the Italian original: *Le antiche civiltà semitiche* (1961). The German translation of this was reviewed in *B.L.*, 1962, p. 60; *Decade*, p. 370. The praise for the book there voiced may be simply repeated for the Czech translation, and indeed it is proper that thanks should be added to the translator for having taken the trouble, with some assistance from other Prague orientalists, to get the texts cited translated afresh from the original languages. In a postscript, Dr Segert provides for the Czech reader general information about the semitic cultures and their contribution to western civilization, about the latest archaeological finds, about the present tasks of semitic studies, about the work of Moscati and about the participation of Czech semitists (pp. 336–42). He has also supplemented Moscati's bibliography with a selection of references to scholarly works by Czechoslovak orientalists (pp. 343–6) which may also be of value to scholars in other countries.

M.B.

OLDENBURG, U.: *The Conflict between El and Baʿal in Canaanite Religion.* (Supplementa ad Numen, Ser. II, Vol. III.) 1969. Pp. xiv, 217. (E. J. Brill, Leiden. Price: Fl. 64)

The subject of the present work is the conflict between El and Baʿal as known from the cuneiform texts found at Ugarit and compared with the fragmentary notices preserved on Hittite tablets and in Sanchuniaton's 'Phoenician History', of which Eusebius gives a summary account in his 'Preparation for the Gospel' (c. A.D. 315). After a detailed discussion of the pantheon and the struggle for supremacy within it, the author reaches the following conclusions: A conflict is supposed to have taken place between El and his family on one side and Ba'al and his associates on the other, whereby El was displaced as monocratic head of the Canaanite pantheon by Ba'al; this conflict was expressed in mythology as a drama of which the central theme was blood-vengeance, whereby the long series of battles, in which Ba'al in spite of defeats and death finally overcomes all opposition, is explained. His battles and death reflect his character and function as a nature-god, which developed considerably from that of the Thunderer riding upon the clouds to become a chthonic deity and also Lord of the Earth. The main difference between Ugaritic mythology, in which El appears humiliated and deposed, and Sanchuniaton's 'History', which depicts him at the summit of his power, reveals different stages in the development of the myth; according to this the revolution in the Canaanite pantheon began in the north and moved southwards as Ba'al usurped the Canaanite El's kingship. This revolution took place c. 2000 B.C. at Ugarit; but El remained supreme according to Sanchuniaton and the account which *Genesis* gives of patriarchal religion until c. 1500 B.C., by which time Ba'al had usurped El's kingship both in the Phoenician states, as the letters from Tell-el Amarna show, and in Palestine, as seen from indications in the book of Judges. Afterwards his cult made its way into the Northern and subsequently even into the Southern kingdom. Thus Yahweh, originally identical with the great semitic creator god El, became involved in the same conflict with Ba'al, in which, however, he was the final victor. Finally, while El and his family represented the original Canaanite pantheon, Hadad and his associates were originally foreign, *viz.* Amorite, deities; thus the religious conflict in the Canaanite pantheon, in which they prevailed, reflects a cultural revolution caused by the Amorite penetration into Canaan. The author argues his case well, and makes a number of good points which will require consideration. An appendix contains fresh translations of several of the relevant texts; here caution must be exercised in following him. His English is remarkably good, though marred by a few solecisms, e.g. 'buildt' (p. 190) and 'princeship' (p. 192); and what does 'who caused his ears to chirp' (p. 198) mean?   G.R.D.

RAPAPORT, I.: *A New Interpretation of §§ 6–8 of the Code of Hammurabi (A Critical Study of a Group of Old Babylonian Laws)*. 1967. Pp. 44. (Privately published for the author, Rabbi's Office, Melbourne: Price: 15s.)

These sections of the Laws of Hammurabi relate to theft from a temple or palace and the acceptance of property from a minor without witnesses or a contract, both punishable by death. The penalty and unusual provisions have led most scholars to consider them mutually contradictory. This monograph offers a highly questionable thesis; it proposes a radical reconstruction of all three sections assuming textual corruption which is unsupported by any manuscript copy or by the earlier identical laws of Lipit-Ishtar which are dismissed as unauthentic and later than those of Hammurabi! The Talmud is

drawn upon in support for details readily knowable from contemporary Old Babylonian texts. The author has not considered the
probability that these were not codified ('usual') legal enactments
but, like much of the Mosaic legal decisions, were specific decisions
in hard cases of which the detail is unrelated (as orally transmitted).

D.J.W.

RINGGREN, H.: *Religionens Form och Funktion*. 1968. Pp. 170. (C. W. K.
Gleerup, Lund. Price: Sw.Kr. 17.50)

This is an introduction in Swedish to the study of religions, intended
for use in Colleges of Education. The book is extremely clear and
up-to-date, displaying a very wide knowledge of its subject. Some
examples are drawn from the Old Testament, but there is no special
concentration on it.   J.V.M.S.

RÖLLIG, W. (ed.): *lišān mitḫurti. Festschrift Wolfram Freiherr von Soden*.
(Alter Orient und Altes Testament, 1.) 1969. Pp. xxviii, 331; pl. VI.
(Butzon und Bercker, Kevelaer, Neukirchen-Vluyn. Price: DM. 51)

The purpose of this new series is stated as being 'to build a bridge
between the Old Testament and the surrounding world', the need for
which will not be disputed. However, with increasing specialization
this is not so easily achieved, and the first volume illustrates the problems. It is a *Festschrift* dedicated to a famous Assyriologist embracing
16 contributions. Some are of considerable length and importance, but
all but one are strictly Assyriological: 13 are philological, mainly
grammatical studies or editions of texts, one is archaeological and
one is devoted to historical geography. The only article from another
field is on Adonis, Attis and Osiris. There is a wealth of material for
Akkadian and Sumerian studies, but the Old Testament scholar
without training in these areas will find little to interest or help him.

W.G.L.

SAGGS, H. W. F.: *Assyriology and the study of the Old Testament*. (An
inaugural lecture delivered at University College, Cardiff, 1968.) 1969.
Pp. 27. (University of Wales Press, Cardiff. Price: 3s. 6d.)

The title makes clear the purpose of this study. After a concise review
of the history of Assyriological studies, Professor Saggs comments
first in general on the relationship of these studies to the study of the
O.T., and then examines the particular contribution of a selection of
royal archives of the 8th century B.C. Assyrian policy and practice
as revealed in this material is carefully related to the biblical evidence
for the same period. Of special interest here is the relating of the
religious practice ascribed to Ahaz to Phoenicia rather than to
Assyria, and the consequences for historical interpretation extracted
from this. In the last part of the lecture, Saggs turns to a familiar
theme, a critique of the dominance of cultic and mythic interpretation
especially in the prophets. The light shed by Assyrian letters on
ordinary thinking in contrast to the stylized presentations of historical
and literary texts is clearly important. But this part of the discussion

begs the question whether the O.T. prophets were or were not religious officials (in some sense) rather than amateurs. In rejecting a particular view as 'not proven', Saggs has ignored the wider range of evidence which has to be assessed.   P.R.A.

QUMRAN STUDIES

ALLEGRO, J. M.: *Rukopisy od Mrtvého moře* (The Dead Sea Scrolls, translated by Mareš, S. and Žilina, M.) 1969. Pp. 214. 37 plates on 27 pages, together with a note about the author and the contents of the book (the pages from 215 onwards are not numbered) (Mladá fronta, Prague. Price: Kčs. 17)

Allegro's well-known book (see *B.L.*, 1957, p. 63; *Decade*, p. 63), has now been translated into Czech, with the omission only of the bibliography. The illustrations have been added on glossy paper. The translators have supplemented Allegro's discussions at some points with footnotes, e.g. on p. 9 on the Jacobites, p. 11 on the establishment of the state of Israel, p. 15 on Sir John Bagot Glubb, etc. At the end of the book (pp. 205–14) there are three appendices to the Czech translation dealing respectively with the formation and divisions of the Bible (including the Apocrypha), the Jewish sects in the period of the Second Temple, and the Jewish months and most important festivals. The Czech reader will be much indebted to the translators for these footnotes and appendices.   M.B.

MACDONALD, J. (ed.): *The Annual of Leeds University Oriental Society.* Vol. VI, 1966–8. *Dead Sea Scroll Studies 1969.* 1969. Pp. viii, 168. (E. J. Brill, Leiden. Price: Fl. 45)

Common to three of the six studies in this volume, which, as the sub-title indicates, is almost entirely concerned with the Dead Sea Scrolls, is a questioning of opinions which have acquired almost the status of dogma. D. Winton Thomas ('The Dead Sea Scrolls: What may we Believe?', pp. 7–20) discusses the uncertainties involved in many areas of research into the scrolls, and makes a plea that the now widely accepted 'orthodox' scholarly view of them should not be allowed prematurely to establish itself. G. R. Driver ('Myths Of Qumran', pp. 23–48) argues that the 'writing tables' found in the *scriptorium* were refectory tables, and *inter alia* offers some comments on Père de Vaux's review of his *Judaean Scrolls*. P. Wernberg-Møller ('The Nature of the Yaḥad according to the Manual of Discipline and Related Documents', pp. 56–81) examines some passages in the *Manual of Discipline* in which the word *yaḥad* occurs, and argues in support of the view that the 'Qumran Community' was not a closed monastic society, but rather was similar to the early Pharisaic *ḥaburot*. Two of the other articles are concerned with biblical exegesis (G. Vermes, 'The Qumran Interpretation of Scripture in its Historical Setting', pp. 85–97; S. Lowy, 'Some Aspects of Normative and Sectarian Interpretation of the Scriptures', pp. 98–163 — the latter not primarily concerned with the scrolls). Finally F. F. Bruce ('Holy Spirit in the Qumran Texts', pp. 49–55) examines the use of the term 'holy spirit' at Qumran, and considers some N.T. parallels.

M.A.K.

APOCRYPHA AND POST-BIBLICAL STUDIES

ADINOLFI, M.: *Questioni bibliche di storia e storiografia.* 1969. Pp. 216. (Paideia, Brescia. Price: Lire 1,800)

This collection of essays by a professor of the Ateneo Antoniano in Rome deals very adequately with such topics as biblical and classical historiography, eloquence and pathos in the second book of Maccabees, the testament of Mattathias in I Macc. 2:49–68, the apparitions in II Macc., chapters 5, 10 and 11, and St Paul at Pozzuoli. Like other productions of the same press it is delightfully printed.   J.M.T.B.

BRUNNER, R. (ed.): *Gesetz und Gnade im Alten Testament und im jüdischen Denken.* (Judaica.) 1969. Pp. 176. (Zwingli Verlag, Zürich. Price: DM. 16)

Three lectures delivered under the auspices of the *Schweizer Evangelischen Judenmission* in Reuti-Hasliberg have here been reproduced as an off-print of *Judaica.* The first by Herbert Schmid briefly surveys Law and Grace in the O.T., with attention to the characteristic terms and with consideration of the Torah in different phases of the literature and at different periods of the history. Kurt Hruby in the second lecture examines Law and Grace in the Rabbinic tradition, dealing *inter alia* with Divine Grace in Man, Grace and Free Will, and Grace in relation to Reward and Punishment. Finally Johann Maier, whose concern is with Law and Grace in the Post-Talmudic era, in the longest of these lectures, presents, with a variety of selected passages from the relevant literature and with appropriate reference to the contributions of its leading exponents, the development of thought relating to the Torah from the Middle Ages through the Enlightenment to the present day. He is at pains to demonstrate the richness of this heritage and its significance for mutual understanding between Jews and Christians.   E.T.R.

BURCHARD, C., JERVELL, J. and THOMAS, J.: *Studien zu den Testamenten der Zwölf Patriarchen.* Drei Aufsätze herausgegeben von W. Eltester. (Beihefte zur Zeitschrift für die neutestamentliche Wissenschaft, 36.) 1969. Pp. VIII, 160. (Verlag Alfred Töpelmann, Berlin. Price: DM. 44)

This volume contains three studies. C. Burchard ('Zur armenischen Überlieferung der Testamente der zwölf Patriarchen', pp. 1–29) gives a preliminary assessment of the forty-five MSS of the Armenian version of T. XII P. known to him (Charles knew of only twelve), and considers the value of the Armenian version in relation to the Greek. J. Jervell ('Ein Interpolator interpretiert', pp. 30–61) argues that the statements in T. XII P. about the fate of Israel-and-the-Gentiles derive in their present form from a Christian interpolator; he discusses the theological significance of these statements and suggests that the first Christian revision of T. XII P. is to be dated at the end of the 1st century. J. Thomas ('Aktuelles im Zeugnis der zwölf Väter', pp. 62–150) argues that the Testaments were originally composed in the pre-Maccabaean period and regards them as an admonition addressed by the Judaean community to the Egyptian diaspora.

M.A.K.

CHRISTIANSEN, I.: *Die Technik der allegorischen Auslegungswissenschaft bei Philon von Alexandrien.* (Beiträge zur Geschichte der Biblischen Hermeneutik, 7.) 1969. Pp. 191. (J. C. B. Mohr (Paul Siebeck), Tübingen. Price: DM. 39; bound DM. 45)

This book examines fully the Hellenistic technique of symbolism and allegorical interpretation and applies it to Philo's exegetical writings. The author's contribution to a better understanding of the Alexandrian exegete is noteworthy but it is perhaps not wholly unnecessary to remark that for a proper appreciation of his achievement, knowledge of his Jewish background is equally essential.   G.V.

FLUSSER, D.: *Jesus,* trans. by R. Walls. 1969. Pp. 159. (Herder and Herder, New York; Burns and Oates, London. Price: $4.95; 45s.)

This is a translation of *Jesus in Selbstzeugnissen und Bilddokumenten* (1968). The author aims to demonstrate the possibility of writing a life of Jesus. Jesus appears as an educated Jew, faithful to the Law and approving the teaching of the Pharisees. He was distinguished by his demand for unconditional love, a new concept of God's righteousness, and the claim that the new age had already begun. He knew himself to be God's servant and recipient of his Spirit. Uniquely close to God, he thought of himself as God's son, gradually becoming convinced that he was also to be the eschatological judge, the Son of Man. He came into fatal conflict with the Sadducees because of his attitude to the temple. Major problems inevitably get summary treatment, but the book is nevertheless stimulating and useful.

M.E.T.

FRIEDLANDER, G.: *The Jewish Sources of the Sermon on the Mount.* (Library of Biblical Studies, ed. H. M. Orlinsky.) 1969. Pp. lviii, 301. (Ktav Publishing House, Inc., New York. Price: $8.95)

This is a reprint of a book first published in 1911, now reissued with an introduction by Dr Solomon Zeitlin. This introduction unfortunately does little to inspire confidence in the book, displaying as it does extraordinary misconceptions about N.T. critical work. This is a pity, since the book — in spite of its polemical approach — is still useful in presenting Jewish parallels to the Matthaean material, provided one remembers that, as Dr Zeitlin remarks, 'Friedlander, in citing the numerous passages from the Rabbinic literature, did not apply critical, historical analysis'.   M.D.H.

GAMBERONI, J.: *Die Auslegung des Buches Tobias in der griechisch-lateinischen Kirche der Antike und der Christenheit des Westens bis 1600.* (Studien zum Alten und Neuen Testament, Band XXI.) 1969. Pp. 356. (Kösel-Verlag, Munich. Price: DM. 82)

This is a history of the use and interpretation of the book of Tobit in the Christian Church from earliest times (the Didache) to the 16th century. It shows how, from the beginning, whatever its position in relation to the Canon, it was regarded as a biblical book and interpretation sought, consciously or unconsciously, to fit it into the

Christian tradition. Indeed at no time was there a clear distinction made between the book in itself and the Christian tradition in which it was embedded. The additional material that is found in the Vulgate (and which may be due to Jerome himself) may be early evidence of this approach to the book, although it is more properly described as moralizing expansion. It had become a Christian book and its interpretation was Christian, even if that meant allegorizing, as it did for Bede and the many who echoed him. The book is valuable not only as a history of interpretation but also as an indirect, but nonetheless important, study of the Canon.

                                                                                          L.H.B.

GAVIN, F.: *The Jewish Antecedents of the Christian Sacraments*, 1928, reprint 1969. Pp. viii, 120. (Ktav Publishing House, Inc., New York. Price: $6.95)

The first of these three lectures, which were originally published in 1928, draws some parallels between the relationship, in O.T. and Rabbinic Judaism and in Christianity, between outward rite and divine activity; the second argues that both the ritual and some aspects of the interpretation of early Christian baptism 'may be found in or explained by' the ritual and interpretation of proselyte baptism; the third presents parallels between some Jewish liturgical forms and early Christian eucharistic liturgies, together with brief remarks about analogies in Judaism to certain other Christian practices. In all the detailed matters discussed here the state of research has advanced considerably since these lectures were first published, and the most useful feature of this reprint is the quite full references to earlier work and to the Rabbinic sources.

                                                                                          C.J.A.H.

GÜTING, E.: *Terumot* (*Priesterheben*.) (Die Mischna I Seder, 6 Traktat, ed. by K. H. Rengstorf und L. Rost.) 1969. Pp. x, 235. (Verlag Alfred Töpelmann, Berlin. Price: DM. 68.00)

Terumot (Heave-Offerings) is the name of the sixth tractate of the first order of the Mishnah called *Zeraim*. The usual translation 'Seeds' is somewhat misleading as the tractates of this order (nos 2–10) are not concerned with seeds as such but with the produce of the soil, the harvest from the agricultural work. It is from this that certain levies are made, most of which go to the temple, the priests, and the levites. They are made only from the soil of the land of Israel which, actually, belongs to God. *Terumah* (cf. Nu. 18:8–14, 19 and Deut. 18:4) was taken from corn (*dagan* = barley and wheat), wine, oil, olives, figs, dates, cucumbers, melons and other fruit of the earth used for human consumption. It is always selected from the best or the most beautiful produce. The separation and delivery of *Terumah* took precedence over all other levies from the soil. A special holiness was attached to *Terumah* which was to be eaten in ritual purity. The tractate, the longest of the whole order, deals with all questions about Terumah in minutest detail. *Terumah* is mentioned hundreds of times in the rest of the Mishnah, which shows that it is a prominent subject of rabbinic discussions. The author of the present edition has admirably fulfilled his difficult undertaking. His presentation is clear and he brings out all the essentials. His style is lucid and makes the study of this tractate easy.

                                                                                          H.K.

HERIKNDSEN, W.: *Israel and the Bible*. 1968. Pp. 63. (Baker Book House, Grand Rapids, Michigan. Price: $1.50)

This pamphlet is primarily concerned with questions involving the relationships between Jews and Christians. It includes a discussion of biblical material which has been thought to be directly related to the current political situation in the Near East, very much tied to a literalistic and conservative viewpoint.   P.R.A.

HENGEL, M.: *Judentum und Hellenismus. Studien zu ihrer Begegnung unter besonderer Berücksichtigung Palästinas bis zur Mitte des 2 Jh.v.Chr.* (Wissenschaftliche Untersuchungen zum Neuen Testament, 10.) 1969. Pp. 692. (J. C. B. Mohr (Paul Siebeck), Tübingen. Price: DM. 137; bound DM. 145)

This is an assessment of the mutual impact of Judaism and Hellenism and the re-shaping of Judaism in consequence. It is concerned chiefly with Palestinian Judaism, but inevitably deals also with that of the Diaspora. It opens with a review of the earliest possible contact of Greek with Jew in Palestine and then deals in minute detail with the period from Alexander to the Maccabaean revolt. There are four chapters. The first (pp. 8–I07) shows how Hellenism exerted a steadily increasing political and economic influence on the inhabitants of Palestine. The ambitions of many leading Jewish families were stirred by the successes of the Greeks in war, administration and commerce. The second chapter (pp. 108–95) surveys the effects of the impact of Greek education and culture on the peoples of Palestine in general and on the Jews in particular. They began to speak Greek, to assume Greek names, and to be educated in the Greek style. Almost inevitably this led to the request that Jerusalem be re-constituted a Greek *polis*. Hengel is at pains here, as throughout the book, to show how uncertain much of the evidence is, and that the actual point at which Jerusalem was so recognized is not clear. Judaism could now be regarded as 'Hellenistic Judaism', with two branches, the Greek-speaking Judaism of the Diaspora and the Hebrew–Aramaic-speaking Judaism of Palestine. Chapter three (pp. 196–463) examines the literature of the period, not only Jewish but also such non-Jewish as treated of the Jews or had any bearing on the question. It is shown that whilst practically no Jewish book exhibits direct dependence on Greek literature there is also no book that cannot be shown to have some echo of Greek thought or ideas, the influence being indirect and largely unconscious. The chapter ends with a full discussion of the community of Essenes at Qumran and its literary output. Even here, where there might be thought to be the strongest resistance to any-thing Greek, there is evidence of Greek influence, e.g. in the very form of their community and in their astrological ideas. The last chapter (pp. 464–570), after sketching the history of the attempt to hellenize Judaism and of the resistance to it, shows how it resulted in an exces-sive zeal for the law, in the development of apocalyptic eschatology, in the hope of a messianic age and in the consciousness, in spite of a continuing nationalism, of being a world-religion.

It is a book to read and return to: it is packed with information, both in the text and in the copious footnotes; the information is carefully sifted and critically examined. This is an important contribution to the subject.   L.H.B.

JOHNSON, M. D.: *The Purpose of the Biblical Genealogies — with special reference to the setting of the genealogies of Jesus.* (S.N.T.S. Monograph Series, 8.) 1969. Pp. x, 310. (Cambridge University Press. Price: 80s.)

Dr Johnson attempts to discover the purpose of the biblical genealogies, and 'the extent to which the genealogical form was utilized by the author of the particular book or source to communicate his characteristic theological convictions'. Half the book is devoted to the O.T. and to later Jewish genealogies. By a detailed examination of the material in the Pentateuch, in Ezra-Nehemiah and Chronicles, the author establishes that the genealogical form was used primarily for apologetic purposes (both nationalistic and theological), and that the material reflects the same theological motifs and tendencies as the sources in which it is found. Examination of the genealogies of Jesus suggests that they, too, reflect the theology of the evangelists, and like the Jewish material, are a form of midrashic exegesis. This is a careful and interesting study which should be useful to both O.T. and N.T. specialists.

M.D.H.

LARCHER, C., O.P.: *Études sur le Livre de la Sagesse.* (Études Bibliques.) 1969. Pp. 442. (Librairie Lecoffre, J. Gabalda et Cie, Éditeurs, Paris. Price: Fr. 78)

Less than justice can be done in a brief notice of the five studies in this volume, presented with much wealth of detail and documentation. The place of the Book of Wisdom in the Christian Church with reference to N.T., Patristic, and subsequent writings is the first subject considered. This is followed by similar examination of the Book's affinities with various parts of the O.T., and with related material in the Book of Enoch, in the literature from Qumran as also in that found in Hellenistic Judaism, notably in Philo. Next dealt with is the influence of Hellenism under the headings of Greek Culture in General, Greek Philosophy, and the Problem of the Sources. The two remaining studies are concerned with the Immortality of the Soul and its attendant themes of reward and punishment in the hereafter, and with Wisdom and Spirit. A full complement of indexes, especially the *Index Analytique*, enchances the usefulness of this indispensable work of reference. Although the author describes these studies as *plutôt théologiques*, there is obviously in them much that will be of interest and value to the O.T. specialist. When, as is promised in the preface, a second volume (to consist of commentary, translation, and full-scale introduction) duly appears to complete the present work, the Book of Wisdom will, by all the tokens, have been superbly treated and most assuredly in keeping with the scholarly tradition of the *Collection d'Études Bibliques*.

E.T.R.

LEVIANT, C. (ed.): *King Artus: A Hebrew Arthurian Romance of 1279.* (Studia Semitica Neerlandica, no. 11.) 1969. Pp. 125. (Van Gorcum, Assen. Price: Fl. 20)

King Arthur's Round Table in an Hebrew translation may at first sight appear to be a *jeu d'esprit* of little importance, but as the scholarly editor and translator shows in his brief introduction this unique copy of the Romance deserves attention on many counts.

The manuscript of 1279 is only found in the Vatican Library. Leviant gives the text and explores the literary background of the Hebrew Arthurian Romance. *Morta Artu* is a secular sermon: biblical scenes blend with Arthurian ones. The heroes of the Old Testament live again, especially David; the Tristan parallels (Joseph) are fascinating. The author lists thirty archetypal situations common to both Jewish and Arthurian stories.

U.E.S.

MACDONALD, J.: *The Samaritan Chronicle No. II (or: Sepher Ha-Yamim) From Joshua to Nebuchadnezzar.* (Beihefte zur Zeitschrift für die alttestamentliche Wissenschaft, 107.) 1969. Pp. 227, 93. (Verlag Alfred Töpelmann, Berlin. Price: DM.70)

The text of the Samaritan Chronicle II is here published for the first time, along with an English translation, an extended introduction and a number of appendices. Of particular importance for Old Testament study will be the comparison here afforded with extensive sections of Joshua, Judges, Samuel, Kings and Chronicles; both the textual criticism of these works and the history of the period they deal with may have fresh light thrown upon them. Even more basic, of course, is the significance of this Chronicle for the Samaritans' own origins and history. Both the links between Samaritans and Jews and the issues which separated them have been more fully explored in recent years, and Macdonald's long-awaited volume will certainly further this study.

R.J.C.

McKELVEY, R. J.: *The New Temple. The Church in the New Testament.* (Oxford Theological Monographs, no. 3.) 1969. Pp. 238. (Oxford University Press, London. Price: 42s.)

This is primarily a New Testament study, and concerns itself with surveying the use of the image of the Temple to describe the Christian Church. The main thesis centres upon a re-examination of texts from the Gospels and Epistles which refer to the Christian community as a temple. The subject is an important one in Jewish–Christian dialogue, and this study provides useful summaries of recent work on the interpretation of the temple in the Old Testament and the Intertestamental Literature. Particular use is made of B. Gärtner's work on the Qumran Scrolls. The work is very competently and carefully done, without attempting any particularly new approach.

R.E.C.

MALINA, B. J.: *The Palestinian Manna Tradition.* The Manna Tradition in the Palestinian Targums and its relationship to the New Testament Writings. (Arbeiten zur Geschichte des späteren Judentums und des Urchristentums, VII.) 1968. Pp. 111. (E. J. Brill, Leiden. Price: Fl. 33)

Fr Malina's thesis contains a careful literary analysis of the O.T tradition relative to the manna in Exod. 16 and of the remaining haggadic and halakhic amplification in Num., Deut., Josh., Pss. and Neh. The biblical research is followed by a study of the relevant sections in the Palestinian Targums with due emphasis on their exegetical innovations. Finally, the manna passages of the N.T. are viewed against the backcloth of the Hebrew Bible seen through its Palestinian Jewish interpretation. On the whole, the work is of real merit though the author might profitably have avoided such generalizations as the claim that *most* Palestinian targumic traditions are pre-mishnaic. An important variant in Neofiti Exod. 16:15 is explained as a scribal error; a different view has been expressed in my contribution to the Matthew Black *Festschrift* (reviewed on p. 8).

G.V.

METZGER, B. M.: *Historical and Literary Studies: Pagan, Jewish and Christian.* (New Testament Tools and Studies, VIII.) 1968. Pp. x, 172, xx plates. (E. J. Brill, Leiden. Price: Fl. 28)

This collection of essays (mostly on N.T. subjects) which have been published previously in various journals, etc., includes a brief note on the inclusion of the 'lost' section of II Esdras in early German editions of the Bible (translated from an Arabic MS.), and a comparison of formulas introducing O.T. quotations in the N.T. and the Mishnah.

M.D.H.

MICHEL, O. and BAUERNFEIND, O.: *Flavius Josephus: De Bello Judaico, Der Jüdische Krieg; Griechisch und Deutsch.* Band II, 2, Buch VI-VII. 1969. Pp. 287. Band III, Ergänzungen und Register, 1969. Pp. XXVIII, 149, one map. (Kösel-Verlag, Munich. Price: DM. 38; DM. 22)

These two volumes complete the edition of the Jewish War. Band I (Books I-III) was published in 1960 and Band II, 1 (Books IV-V) in 1963; neither was noted in the *Book List*. The Greek text, substantially that of Niese with some editorial changes, is printed on the left-hand page with a full critical apparatus at the foot of both pages (fuller than that of Thackeray). The German translation (good and readable where checked) occupies the right-hand page. At the end of each volume of text are fairly full explanatory notes on difficult or important passages. Some of the notes are expanded into 'excursus' form, e.g. no. XII on the use of 'soul' in Josephus, and no. XXIII on the Masada finds and their bearing on Josephus.
English readers will find it most useful for the notes and for the up-to-date information in the Introduction. L.H.B.

The New English Bible: Apocrypha. Library edition. 1970. Pp. xiv, 362. (Oxford and Cambridge. Price: 25s. Also standard edition of whole Bible including Apocrypha: 35s.)

Professor W. D. McHardy writes a short introduction to this new translation of the Apocrypha (for the O.T. see p. 34), to explain the texts used and the general policy of the translators. In particular, it may be noted that the whole text of Esther is printed, so that the additions normally printed alone in the Apocrypha may be read in context. Similarly, the additions to Daniel are clearly indicated as belonging with the book itself. The detailed consideration of the translation cannot be undertaken here. With the production of this

new version and with the increasing emphasis on the need to understand the wider range of writings with which those of the narrower
biblical canon are to be read, it may be hoped that some of the
suspicions surrounding the Apocrypha will be broken down. A new
and readable version will certainly assist in this.   P.R.A.

OESTERLEY, W. O. E., LOEWE, H. and ROSENTHAL, E. I. J.: *Judaism and
Christianity*. Vol. I *The Age of Transition*. Pp. 304; Vol. II *The Contact
of Pharisaism with other cultures*. Pp. 371; Vol. III *Law and Religion*.
Pp. 248. *Prolegomenon* by E. Rivkin. Pp. LXX. 1969. (Ktav Publishing
House, New York. Price: $22.50)

This is a welcome re-issue of the three volumes of Essays relating to
Judaism and Christianity. Vols. 1 and 2 were noticed in the 1938
Book List, p. 12, and vol. 3 in 1939, p. 14. In his Prolegomenon,
Professor Rivkin takes a fresh look at the rise of the Pharisees and
finds that they cannot have come into existence earlier than the
Hasmonean revolt, that they wrote nothing down, but taught in the
form of item-like sayings, and that they had no interest in a messianic
hope. Although they themselves did not uphold the Aaronide
authority, their rise to prominence was due to its disintegration when
the priesthood was Hellenized.   L.H.B.

OESTERREICHER, J.: *Der Baum und die Wurzel*. 1968. Pp. 200. (Verlag
Herder, Freiburg. Price: DM. 20)

Historians, sociologists, theologians and, today, politicians are
variously concerned with the meaning and identity of Israel in both
Jewish and Christian terms. This book, dealing with this issue
primarily from the Christian angle, is of interest to the O.T. scholar
in its reminder that 'the root finds its fulfilment in the crown of the
tree, while the tree itself can only live from its roots'. It was this
apophthegm of Oesterreicher's, no doubt, that led the translator
of his book, *The Israel of God*, to entitle this German version *Der
Baum und die Wurzel*. The text itself is simply a translation of the
earlier version, published in 1963.   W.W.S.

PHILONENKO, M.: *Joseph et Aseneth. Introduction, texte critique, traduction
et notes*. 1968. Pp. 266. (E. J. Brill, Leiden. Price: Fl. 49)

Philonenko's aim has been to present a critical edition of the short
recension of this Jewish pseudepigraphic work together with a fully
annotated French translation. A lengthy introduction outlines the
textual problems, the proselytizing and — allegedly — mystical and
gnostic purport of the novel and its Egyptian background. The date
of composition suggested is the first decade of the 2nd century A.D.
Although the exclusive choice of the short version as the oldest and
most genuine is somewhat arbitrary and the chapter on the 'roman
mystique' debatable, this deserving book will remain a standard work
on the subject for many years to come.   G.V.

PORTEN, B.: *Archives from Elephantine*. 1968. Pp. xxi, 421. (University of California Press. Price: $12.50)

The life of the Jewish colony at Elephantine is here examined from political and economic, religious, and family and communal, points of view. Comparable material from a wide variety of sources is used to illustrate further the Elephantine archives, and the result is an extremely valuable handbook which throws a good deal of light not only on post-exilic Judaism but also on the history of Egypt and more generally of the Persian Empire. A number of disputed questions, especially concerning personal names, are examined in appendices. The texts themselves are not included (save for a further appendix attempting a reconstruction of certain particularly fragmentary passages) but in future this will be a basic accompaniment to the study of the texts in such editions as those of Cowley or Kraeling.

R.J.C.

POULSSEN, N.: *Tobit*. (De Boeken van het Oude Testament, Deel vi/ Boek ii.) 1968. Pp. 56. (J. J. Romen & Zonen, Roermond. Price: Fl. 4.50)

This commentary follows the pattern of the others in the same series; a brief, but well-informed introduction, a translation of the text with footnotes, and finally a list of text changes (a dozen all told). The notes are concise and to the point; they deal with critical and exegetical problems, with folk-lore and literary affinities. L.H.B.

RESE, M.: *Alttestamentliche Motive in der Christologie des Lukas*. (Studien zum Neuen Testament, i.) 1969. Pp. 227. (Gerd Mohn, Gütersloh. Price: DM. 34)

In considering Luke's use of certain O.T. quotations, the author examines their form, and compares the LXX and M.T. He concludes that variations in the Lucan version are generally traceable to Luke's own interests, which have caused him to alter the text, rather than to a particular textual tradition. M.D.H.

RICHARDSON, P.: *Israel in the Apostolic Church*. (S.N.T.S. Monograph series, 10.) 1970. Pp. 257. (Cambridge University Press, London. Price: 80s.)

Richardson's scholarly essay presupposes a wide range of Old and New Testament, to say nothing of patristic, learning to test his thesis that the Christian 'take-over' of the title and prerogatives of Israel took place, not at one fell swoop, but over a considerable period, the first equations of the two not occurring until A.D. 160 in Justin Martyr's *Dialogue with Trypho*. Misunderstanding of this issue, the author emphasizes, has coloured the Church's attitude to Judaism and contributed to antisemitism. W.W.S.

SCHALIT, A.: *Namenwörterbuch zu Flavius Josephus.* (*A complete con-cordance to Flavius Josephus*, ed. K. H. Rengstorf. Suppl. I.) 1968. Pp. 143. (E. J. Brill, Leiden. Price: Fl. 108)

Professor Schalit has produced an indispensable research instrument in compiling the list of all the names of persons and places appearing in the writings of Josephus. Biblical names are accompanied by their Masoretic equivalent and, if different from that used by Josephus, by the form which figures in the LXX. The editor often explains the peculiarities of a name and gives, fairly regularly, bibliographical references. (Strangely none appears under the term 'Essene'.) Several longer notes are placed at the end of the volume, followed by Hebrew and Greek indices of biblical and non-biblical names. G.V.

SCHRECKENBERG, H.: *Bibliographie zu Flavius Josephus.* (Arbeiten zur Literatur und Geschichte des Hellenistischen Judentums, I.) 1968. Pp. 336. (E. J. Brill, Leiden. Price: Fl. 80)

This is a highly useful list of Josephus literature from 1470 to 1968. The titles are arranged chronologically and an appended figure in brackets indicates one of the twenty-five classes to which the publica-tion in question belongs. The editor usually summarizes, in a mini-mum number of words, the general contents of the papers or books. Three indexes (authors, Josephus passages and Greek words) complete the volume. L. H. Feldman's *Scholarship on Philo and Josephus* (1937–62) (Studies in Judaica, Yeshiva University, New York) with its more developed critical comments remains a valuable and necessary supplement to the present work. G.V.

SCHREINER, J.: *Alttestamentlich-jüdische Apokalyptik. Eine Einführung.* (Biblische Handbibliothek, Band VI.) 1969. Pp. 204. (Kösel-Verlag, Mün-chen. Price: DM. 25)

Among the stated aims of the author in this attractively written and produced introduction, which is based upon lectures previously given, are those of making clear the significance of apocalyptic as a forma-tive influence for the understanding of the N.T. and Christian theology, and of stimulating the reader to further study. Details of works generally accepted as apocalyptic, but excluding the Qumran material and the lesser-known writings, are first provided, and are succeeded by chapters on the form and language and on the charac-teristic ideas. The relation to prophecy, wisdom and extra-Israelite influence, spiritual movements in the later O.T. period, and the ideology of the Qumran community are then discussed. There is a concluding note on the motive and objective of apocalyptic teaching, and it is emphasized that the message of apocalyptic is above all a message of hope. E.T.R.

PHILOLOGY AND GRAMMAR

BEYER, K.: *Althebräische Grammatik.* 1969. Pp. 68. (Vandenhoeck & Ruprecht, Göttingen. Price: DM. 9.80)

This is an exceedingly curious booklet. Its express aims are twofold: (1) to free the Hebrew language from the stranglehold exerted by the

Masoretic tradition and to reveal its features in their pristine pre-exilic form; and (2) to demonstrate that the 'original' Hebrew language was much 'clearer' and 'simpler' than the artificial Masoretic structure would suggest and 'hence more suitable for teaching purposes' (p. 7). Most scholars will sympathize with the theoretical exercise adumbrated under (1), but the requirements of scholarship must not be confused with the practical needs of teaching Hebrew. And here most university teachers will still prefer the Masoretic tradition (with all its profound shortcomings) to Dr Beyer's reconstructed version.

It is very odd that no reference whatsoever is made to Z. S. Harris' important study on the linguistic structure of Hebrew in 600 B.C. (*J.A.O.S.*, 1941) which had already accomplished (more than a quarter of a century ago) what Beyer sets out to do. The author asserts (p. 14) that Hebrew had ceased to be a living language before 500 B.C. [*sic*] and that since then the Aramaic vowel system had been imposed upon the consonantal skeleton. His chronology, however, is surely wildly out of focus, and he appears to mistake the natural development of the language in *pre-Christian* times for the death throes induced by an alien linguistic system. Dr Beyer does not seem to allow for the vital distinction between changes due to languages in *living* contact (the situation of Hebrew and Aramaic in post-exilic times) and the graphic and pseudo-phonetic labours of the Masoretes operating upon the consonantal skeleton of a very dead body (carried out close on a millennium after the effective demise). His methodology represents a curious amalgam of old-fashioned ideas with some modern notions and terminological devices. At the same time his collection of material is useful and there are enough hard facts (from p. 34 onwards) in this monograph to make its study worthwhile. Incidentally, what does *unterwandert* (p. 14) mean?   E.U.

BLOMMERDE, A. C. M.: *Northwest Semitic Grammar and Job*. 1969. Pp. xxviii, 151. (Rome, Pontifical Biblical Institute. Price: Lire 2,700; $4.50)

The first part of this rather oddly constructed monograph offers bibliographical references to a number of grammatical phenomena relevant to Hebrew, Ugaritic, and Phoenician, while the second part discusses a few dozen Job passages. There is not a single reference to Torczyner/Tur-Sinai's numerous works on Job, and the bibliography is largely centred on Father Dahood's writings. This book belongs, therefore, to the same literary *genre* as Father Martinez's work (noticed in *B.L.*, 1968, p. 69): its precise purpose is not entirely clear — unless it was composed *ad majorem Dahoodi gloriam* (see Preface). Professor Dahood has obviously many dutiful disciples, but he requires no such testimony to his international standing which is firmly established. He himself could have written this book so much better, though there was, in truth, no need for it to be written at all.

E.U.

DEGEN, R.: *Altaramäische Grammatik der Inschriften des 10.–8. Jh. v. Chr.* (Abhandlungen für die Kunde des Morgenlandes, xxxviii, 3.) 1969. Pp. xviii, 144. (Franz Steiner, Wiesbaden. Price: DM. 34)

This is a valuable book. It is based on a doctoral dissertation and offers a full description of the Old Aramaic language of the inscriptions dating from the 10th to the 8th century B.C. The author explains (p. 2) that the linguistic peculiarities, particularly in the area of the syntax, are sufficiently marked to differentiate this language from later manifestations of Aramaic. Degen introduces the reader to some 20 pages of Old Aramaic texts, among them prominently the Sfire inscriptions, and then proceeds to take us through the graphic system, phonology, morphology, and a detailed description of the syntax. There are also a bibliography and an index.

The author discharges his task with considerable competence, and his book will become an essential part of the equipment of every Semitist and O.T. scholar. The need for a strictly synchronic treatment (p. IX) in a language attested in epigraphic documents only is not, perhaps, overwhelming. A comparative study would have had certain obvious advantages, but it would not be fair to blame the author for adhering to this self-imposed limitation. More doubtful is the peculiar mode of his presentation of the phoneme inventory which follows, without explanation or justification, the teachings of his master, Professor O. Rössler. It is a matter of some satisfaction, especially these days, to have dutiful students, but it remains important to adduce adequate grounds for innovations. The tone of some of the critical footnotes (and in particular the last one in the book) is unnecessarily testy as well as somewhat indecorous in so recent a doctoral candidate.

E.U.

GREENBERG, M.: *Introduction to Hebrew*. 1969 (1965). Pp. viii, 226. (Prentice-Hall, Inc., Englewood Cliffs, New Jersey. Price: 74s.)

This rather brief, but clear, introduction to Hebrew, constructed to lead up to readings from the Joseph story, which was missed by the *Book List* when it first appeared in 1965, has now been reprinted, remedying the unfortunate omission in the first edition of a section on the geminate verbs.

J.V.M.S.

HARRIS, H.: *English Words of Hebrew Origin*. 1969. Pp. 12. (Society for Jewish Study, London)

This paper of general interest, the contents of which are accurately described by the title, was delivered as a lecture to the Society for Jewish Study on 15 April 1969.

J.A.E.

MACUCH, R.: *Grammatik des samaritanischen Hebräisch* (Studia Samaritana, herausgegeben von R. Macuch, Band 1). 1969. Pp. xl, 572. (Walter de Gruyter, Berlin. Price: DM. 220)

This large scale, comprehensive grammar of Samaritan Hebrew, which consists of four main sections — on orthography, phonology, morphology, and syntax — is a work of outstanding importance, which will be indispensable to all students of Hebrew, Massoretic as well as Samaritan, and of the textual criticism of the Pentateuch. The material on which it is based, ranging from the Samaritan Pentateuch to Samaritan literature of the present day, is throughout assembled and ordered in a truly impressive way. The pronunciation of Samaritan Hebrew here adopted is that which the author himself heard from Samaritan authorities during a visit to Nablus in 1965, and his first-hand acquaintance with their pronunciation has enabled him fruitfully to reassess the findings of his predecessors in this elusive field of study. A dictionary of Samaritan Hebrew, which will include all Hebrew words that occur in the volume, is in preparation, and will make good the lack of a philological index in the present work. With this inaugural volume the new series has got off to a fine start.

D.W.T.

MAUCHLINE, J.: *Key to the Exercises in the Twenty-fifth and Twenty-sixth editions of the late Professor A. B. Davidson's Introductory Hebrew Grammar with explanatory notes.* 3rd ed. 1967. Pp. vi, 192. (T. & T. Clark, Edinburgh. Price: 35s.)

Professor Mauchline, who was responsible for the 25th edition of Davidson's grammar (*B.L.*, 1963, p. 71; *Decade*, p. 465), has written this key to it and to the 26th edition. It follows the pattern of the earlier editions of the key, and consists of answers to exercises, detailed notes (which contain much helpful information, even though a few debatable opinions are expressed), and indexes of biblical references, subjects, and Hebrew words and forms. The dangers of cribs are well known, but this work will, if rightly used, be most helpful to the reader, and anyone who works carefully through the notes will learn much about Hebrew usage in the Old Testament.

J.A.E.

MOSCATI, S. (ed.): *An Introduction to the Comparative Grammar of the Semitic Languages.* (Porta Linguarum Orientalium, N.S. VI.) Reprint, 1969 (1964). Pp. 185. (Otto Harrassowitz, Wiesbaden. Price: DM. 28)

This study, a masterly compression of information regarding the languages, their grouping, phonology and morphology (noted in *B.L.*, 1965, p. 65; *Decade*, p. 617) is now reprinted. The work is primarily that of A. Spitaler, E. Ullendorff, and W. von Soden, under the editorship of Moscati.

P.R.A.

PENNACCHIETI, F. A.: *Studi sui Pronomi Determinativi Semitici.* (Pubblicazioni del Seminario di Semitistica. Ricerche 4.) 1968. Pp. 164. (Istituto Orientali di Napoli. Price: 54s. approx.)

After some introductory remarks on the East-Semitic pronouns, the author devotes the bulk of his book to the various uses of *d* and *š* as independent and relative pronouns and as indicators of the genitival relationship and of *m(n)* and *y(n)* as interrogative and indefinite pronouns in the West-Semitic languages; and he then adds some concluding remarks on their classification as 'autonomous' and 'non-autonomous' (these last divided into three sub-classes) pronouns.

Every usage is clearly explained and amply illustrated with examples drawn from all the West-Semitic languages, both ancient and modern, and transliterated into Roman characters; and the source from which each is derived is always given. Thus the student of the Old Testament will find a number of obscure points in the use of the Hebrew pronouns made clear by the examples from the sister languages set over against them and several idioms disapproved of or even 'emended' out of existence by modern writers on Hebrew grammar thereby justified; indeed, both beginner and advanced student will learn much from this well arranged and illuminating treatise on the Semitic pronouns.

G.R.D.

WILLIAMS, R. J.: *Hebrew Syntax: An Outline.* 1967. Pp. 122. (University of Toronto Press. Price: $3.50)

Williams' approach is normative rather than descriptive; his motivation is didactic and he wishes to impart what in Britain has traditionally and best been imparted by the discipline of prose composition. First, parts of speech and, secondly, syntactical clauses are listed according to their English labels; their mode of expression in Hebrew is noted together with, usually, one example from the M.T. The examples remain untranslated, for the meaning is regarded as being clear from the syntactical category in which they are placed. The disadvantages of this method include that of over-elaborate classification and that what purports to be syntax approximates to what is properly lexicography. Many grammatical terms will be unfamiliar (e.g. *telic*, *fientive*, etc.) and confusing (e.g. *pl. of respect* for *pl. of majesty*) to English readers. The familiar terms Absolute and Construct are replaced by 'the more accurate linguistic expressions *Free* and *Bound* (*Forms*)', although infinitives retain their old labels. (In any case, *Free* can hardly be 'more accurate' when it is a mere translation of the Latin term.) Advances in our knowledge are adequately reflected in some parts of the work (e.g. Superlatives), inadequately in others (e.g. *waw* consecutive).

If traditional British methods of teaching Hebrew are retained, this book will be of little use; if the methods of modern linguistics are adopted then this work may be regarded more as a patching up of old wine skins than as a re-bottling of Hebrew.

A.A.M.

ADDITIONAL NOTES ON SCHOOL TEXTBOOKS, ETC.

*BLENKINSOPP, J.: *Genesis 1–11. A Scripture Discussion Outline.* 1968. Pp. 52. (Sheed and Ward, London. Price: 3s. 6d.)

*BLENKINSOPP, J.: *Deuteronomy. The Book of the Covenant. A Scripture Discussion Outline.* 1968. Pp. 54. (Sheed and Ward, London. Price: 3s. 6d.)

*CHALLENOR, J.: *Jeremiah. A Scripture Discussion Outline.* 1968. Pp. 52. (Sheed and Ward, London. Price: 3s. 6d.)

These booklets are included in a new series of 'Scripture Discussion Outlines' under the general editorship of Laurence Bright, O.P.

A general introduction is followed by a more detailed treatment of the biblical text, section by section, with suggestions for further reading and questions for discussion. The first two outlines have set a very high standard. The aim is to make the student think for himself. These outlines should appeal to intelligent Sixth-formers, undergraduates and educated laymen of all denominations. L.A.P.

*BRUEGGEMANN, W.: *Confronting the Bible.* 1968. Pp. 75. (Burns & Oates, London. Price: 10s.)

This 'Resource and Discussion Book for Youth' is one in the American series 'Christian Commitment'. It is designed for eight sessions of confrontation — a 'workshop course', using such tools as standard introductions, commentaries, Bible word books, concordances and modern translations. For many young people the author should make the Bible come alive. G.F.

*CALLISTER, F.: *One World Not Two. An examination of Bible Wonders in the Old and New Testaments.* 1968. Pp. 240. (Religious Education Press, Ltd., Oxford. Price: 17s. 6d.)

This book is intended to help teachers of Religious Knowledge, especially non-specialists, who are perplexed by the miracles and myths of the Bible. A third of the book is devoted to prolegomena, the history of criticism, etc., and rather less than a third to the legends and myths and miracles of the O.T. The treatment is rather discursive but the book contains a wealth of back-ground material for the non-specialist. L.A.P.

*GAUBERT, H.: *The Bible in History.* Volume 1. *Abraham, Loved by God.* 1968. Pp. 195. (Darton, Longman and Todd, London. Price: 21s. 0d.)

*GAUBERT, H.: *The Bible in History.* Volume 2. *Isaac and Jacob, God's Chosen Ones.* 1969. Pp. 204. (Darton, Longman and Todd, London. Price: 21s. 0d.)

*GAUBERT, H.: *The Bible in History.* Volume 3. *Moses and Joshua, Founders of the Nation.* 1969. Pp. 205. (Darton, Longman and Todd, London. Price: 21s. 0d.)

These volumes, under the general editorship of Joseph Rhymer, are a revised edition of the French series *La Bible dans l'Histoire.* The aim of the series being to recreate the historical background of the biblical narrative, it is surprising that two of the seven volumes allotted to the O.T. should be devoted to the Patriarchal Age. Much valuable background material is introduced and the text is generously illustrated by maps, diagrams, photographs and line drawings. The standpoint throughout is deeply conservative. L.A.P.

SMYTHE, B. H.: *Search Book One*. 1966. Pp. 63 (including four page illustrations). (Darton, Longman and Todd, London. Price: 6s. 6d.)

SMYTHE, B. H.: *Search Book Two*. 1966. Pp. 62 (including five page illustrations). (Darton, Longman and Todd, London. Price: 6s. 6d.)

SMYTHE, B. H.: *Search Books One and Two with Teacher's Introduction*. 1966. Pp. xi, 63, 62 (including 9 page illustrations). (Darton, Longman and Todd, London. Price: 16s. 6d.)

These volumes, based on a successful pioneer experiment in using programmed learning in Religious Education, are intended for use by pupils of 9 to 12 years. They will be of interest to both specialist and non-specialist teachers in Primary and Preparatory Schools.

L.A.P.

Book List 1971

GENERAL

ALT, A.: *Grundfragen der Geschichte des Volkes Israel. Eine Auswahl aus den 'Kleinen Schriften'* (Studienausgabe). Ed. by S. Herrmann. 1970. Pp. xvi, 478. (C. H. Beck, Munich. Price: DM. 17.80)

The three volumes of Alt's *Kleine Schriften* are well known (see *B.L.*, 1954, p. 22; 1960, p. 11; *Eleven Years*, p. 559; *Decade*, p. 191); the translation of five of the most important studies into English appeared in 1966 (*B.L.*, 1967, p. 3). The present volume includes those five, but has in addition the further essay on the settlement in Palestine (1939) and one on Joshua (1936). It includes the essays on the rise to prominence of Jerusalem (1925), on David's empire (1950), on the influence of the monarchy on the social development in the two kingdoms (1955), and on the part played by Samaria in the establishment of Judaism (1934). It also includes the study on the place of origin of Deuteronomy (1953). The opening and closing studies are of a more general kind, the one on historical rhythms in the ancient history of Syria and Palestine (1944), and the other on the interpretation of world history in the Old Testament (1959). This last was not included in the *Kleine Schriften*. It is very convenient to have this group of essays in such a form, and much to be desired that the English edition should be complemented by a second volume containing those which it lacks.

P.R.A.

BAUER, J. B. (ed.): *Encyclopedia of Biblical Theology*, 3 Vols. 1970. Pp. xxxiii, 1141 numbered consecutively, 1–382, 385–792, 797–1141. (Sheed and Ward, London. Price: £15·00)

This is a translation, by J. Blenkinsopp, D. J. Bourke, N. D. Smith and W. P. van Stigt, of the 3rd edition of Bauer's *Bibeltheologisches Wörterbuch* (first ed., 1959, noticed in *B.L.*, 1960, p. 3; 2nd ed., 1962, *B.L.*, 1963, p. 3; *Decade*, pp. 183, 397). The one-volume original has become an expensive trio printed in larger type (two columns) on thick paper. Many articles are excellent, e.g. Covenant, Eucharist, Flesh, Kingdom of God, Law, Light, Love, Mediation, Mystery, Spirit, Thanksgiving. Others are disappointing in content and confused in relationship, e.g. those concerned with O.T. cult institutions. Some titles are confusingly rendered, e.g. 'Heathen' for *Heiden* (Gentiles); 'Confession' and 'Preaching' conceal Christological essays which valuably supplement A. Vögtle's fine article 'Jesus Christ'. But there is still no proper treatment of 'Son of Man', and too little on Jesus' resurrection. The Jewish background to the N.T. is somewhat neglected, except for Qumran which is perhaps overplayed. Some articles give disproportionate space to modern Roman Catholic doctrinal anxieties largely alien to biblical theology. The claim to render a unique service in English rests not only on the work's dimensions compared with Richardson or Léon-Dufour, but also on the bibliographies, specially enlarged for the English edition, both in a new supplement (Vol. III, pp. 1015–25) and following the several articles. Granted that the service *is* unique in a work of this scope in English, it must be said that deficiencies remain, serious both in number and in importance, as regards both original English-language works and translations of foreign works.

R.M.

BOTTERWECK, G. J. and RINGGREN, H. (ed.): *Theologisches Wörterbuch zum Alten Testament*. Band I. Lieferung 1 (Spalte 1–128). 1970. (W. Kolhammer, Stuttgart. Price: DM. 16)

The first fascicle of *TWAT* designed to stand alongside the now nearly complete *TWNT* (and its rapidly advancing English translation *TDNT*), reveals at once something of the variety of approaches and the problems of method to which the editors refer in a note printed on the back cover. The dictionary is to be completed in 4 volumes, each to consist of 12 fascicles. If the plan is adhered to, this promises a controlled length and not the ever-expanding one from which *TWNT* has suffered. It involves a wide range of scholars and the editors are assisted by an editorial board consisting of G. W. Anderson, H. Cazelles, D. N. Freedman, S. Talmon, and G. Wallis. The international and interconfessional range will inevitably mean a variety of presentations. The method of arrangement, with articles under the heading of Hebrew words, inevitably presents problems. In this first fascicle, which covers '*āb* (erroneously as '*āw* in the list of contents) to '*āhab* (with the first few lines of '*ōhel*), difference of method may be seen in the very largely linguistic article on '*ādōn* by O. Eissfeldt (cf. also p. 39) by comparison with the much more strongly — and surely rightly — theological articles on '*āb* (H. Ringgren), '*abrāhām* (R. E. Clements), '*ādām* (F. Maass). The disadvantage of working from particular Hebrew words is apparent in the article on '*ebyōn* (G. J. Botterweck), since although this article includes references to other words with equivalent or related meaning, there is no clear place for the discussion of the semantic field to which the word belongs.

There is no doubt that both by their contents and by their bibliographical references, the articles in *TWAT* will prove of very great value. Many will feel regret at the inevitable limitations imposed upon the work; LXX is included — though curiously this is said to be because of the interconfessional nature of the enterprise — Qumran is briefly handled, but not the pseudepigrapha nor the developments into the rabbinic Judaism. (The omission of the N.T. is understandable).

P.R.A.

BOWMAN, J. (ed.): *Abr-Nahrain*, Vol. VIII (1968–9). An Annual published by the Department of Middle Eastern Studies, University of Melbourne. 1969. Pp. ix, 94. Pls. IV. (E. J. Brill, Leiden. Price: Fl. 33)

Four studies are comprised. D. D. Leslie follows up three earlier contributions on the K'aifeng Jews with an investigation of 'The Judaeo-Persian Colophons to the Pentateuch' which date from the 17th century and are currently housed in Cincinnati. A. K. Kazi and J. G. Flynn publish the first part of their annotated translation of al-Shahrastani, *Kitab al-Milal w'al-Nihal*, dealing with the Mu'tazilites, and thereby do a service to students of Islam. In 'Myth and Development' D. Broadribb, applying the methods of depth psychology, suggests that myths are dreams of society, to be classified in eight stages of development from pre- to post-historic. R. C. Dalk analyses the 'Arabic Verb Forms XI-XV' in an interesting though not very deep-going study. The uncertainty found in both form and meaning suggests to me that they are largely artificial creations — as the author notes, they rarely occur in the living language.

D.R.Ap-T.

Vol. IX of *Abr-Nahrain* (1969–70. 1970. Pp. viii, 109. Price: Fl. 33) has also appeared. A copy has not been received, but a list of contents indicates that none of the articles is concerned with O.T. study.

BOWMAN, J. (ed.): *Abr-Nahrain* x (1970–1). 1970. Pp. 133. (E. J. Brill, Leiden. Price: Fl. 33)

Three of the ten articles in this annual have some relevance to Old Testament studies. A. Vööbus reports on recently discovered mss. of the 9th-century Syrian Old Testament commentator Mose bar Kepha; A. Murtonen, 'On the Study of Language and Literature', raises some interesting questions concerning objective criteria in Old Testament study; and H. Klarberg writes on 'Stress Patterns in Spoken Israeli Hebrew'. R.J.C.

*BRUCE, F. F.: *The English Bible. A History of Translations from the earliest English Versions to the New English Bible.* New and revised edition. 1970. Pp. xiv, 264, Pls. 8. (Lutterworth Press, London. Price: £1·75)

The first edition of this comprehensive survey was reviewed in *B.L.*, 1961, p. 5: *Decade*, p. 243. It was published soon after the appearance of the *N.E.B.* N.T. The new edition, appropriately, follows hard on the heels of the *N.E.B.* O.T. and Apocrypha. The principal changes and additions are the discussion of the completed *N.E.B.* and also of other recent English versions, such as the *Jerusalem Bible* and Professor William Barclay's translation of the N.T. Various minor changes have been made in the text, and references to recent literature added. Encyclopaedic in its range, yet eminently readable, it is probably the best introduction of its size to the history of the Bible in English. G.W.A.

COPPENS, J.: *In Memorium Mgr. Gonzague Ryckmans; In Memorium Professor H. H. Rowley.* Offprints from *Jaarboek 1969 van de koninklijke Vlaamse Akademie voor Wetenschappen, Letteren en Schone Kunsten van Belgie.* (Pp. 323–64; 403–7. Each with a photograph.) (In Flemish)

COPPENS, J.: *Monseigneur Gonzague Ryckmans.* Offprint from *Le Muséon* lxxxiii (Louvain, Imprimerie Orientaliste. 1970). (Pp. 5–40, with a photograph.) (In French)

This *Book List* does not normally include reference to articles in periodicals, but the exception may be made in this instance, since the notices of Mgr. Ryckmans contain not only an appreciation of the man and his work (in *Le Muséon* contributed in part by J. Pirenne), but bibliographical lists amounting to more than 400 items (the list in *Le Muséon* appears to be somewhat shorter). The note on Professor Rowley contains only brief bibliographical information. P.R.A.

*DAVIES, G. HENTON and A.B.: *Who's Who in the Bible. Including the Apocrypha.* 1970. Pp. viii, 227. (Teach Yourself Books. English Universities Press, London. Price: 75p)

This is a list in alphabetical order of all the personal names mentioned in the Bible. The biblical reference is given in each case, together with cross-references to other biblical personalities. The most important characters also have a paragraph which sets out the highlights of their careers. J.R.

DURHAM, J. I. and PORTER, J. R. (ed.): *Proclamation and Presence. Old Testament Essays in honour of Gwynne Henton Davies.* 1970. Pp. xx, 316. (S.C.M. Press, London. Price: £4·00)

This collection of essays contains a tribute to Principal Henton Davies and a bibliography, together with fourteen essays. The first by N. W. Porteous, on 'The Limits of Old Testament Interpretation', stands alone under a heading 'Old Testament Hermeneutics'. The remainder are grouped under three headings. First 'The Hexateuch' — G. Widengren on Moses, R. de Vaux on the Tetragrammaton — both summarising and useful critical surveys; J. Weingreen, somewhat fancifully on 'proto-rabbinic' method in the Deuteronomic legislator; O. Eissfeldt on 'Gilgal or Shechem?', a valuable critique of passages which appear to imply actions which take place at both, raising questions about the nature of topographical identification in theological discussion; J. R. Porter on 'The Succession of Joshua', an important consideration of the nature of the relationship now presented between Joshua and Moses. Second, 'The Former Prophets and the Latter Prophets', with D. R. Ap-Thomas on terms for horses; E. Würthwein on the different levels of material in 1 Kings 19: 9–18; W. Eichrodt in a useful contribution to current discussions of the 'covenant' idea, with reference to Isaiah; J. Bright in a critique of Reventlow's approach to the Jeremiah confessions (a comparison may be made with the study by J. M. Berridge, see p. 36); J. Muilenburg on 'Baruch the Scribe'; H. Cazelles on the theme of the return of David, linked to a group of passages including Gen. 49:10. Third, 'The Psalms', with A. R. Johnson considering Ps. 23 and the concept of the 'household of faith' and J. I. Durham on '*shālôm* and the Presence of God'. If the title of the volume appears somewhat arbitrary, there are here some useful contributions to particular problems of interpretation.

P.R.A.

ENGNELL, I.: *Critical Essays on the Old Testament.* Translated and edited by John T. Willis. 1970. Pp. xiv, 303 (S.P.C.K., London. Price: £2·50)

Hitherto, only a comparatively small amount of Engnell's work has been available in English and this has meant that, in many quarters, his contribution to the study of the O.T. has not been fully understood or appreciated. For not the least important of Engnell's achievements was the working out of a consistent critical approach to the O.T. material such as perhaps no scholar since Wellhausen, in a very different way, has attempted. This valuable book should do much to correct the situation. It contains thirteen essays translated from the *Svensk Bibliskt Upplagswerk*, in which Engnell expressed many of his most mature views, since the second edition appeared only a year before his death. Thus English readers will now be able to assess what he really said about such topics as the Pentateuch, the Traditio-Historical Method, New Year Festivals and many others. The translation is readable and generally accurate, but the editorial notes could have been more useful. The editor apologises for the absence of complete bibliographical information in some cases where only a little further research would easily have supplied it. (The volume was published by Abingdon Press, Nashville in 1969 under the title *A Rigid Scrutiny*).

J.R.P.

FRANK, H. T. and REED, W. L. (ed.): *Translating and Understanding the Old Testament. Essays in Honor of H. G. May.* 1970. Pp. 351. 5 plates and 4 figures. (Abingdon Press, Nashville. Price: $11.00)

No more appropriate title could have been given to this volume, having regard both to the work in so many fields of biblical study of the highly regarded scholar whom it serves to honour and also to the content in general of the essays in it.

The editors pay tribute to the many contributions of H. G. May in the areas of theology, archaeology, cartography, and Bible translation; and in the essays which follow the 'Curriculum Vitae', 'Bibliography of Publications', and 'List of Abbreviations', these fields of study are mostly represented.

L. A. Weigle presents an account of 'The Standard Bible Committee' of which H. G. May is now chairman after twenty-five years of outstanding service, whilst on the subject of O.T. translation W. F. Stinespring considers 'The Participle of the Future and Other Matters'. The translation, interpretation, and unity of Jer. 43:1–7 are dealt with by P. A. H. de Boer, 'The Terminology of Adversity in Jeremiah' by J. Muilenburg, and 'The Literary Category of the Book of Jonah' by M. Burrows, which he regards as a satire. In 'Form and Content: A Hermeneutical Application', R. L. Hicks is concerned with the unity of the Scriptures through Christ.

Contributing to the understanding of the O.T. from archaeological and historical standpoints are W. F. Albright on 'Midianite Donkey Caravans', N. Glueck on 'Incense Altars' (illustrated), R. de Vaux, in a very full essay, on 'The Settlement of the Israelites in Southern Palestine and the Origins of the Tribe of Judah', and F. V. Winnett on 'The Arabian Genealogies in the Book of Genesis'.

More within the scope of theology is G. W. Anderson's discussion of the nature of Israel's self-understanding as the people of Yahweh in an essay entitled 'Israel: Amphictyony: 'AM; ḴĀHĀL; 'ĒḌĀH', to which J. P. Hyatt's contribution, 'Were There an Ancient Historical Credo in Israel and an Independent Sinai Tradition?' is not unrelated. Also in varying degree within this field are essays by D. Baly on 'The Geography of Monotheism', W. Harrelson on 'The Significance of Cosmology in the Ancient Near East', H. M. Orlinsky on 'National-Universalism and Internationalism in Ancient Israel', and G. E. Wright on 'Historical Knowledge and Revelation'.

Not only is this *Festschrift* eminently worthy of the one to whom it is offered but also it goes without saying that there is much here of the highest quality to interest and to stimulate the specialist as also the general practitioner in O.T. studies. A general index adds to its usefulness.   E.T.R.

FRIEDRICH, G. (ed.): *Theologisches Wörterbuch zum Neuen Testament* (Begun by G. Kittel). Band IX. Lieferungen 2, 3 and 4. 1970. Each pp. 64. (Kohlhammer, Stuttgart. Subscr. Price: each Lieferung DM. 8)

Lieferung 2 continues *pherō* and its cognates which was begun in Lieferung 1. See especially *prospherō* and *sympherō*. Interesting also are *phoros* and *phortion* (K. Weiss) and (*pro*)*phthanō* (G. Fitzer). More important are *phtheirō* and its cognates (G. Harder) and *phileō* and its cognates (G. Stählin) which extends into Lieferung 3. Especially noteworthy is the study of friendship under *philos* and *philia*. The article on *philosophia* is relevant for Rabbinic Judaism (O. Michel). Lieferung 4 has articles on *phobeō* and *phobos* (G. Wanke/H. Balz), *phrēn* and its cognates (G. Bertram), *phylassō* and *phylaké* (G. Bertram), *phylé* (C. Maurer) and *physis* (H. Köster).   N.W.P.

GEHMAN, H. S. (ed.): *The New Westminster Dictionary of the Bible.* Illustrations ed. by R. B. Wright. 1970. Pp. xi, 1027. 16 maps in colour with gazetteer, taken from Westminster Historical Maps. (Westminster Press, Philadelphia. Collins, London. Price: $10.95; £4·50)

The previous edition of this dictionary, described simply as *The Westminster Dictionary of the Bible* was edited by Gehman in 1944, as the 5th edition of the older work of J. D. Davis (see *B.L.*, 1946, p. 3; *Eleven Years*, p. 3). It was restricted then to less than 700 pages, and the increase in the present edition indicates something of the increase both in the topics which need to be covered and the available range of information. Each proper name is provided with a clear guide to pronunciation. No bibliographies are supplied to the articles, though a few references to discussions of problems are included within them. In general, the work retains its earlier conservative character, with a somewhat uneasy balance between articles which simply relate biblical material as if narratives could be woven together into a coherent story and others which indicate, often rather sketchily, that there are problems and possible alternatives to the conservative view which is most often accepted. An exception is the recognition of a second century date for the book of Daniel, though this stands next to the narrating of the story of Daniel as if it were straight history. Substantial use of archaeological information is not always satisfactorily integrated. Thus the article on Hazor weaves archival information, biblical and non-biblical, together with the statement that the last of four Canaanite temples was destroyed by the Israelites in the second half of the thirteenth century B.C., ignoring the alternative interpretations.

The text is accompanied by photographs, many of them new, but some too small for the detail to be readily discernible, and by some charts and maps in black and white in addition to the colour maps at the end. That such a volume has been produced very largely by the efforts of a single scholar is a cause for admiration; but its wealth of useful information needs to be handled with discretion.   P.R.A.

HARAN, M.: *Biblical Research in Hebrew. A Discussion of its character and trends.* 1970. Pp. 31. (Magnes Press, Jerusalem (distributed by Oxford University Press, London). Price: 20p)

This is the English translation of Professor Haran's inaugural lecture in the Yehezkel Kaufmann Chair of Bible Studies in 1968. It traces the development of biblical scholarship, especially during the last century, as this has appeared in writings in Hebrew, and offers a useful survey of the work of scholars many of whose names have become internationally known. In the final pages, there is a brief discussion of the character of this biblical scholarship in more general terms. An index of writers mentioned is a helpful addendum.   P.R.A.

Internationale Zeitschriftenschau für Bibelwissenschaft und Grenzgebiete.
Vol. 14. (1967–8). 1968. Pp. xiv, 334; Vol. 15. (1968–9). 1969. Pp. xvi,
349. (Patmos-Verlag, Düsseldorf. Price: DM. 68 each)

This well-known bibliographical aid (see *B.L.*, 1961, p. 9; *Decade*,
p. 247; *B.L.*, 1968, p. 6) continues to appear with regularity and to
provide an essential service not only by the listing of periodical
articles, contributions to composite volumes, and also some publications in series, but by giving for a majority of the items a short
summary of content. The clear classification follows the previous
pattern, and this enables a rapid use of the volumes for discovering
items on particular areas of study.   P.R.A.

JOEL, I.: *Index of Articles on Jewish Studies I: 5726 — 1966* (1969).
Pp. xvi, 136. II: 5727 — 1967 (1970). Pp. xviii, 186. (Issued by the
Editorial Board of 'Kirjath Sepher' Bibliographical Quarterly of the
Jewish National and University Library) (The Magnes Press, The
Hebrew University, Jerusalem. Price: $4.00)

This low-priced, year-by-year bibliography is going to prove extremely valuable to students of all branches of Jewish Studies. Over
2,000 articles are grouped in twelve sections. The longest is III. Old
Testament, in twelve subsections (Text and Massorah, Single Books
and Verses, O.T. Religion (in 10 subsections), O.T. and the New
Testament, and the like) and other sections likely to be of interest to
users of this *List* are Apocrypha, Dead Sea Scrolls, Mishnah/
Talmud, etc., Liturgy, Language, and Jewish History. The Foreword,
Table of Contents of course about 80% of the entries are in
English or another European language. There are an alphabetical list
of the periodicals and collections used, subject indices in Hebrew and
English, and two indices of authors, one for Hebrew articles and one
for non-Hebrew articles. At $4.00 ($1.50 for members of the World
Union of Jewish Studies) this is very good value for money.

                                                                J.F.A.S.

KAPELRUD, A. S. and JERVELL, J. (ed.): *Studia Theologica*. Scandinavian
Journal of Theology. Vol. 24, nos. 1 and 2. 1970. Pp. 1–92, 93–182.
(Universitetsforlaget, Oslo. Subscription price: N.Kr. 60.00 per volume)

Only one of the eight articles in this volume is directly concerned with
the O.T. M. Saebø ('Die hebräischen Nomina 'ed und 'ēd — zwei
sumerisch-akkadische Fremdwörter?', pp. 130–41) argues that *'ed*
(Gen. 2:6; Job 36:27) and *'ēd* ('distress, calamity') are both Sumero-
Akkadian loan words, the former corresponding to ÍD/*id*, the latter
to A.DÉ.A/*edû*.   M.A.K.

KREUTZBERGER, M. (ed.): *Leo Baeck Institute New York Bibliothek und
Archiv, Katalog Band I*. (Schriftenreihe wissenschaftlicher Abhandlungen
des Leo Baeck Instituts.) Herausgegeben von Max Kreutzberger unter
Mitarbeit von Irmgard Foerg. 1970. Pp. xli, 623. Pls. XXIII. (J. C. B. Mohr
(Paul Siebeck), Tübingen. Price: DM. 135, DM. 143)

The Leo Baeck Institute in New York, founded in 1955 and named
after the German Chief Rabbi before World War II, has perhaps the
richest collection of Jewish historical publications in the German

language. It has now published the first volume of the catalogue of its library which contains both printed and manuscript material. The first and largest part of the Catalogue brings the historical publications on Jewish communities in pre-Nazi Germany, arranged alphabetically according to districts and townships. The second lists journals, annuals and other periodicals. The last part records the personal and family memoirs most of which are in manuscript. These memorials naturally date mainly from the time of the Nazi persecution; the collection is probably quite unique and consists of 450 items. In each case the content is briefly indicated. An index of 137 pages concludes the volume and is a valuable guide through the Catalogue. The volume is the 22nd in the series of monographs published by the Leo Baeck Institute. H.K.

LEACH, E.: *Genesis as Myth, and other essays*. (Cape Editions, 39). 1969. Pp. 124. (J. Cape, London. Price: hardback £1·05, paperback 40p)

This is a collection of three previously published essays, 'Genesis as Myth', 'The Legitimacy of Solomon' and 'Virgin Birth', which aim at showing that structuralism is as relevant for the interpretation of biblical material as it is for the analysis of present-day primitive societies. This point of parity is explicitly made in the third essay where the author criticizes anthropologists for studiously avoiding a discussion of Jewish and Christian sources. Leach is here drawing out the full implications of one of the major principles of structuralism, that the unconscious patterns of human thought are universal in scope. Distinctions between sophisticated and primitive cultures, although valid in other contexts of study, are here irrelevant. Structuralism is the obverse side of Jungian depth psychology, an explanation of unconscious reasoning in terms of the overt structures of myths, rituals and societies. A much wider application of the structuralist methodology has been made, to linguistics, literary criticism, political and economic history, mathematics, but not always with the same degree of success as in the elucidation of myth and ritual. The narrative of Solomon's succession is interpreted as a mediating link between the Hebraic ideal of endogamy and the historical situation of intermarriage with foreign neighbours. Similarly doctrines of virgin birth blur the disjunction between God and man and point to continuity between the two worlds. Leach does not claim to have exhausted the biblical meaning, only that he has uncovered one of its dimensions. The new and exciting methodology of structuralism, established though not invented by C. Lévi-Strauss, fairly spits and sparkles like a fire-cracker in this splendid volume, which is to be heartily recommended to O.T. specialists. I.B.

Liber Amicorum: Studies in Honour of Professor Dr. C. J. Bleeker. (Studies in the History of Religions: Supplements to *Numen*, xvii.) 1969. Pp. 324. (Brill, Leiden. Price: Fl. 65)

This collection ranges over the general field of the Phenomenology of Religion and the History of Religions, and although lacking a common theme it includes an appropriate emphasis upon C. J. Bleeker's own special field of ancient Egyptian Religion. Of importance in enabling O.T. scholars to see their subject from the perspective of a wider discipline is 'Le Professeur W. B. Kristensen et

GENERAL

l'Ancien Testament' by M. A. Beek. 'Der Schrecken Pharaos' by
S. Morenz also bears on various O.T. passages and 'Muḥammad and
the Qur'an. Criteria for Muḥammad's prophecy' by K. Wagtendonk
valuably argues that the founder of Islam combined the roles of
charismatic judge and classical prophet. The volume includes a list of
C. J. Bleeker's publications and a personal appreciation by G.
Widengren.
I.B.

NEUMARK, D. (ed.): *Journal of Jewish Lore and Philosophy*. Volume I.
(1919); reprint 1969. Pp. 463. (Ktav Publishing House, Inc., New York.
Price: $25.00)

Many will welcome the reissue of this solitary representative of its
species, which was published in 1919 and after a lapse of five years
continued as the *H.U.C.A.* Although marred by an appreciable
number of small printing errors, it contains articles of value which
appear to be not widely known nor otherwise easily accessible.
To mark the occasion there is a reprinting from the *H.U.C.A.* XXXVII
(1966) of a centenary tribute to David Neumark, editor of the volume,
who here contributed an introduction as well as articles on 'The
Beauties of Japhet in the Tents of Sem' and 'Spirit' — both of philo-
sophical interest, and an addendum on 'The Principles of Judaism'.
Essays connected with the O.T. field are: 'Saadia Gaon's Messianic
Computation' (H. Malter); 'Problems of Chronology in the Persian
Period' and 'Ezra the Scribe' (H. Englander); 'The Sources of the
Paradise Story' — in two parts (J. Morgenstern); 'Apocalypse in the
Bible' (J. Rauch); and 'The Origin of Death' (S. S. Cohen). Some of
the articles in the field of Jewish Studies have some overlap with the
O.T.
E.T.R.

NIDA, E. A. and TABER, C. R.: *The Theory and Practice of Translation*.
Helps for Translators prepared under the auspices of the United Bible
Societies, Vol. VIII. 1969. Pp. viii, 220, incl. 18 figs. (E. J. Brill, Leiden.
Price: Fl. 26)

This work appeared at about the same time as the *New English Bible*
O.T. and indeed received a vitriolic review by Margaret Masterman
in the same number of *The Times Literary Supplement* (19th March,
1970); see also *Theoria to Theory* IV (1970), 5–26. The basic ideas are a
development from Nida's *Toward a Science of Translating* (see *B.L.*,
1965, p. 66; *Decade*, p. 618). The book is designed much more for the
practical biblical translator than for the actual biblical scholar;
nevertheless it may for the interested biblical scholar provide a mode
of entry into post-Chomsky linguistics — 'kernels', 'deep structures'
and 'transformations' — which he might otherwise have ignored.

J.B.

NOBER, P., S.J.: *Elenchus Bibliographicus Biblicus*, Vol. 50. 1969. Pp. xx,
741. (Biblical Institute Press, Rome. Subscription Price: Lire 9,000;
$15.00)

The 1969 issue of this invaluable bibliographical aid carries 8,574
entries and more than a hundred pages devoted to indexes enabling
ready reference to be made to its contents. Its compression into a

smaller compass than the previous issue has not lessened its usefulness. Its indefatigable editor is again to be congratulated, and the world of scholarship is deeply indebted to him. The price, regrettably but inevitably, is substantially increased.

P.R.A.

RIESENFELD, H. (ed.): *Svensk exegetisk årsbok*, XXXI. 1969. Pp. 200. (C. W. K. Gleerup, Lund. Price: Sw.Kr. 20)

Only one article in this issue is of direct interest to the *Alttestamentler:* that by J. T. Willis on 'The Structure of the Book of Micah', in which he surveys earlier views of the subject and argues that the final form of the book has a basic coherence: three doom sections (1:2–2:11; 3; 6:1–7:6), each followed by a hope section (2:12–13; 4–5; 7:7–20), with striking parallels within each group of three, and with a marked progression of thought within each of the main parts of the book (1–2; 3–5; 6–7). H. Ljungvik comments (in Swedish) on the proposals for a new Bible translation made by the Swedish Bible Committee of 1963. The remaining articles are on N.T. and patristics.

G.W.A.

*ROWLEY, H. H.: *Dictionary of Bible Place Names*. 1970. Pp. 173. 5 maps. (Oliphants, London. Price: £1·50)

This volume is uniform with the *Dictionary of Bible Personal Names* and the *Dictionary of Bible Themes* (see *B.L.*, 1969, p. 8). It covers the whole Bible, including the Apocrypha, and, while based on the R.S.V., incorporates also some of the variants found in the Jerusalem Bible. Under each place name, a short statement is given of the biblical information available, together with later names for the same place and location and modern identification if these are known. It provides a handy reference-book, and the maps enable geographical positions to be determined where identification is available.

P.R.A.

RYLAARSDAM, J. C. (ed.): *Transitions in Biblical Scholarship*. (Essays in Divinity ed. by J. C. Brauer, Vol. VI.) 1968. Pp. x, 318. (The University of Chicago Press, London, Price: £3·80)

This volume of essays by graduates of the Divinity School of the University of Chicago is devoted to biblical subjects, five on the O.T. and eight on the N.T., together with an introductory essay by J. C. Rylaarsdam on the history of the Chicago school and the work of some of its outstanding scholars. F. C. Prussner writes on the Davidic covenant of 2 Sam. 7 and the problem of unity within O.T. theology which it exemplifies. He recognizes that the royal theology represented a very different stratum of religious and political ideology from that of the amphictyonic traditions. J. A. Wilcoxen studies the element of cultic legend in Jos. 1–6, and D. E. Gowan the theme of the role of the prophets in combating the syncretistic cult in Israel, and the consequences of this in Deuteronomy. A particularly interesting essay is offered by G. W. Ahlström entitled 'Some Remarks on Prophets and Cult' in which he reviews many recent theories about the cultic background of the prophets and puts forward some valuable reappraisals of his own.

R.E.C.

THOMSEN, P.: *Die Palästina-Literatur. Eine internationale Bibliographie in systematischer Ordnung mit Autoren und Sachregister.* Band VII. *Die Literatur der Jahre 1940–1945.* Lieferung 3 (pp. 321–496). Prepared for publication by O. Eissfeldt and L. Rost. 1970. (Akademie-Verlag, Berlin. Price: DM. 58)

The first two fascicles of this volume of the bibliographical survey were noted in *B.L.*, 1970, p. 14. This third fascicle covers the remainder of the history section (up to p. 345); it begins the section on archaeology and covers the general part of this, in which is included the linguistic and inscriptional material (up to p. 450). This is followed by literature dealing with specific sites, which will be completed in fascicle 4, scheduled to appear in December 1970. The value of this bibliography to Old Testament scholarship will be immediately clear.

P.R.A.

TSEVAT, M. (ed.): *Hebrew Union College Annual* XL–XLI. 1969–70. Pp. 580, 30 in Hebrew. Index to Vols. I–XXXIX. (Hebrew Union College, Cincinnati)

It is impossible in this review to do justice to all the 19 essays contained in this volume, dedicated to Nelson Glueck on his 70th birthday. Therefore one has to be selective, and mention those which are more likely to be of interest to the student of the O.T. 'Transliteration and Transcription of Hebrew' (W. Weinberg) examines how Hebrew consonants are represented in various Grammars. 'A Textbook case of adultery in Ancient Mesopotamia' (S. Greengus) considers the interpretation of a Sumerian document published by J. van Dijk in *Sumer* 15 (1959) pp. 12–14. Then there is included a second instalment of 'Old Assyrian texts in the University Museum (2)' (H. Lewy). 'An old Babylonian Forerunner of *Šumma Ālu*' (D. B. Weisberg) gives a transcription and translation of the text of the Old Babylonian tablet BM 113915, which deals with the art of divination connected with birds. 'Isaiah 61' (J. Morgenstern) is a careful study of this chapter of Isaiah, and proposes a date *c.* 440 B.C. 'God and the Gods in Assembly; an interpretation of Psalm 82' (M. Tsevat) studies the text and interpretation of this Psalm, and adds a comparison with Psalm 58. 'Iron Age epigraphic material from the area of Khirbet El-Kôm' (W. G. Dever) gives a careful study, with examples of inscriptions and coins, together with good photographs, of a site west of Hebron. Other articles deal with various aspects of Judaism, some of theological and others of philosophical and historical interests.

E.R.R.

ARCHAEOLOGY AND EPIGRAPHY

BITTEL, K.: *Hattusha. The Capital of the Hittites.* 1970. Pp. 174, pls. 30. (Oxford University Press, London. Price: £4·25)

In these lectures the excavator gives a first, and admirable, account of recent work at Boğazköy. The site with its history and archives is well described and illustrated. The chapter on the Hittite Empire and Egypt is useful for students of O.T. background.

D.J.W.

*CAMPBELL, E. F. and FREEDMAN, D. N. (ed.): *The Biblical Archaeologist Reader* 3. 1970. Pp. xv, 424. (Anchor Books, Doubleday, New York. Price: $2.45)

This third volume of selections from the *Biblical Archaeologist* presents in convenient form some of the most important articles which have appeared there. It is useful to have in the first section the influential articles by G. E. Mendenhall on law and covenant which appeared in 1954, among others which are relevant to the study of Israel's history and institutions in the ancient near eastern context. The second section of the volume contains articles on the Samaria papyri, on Qumran and other literary discoveries of recent years. The third section consists of miscellaneous articles, but includes weights and measures and the Madeba map. Previous volumes in this series were published in 1961 (ed. by G. E. Wright and D. N. Freedman) and 1964 (ed. by Campbell and Freedman); neither was noted in the *Book List*.

P.R.A.

*GRAY, J.: *A History of Jerusalem*. 1969. Pp. xiv, 336, Pls. xxxii, Maps and plans 11. (Robert Hale, London. Price: £3·15)

The book opens with a sketch of the historical geography and archaeological topography of Jerusalem, called 'The Situation and Development of the City'. Eleven chapters then trace the story from Amorite days down to the Divided City of recent times. The author's reputation is a good guarantee of what we may expect here. Obviously much of it is a work of assemblage rather than detailed research, but it appears to be thoroughly reliable as a whole and well abreast of modern knowledge.

D.R.Ap-T.

KUSCHKE, A. and KUTSCH, E. (ed.): *Archäologie und Altes Testament: Festschrift für Kurt Galling*. 1970. Pp. 363. (J. C. B. Mohr (Paul Siebeck), Tübingen. Price: DM. 95)

This impressive volume contains thirty-one contributions. Of most direct interest to O.T. scholars are those by Y. Aharoni on Mount Carmel as the geographical and political boundary of Phoenicia; O. Eissfeldt on Eccles. 3:1–8; F. Ellermeier on ancient oriental stringed instruments; K. Elliger on the identification of Michmethath; G. Fohrer on the temple and cult in the post-exilic period; H. Gese on Hadad's whip and the interpretation of Isa. 28:15, 18; H. Haag on the activities of the prophets Gad and Nathan; A. Jepsen on I Kings 21:27–29; E. Kutsch on the etymology of *berith;* A. Parrot on the earthen altars at Mari; L. Rost on the exercise of jurisdiction at sanctuaries; W. Rudolph on the book of Jonah and the use of (*ha-*)'*elohim* in it; H. Schmid on the religio-historical considerations behind the building of Solomon's temple; T. C. Vriezen on Amos 3:2; H. W. Wolff on the end of the sanctuary in Bethel; G. E. Wright on the significance of Ai in the third millennium B.C.; and W. Zimmerli on 'the year of the Lord's favour' (Isa. 61:1). There is a photograph of Professor Galling, and a full bibliography of his writings, prepared by P. Welten.

D.W.T.

MITTMANN, S.: *Beiträge zur Siedlungs- und Territorialgeschichte des nördlichen Ostjordanlandes*. (Abhandlungen des Deutschen Palästina-vereins.) 1970. Pp. viii, 284, Pls. xxxv + 1 large map (loose). (Otto Harrassowitz, Wiesbaden. Price: DM. 68)

This is, in a way, a continuation of the surface exploration of Trans-jordan begun by Glueck, whose conclusions are sometimes criticized. Mittmann's researches have almost trebled the number of sites examined in northern Transjordan. In addition to classifying the surface pottery, the area's Roman and medieval roads are studied, and a corpus of the Greek and Roman inscriptions found here and in the Hauran is given, consisting mainly of milestones and epitaphs. Finally the attempt is made to reconstruct the area's history during the Israelite period and in the time of the Crusaders. In a way, therefore, this is at least four independent, though not unrelated, studies. For those interested in any one of these fields, the factual matter — well brought together and well indexed — will be the most convenient, if not the only, source of information available about a now rapidly changing area. The usefulness of the work is multiplied several times by the inclusion of the 1:100,000 scale map, on which all finds are plotted.   D.R.Ap-T.

PARROT, A.: *Bible et Archéologie*. 1. *Déluge et Arche de Noé*. 2. *La Tour de Babel*. (Archéologie Biblique, 1–2.) Pp. 121. 1970. (Delachaux & Niestlé, Paris. Price: (approx.) £1·55)

This first volume of the series Archéologie Biblique consists of two studies by Parrot formerly issued separately. The volume on the flood-stories was noticed in *B.L.*, 1953, p. 22 (*Eleven Years*, p. 475); that on the Tower of Babel in *B.L.*, 1954, p. 20 (*Eleven Years*, p. 557); both were translated into English (*B.L.*, 1956, pp. 14f; *Eleven Years*, pp. 721f). The present volume is substantially a reissue, with minor corrections and an up-to-date bibliography, but with no major changes in interpretation.   R.J.C.

PFEIFFER, C. F.: *Jerusalem through the Ages*. (Baker Studies in Biblical Archaeology No. 6.) 1967, reprint 1969. Pp. 94, illus. 34. (Baker Book House, Grand Rapids, Michigan. Price: $1.95, paperback)

The biblical, and pre-biblical, archaeology of Jerusalem cannot be treated adequately on this small scale. That understood, in under 80 pp. the author succeeds remarkably in supplying a clear, well-balanced historical back-cloth to the Jerusalem of today. As such it can be warmly recommended to the intelligent visitor.   D.R.Ap-T.

PFEIFFER, C. F.: *Tell el Amarna and the Bible*. (Baker Studies in Biblical Archaeology No. 2.) 1963. Pp. 75, illus. 18, maps 2. (Baker Book House, Grand Rapids, Michigan. Price: $1.50, paperback)

The last short, fairly general, chapter gives its name to the whole monograph. Otherwise it is mostly a popular account of Akhenaton and his reform. The Letters are dealt with in a chapter on 'The Affairs of Empire', and the Habiru question is sketchily outlined. A praiseworthy attempt to give the layman an uncomplicated outline of the subject. The same author's *Ras Shamra and the Bible* was noticed in *B.L.*, 1964, p. 20; *Decade*, p. 488.   D.R.Ap-T.

*PRITCHARD, J. B. (ed.): *The Ancient Near East: Supplementary Texts and Pictures relating to the Old Testament.* Pp. viii, 274, illus. 113. 1969. (Princeton University Press. Oxford University Press. Price: £7·25)

Owners of the original editions of *ANET* and *ANEP* can now bring both up to date by purchasing this supplement. In addition to the texts added in both 2nd and 3rd editions of *ANET*, it includes the addenda and corrigenda which could not be inserted on to the original printing plates. Well over 100 additional pictures, usefully enlarging and bringing up to date the first edition of *ANEP*, have been included. The inclusion in this supplement of comprehensive indexes covering the whole work greatly eases the task of reference. The main disadvantage of the supplement is that it cannot give us those corrections of the earlier translations which it has proved possible to insert into the plates for the complete new edition. Nevertheless both editor and publishers will be warmly applauded for making this supplement available.

D.R.Ap-T.

THUBRON, C.: *Jerusalem.* Pp. 256, Pls. in col. LXIV, Maps and plans 6, Engravings 13. 1969. (Heinemann, London. Price: £4·20)

This is a travel book by a writer who has taken pains to get at the facts and who shows a real gift for writing them up attractively. His sensitive portrayal is ably backed up by A. Duncan's effective photography — the picture of our Honorary Member, Père de Vaux, is a gem.

D.R.Ap-T.

WELTEN, P.: *Die Königs-Stempel.* (Abhandlungen des Deutschen Palästinavereins.) 1969. Pp. xiii, 198, Figs. 58. (Otto Harrassowitz, Wiesbaden. Price: DM. 44)

Over 800 stamped jar handles have been discovered in Palestinian excavations. The author seeks to classify them here as to type, date and purpose. Three main types are recognized, which are dated as ante-700, *c.* 700 and post 630, respectively. The purpose of all was to brand army rations from four crown properties, and the author discusses the location of *mmšt*. In a section on Judah's foreign relations, the Assyrians are shown to have attacked Judah along the coast road, usually, and the relevance of this fact to the distribution of these jar handles is well worked out. This is a careful and systematic work whose usefulness is considerably enhanced by the Scripture Reference index.

D.R.Ap-T.

YAMAUCHI, E. M.: *Greece and Babylon: Early Contacts between the Aegean and the Near East.* (Baker Studies in Biblical Archaeology No. 3.) 1967. Pp. 115, illus. 62. (Baker Book House, Grand Rapids, Michigan. Price: $1.50, paperback)

The author has cast a very wide net to catch so many instances of putative as well as probable and certain contacts between Semite, Hamite and Japhethite before 400 A.D. He is perhaps a little too indiscriminating for his intended readers. Above all, it seems a pity that he has topped and tailed a very useful, even though uncritical, survey of this important field with some — to this reviewer — rather irrelevant argumentation about the date of the book of Daniel.

D.R.Ap-T.

HISTORY AND GEOGRAPHY

BEN-SASSON, H. H. (ed.): *History of the Jewish People*. Volume One: *The Ancient Times* (Hebrew. Original title: *Tol^edoth 'am Yiśrael bime qedem*). 1969. Pp. xxx, 381, 52 plates. (Devir, Tel Aviv. Price: $6.30)

There are four main sections in this volume. The Beginnings of the Israelite people are treated by A. Malamat (pp. 9–90). H. Tadmor covers the period of the Kingdom, down to the return from Exile and, in effect, the Persian period (pp. 93–173). The third section is written by M. Stern (pp. 177–294) and deals with the Hellenistic period down to the war against Rome and the destruction of the Temple. Finally, S. Safrai's section is entitled 'The Period of the Mishnah and the Talmud' and takes as its chronological framework the time from 70 to 640 C.E. The whole is preceded by a general introduction to the entire work by the general editor (pp. xi–xxx). In addition to the plates there are a number of maps in the text (listed on p. 4); and there is a brief classified bibliography, which includes works both in Hebrew and in European languages. The writers are professional historians in the field and the level is high without being unduly technical. J.B.

EDWARDS, I. E. S., GADD, C. J. and HAMMOND, N. G. L. (eds.): *The Cambridge Ancient History*. Vol. I, Part 1. *Prolegomena and Prehistory*. 3rd ed. 1970. Pp. xxii, 758, with 17 maps, 7 tables and 45 text-figures. (Cambridge University Press. Price: £6·00)

The fascicles which are to make up the new edition of the first two volumes of the *C.A.H.* have been appearing for some years, and they have been noted in the *Book List*, beginning at 1963 (p. 17, *Decade*, p. 411) and ending at 1969 (p. 13). Now the first part of the first volume appears as a whole, with the addition of maps, indexes and chronological tables. The opportunity has been given to contributors to bring their texts up to date and additions have been made to the bibliographies published in the fascicles. Much of this particular volume is concerned with periods which considerably antedate the O.T., though the chapters on early man provide important background. The chapters on language and on chronology are clearly relevant; the latter contains a brief statement about the problems of the early chronology of Israelite history. R. de Vaux's section on 'Palestine during the neolithic and chalcolithic periods' provides the context for the understanding of the excavations of Jericho and other centres whose importance for the O.T. will be brought out in the volumes to come. P.R.A.

*NEGENMAN, J. H.: *New Atlas of the Bible*. Edited by H. H. Rowley. 1969. Pp. 208. (Collins, London. Price: £5·25)

Reference was made in the 1970 *Book List* (p. 21) to an English edition of the Negenman atlas. This has now appeared, in a clear and readable translation by H. Hoskins and R. Beckley. R.J.C.

PFEIFFER, C. F.: *The United Kingdom*. 1970. Pp. 92. (Baker House Press, Grand Rapids, Michigan. Price: $3.95)

This addition to the author's series of textbooks of O.T. history is a summary of the biblical history from the birth of Samuel to the death of Solomon, written from a very conservative standpoint with a marked emphasis on the archaeological background but no critical evaluation of the text. There are two maps and useful photographs and diagrams.

L.A.P.

ROTH, C.: *A Short History of the Jewish People.* Newly revised and enlarged. 1969. Pp. xix, 494. (East and West Library, London. Price: £3·75)

Since the first edition (1935) of this well-known history, Dr. Roth has brought out successive editions, bringing the story up to date, to include the Nazi persecutions, and the establishment of the State of Israel. In this final (fifth) edition he has added pages to cover the Six Days War. The strengths and weaknesses of the book are familiar and do not need extended comment here. It is in the tradition of Jewish historiography despite the author's belief that he was breaking away from it. The history of the biblical period is recounted with a deliberately over-simplified reliance on the biblical traditions as handed down. The value of the book is in its panoramic scope and in its emphasis on social history. His identification of the Qumran sect with the Zealots is reaffirmed without hint that other views might be possible. Many will doubt the wisdom of adding so much of the immediate past. It is inconceivable that this somewhat passionate and uncritical story will not soon need radical revision in the light of a wider perspective. The edition is handsome; the illustrations profuse and fascinating.

D.R.J.

SMEND, R.: *Yahweh War and Tribal Confederation. Reflections upon Israel's Earliest History.* E.T. by M. G. Rogers. 1970. Pp. 144. (Abingdon Press, Nashville. Price: $4.50)

The German original of this book (first edition 1963, second edition 1966) was noted in *B.L.*, 1964, p. 28; *Decade*, p. 496. It is an important study, developing ideas associated with von Rad, Alt and Noth, and making stimulating contributions to the interpretation both of the book of Judges and of the pre-monarchy period in general, and it is good to have an English translation of it, based on the second edition.

P.R.A.

WALLIS, G.: *Geschichte und Überlieferung. Gedanken über alttestamentliche Darstellungen der Frühgeschichte Israels und der Anfänge seines Königtums.* 1968. Pp. 130. 1 map. (Evangelische Verlagsanstalt, Berlin. Price: DM. 24)

This volume contains four essays by Wallis and one study incorporating a series of contributions from a Seminar to the consideration of tribal traditions and history in relation to the Jacob saga, but leading on into the books of Joshua and Judges. The main essays deal with the origins of the kingdoms (an extended form of the author's inaugural lecture), a traditio-historical study of the Samuel materials, the status of the king in Israel — the king viewed as servant and as lord — and a general essay on 'History, Tradition and Traditio-history'. The studies form a useful and unified collection.

P.R.A.

TEXT AND VERSIONS

APTOWITZER, V.: *Das Schriftwort in der rabbinischen Literatur*. Parts i–v. *Prolegomenon* by S. Loewinger. (*The Library of Biblical Studies*. Ed. by H. M. Orlinsky.) First published 1906–15. 1970. Pp. xiv, 406. (Ktav Publishing House Inc., New York. Price: $25.00)

The *Library of Biblical Studies* is going on apace, and each time the re-issue of a classical study, long since unobtainable, is amply justified, and nowhere more than in the present case. The writer of the very useful *Prolegomenon*, Professor S. Loewinger, rightly complains about the neglect of Rabbinic variants in critical editions such as *Biblia Hebraica*, but without Aptowitzer, where could one start? And, humanly speaking, it is not very comforting to learn from Loewinger that there are so many new opportunities of examining sources previously 'unknown or unattainable' (think of the 20,000 Geniza fragments!). No one person can deal with it all, but it is good to have the material at hand, and the old Aptowitzer to set us on the right road.   B.J.R.

A Handy Concordance of the Septuagint. 1970. Pp. 284. (Bagster & Sons, London. Price: £2·50)

The re-issue of this work, first published in the nineteenth century, will fulfil a purpose analagous to that of a pocket dictionary. By modern scholarly standards it often seems arbitrary — in its textual basis, in its omissions, and in the fact that on dogmatic grounds only those books found in the Hebrew canon are referred to. Provided that these limitations are borne in mind, the work will give the non-specialist some useful guidance to LXX usage.   R.J.C.

Biblia Sacra Iuxta Vulgatam Versionem. Ed. by R. Weber, with the assistance of B. Fischer, J. Gribomont, H. F. D. Sparks, W. Thiele. 2 vols. (Genesis-Psalmi; Proverbia-Apocalypsis. Appendix). 1969. Pp. xxi, 1980. (Württembergische Bibelanstalt, Stuttgart. Price: DM. 56)

The publication of this convenient and excellently produced edition of the Vulgate, in series with the Bibelanstalt's *Biblia Hebraica* and *Septuaginta*, is to be warmly welcomed. It is clear, well printed, and careful. The introduction (provided in Latin, German, French and English) is a model of conciseness and clarity, setting out admirably the intention of the edition, the principles upon which the editors have worked, and the nature and limits of the *apparatus criticus*. Jerome's prologues have been included before the books or groups of books to which they belong. The 'Gallican' and 'Hebrew' psalters are printed on opposite pages. The abbreviations are clear, the textual notes easy to follow. For the student of the biblical text, and for the scholar needing a convenient text of the Vulgate for immediate reference purposes, this is exactly right.   P.R.A.

DÍEZ MACHO, A.: *Neophyti 1 Targum Palestinense Ms de la Biblioteca Vaticana*, Vol. i: *Génesis*. 1968. Pp. 137*, 643. (Consejo Superior de Investigaciones Científicas. Price: $45.00)

The long-awaited first volume of the *editio princeps* of the Neofiti Targum is a sumptuous publication. It contains the transcription of this previously unknown Aramaic paraphrase of Genesis, together with a critical apparatus which reproduces the Codex's many marginal and inter-linear variant readings. A Spanish translation prepared by the editor accompanies the original text page by page, followed by a French version by R. Le Déaut (pp. 353–494) and an English one by M. McNamara and M. Maher (pp. 495–642). An introduction of over 130 pages in Spanish describes the ms. and discusses its contents, the date of the recension, its relationship to other targumic traditions, and its linguistic features. The information is exhaustive, though the conclusions often remain arguable. It is hoped that a facsimile edition of the Codex will follow, and perhaps also a *Schulausgabe* which students (and teachers) can afford.   G.V.

GEISSEN, A.: *Der Septuaginta-Text des Buches Daniel, Kap. 5–12, zusammen mit Susanna, Bel et Draco, sowie Esther Kap. 1, 1a–2, 15, nach dem kölner Teil des Papyrus 967.* (Papyrologische Texte und Abhandlungen. Band 5.) 1968. Pp. 313, 4 plates. (Rudolf Habelt Verlag, Bonn)

HAMM, W.: *Der Septuaginta-Text des Buches Daniel, Kap. 1–2, nach dem kölner Teil des Papyrus 967.* (Papyrologische Texte und Abhandlungen. Band 10.) 1969. Pp. 281. (Rudolf Habelt Verlag, Bonn)

967 is of particular importance, being the only surviving witness to the pre-hexaplaric form of the o′ text of Daniel, and Ziegler, in the Göttingen LXX, only had available the fragments of this papyrus in the Chester Beatty Library. Further extensive portions of the same manuscript are fortunately now to be found in the Köln collection of papyri. Both volumes contain introductions and fairly extensive textual commentaries; that by Geissen has 4 plates, but a complete set would be welcome. A further volume, with the Köln fragments of ch. 3–4, is to appear.   S.P.B.

*HUNT, G.: *About the New English Bible.* 1970. Pp. viii, 83. (Oxford University Press, Cambridge University Press. Price: 30p)

This useful little book provides an account of the background and making of the N.E.B., setting out more fully what is stated in its preface, describing the work of the translating and literary panels, explaining the footnotes and commenting on some points of detail. It is very helpful to the general reader to have this information so conveniently set out.   P.R.A.

ORLINSKY, H. M. (ed.): *Notes on the new translation of The Torah.* 1969. Pp. 288. (The Jewish Publication Society of America, Philadelphia. Price: $6.00)

In 1962 the Jewish Publication Society published *The Torah*, a new translation of the Pentateuch in English. The purpose of this volume of *Notes* is to account for significant or interesting departures from the earlier translation published in 1917. In an informative introduction the history of the translation of the O.T. is briefly surveyed, and the failure of traditional translations to bring out the precise nuances of some Hebrew words and phrases is discussed, with numerous examples. The notes are both helpful and instructive, and adequately meet the purpose for which they have been prepared. The reliance placed upon traditional Jewish interpretations is a prominent feature of the translation, and is conspicuously reflected throughout the notes and in the bibliography.   D.W.T.

RÜGER, H. P.: *Text und Textform im hebräischen Sirach.* (Beihefte zur Zeitschrift für die alttestamentliche Wissenschaft, 112). 1970. Pp. 117. (Walter de Gruyter & Co., Berlin. Price: DM. 46)

Described as a preparatory study for the future edition of Ben Sira in BHS, this work contains a very detailed and worthwhile discussion of the variations between (and doublets within) the different Hebrew Geniza fragments (the passages common to B and the Masada fragments, however, are not included). Against (e.g.) Ziegler and di Lella, Rüger finds no evidence for the existence of any back-translations from Greek or Syriac as a source for variants in the surviving Hebrew manuscripts (ch. 51 is not considered here): rather, the variations between the different texts simply represent earlier and later text forms, both of which are reflected in the versions.   S.P.B.

SPERBER, A.: *The Prophets according to the Codex Reuchlinianus.* 1969. Pp. 342. (E. J. Brill, Leiden. Price: Fl. 110)

Here is presented for us the text of *Codex Reuchlinianus* of the Prophets (Former and Latter). This will be welcomed by those interested in the text of the O.T., and in the pre-masoretic vocalization. No doubt we can look forward to further studies based on this edition. The editor does offer a brief explanation of his method of dealing with the text, and points out that a study of his treatment of Hebrew grammar is essential for a proper understanding of this edition. At the same time a more detailed introduction would have been very helpful.   E.R.R.

TALMON, S. (ed.): *Textus: Annual of the Hebrew University Bible Project,* Vol. VII. 1969. Pp. 137 + 12 in Hebrew. 3 plates. (Magnes Press, Jerusalem. Price: £2·20)

The volume opens with a long article by D. W. Gooding on 'Text and Midrash in 3rd Reigns', in which he argues that considerable editorial activity lies behind the Greek text of 1 Kings: with this contrast Shenkel's very different evaluation in his recent book (see *B.L.*, 1970, p. 26). M. Delcor comments on a 'targumic' translation in the LXX of Daniel 3. B. Kedar-Kopfstein collects a considerable number of instances where Jerome's Hebrew *Vorlage* differs in points of detail from MT in Jeremiah. E. J. Revell publishes a new Genizah fragment of Chronicles with Palestinian vocalization. I. Yeivin discusses the divisions into sections in manuscripts of Psalms. N. Fried lists the *sedarim* for Numbers according to the triennial cycle. A second article by Yeivin comments on the new BHS Isaiah, with especial reference to the treatment of accents and massorah. In shorter notes, S. Talmon argues for the LXX reading at Jer. 15: 11; G. R. Driver comments on a phrase in Ps. 118: 27; R. Weiss on 4Q180; and E. Fleischer on the autograph of Sa'id ben Farjoi.   S.P.B.

WICKES, W.: *Two Treatises on the Accentuation of the Old Testament:* (on *Psalms, Proverbs and Job*, and on *the Twenty-one Prose Books*). *Prolegomenon* by A. Dotan. (*The Library of Biblical Studies*. Ed. by H. M. Orlinsky). First published 1881, 1887; 1970. Pp. xlvi, 6, 119, 14, 155. (Ktav Publishing House Inc., New York. Price: $14.95)

The two books by Wickes, despite their being based on wrong presuppositions about the Massorah, are still indispensable for a study of the Hebrew accentuation systems, and Professor Dotan's *Prolegomenon* to the publication is the best introduction to the topic that I have ever seen. One does miss, however, the plate of the page of *Aleppo Codex* which accompanied the original *Twenty-one Prose Books*, and also an explanation of why it was omitted.

B.J.R.

EXEGESIS AND MODERN TRANSLATIONS

ALLEN, C. J. (ed.): *The Broadman Bible Commentary — Vol. I.* General Articles — Genesis, Exodus. 1969. Pp. 472. (Broadman Press, Nashville, Tennessee. Marshall, Morgan and Scott, London. Price: £3·50)

The emphasis of this commentary is stated to be on 'the redemptive message of the Scriptures and on the relevance of Bible teaching to the issues and problems of the present world'. There is little in it that is obscurantist or obtusely dogmatic. C. J. Allen states the point of view of himself and doubtless of many other contributors when he writes: 'A faith that asks no questions is scarcely faith because it seeks no meanings.'

The subjects of the general articles in this volume are: 'The Book of Christian Faith' (C. J. Allen), 'The Scriptures in Translation' (R. G. Bratcher), 'Interpreting the Bible' (J. P. Newport), 'The Geography of the Bible' (B. E. Scoggin), 'Archaeology and the Bible' (J. A. Callaway), 'The Canon and Text of the Old Testament' (B. A. Sizemore, Jr.), 'The History of Israel' (C. T. Francisco), 'The Theology of the Old Testament' (E. C. Rust), 'Contemporary Approaches in Old Testament Study' (J. I. Durham). The art of saying *multum in parvo* is always a difficult one to exercise because of what must be left out to make room for what must be put in. Each of these contributors has made a commendable use of the space allotted to him and has generally succeeded in including the significant aspects of his subject and the central issues of discussion today.

The sections on Genesis (G. H. Davies) and Exodus (R. L. Honeycutt, Jr.) have each a succinct and well-presented introduction and a commentary which will be exegetically helpful and instructive for the general reader, for whose use the commentary is devised. It is a pity that more space was not available for a fuller statement on the Book of the Covenant in Exodus.

J.M.

BJØRNDALEN, A. J. and others: *Første Mosebok. En kommentar* (Gammaltestamentlig Bibliotek, 1). 1970. Pp. 300. (Forlaget Land og Kirke, Oslo)

This commentary is intended for use by students and study groups. It was produced by a group of students in the Menighetsfakultet in Oslo under the direction of their teacher, Mr. A. J. Bjørndalen, who himself contributes a section on the plan and method of the commentary, and a classified bibliography. The general introduction to

Genesis is by K. I. Johannessen. The text is apportioned as follows:
1:1–11:26 (A. J. Bjørndalen); 11:27–15:18 (T. T. Sørensen and H.
Bekker); 25:19–37:1 (H. Harflot and O. Myklebust); 37:2–50:26
(E. O. Båsland and T. Engelsviken). Each section has its own introduction, in which its limits, structure, setting, and literary affiliations
are discussed: and this forms an admirable preamble to the exegetical
treatment. An interesting experiment in co-operation, competently
carried out, has produced a valuable textbook. G.W.A.

BROCKINGTON, L. H.: *Ezra, Nehemiah and Esther*. (New Century Bible.)
1970. Pp. x, 252. (Oliphants, London. Price: £3·25)

The main emphasis of this commentary is strongly historical rather
than theological, so that little attention is given to the overall theology
of the Chronicler, or to the possibility of accounting for the arrangement of Ezra 4 by reasons other than chronological confusion.
Detailed consideration is given to the historical problems associated
with Ezra and Nehemiah (Sheshbazzar is taken as probably an imperial
official; Ezra's mission dated at 398), and to the proper names in the
books. The brief commentary on Esther which is appended makes a
somewhat incongruous and unrelated addition; the book is taken to be
a historical novel from the mid-second century. R.J.C.

BUIS, P.: *Le Deutéronome* (Verbum Salutis: Ancien Testament, 4) 1969.
Pp. 484. (Beauchesne, Paris. Price: Fr. 39)

Fr. Buis is already known for his contribution to an earlier work on
Deuteronomy (*B.L.*, 1964, p. 31; *Decade*, p. 411), and this commentary on the book makes use of the best modern scholarship in presenting a popular, but thoroughly theological, interpretation of it. The
various theories about the origins of the traditions used in the book
are fully discussed, and Buis argues for the probability of some
elements of northern origin in its make-up, and its adoption of the
form of a covenant document derived from political treaties. The
works of Alt, von Rad, Lohfink and McCarthy are utilized very
effectively, and are presented in a very readable form for the student
and general reader. R.E.C.

BURNEY, C. F.: *The Book of Judges with Introduction and Notes* and *Notes
on the Hebrew Text of the Book of Kings with an Introduction and
Appendix. Prolegomenon* by W. F. Albright. (The Library of Biblical
Studies. Ed. by H. M. Orlinsky). (First published 1903, 1918). 1970.
Pp. 38; cxxviii, 528, with 5 maps, 6 plates; xlviii, 384. (Ktav Publishing
House, New York. Price: $19.95)

Two very valuable older works are here reprinted in this series, and
although much has happened since their publication, their detail of
linguistic, textual and archaeological comment remains a source of
rich information. Albright's *Prolegomenon* includes a brief biographical note, and some indications of the development of scholarship in
regard to certain areas covered in these two works. Characteristically
his comments are devoted largely to his own work and that of those
who have been associated with him. P.R.A.

*CHAMBERLAIN, E. (ed.): *Mowbray's Mini-commentary series* (A. R. Mowbray and Co. Ltd., London. Price: 30p each)

TRILLO, J.: *Joshua, Judges, 1 and 2 Samuel, 1 and 2 Kings.* (Mini-commentary, 6.) 1970. Pp. 71

ACKROYD, P. R.: *1 and 2 Chronicles, Ezra, Nehemiah, Ruth, Jonah, 1 and 2 Maccabees.* (Mini-commentary, 7.) 1970. Pp. 65

ROBERTSON, E. H.: *Jeremiah, Lamentations, Baruch, Ezekiel, Isaiah 40–66.* (Mini-commentary, 9.) 1970. Pp. 67

HERKLOTS, H. G. G.: *An Old Testament Dozen.* (Mini-commentary, 10.) 1970. Pp. 70

SIMON, U. E. : *Psalms.* (Mini-commentary, 11.) 1970. Pp. 64

LEAHY, D.: *The Wisdom Literature.* (Mini-commentary, 12.) 1970. Pp. 49

Volumes 5 and 8 of this series were reviewed in *B.L.*, 1970, pp. 35, 36. All the volumes of this useful series, which is based on the text of the Jerusalem Bible, are interesting and informative, succinct but lively, may be unhesitatingly recommended to the general reader, and will be of interest to many with a more professional interest in Bible study.

L.A.P.

*EATON, J. H.: *Psalms* (Torch Bible Paperbacks). 1970. Pp. 318. (S.C.M. Press Ltd., London. Price: 90p)

This is an unchanged paperback reprint of the commentary first published in 1967 (see *B.L.*, 1968, p. 22). M.A.K.

ELLERMEIER, F.: *Qohelet.* Teil I, Abschnitt 1. *Untersuchungen zum Buche Qohelet.* 1967. Pp. xii, 371. Teil I, Abschnitt 2, Einzelfrage Nr. 7. *Das Verbum ḥûš in Qoh 2, 25. Akkadisch ḥâšu(m) 'sich sorgen' im Lichte neu veröffentlichter Texte.* 1968. Pp. 35. (Verlag Erwin Jungfer, Herzberg am Harz.)

These are the first two parts to appear of a comprehensive study of Ecclesiastes which will eventually comprise three parts in, apparently, nine volumes, culminating in the last volume with a new translation. Teil I, Abschnitt 1 is devoted mainly to a general discussion of the problems of interpretation, a new attempt to determine the structure of the book through a detailed study of its formal characteristics and patterns of thought, and a discussion of the problems of translation. An appendix contains one of the 38 *Einzelfragen* of which the bulk will appear in Teil I, Abschnitt 2: an enquiry into the meaning of '*ôlām* in 3: 11 which is held to refer to the unchanging character of human existence. Teil I, Abschnitt 2, Einzelfrage 7 discusses *yāḥûš* in 2:25, concluding that the meaning of the verb *ḥûš* is 'be anxious'. It is clear that the work when completed will be a massive study which, apart from its form, will have all the characteristics of a major commentary.

R.N.W.

ELLIGER, K.: *Jesaja II* (Biblischer Kommentar, Altes Testament XI, 1). 1970. Pp. 1–80. (Verlag der Buchhandlung des Erziehungsvereins, Neukirchen-Vluyn. Price: DM. 7.75; Subscr. DM. 6.50)

This first fascicle of Professor Elliger's commentary on II Isaiah covers 40:1–26. It is closely argued, very detailed, based on wide knowledge of the very extensive literature. There is considerable stress on the forms of the literature, and the sectional divisions of the text. Many of his judgements are controversial, but it is well balanced and clearly written and an extremely valuable commentary whose further instalments will be eagerly awaited.   J.N.S.

GRAY, J.: *I and II Kings. A Commentary.* Second, Fully Revised, Edition. 1970. Pp. xviii, 802, 3 maps. (S.C.M. Press Ltd., London. Price: £8·00)

The first edition of this massive commentary was reviewed in *B.L.*, 1964, p. 34; *Decade*, pp. 502–3. The revised form is 58 pages longer than its predecessor, despite the fact that there are now no indexes. The author has corrected errors, added new material, and re-written parts of his work in the light of further thought, fresh evidence, or recent publications. While there are places where further revision is still desirable (for example, the section on the Greek versions should give due consideration to Barthélemy's work), this new edition of a substantial and important work is greatly to be welcomed. J.A.E.

GROSCH, H.: *Der Prophet Amos* (Handbücherei für den Religionsunterricht, 6). 1969. Pp. 88. (Gütersloher Verlagshaus, Gerd Mohn. Price: DM. 8.80)

This short study is intended for those engaged in teaching religion in schools and in general university courses. It uses the prophet Amos to provide a general introduction to O.T. prophecy. After noting the main features of prophecy it offers a detailed study of Amos 7:10–17; 6:1–8; 5:21–7 and 7:1–9, and concludes with some considerations and suggestions on teaching the O.T. with special regard to the religious and moral issues raised by Amos. The work is based on the best modern scholarship, and assumes little specialized knowledge on the part of the reader. It is well annotated with references to recent literature on Amos, and points connections to wider theological issues. Its main contribution lies in relating a good critical exegesis of the book of Amos to the particular needs of religious education.

R.E.C.

GUTHRIE, D., MOTYER, J. A., STIBBS, A. M. and WISEMAN, D. J. (ed.): *The New Bible Commentary Revised.* 1970. Pp. xv, 1310. (Inter-Varsity Press, London. Price: £3·00)

The first edition of this commentary was published in 1953. In this new edition, which is attractively set out and very reasonably priced, more than half of the articles and commentaries have been re-written. Nevertheless, the criticisms raised against the original in *B.L.*, 1954, p. 33; *Eleven Years*, p. 570, that it was 'designed for readers who have . . . no awareness of the purposes of biblical scholarship', remain valid. The key sections are the article on Authority (G. W. Bromiley) and that on Revelation and Inspiration (J. I. Packer); with the presuppositions there laid down, subsequent discussions of critical and historical problems are for the most part artificial, with the answers effectively determined in advance. There are some exceptions to this general standard, notably a number of articles by F. F. Bruce, who is almost alone in providing any bibliographical aids. R.J.C.

*HANSON, A. and M.: *Job* (Torch Bible Paperbacks). 1970. Pp. 122. (S.C.M. Press, London. Price: 50p)

Most of the re-issues in this paperback series have left the original completely unchanged, but a useful feature of this one is a four-page postscript by the authors, indicating some of the shifts in scholarly opinion since the publication of the original edition, with a note on newly-discovered extra-biblical material bearing on Job and a brief mention of other recent commentaries. The original edition was noticed in *B.L.*, 1954, p. 36, *Eleven Years*, p. 573.   R.J.C.

HAURET, C.: *Amos et Osée:* (Verbum Salutis Ancien Testament, 5) 1970. Pp. 284. (Beauchesne, Paris. Price: Fr. 26.00)

This book does not, in the usual way, begin with an introduction to the books of the Old Testament with which it deals, but in each case the first verse is used as a frame of reference for a brief statement about each prophet and the situation in which he lived and worked. In Professor Hauret's opinion Amos was a sheepmaster rather than a cultic official, and Hosea was called to marry a *qᵉdēšāh* so that his message might be presented symbolically in a household setting as Jeremiah's message was presented by the loneliness of his unmarried state.

The commentary throughout, linguistic, form-critical, exegetical and theological, is well-constructed, crisp and succinct. Textual problems are clearly defined and possible solutions are briefly outlined. The author succeeds very effectively in giving a vivid presentation of each prophet doing a significant job in a hostile and unreceptive community which had no respect for the past nor concern for the future nor inclination to be diverted from present pursuits.   J.M.

HOWARD, J. K.: *Amos Among the Prophets* (The New Minister's Handbook Series) 1967; reprinted 1968. Pp. viii, 119. (Baker Book House, Grand Rapids, Michigan. Price: $2.95). (Also Pickering & Inglis, 1967: *Among the Prophets*)

Dr. Howard writes from a conservative point of view but in a section entitled 'Critical Considerations' he takes account of textual problems and intrusive elements, of redactors and editors. The introduction he provides gives a brief survey of the distinctive work of the canonical prophets as a whole and of that of Amos in particular and of the social environment and political situation in which he exercised it. Textual problems (as in 3:12, 5:10, 5:26) are lightly touched upon, if at all, the main purpose being to interpret each section as a whole. *Nōqēḏ* as a cultic official is not mentioned and some recent lines of study on Amos are passed over. But within the restricted line of presentation the author has chosen for the general reader, he has presented a well-balanced and helpful introduction. A minor point; two words seem to be persistently misspelt: 'Jereboam' and 'apostacy'.   J.M.

JENSEN, I. L.: *Studies in Isaiah and Jeremiah.* (Bible Self-Study Series.) 1968. Pp. 112. (Moody Press, Chicago.)

This is a simple exposition of the life, times and teaching of the two prophets written from a completely conservative point of view.   J.R.

JENSEN, I. L.: *Jeremiah — Prophet of Judgement*. (Everyman's Bible Commentary.) 1966. Pp. 128. (Moody Press, Chicago. Price: 95c.)

This is an expository commentary based on the R.S.V. text and written for the layman. The point of view is conservative throughout.   J.R.

Jubilee Commentary (Hungarian). Fascicles 1–3. 1968–9. (Published by the Press Service of the Budapest Synod of the Reformed Church of Hungary. Budapest XIV, Abonyi-utca 21)

This Jubilee Commentary, issued in Hungarian by the Reformed Church of Hungary, is appearing in fascicles. All the contributors are Hungarian scholars. Its format when complete will be similar to Peake's One-Volume Commentary, two columns to a page; each biblical book receives an introduction and a (very) short bibliography, mostly of books in German, a few in English or Dutch. The standpoint is at once critical and conservative. Fascicle 1 (1968), 131 pages, contains six articles on Introduction to both Testaments. Fascicle 2 (1969), 364 pages, comprises commentaries on N.T. books up to the 2nd Epistle of John. Fascicle 3 (1969) covers Genesis and Exodus, both from the hand of Dr. Kálmán Tóth. The editors, who must study almost wholly in foreign languages, are to be congratulated on producing what will become the standard Commentary for this century in the Hungarian language.   G.A.F.K.

LUCK, G. C.: *Daniel*. (Everyman's Bible Commentary.) 1958. Pp. 127. (Moody Press, Chicago. Price: 95c.)

The author's conservative approach to the critical problems of this book is made clear in his Introduction. Jesus' reference to Daniel in Matt. 24:15 is proof 'that he was a prophet, that he wrote the book attributed to him, and that he prophesied events which were still future at the time Christ spoke.' (p. 11). This last point necessitates a 'great parenthesis' in the prophecies in which God's 'prophetic clock' stopped ticking (p. 104). Belshazzar's descent from Nebuchadnezzar and the historicity of Darius the Mede are accepted without convincing reasons. The commentary offers a general rather than a detailed treatment of the text, with frequent spiritual exhortations.   G.F.

LUCK, G. C.: *Ezra and Nehemiah*. (Everyman's Bible Commentary.) 1961. Pp. 127. (Moody Press, Chicago. Price: 95c.)

This commentary is written from an extreme conservative point of view, which gives no indication that there are any historical problems connected with these books, and does not mention any possible link with the work of the Chronicler. The bibliography and footnotes are confined entirely to works of a similar standpoint.   R.J.C.

McKANE, W.: *Proverbs, a new approach*. 1970. Pp. xxii, 670. (S.C.M. Press Ltd., London. Price £5·00)

This is a remarkable book. Professor McKane deserves our congratulations on writing a work which is erudite, judicious, wide-ranging, and methodologically satisfying.

The book has an excellent introduction which is followed by a detailed study of 'international wisdom' (largely Egyptian and Babylonian-Assyrian). The translation and commentary form the second part of this fine work. There is also a good bibliography.

The transcription is at times a little odd: why should *miš^{e}le* have a *š^{e}wa mobile*? (p. xxi). McKane refers, in his bibliography, to Torczy-ner/Tur-Sinai's commentary on Proverbs, but, in fact, he scarcely seems to have used it — except at second hand (e.g. p. 597 where he misunderstands Torczyner). This is a pity, for Torczyner's book contains many brilliant suggestions, even if occasionally they rub shoulders with very odd ones. This reviewer cannot see that the 'material on the Palestinian background' of Proverbs (p. vii) sheds any significant light on our text (e.g. p. 318).

But Professor McKane is guilty of the eighth deadly sin, i.e. failure to provide an index. Let us hope that in the many future works which we would like to see issuing from his pen he will never again make his readers' task so arduous. Meanwhile, this book represents a fine achievement in which his colleagues will rejoice.   E.U.

NIELSEN, E.: *Deuterozakarja. Nye bidrag til belysning af Zak. 9–14.* 1970. Pp. 77. (G. E. C. Gad, Copenhagen. Price: D.Kr. 15.85)

This booklet is the first one in a new series of monographs by name *Tekst & tolkning* (text and interpretation) issued by the Institute of Biblical Exegesis in Copenhagen. After a short introduction and a summary of the content of Zech. 9–14, there follow in two chapters reviews of the two dissertations Benedikt Otzen: *Studien über Deutero-sacharja*, Copenhagen, 1964 (see *B.L.*, p. 50, 1964; *Decade*, p. 518) and Magne Sæbø: *Sacharja 9–14, Untersuchungen von Text und Form*, 1969 (see p. 45). The reviews are almost identical with the author's objections raised to the dissertations in Aarhus 1964 and in Oslo 1969 respectively.   E.H.

PETITJEAN, A.: *Les oracles du Proto-Zacharie. Un programme de restaura-tion pour la communauté juive après l'exil.* (Études Bibliques). 1969. Pp. x, 502. (J. Gabalda et Cie, Paris; Editions Imprimerie Orientaliste, Louvain. Price: Fr. 88)

This is a commentary on the Hebrew text of the prophetic oracles, as distinct from the visions, in Zech. 1–8: that is, according to the author, 1:1–6, 14b–17; 2:10–17; 3:8–10; 4:6ab–10a; 6:9–15; 7:4–41; 8. The reliability of the Hebrew consonantal text is strongly defended. Almost the whole of these oracles is attributed to Zechariah; some are dated to the period before the building of the Temple. Zechariah was strongly influenced by his prophetic predecessors, but there is also a note of originality in his message, which was fundamentally an announcement of the immediate dawning of a new era in which Zerubbabel as successor of the Davidic kings would reign, with the co-operation of the High Priest Joshua, over a renewed Jerusalem to whose restored temple the nations would flock to worship. There is a full discussion of all the main problems of these passages, and in some cases new solutions are proposed.   R.N.W.

ROWLEY, H. H.: *Job.* (New Century Bible.) 1970. Pp. xvii, 359. (Oliphants, London. Price: £6·00)

Two previous volumes in this series have been noted (*B.L.*, 1968, pp. 23, 29, see also pp. 25, 34). This latest is produced by a new publisher. It follows the pattern of the series, with inevitably short sections of text at the head of the page and notes below. On some pages, this is improved on by the text being printed at the top of the left-hand page only. As was to be expected in any work by the late H. H. Rowley, there is here a wealth of bibliographical information. Alternative renderings for many phrases are given, with references to the names of a multitude of scholars. Where the English version of Dhorme inevitably could give only older information, here the most recent work is taken into account. Rowley is more conservative than many who have written on the problems of the text of Job. Often he leaves the reader to decide among a group of alternatives. It is at the level of exegesis that the work is less satisfying. The relatively short exposition in the Introduction and the short summarising headings do not really provide an adequate discussion of the problems of interpreting the book. The interrelationship between elucidating the meaning of a phrase and the consequences which this has for interpretation is not really worked out. Perhaps it cannot be with a commentary which inevitably devotes almost all its attention to the detail. And perhaps Job is one of those O.T. books where a running exegesis is most needed alongside the detailed discussion. Dhorme and Fohrer both offer more in this respect.   P.R.A.

SABOURIN, L., S.J.: *The Psalms: Their Origin and Meaning.* 1969. 2 vols. Pp. xix, 253; xix, 373. (Alba House, Society of S. Paul, New York. Price: $17.50)

As a commentary on the psalms, this is a disappointing work. Its thirty odd pages of bibliography — containing only works consulted by the author — is certainly an impressive witness to his industry and learning. But to say, as R. A. F. MacKenzie does in the Foreword, that he 'has digested and summarized the results' of modern scholarship is hardly adequate. For both the more general sections, covering the making of the Psalter, the original setting of the psalms, and their religious teaching, and also the sections dealing with the psalms in detail, arranged according to types, consist very largely of the recounting of the views of these scholars. Occasionally, the rejection of one scholar's views by another is noted as convincing, but for the most part the author's own conclusions are exceedingly difficult to find. Digestion implies that the material taken in has become part of the digester. The author's concern to present so large a range of views, though it provides a convenient conspectus of much scholarly work, prevents him from providing the reader with a coherent commentary in which this work is drawn on and used with discrimination.

P.R.A.

SCHULTE, H.: *... Bis auf diesen Tag. Der Text des Jahwisten, des ältesten Geschichtsschreibers der Bibel.* 1967. Pp. 106. (Herbert Reich, Evangelischer Verlag, Hamburg-Bergstedt. Price: DM. 12.00)

Three pages of introduction provide an indication of the basis on which this selection of passages regarded as belonging to the Yahwist have been printed as a continuous narrative. Some of the uncertainties about the presence of the Yahwistic strand in the books of Samuel and Kings are voiced. The text printed is that of the Zurich Bible. A few notes are added to it. It is a useful but now somewhat old-fashioned exercise.

P.R.A.

SOGGIN, J. A.: *Le Livre de Josué*. (Commentaire de l'Ancien Testament, Va). 1970. Pp. 186. (Delachaux et Niestlé, Neuchâtel)

This is a distinguished addition to an already well-established and valuable series, not least because it offers, in the context of this French Protestant enterprise, the work of the excellent Waldensian scholar J. A. Soggin. The commentary is clear, well ordered, and extremely readable. It provides in the introduction not only a clear picture of the problems of exegesis and historical assessment, but also a valuable section on the theological contribution of the book in its biblical context. The bibliographies, both general and particular to individual sections, are full. The views of scholars are carefully expounded, revealing the breadth of study undertaken. There emerges an exposition which stands in the Alt-Noth tradition, but takes full account of a wide range of interpretation and provides a coherent and comprehensive view of the book. Detail of textual and linguistic points enables an adequate translation to be offered and a discussion of the problems of individual passages leads to a clear view of the possible solutions to them.

P.R.A.

Starý zákon/překlad s výkladem: 4. *Jozue — Soudeů — Rút* (The Old Testament/translation with commentary: 4. Joshua — Judges — Ruth). 1969. Pp. 230. (Kalich, Prague. Price: Kčs. 30)

Starý zákon/překlad s výkladem: 7. *Ezdráš — Nehemjáš — Ester* (The Old Testament/translation with commentary: 7. Ezra — Nehemiah — Esther). 1970. Pp. 172. (Kalich, Prague. Price: Kčs. 24)

The new Czech commentary series, noted already in *B.L.*, 1969, p. 27 (1. *Genesis*) and 1970, p. 36 (14. *Twelve Prophets*) is continued in these two volumes (nos. 4 and 7). They have the same format as their predecessors. It may be stressed that this is a co-operative work on an ecumenical basis; both the translation and the commentary are produced as a result of corporate work and the final form is not undertaken by any of the individual contributors. Further volumes are already prepared for the press.

M.B.

*WALTON, R. C. (ed.): *A Source Book of the Bible for Teachers*. 1970. Pp. xxi, 394 (including 11 maps). (S.C.M. Press Ltd., London. Price: £3·15)

This book, replacing *The Teachers' Commentary* (published in 1932 and revised in 1955) reflects recent changes in biblical scholarship and even more recent developments in the theory and practice of religious education. Hence instead of a conventional biblical commentary we have a Source Book for teachers which will meet a widely felt need. An essay on the biblical scholar and his tools is followed by some fifty pages on the needs of the pupils, in accordance with the recent emphasis on 'child-centred' education. Part 3 of the book, devoted to the O.T. is divided into 13 chapters, occupying 124 pages, a third of the whole volume. These essays, covering every aspect of the history and religion of Israel, are of a consistently high quality. Teachers of R.E. will welcome the book as an invaluable vade-mecum. L.A.P.

WATTS, J. D. W.: *Obadiah: A Critical Exegetical Commentary.* 1970. Pp. 78 (Eerdmans Publishing Co., Grand Rapids, Michigan. Price: $3.50)

The author first surveys the variety of scholarly judgement on the nature, unity and date of the Book of Obadiah, traces the history of Israel-Edom relations, defines the focal points of attention of the Book as the punishment of Edom and the Day of Yahweh and takes the view that the book as it stands is liturgically suited for use at a religious festival, probably that of the annual enthronement festival of Yahweh. All this is an orderly and well-discussed thesis, and the commentary which follows will prove helpful to many readers. But the so-called distinctive translation of a corrected and re-arranged text of Obadiah will be criticized, and certainly such phrases as 'stretch your mouth' (v. 12), 'stretch out a hand among his goods' (v. 13), 'on the crossing' (v. 14), and 'it will proceed to be done to you' (v. 15) are either stiffly literal or inelegant, and, in the first example, at least, of indefinite meaning. J.M.

WEBER, J. J.: *Cantiques de l'Office Divin.* 1970. Pp. 128. (Desclée, Tournai. Price: Fr. 19·50)

Monseigneur Weber, the retired Archbishop-Bishop of Strasbourg, now in his eighty-fourth year, has compiled a pleasant and readable French text of the canticles used in the Divine Office, though, in addition to the seventeen used in the Roman Breviary, he has printed no less than twenty-two more, which include seven additional passages from Isaiah, four from Paul, and four from the Apocalypse. The texts are taken from the *Bible de Jérusalem* and the *C.N.P.L.* rendering, and these are accompanied by a short commentary that faces each page of the translation. There is an index of subjects occurring in the canticles, and tables showing the canticles in the order of their authors' names, and in the Breviary arrangement according to the days of the week and the month. J.M.T.B.

VAN DER WEIDEN, W. A.: *Le Livre des Proverbes: Notes Philologiques.* 1970. Pp. 178. (Biblica et Orientalia, Biblical Institute Press, Rome. Price: Lira 2,400 or $4.00)

The book here reviewed is a running commentary on linguistic and philological problems offered by *Proverbs;* these indeed are enough, but the author adds to their number, not always as necessary. His main operative principles are 'the principles of ellipse' and the 'ballast variant' in poetry, and an ample recourse to Ugaritic roots; here he is a follower of Dahood, though in not so extreme a form, and, while not a few of his suggestions will hardly be accepted, many are illuminating. What gain is it to change 'a nagging wife is like water dripping endlessly' into 'like the crumbling (of a house) that drives one out of doors' (Prov. 19:13; cp. 27:15) on the strength of dubiously parallel passages (cp. Baal III* A 17–18 and Eccl. 10:18)? Many of the Ugaritic comparisons, however, are interesting and worthy of notice, as also are a number of other fresh interpretations of various proverbs, some of which may well be considered in any future edition of the New English Bible (e.g. Prov. 7:21, 10:4, 12:27, 14:13, 16:33, 20:8, 22:8, 24:5, 25:20, 28:10, 31:29, 31:31). Several *obiter dicta* on obscure and difficult passages in the Old Testament outside *Proverbs* also deserve consideration (e.g. Jud. 9:9).

G.R.D.

WERNER, H.: *Amos*. (Exempla Biblica, iv). 1969. Pp. 203. (Vandenhoeck & Ruprecht, Göttingen. Price: DM. 12.80)

This is the fourth volume of a series, *Exempla Biblica*, designed for the use of teachers of the O.T. in schools and colleges. A detailed exposition and annotation of the text is followed by a lengthy essay on the place of the book of Amos in the school curriculum. This book is not so much a text-book as a contribution to educational theory.

L.A.P.

WESTERMANN, C.: *Genesis*. (Biblischer Kommentar, Altes Testament, i, 4.) 1970. Pp. 80. (Neukirchener Verlag, Neukirchen-Vluyn. Price: DM. 7.75; subscr. 6.50)

Earlier fascicles were noted in *B.L.*, 1968, p. 29; 1969, p. 27; 1970, p. 37. This fascicle completes the commentary on Genesis 2:1–4a. Then follows a translation of Genesis 2:4b–3:24 with commentary extending to 2:25. The translation is preceded by a full bibliography relating to the passage (4 pages) and is followed by grammatical and text-critical notes. The commentary includes discussion of form and *Sitz im Leben* and longer notes on particular words and phrases such as *'adam* (man=mankind), Eden, tree of life. The two chapters are seen as a complex deriving from a larger collection of oral narratives.

A.S.H.

WEVERS, J. W.: *Ezekiel* (New Century Bible). 1969. Pp. x, 355. (Nelson, London. Now published by Oliphants, London. Price: £3·75)

A careful analysis of the book and of its structure and a discussion of the forms of its material lead into a brief tentative note of the original prophecies as compared with the expansions in the present form of the book of Ezekiel. A good deal of attention is also devoted to this in the detailed notes on individual passages and verses. There is a sensible balance of treatment — a generally cautious estimate of the situation of the prophet, but an awareness of the problems which the book presents. This is done in such a way as to preserve a sense of the unity of the prophetic tradition of Ezekiel, but it may leave the reader wishing (a) that a fuller indication had been given of the place of Ezekiel in the larger prophetic movement — though there are some indications of this — and (b) that at some point there had been a drawing together of the message of the prophet and the nature of its expansion and reapplication. But there is a wealth of information in the commentary, and it may be conveniently used alongside that of Eichrodt as providing for the English reader both technical detail and general comment.

P.R.A.

WILDBERGER, H.: *Jesaja*. (Biblischer Kommentar, Altes Testament, x, 5.) 1970. Pp. 321–400. (Neukirchener Verlag, Neukirchen-Vluyn. Price: DM. 7.75; subscr. DM. 6.50)

This fascicle (see *B.L.*, 1970, p. 38, for the previous one) deals with 8:5–10:15. Wildberger argues that 8:16 is to be understood figuratively and does not refer to a written record of the prophet's message, and that 9:1–6 comes from Isaiah himself. J.A.E.

WOLFF, H. W.: *Dodekapropheten: Amos* (Biblischer Kommentar, Altes Testament, xiv, 8 and 9). 1969. Pp. 265–424. (Neukirchener Verlag, Neukirchen-Vluyn. Price DM. 7.75; subscr. DM. 6.50 each)

The first and second parts of H. W. Wolff's commentary on Amos for the *Biblischer Kommentar* have already been noted in the *Book List* (1968, p. 30; 1970, p. 38). These two parts complete the commentary and deal with Amos 5:1–9:15. The merits of the earlier parts are fully maintained in these. J.M.

LITERARY CRITICISM AND INTRODUCTION

(including History of Interpretation, Canon, and Special Studies)

ACKROYD, P. R.: *The Age of the Chronicler* (The Selwyn Lectures, 1970). A Supplement to *Colloquium* — the Australian and New Zealand Theological Review, 1970. Pp. 60. (Price: $A/NZ. 2.00)

This publication represents the full text of the Selwyn Lectures delivered in 1970 in both New Zealand and Australia. There are three lectures: (i) Political and Social Aspects of the Jewish Community; (ii) the Great Reformers; and (iii) Theological Strands in the Age of the Chronicler. It is valuable to have this period so singled out and treated. Nor is the interest 'merely' an Old Testament one. The author remains aware throughout that many of the problems of the Persian period — for example, the importance of tradition and the need to be 'contemporary' — are not without their relevance to the present day. *The Age of the Chronicler* may be obtained from the Publishers (at 202 St. John's Road, Auckland 5, New Zealand, or Room 2, Third Floor, 511 Kent Street, Sydney 2000) or from the S.P.C.K., London.

R.S.F.

*ACKROYD, P. R.: *Israel under Babylon and Persia*. (New Clarendon Bible, IV) 1970. Pp. xvi, 374. (Oxford University Press. Price: £1·50)

This is a distinguished addition to the *New Clarendon Bible*. While conforming to the general plan of the series, it offers a number of improvements both in structure and execution which make this more than a mere replacement of Lofthouse's *Israel after the Exile*. In particular the author of *Exile and Restoration* has an understanding of the Old Testament traditions which pervades every part of the book. Documentation of course belongs to the Hulsean Lectures which deal with substantially the same ground. Here he has been able to stand back from the material and expound it for students with a mastery and skill, which makes the book as readable as it is reliable. Teachers

of the Old Testament will be grateful for a book which will not
quickly be superseded and which, in these days, with its attractive
lay-out, maps and illustrations, is exceptional value for money.

D.R.J.

*ACKROYD, P. R. and EVANS, C. F. (ed.): *The Cambridge History of the
Bible*, Vol. 1: *From the Beginnings to Jerome*. 1970. Pp. x, 649. 25 plates.
(Cambridge University Press. Price: £4·50)

Earlier volumes of this work were reviewed in *B.L.*, 1964, p. 9;
Decade, p. 477 and *B.L.*, 1970, p. 51. The present volume rounds off a
magisterial enterprise and is concerned with tracing the process by
which the Bible as we know it came into being. It has five sections, on
Language and Script, Books in the Ancient World, the O.T., the
N.T., and the Bible in the Early Church. Of particular interest to
users of the *Book List* will be the chapters on the Biblical Languages by
M. Black, the Biblical Scripts by D. Diringer, Books in the Ancient
Near East by D. J. Wiseman, the O.T. in the Making by P. R.
Ackroyd, Canonical and non-Canonical by G. W. Anderson, the
O.T. Text by S. Talmon, and Bible and Midrash by G. Vermes. The
names of the contributors are sufficient to guarantee the high quality
of the work, which summarizes the present state of scholarship in
these and other areas in clear, non-technical language. Inevitably
there is a fair amount of overlap with Vol. 2, which was conceived
independently of the present book, and a comparison of the two
volumes, for example in their treatments of the O.T. text and versions,
reveals the rapid progress of modern biblical scholarship even in a
comparatively short space of time.   J.R.P.

*ANDERSON, G. W.: *A Critical Introduction to the Old Testament* (Studies
in Theology, 52). 1959; reprint 1970. Pp. viii, 261. (Duckworth, London.
Price: 90p)

This paperback is unchanged from the 1960 reprint of the original
1959 edition (see *B.L.* 1960, p. 24; *Decade* p. 204). The publishers
could usefully have permitted an updating of the bibliography.

P.R.A.

BERRIDGE, J. M.: *Prophet, People, and the Word of Yahweh. An Examina-
tion of Form and Content in the Proclamation of the Prophet Jeremiah.*
(Basel Studies in Theology, No. 4.) 1970. Pp. 226. (EVZ-Verlag,
Zürich. Price: Sw.Fr. 26)

On the basis of a form-critical examination of various passages in the
Book of Jeremiah, Berridge rejects the view of Reventlow that such
passages, where well-known cultic *Gattungen* are employed, hold no
evidence of a 'personal' Jeremiah. It is argued that the prophet,
though often employing cultic forms, did not hold a cultic office and
that it is precisely in the passages in question that the most valuable
evidence of the individuality of Jeremiah is to be found. Berridge
contends that an important key to an understanding of the person of
Jeremiah is provided by the prophet's repeated and diverse confron-
tations with Yahweh's word, and by the consciousness of his solidarity
with the people to whom he ministered during the most critical period
of Israel's history. The work is thoroughly documented and constitutes

an important contribution to the investigation of the problem in question and to the broader issue of the relevance of cultic *Gattungen* in the prophetic literature for the understanding of the ministry and preaching of the prophets. It is regrettable that the book contains so many quotations in German which will render it difficult for the average English-speaking student to read. The index of biblical references deals only with the Book of Jeremiah and would have been more helpful if it had also included the many other biblical references cited in the book, especially as it is the only index provided.

E.W.N.

BLANK, S. H.: *Understanding the Prophets* (Issues of Faith, Vol. 3). 1969. Pp. 138. (University of American Hebrew Congregations, New York. Price: $2.50)

Professor Blank writes a popular account of the prophets' teaching in which the aim is to set out their basic religious ideas and their contributions to man's religious history. The work is aimed at an audience in High School or early University, and offers fresh translations of the many quotations made from the prophets, with an analysis of leading theological and ethical themes. As a popular Jewish interpretation it is of special interest, combining critical modern scholarship with a deep sympathy for the religious relevance of the material discussed. Few basic questions are left unasked, and clear and penetrating answers are offered.

R.E.C.

CONRAD, J.: *Die junge Generation im Alten Testament. Möglichkeiten und Grundzüge einer Beurteilung.* (Aufsätze und Vorträge zur Theologie und Religionswissenschaft, 47.) 1970. Pp. 97. (Evangelische Verlagsanstalt, Berlin.)

This monograph is a modified and much shortened form of a dissertation presented in 1963. It traces the position of the younger members of the O.T. community (mainly the sons) in relation to family life, to education, as illustrated by the Wisdom literature, and in relation to divine choice. It tends to lay most emphasis on the perhaps rather obvious point that the interest in younger members of the community really depends upon the position they are ultimately to occupy.

P.R.A.

*DAVIDSON, R. and LEANEY, A. R. C.: *Biblical Criticism. The Pelican Guide to Modern Theology.* Volume 3. Ed. by R. P. C. Hanson. 1970. Pp. 393. (Penguin Books, Harmondsworth, Middlesex. Price: 40p)

A short section by the general editor introduces the two main parts of this book, dealing with the Old and New Testaments respecitvely. Pp. 25–165 cover the O.T., with notes gathered at the end of the volume. Under the main headings of archaeology, literature, text, religion and theology, Davidson has provided a very readable survey of the main developments of recent years, and a balanced assessment of the position reached. The general reader and the theological student at the beginning of his course will be the most obvious beneficiaries of this short survey. Much has had to be omitted and every topic has had to be handled only briefly, but much can be learnt from this. The sections on religion and theology are particularly helpful. Leaney has a somewhat longer section on the N.T.

                                                                    P.R.A.

DRIVER, S. R. and NEUBAUER, A.: *The Fifty-Third Chapter of Isaiah according to the Jewish Interpreters. Prolegomenon* by R. Loewe. (Library of Biblical Studies. Ed. H. M. Orlinsky). Vol. I. — Texts. II. — Translations. 1970 (First edition 1876). Pp. 572 and 574. (Ktav Publishing House, Inc., New York. Price $22.50)

This is a most welcome reprint of a remarkable work of scholarship produced nearly one hundred years ago and still retaining great value. It was initiated by Pusey and the project was carried out by Driver and Neubauer in a most happy collaboration. The extracts printed and translated include quotations from the LXX, the other Greek translations, the Targum of Jonathan, the Talmuds, the Midrashim, the Zohar and many Jewish scholars such as Sa'adyah, Rashi, ibn Ezra, David Kimchi, Nachmanides, Abarbanel, Halevi, etc. This reprint is introduced by a learned and judicious introduction by Raphael Loewe who, besides making many interesting comments, pleads for a more objective, scientific exposition of the section of Scripture under consideration on the part of Jews as well as of Christians. He points out that some of the extracts printed in Vol. I are now available in an improved text. S. R. Driver's extensive knowledge of Jewish literature comes out impressively in his Preface.

                                                                    N.W.P.

DVIR, Y.: *yiʿudah šel ha-šlihut ba-šem ha-miqra'i* ('Biblical Proper Names and their Mission'). 1969. Pp. 368. (Otsar Hamoreh, Publishing House of the Teachers' Union in Israel, Tel Aviv.)

This unusual miscellany of literary, philological and theological discourse arises out of the thesis that the function (or 'mission') of biblical proper names is to encapsulate, or at least clearly allude to, elements in the legends about those who bear them. This correlation between name and biography is of course well known from the biblical folk-etymologies of names like Abraham, Moses and Jerubbaal; but Dvir argues that the same holds for all the protagonists of Old Testament tradition, whether or not the appropriate folk-etymology is recorded in the text. In the first place, the authors were not historians, but more like prophets. Second, there was only one Moses, one David, one Isaiah and so on, so that a 1:1 correspondence between name and traditional role is possible. Then there is evidence for the practice of giving a man a new and appropriate name later in life, after he has demonstrated his character and abilities. Finally it is most remarkable how often a suitable folk-etymology, often incidentally involving Aramaic and often noted already in the rabbinical literature, is available for biblical proper names. It would be hard to prove that the biblical authors did not select or invent significant names for their heroes and heroines, maybe as part of the Israelite adaptation of foreign material.

Dvir is familiar with the standard works on ancient near eastern proper names by Noth, Ranke, Tallquist, and the rest (although Huffmon (1965) and Gröndahl (1967) are absent); but he is less concerned with historical and comparative linguistics than with the synchronic meaning of names in the context of the Old Testament. What did the author mean by calling the hero of the Midianite wars 'Gideon'? It is less important that there are pagan parallels to the name Deborah than that this is the prophetess who, like a hornet, drove the Canaanites from their land (it is recorded that the inhabitants of Phaselis in Lycia were compelled to leave their land by a plague of bees). Similarly the name Lot, *etym.dub.* according to the lexica and not even mentioned by Noth, is related in rabbinic tradition (and why not earlier?) to Aramaic *luṭ* 'to curse', and thus, for one thing, brands Ammon and Moab as *bne loṭ* 'sons of a curse'. The author knows exactly what he is doing: it is something very different from Noth's *Israelitische Personennamen*, but it is nonetheless valuable as a systematic, if at times rather romantic, study in biblical folk-onomastics.   J.F.A.S.

EISSFELDT, O.: *Adonis und Adonaj.* (Sitzungsberichte der Sächsischen Akademie der Wissenschaften zu Leipzig. Philosophisch-historische Klasse, Band 115, Heft 4.) 1970. Pp. 28, 15 Pls. (Akademie-Verlag, Berlin.)

This monograph provides a complement to the article on *'ādōn* in *TWAT* (cf. p. 6). A brief section is devoted to the consideration of the structure of the form *'adonay*, relating it to the comparable Ugaritic *bʻlny* 'Allherrscher'. Much of the discussion in *TWAT* is devoted to the various approaches to the form *'adonay*. Here it is in the context of a consideration of the relationship between the deity Adonis and his various west-semitic counterparts.   P.R.A.

ERLANDSSON, S.: *The Burden of Babylon: A study of Isaiah 13:2–14:23.* (Coniectanea Biblica, O.T. Series 4). 1970. Pp. 195. (C. W. K. Gleerup, Lund.)

This doctoral dissertation opens with a translation of Isa. 13:2–14:23, with full critical notes on the Hebrew text. There follows a discussion of earlier analytical approaches to Isa. 1–39, and of the composition of 14:24–23:18, as a prelude to a study of the composition and form of 13:2–14:23, its diction and motifs, and its relationship to Jer. 50–51. The conclusion reached is that the linguistic and thematic contents of this section link it closely with generally accepted portions of Isaiah. It originated in connection with the Assyrian expedition against Judah in 701 B.C., and was later modified during the Exile to refer to Babylon. The author shows an excellent knowledge of recent literature and he puts up an able defence of a minority view which merits serious attention.   D.W.T.

*FOSTER, R. S.: *The Restoration of Israel,* 1970. Pp. xi, 239. (Darton, Longman and Todd, London. Price: £3·00)

This is advertised as a textbook on the Exile and Return. Despite too frequent and often unnecessary quotation from other writers, it is a clear and knowledgeable discussion of the main problems, and offers a coherent account of the history of Israel from the time of Josiah to the work of Ezra, based on the biblical evidence. Its virtues are however spoiled by a number of less attractive features. There is a tendency to rest on critical positions with a confidence not warranted by the evidence. There is an underlying old-fashioned literary approach to the prophets, which betrays no awareness of the problems created by traditio-historical and form-critical methods. For this reason the approach to Deutero-Isaiah, the Servant Songs and especially Ezekiel (a Jerusalem prophet whose Babylonian appearance is created by a later editor) will to many seem fundamentally unsatisfactory. Where the author is most original, e.g. in his theory concerning the Samaritans (particularly in Deutero-Isaiah), he appears most arbitrary and unconvincing. Sanballat is everywhere referred to as Sanballet and even the title of H. H. Rowley's essay made to conform. On p. 201 'the King of Arsames' is a grotesque slip. The transliteration is at best odd, at worst wrong.

D.R.J.

*FRETHEIM, T. E.: *Creation, Fall, and Flood. Studies in Genesis 1–11*. 1969. Pp. 127. (Augsburg Publishing House, Minneapolis. Price: $1.75)

This paperback is a careful exposition of the meaning of Genesis 1–11 in the light of modern scholarship written for the layman in non-technical language. Sixth-Form teachers and others will find much in this book of interest to them; the author is a first-rate teacher.

L.A.P.

*GROLLENBERG, L. H.: *Interpreting the Bible*. 1968. Pp. 138. (Paulist Press Deus Books, New York. Price: $1.45)

This paperback, intended for the enquiring layman, and based on twelve discussions presented on the Dutch T.V. network in 1965, is a first-rate book. Rather more than half the contents is devoted to the O.T. The author shows convincingly how only by probing the historical background and the motivation of the biblical authors can we learn to understand better what they have to say to us as Christians today.

L.A.P.

*GROLLENBERG, L. H.: *A New Look at an Old Book*. Translated by R. Rutherford. 1969. Pp. viii, 408. (Newman Press, New York and London. Price: $4.95)

This popular and very readable account of the biblical literature has been translated from the Dutch *Nieuwe kijk op het oude boek* (Elsevier, Amsterdam. 1968). A full coverage of the Bible is not offered but a general survey of the various types of Old Testament (including Apocryphal) writings, with selected illustrations treated with greater detail, and an account of the Gospels. Given originally as lectures in South Africa with the aim of clarifying the effect for the understanding of the Bible of the changed atmosphere brought into the open by Vatican II, the book speaks frankly of historical and theological interpretation, and of the nature of prophetic, apocalyptic and wisdom literature. It is designed for the ordinary reader, and it certainly meets many of the questions which are commonly asked. At times the account is inevitably oversimplified; the comments on the Samaritans (pp. 112f.) are rather antiquated. The illustrations from the prophetic literature are overbalanced towards the earlier prophets, and include neither Second Isaiah nor any later prophet. But the book is stimulating and enjoyable.

P.R.A.

HALS, R. M.: *The Theology of the Book of Ruth* (Facet Books, Biblical Series, 23). 1969. Pp. xii, 78. (Fortress Press, Philadelphia. Price: $1.00)

The thesis of this monograph, whose author acknowledges his indebtedness to von Rad, is that the Book of Ruth is a product of the 'Solomonic enlightenment' and comparable both in style and theology to the Court History of David, the Joseph story in Genesis, and certain narratives of the Yahwist. It shares with them the purpose of illustrating the divine activity in history as continuous and operating through human aspirations and actions rather than sporadically through the older sacral institutions. The analysis of style and structure is perceptive and illuminating, but the theological interpretation appears rather forced, and probably attributes a greater subtlety of mind to the author of Ruth than he actually possessed.   R.N.W.

*HENN, T. R.: *The Bible as Literature*, 1970. Pp. 270 (Lutterworth Press, London. Price: £2·25)

The design of this book is similar to the author's article on the same subject contributed to the revised edition of *Peake's Commentary on the Bible* (edited by M. Black and H. H. Rowley) 1962, of which it is an expanded version. Dr. Henn uses as the basis of his study the Authorised Version as the only English translation likely to rank as a literary monument. He also finds Elizabethan English specially appropriate for translation from Hebrew since both languages were specially sensitive to what nowadays would be called the physical basis of personality. Students of the Old Testament will find particularly interesting the chapter on 'Proverbs and Prophecy' and the analysis of the tragic structure of the stories of Moses and David.

The book is full of interesting literary notes on the influence of biblical imagery on English literature. More rewarding still would have been some attempt to relate literary criticism of the Bible as the littérateur practices it to that of the biblical scholar.   E.J.T.

HENRY, M.-L.: *Prophet und Tradition. Versuch einer Problemstellung* (Beihefte zur Zeitschrift für die alttestamentliche Wissenschaft, 116). Pp. vi, 77. 1969. (Walter de Gruyter, Berlin. Price: DM. 22)

In this study of a subject that has been prominent in recent discussion the authoress endeavours to show that, both in its origin and development, the religion of Israel was primarily indebted to the type of the individual prophetic figure. The divinely called and endowed individual was the central fact from which the religion originated, and through whom it developed. This is evidenced in the early patriarchal traditions, the prophetic call-narratives, and more abundantly in the prophetic literature itself. Thus the clusters of tradition and the established institutions of the religion were subordinate to, and not determinative of, its essential character. Recent attempts to subordinate the prophets to such traditions and institutions are thereby shown to be contrary to the fundamental witness of the O.T. to the nature of Israel's religion.   R.E.C.

JEREMIAS. JÖRG: *Kultprophetie und Gerichtsverkündigung in der späten Königszeit*. (Wissenschaftliche Monographien zum Alten und Neuen Testament, 35.) 1969. Pp. viii, 214. (Neukirchener Verlag, Neukirchen-Vluyn. Price: DM. 33; paper DM. 31)

This *Habilitationsschrift* uses Nahum, Habakkuk and the oracular psalms to clarify the relation of the canonical to the cultic prophets. Nahum is found to have been a prophet of doom comparable to Hosea and Zephaniah, before his words were reconstituted by exilic cult prophets. But Habakkuk is recognized as a cultic prophet in spite of such redaction; characteristic is his discrimination between sinners and righteous within Israel, as opposed to the blanket condemnation uttered by the non-cultic prophets. This is developed as the decisive difference between the two forms of prophecy. The author does well to recognize the value of Habakkuk. Whether he goes far enough in appreciating the contribution of the cult to prophecy is debatable.

J.H.E.

KOOLE, J. L.: *Verhaal en Feit in het Oude Testament*. (Cahiers voor de Gemeente, 1). 1969. Pp. 68. (J. H. Kok, Kampen. Price: Fl. 4.25)

This work by the Professor of Old Testament in Kampen Theological Seminary is the first in a series of 'Pamphlets for the Congregation' which aim at communicating the attitudes and findings of modern biblical study to members of a group of Dutch churches which are traditionally conservative in criticism and literalist in interpretation. 'Story and Fact in the Old Testament' are treated in such a way as to show that the acceptance of the methods and conclusions of criticism in no way diminishes the abiding value of the Old Testament in the Church.

F.F.B.

LIPINSKI, E.: *La liturgie pénitentielle dans la Bible*. (Lectio Divina 52.) 1969. Pp. 117. (Les éditions du Cerf, Paris. Price: Fr. 16)

This is chiefly a study of the setting of the psalms of collective lament, but comparable passages in the prophets are also given a prominent place. An index of the passages treated would have been valuable. The author has succeeded in writing a book which will be useful to specialists while serving a wider public. He adduces materials to depict the services of penitence: the dates, the summons, the mourning rites, the lamenting prayers, the answering assurance of prophetic oracle or priestly benediction.

J.H.E.

*MCELENEY, N. J.: *The Melody of Israel: Introduction to the Psalms*. (Pamphlet Bible Series, 42.) 1968. Pp. 32. (Paulist Press, New York. Price: 50c.)

A brief and clear treatment of the usual introductory questions, ending with a 'self-teaching quiz'. It would be useful in an older school class or a laymen's group. But to complete the Psalter in this series one would have to get a further six pamphlets.

J.H.E.

MARTIN-ACHARD, R.: *Actualité d'Abraham*. (Bibliothèque Théologique, ed. by J.-J. von Allmen.) 1969. Pp. 197. (Delachaux et Niestlé, Neuchâtel. Price: Sw.Fr. 20.50)

The purpose of this book is to present the traditions concerning Abraham together with their later developments and re-interpretations, in order to show how it may be possible to discover their relevance for the present day. After a useful critical survey of the historical, literary and theological problems of the Abraham stories in Genesis, the development of the tradition is traced in the other books of the O.T., the post-canonical literature, the literature of Rabbinical and Hellenistic Judaism, the N.T. and the *Qur'an*. There is abundant reference to recent literature, and the author displays a sober critical judgement which will make the book a useful introduction to the subject.   R.N.W.

MERENDINO, R. P.: *Das Deuteronomische Gesetz. Eine literarkritische, gattungs- und überlieferungsgeschichtliche Untersuchung zu Dt 12–26*. (Bonner Biblische Beiträge, Band 31.) 1969. Pp. xxvi, 458. (Peter Hanstein Verlag, Bonn. Price: DM. 64.50; paper DM. 58.80)

After an introductory chapter which surveys recent literary critical, form-critical and traditio-historical research into Deuteronomy 12–26, Merendino presents a detailed examination of each of the fifteen chapters in question and concludes with a summary of the pre-Deuteronomic traditions underlying these chapters and their Deuteronomic and post-Deuteronomic redaction. Two special sections in the work are devoted to the *to'ēbā* and *bi'artā* passages in Deuteronomy and the centralization passages. An extensive bibliography and complete indices are provided. This is a very important and major contribution to Deuteronomy research and is to be highly recommended.   E.W.N.

MEYER, F. B.: *David*. 1970. Pp. 175. *Christ in Isaiah*. 1970. Pp. 192. (Lakeland Series) (Oliphant, London. Price: 30p each)

These two re-issues were first published in 1895. They are of no scholarly value, and it is not easy to see that they have much worth today as devotional works.   ·   R.J.C.

NICHOLSON, E. W.: *Preaching to the Exiles*. 1970. Pp. vii, 154. (Basil Blackwell, Oxford. Price: £2·00)

The composition of the book of Jeremiah is a notorious problem, to the solution of which this consideration of its prose material is a major contribution. Nicholson's basic contention is that the prose, both the so-called 'biography' and the sermon-like passages, should be ascribed to Deuteronomistic circles, and understood, not as a merely literary process but as a theological application of Jeremiah's words to changing circumstances. Literary and theological considerations in support of this view are adduced, and a final chapter argues that the historical setting of this process was among the exiles in Babylon. At this point the argument is, perhaps necessarily, more speculative, and some doubts remain. But the greater part of the work is extremely convincing. Nicholson sets out his thesis with his customary clarity, and with careful consideration of other views.   R.J.C.

OVERHOLT, T. W.: *The Threat of Falsehood*. (Studies in Biblical Theology, Second Series, 16). 1970. Pp. ix, 110. (S.C.M. Press, London. Price £1·75)

This study in the theology of Jeremiah centres around the book's use of the term *sheqer*. It is seen in terms basically of the nation's false sense of security, of the falsehood of Jeremiah's prophetic opponents, and of the worship of false gods. The particular sections of the book examined in detail are the temple-sermon (c. 7), the conflict between Jeremiah and his opponents (cc. 27–9), and the section concerning the prophets in c. 23, where the widely-held 'moralising' view is rejected as a basis for their being condemned. Instead, this section, like the others, is basically concerned with false security. Brief attention is also given to the use of *sheqer* in other parts of the book, and to its usage elsewhere in the Old Testament. This is a useful contribution to an important theme in Jeremiah.　　　　　　　　　　　　　　R.J.C.

PERLITT, L.: *Bundestheologie im Alten Testament*. (Wissenschaftliche Monographien zum Alten und Neuen Testament, 36.) 1969. Pp. viii, 300. (Neukirchener Verlag. Price: DM. 44; paper DM. 42)

Perlitt challenges the now widely held view that Israel's faith from the beginning centred on a covenant with Yahweh. It is argued that the Old Testament covenant theology was a late development in Israel at the hands of the Deuteronomic authors in the 7th and 6th centuries B.C. as an attempt to meet the crises brought about by the destruction of the two Israelite kingdoms. It was in this period that the theologumena of the covenant with the fathers, the covenant at Horeb, and the Davidic covenant originated. This in turn explains why the 8th-century prophets were silent about the covenant: the terminology of breach of covenant did not exist at that time. This is a stimulating work which will provoke widespread discussion on this central Old Testament problem.　　　　　　　　　　　　　　E.W.N.

REHM, M.: *Der königliche Messias im Licht der Immanuel-Weissagungen des Buches Jesaja* (Eichstätter Studien, N.F. 1) 1968. Pp. xii, 432. (Butzon & Bercker, Kevelaer Rheinland. Price: DM. 48)

We have in this clearly written and well-documented work an examination of the many O.T. passages which might conceivably have contributed to the development of the Messianic Hope in its association with the House of David. Careful attention is paid to important exegetical points and most theories of a political or mythological background, as these arise in each case. By a process of elimination the author recognizes: (*a*) a period of preparation discernible in Gen. 49, Num. 23–24, and 2 Sam. 7: 11–16; (*b*) a basically formative period represented by the Immanuel passages in Isa. 7: 14–16, 8: 5–10, 9: 1–6, 11: 1–9; (*c*) a period of development illustrated by Isa. 32: 15–20, Mic. 4: 14–5: 3, Jer. 23: 5 f., Zech. 3: 7–10, 6: 11–14 in association with Pss. 2 and 110, and, late in the post-exilic period, Zech. 9: 9 f. with its supposed influence upon Ps. 72. Some readers, like the reviewer, will conclude that in his attitude to the Psalter the author has his priorities wrong, and that the Immanuel passages (despite his emphasis upon divine revelation) are rooted in far too thin a soil to have blossomed in the way suggested; but on the whole the book may be warmly recommended as a valuable contribution to the subject.　　　　　　　　　　　　　　A.R.J.

SAEBØ, M.: *Sacharja 9–14. Untersuchungen von Text und Form.* (Wissenschaftliche Monographien zum Alten und Neuen Testament, 34). 1969. Pp. 366. (Neukirchener Verlag, Neukirchen-Vluyn. Price: DM. 41.80, paper DM. 39.80)

Professor Saebø is to be congratulated on a magnificent study of one of the most difficult sections of the O.T. Substantial as his work is, however, it remains for the present incomplete. A further volume will deal with content and background. The present work, as the subtitle shows, is strictly formal in its reference. It falls into two main parts. The first is concerned with the text. It surveys earlier work on the subject and then presents a detailed examination of each chapter in the attempt to determine the original form of the text in the light of the process by which the MT emerged. A strong case is made for the antiquity and general reliability of the MT. The second part is a form-critical analysis, again carried out in great detail. Any attempt at critical appraisal of Professor Saebø's work in a short notice is impossible. Suffice it to say that this volume is a substantial and distinguished contribution to the subject. The promised sequel will be eagerly awaited.   G.W.A.

SCHMITT, GÖTZ: *Du sollst keinen Frieden schliessen mit den Bewohnern des Landes* (Beiträge zur Wissenschaft vom Alten und Neuen Testament, 91). 1970. Pp. 174. (W. Kohlhammer, Stuttgart. Price: DM. 32)

Schmitt sets out to examine those passages (Ex. 23:32–3; 34:12; Jos. 9:1ff. etc.) which prohibit Israel from making any covenant with the Canaanite inhabitants of the land promised to their ancestors. After a careful analysis and comparison of the relevant texts he concludes that the prohibition was originally concerned with the question of possession of the land, and was intended to preclude any limitation of Israel's enjoyment of the land which had been divinely promised to it. The belief in such a prohibition arose after the final settlement, but before the time of David, when it was already operative. Later, especially under the influence of the Deuteronomic movement, it was given a more directly religious explanation in terms of avoiding idolatry, and was combined with a (theoretical) demand for the complete destruction of the original Canaanite inhabitants. This was then linked more widely with a religious hostility towards foreigners which introduced restrictions on trading or intermarriage with them. The study is a useful one connecting with the major theme of Israel's attitude to foreigners, and it includes some useful suggestions, especially concerning the background and ideology of the Settlement narratives.   R.E.C.

SHEED, F. J.: *Genesis Regained.* 1970. Pp. 182. (Sheed and Ward, London and Sydney. Price: £1·65)

The core of this study of Gen. 1–11 is an analysis of Gen. 1–3 against the background of Ancient Near Eastern mythology and in the light of Roman Catholic teaching on creation and original sin. Although stimulating and felicitously expressed, the theological conclusions seem often to move beyond the limits of the text. Does Gen. 2:24, for example, state 'the primacy of divorceless monogamy'? (p. 102). The transliteration of Hebrew words occasionally nods, e.g. p. 47.   R.D.

STADELMANN, L. I. J.: *The Hebrew Conception of the World*. (Analecta Biblica, 39.) 1970. pp. 207. (Biblical Institute Press, Rome. Price: Lire 3,000: $5.00)

Biblical scholars will be grateful to the author of this discussion on the Hebrew conception of the world, for seldom does one find a whole volume devoted to this subject. It contains a full treatment of the Hebrew terms for the world and its various parts. Included in this is the study of the heaven and heavenly bodies, viz. sun, moon, planets and stars, as well as the earth, sea, streams, springs, and the under-world. In addition to the examination of biblical texts, full use is made of relevant material from the literature of the Near East, as well as an etymological study of the terms discussed. A small number of misprints have slipped into the text, yet readers will find this a valuable and stimulating contribution.   E.R.R.

THOMPSON, R. J.: *Moses and the Law in a Century of Criticism Since Graf*. (Supplements to Vetus Testamentum, Vol. XIX.) 1970. Pp. 208. (E. J. Brill, Leiden. Price: Fl. 54; for subscribers to V.T. Fl. 46)

Pentateuchal studies have come a long way since Graf and Well-hausen, and changes and trends of recent work have tempted some scholars to suggest that most of the earlier literary-critical work requires to be undone. This very thorough and well-documented bibliographical essay shows that this is not so, by surveying the rise, progress and triumph of the literary-critical approach to the Penta-teuch. Rightly it centres upon the emergence of the classical docu-mentary theories of literary-criticism, but it also goes on to show the way in which more recent methods of tradition-history, form-criti-cism and redaction-criticism have built upon the earlier work. Thompson concludes that a basic literary-criticism has been, and still is, indispensable to any real advance in Pentateuchal studies. The twenty-five page bibliography is itself of great usefulness, and the work as a whole, which sets out to be no more than a historical survey, is full of interest and insight. By tracing the mutual interaction of scholarship, Thompson shows the greatness and weakness of the work of individual scholars, and draws overall a picture of a real progress within scholarship, which has, contrary to much popular opinion, been of essential religious worth.   R.E.C.

TORREY, C. C.: *Ezra Studies. Prolegomenon* by W. F. Stinespring. (The Library of Biblical Studies, ed. H. M. Orlinsky.) 1970. Pp. xxxiv, 346. (Ktav Publishing House, New York. Price: $14.95)

This was the first of Torrey's major works, published in 1910. In the prolegomenon Stinespring summarizes the main views on the mission of Ezra held prior to Torrey's work, though little mention is made of other more recent contributions. Torrey's own *Composition and Historical Value of Ezra and Nehemiah* (1896) and relevant parts of his other writings are summarized. Stinespring's verdict on this work seems just: 'Though few agree with him, none dare ignore him.'

R.J.C.

TORREY, C. C. and SPIEGEL, S.: *Pseudo-Ezekiel and the Original Prophecy, and Critical Articles. Prolegomenon* by M. Greenberg. (The Library of Biblical Studies, ed. H. M. Orlinsky.) 1970. Pp. xxxix, 261. (Ktav Publishing House, New York. Price: $12.50)

The reissue of this work, first published in 1930, together with that of Torrey's *Ezra Studies* (see previous entry), will enable students to consider again the implications of his reconstruction of the later Old Testament period, which regarded the Exile largely as a fiction inspired by the anti-Samaritan propaganda of the Chronicler. Less than half of the volume here noticed is taken up by Torrey's original work; to it have been added two articles by S. Spiegel with a reply by Torrey, reprinted from *H.T.R.* 1931 and *J.B.L.* 1934–5, and a prolegomenon by M. Greenberg, which gives a brief resumé of Ezekiel criticism and shows that many of Torrey's insights retain their value even if his detailed reconstruction has proved unacceptable

R.J.C.

TUNYOGI, A. D.: *The Rebellions of Israel.* 1969. Pp. 158. (John Knox Press, Richmond, Virginia. Price: $4.95).

Professor Tunyogi discusses the theme of Israel's rebellions against Yahweh and the divine response to them. The discussion concentrates on the Tetrateuch but also briefly examines the theme in the rest of the Old Testament, and in the New Testament, the Apocrypha and the Dead Sea Scrolls. The methodological presuppositions of the work are, however, open to serious question, whilst the inclusion amongst Israel's rebellions of the refusal of Moses' mediation by an Israelite in Egypt struggling with his fellow and of Moses' objections to God at being sent to deliver Israel from Egypt is scarcely warranted.

E.W.N.

WEHMEIER, G.: *Der Segen im Alten Testament. Eine semasiologische Untersuchung der Wurzel brk.* (Theologische Dissertationen, Basel. Band VI. Ed. by B. Reicke.) 1970. Pp. 244. (Friedrich Reinhardt Kommissionsverlag, Basel. Price: Sw.Fr. 17.80)

This doctoral thesis is a careful study of the root *brk* in the Old Testament. It begins with a survey of the use of the root in the other north-west Semitic languages, tentatively suggesting that the sense of 'life-power, potency' underlies the range of usage. The occurrences of the words from the root in the O.T. are then systematically examined, with careful regard for the use and context; this section is classified under the noun and the verbal forms, with a short note on personal names. In the final section an attempt is made at tracing the history of the usage by considering the various main O.T. documents. The more static concept of blessing as life-power is shown to be modified in the O.T. in various ways, particularly in regard to the experience of divine action in the experience of the people. The O.T. background is utilized for some brief comments on N.T. developments. It is a careful and judicious study, showing good knowledge of the literature and representing a further development in particular of the work of C. Westermann.

P.R.A.

LAW, RELIGION, AND THEOLOGY

ALLEGRO, J. M.: *The Sacred Mushroom and the Cross*. 1970. Pp. xxii, 349. (Hodder and Stoughton, London. Price: £3·15)

Anyone who is prepared to believe that Zeus and Yahweh mean spermatozoa (p. 20), that Jesus (derived, of course, from Sumerian) means semen (p. 215), that Sabaoth is penis of the storm (p. 24), that, in fact, there are scarcely any words other than penis, semen, mushroom, and womb — anyone prepared to credit this and a good deal else will find this an absorbing and rewarding work of scholarship.

E.U.

P.S. Linguists have for some time been interested in sentences which are structurally entirely acceptable but fail to give semantic satisfaction. Hitherto they have had to be content with phrases such as 'colourful green ideas are sleeping furiously', but now Mr. Allegro (who wishes his book to be judged as a work of philology) has given them some splendid examples. Among these I would single out for special attention: 'U (meaning, of course, to copulate) is, perhaps, the most important phoneme in the whole of Near Eastern religion. So . . . our earliest records lead us back to a single idea, even a single letter, "U" ' (p. 20).

E.U.

BENTZEN, A.: *King and Messiah*. Edited by G. W. Anderson. 2nd Edition. Pp. 118. (Basil Blackwell, Oxford. Price: £1·50)

Professor Anderson has written a preface for this new edition of *King and Messiah* (see *B.L.*, 1949, pp. 37f; 1955, p. 46; *Eleven Years*, p. 679), and has made some modifications in the notes — largely by way of referring to English translations of foreign works, where these now exist. Otherwise no changes have been made.

M.A.K.

Bibelsyn och bibelbruk. 1970. Pp. 158. (Håkan Ohlssons Forlag, Lund. Price: Sw.Kr. 19)

This is the report of a commission appointed in 1964 by the Bishops of the Swedish Church to examine different approaches to the Bible and to consider the problems of its interpretation and authority. Among its members were Professor B. Albrektson of Åbo and Professor B. Gerhardsson of Lund. The report surveys the field with thoroughness and clarity in the light of the contemporary debate and with reference to the Swedish ecclesiastical and theological tradition. There are three main sections, dealing respectively with 1. different attitudes to the Bible and the reasons for them; 2. the critical approach to the Bible and the attitude of the Church; 3. the Bible as the Word of God. An excellent and compact survey.

G.W.A.

CHILDS, B. S.: *Biblical Theology in Crisis*. 1970. Pp. 255. (The Westminster Press, Philadelphia. Price $8.00)

This book will be found very useful by anyone wishing orientation in the development of biblical theology in the United States during the past twenty-five years and in the way in which it was related to what was happening on the continent of Europe and in Britain. In particular there is a valuable account of what the author calls the 'Biblical Theology Movement', an American phenomenon which represents an attempt to bridge the gulf separating Fundamentalists and Modernists. The chief emphasis was on history and on revelation through the acts of God in history. It was believed that archaeological research, in which America plays a notable part, made it possible to take a more positive view of Israel's history than was characteristic of scholars like von Rad and Noth, though von Rad's emphasis on *Heilsgeschichte* had an obvious influence on American developments which also owed much to the theological teaching of Brunner.

The second section of the book describes in useful detail the reaction which followed as a result of the views of men like Bultmann, Tillich, J. A. T. Robinson, Harvey Cox, the 'death of God' theologians and J. Barr (both in his opposition to the one-sided emphasis on 'revelation through history' and in his studies in biblical linguistics).

Childs's own positive proposal is that a biblical theology ought to be developed in the context of the canon, accepted as that was in faith by the Christian Church on the basis of its experience of its efficacy. A number of detailed examples of theological exposition in the context of the canon are given. There is just a suggestion of artificiality in the treatment.   N.W.P.

GASTER, T. H.: *Myth, Legend, and Custom in the Old Testament: A comparative study with chapters from Sir James G. Frazer's Folklore in the Old Testament.* 1969. Pp. lv, 899. (G. Duckworth, London. Price: £6·50)

Frazerian in concept, methodology and occasionally in style of writing, this volume comprehensively discusses mythical, legendary and ritualistic elements in the O.T. in the light of comparative material from a formidable array of different cultures. Originally commissioned to edit Frazer, the author has produced a separate work on the Frazerian pattern. As a cut and dried source-book it has considerable interest, but in its tendency to confuse description with interpretation and equate similarity and identity it perpetuates an inadequate methodology which should be discarded.   I.B.

*GRAY, J.: *Near Eastern Mythology: Mesopotamia, Canaan, Israel.* Pp. 141, plates in col. xxvi, B. and W. 105, map and chron. table. 1969. (Hamlyn, London. Price: £1·25)

This is primarily a beautiful picture book. In the letterpress the author's well-known interests and viewpoints are succinctly and dogmatically expressed, without what some scholars would regard as the desirable acknowledgement of other interpretations. Mesopotamia, Canaan and Israel (differently named on the jacket) are treated on similar lines: a general introduction to each, followed by sections entitled 'The Religion', 'The Myths', 'The King', for the first two; 'Myth and History', 'The Reign of God', 'The King and the Messiah', for Israel.

This is mainly a recreation volume rather than a work-book, though it has a general (but no scripture) index; on any view it is a remarkable bargain for today.   D.R.Ap-T.

LAURIN, R. B. (ed.): *Contemporary Old Testament Theologians*. 1970. Pp. 223. (Judson Press, Valley Forge. Price: $8.95)

This book contains essays by seven scholars in which the works of modern writers of theologies of the O.T. are described and critically discussed: N. K. Gottwald on W. Eichrodt, G. Henton Davies on G. von Rad, J. N. Schofield on O. Procksch, R. E. Clements on T. C. Vriezen, R. B. Laurin on E. Jacob, J. I. Durham on G. A. F. Knight, and D. A. Hubbard on P. van Imschoot. There are also an introduction by the editor, and indexes of subjects, authors, and biblical passages.

                                                                                                    J.A.E.

LIPINSKI, E.: *Essais sur la Revelation et la Bible* (Lectio Divina, 60.) 1970. Pp. 148. (Les éditions du Cerf, Paris. Price: Fr. 16.50)

This book of essays by a professor in the University of Louvain, while it handles such matters of interest to students of the Old Testament as the relation between revelation and history and between history and myth and the relation of the word of God to the Scriptures, does so in the framework of Roman Catholic theology. Among other essays there is an interesting one on the Promised Land as the heritage of Yahweh of which he gave the usufruct to Israel. It leads up to the thought of Christ as the inheritor of all things. The book concludes with a thoughtful and eloquent study of the theme of the Book of Job.

                                                                                                    N.W.P.

PAUL, S. M.: *Studies in the Book of the Covenant in the light of cuneiform and Biblical law* (Supplements to *Vetus Testamentum*, Vol. XVIII). 1970. Pp. 149. (E. J. Brill, Leiden. Price: Fl. 56; subscr. Fl. 48)

The author first analyzes the Mesopotamian concept of law and then argues that the judicial corpus of the various cuneiform legal codes was contained in a prologue-epilogue framework. He finds the same literary form in the final redaction of Exodus 19–24. But while the prologue-epilogue to the Code of Hammurabi stresses political and economic benefits, that to the Book of the Covenant has an explicitly religious concern. There follows a detailed examination of the legal corpus Ex. 21:2–22:16. Much reference is made to Mesopotamian law and other material. The Book of the Covenant itself is dated to the period immediately before and after the conquest, and is seen as the charter of the newly emerging nation. In two appendices the author deals with the arrangement of the laws in the Book of the Covenant and the formal division of law into casuistic and apodictic categories. Throughout the study cuneiform and biblical law are compared and contrasted.

                                                                                                    A.C.J.P.

RENDTORFF, R.: *God's History: A Way through the Old Testament*. Translated by G. C. Winsor. 1969. Pp. 77. (Westminster Press, Philadelphia. Price: $1.85)

By its translation from the German original of 1962, this short introduction to the O.T. (see *B.L.*, 1963, p. 37; *Decade*, p. 431), with its theological approach and its fresh treatment of the place of the O.T. in the life of the contemporary Church, is now made available to a wider public.

                                                                                                    E.T.R.

ROBERTSON SMITH, W.: *Lectures on the Religion of the Semites. The Fundamental Institutions.* 3rd edition, with an Introduction and Notes by Stanley A. Cook, originally published in 1927, reprinted with a *Prolegomenon* by James Muilenberg (*sic*) (Library of Biblical Studies, ed. by H. M. Orlinsky). 1969. Pp. 28, lxiv, 718. (Ktav Publishing House, New York. Price: $22.50)

We welcome the reissue of Robertson Smith's classic work in so handsome a form. At this time of day it needs no review; but it is good to have from the pen of Professor Muilenburg (whose name is, unfortunately, misspelt on both the cover and the title page) a biographical and bibliographical prolegomenon which puts Robertson Smith's lectures in the context of the history of scholarship.

G.W.A.

ROWLEY, H. H.: *The Faith of Israel.* 1970. (1956). Pp. 220. (S.C.M. Press, London. Price: £1·05)

This paperback reprint of a book already widely known (see *B.L.*, 1957, p. 54; 1962, p. 54; *Decade*, pp. 54, 364), is unaltered except for the appropriate addition of a brief appreciation of the author contributed by N. W. Porteous.

P.R.A.

SMEND, R.: *Die Mitte des Alten Testaments* (Theologische Studien, 101). 1970. Pp. 59. (EVZ-Verlag, Zurich. Price: Sw.Fr. 7.80)

Surveys of the religion and theology of the O.T. have often been dependent on the identification of a 'centre' of the Old Testament, and this short essay seeks to describe how this 'centre' has been described and identified. According to Smend (p. 7), there has been a continual loss of confidence in claims to identify such a centre. Historically, the author looks at the various trends within Old Testament theology which have led to the search for such a centre; and on the other hand he leads up to his own definition of such a centre (as lying in 'Yahweh the God of Israel, Israel the people of Yahweh', p. 54). The fine discrimination, and the deep insights into the history of Old Testament studies, which are known characteristics of the author, are again evident in this study.

J.B.

WHITLEY, C. F.: *The Genius of Ancient Israel. The Distinctive Nature of the Basic Concepts of Israel Studied Against the Cultures of the Ancient Near East.* 1969. Pp. x, 179. (Philo Press, Amsterdam. Price: Fl. 36; $10.00)

The author believes that the distinctive features of the Israelite faith have been insufficiently emphasized in recent comparative study, and seeks to redress the balance. An examination of the views expressed in the O.T. and by Israel's neighbours on such subjects as revelation, the interpretation of history, ethics, God and man leads to the conclusion that, while similarities must be acknowledged, Israel's contribution was in every case the most significant one. The immense scope of the subject has led to some somewhat misleading generalizations. The author is also guilty at some points of special pleading, as when he points to Babylon's fall as a proof of the inadequacy of Babylonian theology. There are a number of inconsistencies in the spelling of proper names and in the indexing.

R.N.W.

WRIGHT, G. E.: *The Old Testament and Theology*. 1969. Pp. 190. (Harper and Row, New York. Price: $6.00)

In this defence of the theological relevance of the Old Testament the author reasserts the views which he expressed many years ago in his *God Who Acts: Biblical Theology As Recital* (1952, see *B.L.*, 1953, p. 65, *Eleven Years*, p. 518), taking issue with his critics and at the same time grappling with the new problems posed by the changed theological climate. He believes that some modern theologians have so overstressed the centrality of Christology that they have lost hold of that apprehension of the 'independence of God' which is the main emphasis of the Old Testament; and this has occurred precisely at a time when this insight is particularly needed to help modern man out of his uncertainty about the very possibility of a meaningful belief in God. The problems of revelation and of the Canon are also discussed.

R.N.W.

THE LIFE AND THOUGHT OF THE SURROUNDING PEOPLES

*BARNETT, R. D.: *Assyrian Palace Reliefs*. 1970. Pp. 45, 20 plates, plus 2 cover plates. (British Museum, London. Price: 60p)

This is essentially a brief guide to the newly rearranged Assyrian sculpture galleries at the Museum. The text is close to that of the earlier *Assyrian Palace Reliefs; and their Influence on the Sculptures of Babylonia and Persia*. (Artia Press, Prague. 1959), not noted in the *Book List*. Two diagrams and a map add to its usefulness. There is a short list of the sculptures in the galleries, and the plates (from photographs by W. Forman) have all been newly made for the volume. This is a pleasing and well-produced handbook whose usefulness extends beyond its value for those who visit the Museum. P.R.A.

BOWMAN, R. A.: *Aramaic Ritual Texts from Persepolis*. (The University of Chicago Oriental Institute Publications, Vol. XCI.) 1970. Pp. 194. 36 plates. (The University of Chicago Press, Chicago)

Over 200 mortars and pestles inscribed in Aramaic with brief formulaic texts of a ritual nature, and dating from the 5th century B.C., were found during the Chicago excavations at Persepolis of 1936–8. The texts, which constitute a valuable addition to the small corpus of Imperial Aramaic, are evidently concerned with some proto-Mithraic haoma ceremony. The book has an extensive introduction and excellent plates.

S.P.B.

BROWN, J. P.: *The Lebanon and Phoenicia: Ancient Texts Illustrating their Physical Geography and Native Industries*. Vol. I. *The Physical Setting and the Forest*. 1969. Pp. xxxix, 220. (The American University of Beirut, Beirut)

This original book provides translations, introductory notes and brief comments for ancient texts derived from both Classical and Near Eastern sources that deal with the physical geography of the area roughly covered by ancient Phoenicia. A number of biblical passages are included, but the chief interest of the book to scholars in the O.T. field will lie, not so much in the mere presence of these, as in their illuminating juxtaposition with non-biblical material. S.P.B.

DIETRICH, M.: *Die Aramäer Südbabyloniens in der Sargonidenzeit.* (Alter Orient und Altes Testament, 7). 1970. Pp. xi, 232. (Butzon und Bercker, Kevelaer, Neukirchen-Vluyn. Price: DM. 58)

The Arameans who invaded Mesopotamia between 1100 and 900 B.C. settled in large numbers in the South, near the Persian Gulf. After the passage of time these tribes became a major political force, and the Merodachbaladan who had dealings with Hezekiah was one of their best leaders. This volume is a painstaking and competent history of these tribes from 700–648, based largely on a fresh study of the royal correspondence of the period, relevant excerpts from which form 'Band 2' (actually the second half of the volume). This is a minute study and presentation of sources rather than a narrative history.

W.G.L.

DUVAL, R.: *La Littérature syriaque.* 1970. Pp. xviii, 430, one map. (Philo Press, Amsterdam. Price: Fl. 48.00)

This is a reprint of the third edition, Paris 1907. It follows reprints by the same publishers of W. Wright's *Short History of Syriac Literature* (1948, 1966) and of Duval's *Traité de grammaire syriaque* (1881, 1969) and his edition of Bar Bahlul's *Lexicon syriacum* (1886–1903, 1970). For the information available, Duval's small history is long superseded by Baumstark (1922) and Ortiz de Urbina (ed. 2, 1965); he antedates all work since Burkitt on the Syriac biblical textual traditions, and the enormous progress in critical editions of Syriac writers, especially in *Patrologia Syriaca* and C.S.C.O. There remains a need for a readable history of the literature, such as Duval provided for his day. He remains reliable, however, on important areas which have been less intensively studied, such as the transmission of Greek learning.

R.P.R.M.

ELLERMEIER, F.: *Prophetie in Mari und Israel* (Theologische und Orientalische Arbeiten, 1). 1968. Pp. 248. (Verlag Erwin Jungfer, Herzberg am Harz.)

This is the most comprehensive study of the prophetic texts from Mari and of their relevance for the Old Testament which has yet appeared. All the relevant Mari texts, 22 in number, are first reproduced in transliteration with translation and philological notes. They are then scrutinized with regard to both form and content in an attempt to form a comprehensive picture of prophecy in Mari, and in a final chapter these findings are then compared with the Old Testament texts. The reader is thus provided with the fullest opportunity to form his own judgement. The similarities between the two prophetic movements emerge with great clarity, although the author seems at times to overstate his case. One of the most interesting features of the book is its insistence that the conclusions of some of the form critics, especially Westermann, may need to be revised in the light of the new evidence. R.N.W.

GARELLI, P.: *Le Proche-Orient asiatique; des origines aux invasions des peuples de la mer.* (Nouvelle Clio: L'Histoire et ses problèmes, 2.) 1969. Pp. 377. (Presses Universitaires de France, Paris. Price: Fr. 24)

The author of this work teaches ancient history at one of the new universities growing out of the Sorbonne, and the book was conceived as a textbook. But it is of a higher calibre than that description might be taken to imply. It covers the history — political, social, ideological, cultural and economic — of Mesopotamia, Syria, Palestine and Anatolia from the earliest times to about 1100 B.C. The material is presented very concisely so that it lacks the charm that may come from a more narrative style, but it informs the reader rapidly. There is a large bibliography of books and articles to which reference is frequently made in the text, and detailed charts of rulers and dynasties are given. The outstanding character of this work is its comprehensive coverage. Every aspect has attention, and 120 pages are devoted to brief essays on topics for which there are only tentative or partial results. These cover a wide range: Sumerian theology, the standard of living, chronology, etc. This is an up-to-date and authoritative work well suited to the Old Testament scholar. A further volume bringing the work up to the middle of the First Millennium B.C. is in preparation.
                                                                              W.G.L.

GOITEIN, S. D. F.: *Jemenica. Sprichwörter und Redensarten aus Zentral-Jemen.* (Leipzig 1934) 1970 reprint. Pp. xxiii, 194. (E. J. Brill, Leiden. Price: Fl. 28)

This well-known early work by Professor Goitein had long been unobtainable, and this is one of the relatively few cases where a photomechanic reprint is not only justified but highly welcome. After a brief introduction dealing with the most basic linguistic elements, this book collects more than 1,400 proverbs and sayings which Professor Goitein took down from Yemenite Jews then recently settled in Palestine. They deal with a great variety of subjects (properly recorded in the helpful index) and are of indirect use to the biblical scholar in so far as they reflect a way of life and a mode of thinking that are richly archaic and imbued with a biblical atmosphere and flavour.
                                                                              E.U.

JAMES, E. O.: *Creation and Cosmology. A historical and comparative inquiry.* (Studies in the History of Religions; Supplements to *Numen.* XVI.) 1969. Pp. xii, 148. (Brill, Leiden. Price: Fl. 38)

Intended as an extension to the discussion of the theme of 'Urzeit' and 'Endzeit' at the Tenth International Congress for the History of Religions in the University of Marburg in 1960, this volume ranges from ancient mythological to modern philosophical and scientific thinking and summarizes the contents of a number of different religious systems. Two main criticisms may be offered. First, compression has resulted in some dubious assertions. The *Enuma elish* cannot be regarded as a coherent account (p. 24), for it is composite and contains blatant contradictions. Tiamat is both a fluid and a solid. Again, the traditional view (p. 42) that Krishna is the 'descent' of the high-god Vishnu in the *Bhagavad Gita* is now being seriously questioned. In the *Gita* as a whole Krishna is more the manifestation of the impersonal Brahman. Secondly, the author's understanding of the relationship between myth and science is unclear. He rejects the view that myth is a pseudo-science, but still holds that it is related to the control of natural forces. The latter view seems to contradict the former. No mention is made of the new interpretation of Lévi-Strauss that myth is a kind of logical model designed to overcome or blur binary oppositions.

I.B.

LAYARD, H. A.: *Nineveh and its Remains*, ed. with Introduction and Notes by SAGGS, H. W. F. (Travellers and Explorers.) Pp. xiv, 299, Pls. IV, Figs. 15, Maps and plans 7. 1970. (Routledge and Kegan Paul, London. Price: £2·75)

For an account of recent archaeological investigation of Nimrud, which Layard mistakenly thought was Nineveh, we have M. Mallowan: *Nimrud and its Remains* (see *B.L.*, 1967, p. 44). A reissue of Layard's classic after well over a century is in no way superfluous, however. It is a historic document in its own right, with an added period charm. So it is regrettable that, in making this short version, the chapter summaries which are a feature of Layard's own abridgement had to be omitted. As recompense, the editor adds a memoir of the author drawn from original sources, and helps to bridge the inevitable gap between his day and ours by means of light annotation. He also includes Layard's visit to the Chaldean Christians which was previously omitted. This was editorial work worth doing, though an unresolved incongruity is the alternation of Austen Henry (literarily best attested) with Henry Austen (*a priori* more natural) as the hero's forenames.

D.R.Ap-T.

MALAMAT, A.: *Sources for Early Biblical History; The Second Millennium B.C.* 1970. Pp. xi, 217. (Academon, Jerusalem)

This chrestomathy, compiled for the Bible History course of the Hebrew University, will be of use to those able to read transliterations and translations of Egyptian, Hittite, and Akkadian texts in Hebrew.

D.J.W.

MCNEIL, W. H. and SEDLAR, J. W.: *The Ancient Near East* (Readings in World History, 2). 1968. Pp. viii, 261. (Oxford University Press, London. Price: 55p)

This selection of translations from Egyptian, Hittite, Hebrew, Assyrian and Persian sources aims to illustrate the development of empires (parts of 1–2 Sam.; 1–2 Kings; Isa. 36–37 and I Esd. for O.T.), laws (arranged under arbitrary rubrics e.g., origins, slavery) and monotheism (Atonism in Egypt, Yahwism in Palestine and Zoroastrianism in Persia). Despite the use of KJV for O.T. it provides some useful initial reading material for introductory classes in ancient history and comparative religion.

D.J.W.

Du Mesnil Du Buisson, R.: *Études sur les Dieux phéniciens hérités par l'Empire romain*. (Études préliminaires aux Religions Orientales dans l'Empire romain, edited by M. J. Vermasseren, xiv.) 1970. Pp. xx, 149. (E. J. Brill, Leiden. Price: Fl. 50)

The present volume contains 4 chapters dealing with (1) the astral deities of the tablets from Ugarit, (2) outlines of Phoenician mythology which Philo Byblius has preserved, (3) the Byblian Pantheon, and (4) Asiatic gods who have made their way into Persian Egypt. At the end is an appendix containing two notes on gryphons and celestial serpents, an alphabetical list of contents and of plates. The numerous line drawings of ancient deities and the scenes in which they are depicted are excellent, as also are the photographic plates at the end of the book. The exploration of the various problems raised by these strange deities and their worship is exhaustive and the references to relevant literature are adequate; but the author's imagination seems here and there to run away with him. The points of most interest to O.T. scholars will be the new explanation which he offers of Psalm 68:7, which will rouse discussion even if it is not finally accepted (pp. 7–21), and of *'ēl bêt'ēl* (Gen. 35:7) to which a number of parallel divine figures or emblems are adduced (pp. 121–7).   G.R.D.

Montgomery, J. A.: *Arabia and the Bible*. Prolegomenon by Gus W. van Beek. 1934; reprint 1969. Pp. xxxi, 207. (Ktav Publishing House, New York. Price: $12.50)

J. A. Montgomery's lectures on Arabia and the Bible were a fine achievement when first they appeared in print and, despite many advances in the relevant areas of scholarship, they have essentially maintained this favourable estimate as being the best introduction to the relationship between Arabia and the world of the Bible. It is quite another question whether they should have been reprinted and whether their distinguished author would have approved of such a course. Dr. van Beek's excellent prolegomenon deals with some new developments and fresh recognitions, and, despite a pronounced transatlantic bibliographical bias, his observations go some way towards bridging the gap of forty years since Montgomery's Haskell Lectures were delivered in 1930.   E.U.

Parpola, S.: *Neo-Assyrian Toponyms*. (Alter Orient und Altes Testament, 6.) 1970. Pp. xxix, 408. (Butzon und Bercker, Kevelaer, Neukirchen-Vluyn. Price: DM. 72)

This is an exhaustive alphabetical list of place- and other geographic names from Late Assyrian texts (*c.* 950–600 B.C.), with full list of passages for each, but without discussion of location. There is a map on which certainly identified places are marked, but this is the only help for the O.T. scholar. Use of the list usually requires some Assyriological training. The material was arranged and printed by computer.   W.G.L.

Segal, J. B.: *Edessa. 'The Blessed City'*. 1970. Pp. xiv, 308, 44 plates. (Clarendon Press, Oxford University Press. Price: £5·00)

Professor Segal gives an excellent survey of the history of Edessa (modern Urfa), richly illustrated from contemporary sources and covering the period down to 1146. Of special interest to users of the *Book List* will be the sections on the Jewish community (pp. 41–3, 100–4); there is only a short discussion of the Peshiṭta Old Testament.

S.P.B.

VON SODEN, W. (ed.): *Reallexikon der Assyriologie und vorderasiatischen Archäologie* III. Lieferung 4: Geschwulst-Gewand. 1966. Pp. 83. 5: Gewand-Girsu. 1968. Pp. 79. 6: Girsu-Götterreisen. 1969. Pp. 79. 7: Götterreisen-Gott. 1969 Pp. 79. 8: Gott-Grenze. 1971. Pp. 79. (Walter de Gruyter, Berlin.)

This major reference work, begun by E. Ebeling, B. Meissner and E. Weidner, is now continued by a new Editorial Board responsible for Sumerian (D. O. Edzard), Akkadian (W. von Soden, W. Röllig), Hittitology (H. Otten), History (D. J. Wiseman) and Archaeology (A. Moorgat, P. Calmeyer). The coverage is complete for Mesopotamian, Hittite, Syrian and Elamite sources. Palestine items are included only where these occur in cuneiform sources. Nevertheless, the articles by specialists are important for O.T. students. The survey and bibliography on Laws (Gesetze), Gilgamesh, god-Lists, god, letter to deities (Gottesbrief), and grave (Grab) are noteworthy. D.J.W.

QUMRAN STUDIES

SEGERT, S.: *Synové světla a synové tmy. Svědectví nejstarších biblických rukopisů.* (The Sons of Light and the Sons of Darkness. The Testimony of the Oldest Biblical Manuscripts.) 1970. Pp. 226, 24 plates. (Orbis, Prague. Price: Kčs. 30)

Except for foreign literature which is difficult to obtain and a few articles in journals, the Czech reader has until now been able to learn about the Qumran discoveries only from the volume by M. Bič, *Poklad v Judské poušti* (*B.L.*, 1961, p. 61; *Decade*, p. 299). Slovak readers have had a translation of the Russian work of I. D. Amusin, *Rukopisy Mrtvého mora* (*B.L.*, 1963, p. 60; *Decade*, p. 454). The more recent results of study have remained virtually unknown. The well-known Prague semitist, S. Segert, has now filled this gap. His book, with a title reminiscent of the famous Qumran War Scroll, provides a comprehensive and thorough survey of the current position of Qumran research. He deals with the external circumstances which led to the discovery of the manuscripts, and then offers a historical survey. The biblical texts in particular are handled in detail, with references to questions of the canon, to apocryphal writings, and to writings which further elaborate biblical texts (Targums, Midrashim, etc.). The reader is given a survey of all the significant kinds of writings which have been found in the Qumran caves. The last two chapters deal with the history of the Essenes and their influence, and in particular that upon Christianity. Segert here takes up a theme of one of his own earlier studies (1955) to point to the similarity between Essenism and the Waldensians and the old Unitas fratrum in Bohemia. The volume clearly provides the most complete and comprehensive information on Qumran in Czechoslovak literature.

M.B.

WILSON, E.: *The Dead Sea Scrolls, 1947–1969*. 1969. Pp. viii, 320. (Oxford University Press, New York. Price: £2·80)

This work, based on articles which originally appeared in the *New Yorker*, is an attempt by a non-Semitist to give the general reader an account of the Scrolls. The first part of the book consists of a slightly revised reprint of the author's *The Scrolls from the Dead Sea* (1955; cf. *B.L.*, 1956, p. 67; *Eleven Years*, p. 774). The second part aims to bring the story up to date; it describes the new documents that have been made available since 1955, and discusses recent developments in the study of the Scrolls. But the comments made in the review of the author's earlier book are still apposite. While the volume gives a vivid description of some of the personalities who are concerned with the Scrolls, it fails to give a balanced account of the scholarly work that has actually been carried out.

M.A.K.

APOCRYPHA AND POST-BIBLICAL STUDIES

BARON, S. W.: *A Social and Religious History of the Jews. Late Middle Ages and Era of European Expansion* (1200–1650). Vol. XIII, 2nd Edition. 1969. Pp. vi, 463. Vol. XIV. 2nd Edition. 1969. Pp. 412. (Columbia University Press, New York and London. Price: $10.00 per vol.)

Vol. XIII deals with the Iberian Inquisition; Marrano dispersion; Humanism and Renaissance; Protestant Reformation. Vol. XIV deals with Catholic reform: Italian conformity; Imperial (Habsburg) turmoil; Thirty Years' War. In all the above subjects discussed the impact of the environment on Jewish beliefs and modes of life is commendably brought out.
For reviews of preceding volumes in the *B.L.* see 1968, p. 60f.

M.W.

BECKER, J.: *Untersuchungen zur Entstehungsgeschichte der Testamente der zwölf Patriarchen*. (Arbeiten zur Geschichte des antiken Judentums und des Urchristentums, VIII). 1970. Pp. viii, 420. (E. J. Brill, Leiden. Price: Fl. 80)

The purpose of this book is to examine afresh the much debated problem of the origin of the Testaments of the Twelve Patriarchs. After considering in two preliminary chapters the text of the Testaments and the Semitic traditions parallel to T. Levi, T. Naphtali and T. Judah, Becker devotes the central and largest part of this book to a detailed examination of the composition and structure of the various sections of the work (the framework; the S.E.R. and L.J. passages; the individual testaments). In a short concluding chapter he discusses the date and the theology of the Testaments, and of the various additions made to them. The author's main conclusions are as follows: (1) The Testaments are in origin Jewish; more precisely, the original Testaments were composed in a Hellenistic-Jewish milieu (possibly Egypt) in the first three decades of the second century B.C., one of their main themes being an exhortation to practice brotherly love. (2) The original Testaments were considerably expanded by the addition of many Jewish passages which also derive from a Hellenistic-Jewish milieu; amongst these additions are to be placed many of the

parenetic passages (which have the form of a Hellenistic-Jewish synagogue homily) and many of the apocalyptic passages. (3) Finally, beginning in the second century A.D., a limited number of Christian additions (which can be identified) were made to the Testaments. In the course of his argument the author pays careful and detailed attention to literary-critical and traditio-historical questions, and for this reason, apart from any other, this book is fundamentally important. As can be seen, this book represents a radical criticism of the views of de Jonge, and a return to the kind of position maintained by Schnapp, Bousset and Charles. Whether Becker's views come to be accepted or not, any future alternative explanation of the origin of the Testaments will have to be based on as detailed a treatment of the evidence as Becker here offers.
M.A.K.

BOGAERT, P.: *Apocalypse de Baruch. Introduction, traduction du syriaque et commentaire.* (Sources chrétiennes, 144–5). 1969. Pp. 528, 283. (Les Éditions du Cerf, Paris. Price: Fr. 110)

Contrary to the normal practice of this series there is a long and important introduction (I, pp. 33–459) and an extended commentary (II, pp. 7–164). The French translation completes Vol. I, while in Vol. II the commentary is followed by a full bibliography and indices. This is a work of basic importance for the study of this apocalypse.
S.P.B.

BOWKER, J.: *The Targums and Rabbinic Literature. An Introduction to Jewish Interpretations of Scripture.* 1969. Pp. xxi, 379. (Cambridge University Press. Price: £3·75)

This very useful volume contains about 90 pages of general introduction to the targumic literature, with a convenient listing of the main writings to which reference is made. The main part of the book contains a translation of Pseudo-Jonathan on selected chapters of Genesis, indicating correspondence to and deviation from the Hebrew. Each chapter so translated is followed by selections from other Targums on the same passage, and by notes giving cross-reference to rabbinic writings and other sources which may usefully be compared. Appendices cover various points of detail, and there is an extensive bibliography and indexes. The value of the book is apparent in its opening up of this very complex but important literature in a way which makes it available to the student of Old and New Testaments, and indeed to anyone interested in the nature and history of interpretation.
P.R.A.

BRAUDE, W. G.: *Pesikta Rabbati, Discourses for Feasts, Fasts, and Special Sabbaths.* Translated from the Hebrew. (Yale Judaica Series, XVIII, 1 and 2). Two volumes, 1968. Pp. xi and vii, 995. (Yale University Press, New Haven and London. Price: $25.00; £11·25)

The present work is the first complete translation of the *Pesiqta rabbati* into any modern language. The author mentions (p. 27 note 40) that only two chapters (*Pisqa* 20 and 26) have so far been translated which is incorrect. Substantial parts were given in German by

Aug. Wünsche (from chapters 20–31, 34–7, and 39–41, also shorter
extracts from chapters 5, 8, and 10), unfortunately in a place where
one does not expect them (in an appendix to his *Midrasch Debarim
Rabba*, 1882, pp. 138–84). We also find hundreds of important
passages in German translation in the great commentary on the N.T.
by Strack-Billerbeck (see index volume pp. 83a–84b). Rabbi Braude
follows largely M. Friedmann's edition of the text with notes (Wien
1880), which is still the most commonly available text on which both
Wünsche and Billerbeck based their translations, but he also uses the
editio princeps (Prague, 1654) and subsequent editions with their
annotations and commentaries as well as the two MS codices Parma
1240 (13th century) and Casanata 3324 (17th century) which, however,
do not contain the whole of the *Pesiqta*. 'Hence the present translation
is based on an eclectic text' (p. 27). The *Pesiqta rabbati*, like the older
Pesiqta (de Rab Kahana, German translation by A. Wünsche 1885)
with which it has some chapters in common, consists of homilies or
discourses, called *Pisqas* or sections, for the feasts, fasts, and special
sabbaths (listed on pp. 909f). A special group of *Pisqas* (nos. 20–4)
deal with the Ten Commandments (also among the excerpts of
Wünsche). The authors of the discourses are Palestinian Amoraim
(3rd and 4th centuries) who occasionally quote Tannaitic authorities.
It was generally accepted (Zunz, Friedman a.o.) that the *Pesiqta r.*
was composed not before the year 850, but more modern scholars,
including the author of our translation, prefer the 7th or even the 6th
century as the date for its redaction. The midrash is not a 'halakhic'
midrash like the oldest midrashim (*Mekhilta, Sifra, Sifre*), but uses
the haggadic method for the interpretation of the Law and makes
ample use of parables and stories. The present translation has
substantial indices, among them a very useful subject index of 45
pages.   H.K.

DENIS, A.-M.: *Introduction aux Pseudépigraphes Grecs d'Ancien Testament*.
(Studia in Veteris Testamenti Pseudepigrapha, ed. A.-M. Denis and
M. de Jonge, Vol. I). 1970. Pp. xxviii, 344. (E. J. Brill, Leiden. Price:
Fl. 85)

This work is intended primarily as an introduction to the Greek texts
of the O.T. pseudepigrapha, and the emphasis throughout is on
textual issues. After setting out his aims in a short preface, the author
examines each of the pseudepigrapha in turn, first those of which we
possess either entire, or fairly complete, Greek texts, then those of
which in Greek we possess only fragments. The author gives a short
description of each pseudepigraph, and then discusses in detail the
Greek evidence and the evidence of such other versions as exist. He
devotes proportionately less space to questions of date, authorship
and composition, and one might wish that it had been possible to
deal with these aspects of Introduction in more detail. The volume
contains a mine of information, and is likely to remain for a long time
an extremely valuable work of reference.
This new series, *Studia in Veteris Testamenti Pseudepigrapha*, is
intended to complement the editions of the Greek texts of the
pseudepigrapha that are currently being published in the series
Pseudepigrapha Veteris Testamenti graece (also edited by Denis and
de Jonge). In addition to the work here noticed a concordance is
already projected; it is to be hoped that its appearance will not be too
long delayed.   M.A.K.

FELDMAN, L. A.: *R. Abraham b. Isaac ha-Levi TaMaKH, Commentary on The Song of Songs*. Based on MSS and Early Printings with an Introduction, Notes, Variants and Comments. (Studia Semitica Neerlandica, No. 9). 1970. Pp. XII, 253. (Van Gorcum, Assen. Price: Fl. 42.50)

The allegorical interpretation of the Song of Songs in which Israel is the beloved bride and God the loving bridegroom is certainly older than Rabbi Aqiba (d. 135) who was the first to voice this opinion emphatically (cf. Mekh. on Ex. 15:2; ed. Lauterbach II, pp. 26f.). 'All the ages of the world are not worth as much as the day on which the Song of Songs was given to Israel; all the *ketubim* are holy, but the Song of Songs is the most holy' (Mishna Yad. 3, 5). Aqiba even anathematized those who sang parts of the Song as erotic ditties at their banquets: 'they will have no share in the world to come' (Tos. Sanh. 12, 10). The number of references to the allegorical explanation of the Song of Songs is quite considerable from R. Aqiba right down to the comments of the Mediaeval rabbis. The author of the present Commentary who lived in the 14th century makes extensive use of all the preceding literature without, however, always indicating his source. His work has, in turn, been used by later Jewish commentators. He proceeds systematically from verse to verse and gives first the direct explanation of the love songs and afterwords the *nistar*, the hidden meaning or, as the editor calls it, 'the occult interpretation', and constantly applies the details of the text to Israel and its history. The edition of the text is exemplary in every respect; the English rendering is pleasing, though now and then unnecessarily paraphrastic.   H.K.

Sifre on Deuteronomy. Published originally by the Gesellschaft zur Förderung der Wissenschaft des Judentums and now re-published by The Jewish Theological Seminary of America (a reprint of Siphre ad Deuteronomium . . . edidit Dr. Louis Finkelstein. Berolini MCMXXXIX). 5729 (1969). Pp. 431. (Ktav Publishing House, New York. Price: $15.00)

The standard text of *Sifre* on Numbers and Deuteronomy for over a hundred years has been that of M. Friedmann, published in 1864 (Vienna). Together with the *Mekhilta* on Exodus and *Sifra* on Leviticus the midrash belongs to the oldest midrashim that have come down to us; they are particularly valuable for the study of the earliest rabbinic teaching and therefore also for the study of the Jewish background of the N.T. A new edition of *Sifre* on Numbers appeared in 1917 (Leipsic), edited by H. S. Horowitz. It was his intention to publish also the remaining Tannaitic midrashim, but he died in 1921. The papers he had left in preparation of a new edition of *Sifre* on Deuteronomy were handed over to Professor L. Finkelstein who revised text and notes. He published his work in October 1939 in Berlin, a month after the outbreak of the Second World War. The book shared the fate of other Jewish publications under the Nazi regime and only a few copies survived. The present edition is a photographic reprint of that of 1939 (printed and bound in Japan). In a new preface Professor Finkelstein explains why he was unable, much to our regret, to incorporate in the new edition the manuscript fragments of the text which have turned up in the past thirty years, but he draws our attention to some articles and books which have appeared in the meantime and are relevant to the midrash.   H.K.

GEIGER, A.: *Judaism and Islam. Prolegomenon* by M. Pearlman. (Library of Jewish Classics, ed. by D. Cohen). 1970. Pp. xxxii, 170. (Ktav Publishing House, New York. Price: $12.50)

Professor M. Pearlman's *Prolegomenon* briefly surveys research following Geiger's epoch-making prize-essay published as *Was hat Mohammed aus dem Judenthume aufgenommen* in 1833 and translated by F. M. Young at the suggestion of Christian missionaries working among Muslims in India in 1896 and published in 1898 under the misleading title *Judaism and Islam* since Geiger confines himself to the Jewish elements in the Qur'an. The reprint is to be welcomed because Geiger's pioneering effort has proved of enduring value and importance both in approach and execution for the understanding of Muḥammad and the Qur'an, and this whether one agrees with his attribution to Judaism of ideas and stories in the Qur'an or assumes Christian transmission. Pearlman rightly singles out S. D. Goitein's researches among others because they largely confirm Geiger's findings on the basis of a considerable amount of source material not yet accessible to Geiger at the time. E.I.J.R.

HARNISCH, W.: *Verhängnis und Verheissung der Geschichte. Untersuchungen zum Zeit- und Geschichtsverständnis im 4. Buch Esra und in der syr. Baruchapokalypse.* (Forschungen zur Religion und Literatur des Alten und Neuen Testamentes, 97.) 1969. Pp. 362. (Vandenhoeck & Ruprecht, Göttingen. Price: DM. 48)

This Marburg dissertation is essentially a systematic exposition of the main theological ideas to be found in IV Ezra and II Baruch. The author rightly maintains that in discussing apocalyptic it is important to take account of the differences between the various apocalyptic writings, and so confines his attention to these two closely related works. He argues that the dialogue form of IV Ezra has a real purpose, and that the words of Ezra give expression to a profound scepticism about the trustworthiness of God's promises to Israel which the author of IV Ezra, whose own views are to be found only in the speeches of the interpreting angel, was concerned to combat. The scepticism about God's promises reflected in the words of Ezra seems to have derived in part from Israel's situation after A.D. 70, and in part from a belief that man is inevitably subject to sin, and therefore incapable of inheriting the promise contained in the law. The author of IV Ezra seeks to meet this scepticism with a dualistic and deterministic view of history. God's promises will be redeemed in the world that is to come; man was not made inevitably subject to sin as a result of Adam's sin, and is capable in this world of fulfilling the requirements of the law — the precondition of the attainment of life in the future world. The author of IV Ezra seems also to have been concerned to neutralize a belief in an imminent end; the end is inevitably coming, but not until the moment determined by God — and man cannot calculate when this will be. The argument and purpose of II Baruch is basically the same as that of IV Ezra. Although this book is at times unnecessarily repetitive, it contains a careful, and in general convincing, exegesis of the two texts. M.A.K.

HAMMERSHAIMB, E., MUNCK, J., NOACK, B. and SEIDELIN, P. (ed.): *De gammeltestamentlige Pseudepigrafer i oversaettelse med indledning og noter.* 5. haefte, 1970. Pp. 509–623 (Gad, Copenhagen; Cammermeyer, Oslo; Gleerup, Lund. Price: D.Kr. 30)

This fascicle contains The Books of Adam (E. Hammershaimb), The Psalms of Solomon (S. Holm-Nielsen) and The Third Book of the Maccabees (N. Hyldahl). The two first fascicles, 1953 and 1956 (4 Ezra, 1 Enoch) were mentioned in *B.L.*, 1957, p. 71 (*Decade*, p. 71), the third fascicle, 1958 (Jubilees, Martyrdom of Isaiah) in *B.L.*, 1959, p. 42 (*Decade*, p. 178), and the fourth fascicle 1963 (Assumption of Moses, 1 (3) Esdras, Letter of Aristeas, Sibylline Oracles), in *B.L.*, 1964, p. 76 (*Decade*, p. 544). A sixth and concluding fascicle (Fourth Book of the Maccabees, Testaments of the XII Patriarchs, Slavonic Enoch, Syriac, Greek Apocalypses of Baruch besides indices) is planned to be issued not later than the beginning of 1972.   E.H.

LAPERROUSAZ, E.-M.: *Le Testament de Moïse* (*généralement appelé 'Assomption de Moïse'*). *Traduction avec introduction et notes.* (Semitica, Vol. XIX.) 1970. Pp. xi, 140. (Adrien-Maisonneuve, Paris)

The acephalous Latin text edited by Ceriani under the title 'Assumption of Moses' has long been recognized as properly belonging to the 'Testament' literature, and the work is here given its more fitting title. The second of the four valuable and important introductory chapters discusses the true relationship of this work to the real, and otherwise lost, *Assumption of Moses* (known only from Patristic quotations). Ceriani's Latin text is usefully reproduced (with chapter and verse references added), and the French translation is accompanied by notes.   S.P.B.

NEUSNER, J.: *Development of a legend. Studies on the traditions concerning Yohanan ben Zakkai* (Studia Post-Biblica, Vol. XVI). 1970. Pp. xvii, 316. (E. J. Brill, Leiden. Price: Fl. 60)

The author, who is principally known for his five-volume *History of the Jews in Babylonia*, began his very productive literary career in 1962 with *A Life of Rabban Yohanan ben Zakkai* in which he attempted to reconstruct the story of the founder of the Yavneh academy on the basis of all the available traditions, ancient and more recent. Here the same traditions are re-examined both in their historical sequence and synoptically according to themes. The approach is that of *Formgeschichte* with a view to tracing the formation of a legend around an historical figure. A pioneering methodological work in rabbinic research.   G.V.

PHILONENKO, M.: *Le Testament de Job. Introduction, traduction et notes.* (Semitica, Vol. XVIII.) 1968. Pp. 78. (Adrien-Maisonneuve, Paris)

Hitherto the only modern translation of the oldest form of the text of *T. Job* was that by Riessler (Kohler's English translation, for example, was based on a later, somewhat expanded, text). Philonenko's useful French translation (with short notes and a succinct introduction) is based on the re-edition of the older text form in *Pseudepigrapha Veteris Testamenti* II (see *B.L.*, 1969, p. 60). An appendix draws attention to some hitherto unknown Coptic fragments of the work.   S.P.B.

SCHALIT, A.: *König Herodes. Der Mann und sein Werk.* (Studia Judaica, Band IV.) 1969. Pp. xvi, 890 (Walter de Gruyter, Berlin. Price: DM. 148)

This is a German translation of a full revision of a Hebrew work (under the same title, in Hebrew) first published in 1960. It is an exhaustive study of Herod's life and reign and contains searching assessments of his character, his thinking (in so far as that can be reconstructed from the sources available) and his achievements. On the biographical side, especially in relation to other leading figures, Antony, Cleopatra, Mariamme, Octavian, etc., there is a close examination of motives and moods, and on the political side a detailed study of the Greek and Roman systems of government as they impinged on or influenced the affairs of Judaea as administered by Herod. Inevitably Schalit has had to follow Josephus as almost the only source for his material, but the abundant and detailed footnotes and additional notes testify to the careful critical handling of the source material. Even where one might differ from Schalit, as one must sometimes where so much is matter for speculation, the reason for the difference is abundantly clear. It is an important re-assessment of Herod.

L.H.B.

SCHECHTER, S.: *Documents of Jewish Sectaries. Vol. I: Fragments of a Zadokite Work. Vol. II: Fragments of the Book of the Commandments by Anan.* (The Library of Biblical Studies, ed. by H. M. Orlinsky.) 1970. Pp. 176. (Ktav Publishing House, Inc., New York. Price: $25.00)

Schechter's editions of the *Zadokite Fragments* and of the Karaite *Book of the Commandments by Anan*, which were originally issued as two separate volumes in 1910, are here republished in a single volume with the addition of a new introduction by J. A. Fitzmyer. Fitzmyer devotes most of his space to a discussion of the *Zadokite Fragments*, and provides a list of corrections and restorations to the text printed by Schechter, as well as a fairly extensive bibliography (both pre- and post-Qumran) of studies of this important document. Though it is convenient to have Schechter's edition of the *Zadokite Fragments* once more available, it is not clear that it was worth republishing.

M.A.K.

STONE, M. E.: *The Testament of Levi. A First Study of the Armenian Manuscripts of the Testaments of the XII Patriarchs in the Convent of St. James, Jerusalem.* 1969. Pp. x, 203. (St. James Press, Jerusalem)

This book contains the texts (with facing English translation) of the two recensions of the Armenian version of *T. Levi*, each based on manuscripts to be found in the library of the Armenian Patriarchate in Jerusalem. The apparatus also incorporates the variants of other manuscripts, derived from Charles, and from the Venice edition of *T. XII Patr.* While the present work is greatly superior to the Venice edition, it by no means represents all the evidence available (see for this Burchard's survey in *Studien zu den Testamenten der Zwölf Patriarchen*, B.L., 1970, p. 72). The texts are prefaced by a long introduction on the relationships between the various Armenian manuscripts used.

S.P.B.

TAYLOR, C.: *Sayings of the Jewish Fathers* (Library of Jewish Classics). With a new introduction by J. Goldin. 1970. Pp. xviii, 183. (Ktav Publishing House, New York. Price: $14.95)

This is a reprint of the second edition (1897) of Taylor's famous study of *Aboth*, together with the Appendix (1900) containing a lengthy catalogue of manuscripts and fragments. The commentary and notes are still of value but the translation, to quote J. Goldin's Prolegomenon, is 'almost unbelievable', a 'lexical servitude'.   G.V.

THYEN, H.: *Studien zur Sündenvergebung im Neuen Testament und seinen alttestamentlichen und jüdischen Voraussetzungen.* (Forschungen zur Religion und Literatur des Alten und Neuen Testaments, 96.) 1970. Pp. 281. (Vandenhoeck & Ruprecht, Göttingen. Price: DM. 40; paper DM. 35)

Studies on the Baptist, on some crucial statements of forgiveness through the death of Jesus, and on the Matthean commission to Peter, are here prefaced by a detailed examination of sin and forgiveness in the O.T. and in 'intertestamental' Judaism, which in fact occupies half the book. The emergence of the idea of sinfulness, and of the 'forgiving, transforming word of grace' (p. 43), is the author's nearest approach to a guiding thread in the later stages of a descriptive survey which is sharply critical of simplifications; earlier, the individualization of originally corporate understandings of guilt and restoration is illustrated in terms both of law and of the cult (where the ritual of admission to the temple is thought to have played an important part). The development in Palestinian and Hellenistic Judaism is documented; in the latter case, use is made of the recently edited *Memar Marqah* and of the interpretative contribution of the LXX translators, as well as of Philo; the influence of the Egyptian mysteries on the latter is briefly discussed. The section on Qumran is largely an extended and valuable treatment of the *Hodayoth*. The chapter as a whole provides a comprehensive critical review of existing work in German which bears on the subject, and the footnotes constitute a useful bibliography. There are two excursuses on *ṣdq* and its cognates (pp. 23 ff, 57 ff.)   C.J.A.H.

WEISS, R.: *Leqet Bibliographi 'al Hashomᵉronim.* 1970. Pp. 23. (Jerusalem, 1970)

The first edition of this select bibliography on the Samaritans was published in 1968, and listed 306 books and articles, about one-third of which were in Hebrew, and divided into twenty-two different categories. An appendix of sixteen further items has now been added, together with a few corrections of wrong references. The work is a useful reference guide for those working on Samaritan studies.

R.J.C.

PHILOLOGY AND GRAMMAR

BROENNO, E.: *Die Aussprache der hebräischen Laryngale nach Zeugnissen des Hieronymus.* 1970. Pp. 214. (Universitetsforlaget i Aarhus. Price: D.Kr. 80.50)

In continuation of his earlier works the author gives in this dissertation a carefully elaborated refutation of A. Sperber's and P. Kahle's theory about the pronunciation of the laryngals. According to these scholars the Tiberian pronunciation of the laryngals is an artificial reconstruction and reintroduction after a period during which they were not pronounced. It must be admitted that Jerome's utterances on the laryngals and his description of them can be misleading, but Broenno adduces clear arguments for his understanding of Jerome's apparently contradictory statements. Jerome was no linguistic historian, but when e.g. concerning *ḥeth* and *'ayin* he speaks of *adspirationes* and *rasura gulae* (i.e. a guttural roughness) and declares that *ḥeth* was pronounced with a double aspiration, this proves, according to B., that Jerome was familiar with the Jewish pronunciation of these sounds as real laryngals.

                                                                                    E.H.

ALSTER, G. and MOSSEL, B. M.: *Hadachlil. Leerboek van het Israëlische Hebreeuws*. 1969. Pp. 491. (Van Gorcum, Assen, Price: Fl. 29)

The authors of *Hadachlil* see the study of Israeli Hebrew not only as the ambition of visitors and immigrants to Israel, but also as an integral part of the study of the Semitic languages. Dissatisfied with the shortcomings of gramophone records, picture-books and other popular teaching aids, they emphasize from the start that Hebrew is a hard language and that they are not going to gloss over the difficulties. There are some pedagogical aids: the definite article is introduced in its 'standard form' on p. 8, and the complications before gutturals are left till p. 60; in the verb-tables the first person singular forms come first; the Hebrew-Dutch vocabulary gives construct as well as absolute; and there are plenty of good exercises. But on the whole, true to its title (*hadachlil* is Hebrew for 'scarecrow'), it retains all the masoretic terminology, introduces vocabulary in a quite haphazard way, and has no index, so that one feels it certainly will scare off all but the most dedicated Dutch students.

                                                                                    J.F.A.S.

ANDERSEN, F. I.: *The Hebrew Verbless Clause in the Pentateuch* (Journal of Biblical Literature Monograph Series, 14). 1970. Pp. 128. (Abingdon Press, Nashville and New York. Price: $3.00)

Part I summarizes and criticizes earlier work on the subject, and explains the methods (worked out under the influence of modern linguistics) used in the present study, and Part II analyzes and interprets the author's findings. The evidence is set out in a systematic way in Part III, and Part IV consists of tables of different types of clause. Finally, there are notes, and an index of biblical references in them and in Parts I and II. This valuable contribution to the study of the Hebrew language shows that some generally-accepted theories need to be revised, and that much can still be learned about Hebrew by such a systematic study of the usage in the Bible.

                                                                                    J.A.E.

BALGUR, R.: *The Basic Word List for Elementary Schools* (in Hebrew). 1968. Pp. 207. ('Otsar Hamoreh', Publishing House of the Teachers' Union in Israel. Price: $4.50)

4,000 words are listed, first, in order of frequency from *'et* (6701 times) down to about 200 words occurring only 5 times in the corpus, and then in alphabetical order with cross-references to the frequency list. This volume bears all the marks of sound scholarship, and will be of immense value, not only to the school-teachers for whom it is intended, but also to anyone learning modern Israeli Hebrew. It will be of interest too, as a comparison with J. D. W. Watts' *List of Words* (Leiden, 1959, 1967, *B.L.*, 1960, p. 57; *Decade*, p. 237; *B.L.*, 1968, p. 70), shows, both to the teacher of biblical Hebrew and Hebraists in general. A preface by Professor Chaim Rabin is translated into English, and there is an adequate English summary of the introduction.

J.F.A.S.

VAN DEN BRANDEN, A.: *Grammaire phénicienne*. (Bibliothèque de l'Université Saint-Esprit, Kaslik – Liban, II). 1969. Pp. x, 164. (Librairie du Liban, Beyrouth)

The author modestly describes this as a grammar for the use of beginners. As such it will indeed be valuable, but, in that it makes good use of the more recent material, notably from Karatepe, not available to Friedrich, it will also be useful to the more advanced, although they may well find themselves in disagreement with van den Branden on several points of detail. Phoenician characters are used throughout.

S.P.B.

COHEN, D. and ZAFRANI, H.: *Grammaire de l'hébreu vivant*. 1968. Pp. xii, 317. (Presses universitaires de France, Paris. Price: Fr. 33.20)

After a brief introductory section on the history of Hebrew up to the present, the grammar is divided into three parts. Part I (pp. 19–48) contains an elementary introduction to phonetics, a description of the 20 consonants and 5 vowels that are distinctive in Modern Hebrew, and an examination of the problems involved in representing these in the traditional script. Part II, 'Les Formes et les Valeurs', starts with the verbal system (pp. 51–126). After definitions of 'racine', 'thème', etc., Hebrew verbs are described in four classes: 'triconsonnes', 'biconsonnes' (CVC and CCV), 'faux-biconsonnes' (e.g. *yašab*, *našak*, *ḥagag*), and 'quadriconsonnes'. This is followed by sections on the noun (pp. 127–79) and the numerals, including dates, measures, etc., (pp. 180–9). Part III, 'Les Constructions' (pp. 193–310), begins with the nominal syntagma (definite article, noun + adjective, etc.), gives compact descriptions of adverbs, interrogation, impersonal constructions and the like, and ends with the nominal sentence, the verbal sentence, and co-ordination and subordination in complex sentences. There are 24 pages of verb tables and two indices.

The authors' aim was to provide both a reference book and a teaching aid, and in this they have been conspicuously successful. The book is imaginative, attractive, and thoroughly business-like. The system of transliteration is simple and effective. The notation C = consonant, V = vowel is of course particularly helpful as applied to a Semitic language. Some traditional terms like nifal, piel, etc. are introduced for continuity, but 'la forme en ni-', 'la deuxième forme radicale' (= piel), etc. are preferred. One minor improvement would have been a bibliography. The appearance of this refreshing new descriptive grammar will be welcomed by Hebraists and Semitists alike.

J.F.A.S.

EISENBEIS, W.: *Die Wurzel šlm im Alten Testament* (Beihefte zur Zeitschrift für die alttestamentliche Wissenschaft, 113). 1969. Pp. xvi, 367. (Walter de Gruyter & Co., Berlin. Price: DM. 80)

This work, which is based on a Ph.D. dissertation presented at the University of Chicago in 1966, is a familiar kind of study of a Hebrew root in the Old Testament. After an account of the meanings of *šlm* in cognate languages, there is a systematic examination of the use of the root in Hebrew, and it is maintained that the fundamental meaning is that of wholeness. Finally, there are a bibliography of works relevant to the Accadian cognate, and indexes of authors' names and biblical references. The author does not discuss the criticisms that have recently been made of such word-studies, and his arguments are sometimes open to question (e.g. the discussion of Zech. 9:10), but the work is clearly very useful both because of its collection and analysis of the material and because of its detailed discussion of numerous passages in the Old Testament. J.A.E.

LESLAU, W.: *Hebrew Cognates in Amharic*. 1969. Pp. ix, 105. (Otto Harrassowitz, Wiesbaden. Price: DM. 30)

This discussion of the degree of lexical overlap will be of interest to those who know Hebrew and are curious to see how many words it has in common with a modern Semitic language of quite different structure. An introduction states some principles of the comparison, and the lists of words are easy to follow, all words being printed both in their native script and in romanization, and the Amharic words being listed in the order of the English alphabet, rather than the indigenous order, which is hard to remember. There is a reverse index starting from the Hebrew. J.B.

MEYER, R.: *Hebräische Grammatik. I. Einleitung, Schrift- und Lautlehre* (Sammlung Göschen, Band 763/763a/763b). 3rd edition, 1966. Pp. 120. (Walter de Gruyter & Co., Berlin. Price: DM. 7.80). *II. Formenlehre, Flexionstabellen* (764/764a/764b). 1969. Pp. 221. (Price: DM. 7.80)

The first edition of this short grammar was written by G. Beer and published in 1915. The second was a complete revision of the work by R. Meyer, and Volume I appeared in 1952 (*B.L.*, 1953, p. 79; *Eleven Years*, p. 532) and Volume II in 1955 (*B.L.*, 1956, p. 75; *Eleven Years*, p. 782). The name of Beer no longer appears on the title-page of the third edition, and it is now being published in three volumes, of which the second deals with some subjects contained in Volume I and some in Volume II of the preceding edition. While the same subjects are still discussed in sections with the same numbers as before and much of the wording in many places, especially in Volume II, remains unchanged, numerous alterations and additions have been made; for example, the discussion of Canaanite languages in section 4 has been completely rewritten, and a paragraph has been added to section 87 in which the presence of enclitic *mem* is recognized in some verses of the O.T. Pp. 218–21 of Volume II contain corrections and additions to Volume I. A remarkably large amount of information has been packed into this valuable work. J.A.E.

O'LEARY, DE LACY: *Comparative Grammar of the Semitic Languages.* (first published 1923) reprint 1969. Pp. xv, 280. (Philo Press, Amsterdam. Price: Fl. 42)

This is, perhaps, the oddest product of the increasingly undesirable reprint industry which the present reviewer has seen. Rinaldi (*le lingue semitiche*, 11) rightly said of the original edition that it was not even up-to-date when it was published in 1923; *a fortiori*, close on 50 years later, much of this unhappy compilation is rather in the nature of a poor joke. Reprint publishers, in their anxiety to make quick gains, are apt to be exceedingly cruel to the memory of scholars who would never have permitted an uncorrected reprint.

The bibliography contains factual mistakes. The text comprises such gems as 'Amharic is not derived from Ge'ez but from a sister language. It is more affected by Arabic and Galla and less by Greek and Coptic' (p. 23); or 'Probably the oldest type of plural is that which shows the reduplication of the singular' (p. 192); or 'The essential difference between [perfect and imperfect] may be regarded as a question of musical *tempo* . . . the command and subordinate statement (imperfect) is in *tempo allegro*' (p. 230).

There are satisfactory introductions to the study of the Semitic languages on the market (foremost among them Brockelmann's *Grundriss* and Bergsträsser's *Einführung*), and it must be hoped that librarians will think twice before investing their meagre funds in a reprint of this nature. E.U.

Proceedings of the International Conference on Semitic Studies held in Jerusalem, 19–23 July 1965. 1969. Pp. 234. (The Israel Academy of Sciences and Humanities, Jerusalem. Price: Fl. 38)

The topics discussed in these papers (in English, French, or German) range over several Semitic languages. The essays of O. Kapeliuk ('Auxiliaires descriptifs en Amharique') and W. Leslau ('Is there a Proto-Gurage?') are concerned with Ethiopian languages, and those of H. Blanc (Semitic *g* and the '*qāl-gāl* Dialect Split') and W. Fischer (problems of syllabic structure) primarily with Arabic, and J. Blau examines 'Some Problems of the Formation of the Old Semitic Languages in the Light of Arabic Dialects'. S. E. Loewenstamm discusses the numerals in Ugaritic, A. F. Rainey some of its uses of prepositions, and J. C. Greenfield its relation to Amurrite and Canaanite. Aramaic questions are considered by M. Z. Kaddari ('Construct State and *dī*-Phrases in Imperial Aramaic') and E. Y. Kutscher ('Two "Passive" Constructions . . . in the Light of Persian'), and S. Morag contributes an interesting essay on the oral traditions of the pronunciation of Aramaic among Yemenite Jews and on the methods to be used in studying them. H. B. Rosén discusses the Hebrew tenses, while more general questions of the verb in Semitic languages are examined by G. R. Driver (some uses of *qtl*), M. H. Goshen-Gottstein (the system of verbal stems), and M. Cohen ('Vue générale du verbe chamito-sémitique'). C. Rabin's essay is concerned with case endings in Semitic languages. A high standard is set in this collection of papers, and it is of great value for the Semitic scholar. J.A.E.

ADDITIONAL NOTES ON SCHOOL TEXTBOOKS, ETC.

*EDGELL, H. A. R.: *Dead Sea Discoveries. An Introduction to the Scrolls from Qumran, Masada and other sites.* 1970. Pp. 52. (Religious Education Press Ltd., Oxford. Price: 40p)

This is a simply written, straightforward, comprehensive and accurate account of the Scrolls and their background, suitable for use in the lower forms of Secondary Schools. It is attractively produced in a limp cover, with maps, silhouette illustrations, a table of dates and a booklist.

L.A.P.

*GAUBERT, H.: *The Bible in History.* Volume 4. *David and the Foundation of Jerusalem.* 1969. Pp. 195. (Darton, Longman and Todd, London. Price: £1·30)

*GAUBERT, H.: *The Bible in History*, Volume 5. *Solomon the Magnificent.* 1970. Pp. 191. (Darton, Longman and Todd, London. Price: £1·40)

The first three volumes of this series were reviewed in the *B.L.*, 1970, p. 86. These two volumes present a fairly straightforward exposition of the biblical text from a conservative but not entirely uncritical standpoint. The life of David is illustrated by citations from the Psalms, since it is held that about half the Psalter may be attributed to him. The text is illustrated by frequent sketch-maps, diagrams, drawings and photographs.

L.A.P.

*JONES, E.: *The Living Word: An introduction to Old Testament Theology.* ('Understanding the Bible' Series, Vol. 3.) 1970. Pp. xi, 136. (Pergamon Press, Oxford. Price: 75p limp cover, £1·00 hard)

This is an excellent introduction to Old Testament theology for beginners, written in simple terms, avoiding technical jargon. It deals with the main aspects under four headings: the Bible and theology; the revelation of God; the response of man; God, man and eternity. The reading lists at the end of each chapter point to fuller treatments of each subject.
Useful for upper secondary forms in school and 'basic' or 'curriculum' courses in colleges of education.

C.A.

Book List 1972

GENERAL

BERLIN, C.: *Index to Festschriften in Jewish Studies.* 1971. Pp. xl, 321. (Ktav Publishing House, Inc., New York. Price: $35.00)

243 *Festschriften* are here indexed, by way of providing a much more complete survey than is available in J. R. Marcus and A. Bilgray, *An Index to Jewish Festschriften* (Hebrew Union College, Cincinnati, 1937) which covered 53 (not included here). Although many of those indexed are concerned with the later periods of Judaism, the inclusion of volumes dealing with O.T. makes this a very valuable guide to a wealth of scholarship which is sometimes in danger of being lost to sight. A complete list of the *Festschriften* (pp. xvi–xl), is followed by an author index (pp. 1–118) and a subject index (pp. 119–319), and two pages of corrections and additions.   P.R.A.

BERNHARDT, K. H. (ed.): *Schalom. Studien zu Glaube und Geschichte Israels. Alfred Jepsen zum 70. Geburtstag dargebracht von Freunden, Schülern und Kollegen.* (Aufsätze und Vorträge zur Theologie und Religionswissenschaft, 51). 1971. Pp. 96, 1 plate. (Evangelische Verlagsanstalt, Berlin. Price: DM. 4.50)

This volume of essays presented to Alfred Jepsen on his seventieth birthday contains eleven essays, many of them quite short. In the longest of them K. H. Bernhardt writes on the historical problems surrounding the campaign of the three kings against Moab in the 9th century referred to in 2 Kings 3: 6ff., and its possible connection with the Moabite Mesha inscription. Miklos Pálfy discusses certain human and psychological aspects of fear in the Old Testament, and G. von Rad looks at the form of the doxology of judgement as seen in the prayers of Ezra 9, Neh. 9 and Dan. 9. H. Ringgren writes on the function of the creation myth in Is. 51:9–11, as establishing a basis of faith for the renewal of Israel. L. Rost contributes some considerations of the meaning of *shalom*, and W. Rudolph writes on the oracle against the nations in Amos 1:3–2:5, arguing for its substantial authenticity, with the exception of parts of the Edom (1:11bß) and Judah (2:4bß) oracles. K. D. Schunck writes on the earliest history of Jerusalem, L. Wächter on the significance of the name Jeshurun, S. Wagner on the conception of divine revelation as illustrated by 1 Sam. 9:15, and C. Westermann on Wisdom in proverbial sayings. Finally W. Zimmerli writes on the prohibition of images in the Old Testament, especially in relation to the golden calf, the bronze snake, the massebah and the ark. In addition there is a fine portrait of A. Jepsen, but no bibliography of his writings.   R.E.C.

BOTTERWECK, G. J. and RINGGREN, H. (ed.): *Theologisches Wörterbuch zum Alten Testament.* Band I. Lieferung 2 (Spalte 129–256). 1971. (W. Kohlhammer, Stuttgart. Price: DM. 16)

Some general remarks on this enterprise will be found in *B.L.*, 1971, p. 6. The present fascicle covers *'ōhel* (continued from fascicle 1) to *'ākal* (to be continued). The articles to which the greatest space is devoted are *'ōhel* (K. Koch), *'ōr* (S. Aalen) and *'iš* (N. P. Bratsiotis). The last of these includes a discussion on the relationship between *'ādām*, *'iš* and *'enōš*, which was not dealt with in the article on *'ādām* in fascicle 1. The lack of an article on *'aharōn* is surprising,

349

since the inclusion of *'abrāhām* in fascicle 1 had led one to suppose that proper names of theological significance would be included. On the other hand it is questionable whether some articles, especially *'aḥᵃrē*, deserve a place in a work of this kind.

R.N.W.

BOTTERWECK, G. J. and RINGGREN, H. (ed.): *Theologisches Wörterbuch zum Alten Testament*. Band I. Lieferung 3 (Spalte 257–384). 1971. (W. Kohlhammer, Stuttgart. Price: DM. 16)

Of the nine complete articles in the present fascicle three are on words of outstanding importance by acknowledged masters in their fields: *'ēl* (F. M. Cross), *'ᵉlōhīm* (H. Ringgren) and *'āman* (A. Jepsen). The article on *'ēl* is remarkable for its very full treatment of the Canaanite background; that on *'ᵉlōhīm*, as one would expect from the author, is a masterly treatment of concepts of god in the ancient Near East; it is here, also, that the distinction in usage between *'ēl*, *'ᵉlōah* and *'ᵉlōhīm* in the Old Testament is discussed. The article on *'āman* deals comprehensively with the important cognates as well as with the forms of the verb itself. The lack of an article on *'ēm* is surprising.

R.N.W.

BOTTERWECK, G. J. and RINGGREN, H. (ed.): *Theologisches Wörterbuch zum Alten Testament*. Band I. Lieferung 4 (Spalte 385–512). 1971. (W. Kohlhammer, Stuttgart. Price: DM. 16)

This fascicle covers *'ānap* (including *'ap*) to *bādād*, and includes important articles on *'ᵃrōn* (H.-J. Zobel), *'ereṣ* (J. Bergman and M. Ottosson), *'ārar* (J. Scharbert), *'ēš/'iššе* (J. Bergman, J. Krecher and V. Hamp), *'āšām* (D. Kellermann) and *'ašrē* (H. Cazelles). Among proper names, *bābel* (H. Ringgren) is included, but not Ephraim, Aram or Asshur. One may doubt whether a long article on *'ᵃrī* and other words meaning 'lion' (G. J. Botterweck) is justified. It is now clear that in some cases (e.g. *'ᵃrī*, and *'ēt/'im* by H. D. Preuss) groups of non-cognate words in the same semantic field will be discussed in a single article under the member of that group which is considered to be the most important, with cross-references.

R.N.W.

*COMAY, J.: *Who's Who in the Old Testament together with the Apocrypha*. 1971. Pp. 448. (Weidenfeld & Nicolson, London. Price: £4·75)

Brief biographical sketches are here given of every character mentioned in the Old Testament (including the Apocrypha). There is little in the text to distinguish this from other works of a similar kind, but the special attraction of the book is the large number of excellent and varied illustrations.

R.J.C.

CASTELLINO, G. R., D'ERCOLE, G. and GAROFALO, S. (ed.): *Populus Dei* Vol. I. *Israel*. 1966. Pp. xv, 651. (Librerio Ateneo, Salesiano, Rome)

The names of the three principal contributors are given in the preface to this scholarly work, which commemorates the priestly golden jubilee of Cardinal Alfredo Ottaviani, the prelate who had the joyful office of proclaiming Paul VI as Pope on 21 June, 1963. All the twelve contributors are or were scholars of repute. Three of them, including, most recently, Roland de Vaux, are now dead. The main distribution of the subject-matter is between the section on Israel's dogmatic and moral structure and her juridical structure. A. Barucq writes at considerable length on the notion of Covenant in the Bible and in Palestinian and Alexandrian Judaism. The priesthood in Israel is discussed by de Vaux in an article running to fifty-five pages, which supplements the account given in his earlier *Les Institutions de l'Ancien Testament*, Vol. II (1960). In the second division of this work the outstanding article is that by G. D'Ercole on 'The Juridical Structure of Israel from the Time of Her Origin until the period of Hadrian' (pp. 389–461).

It is unfortunate that there are no numbers assigned to the contributions, and no helpful list of contents giving the author's name for each essay, together with the pages assigned to it. Presumably there will be an alphabetical index when the second volume appears.

J.M.T.B.

EMANUEL, M. (ed.): *Israel. A Survey and Bibliography*. 1971. Pp. 309. (St. James Press, London. Price: £3·75)

The 25 essays in this volume are concerned with aspects of the life of the modern state of Israel. Of particular interest to readers of the *Book List* will be one by M. Gertner on 'Hebrew Language', tracing its development to the contemporary situation, and a very brief one by M. Mansoor on 'The Dead Sea Scrolls'.

P.R.A.

Eretz-Israel. Archaeological, Historical and Geographical Studies, Vol. x, *Zalman Shazar Volume*. 1971. Pp. xx (English), viii, 282 (Hebrew), 73 plates, and numerous plans and drawings. (Israel Exploration Society, Jerusalem)

The forty papers in this volume, which is dedicated to the President of Israel, are written in Hebrew, but there are English summaries of all except the few that have been, or will be, published elsewhere in English. O.T. scholars will be especially interested in the essays of the following: B. Mazar (excavations in the Old City of Jerusalem in 1969–70), N. Avigad (a burial vault on Mount Scopus from the early first century A.D.), Y. Aharoni (the stratification of Israelite Megiddo), M. Altbauer (the word *semadar* on a jar from Hazor), P. Bar-Adon (a settlement of the Qumran sect at Ain el-Ghuweir), J. Braslavi (En-Tannin in Neh. 2:13), N. Glueck (incense altars), M. Dothan (the Late Chalcolithic period in Palestine), M. Haran (the route of the exodus in the Pentateuch), Y. Yadin (the questionable nature of some opinions about a South Arabian clay stamp at Bethel), S. Yeivin (2 Kings 14:28), B. Z. Lurie (the walls of Jerusalem at the end of the period of the second temple), S. E. Loewenstamm (the investiture of Levi in the Pentateuch), A. Malamat (resemblances between the accounts of the Danite migration to the north and of the exodus and conquest of Canaan), J. Naveh (inscriptions on ossuaries from Jerusalem), B. Oded (the Darb el-Hawarneh route from northern Transjordan to Acco and its importance for O.T. history), L. Finkelstein (an old *Baraitha* on Deuteronomy), Z. Kallai (the kingdom of Rehoboam), J. Kaplan (a Samaritan amulet from Tel Aviv), H. Reviv (some problems in biblical references to non-Israelite cities

and their institutions), A. F. Rainey (surface remains near Machaerus),
E. Stern (seals depicting lions and their bearing on the history of
Judah in the fifth century B.C.), and M. Stern (some questions
concerning the administration of Judaea in the early Roman empire).

J.A.E.

COENEN, L., BEYREUTHER, E., BIETENHARD, H. (ed.): *Theologisches
Begriffslexikon zum Neuen Testament*, Fasc. 10, 11. 1970. Pp. 112, 96.
(Presbyter-Segen, ₚpp. 1009–1120; Segen-Taufe, pp. 1121–1216) (R.
Brockhaus Verlag, Wuppertal. Price: DM. 16.80)

Previous fascicles of this lexicon have been noted (see *B.L.* 1970,
pp. 6 f.); a general description of its hermeneutical purpose was given
in *B.L.* 1968, p. 4. The two latest fascicles contain similarly informative articles on such themes as *Prophet, Reich* (kingdom), *Satan,
Schöpfung, Sklave, Sohn, Sünde*. The editors' concern for the preacher
remains paramount, but the scholarship is none the less careful.

P.R.A.

EYBERS, I. H., FENSHAM, F. C., VAN WYK, W. C. and VAN ZYL, A. H.
(ed.): *De Fructu Oris Sui: Essays in Honour of Adrianus van Selms.*
(Pretoria Oriental Series, vol. IX.) 1971. Pp. viii, 259. (E. J. Brill,
Leiden. Price: Fl. 60)

Sixteen out of the twenty essays in this volume concern various
aspects of the O.T. There are philological studies on $\sqrt{qr}$, *ᶜr*, *ş/ţr*
(H. J. Dreyer), *ᶜrb/ᶜrp* and concept of darkness (J. A. Loader), morphological peculiarities in Qohelet (S. J. Du Plessis), *ᶜakkabiš* (J. P. Van der
Westerhuizen); literary studies on darkness/drought and light/vegeta-
tion in Jeremiah (A. P. B. Breytenbach), composition of the historical
books (Eybers), assonance in O.T. poetry (J. J. Glück), structure of
Deut. 32 (C. J. Labuschagne), the background of Nahum (Van Wyk),
and Psalm 27 (Van Zyl). The remaining items of O.T. interest are on
the Rechabites (L. Bronner), translation (Fensham), the patriarchs as
'village pastoralists' (L. M. Muntingh), Man in the Psalms (J. P.
Oberholzer), Revelation (S. Du Toit), and the use of *bmymr'* in Neofiti
Genesis (W. S. Vorster). It must be confessed that several of the
contributions are rather second-rate.

S.P.B.

GORDIS, R.: *Poets, Prophets and Sages. Essays in Biblical Interpretation.*
1971. Pp. x, 436. (Indiana University Press, Bloomington and London.
Price: $15.00)

This is a collection of fifteen essays by Rabbi Gordis, all previously
published during the period 1940 to 1966, and selected with the
general reader in mind. Six are introductory articles on prophetical
and wisdom books; the remainder cover a wide range of subjects.
The articles on Job and Ecclesiastes in particular are useful as
summaries of views which the author has expressed more fully
elsewhere. Perhaps the most notable article is that entitled 'Quotations
in Biblical, Oriental and Rabbinic Literature', in which the author

presents in detail and with cogency the opinion that many problems of consistency of thought and of continuity can be solved once it is recognized that the authors of the books or passages in question are, for a variety of reasons, quoting from earlier sources, not always with approval. The article entitled 'Primitive Democracy in Ancient Israel', though not convincing to the reviewer, is also of more than ordinary interest.

R.N.W.

GRABNER-HAIDER, A. (ed.): *Praktisches Bibellexikon. Unter Mitarbeit katholischer und evangelischer Theologen.* 1969. Pp. xlvii, 1275, with 8 maps. (Herder, Freiburg-Basel-Vienna. Price: DM. 36)

This is probably the *lightest* bible dictionary with any claim to exhaustive scope; it weighs just 2 lb., measuring 14 × 24 cms × 6 cms thick. In range it corresponds approximately to Haag's *Bibel-Lexikon* (cf. *B.L.* 1969, p. 5), but it has no long articles; it is essentially a hand reference book for quick answers. The entries are classified as (1) 'Realia', (2) Biblical-theological concepts, (3) terms used in Form-criticism and History of Religions, and (4) hermeneutical terms. In these two latter categories this volume goes beyond what is provided in most other comparable works. A useful feature is an index of biblical passages with the articles which can be hoped to illuminate each. Bibliographical material is limited to 6 pages of very general scope. Probably the book's greatest value is as an aide-mémoire to the student and a source of minimum explanations to the layman; it is especially useful to have a handy key to form-critical and 'hermeneutical' jargon (though some was surely hardly worth recording, while there are serious gaps; the rather tendentious article 'Entsakralisierung' is unsupported by any entry on 'Sakral'). Articles on biblical books vary greatly in quality; many of the best are on deutero- or non-canonical books. The restrictions of a brief note without bibliography are handled with varying skill: quite well in (e.g.) 'Thronbesteigungsfest' but sometimes misleadingly. (Who has agreed that 'Jehovist' is the term for the *Zusammenarbeitung* of J and E?) Given the laudable scope of the dictionary, the thin coverage of biblical midrashic themes is a pity. 'Targum' gets only 40 uninformative words, while major themes such as the Binding of Isaac find no place.

R.M.

HEALEY, F. G. (ed.): *Preface to Christian Studies.* 1971. Pp. 354 (Lutterworth Press, London. Price: £3·00)

This work sets out to provide a guide to what is involved in contemporary Christian studies. The thirteen essays include 'The Old Testament' by P. R. Ackroyd (who has also supplied a brief note on 'Language Study and Theology') and 'Inter-Testamental Literature' by F. F. Bruce. Different contributors have interpreted their brief in rather different ways, so that some chapters are general essays on what is involved in a particular area, while others are surveys of present tendencies; but for the most part this should be a useful volume for the interested inquirer.

R.J.C.

Internationale Zeitschriftenschau für Bibelwissenschaft und Grenzgebiete. Vol. 16 (1969–70). 1970. Pp. xv, 411; Vol. 17 (1970–1). 1971. Pp. xiv, 380. (Patmos Verlag, Düsseldorf. Price: DM. 80; DM. 88 respectively)

Well over 2000 items in each of these volumes, covering both Old and New Testaments, show how this bibliographical aid continues to provide both useful summaries of almost all the material mentioned, and also clearly classified and indexed information.

P.R.A.

JENNI, E. and WESTERMANN, C. (ed.): *Theologisches Handwörterbuch zum Alten Testament*, Band I. 1971. Pp. xli, 942. (Chr. Kaiser Verlag, Munich and Theologischer Verlag, Zurich. Price: DM. 62.50; subscr. price DM. 55)

The purpose of *THAT*, of which the first of two volumes, covering *'āb* to *mātay*, has now appeared, is to supplement and enlarge the treatment accorded by the standard lexica to words of theological importance, taking into account modern critical, and especially semantic, approaches to the Old Testament. The editors stress that the book is not intended to be a compendium of biblical archaeology or of the history of religion, and that by 'theological vocabulary' they mean words which are used in referring to the encounter between God and man. This criterion has resulted in a rather curious selection of words: the exclusion of proper names is understandable, but the omission of words like *'ᵃrōn, zebaḥ* and *kōhēn*, while, for example, *'ūlay, bayit* and *mālē'* are included, will lessen the usefulness of the book as a work of reference. The standard of the articles themselves, however, is good, with useful surveys of recent discussion and full bibliographical references. A special feature is the provision at the beginning of each article of a statistical table of occurrences of the word in question in each Old Testament book or source.

R.N.W.

KAPELRUD, A. S. and JERVELL, J. (ed.): *Studia Theologica*, Scandinavian Journal of Theology. Vol. 25, nos. 1 and 2. 1971. Pp. 1–159. (Universitetsforlaget, Oslo. Subscription price: N. Kr. 60, $10.00)

In the first of these two numbers, N. A. Dahl considers Paul's use in Gal. 3:11–13 and Rom. 4 of the principle of solving an apparent contradiction between two texts by adducing a third, and compares it with the use of the same principle by the Rabbis and by Philo. Neither a heilsgeschichtlich nor an existentialist interpretation of either chapter is thus justified, since both correlate 'the situation in a missionary area and Scripture' by means of an established exegetical technique. Ragnar Bring, in an article full of arbitrary statements but not without interest to students of the O.T. theology of election, sees Paul as affirming O.T. salvation history, fulfilled in Christ, in such a way that the O.T. texts he uses 'were in a real sense the words and deeds of Christ' (p. 30), and that 'the law is still in every sense true' (*sic*, p. 56). In no. 2, J. Jervell reviews the evidence for the belief that in the Coming Age a New Torah would be revealed, correcting rather than rightly interpreting the Old, and concludes (pp. 107 f.) that some rabbinic teachings were altered so as to suppress this belief.

C.J.A.H.

JOEL, I.: *Index of Articles on Jewish Studies III:* 5728–1968 (1971). Pp. xviii, 178. (Issued by the Editorial Board of 'Kirjath Sepher', bibliographical quarterly of the Jewish National and University Library) (The Magnes Press, The Hebrew University, Jerusalem. Price: $4.00)

This instalment of the Index lists articles on Jewish studies that appeared in Hebrew in the year 5728, and in other languages in 1968. It also contains additions to Vols. I and II (see *B.L.*, 1971, p. 11). The articles are grouped in twelve divisions of which the longest are III. Old Testament and X. Jewish History. There are also long sections on Mishnah/Talmud, etc., Hebrew Language, and the Archaeology of Palestine. Three good indices make this annual bibliography easy to use. It also costs very little.   J.F.A.S.

KOSMALA, H. (ed.): *Annual of the Swedish Theological Institute*, vol. VII. Pp. viii, 134. 1970. (E. J. Brill, Leiden. Price: Fl. 32)

Following the annual report for 1968–9 there are eight contributions each of direct or indirect interest to readers of the *Book List*. M. C. Lind treats 'The Concept of Political Power in Ancient Israel' and in what sense it was a theocracy. J. H. Eaton discusses 'The King as God's Witness', with special reference to Isa. 55:4. 'Some Aspects of the Theological Significance of Doubt in the O.T.' by R. Davidson opens a field of considerable religious value. G. Ll. Jones gathers together eight examples from Ezekiel, where 'Jewish Exegesis and the English Bible' are seen in contact. A series of lectures propounding the theory of a Qumran-Hebrew *Vorlage* is summarized by J. Carmignac in 'Studies in the Hebrew Background of the Synoptic Gospels'. H. Kosmala writes a learned exposition of Mat. 27:24 f. 'His Blood on Us and Our Children' and is wary of the attempt to base a theory of eternal national guilt thereon. Finally, E. Bammel, '*Gerim Gerurim*', argues a translation, 'proselytes put to the final test', lit., 'dragged around'; and J. van Zijl proveds a useful second list of 28 emendations to Sperber's Isaiah Targum.

It is difficult to think of any other annual which provides quite the same interesting and instructive variety of offerings. Our congratulations to the editor once more, and our best wishes to him in his retirement.   D.R.Ap-T.

*LAYMON, M. (ed.): *The Interpreter's One-Volume Commentary on the Bible, Including the Apocrypha, with General Articles.* 1971. (Abingdon Press, Nashville and New York. Pp. 1386. Price: Regular Edition $17.50. Thumb-index Edition $19.50)

One-volume Bible commentaries are a distinctive *genre* of literature, with an emphasis upon comprehensiveness and the mediating of up-to-date scholarship to non-technical readers. The Interpreter's One-Volume Commentary falls within this pattern and contains an immense wealth of scholarly information contributed by an international, though predominantly American, team of scholars. The names of the contributors are too numerous to mention in a short review, but many are very familiar and highly regarded in the world of biblical scholarship, amply guaranteeing the scholarly status of the work. There are four major sections covering (1) commentaries on the individual books of the Old Testament, (2) the Apocrypha, (3) the books of the New Testament, and (4) a collection of general articles on the historical background, growth and interpretation of the biblical books. Five shorter sections then cover more technical matters of chronology, measures and money, sixteen maps, and two indexes, first to biblical references and secondly to subjects. Altogether this is a remarkably extensive coverage making this a dictionary as well as a commentary. As a general tool for ministers and students it must certainly be a most useful acquisition and very good value for money, even at the disadvantage of being rather a cumbersome book to handle.   R.E.C.

(An English edition is to be published by Collins, London, in September 1972)

MARROW, S. (ed.): *Biblica. Index Generalis. Vol. 26–50 (1945–69).* 1971. Pp. 157. (Biblical Institute Press, Rome. Price: Lire 3,000; $5.00)

The index to vols 1–25 (1920–44) of *Biblica* by A. Bürgi was not noted in the *Book List*. It has now been followed by an index to the next series of volumes, a further valuable tool for bibliographical purposes. Indexes of authors and of books reviewed are followed by subjects, biblical references, and Hebrew, Aramaic and Greek words (the first of these not quite complete, as the preface explains, since only the later articles on 'Hebrew-Ugaritic Lexicography' are here indexed and not those covered in E. R. Martinez, *Hebrew-Ugaritic Index to the Writings of M. J. Dahood* (cf. *B.L.* 1968, p. 69).   P.R.A.

NOBER, P., S. J.: *Elenchus Bibliographicus Biblicus*, Vol. 51. 1970. Pp. xx, 679. (Biblical Institute Press, Rome. Subscription Price: Lire 9,000)

The 1970 issue of this invaluable bibliographical aid carries 8419 entries and more than a hundred pages devoted to indexes facilitating the use of the volume. There is again a decrease in size, with no great decrease in contents. The more modest aim of this *Book List*, with its inclusion only of books where the *Elenchus* covers articles, makes the work of Father Nober all the more to be admired. Biblical scholarship is again in his debt.   P.R.A.

RIESENFELD, H. (ed.): *Svensk exegetisk årsbok*, xxxv. 1970 (1971). Pp. 152. (C. W. K. Gleerup, Lund. Price: Sw.Kr. 20)

Only one contribution in this volume is devoted to an O.T. subject: 'Ein Drache in Babel. Exegetische Skizze über Daniel 14:23–42', by A. K. Fenz, who examines the form and content of the passage, compares it with Dan. 6:2–29, considers possible influence from Dan. 14:1–22 and from other O.T. texts, and finally discusses the *Enstehungsgeschichte* of the passage. Of the remaining articles, G. Friedrich's 'Till kritiken mot semantiken i Theologisches Wörterbuch zum Neuen Testament' (an examination of Professor Barr's criticisms of *TWNT*) is of obvious interest to the *Alttestamentler*.   G.W.A.

ROSENTHAL, E. I. J.: *Studia Semitica.* Volume I: *Jewish Themes*; volume II: *Islamic Themes*. 1971. Pp. xv, 368 and pp. xv, 224. (Cambridge University Press. Price: £3·40 and £2·80)

Of the essays here collected, and published originally over several decades, only one, the first, is directly devoted to the Old Testament ('Some Aspects of the Hebrew Monarchy'). A majority concern rather the history of exegesis and scholarship, especially in mediaeval

Judaism. An Introduction (the same in each volume) helps to explain the relatedness of the Jewish and the Islamic sections. The appearance of the work suffers from the mode of production, which photographically reproduces the widely differing typographies of each of the numerous original publications.

J.B.

Semitics I, ed. by I. H. Eybers, J. J. Glück, R. W. Reynolds. 1970. Pp. ii, 156. (University of S. Africa, PO Box 392, Pretoria, S. Africa. Price: R. 150)

The editors propose to publish one volume annually, consisting of articles on a single theme. The present volume is on 'Figures of Speech', and the ten articles are: *Irony by Way of Attributions* (S. H. Blank), *Aufbrechen von geprägten Wortverbindungen u. Zusammenfassungen von stereotypen Ausdrücken i.d. a.t. Kunstprosa* (G. Braulich, OSB), *Paronomasia and Assonance in the Syriac Text of the Odes of Solomon* (J. H. Charlesworth), *A Liturgy of Wasted Opportunity* (J. L. Crenshaw), *Some Examples of Hyperbole in BH* (I. H. Eybers), *Paronomasia in Biblical Literature* (J. J. Glück), *Ezekiel's Ship: Some Extended Metaphors in the OT* (E. M. Good), *Word and Fulfilment: a Stylistic Feature of the Priestly Writer* (S. McEvenue), *A Perspective on the Use of Simile in the OT* (D. F. Payne), *Oaths in the Qur'an* (G. R. Smith). Vol. II will be on the same topic.

The editors are to be congratulated on successfully launching this new venture and on gathering such an interesting garner of firstfruits for vol. I.

D.R.Ap-T.

Soušek, Z. (ed.): *Brána i klíč*. Soubor starozákonních studií k šedesátinám Professor Dr. Miloše Biče. (*The Gate and the Key*. A Collection of Studies in Honour of the 60th Anniversary of Professor Dr. Miloš Bič.) 1971. Pp. 76. (Kalich, Prague. Price: Kčs. 8)

A group of friends and colleagues of Professor Bič presents here a number of O.T. studies. Mention may be made in particular of: M. Balabán, 'Moc slova a síla mlčení' (The power (*Macht*) of the word and the power (*Kraft*) of silence); J. Heller, 'Elijášova oběť' (Elijah's sacrifice); B. Pípal, 'Hospodinův služebník v exilu' (The Servant of Yahweh in the Exile); R. Nechuta, 'Tvořím zlo — já Hospodin' (I create evil, I, the Lord). For reasons outside the control of those who produced this collection, it was not possible for it to be printed, but only in duplicated form and containing only a rather limited range of contents. But the articles mentioned deserve to be more generally known. The full contents cover twelve studies, the bibliography of Professor Bič, and a dedicatory poem.

M.B.

(A note may be added to this of an article by J. Mánek, 'Composite Quotations in the New Testament and Their Purpose', *Communio viatorum, Theological Quarterly, Prague* (1970, 3/4), pp. 181–8, also offered to Professor Bič on the same occasion in which some Old Testament quotations in the N.T. are discussed; the question is raised as to why they often consist of two or more O.T. passages combined. The answer is found in the prescription of the law in Deut. 19:15 according to which evidence must be deposed by two or three witnesses not by one alone).

Stoebe, H. J., with Stamm, J. J. and Jenni, E. (ed.): *Wort — Gebot —
Glaube. Beiträge zur Theologie des Alten Testaments Walter Eichrodt
zum 80. Geburtstag.* (Abhandlungen zur Theologie des Alten und
Neuen Testaments, 59). 1971. Pp. 334, 1 plate. (Zwingli Verlag, Zürich.
Price: DM. 42)

This volume of twenty five essays was presented to Professor Eichrodt
on the occasion of his eightieth birthday on 1 August 1971.
Besides a portrait of Professor Eichrodt it includes a bibliography of
his publications between 1961 and 1970. C. A. Keller contributes a
study of the concept of faith in the Wisdom of Solomon and
O. Bächli writes on the admission of foreigners to Israel's cultic
community, for which he finds evidence in the stories of Rahab (Jos.
2: 9 ff.) and the Gibeonites (Jos. 9: 9 ff.). W. Rudolph provides a
detailed study of Amos 4:6–13 and H. J. Stoebe examines the
spiritual presuppositions of this prophet. L. Rost suggests that the
Septuagint translation was originally undertaken for juristic reasons
relating to the special legal position of Jews in the Hellenistic state.
Two studies are devoted to the P document, with J. Scharbert
discussing the *toledot* formula and C. Westermann the glory of God.
Two studies are concerned with the book of Exodus, H. Gross
drawing attention to the emphasis on 'believing in' Moses and
W. Zimmerli examining the covenant concept in Exod. 19–34.
Concerning the exilic age E. Vogt studies the question of Ezekiel's
dumbness and paralysis and R. Martin-Achard the hope of Israel's
reunification expressed in Ezek. 37: 15 ff. J. W. Miller attempts a
fresh look at the Servant Songs, particularly seeing in Is. 53 evidence
of the prophet's martyrdom at the hands of the Babylonian authorities. H. Wildberger studies the re-interpretation of the concept of
election as a result of the crisis of the exile. J. A. Soggin and M.
Schmidt write on aspects of the Psalter, and E. Jacob and G. Sauer
on Isaiah. Other essays on broader theological and hermeneutical
issues are contributed by N. W. Porteous, J. J. Stamm, M. Bič,
H. van Oyen and E. Jenni. A. Jepsen contributes some comments on
Jonah and B. Reicke on Joel. Altogether this is a wide-ranging and
distinguished tribute to a great Old Testament scholar.   R.E.C.

Thomsen, P.: *Die Palästina-Literatur. Eine internationale Bibliographie in
systematischer Ordnung mit Autoren- und Sachregister.* Band VII. *Die
Literatur der Jahre 1940–1945.* Lieferung 4 (pp. 497–784). Prepared for
publication by O. Eissfeldt and L. Rost. 1972. (Akademie-Verlag,
Berlin)

For the previous three fascicles of this volume of the bibliographical
survey, see *B.L.*, 1970, p. 14; 1971, p. 15. In this the final fascicle of
the volume, a few pages complete the archaeological section. This is
followed by 'historical geography' (pp. 509–39), 'geography' (pp.
540–70), and 'Syria and Palestine' (pp. 571–661). The index of
authors and subjects covers pp. 662–775, with short Russian and
Greek indices at the end. There is a short list of libraries and manuscripts mentioned in the entries. The range of this bibliography is
immense (a total of over 11,000 entries), going far beyond the biblical
area. Its usefulness to O.T. scholars will be evident.   P.R.A.

WOLFF, H. W. (ed.): *Probleme Biblischer Theologie. Gerhard von Rad zum 70. Geburtstag*. 1971. Pp. 690. (Chr. Kaiser Verlag, Munich. Price: DM. 60)

This tribute, offered to Gerhard von Rad by his former pupils and colleagues shortly before his death, contains 39 articles, all of which, with the exception of those of N. W. Porteous and S. Talmon are by German speaking scholars, many of whose names are as well known in this country as in their own. The emphasis is on Old Testament theology, and, as the editor remarks in the preface, many of the articles owe their inspiration to the theological thinking of von Rad himself. There are also a few articles on non-biblical subjects. The volume also contains an appreciation of von Rad's work by H. W. Wolff, a reprint of a short article by von Rad himself on his understanding of his function as a scholar and university teacher, and a full bibliography of his published works. It is completed by a photograph, and by a foreword by the President of the West German Republic, itself a proof of the high esteem in which von Rad was held by his own countrymen.   R.N.W.

WÜRTHWEIN, E.: *Wort und Existenz: Studien zum Alten Testament*. 1970. Pp. 320. (Vandenhoeck & Ruprecht, Göttingen. Price: DM. 38)

Of the fourteen studies in this volume (most of which have previously appeared in *Festschriften* and periodicals) two date from the period before World War II: 'Vom Verstehen des Alten Testaments' (1935), and 'Gott und Mensch in Dialog und Gottesreden des Buches Hiob', which was written in 1937–8 but is now published for the first time. Most parts of the O.T. are represented. The essays, 'Chaos und Schöpfung im mythischen Denken und in der biblischen Urgeschichte' and 'Der Sinn des Gesetzes im Alten Testament' are followed by five on various aspects of prophecy ('Amos 5:21–27', 'Amos-Studien', 'Der Ursprung der prophetischen Gerichtsrede', 'Jesaja 7:1–9. Ein Beitrag zu dem Thema: Prophetie und Politik', and 'Kultpolemik oder Kultbescheid?') and two on the Psalms ('Erwägungen zu Psalm 73', and 'Erwägungen zu Psalm 139'). In addition to the study of Job, Wisdom is represented by 'Die Weisheit Ägyptens und das Alte Testament', and theology by 'Geschichte und Verantwortung. Vom Menschenbild des Alten Testaments'. The volume ends with a sermon on Gen. 8 f. preached before the University of Marburg: 'Der Lebensgrund'. These are all important studies and most of them are substantial. Together they form a most useful volume.   G.W.A.

ARCHAEOLOGY AND EPIGRAPHY

CROSS, F. M. and STRUGNELL, J. (ed.): *Studies in Memory of Paul Lapp* (Harvard Theological Review 64, 2, 3). 1971. Pp. 129–450. (Harvard U.P., Oxford University Press, London. Price: $5.00)

While this *Book List* does not offer reviews of journals, it is appropriate that a brief note should be given of this volume in memory of Paul Lapp, the outstanding American archaeologist of Palestine, whose work has contributed much to the development of our understanding of the problems and interpretation of archaeology. A short biographical note is followed by a bibliography of Lapp's writings. 18 articles on various archaeological topics have been contributed by a representative group of scholars. Those most relevant for readers of the *Book List* may be noted: 'A Hebrew Cognate of Unuššu/'Unṭ in Isa. 33:8' by D. R. Hillers; 'Kleine Beiträge zur Siedlungsgeschichte der Stämme Asser und Juda' by A. Kuschke; 'The Royal Stamps and the Kingdom of Josiah' by H. D. Lance — an important questioning of assumptions about Josiah's activities; 'Problèmes de la Littérature Hénochique à la Lumière des Fragments Araméens de Qumrân' by J. T. Milik; 'The Original Text of CD 7:9–8:2 = 19:5–14' by J. Murphy-O'Connor; 'The Acrostic Poem in Sirach 51:13–33' by P. W. Skehan; 'La Thèse de l' "Amphictyonie Israélite" ' by R. de Vaux, a fairly devastating onslaught on a theory which has, nevertheless, stimulated much development; it is sad that death has now deprived scholarship of such a charming but outspoken critic; 'A Problem of Ancient Topography: Lachish and Eglon' by G. E. Wright and L. E. Stager. There is also an important general 'Essay on Archaeological Technique' by Kathleen Kenyon.

P.R.A.

GIBSON, J. C. L.: *Textbook of Syrian Semitic Inscriptions*. Vol. I: *Hebrew and Moabite Inscriptions*. 1971. Pp. xi, 119 (Clarendon Press, Oxford. Price £3·00)

This is the first volume of a manual dealing with Hebrew, Moabite, Phoenician-Punic, and Aramaic inscriptions. It is intended to replace G. A. Cooke's 1903 *Text-Book*; and if it is considered essential (despite the existence of Diringer's and Moscati's volumes and some scattered monographs) to collect and republish this epigraphic material, then it certainly was a happy thought to entrust this task to Dr. Gibson who has discharged his assignment with knowledge and competence.

In the title, 'Syrian' Semitic is apt to mislead, and despite the explanation in the Preface I know of no cogent argument against the conventional description of these languages (in the present case Hebrew) as North or North-West Semitic. In the bibliography, Torczyner's 1940 *The Lachish Ostraca* (in Hebrew) has been omitted, although it represents a marked advance on his 1938 English volume. The omission of Bergsträsser's *Hebräische Grammatik* (p. 86) is odd, especially for someone so well versed in linguistic method as the editor of this volume.

A word in the ear of the venerable Clarendon Press: in order to reduce printing costs, it is inevitable that modern off-set processes, cheaper if aesthetically less satisfying, should be used even by our two great university presses. But it may well be doubted whether lithographic reproduction from a typescript is the most suitable method for a standard manual intended for many generations of students where utmost clarity is particularly desirable. True, if 120 pages of photographic reproduction cost £3, the mind boggles at the price orthodox processes of typesetting would have demanded.

E.U.

NAVEH, J.: *The Development of the Aramaic Script*. (The Israel Academy of Sciences and Humanities: Proceedings, Volume V, no. 1.) 1970. Pp. 69 + 12 plates. (The Israel Academy, Jerusalem)

This is a descriptive study, the first of its kind, of the Aramaic script from its beginnings down to the fourth century B.C. Besides the very valuable plates, with tables of scripts, there are marginal line drawings to illustrate the forms of individual letters described. *Multum in parvo*.

S.P.B.

SANDERS, J. A. (ed.): *Essays in Honor of Nelson Glueck: Near Eastern Archaeology in the Twentieth Century.* 1970. Pp. xxv, 406, with portrait and Pls 45 + numerous figs. in text. (Doubleday & Co, Garden City, New York. Price $12.50)

The able editor has here gathered a galaxy of experts from A to Y to write a Festschrift on twenty facets of Near Eastern Archaeology, mainly Palestinian. With so many first-rate contributions it is impossible to mention all or single out any one — except, perhaps, to echo the editor's satisfaction at having here, and at last, a comprehensive ceramic chronology for the Nabatean pottery of Petra (from the pen of P. J. Parr). The rest of the book, too, is indispensable for the biblical archaeologist. Fritz Bamberger contributes a Preface on 'The Mind of Nelson Glueck' and E. K. Vogel a bibliography of his writings. The world of Near Eastern archaeology is poorer and drabber by his death; we are glad that this well-deserved honour came to him during his life.   D.R.Ap-T.

THOMPSON, H. O.: *Mekal, the God of Beth-shan.* 1970. Pp. xii, 217 with 6 illustrations. (E. J. Brill, Leiden. Price: Fl. 44)

This book is a study of the god *Mkl* who, though rarely mentioned directly in literature, seems to have been recognized in various excavations, notably at Beth-shean or, as the author calls it, Beth-shan (although the identity of the two places has been recently doubted). The contents include a description of the archaeological discoveries at Beth-shean, the *stele* of the god *Mkl* and the panel thought to depict him, the gods Nergal and Set and Resheph, the connection of *Mkl* with Cyprus, and concluding remarks and additions. The conclusion that all these gods may be identified is plausible but can hardly be said to have been proved; but the author has the good sense finally to describe his work as a 'tantalizing study'. The text takes the form apparently of brief entries from a card-index, followed by a summary at the end of each paragraph; but, as the entries are apt to be self-contradictory, the conclusions are equally apt to be inconclusive. Indeed, they serve often only to show on what wild guesses much archaeology rests. The philological treatment of the god's name at the end is equally confusing. The book also teems with misprints and other errors which can hardly be called misprints.   G.R.D.

HISTORY AND GEOGRAPHY

ALLEGRO, J. M.: *The Chosen People. A Study of Jewish History from the Time of the Exile until the Revolt of Bar Kocheba.* 1971. Pp. 286, Pl. 24, Figs. 9. (Hodder & Stoughton, London. Price: £3·00)

The importance of the period covered by Mr. Allegro's book is equalled by the complexity of the events and of much of the evidence by which they are attested. To tell the story clearly and convincingly calls for the high degree of narrative skill which Mr. Allegro possesses. His lucid and often vivid prose not only presents the facts but brings the past to life. In this respect the merits of his book are obvious. Some criticisms must, however, be made. It can be argued that, although Mr. Allegro does take some account of the Jewish communities in Babylonia and Egypt, attention is concentrated too much on events and conditions in Palestine. Further his judgements, even when they are most arresting, are sometimes highly questionable (Did Nebuchadnezzar really create both Judaism and the Jewish problem?). His emphasis on the part played by social and political factors in situations and events which have sometimes been regarded as exclusively religious is in itself sound; but many of his dogmatic assertions on religious questions fail to carry conviction, at least to the present reviewer. Finally, the fact that the mushroom cult again rears its erotic head is an unfortunate blemish in a book from whose considerable merits it seriously detracts.

                                                                                        G.W.A.

The Cambridge Ancient History: Revised Edition of Volumes I and II. *Palestine in the Time of the Eighteenth Dynasty* by K. M. Kenyon. Fasc. 69. 1971. Pp. 33 (Cambridge University Press. Price: 30 p.)

After a masterly summary of the archaeological evidence about the relevant period of occupation from some twenty-two sites, less than two pages presents the historical information gleaned from it. It seems a pity that history has been given such a narrow interpretation here; perhaps the wider aspects will find fuller mention elsewhere in the complete volume.

                                                                                        D.R.Ap-T.

*CANSDALE, G.: *Animals of Bible Lands*. 1970. Pp. 256 with 16 illustrations in colour and 25 black-and-white drawings, with 2 maps as end pieces. (Paternoster Press, Exeter. Price: £2·50)

The difficulties besetting the identification of the various beasts mentioned in the Old Testament are many and well known: *e.g.* rarity of words, lack of precise information and typically oriental disregard of scientific accuracy; and the modern Hebraist is rarely a naturalist or the naturalist a philologist. Bochart drew his information from classical literature and Tristram, admirable as an observer of nature, was untrustworthy as an Orientalist. Mr Cansdale, although labouring under the same difficulty as Tristram, nonetheless goes far to bringing him up to date with much new information, and every student of the Bible will learn much from this admirable work. Against this must be set his ignorance of Hebrew which leads him into quoting such nonsense as 'all they that make sluices and ponds for fishes' (Is. 19:10, A.V.), while neglecting to explain 'the fish . . . which stick to thy scales' (Ezek. 29:4 already rightly explained by Tristram as a mollusc). Not a few identifications rest on antiquated philology, *e.g.* 'peacocks' ((1 Ki. 10:22+), 'elephant' and 'hippopotamus' (Jb. 40:15, A.V. and R.V.) although neither has a 'tail rigid as a cedar' or 'takes the cattle of the hills for his prey'. Further, why elephants were made drunk before going into battle (1 Macc. 6:34) is wrongly explained, though known to Aelian (cp. 3 Macc. 5:36–6:21). Most of these errors have long been recognized; but to introduce correct but modern translation into English Bibles is one of the hardest tasks on earth; for many readers, lured by the melodious rhythm of the A.V. (and R.V.), disregard the sense! Nor can the author be blamed for ignorance of recent philological work, which has removed 'hornet' (Exod. 23:28+) and 'snail' (Ps. 58:8) and introduced 'shark' (Ps. 74:14), 'marmot' and 'porcupine' and 'nightjar' (Is. 34:17), as well as the '*ky*-bird' (Job. 39:27). Finally, the illustrations are excellent. May the reviewer hope that the author will not only in due course produce a new edition of a most interesting work but will also dare to use the New English Bible?

                                                                                        G.R.D.

DONNER, H.: *Herrschergestalten in Israel* (Verständliche Wissenschaft, 103), 1970. Pp. x, 123, Pls 5 + Map. (Springer-Verlag, Berlin, Heidelberg, New York. Price: DM. 80, $2.30)

This is a brief, popularly written account of the kings of Israel and Judah, under the chapter-headings: Saul, David, Solomon, Rehoboam, Jehu, Hezekiah, Josiah, Zedekiah. Brief reference is made to the intervening reigns, and some estimate is offered of the significance of each king.   A.S.H.

*EDWARDS, I. E. S., GADD, C. J. and HAMMOND, N. G. L. (eds.): *The Cambridge Ancient History*. Vol. I, Part 2. *Early History of the Middle East*. 3rd ed. 1971. Pp. xxiv, 1058, with 16 maps, 3 tables and 22 text figures. (Cambridge University Press; Price: £8·00)

The first part of this volume was noted in *B.L.* 1971, p. 19; the second part completes it. The fascicles have previously been noted in the *Book List* (from 1963 to 1969). Some revision and up-dating of the material has been possible in the preparing of the complete volume. Of particular interest to readers of the *Book List* will be R. de Vaux on 'Palestine in the Early Bronze Age', K. M. Kenyon on the archaeological sites of Syria and Palestine in the late third and early second millennia, and a number of chapters which deal with the early history of Syria. In addition there is much concerning the early life of Babylonia, Egypt and Anatolia which draws together and clarifies the immense extension of evidence in recent years.   P.R.A.

HARRISON, R. K.: *Old Testament Times*. Pp. xvi, 357; ill. 108; maps 3. 1970. (W. B. Eerdmans, Grand Rapids; Inter-Varsity Press, London. Price $6.95; £2.25)

The biblical account of history is followed conservatively, and other Near Eastern sources are used to supplement and support the biblical narrative in a rather selective way and, sometimes, not quite fairly; e.g., it is true that the story of Sargon I being consigned as a baby to a floating cradle is now extant only in late copies but, in order to support the historicity of the baby Moses story, we are told, 'this event antedated by several centuries the cuneiform legend (c. 800 B.C.) of Sargon I'. Scholars will therefore be not altogether happy to recommend this interestingly written compendium.   D.R.Ap-T.

MAZAR, B. (ed.): *The World History of the Jewish People*. Vol. II. *Patriarchs*. (World History of the Jewish People First Series: Ancient Times). 1971. (W. H. Allen, London. Pp. 306. Price: £8·50)

This beautifully produced volume is essentially a handbook to material relating to the history of Israel intended both for students and the general reader. Produced by a distinguished team of Jewish scholars, it provides general essays on the main fields of study which have a bearing on Israel's origins, and the religious and political history of Palestine in the first three-quarters of the second millennium B.C. The essays are basically descriptive and introductory, rather than attempts to set out new hypotheses. The keynotes are comprehensiveness and cautious judgement. E. A. Speiser writes on Mesopotamian historiography, S. E. Loewenstamm on Ugaritic literature, H. L.

Ginsberg on Northwest Semitic languages and B. Mazar on Canaan
in the Patriarchal Age. This is simply to single out some prominent
essays. Those who are familiar with the field will not find much that is
new, but for the non-specialist the work is admirably done, and seeks
conscientiously to single out factual evidence from the many theories
that have been built upon it. The emphasis is strongly upon archaeological work, and the attention to the problems of the biblical
narratives is thin in comparison. There are useful references for further
research and some excellent illustrations.
                                                                    R.E.C.

NOTH, M.: *Aufsätze zur biblischen Landes- und Altertumskunde.* (ed. by
H. W. Wolff). 2 vols. 1971. Pp. xii, 543; vii, 373 with one plate.
(Neukirchener Verlag, Neukirchen-Vluyn. Price: DM. 180)

Two volumes of studies by Noth have already appeared, gathering his
most important contributions in article form to O.T. problems of a
general and theological nature (cf. *B.L.* 1957, p. 11; *Decade*, p. 11;
B.L. 1970, p. 12). The present two-volume collection covers that
wide area to which Noth devoted so much of his attention, the
problems of history and geography, and of archaeology and its
interpretation. The first volume gathers studies closely related to the
history of Israel in the light of archaeological, geographical and
exegetical discussions; three essays concerned with the contribution
of archaeology, six described as primarily exegetical, but dealing with
particular passages or particular historical or geographical problems;
nine devoted to tribal history and geography, fairly broadly interpreted, and five to the Transjordan area. The second volume is more
concerned with the evidence from outside Israel. It contains two
substantial studies utilizing Egyptian evidence, three relevant to the
history and geography of Syria, and three devoted to the significance
of the Mari texts. All these studies have been published previously,
many of them in *ZDPV*. It is very useful to be able to get a full
conspectus of Noth's contributions to so many different problems
in a convenient form.
                                                                    P.R.A.

WEIPPERT, M.: *The Settlement of the Israelite Tribes in Palestine.* (Studies
in Biblical Theology, Second Series, 21), 1971. Pp. xx, 181. (S.C.M.
Press, London. Price: £3·00)

In welcoming the original German edition of this book (1967), the
reviewer in *B.L.* 1969, p. 44, noted that an English translation was in
preparation, and this has now appeared. The author has taken the
opportunity of this new edition to correct or amplify some of his
views, but no fundamental changes have been made. The translation
of this by no means easy work is accurate and readable and it is good
to have what is clearly a fundamental study now available for
English readers.
                                                                    J.R.P.

TEXT AND VERSIONS

ANAT, A.: *The People's Bible. Pentateuch.* (In Hebrew). 1970. Pp. xii,
1036. (Am Oved Publishers Ltd, Tel Aviv)

The volume is quite unlike anything I have hitherto read. The text,
printed with the conventional printing, has hardly a *maqqeph* but an
abundance of commas, interjections, and question and exclamation

marks. The sentences are in short stichoi, based on a special system of accentuation explained in the preface in some detail. About 250 pages are devoted to terse notes, sometimes of elementary etymology and grammar, at other times of equally elementary exegesis.

B.J.R.

Biblia Hebraica Stuttgartensia. Editio funditus renovata. Ed. K. ELLIGER and W. RUDOLPH. Fasc. 1. *Liber Genesis*, praeparavit O. Eissfeldt, 1969. Pp. x, 85. (Württembergische Bibelanstalt, Stuttgart. Price: DM. 5.80)

The general lines of the new edition are already known (see *B.L.*, 1969, p. 16; 1970, p. 23). Compared with the first fascicles to appear, *Genesis* shows a shrinking of the textual apparatus but an expansion of the amount of Masora and Masoretic apparatus. This material clutters the page and is surely too specialized for the needs of the general student, or even the general scholar, of the O.T.   J.B.

Biblia Hebraica Stuttgartensia. Editio funditus renovata. Ed. K. ELLIGER and W. RUDOLPH. Fasc. 10. *Liber XII Prophetarum*, praeparavit K. Elliger, 1970. Pp. x, 96. (Württembergische Bibelanstalt, Stuttgart. Price: DM. 5.80)

Another fascicle of the new text edition. Has the rethinking for this new project been sufficiently radical? For instance, can annotations in Latin still be of use to students? Why not a series of symbols, meaning 'has been proposed', 'should be read', etc., with a key giving explanations of the symbols in English, German, French, etc.? It is a quaint custom to furnish a bookmark which lists all the Hebrew accents; who ever wanted such a thing?   J.B.

Biblia Hebraica Stuttgartensia. Editio funditus renovata. Ed. K. ELLIGER et W. RUDOLPH. Fasc. 9. *Liber Ezechiel*, praeparavit K. Elliger. 1971. Pp. xii, 95 (Württembergische Bibelanstalt, Stuttgart. Price: DM. 5.80)

For previous issues of *BHS* see *B.L.* 1969, p. 15; 1970, p. 23 and above. This fascicle follows the standard pattern, with fairly substantial textual notes, not surprising in view of the complexities of the Ezekiel text. The masoretic information remains inaccessible pending the full publication of the relevant material.   P.R.A.

FERNÁNDEZ-GALIANO, M.: *Nuevas Páginas del Códice 967 del A. T. Griego (Ez 28, 19–43, 9)* (*P. Matr. bibl. 1*). (Studia Papyrologica, Tomo x, Fasc. 1.) 1971. Pp. 77 and 1 plate. (Barcelona. Price: $5.00)

Ziegler's edition of Ezekiel in the Göttingen Septuagint (1952) had available for the important third century papyrus 967 only the fragments preserved in the Chester Beatty and Scheide collections. Since that date further leaves of the same manuscript have turned up and are now at Cologne, Madrid and Barcelona. The Madrid leaves of 967 are nos 65–6, 75–8 and 91–104 of the codex, and cover Ezekiel 28:19–43:9 (the intermediate leaves, 67–74 and 79–90 have already been published, as part of the Scheide collection). Fernández-Galiano provides a line for line transcription, together with a collation against Ziegler's text. There is an introduction and discussion of a number of points of detail (e.g. treatment of *nomina sacra*).

S.P.B.

GOODWIN, D. W.: *Text-Restoration Methods in Contemporary U.S.A. Biblical Scholarship.* (Pubblicazioni del Seminario di Semitistica: Ricerche V.) 1969. Pp. x, 178. (Istituto Orientale de Napoli, Naples)

The methods are those of Albright, Cross and Freedman, and the book is a critical study of their treatment, in a well known series of articles, of the following O.T. poetic passages: Exodus 15, poetic portions of Numbers 23–4, Deut. 33, 2 Sam. 22/Ps. 18, Ps. 68, and Hab. 3. In the course of four main chapters (dialects of the second millennium B.C., orthographic theory, archaic forms — by far the longest—, and metrical theory), Goodwin is able to show that, in their zeal to find evidence of second millennium features, these scholars have at times failed to live up to the rigorous standards they themselves had set.

S.P.B.

LE DÉAUT, R. and ROBERT, J.: *Targum des Chroniques.* I. *Introduction et Traduction.* II. *Texte et Glossaire.* (Analecta Biblica, 51). 1971. Pp. 179, 219. 2 plates. (Biblical Institute Press, Rome. Price: Lire 10,900; $18.00)

This edition is designed to provide a targum text, with the necessary information in the form of introduction, notes and glossary, so that students can get a clear picture of what a targum is like from reading a continuous text rather than merely gathering bits and pieces from a commentary or textual apparatus. The translation sets out in italics material not in the original Hebrew and thus enables a quick survey of the types of amplification. The introduction provides a brief account of the targum of the books of Chronicles, and in particular of the text here used (of which two leaves are reproduced in facsimile in the plates) — Cod. Vat. Urb. Ebr. 1. — in which the Hebrew of each verse is followed by the Aramaic rendering. Some account is also given of the characteristics of the targum — explanation, theological harmonising, up-dating, adaptation. The work thus provides a very serviceable working text, illustrating the contemporary emphasis on the exegetical significance of the Aramaic targums alongside other ancient versions and commentaries.

P.R.A.

SPERBER, A.: *The Bible in Aramaic, Based on Old Manuscripts and Printed Texts.* Vol. IVA. *The Hagiographa, Transition from Translation to Midrash.* 1968. Pp. viii, 205. (E. J. Brill, Leiden. Price: Fl. 51)

Years have elapsed since the last issue of Sperber's *The Bible in Aramaic* (See *B.L.* 1960, p. 16 for vol. 1, 1961, p. 26, vol. 2, 1963, p. 20, vol. 3; *Decade* pp. 196, 264, 414), and the present book constitutes the first part of the final volume. It contains the text of Targum to Chronicles (based on the Berlin manuscript published also by Beck in 1680 and in Lagarde's *Hagiographa Chaldaice,* 1873), — and the Targum to Ruth in the ben Chayim text from Lagarde, *ibid.* In these texts, Sperber finds a 'gradual inclusion of midrashic elements', and he also includes a number of parallel passages from Chron. and Samuel-Kings (from *Codex Reuchlinianus*). The Targum to Cant., Lam., Eccles, and Esther is based on *MS. Or. 2375* of the British Museum, the first three showing a complete fusion of translation and midrash, the last being wholly midrash, and not straightforward at that. This last issue has done nothing to damp down our eagerness for the final survey.

B.J.R.

EXEGESIS AND MODERN TRANSLATIONS

*Ackroyd, P. R.: *The First Book of Samuel*. (The Cambridge Bible Commentary on the N.E.B.) 1971. Pp. 237. (Cambridge University Press. Price: £2·20, paperback 96p)

*McKeating, H.: *Amos, Hosea, Micah*. (The Cambridge Bible Commentary on the N.E.B.) 1971. Pp. 198. (Cambridge University Press. Price: £2·20, paperback 96p)

*Jones, C. M.: *Old Testament Illustrations*. (The Cambridge Bible Commentary on the N.E.B.) 1971. Pp. 189. (Cambridge University Press. Price: £3·00, paperback £1·40)

These are the first three volumes of the O.T. series of commentaries on the text of the N.E.B., under the general editorship of P. R. Ackroyd, A. R. C. Leaney and J. W. Packer. These commentaries are designed to make the findings of modern scholarship available to the general reader and also to teachers generally and to students in Theological Colleges and Colleges of Education. Each volume may be used independently of the rest, and no knowledge of Hebrew or Greek is presupposed. After concise introductions to the reading of the text, short sections of the text and the relevant commentary are interposed, so that the books may be read consecutively from the first page to the last.

The commentaries are written clearly and concisely to enable the student to appreciate the exact meaning of the original text and its theological significance for the modern reader. The footnotes of the N.E.B. are included in the text, and Professor Ackroyd's commentary in particular pays close attention to textual problems.

Mr. Jones's book is one of three volumes in the series of a more general character. It contains 201 photographs, maps and drawings, providing a comprehensive pictorial background to the O.T. with a detailed commentary on the illustrations.

These volumes reach a high standard of achievement in every respect, and for their purpose could hardly be bettered.   L.A.P.

Allen, C. J. (ed.): *The Broadman Bible Commentary*, Vol. 2 (Leviticus-Ruth), 1971. Pp. 480. (Broadman Press, Nashville, Tennessee; Marshall, Morgan & Scott, London. Price: £3·50)

The main purpose of this commentary is to lay emphasis on the redemptive message of the Scriptures and on the relevance of Bible teaching for the issues and problems of today. Vol. 1 was reviewed in *B.L.* 1971, p. 24.

The Introductions given to the Old Testament books dealt with in Vol. 2 vary considerably in length. A conservative standpoint is commonly taken in them, but questions of source- and literary-criticism are faced and discussed. Occasionally the reader is told that he 'must not be afraid to recognise' this fact or that.

R. E. Clements (Leviticus) deals well, *inter alia*, with the legitimacy of ascribing to Moses rules and regulations whose written form belongs to the time of the exile or later. J. D. W. Watts (Deuteronomy) writes a relatively lengthy introduction which is well-ordered and instructed. W. H. Martin (Joshua) makes effective use of the available archaeological evidence, while J. J. Owens (Judges) has a helpful section on the relation of religious thought and practice to cultic image and act. The Introduction to Ruth (by J. H. Kennedy) might

profitably have been longer in order to take more account of some
recent writing on the subject.

The commentary on each book deals on the whole with essential
contents, omitting minor details. Each book is expounded primarily
as a document of Israel's faith and not simply as a part of the surviving
literature of an ancient people. The general reader should find the
work helpful and clearly written. The bibliography in some cases is
restricted in range, and references to articles in periodicals are few.

                                                                    J.M.

ALLEN, C. J. (ed.): *The Broadman Bible Commentary*, Vol. 3 (1 Samuel to
Nehemiah). 1970. Pp. 506. (Broadman Press, Nashville, Tennessee.
Marshall, Morgan & Scott, London. Price: £4·50)

As was stated in Volume 1 of this commentary (cf. the review in *B.L.*
1971, p. 24), the main interest of it is in religious thought and practice
in the Old Testament. But the contributors fortunately do not
neglect to elucidate the human situation in which the faith had to be
held. The commentary for each of the books dealt with in this volume
reduces textual comments to a minimum but deals clearly and
frankly with problems of interpretation and does not allow scholarship to lapse into silence or subterfuge in the interests of an undisturbed piety. The introduction to 1 and 2 Samuel by Ben F.
Philbeck, Jr. expounds not only a dramatic and critical period in the
history of ancient Israel but outlines how the records of it came into
being, were preserved and were later composed. That to 1 and 2
Kings by M. Pierce Matheney, Jr. and Roy I. Honeycutt, Jr. refers
the stories about Elisha to the borderland between saga and history
and deals *inter alia* with the vexed problem of chronology. The
introduction to 1 and 2 Chronicles by Clyde T. Francisco covers the
essential issues clearly and succinctly and describes the re-establishment
of national institutions in post-exilic Judah. Emmett W. Hamrick
writing on Ezra-Nehemiah, would designate Nehemiah as the father
of Judaism and assesses his work as much more significant than that
of Ezra.
                                                                    J.M.

BREIT, H. and WESTERMANN, C.: *Calwer Predigthilfen*, Band 6. *Ausgewählte Alttestamentliche Texte*. 1971. Pp. 320. (Calwerverlag, Stuttgart.
Price: D.M. 16.50/18.00)

This substantial volume is of a much higher standard than the usual
kind of help offered to preachers. Indeed it is a serious contribution
to the interpretation of parts of the O.T., dealing radically, as it does,
with questions which are as important for the expositor as they are
for the preacher. The discussion by C. Westermann of Genesis 1–11,
in which he claims that these chapters are not just an introduction to
the *Heilsgeschichte* but are part of the framework of the whole
Bible with their emphasis on creation and on mankind in general,
makes absorbing reading. H. Breit, the author of an important book
on Deuteronomy, deals penetratingly with the relevance of the
Elijah stories for Christian preaching, while J. Kühlewein does the
same for the communal laments in the Psalter. The final section by
H. D. Preuss discusses in scholarly fashion the book of Daniel with
interesting suggestions as to the relevance for today of Apocalyptic.
In particular it is maintained against von Rad that there is a closer

connection between apocalyptic and prophecy than between the former and wisdom. The book as a whole is a demonstration of the unsatisfactoriness of preaching on texts or passages taken out of their context and of the tremendous gain for preaching which accrues from the honest study of scripture. N.W.P.

*BRIGHT, L. (ed.): *Scripture Discussion Commentary* 1. *Pentateuch. Genesis 1–11, Genesis 12–50, Exodus, Deuteronomy.* 1971. Pp. 248 (Sheed and Ward, London and Sydney. Price: £1·45)

*BRIGHT, L. (ed.): *Scripture Discussion Commentary* 2. *Prophets* 1. *Amos and Hosea, Isaiah 1–39, Jeremiah, Isaiah 40–66.* 1971. Pp. 214. (Sheed and Ward, London and Sydney, Price: £1·30)

*BRIGHT, L. (ed.): *Scripture Discussion Commentary* 3. *Histories* 1. *Judges, 1 and 2 Samuel, 1 and 2 Kings, Ruth.* 1971. Pp. 182. (Sheed and Ward, London and Sydney. Price: £1·15)

The booklets on Genesis 1–11, Deuteronomy and Jeremiah embodied in this series were reviewed in *B.L.* 1970, p. 85. These commentaries, written to provoke discussion, are lively and intelligent, and should appeal especially to Sixth Formers and their teachers. L.A.P.

CHEYNE, T. K.: *Critica Biblica or critical linguistic, literary and historical notes on the text of the Old Testament Writings: Isaiah and Jeremiah; Ezekiel and minor prophets; Samuel; Kings; Joshua and Judges.* 1970. (1903/4) (Philo Press, Amsterdam. Price: Fl. 60)

The name of Cheyne stands as that of one of the great scholars of the last century, and his contributions to biblical scholarship are undisputed. But the reprinting of this collection of studies from his 'post-Jerahmeelite' period, when he had moved out of sober scholarship into realms of fancy, does nothing to enhance his memory. Scholars who need his earlier work can find it in libraries; his later writings are better forgotten, even though they may preserve some examples of his critical insight. P.R.A.

DELCOR, M.: *Le Livre de Daniel* (Sources Bibliques.) 1971. Pp. 296 (J. Gabalda et Cie, Paris. Price: Fr. 53)

This book is an important addition to the literature on the Book of Daniel. A useful introduction discussing certain of the literary problems, textual questions and literary *genres* is followed by a detailed commentary on the text of Daniel including that of the Greek additions. A wealth of comparative material is furnished, as was to be expected of a distinguished orientalist. Particularly valuable are the references to relevant French books and articles. Much use is made of the evidence from Qumran. On the question of the unity of Daniel Delcor has much sympathy with Rowley's position. He thinks that the second part of the book is to be attributed to one of the Hasidim who makes use of older stories in the first part. He favours the close relation between prophecy and apocalyptic and, while recognizing the elements of wisdom in Daniel, he is critical of the views of Bentzen and von Rad who regard the book as a piece of wisdom literature. He thinks that the author of Daniel took the term 'Son of Man' in Daniel 7 from Ezekiel and, in opposition to Sellin, Noth,

Ginsberg and Coppens, holds that the one like to a Son of Man in Daniel 7 is to be regarded as a symbol of the holy people Israel. Chapter 7 is treated as a substantial unity. It is curious that no reference is made to the admirable commentary by E. W. Heaton in the Torch series or to A. C. Welch's penetrating study of Daniel in *Visions of the End*.

N.W.P.

DUCKWORTH, D., MONGREDIEU, J. G., RYDER, N. (ed.): *Pentateuch: Genesis, Exodus, Leviticus, Numbers, Deuteronomy*. 1970. Pp. xiv, 355. (The General Conference of the New Church, 20 Bloomsbury Way, London, WC1. Price: £1.50; paperback: £1.00)

The intention of this independent translation is to render the MT, without accepting any emendations, whether supported by any or all the Ancient Versions. Yet 'the New Church finds it necessary to translate the Word in the light of its knowledge of the spiritual sense', and it 'is as much a translation of ideas as it is a translation of words'. Much care (since 1892) has been bestowed on the translation — even to changing the inspired text from the Letteris via Ginsburg to BHK and Snaith; but it is difficult to envisage it having a large sale outside the New Church in face of the strong competition.

D.R.Ap-T.

EMMANUEL: *Pour Commenter La Genèse*, 1971. Pp. 391. (Payot, Paris. Price: Fr. 26.70)

The author presents us with a Jewish meditation on Genesis, divided into 613 sections. It is characterized by a spirituality which draws deeply from the wells of traditional Jewish scholarship and modern biblical interpretation, but is slave to neither. Here is an exegete who refuses to accept that all wisdom begins only with modern critical scholarship, and refuses to read the text as anything other than the Sacred Scripture of a believing community and a witness to the mystery of Israel.

R.D.

GERLEMAN, G.: *Esther*. (Biblischer Kommentar Altes Testament. XXI, 1.) 1970. Pp. 80. (Neukirchener Verlag, Neukirchen-Vluyn. Price: DM. 7.75. sub. DM. 6.50)

More than half of this volume is devoted to the introduction to the book of Esther. It contains a survey of the history of interpretation, and discusses the various dramatic presentations of the story. Full treatment is given to the connection between Esther and Exodus, the feast of Purim, and the Greek text. The introduction ends with a very comprehensive bibliography. The commentary section covers chaps. 1–2:2a. This follows the normal pattern, a full translation, *apparatus criticus*, and comments on text and its interpretation. The completion of this work will be eagerly awaited.

E.R.R.

GINSBURG, C. D.: *The Song of Songs and Qoheleth*. (*Library of Biblical Studies*, ed. H. M. Orlinsky). 1970 (1857). Pp. xliv, 528. (Ktav Publishing House, Inc., New York. Price: $22.50)

This reprint of Ginsburg's monumental commentary, first published in 1857, is warmly to be welcomed. Although inevitably critically outdated in many respects, it remains a mine of information. In particular, to anyone interested in the history of exegesis, the introductions to both books are invaluable.

R.D.

HAMMERSHAIMB, E.: *The Book of Amos. A Commentary*. Translated by J. Sturdy. 1970. Pp. 148. (Blackwell, Oxford. Price: £2·25)

The first edition in Danish of this commentary (1946) was reviewed in *B.L.* 1947, p. 21; *Eleven Years*, p. 83; and the second edition (1958) in *B.L.* 1959, p. 17; *Decade*, p. 153. This translation has been made from the third edition (1967), and some corrections and additions have further been made in the English version. The value of such a commentary, based on precise reference to the Hebrew text and designed primarily for students working on Amos as their first prophetic text, is clear. Professor Hammershaimb's work on the prophets is well known. Its approach is that of the school, in part associated with Scandinavia from the time of H. S. Nyberg's *Hosea*, in which reliance upon the correctness of the MT has discouraged the acceptance of emendation, a sound but sometimes overstated reaction to the extremes of some earlier work. The view taken is the conservative one that most if not all the book can be attributed to Amos, though not in the present order and not necessarily in every detail; this includes the last verses of the book. The acceptability or otherwise of these two basic points does not affect the value of the detailed discussion. The volume will be of great value for teaching and study and may be warmly commended. The handling of 7:10 ff. does not satisfy the present reviewer, for the plain sense of the text there makes it seem so much more evident that Amos claims prophetic status as the basis, in effect, of a refusal to do what Amaziah demands. Hammershaimb assumes that his work ended there; did he really go meekly back to Judah? No note is made of the suggestion that 8:14 contains in *derek* a concealed *dôrekā* 'your pantheon', which makes unnecessary a textual emendation apparently accepted here. P.R.A.

HYATT, J. P.: *Exodus*. (New Century Bible). 1971. Pp. 351. (Oliphants, London. Price: £4·50)

The format of this commentary series has altered a good deal with the change of publishers and of general editors. In this volume the RSV text is not printed in full, but a summary is given at the head of each section. There is an introduction which concentrates mainly on literary and other critical approaches to Exodus and on the historical background, four short excursuses within the main body of the commentary (origins of Yahwism; historicity of the 'passover' events; the crossing of the sea; the location of Sinai), and an appendix dealing with the 'natural' explanation of the plagues. All this material, and the many further references given, is useful, though the commentary itself has a somewhat old-fashioned air — the application in detail of modern approaches to the problems of the Pentateuch is less revealing than one might hope. R.J.C.

KAISER, O.: *Isaiah 1–12. A Commentary*. (Old Testament Library) 1972. Pp. xiii, 167. (S.C.M. Press, London. Price: £2·25)

For many years there has been no major commentary in English on the first part of Isaiah. This work will do something to meet the need, though a long delay seems likely before the commentary on chapters 13–39, which has not yet appeared in German, is available. The translation by R. A. Wilson from the second German edition seems to be accurate and is generally clear; the original edition was noticed in *B.L.* 1961, p. 32 (*Decade*, p. 270), and the revised German edition in *B.L.* 1964, p. 36 (*Decade*, p. 504). R.J.C.

Kniha žalmov (The Book of the Psalms). 1968. Pp. 443–604, in addition to the new edition of the Slovak New Testament. (Tranoscius, Liptovský Mikuláš. Price: Kčs. 46)

This is a new edition of the Slovak translation of the Psalms. The first edition appeared in 1952; the second has been fully revised by a translation commission of the Slovak Lutheran church under the leadership of Dr J. Janko. Slovak has only been developing into a written language since last century, and for this reason there are notable linguistic differences between the two editions. Both philologically and theologically the new edition represents a great step forward.

M.B.

El Libro de la Antigua Alianza. I. *Pentateuco y Josué.* 1970. Pp. 422. (El Antiguo Testamento.) (Editorial Bonum, Buenos Aires)

A noteworthy new Spanish translation of the Old Testament has appeared in the first of a projected five volume series. While it applies both the vocabulary and cadence which are more popular and familiar to southern Latin American ears, it is a stately and completely solid piece of work. Initiated and carried out by Armando J. Levoratti, with the assistance of Alfredo B. Trusso, the consultation and revision of the Sociedades Bíblicas Unidas en Latinoamérica under the direction of William W. Wonderly, and the 'imprímase' of Bishop Kemerer of Posadas, this first volume brings to the reader very helpful and reliable footnotes, brief introductions to each book, and a translation favouring the Masoretic readings and yet fully abreast of textual and linguistic studies, the fruits of Father Levoratti's great erudition and industry. Careful scrutiny and comparison will uncover some inconsistencies (e.g., spelling of YHWH) but will also bring the reader pleasure at the care and dedication of the translator. As stated in an excellent review (*Revista Bíblica* xxxii, No. 139; 1971/1; pp. 84–91), if Father Levoratti succeeds in completing his work it will be the first Catholic version of the whole Bible (the New Testament appeared in the third edition in 1970) ever produced by a Latin American. This translation is therefore a milestone in its own right.

W.J.F.

Los Libros Sagrados. Traducción y comentario de los libros del AT. Directores Luis Alonso Schökel, Juan Mateos y José María Valverde; introducciones, notas y comentarios de Luis Alonso Schökel. (Ediciones Cristiandad, Madrid)

I. *Pentateuco:*
  1. *Génesis y Exodo.* 1970. Pp. 370. (Price: 150 pts)
  2. *Levítico. Números. Deuteronomio.* 1970. Pp. 404. (Price:150 pts)

IV. *Profetas:*
  6. *Isaías.* 1968. Pp. 304. (Price: 150 pts)
  7. *Jeremías.* 1967. Pp. 236. (Price: 125 pts)
  8. *Ezequiel.* 1971. Pp. 315. (Price: 150 pts)
  9. *Doce profetas menores.* 1966. Pp. 224. (Price: 125 pts)

V. *Sapienciales:*
  10. *Salmos.* (Texto oficial litúrgico). 1st ed. 1966. 3rd ed. 1971. Pp. 435. (Price: 150 pts)

11. *Proverbios y Eclesiástico.* 1968. Pp. 334. (Price: 150 pts)
12. *El cantar de los cantares.* 1969. Pp. 110 (Price: 60 pts)
13. *Job.* 1971. Pp. 228. (Price: 150 pts)

(In the press: II. *Historia,* 3. *José, Jueces, Samuel, Reyes.* 1972)
(In preparation: II. *Historia,* 4. *Crónicas, Esdras, Nehemías, Macabeos.*
III. *Narraciones.* 5. *Rut, Tobías, Judit, Ester.*
VI. *Varios.* 14. *Eclesiastés, Sabiduría, Baruc, Daniel, Lamentaciones*)

This translation is based on a comparative stylistic analysis of Hebrew forms and the corresponding Spanish literary forms; each biblical book or groups of books is dealt with individually. For example, Cant. is translated in the language of Spanish love songs (as modern poets use in continuity with the long tradition dating back to the XV century); Prov. is translated in the language of Spanish *refranes* and proverbs (which are a rich tradition of folklore and literature). Working strictly together under a director twelve people have already collaborated in the project. There are short and concise commentaries dealing mainly with literary and theological aspects in each volume. The translation of the O.T. will be completed by 1974.

L.A.S.

MAUCHLINE, J.: *1 and 2 Samuel* (New Century Bible). 1971. Pp. 336. (Oliphants, London. Price: £4·50)

This further volume in the series (in which R. E. Clements has replaced H. H. Rowley as O.T. editor) follows the new pattern of not printing the text. It has instead a running commentary, based on RSV, in which points of detail and longer discussions are interwoven. There is a useful bibliography, a general introduction which deals with the questions of literary analysis and sources and with signs of later editing in a cautious manner — too brief to raise wider questions about the relationship between these books and the Deuteronomic History — and with text and historical value, perhaps again too simplified and not raising the more difficult problems of historicity here. The commentary itself is also on the conservative and cautious side, with much useful material but perhaps too little investigation of the theological motivation of the eventual compilation and too little appreciation of the interweaving of themes. The notes on 'Is Saul also among the prophets?' (pp. 100, 143 f.) do not really deal with the issue; the relation of 2 Sam. 24 to the temple site is too readily assumed. The series is unfortunately, like so many others, reaching so high a price as to be too little accessible to the students for whom it is primarily produced.

P.R.A.

NEHER, A.: *De l'hébreu au français: la traduction.* (Collection 'Initiation et méthodes'). 1969. Pp. 173. (Editions Klincksieck, Paris. Price: Fr. 18)

Some thoughts about the matter of translation along with a collection of texts, some of them commented on; all are modern except for a chapter on the biblical Tower of Babel story. The translation offered of this (pp. 49–50) is bizarre, to put it mildly.

J.B.

Rothuizen, G. Th.: *Landscape: a bundle of thoughts about the Psalms (the first fifty)*, trans. by J. F. Jansen. 1971. Pp. 238. (John Knox Press, Richmond, Virginia. Price: $6.95)

The contents of this volume were originally printed as a series of articles in a Dutch religious periodical and subsequently published as a book entitled *Landschap* (J. H. Kok, Kampen. 1965) of which this is a translation. The author is Professor of Ethics at the Theological School of the Reformed Churches of the Netherlands at Kampen. He does not profess to have produced an academic or even a popular commentary on the Psalms, but rather a series of studies containing thoughts suggested by the Psalms. The language is colloquial, and the treatment discursive, with much reference to modern conditions and situations. The works of J. and N. H. Ridderbos provide the somewhat conservative scholarly background to the author's work.

G.W.A.

Schriften der Bibel, literatur-geschichtlich geordnet. Band ii. *Von der Denkschrift Nehemias bis zu den Pastoralbriefen*. 1970. Pp. 337. (Calwer Verlag, Stuttgart; Kösel-Verlag, München. Price: DM. 23)

The first volume of this scriptural anthology was reviewed in *B.L.* 1969, p. 26. The plan of presentation and the principles of selection of the passages presented, as typical of the literature of each period, which were applied in the first volume are applied also in this volume. Only the first part of it calls for comment here; the remainder is concerned with the New Testament. The passages taken from Nehemiah give a clear picture of the reconstruction of Jerusalem and of the faith and morale of the Jews resident in Judah in the second half of the 5th century B.C. The pursuit of wisdom and the temptation to doubt and scepticism in this period and later are illustrated from the Old Testament wisdom literature, and the nature of the apocalyptic hope is exemplified in quotations from the book of Daniel. In addition, some excerpts from the Qumran literature show how the community at Qumran believed that they were living in the days of the end. The selection of passages has been well done, although much has had to be left out which might profitably have been included.

J.M.

Schultz, S. J.: *Deuteronomy*. (Everyman's Bible Commentary) 1971. Pp. 127. (Moody Press, Chicago. Price: 95c)

This brief commentary is homiletic in character, as is suggested by its sub-title, 'The Gospel of Love', and reflects a strongly conservative point of view. In this it is similar to other volumes in the series, but it differs from them in giving some indication of other ways of understanding the Old Testament.

R.J.C.

Seerveld, C.: *The Greatest Song in critique of Solomon; freshly and literally translated from the Hebrew and arranged for oratorio performance.* 1967. (1963). Pp. 104. (Trinity College Bookstore, Palos Heights, Illinois; Wedge Press, Toronto. Price: $5.00)

The somewhat fanciful extended title and the inclusion of woodcut illustrations and musical score should not divert the reader's attention from the fact that a serious attempt is made in this volume to consider the origins and interpretation of the text of the Song of Songs, to see the text as a whole and to interpret it — highly imaginatively — as such. The introductory and commentary material make it clear that the author has made a careful study of the problems. As with others who have attempted dramatic reconstruction of one kind or another — as witness the NEB — the success of the exercise can be judged only by the degree to which it may be seen to illuminate the meaning of what is, on any view, one of the greatest poetic writings in any language, poetry which, like other great poetry, reveals its secrets more to the sensitive than to the pedantic.   P.R.A.

Stará zmluva: Kniha Józuova až 2. kniha Královská (The Old Covenant: Joshua to 2 Kings). 1971. Pp. 406. (Tranoscius, Liptovský Mikuláš. Price: Kčs. 42)

Stará zmluva: 1. kniha Kronická až Veľpieseň (The Old Covenant: 1 Chronicles to Song of Songs). 1971. Pp. 434. (Tranoscius, Liptovský Mikuláš. Price: Kčs. 37,50)

Stará zmluva: Izaiaš, Jeremiaš, Žalospevy (The Old Covenant: Isaiah, Jeremiah, Lamentations). 1971. Pp. 299. (Tranoscius, Liptovský Mikuláš)

After decades of preparatory work by a translation commission under the leadership of Dr J. Janko, these three volumes of the Slovak Bible translation have been published as working tools. Up till now, the Slovak Lutheran church has used in its worship the old Czech Bible of the Unitas fratrum from the 16th century (the so-called Kralicer, from its place of publication, Kralice). In the meantime, Slovak has developed into an independent written language, and a Bible translation in Slovak became an urgent necessity. Since these three volumes are to be regarded as samples, they have been produced only in cyclostyle. The text must be subjected to a further thorough revision, for there are still far too many unevennesses, some of them indeed very unsatisfactory. This is the inevitable result of the time that has elapsed and the variety of collaborators. However, the prophetic volume containing Isa., Jer., Lam. is the best of the three.   M.B.

Starý zákon/překlad s výkladem (The Old Testament/translation with commentary). Appearing since 1968. (Kalich, Prague)

This new ecumenical translation of the Bible into Czech, which is combined at the same time with a commentary series, the first in Czech theological literature, has already been noted in *B.L.*, 1969, p. 27; 1970, p. 36; 1971, p. 32. Since that time three further volumes have been prepared for the press: 2. Exod.—Lev.; 3. Num.–Deut.; and 5. 1, 2 Sam. with 1 Chron. But unfortunately it has not yet been possible for the editors to gain permission for printing. Work is proceeding on the preparation of further volumes.   M.B.

STEVENSON, H. F.: *Three Prophetic Voices*. 1971. Pp. 158. (Marshall, Morgan & Scott, London. Price: £2.00)

The three voices are those of Joel, Amos and Hosea. In a Foreword, Dr. Paul S. Rees affirms that the author 'has taken these three prophets and reactivated them' (which might imply that the books had lain in torpor until this book was written). Mr. Stevenson is conservative in his interpretation, quotes a few selected authors as aids in textual problems, and follows the AV 'except where the RSV is preferable.' He is aware that Joel has been given a post-exilic date by many scholars but accepts 'the substantial evidence for the conservative opinion of a date about 830 B.C.' The aim of the book is exegetical, didactic and devotional; for some readers its theological approach may not be acceptable, but much of its exegetical content will be profitably read. Some of the author's attempts to relate specific aspects of prophetical teaching to religious and social conditions today state the obvious or overstate the relation.　　J.M.

WESTERMANN, C.: *Genesis*. (Biblischer Kommentar. Altes Testament.I, 5) 1970. Pp. 321–400 (Neukirchener Verlag, Neukirchen-Vluyn. Price: DM. 7.75; sub. DM. 6.50)

This fascicle continues from Fascicle 4 to conclude the exegesis of Gen. 3. Then follows a translation of Gen. 4:1–16 with commentary to Gen. 4:1–4a. It contains an extended discussion of 'the knowledge of good and evil' and the 'punishment words'. Consideration is given to later Jewish and consequent Christian use of Gen. 3 which speaks of man's first disobedience, but not of Original Sin in the technical sense. For previous fascicles, see *B.L.* 1971, p. 34.　　A.S.H.

LITERARY CRITICISM AND INTRODUCTION

(including History of Interpretation, Canon, and Special Studies)

BALTZER, D.: *Ezechiel und Deuterojesaja. Berührungen in der Heilserwartung der beiden grossen Exilspropheten* (Beihefte zur Zeitschrift für die alttestamentliche Wissenschaft, 121). 1971. Pp. xvii, 193. (Walter de Gruyter, Berlin. Price: DM. 58)

Is so sharp a contrast to be drawn between the message of Ezekiel and that of Deutero-Isaiah as considerations, e.g., of the different traditions in which they stand and of the differences in their style (priestly legal as opposed to psalm style) would seem to indicate? Both prophets were active during the period of the Exile, and it was out of this situation that the hope of salvation, which in its various aspects was central to their respective messages, arose. The present dissertation, following a lead from W. Zimmerli, subjects to form and traditio-historical criticism as well as to detailed consideration of their content, those passages in Ezekiel and Deutero-Isaiah relevant to salvation history. These are treated under the headings of the New Exodus, Zion-Jerusalem and the Temple, Yahweh's Return, Deliverance and Obedience, the Creative Efficacy of Yahweh's Word, the Davidic Messiah, and the Era of Peace. There results the affirmation of a striking similarity between the basic emphases of Ezekiel and Deutero-Isaiah regarding the hope of salvation, and where within the area of their common agreement significant variations occur these are judiciously evaluated. Note is taken and criticism offered of current discussion relating to this theme, the study as a whole making a most useful contribution to an important subject.　　E.T.R.

BALTZER, K.: *The Covenant Formulary in Old Testament, Jewish and Early Christian Writings.* Trans. by D. E. Green. 1971. Pp. xiii, 222. (Blackwell, Oxford. Price: £3·75)

The original German edition of *Das Bundesformular* (1960) was reviewed in *B.L.* 1962, p. 35; *Decade*, p. 345; the second German edition, revised and with the addition of a bibliography, appeared in 1964, but was not noted in the *Book List*. The translation depends upon the second edition, and has a useful short preface by the author in which he refers to further stages of the discussion of the covenant/treaty question, and shows his appreciation of the criticisms of the limitations of the form-critical approach which have been offered. The first part (pp. 1–93) is concerned with the O.T. material; the second part deals with Jewish and early Christian texts. It is useful to have such a 'foundation' discussion available in English. The translation appears to be careful and readable.   P.R.A

BARTH, H. and STECK, O. H.: *Exegese des Alten Testaments: Leitfaden der Methodik. Ein Arbeitsbuch für Proseminare, Seminare und Vorlesungen.* 2., um Nachträge ergänzte Auflage. 1971. Pp. xii, 108. (Neukirchener Verlag, Neukirchen-Vluyn. Price: DM. 9.50)

A seminar textbook, intended to make clear the principles of method involved in *Textkritik,Literarkritik, Überlieferungsgeschichte, Redaktionsgeschichte, Formgeschichte, Traditionsgeschichte*, etc. A section is devoted to each of these; an effort is made to secure good definitions and to clarify the terminology. Note the diagram on p. 1. There are lists for further reading. The appendices provide in particular a reaction to the recent work of W. Richter. The book is reproduced from typescript, but is clearly set out and legible.   J.B.

BERGQUIST, J. A.: *A Brief Guide to the Old Testament* (Bible Study Series, 1). 1970. Pp. vi, 53 (Gurukul Theological College, Madras)

This booklet is designed for use by students and laymen. It offers short introductory notes on the books of the Old Testament, in general of a rather cautiously critical kind. There are questions inviting further study. The need to educate readers away from too simple a study of the O.T. is evident and this not only in the context of the Indian churches to which this booklet is addressed.   P.R.A.

BEYERLIN, W.: *Die Rettung der Bedrängten in den Feindpsalmen der Einzelnen auf institutionelle Zusammenhänge untersucht.* (Forschungen zur Religion und Literatur des Alten und Neuen Testaments, No. 99.) 1970. Pp. 174. (Vandenhoeck & Ruprecht, Göttingen. Price: DM. 33; DM. 28)

In a characteristically close-knit argument the author of this interesting monograph applies himself to the familiar problem of the 'enemies' referred to so often in the Psalter. His aim, however, is a modest one, for he ultimately restricts himself in this connection to those psalms of the individual where the language not only centres in the thought of Yahweh's protection and judgement but, as he seeks to show, has clear links with Israel's cultic institutions, i.e. Pss. 3, 4, 5, 7, 11, 17, 23, 26, 27, 57, and 63. After offering a useful critique of the theories of H. Schmidt and L. Delekat he tries to elucidate the *Sitz*

im Leben of these psalms by reference to such passages as Exod.
22:7 f., Deut. 17:8–13, 19:16–20, 1 Kings 8:31 f., and Zeph. 3:5,
thinking in terms of a process of litigation which ends in one's use of
the means provided by the cultus for resorting to Yahweh as the final
court of appeal. Some of the passages cited may be of value as
occasionally offering something of a background to the psalms in
question, but the evidence adduced frequently strikes one as somewhat
strained, and it is doubtful if the links are so close as the author
suggests.   A.R.J.

BOECKER, H. J.: *Redeformen des Rechtslebens im Alten Testament*.
(Wissenschaftliche Monographien zum Alten und Neuen Testament, 14).
2. erweiterte Auflage, 1970. Pp. 194. (Neukirchener Verlag, Neukirchen-
Vluyn. Price: DM. 28)

The first edition of this important monograph (1964) was reviewed in
B.L. 1966, p. 32 (*Decade*, p. 652). It has now been republished without
any substantial changes being made, but with two important additions. Pp. 176–183 provide supplementary material, mainly though
not entirely of a bibliographical kind; and three indexes have been
added: Hebrew words and expressions, subjects, and biblical quotations. Since the lack of indexes in monographs of this kind is often a
matter for complaint, it is good to see this improvement, and we may
hope that other monograph authors will follow this example.

P.R.A.

BRIGGS, C. A.: *General Introduction to the Study of Holy Scripture*. 2nd edn.
1970 (= 1900). Pp. xxii, 688. (Limited Editions Library. Baker Book
House, Grand Rapids. Price: $8.95)

This is a reprint, with a brief introduction by C. F. Pfeiffer, of what
was for many years a standard work. The passage of time means that
the value of this reprint will be more for its historical interest than as a
working companion; but because of the extreme thoroughness with
which all that is involved especially in Old Testament study is set out,
there is still a good deal that can help the modern student.   R.J.C.

*BRUCE, F. F.: *Tradition Old and New*. 1970. Pp. 184. (Paternoster Press,
Exeter. Price: £1·25)

Professor Bruce is at his best here 'bringing forth out of his treasure
things new and old'. His main purpose is to clarify the rightful place
of, and attitude to, tradition in the church of today. To do this he
traces its history, with a fulness of references and of good humour,
right back to New Testament times. It includes sections on tradition
within the O.T. and in Judaism and a useful selection on the canon
and text of the O.T. within church tradition and history.   D.R.Ap-T.

CRENSHAW, J. L.: *Prophetic Conflict. Its Effect Upon Israelite Religion*.
(Beihefte zur Zeitschrift für die alttestamentliche Wissenschaft, 124.)
1971. Pp. xiv, 134. (Walter de Gruyter, Berlin. Price: DM. 54)

In this monograph Crenshaw investigates the impact of prophecy
upon Israelite society and the reasons for the decline and cessation

of the prophetic office in the post-exilic period. From an examination of Israel's response to the prophets — Crenshaw finds this response in the numerous quotations and statements of popular belief preserved in the prophetic literature itself — it is concluded that the impact of prophecy on Israelite society was negligible. At no time did the prophets meet with success, save in fiction (Jonah) or in matters of the cult (Haggai and Zechariah). The tension within the prophetic movement itself evidenced the inability of the prophets to validate a message which they claimed to be from God. Furthermore, the claims of prophecy about history were simply not borne out by the experience of the people, whilst the problem of evil found no adequate response in prophetic theology. Consequently, society found prophecy lacking and turned elsewhere for spiritual direction, namely to apocalyptic and wisdom.

This is a stimulating study and a welcome contribution to a highly complex problem. The only adverse comment this reviewer wishes to make concerns the author's arrangement of his material which in places is somewhat confusing and at times blurs the direction in which the overall argument is moving.   E.W.N.

ꓱISSLER, A.: *Das Alte Testament und die neuere katholische Exegese für die Verkündigung und Katechese dargestellt.* (Aktuelle Schriften zur Religionspädagogik, 1). Fünfte Auflage, 1968. Pp. 128. (Verlag Herder, Freiburg. Price: DM. 7.80)

This excellent little book was first published in 1963, and richly deserves its success. In his preface Dr. Deissler tells us that this new edition is 'fast unverändert'. (Cf. *B.L.* 1964, p. 7; *Decade*, p. 475).

                                                                 J.M.T.B.

ꓥHEY, M. A.: *Cyprian and the Bible: A Study in Third-century Exegesis* (Beiträge zur Geschichte der biblischen Hermeneutik, 9). 1971. Pp. v, 696. (J. C. B. Mohr (Paul Siebeck), Tübingen. Price: DM. 54; paper DM. 48)

After an introduction on Cyprian's life and works and the present state of editions, and a chapter summarizing his theological vocabulary and method in scripture study, the main part of the book presents an exhaustive catalogue of Cyprian's O.T. and N.T. quotations and allusions, followed by a chapter listing, in synthetic summaries, 'Cyprian's Biblical Figures: Salvation-History Personages', with a useful excursus on his vocabulary for typology. Fahey had access to Dom R. Weber's forthcoming edition of Cyprian's *Testimonia*; he also gives here a new Index of Cyprian's scriptural quotations and allusions, to correct and replace Hartel's defective index. This book is a reference tool (a model of its kind) rather than a theological study, but at least it shows how constantly Cyprian found Christ himself acting and speaking in the O.T. (cf. A. T. Hanson's thesis about the N.T., *B.L.* 1966, p. 473, *Decade*, p. 667). Fahey does not aim to deal fully with Cyprian's use of Testimonia, and neglects the significance of sequence in these, which might make him think again about Cyprian's relation to his predecessors, and value Rendel Harris's documentation more highly.   R.M.

FARBRIDGE, M. H.: *Studies in Biblical and Semitic Symbolism* (*The Library of Biblical Studies*, ed. H. M. Orlinsky). 1970 (1923). Pp. lxiii, 288. (Ktav Publishing House, Inc., New York. Price: $14.95)

The subject of symbolism is of front-rank importance today both for biblical and Ancient Near Eastern scholars who are concerned with original meaning, and for theologians and philosophers of religion concerned with a contemporary re-interpretation. Unfortunately this book does not add significantly to our understanding of the subject, for without a proper discussion of the relationship of symbols with other types of religious discourse, e.g., images and analogies, the true dimensions remain hidden. H. G. May's *Prolegomenon* (pp. xi–lix), however, makes excellent reading.
                                                                I.B.

FILBY, F. A.: *The Flood Reconsidered*. 1970. Pp. ix, 148. (Pickering & Inglis, London. Price: £1·10)

The starting point of this work is an unquestioning belief in the historicity of the flood story in Genesis. All other flood myths are dependent on the Genesis story; all relevant archaeological and geological phenomena must be explained by relation to it; all 'higher criticism' of Genesis is disallowed. Those who are unconvinced of the basic presupposition will scarcely find anything here which will change their view.
                                                                R.J.C.

FOHRER, G.: *Das Alte Testament*. Zweiter und Dritter Teil. 1970. Pp. 210. (Verlagshaus Gerd Mohn, Gütersloh. Price: DM. 19.80)

The first volume was reviewed in *B.L.* 1970, pp. 46–7. The plan follows the same general lines, with differences dictated by the material. Thus part 2, 'Prophecy and the Prophetic Books', is divided into (a) historical and form-critical introduction; (b) the analysis of the contents of the books; and (c) the message of the prophets. Part 3 deals with the rest of the material: (a) the history of the exilic and post-exilic period; (b) the narrative literature, the poetry, the wisdom books and apocalyptic; (c) the theology, handled in systematic fashion.

The book ends with some significant pointers towards the theological understanding of the O.T. All is written with a simplicity and direct-ness which will be a boon to the students for whom the book is written. Scholars will find the apparatus and detail they require in Fohrer's complementary *Introduction to the Old Testament* (*B.L.* 1970, p. 47; 1969, p 42; 1967, p. 36).
                                                                D.R.J.

FRITZ, V.: *Israel in der Wüste. Traditionsgeschichtliche Untersuchung der Wüstenüberlieferung des Jahwisten* (Marburger Theologische Studien, 7). 1970. Pp. xii, 151. (N. G. Elwert Verlag, Marburg. Price: DM. 33)

A literary-critical analysis of the non-P parts of the Pentateuch dealing with the wilderness period finds J and additions to it, but no indications of E. A detailed traditio-historical treatment of the passages follows, and the conclusion is drawn that a pre-Jahwistic written collection of five traditions (derived from the oral traditions of the southern tribes, and based not on history but on aetiological explanation of phenomena known to them) which has been expanded and reinterpreted by the Jahwist, who has set Moses more firmly in the traditions, and imposed on the material the themes of disobedience and apostasy. There is a great deal of interest in Fritz' work, although his confidence in the reliability of his analysis cannot always be shared.   J.V.M.S.

GERLEMAN, G.: *Aktuella problem i gammaltestamentlig forskning* (Waldenströmföreläsningarna 1971). 1971. Pp. 64. (Gummessons, Falköping)

In his Waldenström Lectures, Professor Gerleman discusses four diverse themes which are related in varying ways to O.T. study; the problem of myth; the Qumran community; the O.T. passages appointed as texts for sermons in the Church of Sweden (a subject to which the author has devoted much attention in recent years as a member of the committee which revised the appointed texts); and the meaning of *šālôm* (which recalls the paper read by the author at the Uppsala Congress of 1971). All these subjects are of great importance (in spite of its special relevance to Swedish conditions, the third is obviously also of wider interest); and the fact that they are handled with Professor Gerleman's acumen gives the book an importance out of all proportion to its size.   G.W.A.

GOLDMANN, C.: *Ursprungssituationen biblischen Glaubens. Eine Einführung in das A.T. für die pädagogische Praxis.* 1970. Pp. 120. (Vandenhoeck & Ruprecht, Göttingen. Price: DM. 12.80)

In this short but valuable book, which is in effect an introduction to the O.T., and is the outcome of much study and reflection, the author has garnered the fruit of his long experience as a teacher of the O.T. He argues that we can rightly understand the perennial interest of the O.T. literarure only when we relate it to the historical situations that originally shaped it, and he illustrates his thesis by detailed reference to the themes of the Patriarchs, the Exodus, the Prophets and the Law. Addressed primarily to teachers, the book will be of interest to a much wider audience.   L.A.P.

GRAY, G. B.: *Sacrifice in the Old Testament, Its Theory and Practice.* With a *Prolegomenon* by B. A. Levine. (*Library of Biblical Studies*, ed. H. M. Orlinsky). 1971. Pp. liii, 434. (Ktav Publishing House, Inc., New York. Price: $16.95)

Gray's book was first published in 1925, three years after his death. It was and has remained a classic, particularly in its treatment of the Theory of Sacrifice. As for the other three sections, Levine in his useful *Prolegomenon* shows how archaeology has caught up with and passed Gray's chapter on the Altar, while much additional light has illumined the Hebrew Priesthood, and the Festivals still lurk somewhat in the deceptive twilight. Yet no study of worship in Israel is complete without the study of this book, and Ktav have done a service to scholarship by making it available with this prologue.

D.R.Ap-T.

GRØNBAEK, J. H.: *Die Geschichte vom Aufstieg Davids (1. Sam. 15–2. Sam. 5). Tradition und Komposition* (Acta Theologica Danica, Vol. x). 1971. Pp. 302. (Munksgaard, Copenhagen. Price: D.Kr. 76)

The author of the present work is one of the most promising of the younger generation of Danish O.T. scholars. The aim of his study is to show that 1 Sam. 15–2 Sam. 5 was originally an independent and self-contained unity describing David's progress towards supreme royal power in Israel and presenting him as the legitimate successor of Saul. 2 Sam. 5 is the natural conclusion of this narrative; but the author differs from the generally accepted view that it begins at 1 Sam. 16:14 by arguing that 1 Sam. 15 marks a new beginning by contrast with the earlier chapters. Judahite and Benjaminite traditions have been conflated presumably in Jerusalem during the period between the capture of Jerusalem and a date not long after the division of the kingdom. The six main sections of the narrative (15:1–16:13; 16:14–19:17; 19:18–22:23; 23:1–27:4; 27:5–2 Sam. 2:4a; 2 Sam. 2:4b–5:25) are subjected to detailed traditio-historical analysis; and the author argues that the older literary-critical treatment must be rejected. The study has been carried out with great ability and discernment and must be regarded as an important contribution to the study of 1 and 2 Samuel. Unfortunately it is marred by an unusually large number of slips.

G.W.A.

HECHT, F.: *Eschatologie und Ritus bei den 'Reformpropheten'. Ein Beitrag zur Theologie des Alten Testaments.* (Pretoria Theological Studies, Vol. 1) 1971. Pp. x, 228. (E. J. Brill, Leiden. Price: Fl. 54)

Hecht examines the classical O.T. prophets from Amos to Jeremiah with a view to determining the nature of the eschatology to which they looked forward and the primary point of their criticisms of the cultus. These features he believes to be interrelated. The threatening eschatology of the prophets is interpreted as an appeal to the fundamental ideal of the covenant which Israel had failed to achieve, necessitating a condemnation of the existing order. The promise of a subsequent renewal of Israel is then interpreted as a pointing forward to the continuing validity of this fundamental ideal of the covenant. The prophets' criticisms of the cultus are also involved since this latter also witnessed to the covenant. The prophets therefore did not reject it totally but only insofar as it ministered to the notion that the covenant ideal was being realised. At many points the author's language is extremely hard to follow, even in the English summary, but the main arguments are of a primarily exegetical nature.

R.E.C.

KELLERMANN, D.: *Die Priesterschrift von Numeri 1:1 bis 10:10 literarkritisch und traditionsgeschichtlich untersucht* (Beihefte zur Zeitschrift für die alttestamentliche Wissenschaft, 120). 1970. Pp. viii, 168. (Walter de Gruyter, Berlin. Price: DM. 48)

This work is a very detailed examination of the growth of the material in Num 1–10, finding P proper (Pᵍ) only in chapters 1, 2 and 4, and tracing (perhaps over-confidently) a complicated process of accretion of later material. Serious doubt is cast on recent claims for an early date for names and numbers in ch. 1. The book provides in effect not only source-analysis but a detailed and useful commentary on the chapters considered.

J.V.M.S.

KILIAN, R.: *Die Verheissung Immanuels Jes. 7, 14* (Stuttgarter Bibelstudien, 35) 1968. Pp. 132 (Verlag Katholisches Bibelwerk, Stuttgart. Price: DM. 8.80)

After a brief statement of the historical situation, a translation and exegesis of Isa. 7:1–17 is given, followed by an examination of the significance of the names, Shear-jashub and Immanuel. Then, under the heading 'Who is Immanuel?' the various interpretations are examined: Messiah, son of Ahaz, mythic, Isaiah's son, children of various mothers, the new Israel, a hidden mystery to hearers and prophet. It is suggested that the last is probable for both mother and son, but that in the existing situation of the disloyalty of Ahaz the sign to the prophet is given a two-fold interpretation (vv. 16 and 17) of doom. Ahaz has departed from the Davidic covenant and Yahweh is no longer his God.
A.S.H.

KILIAN, R.: *Isaaks Opferung: Zur Überlieferungsgeschichte von Gen. 22.* (Stuttgarter Bibelstudien, 44) 1970. Pp. 128. (Verlag Katholisches Bibelwerk, Stuttgart. Price: DM. 12.80)

This contribution to the unceasing analysis of Genesis 22 is entirely concerned with the traditio-historical origins and developing stratification of the narrative. Kilian argues with and against Reventlow's *Opfere deinen Sohn* (cf. *B.L.* 1969, p. 25), for he holds that the cultic saga, which lies behind the Elohist's theological paradigm of temptation, circulated freely at a sanctuary of *'el jir'æ*, and absorbed motifs of sacred pilgrimage as well as human-animal sacrifice a long time before the clan of Abraham appropriated these themes. The tradition thus reached the family chronicle apart from the original aetiological setting and stems from non-Israelite sources. From these beginnings to the post-Elohistic linking of the story to the Temple in Jerusalem over a millennium of literary and cultic history can be made to yield its secrets. Kilian provides a splendid scientific antidote to more speculative approaches to the same material.
U.E.S.

KNUTH, H. C.: *Zur Auslegungsgeschichte von Psalm 6* (Beiträge zur Geschichte der Biblischen Exegese, 11). 1971. Pp. xi, 430. (J. C. B. Mohr (Paul Siebeck), Tübingen. Price: DM. 74 (cloth); 67.50 (paper))

This large-scale analysis of Psalm 6 covers the widest possible field of hermeneutics. The biblical tradition itself in O.T. and N.T. is but a stepping stone to a magisterial survey of centuries of exegesis, ranging from the Alexandrians to the present day. Jewish exegesis is not included, for the focus of the work lies with the Christian schools of interpretation. By concentrating on a relatively short text the reader gains an immediate impression of patristic methods, of medieval convention, and especially of Luther's quite extraordinary labours. Indeed, Luther has 136 pages to himself. The modern era, by contrast, is a little compressed; even so, Kierkegaard, Jaspers, Heidegger, Lipps, Gadamer are usefully brought into the area of discussion, if only to question and elucidate the problem of 'situation'. Dr. Knuth is a thorough and penetrating guide into the history of exegesis. He admits even blatant exegeses as valid in its own right, though he is rightly critical of the finality of the claims of any one method. He always reverts to the authority of the text, based upon the author from whom the interpreter culls his exegesis. But situations vary and condition the apprehension of reality. Knuth distinguishes particularly between the christological and the ecclesiological orientation. Historical viewpoints may demolish both and existential ones create a new dimension. Of this book it may be said in praise that in its end is also its beginning.

U.E.S.

LAURIN, R. B.: *The Layman's Introduction to the Old Testament.* 1970. Pp. 160. (Judson Press, Valley Forge, Pa. Price: $2.95)

This useful paperback is addressed to the non-specialist student, each of the twelve chapters being followed by questions for discussion and a short list of helpful books. It should appeal to Lay Readers and preachers who want a reliable, straightforward and sensible guide to the literature of the O.T.

L.A.P.

LINDBLOM, J.: *Erwägungen zur Herkunft der Josianischen Tempelurkunde.* (Scripta Minora: Regiae Societatis Humaniorum Litterarum Lundensis. 1970–1, 3) 1971. Pp. 82. (C. W. K. Gleerup. Lund. Price:)

This discussion of the origin of the Josianic lawbook (JTU) and its relationship to Deuteronomy (DGB) by the veteran O.T. scholar will be sure of a welcome. He finds that Levites are a main interest in the book and among them he distinguishes four groups all descended from Levi, landless but with the right to function as priests: (i) those scattered in Palestine, not linked to any shrine, poor and in need of charity and protection; (ii) priests at provincial high-places; (iii) priests at the Jerusalem temple; (iv) descendants of Levi who earlier were cultically unattached, had joined the staff at Jerusalem and thus obtained priestly positions; this group, joined perhaps by Levites from the north wrote JTU during the first decade of Manasseh's reign and hid it in the temple. All JTU is in DGB together with a mosaic of fragments from many times and places, some added by the authors of JTU but mainly from the writers of the Deuteronomic historical work during exilic and post-exilic times. There is a short appendix on the Levites by O. Eissfeldt.

J.N.S.

LORETZ, O.: *Studien zur althebräischen Poesie 1: Das althebräische Liebeslied. Untersuchungen zur Stichometrie und Redaktionsgeschichte des Hohenliedes und des 45. Psalms.* (Alter Orient und altes Testament, Band 14/1.) 1971. Pp. x, 85. (Verlag Butzon und Bercker, Kevelaer; Neukirchener Verlag des Erziehungsvereins, Neukirchen-Vluyn. Price: DM. 48; sub. DM. 44)

This handsome production (21 × 29.5 cm.) is directed chiefly to the reconstruction of the original text of the Song of Songs and Ps. 45, with demarcation of the poetic structure and separation of redactional and other additions. The transliterated Hebrew is set out line by line, supposed additions being marked with brackets and footnotes; a German translation is given in parallel, and the total of Hebrew consonants in each line is recorded. After each poem there are brief comments on the form, transmission and content. Footnotes cite a considerable amount of recent work. The chapters of general conclusions are very slight. Unfortunately the recognition of glosses is often only a matter of intuition; in Ps. 45:7, for example, 'God' is simply marked as a gloss which served an allegorical interpretation: God's marriage to Israel.

J.H.E.

Lust, J.: *Traditie, redactie en kerygma bij Ezechiel. Een analyse van Ez. 20.1–26.* (Nerhandelingen van de Koninklijke Vlaamse Academie, Letteren Jaargang 31, No. 65). 1969. Pp. 176. (Koninklijke Vlaamse Academie, Brussels. Price: B.Fr. 367)

After a bibliography and a review of the main opinions on Ezekiel's purpose since J. Herrmann (1924), the author considers the introductory formulae and the term *drš yhwh* (to consult Y.). The prophet uses formulae found also in earlier prophets, but leaves the impress of his personality on them (in this the author supports Zimmerli against von Reventlow). Special attention is given to the terms *'dny yhwh*, ch. 3; *toᶜeba* and *špṭ* ch. 5; *ns' yd* (to take action), ch. 6. In ch. 4 the author treats the division of Ez. 20. He distinguishes 3 oracles, vv. 1–3; 4–26; and 32–44 (27–29 an insertion, 30–31 an editorial notice). The second oracle consists of 4 strophes, each of them beginning with *ns' yd*. A summary in French is added to this valuable monograph.
P.A.H.de B.

McEvenue, S. E.: *The Narrative Style of the Priestly Writer.* (Analecta Biblica, 50). 1971. Pp. xi, 216. (Biblical Institute, Rome. Price: Lire 3,300; $5.50)

The author sets out to redress the balance against the common evaluation of P as an inferior narrator. He deals briefly with the inadequacies of past approaches, which branded P as pedantic, esoteric, dogmatic, etc. By stressing the affinity of the priestly style and children's literature of all ages he opens up a new perspective. His analyses of the Flood narrative, of the Spy story of Numbers 13–14, and of Genesis 17 are detailed and well-informed. By citing Grimm, Kipling, Tolkien *et al.* McEvenue relates the former to fairy-tale dimensions, though P is not the writer of fairy-stories. His history is in a sense 'true' just because he employs very complex techniques. Repetitions, the careful advance from detail to detail, the emphasis on names, selection of details, the writing in panels and many other expressions which serve the imagination, complete a stylistic picture to which form-criticism fails to respond. The new literary criticism, which is here ably developed, takes the story for what it is and as it comes across for our enjoyment.
U.E.S.

*McGeachy, D. P.: *Common Sense and the Gospel. A Study of the Wisdom Books* (The Covenant Life Curriculum, 7). 1970. Pp. 128. (The Covenant Life Curriculum Press, Richmond, Virginia. Price: $1.25)

This book is part of a series designed as the adult study curriculum of a number of churches, mainly Presbyterian, in the U.S.A. It is a study of the meaning and contemporary relevance of the wisdom literature, and contains chapters on Proverbs, Job, Ecclesiastes and wisdom in the New Testament. Its breezy American style may well irritate some British readers, but it is based on sound scholarship and could perhaps be used in older school and adult study groups.

R.N.W.

Many, G.: *Der Rechtsstreit mit Gott (RIB) im Hiobbuch.* 1971. Pp. vi, 275. (Katholisch-theologische Fakultät, Munich)

The main thesis of this doctoral dissertation is that the poem of Job is to be described as a controversy rather than a discussion, and that the speeches both of Job and the friends are free adaptations of the private dispute of the kind which a master settled for his dependents (cf. 29:16) rather than of the covenant *rîb* whose development is found in the prophetical books. The frequent lamentations in the book are part of this *rîb*-pattern. Much of the detailed discussion, particularly of vocabulary, hardly seems relevant to the argument. The book is marred by the difficulty of reading parts of the photocopied typescript, by mistakes in the hand-written Hebrew words — e.g. *ṣāddîq* for *ṣaddîq*. *'ašîtā* for *'āšîtî* — and by a number of misleading biblical references.

R.N.W.

METTINGER, T. N. D.: *Solomonic State Officials. A Study of the Civil Government Officials of the Israelite Monarchy.* (Coniectanea Biblica O.T. Series, 5). 1971. Pp. xiii, 186. (C. W. K. Gleerup, Lund. Price: £3.80)

A comprehensive survey of the Israelite civil service was badly needed. This book is a useful step towards it. The author has read widely and been fortunate in those to whom he turned for help in specialized fields. The argument is clear, the conclusions not always conclusive; and the author's opinion — however candidly offered as such — is not an adequate substitute for the elusive proof.

Six titles are discussed: *sopher, mazkir, re'e hammelekh, 'al-habbayith, 'al-hannisabhim* and *'al-hammas*; but nothing is said of any possible official *oral* tradent. An appended chapter urges Egypt's far-reaching influence on the scribes' college in Jerusalem and on Israelite wisdom.

D.R.Ap-T.

MILGROM, J.: *Studies in Levitical Terminology,* I. *The Encroacher and the Levite: The Term* 'Aboda. 1970. Pp. ix, 110. (University of California Press, Berkeley. Price: $5.50)

This monograph contains two studies, relating to terms in the 'P' work, which the author envisages as the first of a series of contributions on the cultic terminology of the O.T. In the first, the expression *hazzār haqqārēb yûmāth*, occurring four times in Num., is subjected to a detailed examination and the author concludes that it should be translated 'the unauthorised encroacher shall be put to death.' In this case, the death penalty was inflicted by man and this leads the author on to an examination of the phrase *šāmar mishmereth*, which he holds must refer to guard duties, and thus to a discussion of the guard functions of priests and Levites respectively, in the course of which he makes illuminating use of Nuzu and Hittite parallels. The second study seeks to show that *'aboda* in 'P' always refers to physical labour as opposed to its regular post-exilic meaning of cult service and from this he concludes that the *'aboda* passages in 'P' must be preexilic. Perhaps on occasion the author is over-subtle in his exegesis and as a result some of his hypotheses are very speculative: but this is a most careful and exhaustive work and future compilers of O.T. lexica will have to give full consideration to the meanings proposed for the terms he discusses.

J.R.P.

MÜLLER, H.-P.: *Hiob und seine Freunde.* (Theologische Studien, 103). 1970. Pp. 59. (EVZ-Verlag Zürich. Price: Sw.Fr. 6.70)

The author investigates the vexed problem of the relationship between Job and his friends, who, following Fohrer, may be late-comers on the scene and replace the kinsfolk of the original tale. Müller makes use of the considerable haggadic material as given in the Testament of Job and the Targum, R. Aqiba, Arabic legends, the Talmud, and later Rabbis. He switches freely from early Accadian texts to our contemporaries in the biblical, dogmatic, and comparative fields. The result is a rich crop of highly concentrated aphorisms and suggestive ideas. Definitely a monograph for the specialist.   U.E.S.

PASCHEN, W.: *Rein und Unrein* (Studien zum Alten und Neuen Testament, Band xxiv.) 1970. Pp. 219. (Kösel Verlag, München. Price: DM. 54)

This book is primarily an examination of the development in meaning and use of a group of biblical words. It falls into three parts. The first section is concerned with the O.T. concepts of 'clean' and 'unclean'. On the basis of an examination of such roots as *ṭhr* and *ṭm'*, the author concludes that the notion of uncleanness indicates primarily the sphere of death, but also unfitness for the cult and whatever belongs to the worship of foreign deities. In the second section, the Qumran evidence is examined and a very interesting discussion shows how the ideas of 'clean' and 'unclean' in that community are determined by the Covenanters' distinctive interpretation of the Law: 'unclean' here denotes anyone who does not subscribe to that interpretation. The third section discusses Mark 7:14–23 as a development of the *Gattung* of *Reinheitsmaschal* and investigates its theological significance. The whole study is a very interesting one, not least because of its wide-ranging character, but in some respects it hardly ranges far enough. In particular, some fuller discussion of the ancient Near Eastern background of the O.T. would be desirable, and certainly there should be a much more thorough investigation of the LXX evidence than the author gives.   J.R.P.

PAURITSCH, K.: *Die neue Gemeinde: Gott sammelt Ausgestossene und Arme (Jesaia 56–66).* (Analecta Biblica, 47) 1971. Pp. xvi, 289. (Biblical Institute Press, Rome. Price: Lire 4,500, $7.50)

The sub-title is 'Die Botschaft des Tritojesaia-Buches literar-, form-, gattungskritisch und redaktionsgeschichtlich untersucht'. Each section of Isaiah 56–66 is systematically examined in detail from these three points of view, leading to a distinctive, though speculative view of the origin and structure of the book. The main clue is found in 56:3–7. Emissaries from a community of believers in Yahweh (in Babylon) asked about the admission of aliens and eunuchs to the cult community. A prophet (515–510 B.C.) gave an answer. Questions were also asked concerning the fulfilment of the eschatological message of 2 Isaiah and the nearness of Yahweh to his people in the situation of Jerusalem. The answers amount to a reinterpretation of the prophecies of 2 Isaiah. Subsequently a redactor took the oral and the written material and wove it together according to the definite plan of the present book. There is no single author. Theological homogeneity is provided by the redactor. The work belongs to the early post-exilic period, mostly to 521–510 B.C.   D.R.J.

POHLMANN, K.-F.: *Studien zum dritten Esra. Ein Beitrag zur Frage nach dem ursprünglichen Schluss des chronistischen Geschichtswerkes.* (Forschungen zur Religion und Literatur des Alten und Neuen Testaments, 104). 1970. Pp. 164. (Vandenhoeck und Ruprecht, Göttingen. Price: DM. 32)

> This monograph presents in unaltered form a dissertation submitted at Marburg in the winter of 1968–9. It is a very careful examination of the relationship between 1 Esdras (III Ezra) and the canonical books of Ezra–Nehemiah, and between both of these and Josephus. The discussions of the literary (and by implication, historical) problems raised by the canonical books are reviewed, though it is unfortunate that when the work was prepared for publication, account was not taken of some more recent studies which are relevant. The conclusion, already regarded as very probable by a number of scholars, including this reviewer, that the original work of the Chronicler did not contain the Nehemiah material, is here provided with the fullest critical justification. Consequences are briefly drawn for the understanding of the Chronicler's original purpose; there are also clear and useful historical consequences. The careful evaluation of Josephus' material is not the least useful part of this very well-argued study.   P.R.A.

PREUSS, H. D.: *Verspottung fremder Religionen im Alten Testament.* (Beiträge zur Wissenschaft vom Alten und Neuen Testament, v, 12.) 1971. (W. Kohlhammer Verlag, Stuttgart. Pp. 320. Price: DM. 76)

> This thesis by H. D. Preuss is concerned with the basic theme of Israel's distinctive conception of God as it manifested itself in a widespread and subtle rejection of non-Yahwistic gods and cults. The particular subject matter is the holding up of foreign gods to ridicule in a strong polemic which makes use of various techniques of irony, satire, taunts and outright mockery, and which is found extensively throughout the O.T. After outlining the starting point in the first two commandments of the Decalogue, which Preuss sees as historically ancient and as absolutely fundamental to Yahwism, he examines in detail a large number of passages which either implicitly or explicitly exhibit such ridiculing of foreign gods. These passages are brought together in broad historical and literary groups. The work contains much detailed exegesis, and is fully furnished with bibliographical notes and references. There are no particularly new conclusions, save the assertion of the general importance of such a theme to Israelite thought. Nevertheless the bringing together of this material serves to set it in a better perspective, and to bring out very forcibly Israel's consciousness of possessing a very distinctive understanding of God. This very consciousness was more fundamental than the points of attack.   R.E.C.

VON RAD, G.: *Weisheit in Israel.* 1970. Pp. 427. (Neukirchener Verlag, Neukirchen-Vluyn. Price: DM. 28)

> Once again we have to thank von Rad for sharing with us his extensive knowledge and interest in the study of Israel's wisdom literature. He supplies a very full treatment of the background and form of the sayings of the wise men. Of special interest are those sections which deal with idol worship and the cult. Readers will also

be grateful for the penetrating treatment of the book of Job, Ecclesiastes, and the Wisdom of Jesus ben Sira. All students of the O.T. will value and appreciate this further contribution from a scholar who has influenced their thinking about the O.T. for so many years.

E.R.R.

[A French translation: *Israël et la Sagesse.* 1971. Pp. 392. (Éditions Labor et Fides, Geneva. Price: Sw.Fr. 33) has also appeared. An English translation is forthcoming].

VON RAD, G.: *Das Opfer des Abraham.* 1971. Pp. 95, with 4 pictures. (Chr. Kaiser Verlag, München. Price: DM. 8.50)

This splendid little book combines von Rad's well-known analysis and exegesis of Gen. 22 in its first half with comments by Luther, Kierkegaard, and Kolakowski (dated 1965) in its second, rounded off with four black-and-white reproductions of Rembrandt's timeless rendering of the *Aqeda.* A more evocative form of popularisation, based both on scholarship and imagination, can hardly be imagined. The author's widening perspective, with which he views this scandalous narrative of human obedience in its quest for God, stands in inverse proportion to the brevity of his truly remarkable achievement.

U.E.S.

REDFORD, D. B.: *A Study of the Biblical Story of Joseph* (*Genesis 37–50*). (Supplements to Vetus Testamentum, xx). 1970. Pp. xiii, 290. (E. J. Brill, Leiden. Price: Fl. 64; sub. Fl. 56)

The conclusion drawn from this detailed study, in which all the relevant critical techniques are employed, is that the Joseph story is basically a well-constructed tale (*Märchen*) of a characteristically Israelite type, that is, having a historical rather than a purely fictitious theme, composed between 650 and 425 B.C. It contains no traces of the sources J and E, and (*pace* von Rad) is not to be classed as wisdom literature. Various additions, which detract from its original literary perfection, were subsequently made to it, and its final redaction is the work of the Genesis editor (roughly equivalent to P). Some parts of the study are unnecessarily prolix, but the thoroughness with which it has been carried out, together with its full discussion of earlier work, makes it an important contribution to the subject.

R.N.W.

RIDDERBOS, N. H.: *De Plaats van het Loven en van het Bidden in het Oude Testament. Enkele beschouwingen over en naar aanleiding van Psalm 50:14, 15.* 1970. Pp. 39. (J. H. Kok, Kampen. Price: Fl. 2.95)

This lecture, delivered as part of the celebrations of the 90th anniversary of the Free University of Amsterdam, examines the close relation between praise and petition in Ps. 50:14 f. and elsewhere in O.T. Here is found the biblical basis of the statement in the Heidelberg Catechism that prayer is the principal element in thanksgiving. The subject is treated in the context of the history of Israel's religion. 'What God asks is so little' — not our cattle or other property, only our praise and prayer. 'What God asks is so much' — for acceptable praise and prayer can come only from one who is entirely devoted to

God. In Gunkel's words, 'in the background is the thought that what God desires in the last analysis is a heart which, in trouble and good fortune alike, confesses him as the only helper.' F.F.B.

SCHMIDT, L.: *Menschlicher Erfolg und Jahwes Initiative, Studien zu Tradition, Interpretation und Historie in Überlieferungen von Gideon, Saul und David* (Wissenschaftliche Monographien zum Alten und Neuen Testament, 38). 1970. Pp. 246. (Neukirchener Verlag, Neukirchen-Vluyn. Price: DM. 38)

This is a careful exercise in redaction criticism, in which the attempt is made to analyse the original oral traditions within Judg. 6:25–32, 11–24, 1 Sam. 9:1–10:16, the passages containing the proverb 'Is Saul also among the prophets?' and the references in Sam. and Kings to the *nagid*. These traditions are precisely distinguished from the work of various redactors, whose theological purpose is then defined. In the original separate traditions, success is the criterion of the divine activity among men. For the redactors this is insufficient and the explicit commission of Yahweh and the interpretative word of Yahweh is essential. The analysis is carried out with the same precision that we have come to suspect in literary criticism. The consequences for writing the history of the introduction of the monarchy are drawn. There is a long exposition of the meaning of *nagid*, which is taken to indicate a leader of levies in the period before the emergence of the state, among the Rachel tribes. There is also a discussion of the meaning and origin of anointing. D.R.J.

SCHMIDT, W. H.: *Das erste Gebot. Seine Bedeutung für das Alte Testament.* (Theologische Existenz heute, 165.) 1969. Pp. 55. (Chr. Kaiser Verlag, Munich. Price: DM. 5)

This short but thorough study in effect amounts to a plea for a theology of the Old Testament, or better still a biblical theology, which takes as its starting point the first commandment. The author holds that it is this commandment (often of necessity taken with the second commandment) that differentiates Israel from neighbouring ancient oriental religions, acts as her guide line throughout her history, and provides the link between the Old and New Testaments. Without such a commandment Christianity would have degenerated into gnosticism. A.C.J.P.

SCHUTTERMAYR, G.: *Psalm 18 und 2 Samuel 22. Studien zu einem Doppeltext: Probleme der Textkritik und Übersetzung und das Psalterium Pianum.* (Studien zum Alten und Neuen Testament, Band xxv.) 1971. Pp. 241. (Kösel-Verlag, München. Price: DM. 55)

It is to be hoped that the reference in the title to the new Latin Psalter will not deter non-Catholic scholars from using this book: it is in fact a very detailed, and well documented, study of the variants between the two Hebrew recensions of this psalm, and the references to the Psalterium Pianum are only marginal. S.P.B.

SCOTT, R. B. Y.: *The Way of Wisdom.* 1971. Pp. xv, 238. (Macmillan, New York. Price: $7.95)

Scott's *The Relevance of the Prophets* (see *B.L.* 1969, p. 41) has been a much valued guide to the importance of the prophets for nearly thirty years, and his new work is intended to perform an analogous function for the wisdom literature. It examines the place of the wisdom writings both in their Old Testament and in their international context; considers the relation of wisdom to prophecy; and devotes separate sections to Job and Ecclesiastes, and to the features of wisdom piety. A study that brings together recent developments in the understanding of the wisdom writings has long been needed, and this work will fulfil a useful purpose, but a certain diffuseness and tendency to repetition means that the ideal introductory guide to this literature has still to be written.   R.J.C.

SKEHAN, P. W.: *Studies in Israelite Poetry and Wisdom*. (Catholic Biblical Quarterly Monograph Series, I) 1971. Pp. xii, 265. (Catholic Biblical Association of America, Washington, D.C. Price: $9.00)

This first volume in a new series consists of twenty-six studies together with some reviews; they are for the most part reprints, especially from *C.B.Q.*, to which Mgr. Skehan has been a prolific contributor. The main emphasis of the studies is indicated by the title. An editorial statement indicates that the series will normally be devoted to the work of young American Catholic scholars.   R.J.C.

SMART, J. D.: *The Strange Silence of the Bible in the Church*. 1970. Pp. 187. (S.C.M. Press, London; Westminster Press, Philadelphia. Price: £1.05)

The concern of this book with hermeneutical problems places it primarily within the contemporary debate in this area. It handles both Old and New Testaments. Its interest for O.T. scholars will lie both in its handling of the problems raised in contemporary discussion and in its consideration of the nature of biblical interpretation. The divorce between scholarly study and the use of the Bible in church (and synagogue) is a commonly-observed matter for questioning. Professor Smart covers a wide range of questions, not least that of the delicate relationship between objective scholarship and confessional allegiance.   P.R.A.

SOGGIN, J. A.: *Introduzione all'Antico Testamento*. II. *Dall' esilio alla chiusura del Canone alessandrino*. 1969. Pp. 242. (Paidia, Brescia. Price: Lire 2,200)

Professor Alberto Soggin, born in 1926, was a professor in the Evangelical Faculty of Theology in Buenos Aires, and, since 1962, after a sojourn in Jordan, teaches in the Waldensian Faculty in Rome. His second volume of the *Introduzione* presents simply, but with a reasonable amount of detail, the facts and theories regarding the exilic and post-exilic prophets, the hagiographers and the books of the Alexandrian canon. His remarks on the Elephantine papyri are of special interest. A very full bibliography follows upon the text, and he has been able to include some corrections to his first volume (not noted in the *Book List*). One cannot compare this fairly small volume with Eissfeldt or S. R. Driver, but it may introduce a number of readers by easy stages to an understanding of the biblical literature.   J.M.T.B.

STECK, O. H.: *Die Paradieserzählung. Eine Auslegung von Genesis 2, 4b–3, 24.* (Biblische Studien, Heft 60.) 1970. Pp. 131. (Neukirchener Verlag, Neukirchen-Vluyn. Price: DM. 9)

In this survey and evaluation of the present state of scholarly analysis of the Paradise narrative the stress is entirely on German work, including Westermann's commentary; hence the author's approach seems somewhat parochial. An abstract vocabulary, complicated syntax, a running commentary by way of notes as long as the text, and an absence of indices, should not deter the reader from studying this exposition of the Yahwist's methods and aims. Steck holds that literary criticism is here largely unproductive, because the Yahwist, far from being naive, has accomplished a highly integrated story. Three originally independent actors — serpent, woman, man — are placed in Paradise and encounter famous motifs, such as trees, park, cherub, expulsion. The tale is aetiological in a very special way. The Yahwist not only explains what is (tilling the soil in Canaan) but also wishes to shape the true communal life. The reign of David and the problems of the succession favoured such a politico-social concern for the community. But the story transcends also the immediate needs, and the particular serves the universal. The Yahwist's treatment of the making of Man, the trespass and its consequences, shows, when examined in detail, a profound ambivalence: the perfect creation exercises his autonomy in the questionable area of self-destruction. Steck points to the validity of this principle and to the hope beyond Paradise Lost in our day.

U.E.S.

STOLZ, F.: *Strukturen und Figuren im Kult von Jerusalem. Studien zur altorientalischen vor- und frühisraelitischen Religion.* (Beihefte zur Zeitschrift für die alttestamentliche Wissenschaft, 118). 1970. Pp. 235. (Walter de Gruyter, Berlin. Price: DM. 58)

This study is an attempt to explore as thoroughly as the evidence allows the nature and content of the pre-Israelite cultus of Jerusalem. Working from the biblical material and comparing this with the extra-biblical evidence from Ugarit and elsewhere, particularly as to the evidence of divine names, and rituals, Stolz reconstructs a picture of the old Jerusalem pantheon, with its mythology and cult symbols. The first chapter deals with the myth of creation after a conflict with the power, or powers, of chaos, and the second with the motif of a divine conflict with hostile nations. Both are related by the author to the experience of a great experience of cultural transition. Very full studies are devoted to the god El and his many forms in the ancient Near East, and to the god Šalem and his relation to Chemosh, Milcom and to the ritual inheritance which the Israelites took over from Canaan relating to the practice of child sacrifice. Finally all this is briefly discussed in relation to the distinctive adaptations and developments which took place in Israel. As the author admits, much of the study cannot, of necessity, be more than 'more or less probable conjectures', but there is a very full documentation which makes it a valuable basis for further investigation.

R.E.C.

*THOROGOOD, B.: *A Guide to the Book of Amos* (TEF Study Guide, 4). 1971. Pp. x, 118. (S.P.C.K. London. Price: 45p)

The style of this commentary is that of the same publisher's *Guide to Genesis* (see *B.L.* 1970, p. 48). Included in this 'Guide 'are 22 photographs of human situations from many parts of the world skilfully chosen to relate the prophetic world to the life of mankind today. It is intended for readers using English as a second language, but may be warmly commended for schools in this country. A.S.H.

TUCKER, G. M.: *Form Criticism of the Old Testament*. (Guides to Biblical Scholarship: Old Testament Guides). 1971. Pp. xii, 84. (Fortress Press, Philadelphia. Price: $2.50)

This book, the second in a series in which the volume on literary criticism, by Norman Habel, has apparently already been published, is probably the best introduction to the subject which has appeared so far. It makes a clear distinction at the outset between form criticism in the strict sense and other related disciplines such as redaction- and tradition-criticism, and confines itself to a clear and simple account of the purpose and methods of its proper subject, while at the same time pointing out the relationship of form criticism to the critical enterprise as a whole. The author has, probably wisely in view of the space at his disposal, confined his illustrations, which form the bulk of the book, to two *genres*, narrative and prophecy. The final chapter, in which he tries to summarize in a few pages the way in which form criticism has been applied to other *genres*, is the least satisfactory part of the book. This is mainly a book for beginners, but in these days of terminological imprecision the more advanced reader may well find that it helps to clarify his understanding of the subject. R.N.W.

VOGELS, W.: *La promesse royale de Yahweh préparatoire à l'alliance. Étude d'une forme littéraire de l'Ancien Testament*. 1970. Pp. 181. (Éditions de l'Université Saint Paul / Éditions de l'Université d'Ottawa, Ottawa)

The vassal treaties of the ancient Near East are employed here, with particular reference to the Pentateuch and the canonical prophets as represented by Hosea, Jeremiah, Ezekiel, and Zechariah, in an effort to elucidate in connection with the Sinaitic covenant an apparent scheme involving (i) a basic promise of Yahweh's readiness to protect Israel and, following upon the nation's disloyalty, (ii) a fresh promise of such protection with the *rîb* pattern as the decisive stage in the process. The work reads smoothly, and its value is enhanced by an extensive bibliography and the many passing comments on its contents which occur in the footnotes to the text. On the whole, however, one is left with a renewed impression that there is too much of the strait-jacket technique in studies of this kind, and that here again the value of the vassal treaties tends to be exaggerated.

A.R.J.

VOLLMER, J.: *Geschichtliche Rückblicke und Motive in der Prophetie des Amos, Hosea und Jesaja*. (Beihefte zur Zeitschrift für die alttestament-liche Wissenschaft, 119). 1971. Pp. 217. (Walter de Gruyter, Berlin. Price: DM. 62)

This important dissertation examines the oracles of these prophets with particular reference to their allusions to Israel's history. How do they see Israel's history? How far is their historical survey integral to their whole message? How does this relate to the aim of the prophetic word? What is the relation between the word and the tradition,

and what is the origin of the tradition? After an examination of the
various historical references in the three prophets, including translation, and form-critical analysis, their view of history and their relation
to the tradition (Exodus, Zion, Davidic) is examined. The dissertation
starts from and develops the view expressed in G. von Rad's *Old
Testament Theology*, Vol. II.   A.S.H.

WALKENHORST, K.-H.: *Der Sinai im liturgischen Verständnis der deuteronomistischen und priesterlichen Tradition* (Bonner Biblische Beiträge, 33).
1969. Pp. xiv, 170. (Peter Hanstein Verlag, Bonn. Price: DM. 32)

This book is a little narrower than its title suggests. A review of
recent scholarly discussion of the cultic interpretation of the Sinai
traditions is followed by a very full literary analysis of the P traditions
of the institution of the cult in Ex. 29 and in Lev. 8 and 9, as a result
of which it is argued that it is Lev. 8 and 9 which represent the older
form of the tradition, on which Ex. 29 is based. Only very briefly
at the end is a contrast drawn with the Deuteronomic understanding
of the Sinai event. The points made are interesting, but could with
advantage have been presented more briefly.   J.V.M.S.

WANKE, G.: *Untersuchungen zur sogenannten Baruchschrift*. (Beihefte zur
Zeitschrift für die alttestamentliche Wissenschaft, 122.) 1971. Pp.
viii, 156. (Walter de Gruyter, Berlin. Price: DM. 42)

Wanke re-examines and challenges the widely held view that the
narrative material in the book of Jeremiah is the work of one author
who is in all probability to be identified with Baruch. He isolates
three blocks of material and argues that from the point of view of
origin, structure and purpose they were originally separate from each
other. These three groups of texts are: (1) 19:1–20:6; 26–29; 36;
(2) 37–43; (3) 45; 51:59–64. Of these the third does not belong
strictly speaking to the narrative material but constitutes a small
complex of tradition probably based upon sayings of Jeremiah. The
basis of 37–43 is a series of smaller units which both individually and
as a group are the work of one author. The first group has a more
complex history behind it: the earliest material here is in chapters
26–28, 36 and is the work of one author; the remaining material in
this group was developed subsequently. It is argued that 37–43 is
more plausibly seen as the work of a member of Gedaliah's 'colony'
at Mizpah than as the composition of Baruch, whilst there is as
much to be said against as in favour of attributing 26–28, 36 to
Baruch. Wanke then outlines a number of issues, traditio-historical
and form-critical as well as historical, with which future research in
the problem on hand will have to reckon, and the book concludes
with a brief statement of the theological purpose of the three blocks of
material isolated from the narrative material as a whole in Jeremiah.

E.W.N.

WERNER, H.: *Uraspekte menschlichen Lebens nach Texten aus Genesis 2–11*
(Exempla Biblica, 5). 1971. Pp. 226. (Vandenhoeck & Ruprecht,
Göttingen. Price: DM. 19.80)

The series to which this book belongs is designed primarily for
religious instruction in schools. This volume contains a valuable,
scholarly presentation of the material in the J tradition in Genesis 2–11

on the nature of man. Critical problems are clearly indicated. Judicious use is made of comparative material from extra-biblical sources, the relevant parts of the Gilgamesh Epic, for example, being printed side by side with sections from the J and P versions of the flood tradition.

R.D.

WHALLON, W.: *Formula, Character, and Context: studies in Homeric, Old English and Old Testament Poetry*. (Published by the Center for Hellenic Studies, Washington, D.C.) 1969. Pp. 225. (Harvard University Press, Cambridge, Massachusetts. Price: $10.00)

The purpose of this work is to show that the Homeric epithets are significantly true to the individual characters to which they are applied, while those applied to the heroes of the Iliad influenced their characterization; that the 'kennings' for *Beowulf* rank high in relevance to context but low in economy when compared with the epithets assigned to Homeric heroes and that the poetic fiction of *Beowulf*, though reformed, has not been converted by indebtedness to Scripture and liturgy, inasmuch as the religious elements are actually those of a barely reformed Germanic heathenism, and, finally, that no element in the poetry of the Old Testament is more likely than not to have been created for the passage in which it now appears and that biblical poetry has its frame of reference in the prose. This conclusion follows from the two facts: that Hebrew poetry lacks distinctive characterization and consists of non-naturalistic speech while at the same time it refers only vaguely to its context. Thus Jesus was a traditional poet but he was also a scholar. The latter point can be recognized in his use of the Old Testament, especially when the authority whom he is quoting is named, *e.g.* Isaiah or a Psalmist; and many other sayings contain half or entire verses of poetry which, though not announced as from the Old Testament, call it to mind; the former suggests that he was in the line of the traditional poets, whether reworking old lines or coining fresh ones to suit the immediate situation in the traditional form, often indicated by parallelism of thought. How much was appropriated and how much original cannot now be said, just as it is unclear whether the oral poem, his own work or that of any other speaker, was formally dictated, as some of Jeremiah's teaching was dictated to Baruch; possibly only the Beatitudes spoken in the Sermon on the Mount, although they exist in two slightly differing versions, may have been taken down from dictation. The argument, though over elaborated and much of it barely relevant, is interesting and well worth consideration.

G.R.D.

WHEDBEE, J. W.: *Isaiah and Wisdom*. 1971. Pp. 172. (Abingdon Press, Nashville and New York. Price: $5.95)

The author makes a valuable contribution to the understanding of the relation between the prophets and the wisdom literature. As far as Isaiah is concerned, the influence of the wisdom material is to be seen in his use of parable, proverb, and other didactic forms. It is also pointed out that there is a connection between the 'Woe' oracles and the wisdom literature. This also forms the background to Isaiah's use of the term 'counsel'. This penetrating study will be welcomed by students of both prophetic and wisdom literature.

E.R.R.

WHYBRAY, R. N.: *The Heavenly Counsellor in Isaiah xl. 13–14. A Study of the Sources of the Theology of Deutero-Isaiah.* (S.O.T.S. Monograph Series, 1). 1971. Pp. viii, 91. (Cambridge University Press. Price: £2·20)

This little book merits a warm welcome as the first of the new monograph series of the S.O.T.S. and it sets a high standard for the following monographs. Dr. Whybray offers a detailed examination of two verses in Isaiah 40 in which he puts all the terms used under the microscope and discusses the possible sources for the idea of the heavenly counsellor. While recognizing that the prophet must have been familiar with the Israelite tradition of the heavenly council, he comes to the conclusion that the verses in question imply a warning against taking over ideas associated with the Babylonian pantheon such as might suggest a limitation of the power of Yahweh. Dr. Whybray's argument is persuasive. Perhaps, however, where on pp. 10 and 29–30 he discusses 'the vocabulary of instruction' he should have allowed for the necessity under which a Hebrew poet lies of finding synonyms; one must not press too much distinctions of meaning but should recognize that a certain overlapping of spheres of ideas is not altogether surprising. It is a little odd that no account is taken of Muilenburg's masterly commentary in the Interpreter's Bible.

N.W.P.

WILLI, T.: *Herders Beitrag zum Verstehen des Alten Testaments.* 1971. Pp. viii, 152. (J. C. B. Mohr (Paul Siebeck), Tübingen. Price: DM. 19)

To be reminded of Herder's outstanding greatness in pioneering modern methods of understanding the O.T. is something for which one remains grateful, especially if it is done with the clarity and critical insight which the author brings to this monograph. We watch the genius, who combined science with piety in a rare blend, working in the areas of language, orientalism, literary forms, and, above all, the impact of history on the Word, and of the Word on history. In a way, our problems, especially in the interpretation of the O.T., seem to be continuous with Herder's initial explorations. Willi does not force modern approaches upon Herder, but lets him speak for himself. The result is a very human document which must please every biblical humanist. A pity that the offset print of very small type tries the weary eye and makes the excellent documentation almost unreadable.

U.E.S.

WILLI-PLEIN, I.: *Vorformen der Schriftexegese innerhalb des Alten Testaments. Untersuchungen zum literarischen Werden der auf Amos, Hosea und Micha zurückgehenden Bücher im hebräischen Zwölfprophetenbuch.* (Beihefte zur Zeitschrift für die alttestamentliche Wissenschaft, 123) 1971. Pp. viii, 286. (Walter de Gruyter, Berlin. Price: DM. 88)

Recent work on the prophets has shown the great importance of the secondary additions to the text, including glosses, elaborations and applications of the prophet's original words, as a very fundamental interpretative procedure which belongs essentially to the growth of the O.T. as a sacred canon. This thesis examines in great care and detail the passages in Amos, Hosea and Micah which are to be regarded as secondary, with a view to examining their interpretative intention and presuppositions. Each such text is examined separately, and evidence sought as to the period of its origin and its particular purpose. Then overall a general summary is given setting out a sketch of the growth of the particular book into its present form, with attention given to the religious concerns of each age. Thus the prophetic word is seen to possess a living history as further prophetic-type developments of it were made over a very extended period. Much of the detail in the thesis necessarily remains very controversial, and frequently only broad general arguments can be adduced in reconstruction of the setting of any particular individual addition. Worthy of note are the author's arguments against H. W. Wolff's emphasis upon the Deuteronomic features of the editing of Amos and Hosea. Altogether this is a very useful study of these eighth century prophets, which makes a contribution towards solving some exceedingly difficult questions.

R.E.C.

LAW, RELIGION AND THEOLOGY

*ANDERSON, B. W.: *The Unfolding Drama of the Bible: Eight Studies introducing the Bible as a Whole*. 2nd ed. 1971. Pp. 218. (Association Press, New York. Price: $1.75)

Although the present reissue of this study guide is described as the second edition, earlier forms of it (none of which were noticed in *B.L.*) appeared in 1952, 1953, and 1957. The general plan remains the same; but changes have been made in the text and in the biblical passages for study; and there are useful bibliographical additions. There are seven study sections spanning the entire Bible. Questions for group discussion are provided; and there are also general suggestions for study leaders. The O.T. sections deal with Creation, the Exodus and Sinai, Jeremiah and the Fall of Jerusalem, the Return, and the People of the Torah. There is rich theological content in this imaginatively written booklet.

G.W.A.

BUCHANAN, G. W.: *The Consequences of the Covenant*. (Supplements to Novum Testamentum, xx.) 1970. Pp. xviii, 342. (E. J. Brill, Leiden. Price: Fl. 84; sub. Fl. 72)

'Conquest theology', and the particular form of it embodied in what this writer believes to be the teaching of Jesus that the Kingdom of God meant the liberation and restoration of Solomonic Israel-Judah and the 're-establishment of Jerusalem as the capital of all the twelve tribes of Israel' (p. 82), form an extremely tenuous framework for this collection of fragments of research into a very wide range of biblical subjects. Sections on the geographical extent of Israel at different periods (chapter 3), and on the alleged 'sabbatical eschatology' of Isaiah and Jeremiah, may have some curiosity value for readers of this *Book List*; and those whose special interests lie in the Judaism of the N.T. period will be intrigued by the listing side by side, in a chapter on 'covenantal sectarianism', of the known sects of that period and the 'sect of St Matthew' and the 'sect of St John', i.e. the communities for which the First Gospel and 1 John were written. The very widely ranging bibliography is the most useful part of the book.

C.J.A.H.

COHN, H. H. (ed.): *Jewish Law in Ancient and Modern Israel. Selected Essays.* 1971. Pp. xxxiv, 259. (Ktav Publishing House, Inc., New York. Price: $12.50)

This volume of essays reprinted from *The Israel Law Review* and *Scripta Hierosolymitana* mainly concerns the conflict between the divine Jewish law and the secular legislation of the new state of Israel. In addition there are essays on 'The Goring Ox in Near Eastern Law' (R. Yaron), 'The Penology of the Talmud', and 'Reflections on the Trial and Death of Jesus' (both by the Editor). While most of this volume does not directly concern the O.T. specialist, it does amply illustrate the essentially pragmatic approach of Jewish lawyers in the face of new situations from O.T. times onwards. It is this approach that is now in question.   A.C.J.P.

EICHRODT, W.: *Religionsgeschichte Israels* (Dalp-Taschenbücher, Band 394 D). 1969. Pp. 146. (Francke Verlag, Bern und München. Price: Sw.Fr. 4.80, DM. 3.80)

Although in brief pocket book form, this outline history of Israel's religion bears the hallmark of its author's insights and expertise. It is a new and expanded treatment of a contribution published originally in *Historia Mundi* II (Francke Verlag, Bern, 1953), 377–448, and deals with the religion in the usual order of the periods of the Patriarchs (only briefly, and with a following section on the Covenant), the Settlement, and (at greater length) the Monarchy, and the Exile and after. A comprehensive bibliography completes the work.

E.T.R.

FLÜCKIGER, F.: *Theologie der Geschichte. Die biblische Rede von Gott und die neuere Geschichtstheologie.* 1970. Pp. 208 (Rolf Brockhaus, Wuppertal. Price: DM. 14.80)

The main essay, entitled 'Prophetie und Geschichte', forms the first half of the book. Though concerned as much with the New Testament as the Old, and indeed written from the standpoint of dogmatics, this is of direct interest to the theologian of the O.T. It is written with clarity, without too much academic in-fighting and with frequent and apt biblical illustration. The main point is that while revelation is correctly understood as occurring in and through history, it can only be understood as act of God through the prophetic word. From this point of view a correction of Pannenberg's thought is possible. The author agrees with Pannenberg that *Heilsgeschichte* is not a special kind of history and may be located anywhere in world history. He disagrees with Pannenberg's equation of revelation with world history. The otherwise hidden meaning of secular events becomes knowable through faith awakened by prophetic illumination. The implications of this principle are worked out with skill, and provide a strong defence of essential orthodoxy against some modern deviations. There are also essays on the theology of Pannenberg, 'God is dead', 'Evil in society' and 'Anti-semitism in the Church'.

D.R.J.

KAUFMANN, Y.: *Connaître la Bible* (Sinaï. Collections des Sources d'Israel). 1970. Pp. 400. (Presses Universitaires de France, Paris. Price: Fr. 30).

It is not explicitly stated either in this volume or in the publisher's note accompanying it that this French text is a translation from the

English version (*The Religion of Israel*, 1960. See *B.L.* 1961, p. 48; *Decade*, p. 286). But this appears to be the case. It covers the period from the beginnings to the Babylonian exile, and includes some considerable discussion of the nature and formation of the biblical material. It may be doubted, however, whether the French title is as good as the English, and it will certainly mislead some readers into expecting a work of introduction.

P.R.A.

KAUFMANN, Y.: *The Babylonian Captivity and Deutero-Isaiah*. (*History of the Religion of Israel*, Vol. IV, Chapters 1, 2.) Translated by C. W. Efroymson. 1970. Pp. xvi, 236. (Union of American Hebrew Congregations, New York. Price: $7.50)

The English translation of an abridgement of Kaufmann's *Religion of Israel* (Vols I-III, based upon the first seven volumes of the original. 1960, 1961. See *B.L.*, 1961, p. 48; *Decade*, p. 286). This volume offers the first part of what is intended to be a rendering of the whole of Vol. IV (VIII); when the complete work is available an index and list of passages quoted is promised. This is particularly necessary in view of the presentation. For this volume consists of a chapter dealing with the conditions of the exilic age, another dealing with Deutero–Isaiah, two appendices, bibliography and notes. The section on Deutero–Isaiah is very diffuse, partly more detailed commentary, partly sections on different topics. As in the earlier books, there is much comment on points of detail which is of considerable interest; but far too much rather unprofitable polemic with often somewhat outmoded views, particularly designated as 'Liberal-Protestant'. Isa. 40–66 (plus 34–5) is treated as a literary unity, and considerable attention is devoted both in the text and in one appendix to demonstrating this unity of style and language. With all the rejection of Christian scholarship which goes on, it is strange to find that the notion of 'Servant Songs' remains as if it were an established tenet of scholarship.

P.R.A.

KELLERMANN, U.: *Messias und Gesetz. Grundlinien einer alttestamentlichen Heilserwartung: eine traditionsgeschichtliche Einführung.* (Biblische Studien, Heft 61). 1971. Pp. 142. (Neukirchener Verlag, Neukirchen-Vluyn. Price: DM. 11; sub. DM. 10)

This is an attempt to throw light on the attitude of the New Testament writers to the Law and its relevance for the Christian by investigating the O.T. and inter-testamental background. The development of the concepts of Law and Messiah (in the broad sense) is traced in a rather breathless survey of the relevant texts. The results are mainly negative: only rarely do the two concepts appear together in a significant relationship. The survey itself is not, however, without interest, although in some places arguments are based on debatable presuppositions.

R.N.W.

KOCH, K.: *Ratlos vor der Apokalyptik. Eine Streitschrift über ein vernachlässigtes Gebiet der Bibelwissenschaft und die schädlichen Auswirkungen auf Theologie und Philosophie.* 1970. Pp. 120. (Gütersloher Verlagshaus Gerd Mohn, Gütersloh. Price: DM. 12.80)

This book, which is perhaps of more interest to N.T. scholars and systematic theologians than to O.T. scholars, takes its starting point from what its author describes as a renaissance of apocalyptic, a renaissance typified by the writings of E. Käsemann and W. Pannenberg: its main aim, to which the two central chapters are devoted, is to give a critical (but not exhaustive) survey of recent German discussions dealing with the place of apocalyptic in the life and preaching of Jesus and the Early Church on the one hand, and in contemporary theology on the other. From this survey the author concludes that the normal methods of historical criticism have generally not been applied in the case of apocalyptic, that those who have written about apocalyptic have done so by and large on the basis of an inadequate understanding of its nature, and that it is essential, if progress is to be made in the N.T. and doctrinal fields, that this situation be remedied. However, the preliminary chapters of the book are of direct interest to the O.T. scholar. Here the author gives a short, but valuable, sketch of apocalyptic, and discusses the writings on apocalyptic of M. Noth, O. Plöger and G. von Rad. He also assesses the contributions of English and American scholars in this area of study. An English translation is now available, cf. p. 81.

M.A.K.

KRAUS, H.-J.: *Die biblische Theologie: Ihre Geschichte und Problematik.* 1970. Pp. xiv, 408. (Neukirchener Verlag, Neukirchen-Vluyn. Price: DM. 44)

Professor Kraus, whose history of the critical study of the O.T. is well known (*Decade*, p. 10; *B.L.* 1970, p. 50), has now produced what is in some sense a companion volume on biblical theology. The pre-supposition of the work is that the time has come to produce a biblical theology which would transcend the division between O.T. and N.T. theologies which, in the main, has prevailed since the beginning of the 19th century. The volume under review is not intended to be such a work, but rather a clearing of the ground to see whether and how it could be produced. As the title indicates, both the history of the discipline and current methodological problems are discussed. The historical treatment begins at the Reformation, but it does not continue in unbroken perspective right down to the present day. After the development of biblical theology has been traced down to the end of the 19th century, there is a survey of O.T. theology in relation to the N.T. from G. L. Bauer to G. von Rad, followed by a similar survey of N.T. theology in relation to the O.T. from F. C. Baur to R. Bultmann. The dogmatic treatment of the relationship between the Testaments is then surveyed from Scheiermacher (with some preliminary observations on Semler, Lessing, Hamann, and Herder) to Tillich. Finally, some 100 pages are devoted to those problems which arise in the relationship between biblical study and dogmatic theology.   G.W.A.

KUSKE, M.: *Das Alte Testament als Buch von Christus. Dietrich Bonhoeffers Wertung und Auslegung des Alten Testaments.* 1971. Pp. 140. (Vanden-hoeck & Ruprecht, Göttingen. Price DM. 21)

This book represents an important contribution to the understanding of Dietrich Bonhoeffer's interpretation and use of scripture and, as such, it throws considerable light upon his developing theological position. The author clearly shows that Bonhoeffer changed his views in certain respects. The discussion will help readers to under-stand what Bonhoeffer meant by his claim that Christ is the centre of the Bible and that each Testament must be read in the light of the other. He was deeply influenced by Barth, but his view of the Old Testament must not be equated with that of W. Vischer. It is useful to have a clarification of what Bonhoeffer meant by religion in the expression 'religionless Christianity', viz. religiosity. This has its importance for Old Testament theology.   N.W.P.

LIEDKE, G.: *Gestalt und Bezeichnung alttestamentlicher Rechtssätze* (Wissenschaftliche Monographien zum Alten und Neuen Testament, 39). 1971. Pp. 234. (Neukirchener Verlag, Neukirchen-Vluyn. Price: DM. 36. sub. DM. 32.40)

The work here reviewed was originally a dissertation presented at the University of Heidelberg in 1968. It now appears as something far beyond that; it is a careful examination of the two classes in law, setting out first the offence and second the consequences for the offender, those called by Alt *der kasuistische Rechtsatz* and *der apodiktische Rechtsatz*. These are exhaustively examined both in the O.T. and in the Scrolls from Qumran and elsewhere in the ancient east, notably in the Assyrio-Babylonian and in Hittite law-codes. All the technical terms are fully examined and their meanings carefully defined; nor are their differences overlooked (such as those of 'if/when a man . . .' and 'a man who . . . does such and such an act' or 'one committing an act') for the light which they shed on literary sources. There are also special digressions on several legal terms such as *šapaṭ*, and *mišpaṭ*, *ḥaqaq*,*ḥoq* and *huqqah*, and *torah*. A few errors have been noted, but the study is a model of its kind. The technical German idiom may occasionally be a case of difficulty to English readers; they however ought especially to read it with care since the problems raised in it are as yet insufficiently discussed in English works.   G.R.D.

MAUSER, U.: *Gottesbild und Menschwerdung. Eine Untersuchung zur Einheit des Alten und Neuen Testaments.* (Beiträge zur Historischen Theologie, 43.) 1971. Pp. vii, 211 (J. C. B. Mohr (Paul Siebeck), Tübingen. Price: DM. 32 (paper); 38 (cloth))

This study of the relation between the Old and New Testaments is of particular interest because as it criticizes both Bultmann and Zimmerli for their differing employment of the category of promise and fulfilment. In brief the argument of the book is that the essential unity of the Bible consists in its witness to incarnation. Anthropomorphism has often been regarded as due to an unspiritual view of God. On the contrary the author would plead for the theomorphism of man. After a discussion of the views of Xenophanes and Philo and certain tendencies of modern theology, Mauser divides his book into two main sections. In the first (Chapters III and IV) he subjects the prophecies of Hosea and Jeremiah to a detailed examination with a view to demonstrating that these prophets may be regarded as a parable of God's self-identification with Israel and the struggle between judgement and mercy which that involves. In particular it is argued that the Confessions of Jeremiah are wrongly interpreted as revealing a struggle between the humanity of the prophet and the will of God. The author then turns to the new Testament and examines the Pauline Epistles. In opposition to Bultmann's neglect of the Jesus of history he claims that Jesus' life as well as his death and resurrection is to be regarded as an act of God. In Christ the incarnation of God in the world is complete. The New Testament section contains some detailed and difficult argument and the whole book is a serious contribution to biblical theology.   N.W.P.

NEVILLE, G.: *City of our God. God's presence among his people.* 1971. Pp. ix, 118. (S.P.C.K., London, Price: £2.10)

This work examines the idea of Jerusalem in the Old and New Testaments, and in some of the pseudepigrapha, in order to bring out the way in which God's presence among his people was there envisaged. Two especial dangers, of localisation and of supposing Jerusalem to be inviolable, are found to be present; and various suggestions are then made for the contemporary Christian community preparing to encounter God's presence. Some interesting points are made; but the O.T. sections suffer from too schematic a presentation and from an apparent lack of knowledge of recent treatments of the same theme.   R.J.C.

NIELSEN, E.: *Det gamle Israels religion.* 1971. Pp. 153. (G.E.C. Gad, Copenhagen. Price: D.Kr. 36,80)

The author has preferred to give the subject neither a purely historical nor a systematic treatment, but after two introductory chapters, with a short survey of the history of Israel and the writings of the Old Testament, five chapters follow containing the religion in (1) the epic literature, (2) the cult lyrics, (3) the laws, (4) the prophetical literature, and (5) the wisdom literature (i.e. the Proverbs, the Book of Job and Gen. 1–11). The book is an enlarged and improved edition of E. Nielsen's contribution to *Illustreret Religionshistorie* ed. J. P. Asmussen and J. Laessoe, 1968, and will undoubtedly be much used by teachers as well as by students of theology.   E.H.

PEARCE, V. E. R.: *Who was Adam?* 1969. Pp. 151. (Paternoster Press, Exeter. Price: £1·25)

The author describes his work as 'a scientific exercise to meet the propaganda of those who say, "Science disproves the Bible"' (p. 87). Its premise is a strictly conservative approach to the text, justified, inter alia, by archaeology. The quotations from biblical scholars at this point are tendentiously selective. Social anthropology is invoked to prove that Adam in Gen. 2–3 is New Stone Age Man, while the Adam of Gen. 1 is Old Stone Age Man.

Similarly, genetics provide us with the clue as to how the Word was coded in the D.N.A. of the Virgin Mary. The book will delight those who believe this to be a useful kind of apologetic. Biblical scholars will regret that nowhere is there any attempt to discuss the nature of the material in the early chapters of Genesis.   R.D.

PHILLIPS, A. C. J.: *Ancient Israel's Criminal Law.* 1970. Pp. viii, 218. (Blackwell, Oxford. Price: £3·00)

Among the vast literature dealing with the Ten Commandments, the sub-title of this book, 'A New Approach to the Decalogue', does not claim too much. The author argues that the Commandments were the stipulations of a covenant actually entered into at Sinai and thus so fundamental were they to the nation's existence that any breach of them endangered the whole covenant relationship and so must be punished, by the public agents of the community, with death. Hence the Decalogue has a clearly marked unity, it was Israel's criminal code, and, unlike all other ancient Near Eastern legal systems, Israel's law clearly distinguished between crimes and torts. This theory is developed with great vigour and acuteness, but it leaves a great many questions to be answered. Apart from the legal problem and the somewhat forced interpretation that his thesis compels Dr. Phillips to put on some of the Commandments — e.g. the tenth — his argument is closely linked with a particular, and perhaps rather over-simplified, view of Israel's historical development. For example, is the existence of a pre-monarchial amphictyony, which is essential for his thesis, quite so obvious and unquestionable as he seems to suppose? Nevertheless, this is a very able and stimulating study which illuminates many aspects of the Decalogue and of Israel's legal and religious development.   J.R.P.

PIXLEY, J. V.: *Pluralismo de tradiciones en la religión bíblica*. 1971. Pp. 133. (La Aurora, Buenos Aires)

This volume appears in a series entitled Cuadernos de Contestación Polémica. The stated intention of the author, Dean and Professor of Old Testament at the Seminario Evangélico de Puerto Rico, in San Juan, is to describe the variety of Old Testament traditions, in order to enable better dialogue with a world of religious pluralism today, especially that found in Latin America.

Little attempt is made to relate the chapters to each other, to draw conclusions and comparisons between the traditions, or to fashion the material so as best to address or confront the modern scene. The general tone of the book is descriptive and not argumentative. Actually, what the book offers is a recapitulation of major theological issues in several sectors of Israel's history and thought, viz., tribal religion, agrarian religion, Israelite mythology and its sources, religion of the state (king and capital city), religion of intellectuals (wisdom), and prophetic religion. The synthesis worked out in the brief compass of each chapter is interesting and well-done, up-to-date, and modestly documented. Each reader will find issues upon which to disagree with the author, whether in interpretation or selection of material; this is nevertheless an important contribution to the Latin American literature on the Old Testament.   W.J.F.

REVENTLOW, H. GRAF.: *Rechtfertigung im Horizont des Alten Testaments* (Beiträge zur evangelischen Theologie, Band 58). 1971. Pp. 164. (Chr. Kaiser Verlag, München. Price: DM. 24.50)

The subject was evoked by the failure of the world Lutheran assembly at Helsinki in 1963 to see the relevance of the O.T. for the key theological concept of justification. The paucity of justification language in the O.T. must not blind the reader to the presence of the principle *passim*. Accordingly it is possible to understand the O.T. as a whole from this standpoint. Covenant and justification are regarded as correlative terms and recent approaches to the O.T. on the basis of the idea of covenant are comprehensively surveyed. The author leans heavily on the thesis that *şedek* means basically the right order-ing of the world. Justification is not therefore an individual matter only. The justification of God's people is demonstrated in J, the deuteronomic history, Hosea, and most persuasively in Ezekiel. There is also a long section on individual justification in the Psalms, in which issue is joined with von Rad. The final section deals with the bearing of all this upon Christian theology (including an important section on the representative mediator) and reveals the author at home in both the N.T. and Dogmatics. A unique book of its kind.

D.R.J.

SCHMID, H. H.: *Frieden ohne Illusionen. Die Bedeutung des Begriffs schalom als Grundlage für eine Theologie des Friedens.* 1971. Pp. 64. (Theologischer Verlag, Zürich. Price: Sw.Fr. 6.80)

This is a short popular study of the concept of *shalom* in the Old Testament, stressing its special religious quality and positive meaning. After a brief survey of ideas of peace in Egypt and Mesopotamia the author shows the various areas of life in which *shalom* was important. The notion of world peace as a part of the content of Israel's hope is especially brought out. *Shalom* is seen as a comprehensive concept ranging far beyond the political and military spheres, and relating to the whole social order. On the basis of this study the author raises various questions relating to modern political and social problems.

R.E.C.

SEIDEL, H.: *Das Erlebnis der Einsamkeit im Alten Testament. Eine Unter-suchung zum Menschenbild des Alten Testaments.* (Theologische Arbeiten, Band 29). 1969. Pp. 184. (Evangelische Verlagsanstalt, Berlin. Price: DM. 13)

A dissertation presented in 1963 is here published in revised form. It examines the theme of solitude and loneliness in the O.T. on the basis of the Psalms of the Individual, Job and the experiences of prophets and other figures. The treatment links readily with aspects of psychology, sociology and philosophy, but does not seem to add much to our understanding of the O.T. texts. It is concluded that the Israelite's experience of solitude was bound up with his religious experience and was therefore distinctive. It is interesting that the general bibliography on solitude lists 45 works in German against 2 in English; on the theology of solitude there are listed a further 27 works in German and 2 in English.

J.H.E.

STUHLMUELLER, C.: *Creative Redemption in Deutero-Isaiah* (Analecta Biblica, 43.) 1970. Pp. xii, 300. (Pontifical Biblical Institute, Rome. Price: Lire 4,500. $7.50)

This long and detailed work comprises three sections. Part one deals with the purpose and method of the investigation and discusses among other things the importance of creation faith in Deutero-Isaiah, the literary genre of the poems on creative redemption, and Hebrew syntax in relation to these poems. Part two discusses how Deutero-Isaiah viewed Israel's traditions within the context of the problems of the exile and expanded and transformed those traditions into his message of 'creative redemption'. The discussion in this second part centres on the New Exodus theme (chapter four) and on Yahweh as *gō'ēl* and Israel as Yahweh's elect people (chapter five).

Part three investigates the 'doctrinal motifs' peculiar to Deutero-Isaiah and includes chapters on 'Yahweh, First and Last, as Creative Redeemer', 'the Creative Word of Yahweh', 'Redemption in its Cosmic-Creative Aspects', and 'Creation Vocabulary in the Book of Consolation'.

E.W.N.

VRIEZEN, T. C.: *An Outline of Old Testament Theology.* 2nd ed., 1970. Pp. 479. (Blackwell, Oxford, Price: £5)

In the last twenty years or so Vriezen's *Outline* has rightly established itself as one of the most penetrating treatments of O.T. theology, and has been translated into many languages. The third Dutch edition appeared in 1966 (not noticed in *B.L.*), and forms the basis of this translation. By comparison with the earlier editions, there are brief additional comments on methodology in the first part, and an extensive recasting of the second part, on content. What were formerly the last five chapters have now been brought into three, in a different order and in places substantially revised, with considerable additional stress on the idea of Israel as the community of God. The first Dutch edition was reviewed in *B.L.*, 1950, p. 70; *Eleven Years*, p. 287, and the English translation in *B.L.*, 1958, p. 41; *Decade*, p. 117.

R.J.C.

WATTS, J. D. W.: *Basic Patterns in O.T. Religion.* 1971. Pp. 162. (Vantage Press, New York. Price: $4.50)

In this study the author seeks to understand the religion of the O.T. as the record and as an amalgam of three basic types which he calls 'forms' and which he links with Abraham, Moses and David respectively. While aimed primarily at the student, and though differences of opinion on some points must be expected, the constant search for a plausible *Sitz im Leben* provides a useful brake on the wilder hypotheses of some authors.

D.R.Ap-T.

WEINREB, F.: *Der göttliche Bauplan der Welt. Der Sinn der Bibel nach der ältesten jüdischen Überlieferung.* 1969. Pp. 396. (Origo, Zurich. Price: DM. 29)

This modern kabbalistic meditation on the Pentateuch, an abridged German version of a Dutch original, draws its chief inspiration from old-fashioned *gematria*. Written by an expert in mathematical statistics, who is also a Hasid, it offers a key to the mysteries of spiritual life by deciphering a divine blueprint of the universe.

G.V.

WIDENGREN, G.: *Religionsphänomenologie.* 1969. Pp. xv, 684. (Walter de Gruyter, Berlin. Price: DM. 38)

This is an enlarged version of the second edition of the author's Swedish work published in 1953 under the title, *Religionens värid.* (See *B.L.* 1946, p. 54; *Eleven Years*, p. 54 for review of the first ed., and *B.L.* 1954, *Eleven Years*, p. 617 for review of the second ed.) Professor Widengren defines the Phenomenology of Religion as a systematic synthesis as opposed to the History of Religion which provides an historical analysis. The book ranges over the wide field of the structure and manifestation of religion, and illustrations are found in Semitic, Iranian and Indian religions. Perhaps the book tends more towards phenomenological description than phenomenological illumination of inner meaning, and a topic such as the Formation of the Canon belongs to another context, but the author's sure knowledge and original ideas will commend this book to everyone with a specialist interest in this contemporary subject.   I.B.

WOLFF, H. W.: *Menschliches. Vier Reden über das Herz, den Ruhetag, die Ehe und den Tod im Alten Testament* (Kaiser Traktate, 5). 1971. Pp. 80. (Chr. Kaiser Verlag, München. Price: DM. 6.80)

Two of the four occasional addresses here presented (on the Sabbath and on Marriage) are in effect sermons, and the remaining two are lectures delivered respectively at a Jesuit gathering and at a conference of ministers and doctors. They provide a serious and stimulating study of their subjects and serve to whet the appetite for a more considerable work in the field of O.T. anthropology which the author tells the reader is shortly to follow.   E.T.R.

ZIMMERLI, W.: *Man and his Hope in the Old Testament* (Studies in Biblical Theology, Second Series 20). 1971. Pp. 174 (S.C.M. Press, London. Price: £2·25)

How the Jewish and Christian hope, so different from the Greek, was created, maintained, purified and strengthened is presented in this valuable study. The vocabulary is studied, but the main part of the book analyses the concept in the wisdom literature, Psalms, the various strands in the Pentateuch, historical literature, prophets and apocalyptic. Finally the author discusses what has been in his mind throughout, the 'great philosophical masterpiece' by Ernst Bloch, *Das Prinzip Hoffnung*. While acknowledging Bloch's understanding of the O.T. as repudiating the static outlook in its demand to hear and act anew, he shows that Bloch has misunderstood the movement of O.T. thought as an 'exodus from Yahweh into full humanity'.

                    A.S.H.

ZIMMERLI, W.: *Die Weltlichkeit des Alten Testaments* (Kleine Vandenhoeck-Reihe, 327). 1971. Pp. 162. (Vandenhoeck & Ruprecht, Göttingen. Price: DM. 8.80)

This little paper-back contains eleven public lectures delivered in the summer semester of 1970 in the University of Göttingen. Like everything from Professor Zimmerli's pen, this treatment of an important subject deserves the closest attention. It represents an uncompromising criticism by one of the most distinguished living O.T. scholars of Bultmann's well-known contention that the O.T. is a history of 'failure' because of its 'worldliness' and is fulfilled in the N.T. only by being 'entweltlicht'; what God is doing must be understood in a radical, otherworldly, eschatological sense. Zimmerli insists that Christianity has first and foremost a relevance to this world which must not be overlooked through a failure to recognize that the world which is opposed to Christ is so called in a special sense of the word 'world'. The allegorizing and ascetic tendencies in the mediaeval Church sprang from misunderstanding with regard to the 'worldliness' of Christianity. Israel was summoned by the prophets to obedience in this world and for the sake of the nations. Certainly the cross of Christ represents a going beyond the O.T., not in the sense, however, that the world is rejected, but in the sense that it is redeemed. It is wrong to oppose gospel and law. The book is full of penetrating insights and many familiar topics are illuminated — man's task in the world of God's creation, Israel's relation to its enemies and to its land, the human relationships within Israel, Israel's understanding of life and death and so on. Zimmerli uses the category of promise and fulfilment in a different sense from that advocated by Bultmann.

N.W.P.

THE LIFE AND THOUGHTS OF THE SURROUNDING PEOPLES

GIVEON, R.: *Les bédouins shosou des documents égyptiens* (Documenta et Monumenta orientis antiqui, 12). 1971. Pp. xviii, 278. Pls. 19. (E. J. Brill, Leiden. Price: Fl. 96)

This comprehensive study of 60 texts referring to the Shōsu nomads shows they lived and moved in the Delta, Palestine, Syria and Transjordan only in the period Tuthmosis II–Ramesses III. Their identification with SA.GAZ/hapiru, Sutu or Seth is rejected. It is suggested that the Hebrews may have been a small group associated with Shōsu migrants and so not specifically noted by the Egyptian scribes. The coincidence in the period of activity, the way of life and the routes traversed by both Shōsu and Hebrews is taken as evidence for dating the Exodus traditions to Dynasty XIX. This volume is therefore important for both O.T. and Egyptological studies.

D.J.W.

GRESSMANN, H. (ed.): *Altorientalische Texte zum Alten Testament*. 1970. (1926). Pp. x, 479. (Walter de Gruyter, Berlin. Price: DM. 60)

This is a further reprint of the second edition of this standard work of reference, originally published in 1909, second edition substantially revised in 1926, reprint 1965. There is no doubt of the usefulness of the collection of texts, but one may wonder whether it would not have been more valuable, after 45 years, to have had a new edition incorporating at least some of the more recent material. 100 pages of Egyptian texts and 340 of Mesopotamian, are matched by only 20 of 'north-semitic', and, at the very least, one misses the Ras Shamra material, and indeed much more than this. Reprints are no doubt useful and profitable; new editions more likely to contribute to a proper contemporary understanding.

P.R.A.

HARRISON, R. K.: *The Ancient World*. (Teach Yourself Books). 1971. Pp. ix, 162, 12 plates. (English Universities Press, London. Price: 55p)

The history of the ancient Near East, plus Greece and Rome, from the time of the Sumerians to the Christian era, is here described clearly and succinctly. However, the general reader may find the first chapter, which deals with prehistory and the earliest cultures, rather heavy going. Also, while there are several clear maps, some of the place names mentioned in the text are not to be found on them.

J.W.R.

PARPOLA, S.: *Letters from Assyrian Scholars to the Kings Esarhaddon and Assurbanipal*, Part I: Texts (Alter Orient und Altes Testament, Band 5/1). 1970. Pp. xxi, 341. (Butzon und Bercker, Kevelaer and Neukirchener Verlag, Neukirchen-Vluyn. Price: DM. 72)

The royal Assyrian correspondence of the 7th century B.C., though first published by R. F. Harper in cuneiform from 1892–1914, has not hitherto been adequately translated. S. Parpola, and his mentor K. Deller, have long been working on letters in the Assyrian dialect, collating, joining broken pieces, and studying the grammar. The first results are found in this edition, with full translation, of letters from scribes, several types of magician, and physicians. They give a fascinating picture of daily life in the court as influenced by its expert advisers. The work is of a high scholarly calibre, and the translations usable by O.T. scholars.

                                                                    W.G.L.

WILHELM, G.: *Untersuchungen zum Hurro-Akkadischen von Nuzi* (Alter Orient und Altes Testament, Band 9). 1970. Pp. x, 108. (Butzon und Bercker, Kevelaer and Neukirchener Verlag, Neukirchen-Vluyn. Price: DM. 38)

The Nuzi tablets, well known to O.T. scholars for alleged parallels with the social customs of the patriarchal narratives, are written in a dialect of Akkadian. This was the subject of quite a number of articles in the 1930s, and the present study is a competent presentation of the phenomena by a young scholar who has the advantage of the current level of knowledge of Hurrian (Horite), a language which has strongly influenced the Nuzi dialect.

                                                                    W.G.L.

QUMRAN STUDIES

AMUSIN, I. D.: *Teksty Kumrana, vypusk 1*. (The Texts of Qumran, Part I.) (Pamjatniki pismennosti Vostoka XXXIII, 1 = Monuments of the Literature of the Orient XXXIII, 1.) 1971. Pp. 496. ('Nauka', Moscow. Price: Rubls. 2.02)

This represents the first Russian publication of the Qumran texts, and in particular of the commentaries and florilegia, together with some supplementary fragments. In the first part of the book, the well-known Leningrad orientalist provides a full account of the finds in the Judaean desert in general, but especially of those in the Qumran caves, and he includes valuable excursuses on the extracanonical literature of Judaism and on rabbinic writings. He also gives a thorough account of the Essene sect and the surviving literature concerning it, in particular in the writings of Philo, Pliny and Josephus. The author is excellently well informed concerning all the problems, and his work will provide a mine of information to all who read Russian. His reflections on the date of origin of the various writings from Qumran will also prove stimulating to specialists. The second part of the book is devoted to translation of and comments on the writings mentioned above. An astonishing acquaintance with literature which has appeared outside Russia is shown. Finds after 1966 and the literature relevant to these is covered in an addendum. An extensive bibliography is appended from which it may be seen that the Soviet scholar has concerned himself very fully with these historic discoveries for years. Under his own name there are 25 titles, mainly studies in journals, in addition to a further five which have appeared abroad.   M.B.

JONGELING, B.: *A Classified Bibliography of the Finds in the Desert of Judah, 1958–1969.* (Studies on the Texts of the Desert of Judah, VII). 1971. Pp. xiv, 140. (E. J. Brill, Leiden. Price: Fl. 48)

The author of this bibliography, which covers the years 1958–1969, notes that it forms a continuation of the work of W. S. LaSor, *Bibliography of the Dead Sea Scrolls, 1948–1957* (see *B.L.*, 1960, p. 49; *Decade*, p. 229). The material has been arranged under thirteen headings (although the same work can appear under more than one heading), and there is an author index. Dr. Jongeling does not claim that his work is exhaustive, but this is nonetheless an extremely useful tool for all those working in the field of Qumran studies.   M.A.K.

KAPELRUD, A. S.: *Dødehavsrullene. Funnene som kaster nytt lys over Bibeln og Iesu samtid.* 1971. Pp. 155 and 8 plates and maps. (Universitetsforlaget, Oslo. Price: N.Kr. 20)

The original version of this book, only slightly shorter, was warmly greeted in the *Book List* (1957, p. 66; *Decade*, p. 66), and though many of the book's virtues still remain, one wonders why it is necessary nowadays to repeat so much of the story of the discovery and the description of the scrolls and such topics and to say so little about what has happened to the interpretative and controversial aspects of the study.   B.J.R.

APOCRYPHA AND POST-BIBLICAL STUDIES

ALBECK, C.: *Einführung in die Mischna* (Studia Judaica, Bd. 6.) 1971. Pp. viii, 493. (Walter de Gruyter, Berlin. Price: DM. 68)

C. Albeck was one of the last leading representatives of the classic type of rabbinic scholarship. This *Introduction*, originally published in Hebrew in 1960, appeared as a companion volume to the author's six volume edition of the text of the Mishnah (1952–1958). The work embodies a traditional-academic approach to Talmudic learning and includes a full exposition of issues such as oral teaching, midrashic and mishnaic methods, the redaction of the present Mishnah, its language, and a survey of its authorities and interpreters. The study thus contains in the form of raw materials all that is necessary for a modern historico-critical investigation of the oldest of the rabbinic codes.   G.V.

APPEL, G. (ed.): *Samuel K. Mirsky Memorial Volume. Studies in Jewish Law, Philosophy, and Literature.* 1970. Pp. 285 + 316. (Ktav Publishing House, Inc., New York. Price: $12.50)

The volume is divided into two parts, one in English and one in Hebrew and contains altogether 36 articles and a bibliography of

Rabbi Mirsky. The contributions are concerned, as the title indicates, exclusively with Jewish rabbinical questions, such as Halakhah, Haggadah, philosophy, and history. It does not contain any biblical studies in the narrower sense, except one on a medieval rabbinical view of Proverbs 31:10–31 by K. A. Feldman, and another one of Ruth by B. M. Lerner, both in Hebrew. For those who are interested in the study of the Haftaroth (readings in the Synagogue from the Prophets) attention may be drawn to an article by Rabbi M. Luban on 'Triennial Haftorot' (in English).   H.K.

BLACK, M. (ed.): *Apocalypsis Henochi Graece.* DENIS, A.-M. (ed.): *Fragmenta Pseudepigraphorum Quae Supersunt Graeca una cum Historicorum et Auctorum Judaeorum Hellenistarum Fragmentis.* (Pseudepigrapha Veteris Testamenti Graece III). 1970. Pp. viii, 246. (E. J. Brill, Leiden. Price: Fl. 96)

The two most important sources for our knowledge of the Greek text of Enoch are Codex Panopolitanus (covering chapters 1–32) and the Chester Beatty-Michigan Papyrus (covering, with some gaps, 97.6–107.3). In the first part of this volume Professor Black for the first time publishes these two texts together, along with all the other evidence for the Greek text of Enoch. The edition is based on a fresh collation of the relevant manuscripts. In the second part of this volume Father Denis gathers together the Greek fragments of the 'lost' Jewish pseudepigrapha, and of Jewish historians and Jewish hellenistic authors. The texts are quoted from printed editions, and other ancient translations are given in parallel where appropriate. This work thus forms an indispensable companion to the author's valuable *Introduction aux Pseudépigraphes Grecs d'Ancien Testament* (see *B.L.*, 1971, p. 60) which dealt in the second part with *Les fragments de pseudépigraphes perdus*, and in the third with *Historiens et auteurs littéraires*. (For earlier volumes in the series *Pseudepigrapha Veteris Testamenti Graece* see *B.L.*, 1969, p. 60).   M.A.K.

DALMAN G.: *Jesus-Jeshua. Studies in the Gospels.* Trans. P. P. Levertoff. 1971 (1929). Pp. xii, 256. (Ktav Publishing House, Inc., New York. Price: $12.50)

This is a reprint of a study of the form of Aramaic that was in use in home and synagogue at the time of Jesus chiefly in the interests of establishing more exactly the meaning of some of the sayings of Jesus. Of special interest is the discussion of the acts and sayings of the Passover meal.   L.H.B.

DAVENPORT, G. L.: *The Eschatology of the Book of Jubilees.* (Studia Post-Biblica, xx). 1971. Pp. viii, 124. (E. J. Brill, Leiden. Price: Fl. 36)

The purpose of this Vanderbilt doctoral dissertation is to provide an analysis of the eschatology of Jubilees. The author argues that three stages may be traced in the development of the present book, and that the eschatological ideas of each stratum are to be distinguished. The original work, comprising the major part of the angelic discourse 2:1–50:4, was primarily concerned to teach law, but nonetheless presupposed the idea of a judgement when unfaithful Israelites and

Gentiles would be punished. This work, written at the end of the third or the beginning of the second century B.C., was elaborated early in the period of the Maccabaean struggles (c. 166–160) by a redactor who added 1:4b–26; 23:14–20, 21–31 and 50.5. These additions were explicitly eschatological, and altered the whole thrust of the book; they saw Israel as continuing in a state of exile because of her failure to obey the law, but expressed the hope that God was about to bring a true end to the exile. Finally, during the periods of office of either Simon or John Hyrcanus, a second redactor, working at Qumran, added 1:10b, 17a, 27–28, 29c; 4:26; 23:12; 31:14 and possibly 50:6–13 — passages which emphasized the centrality of the sanctuary in the face of what the redactor saw as its desecration. The discussion, although not always completely convincing, is interesting and valuable. One unsatisfactory feature, however, is that the footnotes tend to overwhelm the text; large parts of the material in the footnotes could well have been omitted, whereas other parts are important for the argument, and ought to have been in the text.

M.A.K.

ECKERT, W., LEVINSON, N. P. and STÖHR, M. (ed.): *Jüdisches Volk — gelobtes Land.* (Abhandlungen zum christlich-jüdischem Dialog, vol. 3). 1970. Pp. 335. (Chr. Kaiser, München. Price: DM. 19.80)

The Arnoldshain conferences on Jewish-Christian concerns have already become famous. This volume continues to record contributions by distinguished contributors from both sides. The central position accorded to the land of Israel in biblical studies is perhaps unprecedented and certainly opens a totally new perspective to the eyes of scholars, especially in the area of the N.T. O.T. studies, by way of contrast, had never lost their firm hold on the life and language of the people, the history and climate of the land. In this symposium four articles, by S. Talmon, R. Rendtorff, G. C. Macholz, and H. Schmid, deal specifically with the pre-Christian dialectic of the land and history, as reflected in the significance of Jerusalem, the people of God, and the Messianic restoration. The value of these studies lies not so much in their technical expertise as in the light which they throw upon one of the most burning issues of our day. This is an exciting document by scholars of the first order.

U.E.S.

FINKELSTEIN, L.: *New Light from the Prophets.* 1969. Pp. 151. (Vallentine, Mitchell, London. Price: £1·50)

L. Finkelstein, scholarly editor of *Sifre* on Deuteronomy, is of the opinion that a good number of pericopae in that midrash, and in rabbinic literature at large, originated in pre-exilic times. Here is an example of his argument. *Sifre*-Deuteronomy 342 asserts that *all* the prophecies start with reproaches and finish with words of consolation, but quotes only Hosea, Joel, Amos, Micah and Jeremiah; it omits Isaiah and Ezekiel. Hence it is 'highly probable, if not certain' that the passage dates to the early sixth century B.C. The claim 'that portions of the Rabbinical tradition were actually composed by the contemporaries of the Prophets or even the Prophets themselves', advanced in the Foreword, will, in the opinion of the reviewer, do a great deal more than 'startle the reader'.

G.V.

FITZMYER, J. A.: *The Genesis Apocryphon of Qumran Cave I. A Commentary* (Biblica et Orientalia, 18A). 2nd edition, 1971. Pp. xvi, 260. (Biblical Institute Press, Rome. Price: Lire 3,900 or $6.50)

The first edition of this work was reviewed in *B.L.* 1967, p. 45, where it was described as 'indispensable for all further study'. The new edition, which is twenty-eight pages longer, reconsiders some questions and adds references to recent literature.   J.A.E.

GASTER, M.: *Studies and Texts in Folklore, Magic, Mediaeval Romance, Hebrew Apocrypha and Samaritan Archaeology. Prolegomenon* by T. H. Gaster. 3 vols. Pp. xliv, 1356 (+1–278 in Hebrew). 1971 (Ktav Publishing House, Inc., New York. Price: $25.00)

These studies, first published in 1928, illustrate many fascinating byways, but are more a memorial to a remarkable polymath than a contribution to current scholarly issues. In the prolegomenon T. H. Gaster brings out both the strengths and the limitations of his father's wide-ranging interests.   R.J.C.

GINZBERG, L.: *A Commentary on the Palestinian Talmud. A Study of the Development of the Halakah and Haggadah in Palestine and Babylonia.* (Texts and Studies of the Jewish Theological Seminary of America 10, 11, 12, and 21.) 1971. 3 volumes. Pp. lxxii, xvi, 420; 325; 444; [Vol. 4: Arranged and Edited Posthumously by D. Halvini. 1961. Pp. viii, 280.] (Ktav Publishing House, Inc., New York. Price: $60.00)

Louis Ginzberg who died in 1953 had an indelible name in Jewish learning; the late I. N. Epstein (Jerusalem) once surnamed him the 'prince of the scholars'. G. is well-known as the author of '*The Legends of the Jews*' in six vols., 1909–28, with index volume, 1938, which have often been reprinted ever since. The first three vols. of his Commentary on the Pal. Talmud, actually only on the first tractate Berakot which deals with the Shma', the prayer, and the benedictions, were issued in 1941; a fourth volume, completing the commentary on Berakot, was published in 1961. The first three volumes which were exhausted, have now been reprinted. The work is written in Hebrew. It is of eminent importance both for its subject matter and its method of approach to the problems of the Pal. Talmud which is somewhat incorrectly called Yerushalmi in the Hebrew language. The Pal. Talmud differs from the more widespread and authoritative Babylonian Talmud, or *the* Talmud, not only in language — they are written in two different dialects of Aramaic — but also in respect of its often divergent opinions in its legal and haggadic matters. G.'s Commentary is preceded by a most instructive introductory essay on this particular theme in English (60 pp.). It is needless here to emphasize the value of the Yerushalmi for the study of the background of the N.T. and early Christianity. Unfortunately only a French translation of the Yerushalmi exists (by Moise Schwab, 11 vols., 1878–89) apart from a German rendering of its haggadic components (by Aug. Wünsche, 1 vol., 1880). The Commentary is beautifully printed on large paper.   H.K.

HERFORD, R. J.: *Talmud and Apocrypha. A comparative study of the ethical teaching in the Rabbinical and non-Rabbinical sources in the early centuries.* 1971 (1933). Pp. 323. (Ktav Publishing House, Inc., New York. Price $10.00)

This reprint of a standard work on Jewish ethical teaching is to be welcomed. For previous notice see *B.L.* 1934, p. 10. L.H.B.

HRUBY, K.: *Die Synagoge. Geschichtliche Entwicklung einer Institution.* (Schriften zur Judentumskunde, Band 3). 1971. Pp. 115. (Theologischer Verlag, Zürich. Price: Sw.Fr. 16,80)

This is the third volume in a series intended to remedy the lack of truthful information about the Jews and Judaism. In the present little volume, Professor Hruby, a Hebrew-Christian and now, after the death of Robert Brunner, the main editor of the quarterly 'Judaica', introduces the theological student and the intelligent Christian reader to the history of the institution of the Synagogue from its early beginnings onward, and deals mainly with the building itself, its orientation, its situation, its inside, its officers, the participation of women in the service, the synagogue in the N.T. and related questions, its relationship to the Temple, its sanctity, and the relationship between Synagogue and Church. It goes without saying that within so small a compass one cannot expect a full description of the Synagogue and its service. Three short excursuses have been added to the book: on ritual ablutions, on the early rabbinical literature, and on the synagogue in Massada. H.K.

JAMES, M. R.: *The Biblical Antiquities of Philo. Prolegomenon* by L. H. Feldman. (*Library of Biblical Studies*: Translations of early Documents series I: Palestinian Jewish Texts (Pre-Rabbinic)). 1971 (1917). Pp. clxix, 280. (Ktav Publishing House, Inc., New York. Price: $19.95)

Pseudo-Philo's *Book of Biblical Antiquities* is a first century A.D. Jewish midrash on Old Testament history from Adam to Saul surviving in a Latin translation only. Neglected by scholars until the 1950's, it has since recovered its rightful place in inter-Testamental literature. In the present volume M. R. James's valuable but antiquated introduction, translation and commentary, originally published in 1917, is brought up to date by L. H. Feldman. In a Prolegomenon of 170 pages he presents a full picture of the *status quaestionis* in which account is taken of the literature of the last twenty years, including unpublished doctoral dissertations. In addition, he provides every possible supplement to James's exegetical notes. Thus, even though no new solutions are advocated in it, the use of this volume is from now on imperative for any student of *Liber Antiquitatum Biblicarum*.

G.V.

KIPPENBERG, H. G.: *Garizim und Synagoge.* (Religionsgeschichtliche Versuche und Vorarbeiten, xxx). 1971. Pp. xiv, 374. (Walter de Gruyter, Berlin. Price: DM. 88)

This is a major work on the Samaritans, with special emphasis on the Aramaic period (the sub-title is *Traditionsgeschichtliche Untersuchungen zur samaritanischen Religion der aramäischen Periode*), but with considerable bearing on the earlier history of the community. An introductory section comments critically on the relevant literature, both editions of ancient texts and modern studies. The main body of the book is then divided into two roughly equal parts. It is the first which will be of the more direct concern to the O.T. scholar. Here the history of the Samaritans down to the Byzantine period is traced. The origins of the community as a distinctive religious group are placed in the Hellenistic period, with special emphasis laid on the disputes within Judaism in the second century B.C. concerning priesthood. The second part of the book then examines a number of Samaritan religious traditions, with special reference to the Aramaic literature (in particular *Memar Marqa* and various liturgical works) and attempts to elucidate their history. In a number of instances it is claimed that these traditions can be traced back before the Christian era. In all, this is one of the most important and interesting of the many recent works on the Samaritans.

R.J.C.

LACHS, S. T. and PASSOW, I. D. (ed.): *Gratz College Anniversary Volume 1895–1970.* 1971. Pp. 278 + Hebrew. (Ktav Publishing House, Inc., New York. Price: $12.50)

This jubilee volume, celebrating the 75th anniversary of the foundation of an important Jewish educational institution in Philadelphia, assembles twenty-four papers covering mostly the domain of Judaica. Users of the *Book List* might note in particular essays by S. N. Kramer (a Sumerian text on the city of Kesh); C. H. Gordon (Virgil and the biblical world); W. Chomsky (Hebrew pronunciation) and S. D. Goitein (Cairo Geniza).

G.V.

LENTZEN-DEIS, F.: *Die Taufe Jesu nach den Synoptikern. Literarkritische und gattungsgeschichtliche Untersuchungen.* (Frankfurter Theologische Studien, 4.) 1970. Pp. 324. (Verlag Josef Knecht, Frankfurt am Main)

This study examines exhaustively all possible traditio-historical influences on the present form of (principally) the Markan baptism-narrative. It is of interest to readers of this *Book List* because of its full and careful use of recent 'gattungsgeschichtlich' studies in German, of which its footnotes provide a useful bibliography: many of the works mentioned deal principally with *Gattungen* found in the O.T., though Lentzen-Deis' main positive argument is based on studies of the Targum, in which he claims to establish the existence of a *Gattung* which he calls the 'Deute-vision' (i.e. a vision which conveys the interpretation of an event which it accompanies). The author points to an extremely fruitful form of study of the Targums in their bearing on the interpretation of the N.T.

C.J.A.H.

MAIER, G.: *Mensch und freier Wille nach den jüdischen Religionsparteien zwischen Ben Sira und Paulus* (Wissenschaftliche Untersuchungen zum N.T., 12). 1971. Pp. vii, 426. (J.C.B. Mohr, Stuttgart. Price: DM. 40 (paper); 46 (cloth))

This is a detailed study of the ways in which man's free will was regarded by the different parties within Judaism during the period from Ben Sira to Paul. Of necessity it also discusses their recognition of the problem of predestination. It is a thoroughly scholarly treatment.

L.H.B.

MANN, J.: *The Bible as Read and Preached in the Synagogue. A study in the cycles of the readings from Torah and Prophets, as well as from Psalms, and in the structure of the midrashic homilies.* Vol. 1. *The Palestinian Triennial Cycle: Genesis and Exodus, with a Hebrew section containing manuscript material of Midrashim to these books. Prolegomenon* by B. Z. Wacholder. (*The Library of Biblical Studies*, ed. by H. M. Orlinsky). 1971. Pp. xci, 574, 346 (Hebrew) (First published 1940). (Ktav Publishing House, Inc., New York. Price: $29.50)

Students of the genizah manuscripts, of New Testament-synagogal affinities, of Rabbinic-midrashic studies, and of the massoretic textual transmission have all had reason to depend on Mann's *Bible as Read in the Synagogue*, since its first publication in 1940, and its basic contribution still persists. Therefore we welcome its inclusion in the invaluable series of the *Library of Biblical Studies*. But also important, not least as a contemporary corrective to some of Mann's less safe information, is the comprehensive survey offered by Professor Wacholder in his *Prolegomenon*.   B.J.R.

MARBÖCK, J.: *Weisheit im Wandel: Untersuchungen zur Weisheitstheologie bei Ben Sira.* (Bonner Biblische Beiträge, 37). 1971. Pp. xxvii, 192. (Peter Hanstein, Bonn. Price: DM. 28.80)

Recent work on the Wisdom of Ben Sira (Ecclesiasticus) has of necessity been selective, and Marböck chooses to examine the place of Ben Sira in the literary and theological development of Jewish wisdom literature. 1:1–10 and 24 are considered in great detail as key passages and, to a lesser extent, 4:11–19, 6:18–37, 14:20–15:10, 38:24–39 and 51:13–30. There is useful discussion of various theological points arising from the hellenistic culture of the time, and Haspecker's *Gottesfurcht bei Jesus Sirach* (see *B.L.* 1968, p. 63) is subjected to considerable criticism. Ben Sira is seen to link earlier theology of wisdom's place in creation with the election traditions of Israel for the first time. The bibliography and biblical index are well drawn up.   J.G.S.

MICHEL, O., SAFRAI, S., LE DÉAUT, R., DE JONGE, M. and VAN GOUDOEVER, J.: *Studies on the Jewish Background of the New Testament.* With a preface by H. van Praag, 1969. Pp. viii, 86. (Van Gorcum & Co., Assen. Price: Fl. 9.90)

The five essays in this collection, which is stated to be the forerunner of a new series *Compendia rerum iudaicarum ad Novum Testamentum*, are intended to demonstrate the extent of the interrelationship between Jewish and Christian history and literature in the first Christian century. The papers were given originally at a Jewish/Christian conference held at Hilversum in 1967. Three of them (by O. Michel, S. Safrai and R. le Déaut respectively) are primarily of interest to N.T. scholars and use Jewish material to elucidate the meaning of the N.T. text. Otherwise, M. de Jonge ('The Role of Intermediaries in God's Final Intervention in the Future according to the Qumran Scrolls') stresses the diversity and flexibility of the ideas held at Qumran about the 'intermediaries' in God's final intervention in history, while J. van Goudoever ('The Significance of

the Counting of the Omer') makes use of Dan. 10–12 in an attempt to explain how it came about that in Christian tradition the period from Easter to Pentecost is a time of joy, whereas in Jewish tradition the period from Passover to the Feast of Weeks is a time of restraint and mourning.
                                                            M.A.K.

Die Mischna. Text, Uebersetzung und ausführliche Erklärung mit textkritischen Anhängen. Herausg. von K. H. Rengstorf und L. Rost.
BOERTIEN, M.: *Nazir (Naziräer).* 1971. Pp. vii, 243. (Walter de Gruyter, Berlin. Price: DM. 68)
KRUPP, M.: *'Arakin (Schätzungen).* 1971. Pp. x, 161. (Price: DM. 48)

The Mishnah has 63 tractates. There is a handy translation of the whole Mishnah into English by Canon Herbert Danby (1933, reprinted many times since). The vast German undertaking brings a critical edition of the Hebrew text with a German translation, a useful introduction, a substantial running commentary, and a text-critical appendix. The publication is invaluable for the student of Rabbinics, but it will be hardly possible for a private person to acquire it. Here are two further contributions to the whole work.
The tractate Nazir, the fourth in the third order called Nashim has nothing to do with women in particular, but with a person, male or female, who dedicates him- or herself to the Lord. The law of the Nazir will be found in Num. 6:1–21. During the whole period of the vow that person had (1) to abstain from drinking wine, in fact from drinking or eating anything which comes from the vine, (2) he must not shave his head, and (3) he must keep ritually clean and especially not touch or go near a corpse. The tractate deals with the regulations of the Nazirite vow in all details in eight chapters, whilst the ninth gives some directions with regard to women and slaves, answers two specific questions, and affirms that Samson and Samuel were Nazirites. The commentary also discusses the vows of Samuel and the apostle Paul. — The tractate 'Arakin, 'Valuations', the fifth in the fifth order of the Mishnah, called Qodashim, determines the amounts to be paid when one has vowed to God a person or the equivalent of a person. The biblical basis for this valuation is Lev. 27:2–15. Chapters 7 and 8 fix the rules for the valuation of fields or parts of fields, whether inherited or bought, mentioned in vv. 16–29. The last chapter of the tractate discusses certain problems arising from Lev. 25:15 f. and 25 ff. — Both authors have lived in Israel for some time and have been able to collect expert information and advice. The tractate 'Arakin is a doctoral dissertation, whilst the editor of the other tractate, who is now Professor in Amsterdam, has based his work on a dissertation in which he considers philological points more closely.
                                                            H.K.

MULDER, M. J.: *Het Meisje van Sodom. De targumim op Genesis 18: 20, 21 tussen bijbeltekst en haggada.* 1970. Pp. 38. (J. H. Kok, Kampen. Price: Fl. 2.95)

This inaugural lecture delivered in the Faculty of Letters of the Free University of Amsterdam examines the development of the story of the girl Peleṯith whose cry, according to the Pseudo-Jonathan Targum on Gen. 18:21, was heard by God. She is the pious girl who, according to a haggada preserved in TB *Sanh.* 109b, was convicted of the crime of feeding the hungry and punished by being smeared with honey and exposed to be devoured by bees, Heb. *rabbah* ('great') in Gen. 18:20 being read as Aram. *riba* ('girl'). Further elaborations of the story are traced in the *Sefer Hayyashar*, *Pirqe de-Rabbi Eliezer* and elsewhere. In some of these she is a daughter of Lot, betrothed (*kalah*, 'altogether', in Gen. 18:21 being read as *kallah*, 'bride') to a man of Sodom. Mulder is inclined to see the story as an imaginative development of the reading *hakkeṣa ʿaqathah* (as against the variant *hakkeṣa ʿaqathamah*) in Gen. 18:20, understood as 'if according to *her* cry . . .', together with the other revocalizations mentioned; we must also allow for the influence of a folklore motif.   F.F.B.

NEHER, A.: *L'exil de la parole.* 1970. Pp. 259. (Éditions du Seuil, Paris. Price: Fr. 21)

In this remarkable essay the author listens with existential concern to the divine silence from the beginnings to the extermination at Auschwitz. His method is all-inclusive: biblical structuralism and semantics speak dialectically to Rabbinic and modern authors, and they, in turn, evoke and question the eternal silence. Built into this highly complex edifice, moreover, is also the polemic of Christian claims of fulfilment and the Jewish hope of 'not yet'. Neher shows great sensitivity to the literary veiling of the eclipse of God, the mask of reality. The dialogue with God implies, in the Hassidic understanding of the *Shema*, norms of silence which cannot be broken. So far the prelude of the great negative polarities without which God cannot be known. Neher proceeds to examine selected biblical passages, such as Gen. 1, Psalm 22, the tragic Saul, seen in the light of comparative data (Oedipus, Odysseus), so that the vignettes may throw up the dimensions of silence. Abraham, tested in silence, is the pioneer of the Noosphere, the decisive mutation, in which creation becomes history. But the progress into, and by, the Word breaks, and Auschwitz is the symbol of the silence after the Word. In the second section Wiesel, Adorno, Bloch, Susman *et al.*, are cited to pinpoint the theological problems of 'no God's land', which, in turn, are submitted to the words, dreams and reality, as given in prophecy and wisdom. The Jew can say Yes to death and martyrdom, and yet hope *because* of the silence of the hidden God.

Neher has written this book 'from the heart to the heart'. While relating biblical themes to modern philosophy and contemporary writing he has tended to belittle, if not ignore, the apophatic tradition in Christianity. Yet, set to the key of 'Nevertheless — Perhaps' of the music of our times, he has made an important contribution to the Theology of Hope.   U.E.S.

NEUSNER, J.: *Aphrahat and Judaism. The Christian-Jewish Argument in Fourth-century Iran* (Studia Post-Biblica, XIX). 1971. Pp. xvi, 265. (E. J. Brill, Leiden. Price: Fl. 56)

Nine, and selections from a tenth, of Aphrahat's Syriac 'Demonstrations' (dated 336–345) are here translated (all but two for the first time into English), with an introduction and three subsequent chapters on Aphrahat in relation to Judaism, to rabbinic writers and to other church Fathers. Neusner adopts Morton Smith's analysis of literary parallels and shows, by means of detailed comparative tables of O.T. proof texts, that Aphrahat is largely independent of both Rabbis and earlier Fathers; the Judaism he knew was probably that of Adiabenian converts, not of Babylonian rabbinic type. This book is useful to the historian of O.T. exegesis, but it exaggerates Aphrahat's isolation as regards Testimonia and his lack of allegorism. There is more to be said about Aphrahat as a midrashist.   R.M.

NEUSNER, J. (ed.): *The Formation of the Babylonian Talmud. Studies in the achievements of late nineteenth and twentieth century historical and literary critical research.* (Studia Post-Biblica, XVII). 1970. Pp. xii, 187. (E. J. Brill, Leiden. Price: Fl. 36)

Jacob Neusner's avowed aim is to set Talmudic studies on an academically respectable basis and to substitute for traditional attitudes modern research methods tested and found valid in the fields of O.T., N.T., ancient history and comparative religion. His Foreword is followed by eleven essays by members of his graduate seminar at Brown University, which summarize and assess the most important solutions offered by Jewish historians and literary critics to the question of the composition of the Babylonian Talmud. Readers interested in the subject, but unfamiliar with modern Hebrew, the language of most books on Talmudic matters, will find the present volume particularly useful and welcome.   G.V.

PREUSS, J.: *Biblisch-talmudische Medizin. Beiträge zur Geschichte der Heilkunde und der Kultur überhaupt.* Introduction by Sussmann Muntner. 1971. Pp. lxxxviii, 735. (Ktav Publishing House, Inc., New York. Price: $25.00)

This book is a verbatim reprint of the first edition (1911); a few reprints have already appeared in Germany after the author's death (1913). It is still the only comprehensive study on the ancient Jewish knowledge of diseases and their treatment to which the author had made many contributions during his lifetime (see the list at the end of the foreword entitled: Julius Preuss — Father of Hebrew Medical Research). The first chapters of the book deal with general matters such as the physician, anatomy and physiology, pathology, therapy, and surgery; then the book discusses the specific defects and diseases of the body, namely of the eyes, teeth, ears, and nose. These chapters are followed by others on the nervous ailments and mental derangements, skin diseases, gynaecology, and childbirth, on pharmacology, nursing, and forensic medicine. The book has a further section on hygiene dealing with the dietary and purity laws, including some remarks on the hygienic effect of circumcision which has already been discussed in a supplement added to the chapter on surgery, and finally there is a chapter on dietetics. It is impossible here to present details of the huge material collected in this work which is important for the study of man in the Bible as well as in the post-biblical literature and that of the Rabbis where we find an overwhelming amount of facts. The book contains a bibliography (16 pp.) which, unfortunately, has not been brought up to date and ends with the first decade of our century; but it has an ample index of the references to the Bible (O.T., Apocrypha, N.T.), the Mishna, the Talmudim, the Tosefta, and the Midrash rabba (24 pp.). An Introduction by

S. Muntner (in English, 26 pp.) has been added to this new reprint and also a list of the Hebrew and Aramaic equivalents of medical terms (with English translation, 53 pp.). Some readers might have wished for a translation of the whole work, but, luckily, the German of this book is, compared with that of some theology books, comparatively simple.   H.K.

REESE, J. M.: *Hellenistic Influences on the Book of Wisdom and its Consequences.* (Analecta Biblica, 41.) 1970. Pp. viii, 197. (Biblical Institute Press, Rome. Price: Lire 3,000 or $5.00)

This interesting work begins with a study of the vocabulary and style of Wisdom in so far as they diverge from anything found in the Old Testament, attributing the differencies to Hellenistic influences. Its author wrote with the conviction that contemporary Jewish culture needed to put forth its ideals in a sophisticated literary style and, in order to show that the old revelation was still significant for Jews living in a cosmopolitan society, deliberately used technical terms derived from Greek learning, pagan literary traditions and Hellenistic rhetorical devices, even when condemning paganism for failing to recognize the one Maker of the universe. The writer next examines the literary genres of Wisdom, of which the principal is the 'protreptic', long employed by Greek sophists as a means of attracting students to the pursuit of oratory and political studies and by Hellenistic rhetoricians in teaching that exhortations must appeal to other human faculties besides pure intellect. He goes on to argue that the unity of Wisdom is proved by the theological homogeneity of its themes and the 'flash-backs', *i.e.* literary reminiscences uniting the various parts of the book, embodying a personal interpretation of history and contemporary theology in an artificial style fitting into the educational literature of the Hellenistic age and offering a vision of the Judaism of a cultured and religious few who looked for a divine apocalyptic intervention foreshadowed in the long past manuals of sacred history and who believed in the endless reign of the just with God. Finally, the ultimate purpose of Wisdom is shown to have been that of preparing well educated Jewish students to live in a Hellenistic society whose cultural level required a sophisticated presentation to provide them with religious insights to build a bridge between their revealed faith and the beliefs and theories of their cultured pagan fellow-citizens. The writer's case is well argued and he shows a deep and extensive acquaintance with the latest researches into Greek Hellenistic literature, much of it not too well known, which greatly increases the value of his work. It may be whole-heartedly recommended though the text is marred by a number of misprints.   G.R.D.

RENGSTORF, K. H. (ed.): *Theokratia. Jahrbuch des Institutum Judaicum Delitzschianum.* I 1967–1969. 1970. Pp. 223. (E.J. Brill, Leiden. Price: Fl. 64)

This is the first volume of a yearbook issued by the 'Delitzschianum' which was founded in 1886, dissolved in 1935, and re-opened in 1948 in Münster i.W. The contributors are Jewish as well as Christian scholars. The first article comes from Abraham Schalit (Jerusalem) on the conquest of the townships of Moab by Alexander Yannai as listed by Josephus. The author shows that the list is not a historical document, but of literary origin, and taken over from Isa. 15 (Jer.

[LXX] 31). H. Schreckenberg makes some remarks on the text of Josephus, mainly the Antiquities. K. H. Rengstorf who is the main editor of 'Die Mischna' and also of the 'Rabbinische Texte' deals with the fundamentals and methods in the treatment of rabbinical texts. B. Brilling, of whose writings the volume gives a bibliography, discusses Jewish medieval tombstone inscriptions in Breslau (Silesia); in another article he writes on the relations between the general organization of Polish Jews and the political and trade authorities in Breslau under Frederic II. There are biographies of two modern prominent Jews of German origin, Alfred Wiener who established the Wiener Library, and Kurt Wilhelm who at the end of his life became the Chief Rabbi of Sweden. The volume also contains two short notes on tannaitic texts and one N.T. essay on loyalty as taught by Paul in Rom. 13.

H.K.

ROST, L.: *Einleitung in die alttestamentlichen Apokryphen und Pseudepigraphen einschliesslich der grossen Qumran-Handschriften.* 1971. Pp. 150. (Quelle & Meyer, Heidelberg. Price: DM. 28)

Professor Fohrer's new edition of the Sellin-Rost *Einleitung in das Alte Testament* (see *B.L.*, 1967, p. 36; 1969, p. 42; 1970, p. 47) was by agreement limited to a discussion of the canonical books of the O.T., and in his preface Professor Fohrer noted that Professor Rost himself intended to publish a separate volume dealing with the extra-canonical writings. That separate volume has now appeared. The work is primarily a text-book for students, and covers the apocrypha, pseudepigrapha and Qumran writings in a straightforward and fairly conventional manner. The bibliography is intended to supplement Eissfeldt, not to be a substitute for it, and thus, apart from standard text-editions and commentaries, refers mainly to monographs and articles published in the last decade. Although the treatment is at times rather unsatisfactory (e.g. the section on the Testaments of the Twelve Patriarchs), in general this is a useful introduction to the writings of the intertestamental period.

M.A.K.

SCHMID, H.: *Die christlich-jüdische Auseinandersetzung um das Alte Testament in hermeneutischer Sicht* (Schriften zur Judentumskunde, 1). 1971. Pp. 55. (Theologischer Verlag, Zürich. Price: Sw.Fr. 8.50)

This expanded lecture is subdivided into sections on (1) the formation of the O.T. canon, and on the Jewish-Christian debate in the periods of (2) the N.T., (3) the early Church, (4) the middle ages, (5) humanists and reformers and (6) modern times. The booklet's value is reduced by its inexplicable neglect of too much important recent work, especially in sections 1, 2, 3 and 6.

R.M.

SCHUBERT, K.: *Die jüdischen Religionsparteien in neutestamentlicher Zeit.* (Stuttgarter Bibelstudien, 43). 1970. Pp. 76. (Verlag Katholisches Bibelwerk, Stuttgart. Price: DM. 6.80)

This short book is intended by Schubert as a popular summary of his earlier writings dealing with Jewish religious parties in the N.T. period. The author traces the origins of the parties in the events of the second century B.C., and then discusses the distinctive features of the Pharisees, the Sadducees, the Essenes, the Zealots and the Sicarii. The account is in general reliable, and the author provides some useful and up to date bibliographical information. But whether the evidence justifies the author's suggestion that the Pharisees are so named because they are 'separated' from the Hasidim seems to me uncertain.

M.A.K.

WICKS, H. J.: *The Doctrine of God in the Jewish Apocryphal and Apocalyptic Literature.* Introduction by R. H. Charles. 1971 (1915). Pp. xi, 371. (Ktav Publishing House, Inc., New York. Price: $14.96)

The volume traces three ideas, the transcendence, justice and grace of God, through the books of the 'intertestamental' period and allows the references to speak for themselves. A reprint of the 1915 edition.

L.H.B.

PHILOLOGY AND GRAMMAR

BARR, J.: *Bibelexegese und moderne Semantik: theologische und linguistische Methode in der Bibelwissenschaft* (translated by E. Gerstenberger). 1965. Pp. 308. (Chr. Kaiser Verlag, Munich. DM. 25)

This translation of *The Semantics of Biblical Language* has a foreword by Professor H. Conzelmann.

BARR, J.: *Semantica del Linguaggio biblico.* 1968. Pp. xxxviii, 436. (Società editrice il Mulino, Bologna)

This Italian translation is by P. Sacchi, and the translator provides an interesting and critical discussion. 'Problemi teologici e problemi linguistici nell'opera del Barr', pp. vii-xxxviii.

BARR, J.: *Sémantique du langage biblique.* 1971. Pp. 346. (Bibliothèque des sciences religieuses: Aubier Montaigne, Éditions du Cerf, Delachaux et Niestlé, Desclée de Brouwer, Paris. Price: Fr. 49)

This French translation is by D. Auscher and J. Prignaud; it contains (pp. 9–14) a brief additional preface by the author, which reviews some of the literature on the subject since the original appearance of the book, and there are some additions to the footnotes.

BLAU, J.: *On Pseudo-Corrections in Some Semitic Languages.* (Publications of the Israel Academy of Sciences and Humanities: Section of Humanities). 1970. Pp. 153. (Jerusalem Academic Press, Jerusalem, 1970. Price: Fl. 27)

The term 'Pseudo-corrections' has been coined by Professor Blau for the correction of speech forms under the influence of contact between a prestigious and a less prestigious language. To students of the O.T. whose knowledge of Semitic languages is confined to Hebrew this work will be of peripheral interest, since, as Professor Blau remarks, 'our knowledge of Hebrew dialects in biblical times is extremely restricted'. But those who have studied Comparative Semitics —

happily they are growing in number — will find this small volume stimulating and suggestive. Blau's chapter on Arabic is, as one would expect, admirable; he has a helpful discussion of 'Pseudo-corrections' in Aramaic, and interesting remarks on Modern Hebrew. This book illustrates excellently a trend of philological research which will undoubtedly increase in importance.   J.B.S.

FOHRER, G.: (with HOFFMAN, H. W.; HUBER, F.; VOLLMER, S.; WANKE, G.): *Hebräisches und aramäisches Wörterbuch zum Alten Testament.* 1971. Pp. x, 332. (Walter de Gruyter, Berlin. Price: DM. 28)

There is no question that this little dictionary fulfils a need, and one can only hope that a parallel work in English will be available quite quickly. It is simply an ordinary student's dictionary, without etymology, not much guess-work, and merely a modicum of grammar. Of course, lexicographers will be occasionally annoyed; e.g. the ubiquitous *ḥesed* duly has its various meanings, but *yada'* only means 'know' and its nuances. The treatment of prepositions, especially those consisting of composite forms, might be looked at again in preparing for the next edition.   B.J.R.

HOLLADAY, W. L.: *A Concise Hebrew and Aramaic Lexicon of the Old Testament.* 1971. Pp. xx, 425. (E. J. Brill, Leiden. Price: Fl. 56)

This is a very serviceable shortened version of the Koehler-Baumgartner *Lexicon in Veteris Testamenti Libros* (1953; cf. *B.L.*, 1969, p. 65 for references), with its *Supplementum* (1958; cf. *B.L.*, 1959, p. 44: *Decade*, p. 180), and of its now-appearing third edition, of which the first fascicle appeared in 1967 (*B.L.*, 1969, p. 65). This third edition has dispensed with the English renderings, sensibly enough. The availability of an English version will be particularly helpful to students.

The shortened version is dependent upon the third edition so far as it is in print, and upon the manuscript of the next part as far a *samekh*; for '*ain* to the end and for the Aramaic, Holladay has used the first/second edition. The disadvantages are obvious, but the delay in the completion of the full third edition, unavoidable because of the death of Professor Baumgartner who was making the revision, inevitably means incompleteness and also that the very necessary corrections to the earlier editions are not yet all available. When the full third edition is available, we may perhaps hope that the concise form will be revised to bring it up to date. In the meantime, this lexicon will serve a very useful purpose; reference can be made from it to the larger work for fuller information, and pending the appearance of the revised Oxford Lexicon, valuable help is provided for the student of the language.   P.R.A.

KOSOVSKY, B.: *Otzar Leshon Hatanna'im* (sic), Vol. 1. 1971. Pp. 413. (Jewish Theological Seminary of America, Jerusalem. Price: $17.50)

This is a concordance, not to Tannaitic literature in general, but to *Sifre* in Numbers and Deut. only; the first volume covers only *Aleph* (!). The principles are like those of Mandelkern: separate entries are given for a word independent, for it with the article, with prepositions, with each of the suffixes and so on. It is a principle good for minutiae but poor for a semantic overview. Will not the enormous size of such a work when eventually completed be disproportionate to its usefulness?

J.B.

MURAOKA, T.: *Emphasis in Biblical Hebrew*. 1969. Pp. viii, 180 + 15 (Hebrew). [Obtainable from Thornton, Oxford; Brill (Leiden); Harrassowitz Wiesbaden; T. Wever (Franeker, Netherlands). Price: £1·50 (approx.)]

This is a Ph.D. dissertation prepared under the supervision of Professor C. Rabin and presented at the Hebrew University in 1969. There is a Hebrew summary, but most of the work is in English which, despite some unidiomatic expressions, is a remarkable and admirable achievement for a Japanese working in Israel. The author examines the ways in which emphasis (a term which, he stresses, needs to be defined because it can be used in different senses) is expressed in the Hebrew Old Testament, and gives a bibliography. This work makes a valuable contribution to the study of Hebrew and of the Old Testament and shows how fresh light can be shed on a familiar book by the use of systematic methods.

J.A.E.

VOGT, E. (ed.): *Lexicon Linguae Aramaicae Veteris Testamenti Documentis Antiquis Illustratum*. 1971. Pp. xiii, 192. (Pontifical Biblical Institute, Rome. Price: $11.50. Lire 6,900)

This volume completes the late F. Zorell's *Lexicon Hebraicum et Aramaicum Veteris Testamenti*, the Hebrew part of which was published in 1959. Aramaic passages from the Old Testament are generously quoted and translated into Latin. The illustration from ancient documents is as full and, wherever Aramaic words used in the Old Testament appear also in the Old Aramaic inscriptions, in the Imperial Aramaic papyri of the Cowley, Kraeling and Driver collections and of the Story of Ahikar, and in the Dead Sea Scrolls — notably the Genesis Apocryphon —, the relevant passages are quoted and translated. This contextual approach dominates the work and there is little of the philological material of Baumgartner's earlier work in Köhler's *Lexicon in Veteris Testamenti Libros* (1953, 2nd ed. 1958). Vogt's lexicon thus complements excellently the approaches of Baumgartner and Driver, and sets the newly discovered texts side by side with the biblical material very helpfully. However, it is not to be regarded as a general dictionary of pre-Christian Aramaic, as words that do not appear in the Old Testament are not cited. There is a short introduction describing the method and the extra-biblical material and a Latin-Aramaic vocabulary at the back.

J.G.S.

ADDITIONAL NOTES ON SCHOOL TEXTBOOKS, ETC.

*LORD, E. and WHITTLE D.: *A Theological Glossary*. 1969. Pp. vii, 134. (Religious Education Press, Oxford. Price: 75p)

This is an introduction (ranging from 'a priori' to 'Zwinglianism)' to the kind of theological and philosophical technical terms, foreign words and phrases and abbreviations which are so often produced without explanation, to the mystification of the non-specialist reader.

It also tries to give objective summaries of the theological positions associated with certain well-known names of the past and present. In such a short book attempting a task of this size anyone can, of course, spot omissions; nevertheless the definitions are clear and concise, and there is a useful addition in the form of an alphabetical list of 'names and dates of persons mentioned'.   E.B.M.

*MOWVLEY, H.: *The Testimony of Israel*. ('Understanding the Bible' Series, Vol. 1). 1971. Pp. xi, 164. (Religious Education Press, Oxford. Price: 90p)

*TOMES, R.: *The Fear of the Lord*. ('Understanding the Bible' Series, Vol. 2). 1971. Pp. xi, 139. (Religious Education Press, Oxford. Price: 90p)

These are two in a six-volume series under the general editorship of Edgar Jones. Vol. 3 was published in 1970 (see *B.L.* 1971, p. 70). *The Testimony of Israel* gives an introduction to the various types of O.T. literature and to techniques of studying them, and adds some basic information regarding individual books. *The Fear of the Lord* examines O.T. religion from the patriarchal period onwards. Both books give excellent suggestions for further reading, which counterbalance the occasional over-generalisations which are inevitable in such brief works. Written with VIth Forms, Colleges of Education and first year theological students in mind, they will also be helpful to the non-specialist teacher of religious education.   E.B.M.

*RHYMER, J.: *The Babylonian Experience. A way through the Old Testament:* 4. *The Exile.* 1971. Pp. 150. (Sheed and Ward, London and Sydney. Price: 80p)

This book explains, simply but clearly, the influence of the Exile on the development of Judaism, with frequent quotations from the biblical literature, especially Ezekiel, in the translation of the Jerusalem Bible. There are no references to other than biblical literature, and no bibliography.   L.A.P.

Book List 1973

GENERAL

BERLIN, C. (ed.): *Studies in Jewish Bibliography, History and Literature in honour of I. E. Krieg.* 1971. Pp. 587, 139. (Ktav Publishing House, New York. Price: $25)

This Festschrift contains 35 contributions in English and 8 in Hebrew by Jewish scholars in America, Europe, and Israel on medieval rabbinic and a few modern topics. No doubt the student of Judaism will be richly rewarded by the great variety of offerings. There are, however, only few articles in this collection which concern or touch upon the O.T. We mention an article on 'The Rebellions during the Reign of David' by M. A. Cohen, a short study on 'The Order of the Books' of the Bible by N. M. Sarna, a bibliographical note on 'Rashi's Commentary on the Pentateuch and on the Five Scrolls, 1538' by M. Schmelzer, and another note on 'A Suggested Source for Some of the Substitute Names for YHWH' by F. Zimmermann. The Hebrew section does not contain any article relevant to the O.T.   H.K.

BOTTERWECK, G. J. and RINGGREN, H. (ed.): *Theologisches Wörterbuch zum Alten Testament.* Band I. Lieferung 5 (Spalte 513–640). 1972. (W. Kohlhammer, Stuttgart. Sub. price: DM. 16)

This fascicle (cf. *B.L.* 1972, p. 5) begins with the final part of the article on *bādād* and ends with the first part of that on *bākāh*. The article on *bō'* includes a treatment of *'ātā*, and that on *bzz* also deals with *šālāl*. By far the largest amount of space is given to *bō'* (H. D. Preuss); one may doubt whether the ubiquity of this word in the Old Testament, which ensures its presence in a variety of religious and theological contexts, really confers on the word itself a theological significance proportionate to the length of the article. The long article on *bᵉhēmā* arouses similar doubts. Other major articles include those on *bāḥar* (mainly by H. Seebass), *bāṭaḥ* (A. Jepsen), *bîn* (H. Ringgren) and *bayit* (H. A. Hoffner). In the last of these it is disappointing that significant place-names like Bethel and Bethlehem receive no individual treatment. As in earlier fascicles the back cover has an index of subjects covered in the fascicle; presumably a subject-index to the whole work will eventually be provided.   R.N.W.

BOTTERWECK, G. J. and RINGGREN, H. (ed.): *Theologisches Wörterbuch zum Alten Testament.* Band I. Lieferung 6/7 (Spalte 641–896). 1972. (W. Kohlhammer, Stuttgart. Sub. price: DM. 32)

This double fascicle runs from *bākāh* to *gᵉbûl*, and no word of theological importance appears to have been omitted. There is, probably wisely, some flexibility in the presentation of the material: for example under *b'r* (H. Ringgren) all roots having this spelling are taken together, whereas *bāśār*, 'flesh' (N. P. Bratsiotis) is treated separately from the article on *bśr* (*biśśēr*) (O. Schilling). *bēn, ben-'ādām* and *bat* have each a separate article. Again, of possibly the two most important articles, *bᵉrît* was entrusted to a single author (M. Weinfeld), while *bārā'* is divided between four, enabling more specialist treatment of such aspects as the Egyptian (J. Bergman) and Mesopotamian (H. Ringgren) backgrounds. The quality of the contributions remains high, and the bibliography well chosen within the limits of space.   R.N.W.

BOWMAN, J. (ed.): *Abr-Nahrain XII, 1971–72*. Pp. viii, 117, pl. IV. 1972. (E. J. Brill, Leiden. Price: Fl. 32)

Nine of the twelve contributions were read as papers at the XXVIIIth International Congress of Orientalists at Canberra. The appeal is more tó the Arabist than to the O.T. scholar. A. Dotan in 'Vowel shift in Phoenician and Punic' deals with the *a* to *o* phenomenon, and A. Vööbus gives a summary of the 'Discovery of important Syriac MSS on the canons of the Ecumenical Councils' treated more fully in his book.   D.R.Ap-T.

CAQUOT, A. and PHILONENKO, M. (ed.): *Hommages à André Dupont-Sommer*. 1971. Pp. xiii, 559. (Librairie d'Amérique et d'Orient, Adrien-Maisonneuve, Paris. Price: Fr. 260)

If the literary *genre* of *Festschriften* has to continue to exist, then the present one dedicated to A. Dupont-Sommer is an excellent one by any standard. It is sub-divided into six sections dealing with the history of the Ancient Orient and Semitic epigraphy, Linguistics, Biblical studies, Qumran studies, Judaism during the Roman period, and Karaism — followed by a list of D-S's publications. Most contributions are of central interest to Semitists and O.T. scholars alike. There are two significant posthumous articles by the deeply lamented D. Winton Thomas and by the brilliant R. de Vaux. It is not clear to me why Sir Godfrey Driver is so often misrepresented as Geoffrey (p. ix).   E.U.

Cesty k pramenům/Biblická archeologie a literární kritika (*The Ways of approach to the sources / Biblical Archaeology and Literary Criticism*), translated by M. Freiová and others. 1971. Pp. 225. (Vyšehrad, Prague. Price: Kčs. 21)

This volume contains three translations. First, there is W. F. Albright's *Recent Discoveries in Bible Lands* (originally published as a supplement to R. Young, *Analytical Concordance* 1936, revised 1955; and separately in 1956; *B.L.* 1957, p. 15; *Decade*, p. 15), *Poznatky starozákonní archeologie*, pp. 15–119. Second, J. Steinmann, *La critique devant la Bible*, translated from the German version: *Die literarische und historische Kritik des biblischen Textes*, by J. Myslivec and J. Sokol (*Literární a historická kritika biblických textů*), pp. 121–205. Third, K. Schubert, *Problém historického výkladu* ('The Problem of historical interpretation') pp. 207–25, from the German *Kerygma und Geschichte*. The aim of the volume is to make a wider circle of readers acquainted with the results of modern biblical scholarship, and so to help them to penetrate more deeply into the biblical message.   M.B.

EISSFELDT, O.: *Kleine Schriften zum Alten Testament*. Herausgegeben von K.-M. Beyse und H.-J. Zobel, n.d. (1972?). Pp. 482. (Evangelische Verlagsanstalt, Berlin)

This volume contains an excellent selection of studies from the first four volumes of Eissfeldt's *Kleine Schriften*, and three which will presumably be included in the fifth volume (viz., 'Die Lade Jahwes in Geschichtserzählung, Sage, und Lied', 'Israels Religion und die

Religionen seiner Umwelt', and 'Der kanaanäische El als Geber der den israelitischen Erzvätern geltenden Nachkommenschaft und Landbesitzverheissungen'). The criterion for the selection of these essays out of the entire corpus has been their direct bearing on O.T. study. They are arranged in five groups: exegetical (12 essays), those dealing with questions of introduction (4), historical (3), those on theology and the history of religion (14), and biographical (3).

For notices of the volumes of *Kleine Schriften* see *Book Lists* 1962, p. 5 (*Decade*, p. 315), 1964, p. 7 (*Decade*, p. 475), 1967, p. 5, and 1969, p. 4.   G.W.A.

FRIEDRICH, G. (ed.): *Theologisches Wörterbuch zum Neuen Testament* (begun by G. Kittel). Band IX. Lieferungen 5–9. 1971–2. Each pp. 64. (Kohlhammer, Stuttgart. Sub. price: Each Lieferung DM. 8.80 up to No. 7, then raised to DM. 9.50. There will probably be two more Lieferungen to complete Vol. IX and the whole work)

Lieferung 5 continues *physis* with section on usage in LXX to Josephus (H. Köster). *Phōnē* and cognates. *Qōl* in O.T., in Palestinian Judaism, in Rabbinic writings and in Hellenistic Judaism. On p. 299 note on Aramaic *sumphonyah. Symphonia* in O.T. and in Judaism. (O. Betz). *Phōs* and cognates. The word-group in O.T. *'ōr, ma'ōr; nēr, nōgah, nagoah, nahar, yapha'*: in Judaism, Qumran and Rabbinic writings. Important for Gnosis (H. Conzelmann).

Lieferung 6. Chairō and cognates. O.T. *samah, hadah,* etc. Judaism, Rabbinic writings and Philo. *Charis.* In LXX usually translated by *hēn.* Section on *hanan* and cognates. Also *hesed* (W. Zimmerli). *Hanan* and *Hesed* in Judaism, Qumran, Testaments of Twelve Patriarchs and Rabbinic Writings and representation in LXX and N.T. (H. Conzelmann).

Lieferung 7. Charis continued. *Charisma* in LXX; sometimes represented by *hesed* in Judaism. *Eucharisteō* and cognates. *Eucharistia* translated by *tōdah* (H. Conzelmann). *Cheir* and cognates; *yad* in O.T. and Post-Biblical Judaism. Especially 'the hand of God' (E. Lohse). *Cherubin. Kerūbim* in O.T. and Post-Biblical Judaism (E. Lohse). *Chēra.* Section on 'widow in O.T.' (G. Stählin).

Double-Lieferung 8/9, Chēra continued. *Chilias / chilioi*; correspondences in O.T. and Judaism (E. Lohse). *chōīkos.* O.T. *'apar.* (W. Schweitzer). *Chrēstos* and cognates; LXX and Jewish literature (K. Weiss). *Chriō, christos* and cognates; *mašah* and *mašiah* in O.T. Anointing of king, etc. (F. Hesse). *mašiah* in late Judaism, in Apocrypha and in Pseudepigrapha (A. S. Van der Woude and M. de Jonge), in Qumran and Rabbinic writings (A. S. Van der Woude), in Philo and Josephus (M. de Jonge). *Christus* in N.T. (W. Grundmann). *Chronos* begins (G. Delling).   N.W.P.

GUTMAN, J. (ed.): *No Graven Images, Studies in art and the Hebrew Bible.* 1971. Pp. lxiii, 599. (Ktav Publishing House, New York. Price: $25)

This volume is a very valuable collection of articles (some illustrated) on various aspects of religion and art (Jewish and early Christian) which have appeared mostly in American and continental journals, some of them not easily obtainable. The editor contributes a number of articles on Jewish art including 'The "second commandment" and the image in Judaism' which provides a much-needed corrective

to the still common assumption that Judaism has been uniformly
hostile to the visual arts. Other important contributions are by
I. Abrahams, 'The Decalogue in Art'; H. Riesenfeld, 'The Resurrection in Ezekiel XXXVII and in the Dura-Europos paintings';
W. Stechow 'Jacob blessing the sons of Joseph from early Christian
times to Rembrandt'; C.-O. Nordström 'The water miracles of Moses
in Jewish legend and Byzantine art'; K. Weitzmann 'The question of
the influence of Jewish pictorial sources in Old Testament illustration';
and A. Werner on the Jerusalem windows of the Jewish painter
Chagall. This book is of first importance to Jewish and Christian scholars interested in the art and iconography of their religious traditions.

E.J.T.

Internationale Zeitschriftenschau für Bibelwissenschaft und Grenzgebiete.
Vol. 18. (1971–2). 1972. Pp. xiv, 445. (Patmos Verlag, Düsseldorf.
Price: DM. 96)

The increase in this issue to over 3,000 items, covering both Old and
New Testaments, is an indication both of the growth in biblical
studies and of the measure of completeness attained in this essential
bibliographical aid.

P.R.A.

KAPELRUD, A. S. and JERVELL, J. (ed.): *Studia Theologica*, Scandinavian
Journal of Theology, Vol. 26, no. 1. 1972. Pp. 1–61. (Universitetsforlaget,
Oslo. Subscription price: N.Kr. 60, $10)

There are two N.T. articles in this fascicle and one O.T.: J. T. Willis,
'Cultic elements in the story of Samuel's birth and education' (pp.
33–61), an interesting study of various approaches which have been
made to 1 Sam. 1–3 and of the problems of interpreting this material,
both with reference to its content and in relation to what precedes and
follows. There is much useful comment and footnotes rich in suggestions and bibliographical information.

P.R.A.

KOCH, K. (ed.): *Um das Prinzip der Vergeltung in Religion und Recht des
Alten Testaments.* (Wege der Forschung, Band cxxv.) 1972. Pp. xiv, 458.
(Wissenschaftliche Buchgesellschaft Darmstadt. Price: DM. 55.20)

This collection of essays on the theme of retribution in the O.T.
published severally between the years 1931 and 1961 offers a valuable
aid to students of its thought. The Editor is Professor Koch of
Hamburg and, in addition to himself, the authors whose work is
reprinted in the book are H. Gunkel, J. Pedersen, K. H. Fahlgren,
F. Horst, H. Gese, W. Preiser (a lawyer), J. Scharbert, J. Weismann,
A. Alt and H. Graf Reventlow. An introduction by Koch makes
clear the purpose of the publication which is to introduce readers to an
extended debate on a subject of considerable theological importance.
Until about a generation ago it was assumed that the concept of
divine retribution was characteristic of the O.T., though after
Wellhausen there was some doubt as to when it became dominant.
Then, especially in Scandinavia, the view was put forward by
Pedersen, Mowinckel and Fahlgren that a series of ethical terms in
Hebrew expressed both cause and consequence and that one should
recognize the presence of a synthetic view of life in the O.T. according

to which wickedness had an inevitable consequence in the nature of things and did not require a retributory act from outside. This order of human existence was under God's supervision, as it owed its creation to him. Von Rad accepted this view of things and today it is strongly represented in this book by Horst, Scharbert, Gese and Reventlow. The general impression left on one reader is that the method of the Procrustes bed is unsuitable for dealing with O.T. thought. Volumes similar to this on other themes would be useful.

N.W.P.

NEUSNER, J. (ed.): *Religions in Antiquity: Essays in Memory of Erwin Ramsdell Goodenough*. (Studies in the History of Religions: Supplements to Numen, XIV). 1968 (reprinted 1970). Pp. x, 688 and a portrait. (E. J. Brill, Leiden. Price: Fl. 94)

The variety and interest of this collection of essays in memory of E. R. Goodenough is a fitting indication of the importance for the study of Judaism of Goodenough's writings, and particularly of the stimulus provided by his *Jewish Symbols in the Greco-Roman Period*. The thirty articles in the collection are divided into four groups (Biblical studies; Apocrypha and Pseudepigrapha; History of Judaism; Symbolism and History of Religions), and of these the following deal directly with O.T. topics: B. A. Levine, 'On the Presence of God in Biblical Religion'; W. Harrelson, 'The Celebration of the Feast of Booths according to Zech. 14:16–21'; H. S. May, 'Psalm 118: The Song of the Citadel'. Otherwise, while the majority of the articles should prove of general interest to O.T. scholars, they are of much greater relevance to scholars concerned with the N.T., with Judaism and with the History of Religions. In addition to the above the volume contains three appreciations of Goodenough, an article by him (with A. T. Kraabel) entitled 'Paul and the Hellenization of Christianity', a bibliography of Goodenough's writings (compiled by Kraabel), and biblical and general indices.

M.A.K.

NOBER, P., S.J.: *Elenchus Bibliographicus Biblicus*, Vol. 52. 1971. Pp. xx, 781. (Biblical Institute Press, Rome. Sub. price: Lire 9,000)

Readers of this *Book List* are already familiar with the invaluable bibliographical aid provided in this annual *Elenchus*. of which the 1971 issue follows the familiar pattern. It is not the least of its values that it contains many references to reviews, giving ready access to critical assessments of books, and that it includes notes of dissertations. Father Nober again deserves the gratitude and praise of the scholarly world.

P.R.A.

REUMANN, J. (ed.): *Understanding the Sacred Text. Essays in Honor of Morton S. Enslin on the Hebrew Bible and Christian Beginnings*. 1972. Pp. 256, 1 plate. (Judson Press, Valley Forge, Pa. Price: $15)

Five essays in this *Festschrift* are devoted to the Hebrew Scriptures; eight to the Gospels and Christian Origins. There is a biographical note and a select bibliography of Enslin's writings. S. Sandmel, 'The Ancient Mind and Ours', continues his concern with what he regards as the haggadic quality of much biblical material — often with a sound antidote to the pedestrian ways of commentators. B. S. Childs, 'Midrash and the O.T.', continues the related investigation of this helpful descriptive category for the understanding of re-interpretation. H. M. Orlinsky, 'Nationalism-Universalism in the Book of Jeremiah', provides a further, somewhat one-sided, corrective to oversimple universalistic interpretations. W. F. Stinespring, 'Some Remarks on the N.E.B.', compares this translation's handling of certain grammatical and syntactical usages which he has elsewhere discussed in other modern versions. J. B. Pritchard, 'Sarepta in History and Tradition', gathers the references, biblical and non-biblical, to this coastal city. The O.T. part of the volume thus provides some useful and stimulating contributions.   P.R.A.

RIESENFELD, H. (ed.): *Svensk exegetisk årsbok*, xxxvi, 1971 (1972). Pp. 192, 6 figs. (C. W. K. Gleerup, Lund. Price: Sw. Kr. 20)

This excellent issue begins with three articles on O.T. themes. In 'The Background of Joshua iii–v', J. R. Porter presents an interpretation of these chapters in cultic terms, as reflecting a pre-Israelite spring New Year festival at Gilgal. S. Erlandsson contributes an investigation of the historical background of Isa. 11:10–16, in which he argues that the historical and geographical allusions in the pericope are best explained in terms of the Assyrian campaigns and deportations at the end of the eighth century. M. Ottosson's article, 'Hexagrammet och pentagrammet i främreorientalisk kontext', is a well documented account of the archaeological and palaeographic evidence for the use in ancient times of the shield of David and the seal of Solomon, as seen in the light of ancient Near Eastern astral symbolism. The remaining major articles deal with inter-testamental and New Testament subjects. M. de Jonge surveys recent studies on the Testaments of the Twelve Patriarchs. J. Neusner writes on the Rabbinic traditions about the Pharisees before A.D. 70. B. Gerhardsson discusses Matt. 6:1–6, 16–21. J. Hjärpe examines Arabic parallels to the *logion* about 'pearls before swine'. L. Hartmann considers the significance for early Christology of baptism in the name of Jesus. Among the other items in the issue is an obituary of Père Roland de Vaux by L.-M. Dewailly. All the articles mentioned are in Swedish, except those by Porter and de Jonge, which are in English.

G.W.A.

SAEBØ, M. (ed.): *Israel, kirken og verden.* Nordisk teologkonferanse Utstein kloster 1971. 1972. Pp. 230. (Forlaget Land og Kirke, Oslo. Price: N.Kr. 40)

Theologians from Denmark, Finland, Norway, and Sweden participated in the conference at Utstein Prionzin, Norway, of which this book is the record. As the title indicates, the theme of the conference was the relationship between Israel, the Church, and the world. After a brief foreword of welcome by O. Hagesaether, Bishop of Stavanger, the scope and intention of the discussion are indicated in a prefatory survey by the editor. Three papers treat of the O.T.: B. Albrektson writes on the election of Israel and Israel as the people of God; B. Johnson discusses prophecy and fulfilment; and M. Saebø summarizes what the O.T. says about Israel's future. Two N.T. essays are devoted to the presentation of the fulfilment of the promises and of Israel's future in the Gospels (S. Aalen), and Paul (N. A. Dahl). The essays by S. Granild on the people of Israel and the land, and by R. Prenter on the people of Israel and worship treat the O.T. and N.T. material consecutively and comparatively. G. Hedenquist's paper on the people of Israel and the state is concerned with the contemporary situation. A. Torm writes on the relations between Church and Synagogue. G. Lindeskog contributes a documented study of discussions between Christians and Jews since 1913. The volume includes biographical data about the contributors and a select bibliography. G.W.A.

SANDMEL, S. (ed.): *Hebrew Union College Annual.* XLII. 1971. Pp. 278 + 23 in Hebrew. (Hebrew Union College, Cincinnati)

The first 94 pages of the volume are allocated to 'Bibliography of Holy Land Sites' (E. K. Vogel). Sites are listed in alphabetical order, and for each one there is a comprehensive bibliography, drawing attention to articles discussing the excavations which have been undertaken at each site. The bibliography will be of great assistance in the tracing of articles in various journals and books. The view that the golden calves erected by Jeroboam I were intended to be variations upon the cherubim, pedestals upon which the invisible Yahweh rode, is challenged in 'The Golden Calf' (L. R. Bailey). The argument may not convince every reader, yet the article is worthy of careful study. 'Esther 9:29–32: The genesis of a late addition' (S. E. Loewenstamm) demonstrates the complex process which underlies the composition of this section of Esther. In 'The oldest Greek Text of Deuteronomy' (G. Howard), it is argued that, as far as Deuteronomy is concerned, the Codex Alexandrinus (A) preserves a more ancient form of text than Codex Vaticanus (B). 'Studies in Hebrew Verb Formation' (J. Blau) examines the Hebrew cohortative and its Semitic correspondence, the origin of the *pôlel | pô'el* themes of *'ayin waw/yodh* and double *'ayin* verbs, and the original vocalization of the perfect of Hebrew *pi'ēl* and *hiph'il*. Two articles are of interest to the Qumran specialist, namely, 'The employment of Palaeo-Hebrew characters for the divine names at Qumran in the light of Tannaitic sources' (J. P. Siegel), and 'The Qumran Hebrew original of Ben Sira's concluding acrostic on Wisdom' (I. Rabinowitz). The article 'Liability for mere intention in early Jewish Law' (B. S. Jackson) contains, together with other interesting material, a very full discussion of the interpretation of the tenth commandment. The use of the computer for Semitic studies is discussed in 'Transliteration and a "Computer-Compatible" Semitic Alphabet' (E. A. Goldman, H. D. Uriel Smith, R. D. Tanenbaum). The other articles in this volume are 'Are there fictitious Baraitot in the Babylonian Talmud?' (L. Jacobs); 'Visibility of the New Moon in Cuneiform and Rabbinic Sources' (Ben Z. Wacholder and D. B. Weisberg); 'Longevity, the Rainbow, and Immanuel of Rome' (D. Goldstein). The article in Hebrew by M. Pelli deals with the work of Saul Berlin. E.R.R.

SCHWAB, M.: *Index of Articles Relative to Jewish History and Literature Published in Periodicals, from 1665 to 1900* (Augmented Edition). 1971. Pp. xvi, 539, 409–613. (Ktav Publishing House, New York. Price: $39.50)

This volume contains a reprint of Schwab's *Répertoire des Articles* in the form in which it finally appeared in print in 1923, together

with the two indices (subjects and Hebrew words) as they were originally lithographed from the author's handwritten manuscript in 1900.
B. Wachstein's list of corrections is also included, and an introduction
and edited list of abbreviations are by Z. Szajkowski. The *Répertoire*
itself is arranged alphabetically by authors and, besides demonstrating
the fact that before the twentieth century few scholars devoted much
time to articles other than book-reviews, it gives easy access to a less
familiar side of the work of scholars whose influence on, and enduring
importance for, modern research are nowadays coming to be increasingly recognized.

J.F.A.S.

SPIEGEL, Y. (ed.): *Psychoanalytische Interpretationen biblischer Texte.* 1972.
Pp. 274. (Chr. Kaiser Verlag, Munich. Price: DM. 35)

The volume contains 21 contributions ranging in date from 1916 to
1968 by 20 different writers, with an introductory essay and a bibliography supplied by the editor. Both this essay and the contribution by
H. Harsch ('Psychological interpretation of biblical texts?') invite by
their questioning approach the attention of biblical scholars to the
need to understand what has been written by those trained in psychoanalysis on questions of biblical interpretation. It is an area in which
it has been all too easy for biblical scholars to dismiss what has been
written, and it is proper that there should be a reminder of both the
seriousness of the discussion and of its recognized limits. Most of the
essays are directed to O.T. problems, though wider questions are
raised; the range includes sacrifice, atonement, dreams, the Samson
saga, sabbath, prophetic consecration, the crossing of the sea. There
is clearly much to be derived from a serious study of an area inevitably
somewhat unfamiliar, since most of the publications have appeared
originally in journals and books devoted to psychoanalysis and
related fields. The strong Jewish contribution is noteworthy. All the
contributions appear here in German; nine were originally published
in English.

P.R.A.

Studies in the Religion of Ancient Israel (Supplements to *Vetus Testamentum*, Vol. xxiii). 1972. Pp. 181. (E. J. Brill, Leiden. Price: Fl. 54)

The articles assembled here are varied. H. Ringgren issues a somewhat
discursive but salutary warning on the difficulties inherent in the
attempt to discover parallels between the religion of Israel and her
neighbours. J. A. Soggin offers a study of the monarchy, particularly
of its origin and the syncretistic features it embodied, concluding that
it was therefore only when the monarchy perished that it could
become transformed into a messianic hope. P. A. H. de Boer has two
essays; on the *leḥem pānîm* which he translates 'facial bread' and
thinks originally indicated a loaf stamped with the face of Yahweh;
and on *rêaḥ nîḥōaḥ* and the idea of 'God's fragrance'. W. Zimmerli
seeks to analyse the *proprium* of prophecy in the Old Testament and
finds it in the inexorable application of the covenant demand of
Yahweh to the great historical catastrophes, leading to the recognition
that Israel's standing is not in her own righteousness, despite the
promise of blessing (J) and of the divine Presence (P), but in the
mercy of God. D. J. McCarthy studies *berît*-making in the
Deuteronomistic history, finds that the picture is by no means
uniform, and concludes that the translation 'covenant' may stand.

There is a substantial study of the Passover Sacrifice by M. Haran, weighing up the relation between the narrative of the passover in Egypt and the ritual provisions of the pentateuchal sources, and the connection between the passover offering and the temple. H. D. Preuss, in an important study, asks whether the specific Yahweh faith exerted any decisive influence on the old wisdom tradition of Israel, and finds that the expressions used in that tradition do not go beyond those of analogous texts in near eastern wisdom generally. He finds his thesis confirmed by an examination of the expression 'the fear of Yahweh', which means wisdom implemented, and is not in itself a sign of the specific Yahweh faith. R. B. Y. Scott takes up the same problem, as raised by von Rad who sees a religious depth in the old wisdom, and W. McKane who distinguishes within Proverbs between the empirical wisdom concerned with education for government, and Yahweh piety. He comes down on the side of McKane and develops his distinction further. The final essay is P. R. Ackroyd's study of the theme of the Temple vessels as a theological pointer, valid independently of the question of historicity, by which the historians indicate the continuity, through disaster, of the people of God. Altogether a good collection. D.R.J.

DE VAUX, R.: *The Bible and the Ancient Near East.* 1972. Pp. 284. (Darton, Longman and Todd, London. Price: £4.50)

There are fifteen articles in this book, chosen by Père de Vaux, from the twenty-eight included in his *Bible et Orient* (*B.L.* 1968, p. 10). The translation is by D. McHugh, and J. McHugh has occasionally added references to works in English in the footnotes and explanatory notes. A.S.H.

WEVERS, J. W. and REDFORD, D. B. (ed.): *Studies on the Ancient Palestinian World presented to Professor F. V. Winnett on the occasion of his retirement 1 July 1971* (Toronto Semitic Texts and Studies, 2). 1972. Pp. xii, 171, pls. 7, plans and drawings 4. (University of Toronto Press; Oxford University Press, London. Price: £5)

This book contains a list of Professor Winnett's publications, and eleven essays in his honour, J. B. Pritchard discusses an incense burner from Tell es-Sa'idiyeh, W. L. Reed the history of Elealeh, and A. D. Tushingham three Byzantine tombstones from Dhiban. E. J. Revell argues that accent signs in biblical manuscripts with Palestinian pointing are used to mark stressed syllables. J. W. Wevers examines the textual affinities of the Arabic translation (one of at least four) of Genesis which is best represented in manuscript Arab 9 in the Bibliothèque Nationale and which was made from the LXX. R. J. Williams considers energic verbal forms in Hebrew. W. S. McCullough surveys Israelite eschatology from Amos to Daniel. R. C. Culley discusses recent work on the historical reliability of oral tradition and its bearing on O.T. study. N. E. Wagner draws attention to the variety of opinion about the extent of the pentateuchal source J, and questions the view that J's portrayal of the patriarchs has its background in the time of David and Solomon. D. B. Redford, while doubting whether Solomon's system of court officials was based on an Egyptian model, argues that, directly or indirectly, his methods of taxation were. A. K. Grayson publishes and discusses an Accadian text of Sin-sharra-ishkun, one of the last kings of Assyria. There is no index. J.A.E.

ARCHAEOLOGY AND EPIGRAPHY

AVIGAD, N.: *Beth She'arim III: The Archaeological Excavations during 1953–1958. The Catacombs 12–23.* 1971. Pp. xvi, 218, pl. LXXIV, figs. 131. (Israel Exploration Society, and Mosad Bialik, Jerusalem)

Apart from the title and contents pages and such words as Plan and Section on drawings, this volume is wholly in Hebrew — unlike vol. 1, 2nd edn, 1957, and vol. 2, 1957 (*B.L.* 1958, p. 13, *Decade*, p. 89). In addition to the catacombs in the title, catacomb 31 and a number of outside tombs from this large necropolis of pious Jewry are reported on. As the preliminary reports in *IEJ* 4–9 (1954–59), and the survey in *Antiquity and Survival* II (1957), showed, these catacombs and their contents shed considerable light on Jewish life in Palestine mainly, if not exclusively, between A.D. 200 and 350.   D.R.Ap-T.

DEVER, W. G., LANCE, H. D., WRIGHT, G. E., and SHAFFER A., with a Preface by GLUECK, N.: *Gezer I: Preliminary Report of the 1964–66 Seasons.* (Annual of the Hebrew Union College Biblical and Archaeological School in Jerusalem, Vol. I). 1970. Pp. viii, 113, 24 pp. listings and drawings of pottery and objects, 25 pp. plates, 13 plans and sections in cover slip-case. (H.U.C. Biblical and Archaeological School, Jerusalem)

Many years of fruitful excavation have been spent at Tell Jezer by W. G. Dever and his team. Here we have the evidence on which other archaeologists can begin to evaluate the real significance of the site and test the conclusions put forward in more popular accounts. Gezer is a site of such importance that a full-scale excavation, such as this, with the latest techniques cannot fail to make an essential and significant contribution to our archaeological knowledge of this whole area, when published. Already every century from Herod back to the sixteenth century B.C. has been evidenced, and all workers in this field will need this well-produced technical report.

D.R.Ap-T.

DRIJVERS, H. J. W.: *Old-Syriac (Edessean) Inscriptions* (Semitic Study Series, New Series, III). 1972. Pp. xviii, 117. (E. J. Brill, Leiden. Price: Fl. 26)

The editor's purpose has been to publish in one book all the Syriac inscriptions (67 in number, of which some have not been published before) from the first three centuries A.D. that have been found in or near Edessa; he has also included three inscriptions and a papyrus from Dura Europos, and four legends of coins. After a general introduction, each text is printed in Syriac type, together with a brief description and references to relevant literature, and there are indexes of names of people, deities, months, etc., and a glossary. It is a pity that a work written in English transcribes *yodh* by *j* rather than *y*, and that the strange form 'Edessean' is employed, but these are minor defects. The publication of this collection of early Syriac texts is very welcome.   J.A.E.

*FRANK, H. T.: *An Archaeological Companion to the Bible.* 1972. Pp. 334, over 100 ill. and sketchmaps. (S.C.M. Press, London; Abingdon Press, Nashville. Price: £3.75, $12.50)

This substantial volume succeeds very well in providing a sober, factual survey of archaeological discoveries relating to the Bible which are woven into a chronologically arranged framework of history in eight main periods. The illustrations are functional rather than glossy, and the indexes of scripture references and names make the book easy to use. It can be warmly recommended for the general reader. (Its American title (1971) is *Bible, Archaeology and Faith*.)

D.R.Ap-T.

FREEDMAN, D. N. and GREENFIELD, J. C. (ed.): *New Directions in Biblical Archaeology*. (1969) 1971. Pp. xxiv, 211 with 57 illustrations. (Doubleday and Co. Inc., Garden City, New York. Price: $2.15)

This collection of essays, whose original appearance in 1969 was not noted in the *Book List*, has now been issued in paperback; it contains thirteen studies, some of which have appeared elsewhere, though in some instances, as for example F. M. Cross's study of the Daliyeh papyri, they have been revised. It is a useful review of important recent work, e.g. at Ashdod and Arad, and in particular contains a group of studies of Qumran, including a bibliographical survey.

P.R.A.

*HARKER, R.: *Digging up the Bible Lands*, 1972. Pp. 126. (The Bodley Head, London. Price: £1.95)

This is one of the 'Bodley Head Archaeologies', a series edited by Magnus Magnusson and apparently intended for younger readers. The eight sites chosen — Ur, Babylon, Nineveh, Jericho, Jerusalem, En-gedi and Qumran — by no means cover all the Bible lands, but they relate to material from the Patriarchs to Bar Kokhba and to archaeological work from the 1830s to the 1960s. The author, a journalist, writes simply yet never patronisingly, and his enthusiasm and love for his subject compensate for an occasional lack of scholarly caution. Attractively produced, with line drawings and photographs, this book gives a fascinating introduction to archaeology and should encourage many of its readers to a deeper interest.

E.B.M.

*KENYON, K.: *Royal Cities of the Old Testament*. 1971. Pp. xii, 164. pl. 103, text figures 28. (Barrie and Jenkins, London. Price: £4)

This volume may be said to have developed from a lecture given on the same subject as the title on the occasion of the centenary of the Palestine Exploration Fund in 1965, and those who heard the lecture will be among the first to welcome this much fuller and well-illustrated exposition. It has all the advantages of being a carefully accurate but non-technical description of the results of archaeological work at Jerusalem, Samaria, Hazor and Megiddo (with other incidental matter) and of being a rounded discussion on a limited but very important area for biblical study. Essentially it covers only the period from David to the fall of Judah; it sheds much light on the relationship between buildings unearthed by excavation and the development of royal and other institutions. The whole is made vivid by the clear plates and figures in which, almost without exception, the points being made in the text can be immediately observed. (The exceptions are only in one or two of the plans which have numerals and signs not easy to pick out, and in one or two photographs of a more general kind.) There are points on which an Old Testament scholar must disagree — 598 B.C. for Jerusalem's first fall is one, anachronistic references to the Samaritans another, occasional oversimplified use of the Chronicler's writings a third. But these are small points compared with the values which may be derived from such an excellent piece of scholarly popularisation.

P.R.A.

MAZAR, B.: *The Excavations in the Old City of Jerusalem near the Temple Mount: Preliminary Report of the Second and Third Seasons, 1969–1970*, together with BEN-DOV, M.: *The Omayyad Structures near the Temple Mount: Preliminary Report.* 1971. Pp. 44, pl. XXXII, figs. 20 with fold-out section and plan. (The Institute of Archaeology, Hebrew University, and The Israel Exploration Society, Jerusalem)

No preliminary report could be more attractively produced. The text has been most competently Englished by R. Grafman from articles which first appeared in *Eretz-Israel* 10 (1971), and the plates are marvels of clarity. The importance of the finds around the S.W. corner of the Haram deserves this treatment, and no account of Herod's Jerusalem and Temple, or of the magnificent later Omayyad interlude, will be adequate which does not now take account of these excavations and their sequel — whatever the final decision may be on matters of detail.

D.R.Ap-T.

HISTORY AND GEOGRAPHY

BIØRN, S.: *Lad os opbygge Jerusalems mure. Topografiske problemer i Nehemjabogen.* (Tekst og tolkning, 2). 1971. Pp. 100. (G.E.C. Gad, Copenhagen. Price: D.Kr. 20.70)

With a quotation from Neh. 2:17, as the title, the theme of the book is stated. The author first shows that an exegetic investigation of Neh. 2, 3 and 12, such as that undertaken by Millar Burrows, does not lead to any solution of the topographical problems. Only by combining the description of locations in the text with the results of archaeological investigations, is it possible to overcome the problems. He has therefore undertaken to examine all of the material which excavations in Jerusalem have brought to light up to the year 1968. He comes to the conclusion that Nehemiah's nocturnal investigations of the walls (Neh. 2:11–18) take place from 'the gate of the valley' southwards along the eastern slope of the Tyropoeon valley, and moving in a counterclockwise direction, he rides around towards the city's most southern point. At the eastern side he continues on foot to investigate the slope towards the Kidron valley, after which he turns back along the same way. — S.B. maintains that Jerusalem in Nehemiah's time lay on the small eastern hill between Kidron and Tyropoeon, and, as such, did not include the western hill. In a concluding note, he does, however, remark that some of his results must be modified because the archaeological finds of 1969ff. seem to indicate that in pre-exilic times, building occurred on the western hill. The book is well supplied with photographs, drawings, and maps.

E.H.

*BRIGHT, J.: *A History of Israel* (Old Testament Library). 2nd ed. 1972. Pp. 519, 16 plates. (S.C.M. Press, London. Price: £4)

The first edition of Bright's history was reviewed in the *B.L.* 1960, p. 12 (*Decade* p. 192), and the second edition adheres to the general scheme of the first. Corrections have been made and some sections have been rewritten (e.g. 'Patriarchal Customs Against the Background of the Second Millennium', pp. 71f. in the first edition and pp. 78f. in the second), but Bright has not shifted from his main positions and has reproduced the substance of his earlier conclusions. The work will continue to be a useful manual for students. W.McK.

DALMAN, G.: *Jerusalem und sein Gelände, mit einer Einführung von Karl-Heinrich Rengstorf und mit Nachträgen auf Grund des Handexemplars von Peter Freimark.* 1972. Pp. xi, x, 402, 40 photos, 1 plan. (Georg Olms Verlag, Hildesheim and New York. Price: DM. 69.80)

Who in his senses would pay this price for an unrevised, forty-year-old, pocket-size description of Jerusalem and its surroundings? It is true that a list of Dalman's later annotations has been appended, but not even printer's errors listed in the original 1938 edition have been corrected; and though many of the 1918 German airforce photos are remarkably clear, considering their vintage and form of reproduction, there are now better ones available. The willing buyer must be one who values Dalman's thorough personal knowledge of the Jerusalem area at the turn of this century, before the old order changed, and who hopes perhaps to find here an overlooked clue to a still more ancient past amid the Arabic names so plentifully quoted.

D.R.Ap-T.

KUDLEK, M. and MICKLER, E. H. (ed.): *Solar and Lunar Eclipses of the Ancient Near East from 3000 B.C. to 0 with Maps* (Alter Orient und Altes Testament-Sonderreihe, Band I). 1971. Pp. ix, 199. (Verlag Butzon & Kevelaer. Neukirchener Verlag des Erziehungsvereins Neukirchen-Vluyn. Price: DM. 80)

Eclipses referred to directly or indirectly in ancient texts, can be precisely dated, the time of day when they occurred, their magnitude and duration accurately computed, so that a convenient series of eclipse tables and maps for the ancient near east could obviously be a valuable reference book. With modern printing techniques and advances in astronomy it would not be hard to improve on the pioneering work of Oppolzer (1887) and Neugebauer (1931), and this Kudlek and Mickler have attempted to do. The main part of the book consists of 157 pages of computer output giving details of all solar eclipses observable at Persepolis, Babylon, Ninive, Hattusa, Jerusalem, Memphis and Thebes during selected periods appropriate to each, and all lunar eclipses observable at Babylon between 2970 B.C. and A.D. 58. A rather fuller and less abstruse introduction and a more congenial computer programme would have saved the non-specialist reader, for whom such a book is clearly intended, a great deal of trouble. There are 39 maps showing the computed tracks of totality or annularity of solar eclipses in the region, but again, although clearly and attractively presented, they would have been far easier to consult if year B.C. or A.D. were given instead of Julian Day Numbers (2nd April, 303 B.C. instead of JDN 1610843). There are several printing errors and infelicities in the English of the three-page introduction.

J.F.A.S.

MAZAR, B. (ed.): *The World History of the Jewish People*. Vol. III. *Judges* (World History of the Jewish People, First Series: Ancient Times). 1971. Pp. xviii, 366. (W. H. Allen, London. Price: £8.50)

The present book is a direct continuation, developing the same themes, of vol. II of this series, which was reviewed in *B.L.* 1972, p. 19, and it continues the high standards of its predecessor. It falls into three sections: the first deals with the history, society and religion of Canaan in the Egyptian New Kingdom period, the second with the exodus, the conquest and settlement of Palestine by the Israelites and the period of the Judges, and the third with Israelite society and culture in the pre-monarchical period. As with the preceding volume, there is great emphasis on the archaeological evidence, but the O.T. material itself also receives full discussion. A valuable feature of this series is that it makes available, for those who do not read modern Hebrew, the findings of some of the important scholarly work being published in Israel. As might be expected, the overall approach, although always sane and cautious, is generally 'conservative' and inevitably not everyone will agree with the reconstruction of such highly debatable subjects as e.g. the exodus and the work of Moses. On the other hand, the very full treatment of early Israelite society and institutions is of great value and it is perhaps not too much to say that this volume provides the best general survey at present available of the period with which it deals. J.R.P.

ORLINSKY, H. M.: *Understanding the Bible through History and Archaeology*. 1972. Pp. ix, 292. (Ktav Publishing House, New York. Price: $7.95)

The basic text of this book is that of Orlinsky's *Ancient Israel* (1954, see *B.L.* 1954, p. 23; 1955, p. 23; *Eleven Years*, pp. 560,656; 1960, see *B.L.* 1961, p. 22, *Decade* p. 260), with some few small modifications and updating of bibliographical material. But the difference in this presentation is that alongside the text of that survey of Israel's history there are printed the English and Hebrew texts of relevant passages. The reader is thus invited to consider the relationship between the account being given by a modern scholar and the texts which provide his most important primary source. In addition there is illustration by pictures and charts, and suggestions for further study. This is essentially designed as a work-book, and it has evident value. Its great risk — though this is one against which the reader is warned at the outset — is that it may be supposed that the accompanying texts are historical texts, whereas it is often clear that their significance lies in the interpretation they offer; and there are inevitably instances where, for example, the linking of a prophetic passage with a particular moment is open to question. But it does encourage the reader to consider the text and not to bypass references to it. P.R.A.

DE VAUX, R.: *Histoire Ancienne d'Israël: Des Origines à l'Installation en Canaan* (Études Bibliques). 1971. Pp. 674. (J. Gabalda, Paris. Price: Fr. 100)

It is sad to think that this book represents de Vaux's final contribution to the study of the earliest period of Israelite history from the origins of Israel to the settlement in Canaan. It is the first of a projected history of Israel in three volumes. Volume two would have carried the history as far as the end of the pre-exilic period — part of this will in due course be available — and volume three was to have dealt with the exilic and post-exilic periods up to the conquest of Syria-Palestine by Alexander the Great. Some of us are particularly grateful to Père de Vaux for having reinforced in volume one the field of study which he covered in a series of articles in *Revue Biblique* 53 (1946); 55 (1948); 62 (1965) and in articles published elsewhere. He sees himself as a mediator between Bright and Noth (p. 9), but this is not the impression which is gained from his earlier work on the patriarchal narratives. There he would seem to be nearer to Bright than to Noth, and, although this final, exhaustive consideration of the patriarchal narratives is marked by greater reserve, he is still a seeker after the historical patriarchs in a sense which does not apply to Noth.

W.McK.

YEIVIN, S.: *The Israelite Conquest of Canaan* (Uitgaven van het Nederlands Historisch-Archaeologisch Institut te Istanbul, XXVII). 1971. Pp. xvii, 301. 12 maps. (Nederlands Historisch-Archaeologisch Institut, Istanbul)

This is a very detailed exposition of evidence concerned with the period of conquest and settlement. The first part sets out the evidence, with an examination of biblical material, genealogical information, extra-biblical sources and archaeological evidence (pp. 1–68). The second part offers a synthesis, described as 'a working hypothesis' both on the entry and conquest and on the settlement (pp. 69–124). Appendices set out the tribal genealogies fully (pp. 126–233), and discuss other matters quite briefly. There is a wealth of information, and valuable reference to a very wide range of scholarly discussion. The tentative conclusion is of a conquest spread over about a century from the late fourteenth to late thirteenth century B.C. There are many points at which the author acknowledges the hypothetical nature of his reconstruction, but he endeavours to show its coherence. Questions inevitably arise in regard to the interpretation of the archaeological evidence, on so much of which there are markedly divergent views. The use of genealogical material without an adequate consideration of how far it may properly be employed in relation to history points to the need to consider the fuller investigation of this which has been undertaken by R. R. Wilson, *The Biblical Genealogies* (Diss. Yale, 1972). There is, however, much to stimulate discussion, and a full endeavour to deal with the complexity of the biblical material in this comprehensive work.

P.R.A.

TEXT AND VERSIONS

Biblia Hebraica Stuttgartensia. Editio Funditus Renovata. Ed. K. ELLIGER and W. RUDOLPH. Fasc. 4. *Josua et Judices*, praeparavit R. Meyer, 1972. Pp. x, 89. Fasc. 8. *Liber Jeremiae*, praeparavit W. Rudolph, 1970. Pp. x, 116. (Württembergische Bibelanstalt, Stuttgart. Price: DM. 5.80 each)

These two further fascicles of *BHS* follow the same pattern as those which have already appeared. These were noted in *B.L.* 1969, p. 16 where the principles of this edition were set out and discussed; *B.L.* 1970, p. 23; and *B.L.* 1972, p. 21.

R.J.C.

DIRKSEN, P. B.: *The Transmission of the Text in the Peshiṭta Manuscripts of the Book of Judges* (Monographs of the Peshiṭta Institute Leiden, I). 1972. Pp. 112. (E. J. Brill, Leiden. Price: Fl. 28)

This monograph is intended to accompany the critical edition of the Peshiṭta on Judges, which is to be published presently by the Peshiṭta Institute. Much of the material to which this study refers is therefore not yet available; nevertheless, Dirksen has written in such a way that his arguments can largely be followed, even if their full implications will not be appreciated until the edition itself is published.

Nearly sixty MSS containing the Syriac Judges are listed and described. The investigation of the MS. inter-relations is conducted with a painstaking thoroughness that must be admired. The MSS are discussed in the following order: Ancient (i.e. the six oldest MSS, dating from cent. vi-ix, plus a few of their descendants), Western, Eastern, Massoretic. Some portions of the discussion will prove more helpful than others. For example, detailed figures and lists are given of the places in which each of the 'ancient' MSS agrees with another against the rest, and so on for all attested permutations; but how clear an impression does all this enable us to form of the actual historical relationships? Most of his material, however, is far more illuminating. The terms 'Western' and 'Eastern' just used refer to provenance rather than text, because it is one of Dirksen's most striking conclusions that, in Judges, western and eastern textual traditions distinct from each other do not exist — against findings in studies of Pesh. to Psalms, Isaiah and Wisdom, that two such distinct text-types could be identified. He considers it more appropriate to make a division between the 'ancient' MSS and the rest, which attest two different types of text, such that the older reading is sometimes preserved in the former, sometimes in the latter type (despite its relatively late attestation). These views are largely reminiscent of those of B. Albrektson in his study of Lamentations (1963).

While this study teaches us a great deal about the later history of the text, virtually nothing is said of the earlier stages (before cent. vi). Whatever views the author had formed — even if they had been somewhat speculative — on the history of the text in this earlier period, would surely have been well worth reading. I should also have liked to see some of the patristic evidence, and also more reference to the Hebrew, which to me seems central to a discussion of the Pesh. MSS. It is accepted today that relationship between MSS is proved not by agreement in readings as such, but by agreement in unauthentic readings; the Hebrew text is a valuable criterion for deciding which out of a set of rival readings is the oldest; greater attention to that criterion might well have uncovered more about the historical relations within the tradition. These few criticisms, however, might be perhaps more justly directed against the policy of the Peshiṭta Institute than against Dirksen himself, who is to be congratulated on a meticulously formulated and exceedingly valuable study.

M.P.W.

FERNANDEZ MARCOS, N. and SAENZ-BADILLOS, A.: *Anotaciones criticas al texto griego del Genesis.* 1972. Pp. 127 (Textos y Estudios 'Cardenal Cisneros', Madrid-Barcelona)

This is a useful and worthwhile contribution to LXX textual studies. The booklet contains three chapters: ch. I provides collations of papyri and a selection of manuscripts not available to Brooke-McLean in their edition of 1906; the collations are given in full for Gen. 1–10, while for 11–50 only a selection of the more important variants are given. Ch. II studies the manuscript groupings, and ch. III the text of Genesis used by Theodoret.   S.P.B.

GORDIS, R.: *The Biblical Text in the Making. A Study of the Kethib-Qre.* Augmented edition with a *Prolegomenon* by R. Gordis. 1971. Pp. lvi, 219. (Ktav Publishing House, New York. Price: $14.95)

The first edition of this work, 1937, was a significant contribution to the study of *K.-Q.*, and its re-issue, together with a lengthy article by the same author, is very welcome. The emphasis in the main part is on the history of the *K.-Q.*, with its pre-Akiba existence, and is reinforced in the Prolegomenon by means of criticisms of divergent views and by drawing further support from the Scrolls — both Murabba'at and Qumran.   B.J.R.

JACQUES, X.: *Index des mots apparentés dans la Septante* (Subsidia Biblica, 1). 1972. Pp. xiv, 233 (Biblical Institute Press, Rome. Price: Lire 4,500, $7.50)

This will prove an invaluable tool for all who have a serious interest in the Septuagint (or, for that matter, the history of the Greek language in the Hellenistic period). The author, who has already provided a similar work for the Greek N.T., has in mind primarily those interested in studying the semantic fields of individual words or groups of words, but there are certainly many other uses to which this work can be put with great profit. A short but clear introduction sets out the principles and self-imposed limitations of the book. Words are listed in alphabetical order under their simplest form; thus, for example, the 40 words incorporating the element *dik-* are found listed under *dikē*. By a simple set of symbols the compiler indicates whether or not a word listed occurs in each of the four groups, Pentateuch, historical books, poetical / wisdom books, and prophets. The work has been compiled on the basis of Hatch-Redpath's *Concordance*, and so this means that words which only occur in the 'original' LXX of sections such as Kingdoms βγ and γδ are not included, since these feature only in the apparatus of the standard editions.

S.P.B.

(*Peshiṭta*): *The Old Testament in Syriac according to the Peshiṭta Version*, edited on behalf of the International Organization for the study of the Old Testament by the Peshiṭta Institute of the University of Leiden (ed. by P. A. H. de Boer and W. Baars). *General Preface.* 1972. Pp. xxiii, and part IV, fasc. vi (*Cantica sive Odae — Oratio Manasse — Psalmi Apocryphi — Psalmi Salomonis — Tobit — I (III) Ezrae.*) 1972. Pp. xvi, 35; vii, 9; x, 12; vi, 27; xiv, 55; xix, 53. (E. J. Brill, Leiden. Price: Fl. 96)

The sample edition of 1966 (see *B.L.* 1968, p. 18) has now been followed up by the first full section of the edition together with the general preface. The principles set out in the sample edition are here followed, the general preface providing a fuller and revised statement of these. The edition itself is divided up in its pagination into separate

sections for the various books covered in the volume. These have
been edited by various scholars: H. Schneider (Canticles or Odes);
W. Baars (Apocryphal Psalms — work undertaken to complete a
beginning made by M. Noth before his death in 1968; and Psalms of
Solomon); J. C. H. Lebram (Tobit); W. Baars and J. C. H. Lebram
(1 (3) Esdras). The range of detailed information provided in this
edition is indicated by the complexity of the preface in which the
presentation of the text and apparatus is explained; but it represents
an achievement of concision in making available so great a wealth of
readings and in assessing them. Of the books here edited, Tobit alone
appeared in the sample edition of 1966 and is here presented in a
significantly revised form. The care devoted to this work and the
skill of both the general editors and of the contributors make this
publication a very notable achievement.
                                                                    P.R.A.

Schreiner, J. (ed.): *Wort, Lied und Gottesspruch. Beiträge zur Septuaginta*
    (Forschung zur Bibel, 1). 1972. Pp. 215. (Echter Verlag, Würzburg)

This is the first half of a two-volume *Festschrift* dedicated to the great
Septuagint scholar J. Ziegler. As the sub-title implies it is almost
entirely devoted to (very varied) aspects of the LXX (15 out of 19
contributions, ranging from a fine one on P. Bodmer 24 and Origen
(D. Barthélemy) to the fate of Enoch in the LXX (A. Schmitt)).
Articles which will have a rather wider interest include ones on creation in the LXX (G. Bertram), Rabbinic statements on the origins of
the LXX (K. Müller), the list of officials in LXX 1 Kings 2:46h
(M. Rehm), flesh, spirit and soul in the LXX Pentateuch (J.
Scharbert), and the Philistines in the LXX (R. de Vaux). Those which
fall outside Septuagint studies concern the role of oracular priests
in the Semitic religions (M. Delcor), Israel in the Hellenistic period
(R. Hanhart), Tobit (L. Ruppert), and a N.T. textual subject.

                                                                    S.P.B.

Strack, H. L.: *The Hebrew Bible — Latter Prophets, The Babylonian
    Codex of Petrograd. Edited with Preface and Critical Annotations.
    Prolegomenon* by P. Wernberg-Møller. (*The Library of Biblical Studies.*
    Ed. by H. M. Orlinsky.) First published 1876. 1971. Pp. xv, xix-xxii,
    1–38, (1)–(8), 225. (Ktav Publishing House, New York, 1971)

Originally, and better-known under this title, *Prophetarum Posteriorum
Codex Babylonicus Petropolitanus* appeared as a publication of first
importance, but since that time its prestige has varied. Nevertheless,
it is indispensable for the history of the text, and its secrets are still
worth probing. The present edition, very well worth-while for the
actual text, is still more valuable because of the fascinating account
of the manuscript given in the *Prolegomenon*.
                                                                    B.J.R.

Tov, E.: *ṭeksṭim nibḥarim mi-tok ha-ʿibbudim šel targum ha-šibʿim* (Selected
    Texts from the Revisions of the Septuagint). 1970. Pp. 28. (Internal
    Publication for students of the Hebrew University, Jerusalem. Price:
    Isr. £5.00)

Photostatically reproduced pages from works by Barthélemy,
Ziegler, Gooding and others, most of them published during the
last twenty years.
                                                                    J.F.A.S.

Tov, E.: *ha-targumim ha-yavaniim veha-laṭiniim šel ha-miqra* (The Greek and Latin Translations of the Bible). 1971. Pp. 43. (Internal Publication for students of the Hebrew University, Jerusalem. Price: Isr. £4.00)

> Photostatic reproductions of pages from original manuscripts and modern editions, as well as from Lagarde, Swete, Kahle and others. Relevant source material from post-classical and rabbinic literature is also given, some of it, like the Letter of Aristeas, in a modern Hebrew translation.   J.F.A.S.

Weiss, M. R.: *mi-baʿyot ha-nosaḥ šel ha-miqra* (Some problems concerning the Text of the Bible). 1972. Pp. 58. (Internal Publication for students of the University of Tel Aviv, Jerusalem. Price: Isr. £5.00)

> Part I 'Parallel Texts' consists of five passages from II Sam. printed alongside the corresponding passages in I Chron. and Ps. 18. Part II contains photostatic reproductions of pages from two editions of the Samaritan Pentateuch in Hebrew script and comparisons with MT. Part III is devoted to the Qumran material and includes references to the work of Allegro, Skehan, Sanders, Cross and others, together with photostatic reproductions of six plates from *The Dead Sea Scrolls of St Mark's Monastery*.   J.F.A.S.

Ziegler, J.: *Sylloge. Gesammelte Aufsätze zur Septuaginta* (Mitteilungen des Septuaginta-Unternehmens, x). 1971. Pp. 678. (Vandenhoeck & Ruprecht, Göttingen. Price: DM. 86)

> In the course of his admirable work in editing seven volumes of the Göttingen Septuagint, Professor Ziegler has produced a considerable number of detailed studies on, in particular, the transmission of the LXX. These, with the exceptions of his longer works on Isaiah (1934) and Jeremiah (1958), are all (28 in number) most usefully reprinted in the present volume, which also fittingly contains one companion article (on Ezekiel) by P. Katz. Alongside the running pagination, that of the original articles is also given, and Dr. P. Hugger has further added to the value of the book by providing an index of Greek words.   S.P.B.

EXEGESIS AND MODERN TRANSLATIONS

Auvray, P.: Isaïe 1–39 (Sources Bibliques). 1972. Pp. 338. (J. Gabalda et Cie, Paris. Price: £8.40)

> The form of this commentary is of the usual pattern. It begins with an Introduction containing brief notes on the text (MT, IQIsa, LXX), composition of the book, some notes on the life and times of Isaiah, and some notes on the main themes in these chapters. Then follow translation, textual comments, and exegetical comments. The translation is deliberately literal rather than dynamic in order to convey to the reader some awareness of the Hebrew modes of speech. The commentary contains some extended notes on features of particular importance, e.g. on 7:14 where the translation has 'jeune fille' and the note suggests 'demoiselle d'honneur' as a better equivalent. One could have wished for some discussion of the historical difficulties in Isa. 36–37. This is a useful commentary, especially for theological students.   A.S.H.

*BALDWIN, J. G.: *Haggai Zechariah Malachi* (Tyndale Old Testament Commentaries). 1972. Pp. 253. (The Tyndale Press, London. Price: £1.20; paperback 95p)

Miss Baldwin has written a most useful Commentary, judiciously weighing the considerable critical work that has been done on these prophets in recent years. The conservative tendency in her judgment is always based on open discussion of the issues, and her knowledge of the literature is such that her book forms an invaluable pocket clearing-house for scholars. Inevitably it has a somewhat eclectic character. She takes on Lamarche's chiastic theory of the structure of Zech. 9–14, and one wonders what the readership of the series will make of this and much else of the scholarly apparatus. But her handling of the many difficulties in the way of the layman help to establish the author among the recognized interpreters of these prophets.

D.R.J.

*BRIGHT, L. (ed.): *Scripture Discussion Commentary* 4. Prophets II, Exekiel, Daniel, Minor Prophets, 1972. Pp. 284. (Sheed and Ward, London. Price: £1.15)

*BRIGHT, L. (ed.): *Scripture Discussion Commentary* 5. Histories II, Joshua, 1 and 2 Chronicles, Ezra and Nehemiah, 1 and 2 Maccabees. 1972. Pp. 215. (Sheed and Ward, London. Price: £1.30)

*BRIGHT, L. (ed.): *Scripture Discussion Commentary* 6. Psalms and Wisdom, Psalms, Job, Proverbs, Ecclesiastes, Sirach, Wisdom. 1972. Pp. 248. (Sheed and Ward, London. Price: £1.45)

These three volumes complete a series of O.T. commentaries written expressly to provoke intelligent and informed discussion, with special reference to life in the world and church of today. The authors are R.C., but their approach is not sectarian, and Sixth Formers in particular and adult study groups should find these volumes an aid to lively and profitable discussion.

L.A.P.

*CLEMENTS, R. E.: *Exodus* (The Cambridge Bible Commentary on the N.E.B.). 1972. Pp. viii, 248. (Cambridge University Press. Price: £2.20 (cloth), 96p (paper))

This valuable addition to the Cambridge Bible Commentary presents a careful and instructive commentary on the meaning of the text, with particular reference to the use of the four main sources and the historical and religious background of the book.

L.A.P.

*CUNLIFFE-JONES, H.: *Deuteronomy* (Torch Bible Paperbacks). Fifth Impression 1972. Pp. 192. (S.C.M. London. Price: 80p)

A paperback reprint of the earliest of the Torch Bible Commentaries, first published in 1951 (see *B.L.* 1952, p. 31; *Eleven Years*, p. 402).

E.B.M.

*DALE, A. T.: *Winding Quest; the Heart of the Old Testament in Plain English.* 1972. Pp. 432. (Oxford University Press. Price: £4 (cloth), £2 (paper))

This, like its N.T. predecessor 'New World', is a selection of material grouped around five central themes which, beginning with the institution of the Israelite monarchy, make sense for the reader by differentiating between story, history, poetry, etc. The author simplifies, paraphrases and occasionally, where explanation is deemed essential, enlarges on the text; most of the book is aimed at a reading age of twelve years but in the last two sections the vocabulary is widened without any obvious loss of intelligibility. Beautifully produced, with attractive art work, this book should go far towards achieving its declared aim of helping ' ... young people to read the Bible with pleasure and understanding'. The difficulty is of course the price; the hardbacked edition will be beyond the reach of the average school Religious Education department, and the paperback is unlikely to stand up to much hard usage.   E.B.M.

*DALE, A. T.: *The Bible in the Classroom.* 1972. Pp. 96. (Oxford University Press. Price: 75p)

A handbook to the author's 'New World' and 'Winding Quest', this is a much needed and refreshingly positive discussion of reasons for and methods of the use of biblical material in school.   E.B.M.

GIVATI, MEIR: *ha-sefer ha-ḥamiši; pirqe ʿiyyun beʾsefer deʾvarim* (Deuteronomy: The Fifth Book of the Pentateuch). 1970. Pp. 124. (Otsar Hamoreh, Publishing House of the Teachers' Union in Israel, Tel Aviv)

This is a brief investigation of some problems concerning the Book of Deuteronomy, chiefly its unity and relationship to other law-codes. The author concentrates on the final form of the Pentateuch and supports his argument with tabulations of parallels (pp. 22–46), 'frequent expressions which have a distinctive meaning in Deuteronomy' (pp. 97–100) and a selection of quotations from mediaeval Jewish commentaries (pp. 86–96). The last 22 pages contain some practical suggestions on how to teach Deuteronomy in schools and colleges and a very brief bibliography.   J.F.A.S.

HILLERS, D. R.: *Lamentations* (The Anchor Bible, 7A). 1972. Pp. 116. (Doubleday and Company, Garden City, New York. Price: $6)

This is a very useful addition to the Anchor Bible series. Critical questions are succinctly but judiciously discussed in the Introduction. The book is treated as an intelligible unity, though a wise agnosticism is expressed on questions of authorship and the precise theological *sitz im leben* of the poems. The translation is occasionally a somewhat uneasy coalition of the traditional and the colloquial (e.g. 1:5), but the commentary throughout is helpful both linguistically and theologically.   R.D.

KESSLER, W.: *Gottes Mitarbeiter am Wiederaufbau. Die Propheten Esra und Nehemia* (Die Botschaft des Alten Testaments, 12, IV). 1971. Pp. 140. (Calwer Verlag, Stuttgart. Price: DM. 14.50)

A considerable proportion of the volumes in this popular commentary series has now appeared. The volume contains a sound translation of the text, with a very small number of notes on the text itself, and a commentary which is primarily directed towards the theological significance of the text for the contemporary situation. The titles of the volumes are clearly chosen with this in mind, though no justification appears to be produced for describing Ezra and Nehemiah as prophets. There is awareness of the literary and historical problems of the period, though these tend to be less taken into account in the commentary than is desirable. The volume concludes with a note on the later estimates of the two, curiously ignoring the Nehemiah tradition in 2 Macc. 1 and taking no account of Josephus; and a short study of the books' message. A useful but not very exciting volume.

P.R.A.

Los Libros Sagrados. Traducción y comentario de los libros del AT. Directores Luis Alonso Schökel, Juan Mateos y José María Valverde; introducciones, notas y comentarios de Luis Alonso Schökel. (Ediciones Cristiandad, Madrid). II. *Historia*, 3. *José, Jueces*; *Samuel*; *Reyes*. 1973. Pp. 274, 272, 288. (Price: 150 pts each part)

For details of this series, see *B.L.* 1972, p. 28.

L.A.S.

MAILLOT, A. AND LELIÈVRE, A.: *Les Psaumes. Traduction, notes et commentaires.* Deuxième édition entièrement revue, et mise à jour. Psaumes 1 à 50. 1972. Pp. 323. (Editions Labor et Fides, Genève. Price: £2.90; 3.60)

The first edition of this commentary appeared in 1961, and was reviewed in *B.L.* 1967. p. 24. The second edition follows the same pattern as the first, but the translation and the textual notes in the *apparatus criticus* have been revised. Additions have also been made to the general commentary.

E.R.R.

Pismo Święte Starego Testamentu, II.1; *Księga Kapłańska* / wstęp — przekład z oryginału — komentarz — ekskursy (*The Holy Scripture of the Old Testament*, II, 1; *Leviticus* / Introduction — Translation from the Original — Commentary — Excursuses) under the direction of Professor S. Łach, Counsellor of the Papal Bible Commission. 1970. Pp. 344. (Pallottinum, Poznań, Warsaw)

This particular volume on Leviticus (*Księga Kapłańska*) belongs to a commentary series planned on a large scale and produced by Catholic biblical scholars under the direction of Professor S. Łach. An extensive bibliography is offered first, beginning with the Church Fathers and leading up to the current state of research. This includes monographs and the like as well as commentaries (pp. 5–19). The translation of the biblical text itself is preceded by a detailed historical and critical introduction with excellent discussions of particular problems (pp. 21–112). The translation which follows is provided with a commentary in which particular attention is devoted to ideas which are of theological importance (pp. 113–290). The volume concludes with special excursuses on atonement, sacrifice, sin etc. (pp. 291–331), together with indexes of names and subjects, as well as a list of Hebrew terms which are the subject of detailed discussion (pp. 332–41). The reviewer is aware that the volumes on Numbers *Księga Liczb*) and Deuteronomy (*Księga Powtórzonego Prawa*) have appeared but these have not been available to him. The whole series is in active preparation. If the remaining volumes are of the same quality as this on Leviticus, there will be good reason to congratulate the editor, for this will be a work which has no parallel up to the present either in Poland or in the whole Slavonic language area.   M.B.

VON RAD, G.: *Das erste Buch Mose. Genesis* (Das Alte Testament Deutsch, Neues Göttinger Bibelwerk). 1972. Pp. 362. (Vandenhoeck & Ruprecht, Göttingen. Price: DM. 19.80; subscr. DM. 16.80)

German editions of this now standard and stimulating commentary have been noted in *B.L.* 1950, p. 40; 1952, p. 36; 1954, p. 41 (*Eleven Years*, pp. 257, 407, 578), the English translation of 1961 in *B.L.* 1962, p. 31 (*Decade*, p. 341) and the French translation in *B.L.* 1969, p. 25. This ninth German edition, bibliographically updated and revised in points of detail by the author, is published posthumously. It will long remain an indispensible tool for both scholar and preacher.   R.D.

VON RAD, G.: *Genesis: A Commentary* (The Old Testament Library). 3rd edition, 1972. Pp. 440. (S.C.M. Press, London. Price: £4)

This third edition of von Rad's commentary on Genesis is based on the ninth German edition, the last work which von Rad compleed before his death. In the German edition von Rad extensively revised the introduction and the commentary on the early chapters of Genesis, but in general made only minor amendments to the commentary on the later chapters. The translation in this new English edition follows von Rad's revision in the case of the introduction and the commentary on chapters 1–11, and the text for these sections has been completely reset. Thereafter, however, in order to cut costs, only the kind of alterations possible in a photographic reproduction have been incorporated into the text. (For *B.L.* references, see preceding note).   M.A.K.

*ROBINSON, J.: *The First Book of Kings* (The Cambridge Bible Commentary on the N.E.B.). 1972. Pp. xi, 259. (Cambridge University Press. Price: £3.60 (cloth), £1.50 (paper))

*WHYBRAY, R. N.: *The Book of Proverbs* (The Cambridge Bible Commentary on the N.E.B.). 1972. Pp. x, 197. (Cambridge University Press. Price: £2.20, $6.95 (cloth), £1.00 (paper))

These two additions to a valuable series fully maintain the high standard set by the introductory volumes, reviewed in *B.L.* 1972, p. 23. The introductions and commentary are brief and to the point, lucid and illuminating, and based on sound but unobtrusive scholarship.   L.A.P.

RUDOLPH, W.: *Joel. Amos. Obadja. Jona* (Kommentar zum Alten Testament, XIII.2). 1971. Pp. 384. (Gütersloher Verlagshaus Gerd Mohn, Gütersloh. Price: DM. 98)

That W. Rudolph's skill and perceptiveness as a commentator is in no way diminished is well evidenced in this further volume from his pen on four of the Minor Prophets. The most important part of it is his interpretation of Amos, and here, as with his previous study of Hosea (*B.L.* 1967, p. 25), his divergences from the views of H. W. Wolff are marked. Rudolph regards far fewer passages as inauthentic than does Wolff, and he defends the substantial authenticity of the Tyre, Edom and Judah oracles in 1:9–12 and 2:4f., as well as the promises of 9:11–15. The doxologies he regards as used by Amos but not composed by him, so that very little of the book is regarded as not stemming directly from the prophet himself. Rudolph admits that there has been some redactional work, but does not regard this as sufficient to allow us to speak either of an Amos school, or of a substantial Deuteronomistic redaction (*pace* Wolff). On the question of Amos' background Rudolph rejects the idea that he ever functioned as a cultic prophet, or that his language is particularly cultic. On the other hand, whilst welcoming the changed emphasis in the attempt to see a strong influence upon the prophet from the old 'clan wisdom', Rudolph suggests that this too has been overdone. Of the other prophets Joel is regarded as a late pre-exilic composition, whilst the interpretations of Obadiah and Jonah follow more familiar critical lines. Undoubtedly this volume is a very lasting contribution to O.T. studies.

R.E.C.

SABOTTKA, L.: *Zephanja, Versuch einer Neuübersetzung mit philologischem Kommentar* (Biblia et Orientalia, 25). 1972. Pp. xx, 177. (Biblical Institute Press, Rome. Price: Lire 3,900, $6.50)

This work, which was prepared under the guidance of Fr M. J. Dahood, contains a translation of Zephaniah, a transliteration of the emended Hebrew text on which it is based, and philological and textual notes (and notes on some other subjects that interest the author). There are also a bibliography, and indexes of authors' names, subjects, Semitic words, and references to the Bible and other ancient Near Eastern writings. In his treatment of the Hebrew text, Sabottka makes extensive use of Dahood's theories, which he appears usually to accept wholeheartedly. Although he often refers (somewhat unsystematically) to the principal ancient versions, he neither gives a general description of their characteristics in Zephaniah nor even states which editions he has used.

J.A.E.

VAN SELMS, A.: *Jeremia*. Deel I. (de Predeking van het Oude Testament, ed. A. van Selms and A. S. van der Woude). 1972. Pp. 301. (G.F. Callenbach, Nijkerk. Price: Fl. 35)

Three volumes in this commentary series, including the two on Genesis also by van Selms, were noted in *B.L.* 1968, p. 27. The present volume contains the first half of the Jeremiah commentary, reaching the end of ch. 25. Like its predecessors, it is particularly directed towards the exposition of the O.T. in preaching; but this is grounded in a careful examination of the text and its interpretation in detail, each section being divided into detailed discussion, followed by a literary analysis and by the preaching exposition. In addition there are eight excursuses, providing more detailed comment on various points.

It is the first of these excursuses which presents a theory concerning the MT and LXX forms of Jeremiah; it is postulated that Baruch, having written the second scroll (ch. 36) with its supplements, continued to add further material. In Egypt, before or after the death of his master, he prepared a 'fair copy' for the Babylonian Jewish community in which hope was held to lie; this was to be the basis of the MT. The rough copy remained in Egypt to provide the basis for the LXX. Subsequent modifications in both and some degree of assimilation may be observed. This theory is tested out in the individual sections of the commentary. It is an interesting if purely hypothetical way of arguing out the problem. Another excursus suggests that the Scythians were the 'enemy from the north', employed as mercenaries by the declining Assyrian power. Others deal with such matters as the literary presentation of the argument.

There is adequate reference to the literature; there is careful discussion of problem passages. The volume is dedicated to the Society for Old Testament Study. A useful contribution to the Jeremiah literature.

P.R.A.

SOGGIN, J. A.: *Joshua*. Translated by R. A. Wilson. 1972. Pp. xvii, 245. (S.C.M. Press, London. Price: £3.25)

The original French edition of this commentary was warmly welcomed in *B.L.* 1971, p. 32: the translator and publisher are to be congratulated on the speedy appearance of the English version. Opportunity has been taken to correct a number of slips and errors, although some still remain. Additions have also been made to the bibliographies and footnotes, but there is perhaps still inadequate notice of works in English, e.g. J. Gray's volume in the New Century Bible is not listed among the standard commentaries on pp. xv-xvi. The RSV text is reproduced, emended where necessary in the light of Soggin's own translation. In general, the English translation is clear, accurate and readable, but the exact nuances of the French are sometimes missed, e.g. on p. 81, 'fermante et renfermée' is not 'closing and reclosed' but 'closing (the way to those seeking to enter) and closed (to those wishing to go out).'

J.R.P.

*TAYLOR, K.: *The Living Bible Paraphrased. The Bible in everyday language for everyone*. 1971. Pp. 1436. (Hodder and Stoughton, London. Price: £1.00)

This is a single volume edition of paraphrases of biblical books which have been published in seven sections from 1962 to 1970 by Tyndale House Publishers. It is published with the name of one particular paraphraser, but it is made clear that the work underwent considerable revision with the advice of experts in Greek and Hebrew. One may welcome the deliberate use of the word 'paraphrase', since this makes it clear that there is recognized to be an element beyond what is more strictly defined as translation. Every translation, unless it is a mere crib, involves choice between alternatives, even if some of the alternatives appear (as they do here) in footnotes. The result is a fairly colloquial and attractively set out text, readable and convenient. It does not attempt to compete with recent new translations, but it offers many insights and suggestions.

P.R.A.

Today's English Version (Old Testament)

Sing a New Song 1972. Pp. 218 (Collins, Fontana paperback. Price: 20p)

The Psalms for Modern Man. 1970. Pp. 218 (American Bible Society. Price: 20c)

'Tried and True'. Job for Modern Man. 1971. Pp. 89 (American Bible Society)

> The appearance of the first sections of the O.T. in this version, already known from the N.T. Good News for Modern Man, is of considerable interest. It is a new translation, not a revision; it attempts to put the text into simple and vigorous English. It is colloquial often without being cheap. It is often paraphrase rather than close translation; but then this is one of the functions of translation, if it is to convey a clear meaning to the reader. It invites reading and enjoyment.

P.R.A.

VERKUYL, G., et al.: *The Modern Language Bible. The New Berkeley Version in Modern English*. Revised edition, 1969 (4th printing 1971). Pp. viii, 944 (O.T.), 291 (N.T.). (Zondervan Publishing House, Grand Rapids, Michigan. Price: $8.95)

> This is a revision by a team of Conservative Evangelical scholars of the translation of the Bible made by the late G. Verkuyl, of which the N.T. first appeared in 1945, and the O.T. in 1959. The translation is in modern English, although some archaisms, such as 'ye' in Isa. 40:1, have been preserved. The attitude towards the text and meaning is very conservative, e.g. *'almāh* in Isa. 7:14 is translated 'virgin'. Although a full commentary is not provided, there are numerous notes which comment on the text, and some of which have a homiletical character. For example, it is said of Ps. 13:1, 'David had lost his fellowship with God: time seemed so long!'; the note on Isa. 6:13 explains how turpentine is obtained from the terebinth; the second, third, and fourth kingdoms in Dan. 2 are identified with the Persian, Macedonian, and Roman empires; Zech. 11:5 is said to contain 'Greed, cruelty, and hypocrisy in one brief sentence'. The translators have recorded before many chapters the dates that they believe to be appropriate. The copy reviewed is a paperback.

J.A.E.

VUILLEUMIER, R. and KELLER, C.-A.: *Michée, Nahoum, Habacuc, Sophonie* (Commentaire de l'Ancien Testament, XIb.). 1971. Pp. 222. (Delachaux et Niestlé, Neuchâtel. Price: S.Fr. 42 (cloth), S.Fr. 36 (paper))

> This beautifully printed commentary offers the text in French transla-tion, a concise critical exegesis and ample footnotes of textual evidence and useful bibliography. Hebrew and Greek types are used and techni-cal details are given with reasonable fullness. The Rabbinic com-mentators have been consulted. Micah is treated by Vuilleumier, the rest by Keller. The most distinctive position adopted is to date Nahum just after the fall of Thebes in 663. Almost all the prophecies are accepted as pre-exilic and the contribution of the festal tradition is recognized. This commentary will be regarded as standard reading on these difficult but rewarding prophets. (It can be affirmed that 'H. J. Eaton' and 'J. H. Eaton', whose opinions fortunately do not greatly diverge, are but manifestations of the present writer.)

J.H.E.

WIJNGAARDS, J.: *Deuteronomium* (De Boeken van het Oude Testament, Deel II/Boek III). 1971. Pp. 360. (J. J. Romen & Zonen, Roermond.

This commentary on Deuteronomy is prefaced with a comprehensive introduction discussing the origin and composition of the book, its relationship with the Deuteronomic history and with the Tetrateuch and the points of contact between it and other Old Testament books. The central body of Deuteronomy (5:1–28:68; 31:9–13; 32:1–43) is traced to a festival of covenant renewal involving a procession from Succoth to Shechem in the premonarchical period. The commentary itself is accompanied by a translation of the book. Each major division in Deuteronomy is discussed and then each individual passage is carefully analysed and explained. Though the author's views on the origin of the book will not appeal to everyone, this will prove a valuable addition to the already existing commentaries on Deuteronomy.   E.W.N.

WILDBERGER, H.: *Jesaja* (Biblischer Kommentar, Altes Testament, x, 6). 1972. Pp. i-viii, 401–95. (Neukirchener Verlag, Neukirchen-Vluyn. Price: DM. 65; subscr. DM. 58.50, for whole volume)

This fascicle (see *B.L.* 1971, p. 35, for the previous one) continues the commentary to the end of chapter 12, and contains the prefatory pages, the indexes of biblical references, names and subjects, and Hebrew words, and also a list of corrections for the first volume, which is now complete. Among much that is interesting, special attention may be drawn to the discussion of the description of the invader's march in 10:27–32, and the defence of the Isaianic authorship of 11:1–9.   J.A.E.

LITERARY CRITICISM AND INTRODUCTION

(including History of Interpretation, Canon, and Special Studies)

*ACKROYD, P. R.: *Exile and Restoration.* 1972. Pp. xv, 286. (S.C.M. Press, London. Price: £2)

This 'Study Edition' of the work first published in 1968 is unchanged save for a small number of verbal modifications in the text and some updating of the bibliographical references in the footnotes. For the original edition, see *B.L.* 1969, p. 28.   R.J.C.

ACKROYD, P. R.: *Israeli Logon Ka Hihas* (*Purana Niyam Kal*) (*The People of the Old Testament.* Hindi Transl. by C. W. David). Pp. xvi, 206. (Hindi Theological Literature Committee, Dehra Dun, U.P. Price: Rs. 6.00)

The translation is intended for the use of Indian theological students, based upon a revised text of the book, published in 1959 (*B.L.* 1959, p. 8; *Decade*, p. 144)

AHLSTRÖM, G. W.: *Joel and the Temple Cult of Jerusalem* (Supplements to *Vetus Testamentum*, XXI). 1971. Pp. xii, 151. (Brill, Leiden. Price: Fl. 60; sub. Fl. 52)

The main problems of the Book of Joel are covered in seven chapters. The book is considered a unity, reproducing the words of a cult-prophet around 500 B.C.; it is hardly a 'liturgy' but uses liturgical forms; prompted by a plague of locusts, Joel may have addressed the assembly at a festival, speaking before a day of penance (1.2–2.17) and after it (2.19–4.21). This useful examination of Joel should be read also for its treatment of wider issues, such as 'Aramaisms', the Day of the Lord, syncretism in the Second Temple and prophecy in the cult.

J.H.E.

ANDERSON, G. W.: *A Critical Introduction to the Old Testament* (Studies in Theology, 52). 1959; Seventh Impression, 1972. Pp. viii, 262. (Duckworth, London. Price: £1.25)

This Seventh Impression of Professor Anderson's well-known and valuable *Introduction* is a further paperback reprint of the original 1959 edition. The text remains unchanged, but the Bibliography has now been completely revised (see *B.L.* 1960, p. 24; *Decade*, p. 204; *B.L.* 1971, p. 36).

M.A.K.

ASHBY, G. W.: *Theodoret of Cyrrhus as Exegete of the Old Testament.* 1971. Pp. v, 173. (Publications Department, Rhodes University, Grahamstown. Price: R. 6.00)

The exegetical work and method of Theodoret (393 – c.466) is here surveyed as the most substantial extant example of Antiochene O.T. exegesis. Cyril of Alexandria is used as foil, Theodore of Mopsuestia (where possible) for comparison. It is a pity that the comparison did not include Ephrem, who exemplifies the same method in Syriac, and could help to show that Theodoret's tradition has not yet grown so far apart from the targumic and midrashic origins of Syrian exegesis; this is the cradle of the typological method which the author expounds well but somewhat drily.

R.M.

BARTHES, R., BOVON, F., LEENHARDT, F. J., MARTIN-ACHARD, R., STAROBINSKI, J.: *Analyse Structurale et Exégèse Biblique. Essais d'Interprétation* (Bibliothèque Théologique). 1971. Pp. 121. (Delachaux and Niestlé, Neuchâtel. Price: S.Fr. 22)

This book is the result of inter-disciplinary discussions arranged by the Protestant Faculty of the University of Geneva. Its intention is to stimulate discussion about the possibility of the use of structural analysis as an aid to biblical exegesis, and it consists of an introductory chapter and four essays, two on Gen. 32:23–33 and two on Mark 5:1–20. In the two O.T. essays the story of Jacob's wrestling with the 'angel' is first analysed by R. Barthes from the point of view of structural analysis and then, quite separately, subjected to a detailed study along the familiar lines of biblical exegesis by R. Martin-Achard. No conclusions are drawn: it is left to the reader to compare

the two methods and form his own judgement. This form of presentation is an interesting one which would have been more effective if the
literary analysts had tried to avoid the mass of technical jargon which
makes their contributions difficult to follow for the non-specialists,
for whom the book is intended.   R.N.W.

BEAUCHAMP, P.: *Création et séparation: étude exégétique du chapitre premier
de la Genèse.* 1969. Pp. 423. (Bibliothèque des sciences religieuses, Paris.
Aubier Montaigne; Éditions du Cerf; Delachaux & Niestlé; Desclée
De Brouwer. Price: Fr. 44.75)

Perhaps fitly to be described as the first major product of French
structuralism to appear on the O.T. scene, this work is a fresh and
highly original approach to the creation story. A very detailed exegesis
is offered, enlivened after the structuralist manner with occasional
diagrams. As the title implies, the aspect of separation is made central
to the story, and surely rightly. This leads on to considerable discussion of the verbal expressions involved (ch. 3), to the general priestly
mode of thought, as seen in documents like Chronicles (ch. 4),
to other related cosmological texts (ch. 5), and to a final discussion
of the literary genre and function of the Heptameron (ch. 6). The
several papers given at the Uppsala congress testify to the interest
likely to attach to this approach in coming years.   J.B.

BEYSE, K.-M.: *Serubbabel und die Königserwartungen der Propheten Haggai
und Sacharja. Eine historische und traditionsgeschichtliche Untersuchung*
(Aufsätze und Vorträge zur Theologie und Religionswissenschaft, 52).
1971. Pp. 108. (Evangelische Verlagsanstalt, Berlin. Price: DM. 13.50)

This short, carefully argued study examines the problems of the
restoration period with a particular concern for the royal expectations
associated with the figure of Zerubbabel. It therefore includes a
consideration of the evidence of Ezra 1–6 alongside that of the
prophetic books, and attempts an assessment of the person of
Zerubbabel. The supposition that Zerubbabel died between the
completion of the temple and its dedication appears somewhat
farfetched. Of greater significance is the precise delineation of the
character of those sections of the two prophetic books relevant to the
theme, in which a careful distinction is made between the differing
emphases of the two prophets. This is a study which sheds further
light on a difficult period.   P.R.A.

BLENKINSOPP, J.: *Gibeon and Israel. The Role of Gibeon and the Gibeonites
in the Political and Religious History of Early Israel* (S.O.T.S. Monograph
Series, 2). 1972. Pp. xi, 152. (Cambridge University Press. Price:
£3.60, $11.50)

Considerable attention has recently been paid to Gibeon from the
archaeological side, since the important excavations there of J. B.
Pritchard. But there has been no traditio-historical study of Gibeon
and its associated cities and population since Bruno's work of 1923.
This monograph is therefore to be welcomed and will take its place
alongside other similar investigations of sanctuaries, which have
proved so fruitful for the reconstruction of Israel's early history and
cult. Perhaps its most valuable contribution is the demonstration of

the close connection of the Gibeonites with, on the one hand, the Hurrians and, on the other, various groups within Israel: its most original suggestion is that the home of the ark, after its return from Philistia, was at Gibeon rather than at Kiriath-jearim and that Saul attempted to make Gibeon his capital. As the author himself recognizes, many of his hypotheses are inevitably highly speculative and not all are equally persuasive. Occasionally, the mass of detail makes it difficult to see what precisely is being said — e.g. in chapter 3, it is not clear whether the treaty of Josh. 9 is to be dated in the early part of the Amarna age or after its close. The bibliographical information is of great value but it is a pity that, in a book which the dust-jacket claims 'is likely to become a standard work of reference,' the General Index should be so incomplete, especially with regard to the authorities cited.

J.R.P.

CAZELLES, H.: *Écriture, Parole et Esprit: ou trois aspects de l'herméneutique biblique.* 1970. Pp. 176. (Desclée, Paris. Price: Fr. 19)

Fittingly dedicated to the memory of a theologian, an orientalist and a philosopher, this attractive little book covers wide fields of interest. A first part surveys the modern development of hermeneutics, giving special note to Heidegger, to the German theological and philosophical tradition, and to the Anglo-Saxon and French contributions. A second part is devoted to 'Hermeneutics and Life in the Spirit'; putting it in another way, it is about the comprehension of the Bible within the universe of today. The third part treats the various kinds of 'criticism' — textual, literary, historical and theological — involved in exegesis. Everywhere there is evidence of wide knowledge and good taste, and of an ability, rare among biblical specialists, to relate scholarship to the general currents of modern thought, including sociology, linguistics and structuralism. The place of the O.T. is constantly kept in mind.

J.B.

DEMARAY, D. E.: *Bible Study Source-Book.* 1972. Pp. xviii, 380. (Zondervan Publishing House, Grand Rapids, Michigan. Price: (paper) $3.95)

This is a second printing of a book which was first published in 1964 as 'Cowman Handbook of the Bible'. It is a vade-mecum covering both the Old and New Testaments written from a strongly conservative viewpoint for the general reader. It deals with the canon, biblical manuscripts and English translations as well as giving a brief summary of each book of the Bible and a compendium of such background information as the author considers most useful to his readers. No attempt has been made to bring the book up to date for this second printing. In the section dealing with English translations there is no reference to the Jerusalem Bible or to the O.T. of the N.E.B. Some of the archaeological material is dated, and the description given of the current political situation in Jerusalem is that which existed before the six day war of 1967.

J.R.

DIEPOLD, P.: *Israels Land* (Beiträge zur Wissenschaft vom Alten und Neuen Testament, 95). 1972. Pp. 236. (W. Kohlhammer, Stuttgart. Price: DM. 37)

Diepold's thesis is essentially an enquiry into the fundamental character and development of the Deuteronomic theology as it can be traced through the book of Deuteronomy, the Deuteronomic History and the Deuteronomic passages in the book of Jeremiah. The particular subject dealt with is the theological interpretation of Israel's land as Yahweh's gift and its loss through the removal of Judah into exile in Babylon on account of the people's disobedience to the law of the covenant. The whole enquiry pivots around the question of the extent to which the Deuteronomic movement maintained a hope of the people's return from exile, and especially the extent to which this is evident in the Deuteronomic History. Diepold sees a development in which the original Deuteronomy threatened the loss of the land as a punishment if Israel should prove disobedient and the Deuteronomic Historian(s) interpreted Judah's downfall as a confirmation of this. The prophet Jeremiah however had preached the hope of a return and this was subsequently taken up and developed by the Deuteronomic editors of his prophecies. Finally a redactor revised the Deuteronomic History to incorporate this element of hope. Altogether the thesis is very interesting and competently done. R.E.C.

DIETRICH, W.: *Prophetie und Geschichte: Eine redaktionsgeschichtliche Untersuchung zum deuteronomistischen Geschichtswerk* (Forschungen zur Religion und Literatur des Alten und Neuen Testaments, Heft 108). 1972. Pp. 158. (Vandenhoeck & Ruprecht, Göttingen. Price: DM. 36 (cloth), DM. 32 (paper))

On the basis of a detailed analysis of a number of passages, taken mainly from the books of Kings, the author argues that there were three main stages in the composition of the Deuteronomic history. The first stage was the work of a historian (DtrG) who, it is maintained, composed his history shortly after 586 B.C. The second stage was the work of a redactor (DtrP) to whom the marked interest in prophecy which now permeates the literature in question is to be assigned. The third and final stage was carried out by an author designated by Dietrich as a 'nomistic' redactor (DtrN) who worked shortly after the rehabilitation of Jehoiachin, that is, about 560 B.C. This is a stimulating study, though one is left with the feeling that the analysis of the texts discussed is rather too refined to be credible.

E.W.N.

ELLUL, J.: *The Judgment of Jonah.* 1971. Pp. 103. (William B. Eerdmans, Michigan. Price: $1.95)

This is a translation by G. W. Bromiley of the author's *Le Livre de Jonas* (Cahiers Bibliques de Foi et Vie, Paris, n.d.). The original has not been reviewed in *B.L.* The author observes the reference to 'the prophet Jonah' in the teaching of Jesus and recognizes the book as prophetic in the biblical sense. It portrays man in his relations with God and God in his dealings with man; as such it points forward to Christ. The historical and other improbabilities in the narrative are irrelevant to its message. The water and the fish are symbols of destruction. The psalm is integral to the book as an appeal to God from perdition and death. The 'sign' of Jonah is genuinely that of death and resurrection. The R.S.V. text is quoted before each section and followed by running commentary, mainly theological. The author is Professor of the History and Sociology of Institutions of the University of Bordeaux. A.S.H.

DE LA FUENTE, O. G.: *La Busqueda de Dios en el Antiguo Testamento*. 1971. Pp. 591. (Publicaciones de la Fundacion Juan March, Guadarrama)

This erudite work quotes in the first lines of the introduction a sentence of the Jerusalem Bible that explains its purpose: 'In the O.T. this "seeking Yahweh" is an imperative necessity of man's religious life; in the New Testament the equivalent is "to seek the Kingdom" Mt. 6:33.' (*Jerusalem Bible*, E.V., p. 1483, on Amos 5:4, note d.) The first part is concerned with consulting God, and the phrase is traced through the Ancient East in Egypt, Assyria, Babylonia, Hittite religion, and Canaan, from which follow chapters on consultation of Yahweh by means of the priesthood, the technique of such consultation and seeking God by means of the prophets. The second part, on seeking God, contains chapters on impetrative prayer, the place of the psalms, and true and false consultation as illustrated in the prophetic books. One chapter is devoted entirely to consulting God as it is found in Chronicles. The author has evidently taken immense pains to illustrate his thesis, and more than twenty pages are devoted to a bibliography and a list of commentaries.

J.M.T.B.

FUSS, W.: *Die deuteronomistische Pentateuchredaktion in Exodus 3-17* (Beihefte zur Zeitschrift für die alttestamentliche Wissenschaft, 126). 1972. Pp. xii, 406. (Walter de Gruyter, Berlin. Price: DM. 98)

This study of Exod. 3-17 attempts a fresh literary-critical analysis of the earlier source material of the chapters which have usually been apportioned by scholars between J and E. Fuss argues that the J narrative from Judah and the E narrative from the Northern Kingdom were combined by a redactor of the Deuteronomic school into a kind of 'harmony'. The work of this redactor, usually dubbed R^{JE}, is claimed to have been much more extensive and editorially more constructive than has previously been accepted. Fuss proceeds by way of detailed comparisons of vocabulary usage and literary style, basic concepts and general theological intention, familiar enough to literary-critical analysts. The basic idea of a more thoroughgoing redaction criticism is constructive enough, but the avid pursuit of analyses make it hard to trace the overall consequences of such an approach. Little is said about the overall goal of such a redaction, and no adequate consideration is given to the possibility that we are faced here with a series of redactions.

R.E.C.

GLASSER, E.: *Le Procès du Bonheur par Qohelet* (Lectio Divina, 61). 1970. Pp. 218. (Les Éditions du Cerf, Paris. Price: Fr. 24)

This volume offers a new translation of Ecclesiastes with a commentary, and is primarily addressed, like others in the series, to non-specialists. The author finds a certain progression of ideas in the arrangement of the main sections of the book, but less in the more detailed arrangement. He sees Qohelet as handicapped by the limitations of the Hebrew language in his attempt to formulate a philosophy of human life; this accounts to some extent for the occasional apparent contradictions of thought. Qohelet was a realist but not a pessimist: in spite of the precarious character of human life and the lack of any apparent interest on the part of God in rewarding men as they deserve, he taught that the fear of God was still worthwhile and that life could and should be lived to the full. While it cannot be said that the author offers any radical new solution to the problems of Ecclesiastes, he has written a readable and witty study which ought not to be ignored.   R.N.W.

GRAY, G. B.: *The Forms of Hebrew Poetry considered with special reference to the criticism and interpretation of the Old Testament. Prolegomenon* by D. N. Freedman. 1972 (1915). Pp. lx, 303. (Ktav Publishing House, New York. Price: $14.95)

It is not surprising that G. B. Gray's book on the Forms of Hebrew Poetry has again appeared in a verbatim reprint. It was first published in 1915 after a season of intensive metrical studies which began with Ed. Sievers' publications. The author does not deal so much with historical details of the metrical studies, but rather with the elements which create biblical Hebrew poetry. The book is divided into eight chapters. He restates the early fundamental discovery of parallelism by Bishop Lowth (1752) and then reviews the problems of rhythm, metre, and structure (forms of versification). In an important chapter (VI) he surveys critically the views of Sievers and Duhm in their bearing on text criticism and interpretation. In the last two chapters (VII and VIII) he discusses some alphabetic poems. The author emphasizes that his studies deal mainly with the formal elements, for he realises that the study of them is relevant to the study of the O.T.; he is aware that Hebrew metre 'is a subject which still presents many obscurities and uncertainties' (p. 240). His cautioning is still valid today. Nearly sixty years have passed since and we are grateful to the editor for his *Prolegomenon* (50 pp.) in which he gives not only an introduction to the book, but also a survey of the study of Hebrew poetry since that date to which he adds a very useful bibliography. (The translation of Lowth's *De Sacra Poesi Hebraeorum* into English by G. Gregory appeared in London already in 1787, in the year of Lowth's death, not in 1835 as indicated on p. liv.)   H.K.

GRISPINO, J. A.: *The Bible Now!* 1971. Pp. ix, 138. (Fides Inc., Indiana. Price: $1.25)

Ten short articles, seven reprinted from *Current Scripture Notes*, on topics relating to biblical scholarship and Catholic teaching. Written in a clear, straightforward and non-technical style, these might serve as a useful summary or introduction.   E.B.M.

HAAG, E.: *Der Mensch am Anfang. Die alttestamentliche Paradiesvorstellung nach Gn 2–3* (Trierer Theologische Studien, Band 24). 1970. Pp. vii, 209. (Paulinus-Verlag, Trier. Price: DM. 38)

This is a careful and detailed study of Gen. 2–3; Ezek. 28 and of the traditions which lie behind them. The author is particularly concerned to make the point that despite affinities with mythological themes which originated outside Israel, the theological content of these chapters is firmly based upon Israelite beliefs which are characteristic of the O.T. as a whole. The attempt to find points of comparison with O.T. material at every point is sometimes rather forced; but on the whole this is a worthwhile exercise. There is a useful bibliography.
                                                                                                        R.N.W.

*HAYES, J. H.: *Introduction to the Bible*. 1970. Pp. xvi, 515. (Westminster Press, Philadelphia. Price: $9.95)

This work is introduction in the popular, rather than *Einleitung* in the technical sense. After a brief section on the background to biblical study, including a consideration of the principles of biblical criticism, the main parts of the book give an introduction to the Old and New Testaments by means of a chronological outline which provides the structure within which the literature and its problems are discussed at appropriate points. There are many books of this kind, but this is one of the best of them, with a very fair and balanced presentation, clear style, and attractive illustrations. The least satisfactory part is the very sketchy presentation of the later O.T. period.   R.J.C.

(An English edition appeared in May 1973, published by S.P.C.K., London. Price: £2.95)

HENDRICKS, H. G.: *Elijah: Confrontation, Conflict and Crisis*. Pp. 64. 1972. (Moody Press, Chicago. Price: $1)

This is a booklet of five good hot-gospel sermons fairly based on incidents in Elijah's life-story. It should be religiously helpful.

D.R.Ap-T.

JAGERSMA, H.: *Leviticus 19. Identiteit — Bevrijding — Gemeenschap* (Studia Semitica Neerlandica, 14). 1972. Pp. 165. (Assen: Van Gorcum & Comp. N.V. Price: Fl. 25)

This monograph in Dutch, with an eleven-page summary in English, consists of a detailed discussion of Lev. 19, which the author sees as a distinct unit within the 'Holiness Law'. After a brief survey of research into the 'Holiness Law' since 1877 and a new translation of this particular chapter, the main part of the book is made up of a form-critical analysis and a valuable exegesis of the material under discussion. From this, the writer concludes that the chapter is made up of three originally separate sections, each of which in turn was built up from other smaller independent collections, and which are linked with a wide range of other biblical traditions and material, so that it can even be asked whether Lev. 19 is not to be considered as a summary of the main ideas of the whole of the O.T. These sections were put together towards the end of the exilic period in circles where the hope of a speedy return was very strong, and together they form a kind of programme for the restored community, based on the three theological terms of the author's subtitle — the people's identity constituted by the command to be holy, the remembrance of the deliverance from Egypt, and the notion of the community. Even if many questions remain unanswered and the discussion seems sometimes over-subtle, this study is an important contribution to the increasingly common approach to Lev. as a work that can best be understood in the wide setting of the whole life of the post-exilic community.

J.R.P.

KLOPFENSTEIN, M. A.: *Scham und Schande nach dem Alten Testament: eine begriffsgeschichtliche Untersuchung zu den hebräischen Wurzeln bôš, klm und hpr* (Abhandlungen zur Theologie des Alten und Neuen Testaments, 62). 1972. Pp. 217. (Theologischer Verlag, Zurich. Price: DM. 27.00)

The title is self-explanatory: the study of a semantic field, investigated through separate treatments of the three roots named, plus an appendix on *qalā, qalôn* etc. The words have roots in different realms: *bôš* belongs to the sexual, *klm* (basically 'point to, indicate') is rather legal; *hpr* comes closer to the painful embarrassing effect of a bad social situation. Material from other Semitic languages is offered, thickly packed in small print. Considerable attention is given to Pedersen's ideas; the general conclusions are brief. A careful and solid study.   J.B.

KOCH, K.: *The Rediscovery of Apocapyptic. A polemical work on a neglected area of biblical studies and its damaging effects on theology and philosophy* (Studies in Biblical Theology, Second Series, 22). Translated by M. Kohl. 1972. Pp. 160. (S.C.M. Press, London. Price: £2.25)

This is an English translation of the work reviewed in *B.L.* 1972, p. 55.   M.A.K.

*LACE, O. J. (ed.): *Understanding the Old Testament*. 1972. Pp. x, 191. (Cambridge University Press. Price: £2.20, paperback 96p)

*MELLOR, E. B. (ed.): *The Making of the Old Testament*. 1972. Pp. x, 214. (Cambridge University Press. Price: £2.20, paperback 96p)

These are two introductory volumes in the Cambridge Bible Commentary on the N.E.B. (See *B.L.* 1972, p. 23). In the first D. R. Ap-Thomas provides an illuminating and concise account of the geographical, archaeological and historical background of the O.T. and Apocrypha, and the editor, under the heading of 'The History and Religion of Israel', deals in an interesting and non-technical fashion with the life and thought of the peoples of the O.T.

The second book is a compendium dealing with the literature of the ancient Near East relevant to the study of the O.T., the literary forms of the O.T., the modern critical study of the O.T., the Apocrypha and Pseudepigrapha, the development of the canon, the relation of the modern English text to earlier versions, and the use of the O.T. by Jews and Christians.   L.A.P.

McCARTHY, D. J.: *Old Testament Covenant. A Survey of Current Opinions*. 1972. Pp. viii, 112. (Basil Blackwell, Oxford, and John Knox Press, Richmond, Virginia. Price: £1.50, $3.95)

Professor McCarthy's study is a survey of the intense concern with O.T. ideas and forms of covenant that has developed in the past fifteen years from comparisons with secular vassal treaties. The related philological questions and the covenant material in the various parts of the O.T. legal and prophetic literature are examined in separate sections. A survey is offered of the wide varieties of opinion about the historical and theological conclusions drawn from comparison with vassal treaties. Whilst being himself a cautious supporter of the view that such treaties have decisively influenced O.T. patterns and ideas, McCarthy is very critical of the enthusiastic excesses of other scholars in this field. The survey and the bibliography are excellent as a guide and basis for further research, even though few questions are solved here.   R.E.C.

MARCOLINO, V.: *Das Alte Testament in der Heilsgeschichte. Untersuchung zum dogmatischen Verständnis des Alten Testaments als heilsgeschichliche Periode nach Alexander von Hales* (Beiträge zur Geschichte der Philosophie und Theologie des Mittelalters, N.F. Band 2). 1970. Pp. vii, 370. (Aschendorff, Münster, Westfalen. Price: DM. 58)

This elaborate study of the important place given to *Heilsgeschichte* in the thought of the thirteenth-century Franciscan theologian Alexander of Hales is interesting for the light it sheds on movements in Roman Catholic theology today. The influence of men like Bultmann, Cullmann and von Rad is obvious. Alexander of Hales was a disciple of Peter Lombard and owed something to Hugo of St. Victor. He held that *Heilsgeschichte* was God's *opus restaurationis* and represented an essential part of theology. It is instructive to see him facing up to the problem of the relation of the Old Testament to the New, safeguarding the unique contribution of the latter while claiming a significant place for the former. The author recognizes the danger of allegorical and anagogical interpretation of the O.T., but he pleads for a measure of pneumatic exegesis, if pure *historismus* is to be avoided.   N.W.P.

MÜLLER, M.: *Messias og 'Menneskesøn' i Daniels Bog, Første Enoksbog og Fjerde Ezrabog*. (Tekst og olkning, 3). 1972. Pp. 94. (G.E.C. Gad, Copenhagen. Price: D.Kr. 19)

In this study the author has undertaken to investigate various conceptions involved in the expression the Son of Man, partly from the canonical writings of O.T., and partly from the pseudepigraphical writings of 1 Enoch and 4 Ezra. He maintains that in Judaism there cannot be shown to have been a special complex of conceptions about the Son of Man, which can be differentiated from the conception of the Messiah, or which is from a different origin than the conception of the Messiah. He who appears as the Son of Man in Dan. 7, has his background in the Ras Shamra texts in the conception of Baal, who has assumed the power from El. In contrast to Dan. 7 the Son of Man in 1 Enoch is clearly conceived as an individual redeemer, not simply a symbol or collective idea. The foundation for 1 Enoch 37–71 is the expression 'as a Son of Man' in Dan. 7, but the expression should not be understood terminologically. In 4 Ezra 13, he interprets the 'man' as Messiah and concludes that the designation 'man' is a result of the author's making use of Dan. 7, which he interprets messianically. In the book's concluding chapter, he sketches an outline up to the N.T. use of the Son of Man. When used by Jesus it is the common Aramaic form of expression for the pronoun 'I'.   E.H.

NEHER, A.: *L'Essence du Prophétisme*. 1972. Pp. 322. (Calmann-Lévy, Paris. Price: Fr. 27)

This distinctively Jewish interpretation of the prophets first appeared in 1955 (see *B.L.*, 1956, p. 50; *Eleven Years*, p. 757) and has now been re-issued with only minor emendations. An English translation, *The Prophetic Existence*, published in 1969, has not been noticed in the *Book List*. R.J.C.

NOTH, M.: *A History of Pentateuchal Traditions*. Trans. with an introduction by B. W. Anderson. 1972. Pp. xii, 296. (Prentice-Hall, Inc., Englewood Cliffs, N.J. Price: £6)

All teachers of the O.T. to English-speaking students will rejoice at the belated appearance in English of Martin Noth's epoch-making *Überlieferungsgeschichte des Pentateuch* (*B.L.* 1950, p. 45; *Eleven Years*, p. 262). The translation, which is excellently done as far as the reviewer is able to judge, is based on the original edition of 1948, and is preceded by an introduction by the translator entitled 'Martin Noth's Traditio-Historical Approach in the Context of Twentieth-Century Biblical Research' and by a short preface to the English edition, written by Noth himself in 1966. R.N.W.

VON RAD, G.: *Wisdom in Israel*. Translated from the German by J. D. Martin. 1972. Pp. xiv, 330. (S.C.M. Press, London. Price: £3.75)

It is good to be able to welcome the early appearance of this English translation of von Rad's *Weisheit in Israel* (for which see *B.L.* 1972, p. 44). M.A.K.

REISER, W.: *Eine Frau wie Ruth: Ein biblisches Buch wird aktuell*. 1972. Pp. 77. (Theologischer Verlag, Zürich. Price: DM. 7.80)

This is a book for the preacher and teacher. The biblical book offers insight and guidance for six problem-situations in the modern world: the mother-in-law / daughter-in-law relationship, mixed marriages, industry, immigrant labour, the man/woman relationship, human freedom and divine order. A.S.H.

*RICHARDSON, A.: *Preface to Bible Study*. Revised Edition 1972. Pp. 128. (S.C.M. London. Price: 55p)

An up-to-date list of sources has been added to this useful and popular book (first published in 1943) but the text apparently remains unaltered; it is a pity that anachronisms, such as the reference to the Institute of Christian Education, could not have been removed.

E.B.M.

RICHTER, W.: *Exegese als Literaturwissenschaft. Entwurf einer alttestamentlichen Literaturtheorie und Methodologie*. 1971. Pp. 211. (Vandenhoeck & Ruprecht, Göttingen und Zürich. Price: DM. 25)

The author brings to exegesis the norms of modern linguistics. In a dispassionate way he dismisses the traditional four methods of literary, allegorical, moral, and anagogical approaches, and argues against a complementary explicit-implicit sense of scripture. Instead he formally classifies the O.T. as literature which can only be taken seriously if its component parts are subjected to objective methods of study. Presuppositions and models of the past are no help, except as a warning that a false method must bring useless results. Richter then examines in detail the structure and validity of the critical functions which we apply today. He distinguishes between *Form-* and *Gattungskritik*, and also regards *Redaktionskritik* as separate from *Traditionskritik*. Given the priority of *Literarkritik* Richter presents us with a clear-cut model of five ways. His particular concern is to investigate the interrelations, not only between these five ways but also as they emerge within each method in their application to a unit of the text. His treatment is theoretical, and it comes almost as a surprise that he disdains the last step in modern analysis, i.e. the reduction of units into codes which can be programmed into a computer.

One may ask whether Richter's confidence in planned methodology is not misplaced. Modern literary criticism is not always quite so distant from, and uninvolved in, the subject matter. Richter devotes his last chapter to what he calls 'exegesis immanent in the text', but it must be confessed that his abstractions (e.g. the meaningless distinction between *Inhalt* and *Gehalt*) darken the perspective. If this book is more than an academic exercise of great expertise and with an excellent bibliography, the prospect for exegesis must be bleak. It is a curious fact that biblical literature gains little from this treatment, whereas Homer, Virgil, Dante, Shakespeare and Goethe often appear to us in a new light. Richter's trouble, which frankly is sheer boredom, may yet help him and many others to press on to a methodology which is both scientific and creative. It should not be impossible.

U.E.S.

RICHTER, W.: *Die sogennanten vorprophetischen Berufungsberichte. Eine literaturwissenschaftliche Studie zu 1 Sam. 9, 1–10, 16, Ex 3f. und Ri 6, 11b–17* (Forschungen zur Religion und Literatur des Alten und Neuen Testaments, 101). 1970. Pp. 203. (Vandenhoeck & Ruprecht, Göttingen. Price: DM. 36 (cloth), DM. 31 (paper))

An analysis of the structure, form and literary history of these texts leads to the conclusion that they exemplify a standard form of call-narrative, which is also that of the call-narratives to be found in the canonical books of the prophets. The fact that this pattern is applied equally to the call of prophets and to that of military 'saviours' is taken as an indication that prophets were involved together with military leaders in the early days of the Holy War, which constitutes the *Sitz im Leben* of the literary type. These texts were composed and handed down at first in prophetical circles in the north, but the pattern later came to be applied to southern prophets as well. The thesis — which is to be supplemented by a further study of the call-narratives of the canonical prophets — is argued rigorously and minutely: this is not a book for the casual reader. Not all readers will be convinced that the pattern is too specific in its details to have developed independently in different circles; but the author's method of work is to be highly commended.

R.N.W.

SANDERS, J. A.: *Torah and Canon*. 1972. Pp. xx, 124. (Fortress Press, Philadelphia, Pa. Price: $2.95)

The growth of interest in the understanding of the canon as a key concept in biblical study is usefully expressed in the initial essay in this volume, where the value of such study is related to theological interpretation in the contemporary situation. What follows in the survey of the literature is often illuminated by important insights into the nature of the O.T. material and into ways in which it may be interpreted; but there is a certain uneasy compromise between a popular book on the O.T., in which there are too many assumptions and unprovable assertions, and a scholarly discernment of a line along which further study may profitably be pursued. The combining of two different styles in the one volume could mean that this more important aspect will not be as clearly picked up as we could wish. The theme itself is of very great importance.   P.R.A.

SANDERS, P. S. (ed.): *Twentieth Century Interpretations of the Book of Job. A Collection of Critical Essays*. 1968. Pp. x, 118. (Prentice-Hall, Inc., Englewood Cliffs, N.J. Price: $1.40)

The particular interest of this collection of essays is that it appears as one of a series of such collections devoted to literary works ranging from Shakespeare to T. S. Eliot. The editor has written a general introduction designed in the main to indicate to the student of literature the nature and problems of the book of Job, and he has then selected ten essays, including older studies by G. B. Gray and A. S. Peake, and others by such well-known writers as Gilbert Murray and A. J. Toynbee and a number by specialists in English literature and the like. The bringing together of such varied approaches is of particular interest at a time when there is a new urge for the study of the O.T. as literature.   P.R.A.

SAWYER, J. F. A.: *Semantics in Biblical Research* (Studies in Biblical Theology, Second Series, 24). 1972. Pp. xii, 146. (SCM Press, London. Price: £2.25)

In this important book, Dr Sawyer argues for the importance of semantic and other techniques known to modern Linguistics, in O.T. study. The reader is introduced to linguistic concepts such as context, semantic fields, synchronic description and transformational grammar, and the usefulness of these categories and procedures is illustrated with reference to the verb *hōšīa'* and its associated field. The linguistic position taken can be described generally as neo-Firthian, with dependence on writers such as Lyons. Dr Saywer makes a strong case for the view that semantic techniques must play their part in the translation and interpretation of O.T. Hebrew. He also argues that whereas the teaching of biblical Hebrew is too often 'adorned with the Akkadian tense-system, the structure of Arabic nouns and a good deal of comparative semitic phonology', these things are by no means indispensable for a proper linguistic description of Hebrew. The book deserves the closest attention from all teachers and interpreters of the Hebrew O.T.   J.W.R.

SCOTT, R. B. Y.: *The Way of Wisdom*. 1972. Pp. 238. (Macmillan, London. Price: £1.30)

This work, noticed last year (see *B.L.* 1972, p. 46), is now also distributed in an English paperback edition.   R.J.C.

SEYBOLD, K.: *Das davidische Königtum im Zeugnis der Propheten* (Forschungen zur Religion und Literatur des Alten und Neuen Testaments, 107). 1972. Pp. 183. (Vandenhoek & Ruprecht, Göttingen. Price: DM. 38 (cloth), DM. 34 (paper))

This is a well-ordered and thoroughly documented study of a subject often discussed; new insights into it are hard to come by. Justifiably the author maintains that the charismatic kingship of the house of David had its setting within the *Heilsgeschichte* tradition concerning the people Israel. The historical fact of the establishment of the Davidic empire was interpreted as authenticating the charisma on David and his house, a charisma which was not later lost because of the failure of any ruling member of that house. Prophets defined the nature and the responsibilities of such rule, temple ceremonies upheld it, and the division of the empire did not extinguish it. The author's review of the relevant evidence in the canonical prophets is judiciously done, but the absence of supporting evidence in, for example, Isa. 40–66 (only 55:1–5 is quoted), Joel and Malachi might have been noted at greater length as showing the effect which historical events can have on theological beliefs — although these beliefs may have a later renaissance.   J.M.

SHAW, M. W.: *Studies in Revelation and the Bible*. 1971. Pp. 92. (Catholic Seminary, Indianapolis.)

Of the four main sections of this book, the first is on 'Revelation in the Ancient Near East' and the second on 'Covenant-Revelation in the Old Testament.' The remainder are concerned with the Fourth Gospel and the Pauline writings. The material in the first section covers familiar ground as it relates to Kingship, Priesthood, Prophecy and Wisdom, but one feels a need to have the word 'revelation' more carefully defined. The second section takes note of what various scholars have said on the covenants with Israel and David.   A.S.H.

SMITH, MORTON: *Palestinian Parties and Politics that shaped the Old Testament* (Lectures on the History of Religions sponsored by the American Council of Learned Societies: New Series, no. 9). 1971. Pp. viii, 348. (Columbia University Press, New York and London. Price: £4.25)

Partisan spirit seems to be taken in this book to be the hermeneutical key to the O.T.; its origin and its transmission alike were guided by party loyalties. After a general introduction, there is a study of religious parties before 587, one of 'hellenization' (quotation marks are used by the author), and one of the survival of the syncretistic cult; there follow chapters surveying the history from Nebuchadnezzar to Nehemiah, in Nehemiah's time, and down to Antiochus Epiphanes. An appendix attacks Alt's account of the Samaritans. There are some interesting cross-references to developments in Greece. Regrettably, the tone used is sometimes cynical, flippant and contemptuous, and notably so in the depiction of Nehemiah.   J.B.

STOLZ, F.: *Jahwes und Israels Kriege: Kriegstheorien und Kriegserfahrungen im Glauben des alten Israels* (Abhandlungen zur Theologie des Alten und Neuen Testaments, 60). 1972. Pp. 211. (Theologischer Verlag, Zürich. Price: DM. 29)

Stolz's nomenclature ('Yahweh's War', 'Israel's War') is connected with the circumstance that he does not employ the hypothesis of amphictyony, and envisages separate, tribal experiences of Yahweh as the one who leads and gives victory in war, rather than 'holy war' with an organizational coherence and established procedures. Nor does he accept that the Song of Miriam (Ex. 15:20 f.) is an archetypal experience of Yahweh as warrior to which all other experiences can be related. Instead of holding that 'holy war' is an amphictyonic activity he supposes that these discrete, tribal experiences of Yahweh as the one who gives effective help in war are a unifying force which promotes the formation of an Israelite consciousness.

His comprehensive review of texts leads him to the conclusion that the establishment of the Jerusalem cult and the concept of Yahweh as warrior consonant with its ideology mark a significant modification of the earlier beliefs and experiences which are traceable up to the time of Saul. In this earlier phase Yahweh as warrior is related to discrete historical events, while in Jerusalem (in the Psalms) the representation belongs to a cultic-cosmic framework, even if historical references are present. In the post-Jerusalem period the more the theory of 'Yahweh's war' is elaborated, the greater the distance between the theory and actual, historical attitudes, with the theorizing reaching its final stage in Deuteronomy.   W.McK.

VETTER, D.: *Jahwes Mit-Sein — ein Ausdruck des Segens.* 1971. Pp. 45 (Calwer Verlag, Stuttgart. Price: DM. 4.80)

The author examines the 103 occurrences in the O.T. of the formulae which express the divine presence with Israel or individual members of it, with the use of the words *'eṭ* and *'im*. No difference in meaning is found between expressions using *'eṭ* and those using *'im*, and it is argued that in the contexts of the expressions, there is a close connection between the idea of the divine presence and the idea of blessing. The author thus concludes, following Westermann, that promises of the divine presence refer primarily to God's continual grace towards Israel, rather than to specific acts of grace.   J.W.R.

WEIDMANN, H.: *Die Patriarchen und ihre Religion im Licht der Forschung seit Julius Wellhausen* (Forschungen zur Religion und Literatur des Alten und Neuen Testaments, 94). 1968. Pp. 186. (Vandenhoeck & Ruprecht, Göttingen. Price: DM. 28 (cloth), DM. 24 (paper))

This is a dissertation by a young scholar whose death followed shortly after its acceptance by the University of Marburg. It is a careful critical survey of the field indicated by its title, but its usefulness is lessened by the fact that the author confined himself mainly, though not exclusively, to German scholarship. E. Würthwein explains in a preface that a final chapter on the contribution of archaeology, especially American, to the understanding of the patriarchs and their religion has been omitted because it was known that the author had intended to expand it before publication. This amputation, together with the failure to take account of the work of such non-German scholars as de Vaux, gives the work something of the character of a torso, although its quality is excellent within its limits.

R.N.W.

WEINFELD, M.: *Deuteronomy and the Deuteronomic School.* 1972. Pp. xviii, 467. (Clarendon Press, Oxford. Price: £9)

The thesis of this book is that 'deuteronomic composition is the creation of scribal circles which began their literary project some time prior to the reign of Josiah and were still at work after the fall of Judah' (p. 9). An investigation of the style, literary methods, theology and didactic aims of Deuteronomy and the other writings of the 'deuteronomic school' shows that the authors had access to and made use of a 'vast reservoir of literary material' whose influence upon them has led to a number of different theories about their identity, but which permits only one conclusion: that they belonged to the scribal class and held public office. The author reaches a number of other conclusions which will certainly arouse great interest and controversy, e.g. that the Deuteronomists 'paved the way for the synagogue' and that it was they who were the redactors of the Priestly document. This is a solid piece of work which deserves serious attention. Among its most interesting features are a discussion of Deuteronomic 'humanism' and a detailed appendix on Deuteronomic phraseology.

R.N.W.

WESTERMANN, C.: *Genesis 1–11* (Erträge der Forschung, Band 7). 1972. Pp. xxv, 108. (Wissenschaftliche Buchgesellschaft, Darmstadt. Price: £2.50)

This valuable study originated in the work of a seminar in Heidelberg, in which R. Albertz, E. Ruprecht, R. Ficker, and Frau Westermann participated. The work of literary-, form-, and traditio-criticism is summarised in seven main sections: Genesis 1–3, 4:2–16, the Genealogies, 6:1–4, the Flood, Noah the vine-grower and his sons, the Tower of Babel. These chapters of Genesis set before us not merely Israel's pre-history, but a theological understanding of all mankind under the curse. This is seen in the way in which both J and P have preserved and modified previously existing material. We are promised a further book on Gen. 12–50.

A.S.H.

WESTERMANN, C.: *Tisíc let a jeden den* (Tausend Jahre und ein Tag), translated by M. Šourek. 1972. Pp. 210. (Kalich, Prague. Price: Kčs. 25)

In this book, originally published in 1957, E.T. from 2nd ed. 1959, published in 1962, (*B.L.* 1962, p. 57; *Decade*, p. 367), Professor Westermann introduces the reader to the thousand year long history of the O.T. in order to point to the relevance of the O.T. message for modern man. At the end of that thousand years stands the one day, that of the crucifixion and resurrection of Christ. The translation has been amplified for the Czech reader by the addition of a few footnotes; some short passages which are concerned with purely German problems, have been omitted.

M.B.

ZENGER, E.: *Die Sinaitheophanie. Untersuchungen zum jahwistischen und elohistischen Geschichtswerk* (Forschung zur Bibel, 3). 1971. Pp. 304. (Echter Verlag Katholisches Bibelwerk, Würzburg. Price: DM. 24)

This study of the sources of the account of the Sinai theophany in Exodus 19–20, 24 and 32–34 pursues a distinctive and fresh approach by its emphasis on the extent and purpose of the work of redactors. Zenger accepts an analysis of the familiar J and E sources which he believes were redacted into a 'Jehovistic History work' in the reign of Hezekieh after the fall of the Northern kingdom. Into this two further additions were incorporated, Exod. 24:9–11 and the 'cultic' decalogue of Exod. 34: 11–26. This document then underwent two Deuteronomic redactions, the first interpreting the Sinai event in terms of the covenant theology of Deuteronomy and the second, after the exile, inserting the Book of the Covenant. The P material was then later added to this, and some further additions were also made.

The work is set out with exemplary clarity and with the greatest attention to the work of other scholars which is shown in useful synopses. The overall emphasis on redaction rather than upon the analysis of separate source documents is constructive, even though Zenger in no way minimises the importance of recognizing these early sources. He claims however, with some justice, that too often scholars have thought they have detected sources when in fact they were dealing with redaction.　　　　　　　　　　　　　　　　　R.E.C.

LAW, RELIGION AND THEOLOGY

CHARLEY, J.: *Fifty Key Words: The Bible.* 1971. Pp. 69. (John Knox Press, Richmond, Virginia and Lutterworth Press, London. Price: $1.65, 60p)

The focus of interest of this biblical wordbook is the N.T. with only incidental reference to O.T. usage. About 500 words are devoted to each article and this brevity limits the usefulness of an otherwise competent book.　　　　　　　　　　　　　　　　　L.A.P.

FIELD, M. J.: *Angels and Ministers of Grace.* 1971. Pp. 135. (Longman, London. Price: £2)

This book is a study by an anthropologist who has observed some parallels between some of the biblical narratives and stories told in West Africa. Thus he sees the Lord to have been originally a human landlord, and the angels his land agents dealing with nomads seeking to settle. At a later stage the former two were regarded as supernatural beings. Moses 'seems to have used hallucinogenic fumes to help him hear the voice of his god.' Ezekiel too was under the influence of a drug! The treatment of the biblical material continues into the N.T.

　　　　　　　　　　　　　　　　　A.S.H.

FOHRER, G.: *Theologische Grundstrukturen des Alten Testaments* (Theologische Bibliothek Töpelmann, 24). 1972. Pp. x, 276. (De Gruyter, Berlin, New York. Price: DM. 38)

This highly readable book of moderate proportions attempts the Everest of Old Testament studies, and if it does not reach the summit will provide many lessons for future expeditions! After an initial glance at some hermeneutic problems (a weak section), the author spends the first third of the book in a mainly descriptive discussion of the Old Testament faith. The emergence of this faith is traced as an attitude to existence forged in dialectic with other attitudes to existence which are partly rejected and partly assimilated. The world of magic is given a role in this dialectic which many will think exaggerated. The central point of a theology of the Old Testament is identified in two conceptions, the sovereignty of God and the fellowship between God and man, regarded as the two foci of an ellipse. This centre is then seen as the impetus of a series of transformations, illustrated by the history of institutions like circumcision and the altar, and by the interpretation of traditions to be found notably in Genesis, the wisdom literature and prophecy. Next the developments of this faith are studied in the personal structure of belief, the relation of God to history and nature and the characteristic pattern of God's relation to man. The final section is a study of various applications of this faith, *inter alia* to politics (the duty of obedience and the right to rebel), social affairs and technocracy. This tends to be an effort to make direct application to modern life. It both ignores the necessity of another kind of dialectic (with Marxists, psychologists and sociologists) and jumps the hermeneutical problem. No doubt the kind of exercise carried out in this book ideally requires a sensitivity as finely tuned to systematic theology and contemporary attitudes to existence as to the faith of the Old Testament. Nevertheless a warm tribute to Fohrer for attempting a book which will completely satisfy few, but will help us all.

D.R.J.

GUNNEWEG, A. H. J., KAISER, O., RATCHOW, C. H., WÜRTHWEIN, E.: *Der Gott der mitgeht. Alttestamentliche Predigten.* 1972. Pp. 141. (Gütersloher Verlagshaus Gerd Mohn, Gütersloh. Price: DM. 12.80)

This stimulating little volume of sermons on O.T. texts by a group of distinguished scholars is preceded by a thoughtful introductory essay on the contemporary relevance of the O.T. by Professor Otto Kaiser of Marburg. Understandably his thought reveals the influence of Bultmann's theology. The sermons themselves are very much to the point and are models of brevity.

N.W.P.

HUNTER, J. E.: *World in rebellion.* 1972. Pp. 142. (Moody Press, Chicago. Price: $1.95)

The spirit of rebellion in human society is seen to be the product of satanic influence, beginning in Genesis 3. Evil is apparently triumphant but the divine power of salvation is available to those who whole-heartedly seek God. Illustrative material is drawn from O.T. and N.T. The book is informed with a warmly evengelical spirit.

A.S.H.

JACKSON, B. S.: *Theft in Early Jewish Law.* 1972. Pp. xviii, 316. (Clarendon Press, Oxford. Price: £5.50)

This study deals with the law of theft of property (theft of persons is not considered) from the earliest biblical times to the end of the Tannaitic period. After considering the principal biblical words used for misappropriation of property, Jackson, first by examining the biblical material, and then its interpretation and elaboration in the post-biblical period, deals in turn with the biblical offences, the penalties, the means of self-help, and the procedures adopted for identifying the thief. He concludes his study with the suggestion that the more lenient Tannaitic law results from a desire to keep the offender outside Roman jurisdiction. Throughout the book, early Jewish law is compared with both other ancient Near Eastern law, as well as Greek and Roman practice. This is a valuable study which again emphasises that there is nothing abstract about early Jewish law, but that it had its origin and development in the everyday life situation of the people among whom it was practised. It can then only be studied as law. A.C.J.P.

LAURIN, R. B. (ed.): *Contemporary Old Testament Theologians*. 1970. Pp. 223. (Marshall, Morgan and Scott, London. Price: £4.25)

The American edition of this useful collection of critical essays was noted in *B.L.* 1971, p. 50. It is now available also in this English edition. P.R.A.

OIKONOMOU, E.: *He Phainomenologia tes Atheias kata ten Palaian Diatheken*. 1972. Pp. 24. (Reprint from *Theologia*, Athens)

This inaugural lecture delivered in the University of Athens on 7 May 1971, addresses itself to the question: 'Is there a problem of atheism in the O.T.?' Not exactly a problem, but a phenomenon: 'atheism' in the O.T. stands over against the knowledge of God. As the pious man cultivates the knowledge of God, so the 'atheist' gives it no place in his life, and is therefore revealed as a *nabal*. Such 'atheism' manifests itself in putting God to the test in respect of his presence ('Is Yahweh among us or not?'), his power ('Can God furnish a table in the wilderness?') and man's claim to autonomy over against him ('you shall be as God'). F.F.B.

SHEEHAN, J. F. X., S.J.: *The Threshing Floor. An Interpretation of the Old Testament*. 1972. Pp. xii, 208. (Paulist Press, New York — Paramus — Toronto. Price: $3.95)

Designed as a kind of first reader to O.T. studies, this book covers a wide range of themes and motifs from the O.T. literature as seen through the eyes of modern scholars. Most of the major theological themes appear, although the approach is selective and has been governed by a concern for general interest and relevance. There is plenty of apt illustration, perhaps rather too directly related to the American scene, but on the whole the book is very well done. It is attractively written, and is very alive theologically. It achieves very well its purpose of stimulating an intelligent interest. R.E.C.

SIEGWALT, G.: *La Loi, chemin du Salut. Étude sur la signification de la loi de l'Ancien Testament* (Bibliothèque Théologique). 1971. Pp. 261. (Delachaux et Niestlé, Neuchâtel. Price: S.Fr. 51)

This is a re-examination of the view that the relationship between the Old and New Testaments is properly and adequately described in terms of the opposition between Law and Gospel. The author's conclusion is that in spite of apparent divergences and contradictions, the two Testaments are basically in agreement internally and with each other in rejecting a 'pharisaic' view of the Law and in understanding it as the consequence rather than the presupposition of the covenant between God and Israel, and so as a help towards salvation rather than as a burden. The treatment of the O.T. material at least is very generalized and hardly does justice to its complexity. The tortuous style makes this a wearisome book to read.   R.N.W.

VAWTER, B.: *Biblical Inspiration* (Theological Resources). 1972. Pp. xii, 195. (Westminster, Philadelphia, and Hutchinson, London. Price: $9.95)

The origins, development, and varieties of the idea that God is the author of the Bible are traced from the implications of the formation of a canon, and the background and meaning of 2 Tim. 3:16, through the Fathers to Aquinas and on to Vatican 2, with a 19-page judicious survey of Protestant views up to the present. The author brings out the importance at an early period of the phenomenon of prophecy as a model for the concept of inspiration, and at a later point the gradual recognition by the Roman magisterium of the importance of literary types in interpreting inspiration. The closing chapter pleads for finding the revelatory value of the Bible in its relation to the community of faith, and the author does not disguise his regret towards much traditional doctrine about inspiration; but his work is scholarly and well-documented, with well-judged excursions into greater detail than the scale of the book permits overall. There is a full bibliography in addition to 8 pages of notes. This work is important for all those whose interests in any way relate to the history of the interpretation of the Bible.   C.J.A.H.

WENHAM, J. W.: *Christ and the Bible*. 1972. Pp. 206. (Tyndale Press, Intervarsity Press. Price £1.35 (cloth), 75p (paper))

This book, the first of a series of four, by the Warden of Latimer House, Oxford, is an able and vigorous plea, in the tradition of B. B. Warfield, for recognition of the verbal inspiration of the Bible. Christ accepted the O.T. without qualification as the Word of God. Christ was inerrant. Christ gave the Apostles their authority. They confirm Christ's view of the O.T. and their authority extends to the N.T. as well. Few concessions are made to meet modern objections and difficulties. In matters of history the Bible is, *ex hypothesi*, accurate from beginning to end, even in trifling details. So important is this that Zechariah the son of Barachiah is given three and a half pages. By those who are able to accept the author's *a priori* method of reasoning the book will be warmly welcomed and the promised sequel eagerly awaited.   N.W.P.

WILLIAMS, J. G.: *Ten Words of Freedom*. 1971. Pp. xiii, 226. (Fortress Press, Philadelphia. Price: $4.95)

Professor Williams has had the idea to use the Ten Commandments as a starting point for expounding the Faith of Israel. Within this self-imposed brief, he manages to range widely from modern theism, and revelation, through the special features of the Exodus faith, to the practice of religion and modern ethical problems. The aim is not impossible and there are many good things in the book. But it had to be done superbly well to be successful. As it is, the book falls between all the stools! It fails to provide a satisfactory exposition of the Commandments; it offers no light on the problems they raise and shows no familiarity with recent books of importance. It contains too many inaccuracies to list here and altogether fails to control disparate discussions with adequate scholarly discipline. The design is too ambitious, requiring an immense expertise. The beginner will not be adequately helped and the scholar will be irritated. This is the premature birth of something potentially good.

D.R.J.

ZIMMERLI, W.: *Grundriss der alttestamentlichen Theologie* (Theologische Wissenschaft, 3). 1972. Pp. 223. (W. Kohlhammer, Stuttgart. Price: DM. 22)

A series of eighteen volumes is planned under the title 'Theologische Wissenschaft', with a subtitle which makes their purpose plain: 'Sammelwerk für Studium und Beruf'. Three of these are to be devoted to the O.T., the other two being R. Smend, *Entstehung des Alten Testaments*, and A. H. J. Gunneweg, *Geschichte Israels bis Bar Kochba*. Two volumes corresponding to Zimmerli and Smend are assigned to the N.T.

The excellence of Professor Zimmerli's volume is just what would be expected of him. It attempts no elaborate theory about O.T. theology, but, as befits a textbook, presents the material in a reasonable order — the nature of God as he reveals himself to Israel, the divine gifts to his people in well-being and charismatic leadership, the demands which he makes upon them, the nature of Israel's life in response. The final section is entitled 'Crisis and Hope' in which there is offered what is both an overall survey of Israel's religion and an examination of the relationship between belief and experience as these are presented in the primeval story, the narratives, the prophetic writings and apocalyptic, culminating in a brief statement on the 'Openness of O.T. proclamation'. Each of the many sections is full of careful survey and precise suggestions of interpretation. There are useful bibliographies, mainly of German works as would be expected in such a textbook. Somewhat surprising is the cursory attention devoted to the Chronicler, still so undervalued in O.T. theologies. The stress throughout is on positive evaluation, and on the under-standing of O.T. theology as a subject for itself, without superficial linkages being made to N.T. themes. The result is much more than a students' handbook; it is a valuable, concise survey of the whole field.

P.R.A.

THE LIFE AND THOUGHT OF THE
SURROUNDING PEOPLES

CASSUTO, U.: *The Goddess Anath. Canaanite Epics of the Patriarchal Age. Texts, Hebrew Translation: Commentary and Introduction, translated from the Hebrew by Israel Abrahams.* 1971. Pp. xii, 194 with 1 frontice-plate and 8 photographic plates. (Magnes Press, Jerusalem, the Hebrew University)

The late Professor U. Cassuto's *Hā-'Ēlā 'Anāth*, (1951; see *B.L.* 1952, p. 60, *Eleven Years*, p. 431. Reprints, 1953, 1958, 1965), has long been known to scholars as one of the best early attempts to bring together the chief pieces of the longest poem, that called 'Anat or Ba'al into a connected poem. Unfortunately, buried in the modern Hebrew jargon, very few English students or other interested people read it or even knew it. It contains a long introduction on the Ugaritic writings and their relationship to the Old Testament and on the Epic of Baal. This is followed by the text of Tablets V and VI in English transliteration and a translation into (as far as possible) biblical Hebrew; and each section is followed by notes, for the most part philological, with special reference to biblical words and phrases, customs and beliefs, and so on. Although still a pioneering work, it remains useful for scholars and invaluable for students, in spite of all recent discoveries. Dr. I. Abrahams, Emeritus Professor of Bible at Cape Town, has produced an excellent translation with which one can rarely disagree, as when he renders *qlm* 'swift ones' and *mhrm* 'fast ones', which now in ordinary English usage means young men who are 'keen on the girls'! May the words not mean 'skilled' (i.e. officers; cp. e.g. '*mhr* young hero') and 'light' (i.e. private soldiers; cp. Bab *qallu* and Hebr. *qal* 'light-armed')? These are trivialities; what is important is that Cassuto's work retains its value, and that the translator has put all interested in the background of the O.T. in his debt for an outstanding contribution by making it accessible to everyone.

G.R.D.

FISHER, L. R. (ed.): *Ras Shamra Parallels. The Texts from Ugarit and the Hebrew Bible. Vol. 1.* Analecta Orientalia, 49. 1972. Pp. xxiii, 537. (Pontificium Institutum Biblicum, Rome)

This is the first of three proposed volumes which will assemble the different types of comparison that have been drawn between the Hebrew Bible and Ugaritic literature. Most of this volume is taken up by a large chapter (II) from M. J. Dahood, S.J., and it is the fullest statement he has so far made about the theory of fixed pairs of words in Hebrew and Ugaritic poetry. More than 600 such pairs are described here. A. Schoors has written Chapter I entitled 'Literary Phrases' and J. H. Sasson in Chapter III discusses 124 common nouns which may be defined as animal, vegetable or mineral. The actual title, 'Flora, Fauna and Minerals' is more restricting but it is typical of the completeness of this work that words for a jar, milk, ointment and even the Kathirat are still discussed. The book appears to have been cursorily proof-read and so the well-planned indices should be used with care.

M.E.J.R.

HALDAR, A.: *Who were the Amorites?* (Monographs on the Ancient Near East, No. 1). 1971. Pp. viii, 93. (E. J. Brill, Leiden. Price: Fl. 25)

In this closely-argued, but not altogether convincing monograph, Haldar suggests that the Sumerian *mar.tu* and the Akkadian *amurrum* refer to the 'westland' between the Euphrates and the Mediterranean and derive from the name of the city Mari which from the Babylonian-Assyrian standpoint was the gateway to the west. 'Amorite' is therefore a geographic, not linguistic or ethnic, term. Haldar discusses why early sites in Syria and Iraq were settled and abandoned; people moved when factors such as deforestation, erosion, volcanic activity or minor climatic fluctuations affected an area's water supply. The Amorites began to move from the 'westland' in the mid-third millennium B.C. They were never nomads, but became travelling traders. Descriptions of them as 'not knowing grain' and 'not having a house', indicate not Amorite nomadism but Sumerian scorn for foreign travellers and their ways. *adda/abum* ('chieftain'), *dāwidūm* (military leader), *gāiūm* (cp. Heb. *gōi*) and other such terms used of the Amorites do not necessarily suggest a nomadic organisation. The tradition of their mountain homes accords with settled, not nomadic origins, for the earliest settlements were on the mountain slopes where the rainfall was higher. The relationship between the historical and biblical Amorites is not fully explored. Haldar too easily accepts Albright's caravaneering Abraham (adding that the line between a large trading caravan and a military expedition was a narrow one), and too easily rejects Kenyon's view of the termination of EB at Jericho by Amorite tribally organized 'semi-nomadic pastoralists'. He argues for Amorite skill in metallurgy, which, if correct, might throw new light on the rise of the MB I (Kenyon: IIA Albright) civilization, which according to Kenyon was produced by the amalgamation of Amorites with a pre-existing, more civilized population, and according to de Vaux by the previous arrival of other groups (who destroyed the EB cities) from copper-producing Anatolia or the Caucasus. More needs to be said here. J.R.B.

*HARRIS, J. R. (ed.): *The Legacy of Egypt.* 2nd ed. 1971. Pp. xii, 510. 24 plates. (Clarendon Press: Oxford University Press. Price: £2.50)

The first edition of this work, edited by S. R. K. Glanville in 1942, was reviewed in *B.L.* 1946, p. 4 (*Eleven Years*, p. 4). The second, completely revised, edition curiously makes no reference to the reasons for the very substantial differences in structure between the two editions. One chapter title they have in common is 'Egypt and Israel', in the earlier edition by W. O. E. Oesterley, here by R. J. Williams. This is clearly the centre of interest for O.T. scholars, and there is much both on administrative and on literary relationships. But in fact the chapter on 'Literature' by G. Posener contains a great deal which is equally relevant, and indeed there is considerable overlap, and some overlap too into the chapter on 'Language and Writing' by J. Czerny. C. H. Roberts writes again in the new edition on 'The Greek Papyri', an area in which there is much to add, and also of much interest to O.T. studies. R. A. Parker on 'The Calendars and Chronology' is another study of particular relevance. But the whole volume, like its predecessor, offers a very rich survey of material which is of interest for itself as well as for its points of contact with the O.T. world. P.R.A.

HEIDENHEIM, M.: *Bibliotheca Samaritana*. 1971. Pp. lii, 98; xlviii, 230; xl, 212, 124. (Philo Press, Amsterdam. Price: Fl. 120)

The three sections of Heidenheim's *Bibliotheca Samaritana*, originally published in 1884, 1885 and 1896, are here republished as a single volume, but otherwise unchanged. The texts reproduced are the Samaritan Targum on Genesis; Samaritan liturgical texts (17 in all, some of them fragmentary); and the Memar Marqah. Each has an extended introduction and there is a German translation of Marqah. The more important of these texts are available in more recent and reliable editions — Heidenheim's editorial work was much criticised even in his own day — and it is not easy to see what useful purpose will be served by this reissue, which has no contemporary comment of any kind.   R.J.C.

DE MOOR, J. C.: *The Seasonal Pattern in the Ugaritic Myth of Ba'lu according to the Version of Ilimilku* (Alter Orient und Alten Testament, Bd. 16). 1971. Pp. x, 321. (Butzon & Bercker, Kevelaer, Neukirchen-Vluyn. Price: DM. 72. Subscription price: DM. 66)

*DE MOOR, J. C.: *New Year with Canaanites and Israelites*. 1972. Part One: *Description*. (Kampers Cahiers, No. 21). Pp. 31. Part Two: *The Canaanite Sources*. (Kampers Cahiers, No. 22). Pp. 35. (J. H. Kok, N.V., Kampen. Price: Fl. 5.50 each)

The Baal story from Ugarit is recorded on several clay tablets but the scribe has left no indication of their sequence. How to interpret frequent unknown words is thus complicated by the uncertainty of the context, and the writer in the larger work here noted has attempted to solve the problem in a rather unusual way. He has examined recent official records from meteorological offices to show that the monthly pattern of rain and drought, of wind and calm changes little from year to year. By isolating allusions to the weather in the story, he is able to suggest to which month a given incident would have referred. Although this often involves new translations which are dependent on far from certain philological comparisons, this new attempt to explain what these texts really signified for the worshippers is a very thorough piece of work. There are abundant biblical references which are carefully indexed, as are the citations from other ancient Near Eastern and Classical sources.

Some of these ideas are developed in a more popular style in two booklets concerned with when the New Year celebrations of ancient Palestine took place. The discussion in Part One is untidy with far too much material condensed into footnotes, but Part Two contains a convenient anthology of Canaanite texts about harvest festivals.   M.E.J.R.

ROBERTS, J. J. M.: *The Earliest Semitic Pantheon. A Study of the Semitic Deities Attested in Mesopotamia before Ur III*. 1972. Pp. xvii, 174. (The Johns Hopkins University Press, Baltimore and London. Price: £5.40)

The earliest attested Semitic language is Old Akkadian, known from the second half of the third millennium B.C. in Mesopotamia, and the oldest attested Semitic deities are known from the same sources. Semitic personal names form the bulk of the material, since Semitic literary remains are almost non-existent for this period. The author of this revised Harvard thesis has systematically collected all the theophorous names and has presented them, each with translation, in an ordered list, with such conclusions as the names justify. This is a sound piece of fundamental research which O.T. scholars can use. However, it would be well to point out that the 'pantheon' referred to is already under Sumerian influence in some matters, such as the deified city, and the occurrence of some Amorite elements is another matter of interest.

W.G.L.

STARK, J. K.: *Personal Names in Palmyrene Inscriptions*, 1971. Pp. xx, 152. (Clarendon Press, Oxford. Price: £6)

Much work has recently been done on the Aramaic dialects in the Nabataean and Palmyrene inscriptions, notably by Cantineau (1930, 1932, 1935) and Rosenthal (1936); and all the words, apart from proper names, are included in Jean and Hoftijzer's *Dictionnaire des Inscriptions sémitiques de l'Ouest* (1965). Dr. Stark's work is a welcome addition to this list. Part I gives a complete (so far as one can see) catalogue of all known personal names, including those drawn from the Persian, Greek and Latin languages, with philological explanations of their meanings. It is, however, a pity that much is made needlessly obscure by transliteration. If Hebr.-Aram. fount had been used, he might have discovered the $T(Y)M$ in such names as $T(y)m$-$Ba'al$, which he rightly interprets as having the same meaning as 'bd-$B'l$ 'servant of Baal', comes from the same root as the Arab. *taymu(n)* 'slave' and *tîmatu(n)* 'sheep kept at home for milking and not let loose for pasturage' and that the Hebr. *tām* 'leading a settled life', a tent-dweller as distinct from one roaming the open country, is from the same root (Gen. 25:27; see N.E.B.); for Jacob, who survived Esau, was far from 'perfect' (R.V. marg.)! Appendices contain a number of improved readings, a list of Palmyrene names recently found at Dura-Europos, and also of Persian, Greek and Latin names adopted by Palmyrenes of either sex, as well as a concordance of modern works cited in the text (followed by a huge list of the abbreviations used for them). Finally the author adds on p. xvii a list of his transliterations of the Hebrew and Arabic and even Greek alphabets. The work indeed, as careful as it is thorough, will be indispensible not only to the narrow specialist in Palmyrene but also to all concerned with West-Semitic studies.

G.R.D.

WHITTAKER, R. E.: *A Concordance of the Ugaritic Literature*. 1972. Pp. vi, 660. (Harvard University Press, Cambridge, Mass. Price. $27.50)

Every Ugaritic word that has so far been attested in published texts is cited in this concordance as well as some of those that are proposed restorations in damaged passages. They are cited together with the words that precede and follow them and most quotations consist of some twenty-five words in all. There should be no omissions for it has been compiled by computer. Since no attempt is made at translation, homographs are not distinguished, so that a careful analysis of entries like *l* is needed before utilizing this material for vocabulary investigations.

M.E.J.R.

QUMRAN STUDIES

VAN DER PLOEG, J. P. M. and VAN DER WOUDE, A. S.: *Le Targum de Job de la Grotte XI de Qumrân*. Edited and translated with the collaboration of B. Jongeling. 1971. Pp. viii, 131, including 16 pls. (Brill, Leiden. Price: Fl. 120)

Here at long last is the impatiently awaited edition of the alas! fragmentarily preserved text of the Targum on Job, ideally edited by scholars of international reputation. It contains a brief *avant-propos* thanking those who have aided the editors in any way, followed by a list of abbreviations and an introduction describing the discovery of the pieces by Beduin in 1956 in a cave situated about 4 kms. from the ruins at Qumran, the seriously damaged state of the document, the orthographic peculiarities of the scribe, the Aramaic dialect used and its relation to the Targumim already known with especial reference to its value as an interpretation of the original poem of Job. The text follows, the Aramaic version and a French translation facing one another on opposite pages with brief philological notes at the bottom of each, followed by a concordance of practically every word with references to the passages in which they occur; all this is followed by marvellously clear photographic plates of the grotto and its situation and of every piece of text however small. The fragments range from 1¼ inches either way showing half a dozen words (some few even less than that) followed by eight pieces presenting whole lines and portions of the flanking columns; these all come from the lower part of the column but in no case preserve either top or bottom of the column. The skill shown by the editors in identifying every single piece and arranging them in their proper order according to the order of the Hebrew text is uncanny; for it is difficult to be absolutely sure of the identity of the work before the appearance of 'Bild[ad the Shuhite]' in col. ix, line 5 and of Job himself and '[Elihu the Buzite of the] family of Ram' in col. xx lines 6–7. The rest then runs on clearly enough, and the fragmentary earlier parts could each be fitted into its proper place with almost complete certainty. The translation and brief notes are admirable, and there is scarcely a word in either with which a reviewer can disagree or where he can find fault; but he may perhaps be allowed to call attention to the *kiy*-bird (Job 39:27) which has recently been identified as the '(Egyptian) vulture' (*P.E.Q.* 104 (1972) pp. 64–66) and is here represented by the Aramaic '*ôzâ* 'black-eagle', as the editors render it (col. xxxiii, 9).

This is a beautifully produced volume, with text, translation, and illustrations spaciously set out.

G.R.D.

ROSENBLOOM, J. R.: *The Dead Sea Isaiah Scroll: A Literary Analysis. A Comparison with the Masoretic Text and the Biblia Hebraica*. 1970. Pp. 88. (William B. Eerdmans, Grand Rapids, Michigan. Price: $4.50)

This study examines the variants from M.T. in IQIsa., and suggests that usually the latter is a deliberate simplification to meet the needs of a particular audience. It is recognized, however, that in some instances the Scroll offers a better reading, e.g. 2:11; 8:2; 30:20. The number of variants that are noted is by no means complete, but the book will be helpful to those who are beginning their studies of textual criticism of the Hebrew text.

A.S.H.

TUINSTRA, E. W.: *Hermeneutische Aspecten van de Targum van Job uit Grot XI van Qumran.* 1970. Pp. 114. (Available from the Zendingshoge-school, Oegstgeest, Leiden, Holland. Price: Fl. 15)

This work, dealing with the hermeneutical aspects of the Job Targum, is a University of Groningen thesis prepared under the supervision of Dr. A. S. van der Woude. This is the first major discussion of the Job Targum and the author had access to all the material for the *editio princeps* which only appeared in 1971.

Dr. Tuinstra analyses in detail the text of the targum of Job found at Qumran. He compares the Qumran text with the Hebrew text, concluding that the minor deviations from the MT are the result of translation rather than of a different vorlage. The targumist approached the MT with a different point of view hence some modification: (1) greater emphasis on the sovereignty of God and the force of the creative word; (2) more stress on the judgement of the godless; (3) delineation of the character of Job not only as a righteous sufferer but also as one upon whom knowledge is bestowed and who acts as a special agent of God. Tuinstra argues that the Teacher of Righteousness may have acted as a model for the figure of Job in the targum. Other questions such as the relation of this targum to the LXX (both independent translations of the Hebrew), the Essene Community (possibly the targum stems from there), and whether this could be the targum ordered to be concealed by Gamaliel the elder (quite possibly it was), are competently discussed.   E.G.C.

APOCRYPHA AND POST-BIBLICAL STUDIES

CORRÉ, A. D.: *The Daughter of my People. Arabic and Hebrew Paraphrases of Jeremiah 8.13–9.23.* 1971. Pp. ix, 119. (E. J. Brill, Leiden. Price: Fl. 32)

The basic content is explained by the title. The texts are mediaeval midrashic expansions, somewhat in the mood of the Book of Lamentations. The main part is taken up by the Judaeo-Arabic texts, four versions being set in parallel columns, with notes and translations following; a comparable Hebrew version is added at the end. The introduction is rather scrappy. For O.T. studies, marginal; more significant for Judaeo-Arabic.   J.B.

DANCY, J. C. (ed.): *The Shorter Books of the Apocrypha* (The Cambridge Bible Commentary on the N.E.B.). 1972. Pp. 253. (Cambridge University Press. Price: £3.60 (cloth), £1.50 (paper))

This commentary follows the general lines established in this series (see pp. 24, 27 and *B.L.* 1972, p. 23). The editor writes on Tobit, Judith, Baruch and the Letter of Jeremiah, and the Prayer of Manasseh, while the additions to Esther are commented on by W. J. Fuerst, and those to Daniel by R. J. Hammer. It is many years since a commentary has appeared in English on any of these books, and this work will fulfil a useful purpose.   R.J.C.

FINKELSTEIN, L.: *Pharisaism in the Making*. 1972. Pp. xx, 459. (Ktav Publishing House, New York. Price: $19.95)

This volume includes twelve papers originally published in five different journals between 1925 and 1969. In fact, except for two more general studies dated to 1958 and 1969, all the learned papers are more than thirty years old. Having been photo-mechanically reproduced, they are un-revised and reflect five distinct typographies. They are preceded by a new Introduction whose recurring theme is that the common claim of the articles, viz. the pre-Maccabaean and partly pre-exilic origin of a substantial part of rabbinic literature, is more than ever valid today. Professor Finkelstein has argued this thesis explicitly in *New Light from the Prophets* (see *B.L.* 1972, p. 67) and now asserts that it is archaeologically confirmed by the Dead Sea Scrolls. The reviewer finds the less speculative papers on Jubilees and various liturgical topics of greater interest.

G.V.

FRANCE, R. T.: *Jesus and the Old Testament. His application of Old Testament passages to himself and his mission*. 1971. Pp. xii, 286. (Tyndale Press, London. Price: £2.75)

The author reviews, noting their relation to the MT and the LXX, the O.T. quotations and allusions attributed to Jesus in the synoptic gospels, and compares the emergent principles of interpretation (which include both the Messianic and the typological, the latter in relation to the Church and to Israel) with those of Qumran, the Pseudepigrapha, Rabbinic Judaism, and early Christianity, including the Fathers up to the fourth century. He concludes that a christological 'single coherent scheme' renders Jesus' use of the O.T. 'not only original' but 'revolutionary'. Isa. 53 is defended against recent criticism as the source of Jesus' self-understanding, and Dan. 7, for this author, contributed solely to the elements of authority and future glory in Jesus' conception of Messiahship. Many readers of this *Book List* will find the somewhat brief treatment of many passages less than convincing (the book is a partly popularized version of a doctoral thesis), and will be irritated by the blanket assumption of the historicity of Jesus' words as reported in the synoptic gospels. They will nevertheless find value in, especially, Dr France's analysis of the varying degrees of approximation in the gospel quotations and allusions to the MT and to the LXX and other versions, and his discussion of some of the passages dealt with from Zech. 9–14. The analysis of the alleged use of texts from the latter chapters in the Qumran material is particularly interesting.

C.J.A.H.

GOLDIN, J.: *The Song at the Sea, being a Commentary on a Commentary in Two Parts*. 1971. Pp. xxii, 290. (Yale University Press, New Haven and London. Price: $10, £4.50)

The commentary on which this book is a commentary is that part of the midrash Mekhilta which is called Shirta, the ancient rabbinic word for word explanation of the 'Song of Moses at the Sea', Ex. 15:1–21. The present work is divided into two parts: (1) a general discussion of both the biblical text and the text of the midrash and (2) a translation of the midrash with a running commentary. The translation is new, the two older ones being the one in German by J. Winter and A. Wünsche with additions by L. Blau, 1909, and the other in English by J. Z. Lauterbach accompanying his text edition, 1933–35 (both of them are translations of the whole Mekhilta). The theme itself, the redemption of Israel from Egyptian bondage, is many times recounted and referred to in the Bible. It has central significance for the Jewish religion (Siddur and Machzor) and is still today annually commemorated at Passover (Passover Haggadah). The book is well indexed (40 pages).   H.K.

HAMMERSHAIMB, E., MUNCK, J., NOACK, B., and SEIDELIN, P. (ed.): *De gammeltestamentlige Pseudepigrafer i oversaettelse med indledning og noter.* 6. haefte, 1972. Pp. 625–76. (Gad, Copenhagen; Cammermeyer, Oslo; Gleerup, Lund)

This appears to be only part of the planned last fascicle of the edition of the pseudepigrapha which has been appearing in Danish since 1953 (cf. *B.L.* 1971, p. 63 for references to previous fascicles). It contains introduction, translation and notes to 4 Maccabees (N. Hyldahl) and the Greek Apocalypse of Baruch (E. Hammershaimb). The introductions are short but adequate; notes include textual and general comments; and there are useful bibliographical lists.   P.R.A.

HOEHNER, H. W.: *Herod Antipas* (Society for New Testament Studies, Monograph Series 17). 1972. Pp. xvi, 440. (Cambridge University Press. Price: £7)

This is a careful, well-documented account of the life and reign of Herod Antipas. In the course of the discussion full and detailed notes are included, both in the text and in footnotes, on matters of critical importance, notably all references to Herod in the N.T. O.T. scholars will welcome the book as supplementing the story of the Herods, and as throwing some light on the Palestinian scene in the early years of the Christian era.   L.H.B.

JANSSEN, E.: *Das Gottesvolk und seine Geschichte. Geschichtsbild und Selbstverständnis im palästinensischen Schrifttum von Jesus Sirach bis Jehuda ha-Nasi.* 1971. Pp. 212. (Neukirchner Verlag, Neukirchen-Vluyn. Price: DM. 36)

The title of this study is somewhat ambiguous, but the subtitle describes its contents more adequately. The author surveys the understanding and interpretation of O.T. history during post-biblical times (200 B.C.–A.D. 200), that is, as it presents itself in the books of Ben Sira and 1 Macc., in the apocalyptic literature (Daniel, Eth. Enoch, Test. Levi, Apoc. of Abraham, 4 Ezra, Syr. Baruch), and in the Ass. Mosis, the Damascus Document and the early Rabbinic literature — always with a view to the self-understanding of Judaism among the various groups and prominent individuals. A bibliography is added to the book.   H.K.

DE JONGE, M. (ed.): *Testamenta XII Patriarchum edited according to Cambridge University Library MS Ff.1.24* (Pseudepigrapha veteris testamenti Graece, I). 2nd edition, 1970. Pp. xxii, 86. (E. J. Brill, Leiden. Price: Fl. 16)

The fact that there should so soon be a need for a second edition of this text of the *Testaments of the Twelve Patriarchs* is an indication of

the revival which has occurred in studies of the *Testaments*, a revival
stimulated in no small part by the work of the editor himself. De
Jonge is currently engaged in the production of a major new critical
edition of the Greek text of the *Testaments*, and his purpose in the
second edition of the present work (which he describes as an *editio
minima*) remains, as before, to provide a working tool for the use of
scholars to assist them in interpreting the confused mass of evidence
in Charles' edition of the text. The major change in the second edition
(the first, 1964, was not noticed in *B.L.*) is to be found in the introduction where de Jonge is able to provide fuller and more up-to-date
information about the Greek, Armenian and Slavonic versions.
In the text itself, which is a transcript of the manuscript which de
Jonge regards as the best single witness, Cambridge MS Ff. 1.24,
only minor corrections of mistakes have been made. (For the other
volumes in this series see *B.L.* 1969, p. 60; 1972, p. 66.)   M.A.K.

LEIPOLDT, J. and GRUNDMANN, W. (ed.): *Umwelt des Urchristentums.*
Vol. I, *Darstellung des neutestamentlichen Zeitalters.* 2nd edition, 1967.
Pp. 528. Vol. II, *Texte zum neutestamentlichen Zeitalter.* 1967. Pp. 426
and a separate map. Vol. III, *Bilder zum neutestamentlichen Zeitalter.*
1966. Pp. 274 (including 205 pages of plates). (Evangelische Verlagsanstalt, Berlin. Price: DM. 22, 23 and 25)

This three-volume work by a team of authors sets out to provide an
account of the world in which Christianity had its beginnings. In the
first volume H. Ristow writes on Roman history from the Gracchi to
Domitian, G. Haufe on Greek popular religion and on the Mystery
religions, G. Hansen on emperor worship and on Greek philosophy,
W. Grundmann on Palestinian Judaism, H. Hegermann on Hellenistic
Judaism and H.-M. Schenke on Gnosticism, while in a concluding
chapter Grundmann discusses early Christianity in the context of the
contemporary religious situation. The second volume provides a
valuable selection of texts, chosen by the same writers, and arranged
according to the chapter order of the first volume. In the final volume
J. Leipoldt presents a series of pictures (with a commentary) which
illustrate vividly the religious world of the Hellenistic and Roman
periods, and form a fitting complement to the material contained in
the earlier volumes. Though intended as a handbook, this useful
work presents a mass of information at a serious level, and it would
be good if something on the same scale were available in English.

                                                                M.A.K.

MCNAMARA, M.: *Targum and Testament. Aramaic Paraphrases of the
Hebrew Bible: A Light on the New Testament.* 1972. Pp. 227. (Irish
University Press, Shannon. Price: £3)

Part One of this valuable introduction lucidly compresses a good
deal of information not easily accessible to students about the
literature and worship of the Judaism of the early Christian centuries,
and in particular about the language, character and date of the
targums. Part Two, in some measure presenting the exegetical
findings of the author's *The New Testament and the Palestinian Targum
to the Pentateuch* (1966. See *B.L.* 1968, p. 18) but adding new material
as well as supplementing ground already covered, describes the
theology of the targumists as it relates to the N.T. An appendix
offers an introduction to all the extant targums, with a succinct

gazetteer to Neofiti. Judgements are cautious, though the writer's early dating of Targum Neofiti is briefly defended against the criticisms of Fitzmyer. The tenuous nature of our knowledge of the first-century synagogue lectionary is stressed. This work is indispensable for students of the Judaism of this period, of the N.T. in its relation to its Palestinian background, and of the history of the interpretation of the O.T. Its attractive presentation, both in style and format, is to be commended. One page each of Neofiti and Pseudo-Jonathan is reproduced, and there are indices.   C.J.A.H.

Le Moyne, J.: *Les Sadducéens* (Études Bibliques). 1972. Pp. 464. (Paris, Librairie Lecoffre, J. Gabalda et Cie)

The first part of the book is a thoroughgoing study of all the literary traditions relevant to the Sadducees — the New Testament, Josephus, Rabbinic literature — but in the end the conclusion is reached that it is all nebulous and uncertain and that even the name cannot be satisfactorily explained. The second part attempts, on the basis of the very slender evidence, to build up a picture of the Sadducees as a religious group, part priestly, part lay, of which the Boethusians formed an inner, or separate group, and which primarily held fast to the written law, but of necessity did develop some traditional law as occasion demanded.   L.H.B.

Neusner, J.: *Rabbinic Traditions about the Pharisees before 70*. 3 volumes. I. *The Masters*. II. *The Houses*. III. *Conclusions*. 1971. Pp. xvi, 419; xiv, 353; xvi, 427. (E. J. Brill, Leiden. Price: Fl. 88 each)

The literary prolificity of Neusner is due to the quickness of his mind filled with novel ideas, to his almost compulsive working habits, and to his readiness to release his discoveries at once, without applying successive layers of polish. The three volumes under review are epoch-making. Not only is it the first time that modern form-critical and redaction-critical methods have been applied to large segments of rabbinic literature (the sayings of the early Pharisees from Simeon the Just to Simeon ben Gamaliel I and those ascribed to the Schools of Hillel and Shammai), but the last volume offers, in addition, a systematic presentation of rabbinic types or *Gattungen*, and of the most essential redactional patterns. Moreover, ch. xx entitled 'Verifications', attempts to devise a means to determine the historical *terminus ante quem* of the various traditions by discovering their earliest attestations. Some of Neusner's theses may be improved, but none of them must be ignored; neither can future Talmudic studies rate as academically respectable without confronting the findings of *Pharisees*.

Old and New Testament scholars are strongly advised to read the Bibliographical Reflections (vol. III, pp. 320–68). Most modern Jewish works come under the heading of 'Pseudo-critical studies', and the bulk of the essays on the Pharisees written by Christian authors qualify only as 'Theology in historical guise'. Very few escape unscathed, but among them are I. Lévi, E. Schürer and G. F. Moore.

G.V.

POTIN, J.: *La fête juive de la Pentecôte. Etude de textes liturgiques. Commentaire + Textes* (Lectio Divina, 65). 2 vols. 1971. Pp. 328, 79. (Éditions du Cerf, Paris. Price: Fr. 73)

The author sets out, in the footsteps of R. Le Déaut and his pioneering work, *La nuit pascale* (1963), to chart the Feast of Weeks in Jewish literature. The basis of the enquiry is the Palestinian Targumic version of Ex. 19–20. (The text of these two chapters, according to all the available manuscripts, constitutes vol. II.) Potin starts with an outline of contemporary views on the Targums followed by a full commentary on the Aramaic paraphrase of Ex. 19 and 20. In Part II, other O.T. texts (Dt. 16, Num. 28, Lev. 23, Ex. 24, Hab. 3, Ez. 1, Pss. 29, 68, 77, 18) connected with the same festival are analysed in their Targumic form. Finally, in Part III, the theological contents of the texts, and consequently the religious significance of Shavu'oth, are distinguished, and the N.T. account of Pentecost considered against them. Apart from a far too credulous attitude towards the over-all antiquity of the Targums, and an occasional uncritical acceptance of certain dogmas of academic orthodoxy (e.g. *Memra* as a 'habitual substitute' for YHWH), this book constitutes an interesting new approach to the study of the early post-biblical phase of one of the major liturgical feasts of Judaism.

G.V.

SANDMEL, S.: *Philo's Place in Judaism: A Study of Conceptions of Abraham in Jewish Literature* (Augmented Edition). 1972. Pp. xx, 232. (Ktav Publishing House, New York. Price: $14.95)

This volume contains the fourth version of Professor Sandmel's doctoral thesis completed originally under the supervision of the late E. R. Goodenough. It first appeared in two separate instalments in *HUCA* 1954 and 1955, and was published in book form under the present title in 1956. The Ktav reprint includes an additional bibliographical note on Philonic research since 1956; a discussion, resulting in a negative judgement, of Philo's relation to Gnosticism; and a new subject index (compiled by D. P. Burrows). Thus the 'Augmented Edition', as sceptical as its predecessor concerning any substantial Palestinian influence on Philo, offers to scholars an improved, lively and controversial instrument of research.

G.V.

SANDMEL, S.: *The Several Israels and an Essay: Religion and Modern Man*. 1971. Pp. xii, 160. (Ktav Publishing House, New York. Price: $6.95)

The author whose name is well-known among Christian theologians who concern themselves with the relationship between Judaism and Christianity has written a number of books on that subject from his personal Jewish point of view. The present volume contains four lectures delivered at Duke University on the name of Israel as applied to three different groups in history. (1) 'The Hebrew Israel', the name of the elect people of the O.T. At the end of this chapter he draws our attention to the conflict between the two principles of particularism and universalism and their practical bearing on the 'living situations for men'. He does not answer the 'burning questions' which arise here, but insists that 'we must keep them constantly before us'. (2) 'The Christian Israel' as the new spiritual Israel in contradistinction to the Israel of the flesh. He ends his description with a consideration of the conflict between the 'authentic super-naturalism' of the Church and the 'authentic naturalism' of modern man who in his dedication to freedom is 'persuaded by values', not by 'authorized persons'. (3) 'The State of Israel': He describes briefly the facts and forces which led to the establishment of the new State. The author is a loyal American and as such a non-Zionist but is nevertheless 'also passionately concerned for the State of Israel'. As a universalist he is bound to take a critical view of the present situations within the State but he prefers not to be very explicit. (4) The last lecture introduces the quest for 'The True Israel' in our disunited modern world of nationalisms. The author finds the answer in the light of Isa. 49:6, 61:1, 2a, 58:6–10. An essay 'Religion and Modern Man' concludes the book.   H.K.

SCHÄFER, P.: *Die Vorstellung vom Heiligen Geist in der rabbinischen Literatur* (Studien zum Alten und Neuen Testament, XXVIII). 1972. Pp. 186. (Kösel-Verlag, München. Price: DM. 55)

The author presents in this Freiburg i.B. D.Phil. thesis an extremely valuable survey of the whole rabbinic evidence relative to the 'spirit of holiness'. Successive chapters are devoted to prophecy, revelation, the cessation, the intermediary activity and the eschatological return of *ruaḥ ha-qodesh*. Each individual passage is subjected to a brief literary, historical and doctrinal analysis so that, in addition to its contribution to an important subject of Jewish religious thought, the volume provided with a good index is also a useful work of reference. British readers may note the custom on the Continent of enabling promising young scholars in Hebraica and Judaica to study at the Hebrew University, and also the interesting fact that the publication of a thesis on rabbinic theology has been financed by the Volkswagen Foundation.   G.V.

The Study of Judaism. Bibliographical Essays (introduced by J. Neusner). 1972. Pp. 229. (Ktav Publishing House, New York. Price: $12.50)

It should be noted that the title of this book is *The Study of Judaism* and that it does not deal with historical aspects of the Jewish people, except in its last two chapters (VII and VIII), the one on (mainly) the American scene and the other on modern Anti-Semitism and the Holocaust. It is written by various American authors under special headings: Judaism in N.T. times, Rabbinic sources, Judaism on Christianity as well as Christianity on Judaism, and modern Jewish thought. These short essays are intended to be an introduction to the bibliographies which list many hundreds of works by Jewish and Christian authors. It is a recommendable vade-mecum for any student of Judaism, Jewish or Christian, for both beginners and advanced students.   H.K.

SUARÈS, C.: *The Song of Songs. The Canonical Song of Solomon Deciphered according to the Original Code of the Qabbala*. 1972. Pp. 161. (Shambala, Berkeley — Routledge & Kegan Paul, London. Price: £2.80)

The fact that the Song of Songs was declared canonical and holy led many commentators, Jewish and Christian, from that date down to our days to interpret it allegorically in every detail. The author of the present publication, however, maintains that all interpretations so far, whether literal or allegorical, are quite beside the mark, and the title should read 'The Residue of Residues, or Quintessence of Quintessences'. He offers his own secret interpretation on the basis of his 'original code of the Qabbala' (the 'Autiot') and reveals the only true meaning of the Song. Unfortunately being 'obliged to use our language in order to make himself understood, he cannot offer the reader the truth of Genesis, but only images of that truth'. A most peculiar book.

H.K.

WEINREB, F.: *Die jüdischen Wurzeln des Matthäus-Evangeliums.* 1972. Pp. 216. (Origo Verlag, Zürich. Price: S.Fr. 16.80)

This is the first volume, reaching Mt. 4:16, of tape-recorded informal talks loosely related to the text of Mt., in which the Jewish author applies exegetical techniques from the Kabbalah — mainly gematria — to arrive at devotional reflections which are partly existentialist and partly neo-platonic in flavour.

C.J.A.H.

PHILOLOGY AND GRAMMAR

BANGE, L. A.: *A Study of the Use of Vowel-Letters in Alphabetic Consonantal Writing.* 1971. Pp. 4*, x, 141, iv. (Verlag UNI-Druck, Munich)

This book is the unrevised text of an Oxford D.Phil. thesis written under the supervision of Sir Godfrey Driver in 1961–62. Although ten years old, it has considerable value as it provides the only comprehensive counter to the views propounded in Cross and Freedman, *Early Hebrew Orthography* (1952). In summary, it is argued that all letters were full consonants before 1000 B.C., then followed a period when *he, waw,* and *yod* were used after accented vowels to indicate the final element of a diphthong (termed 'off-glides'), and *aleph* as a 'glottal stop after short accented vowels in final open syllables'. This function had weakened by about 600 B.C. when these letters began to be used in closed or unaccented open syllables as simple vowel-letters (as clearly in the Lachish Ostraca). The evidence produced from all early Phoenician, Aramaic, and Hebrew inscriptions appears to support the thesis, and, if sustained, aids interpretation of the Gezer Calendar, Siloam Inscription, and other texts. A similar development in South Arabian is noteworthy.

A.R.M.

FONTINOY, CH.: *Le duel dans les langues sémitiques* (Bibliothèque de la Faculté de Philosophie et Lettres de l'Université de Liège, Fascicule clxxix). 1969. Pp. xviii, 255. (Société d'Édition 'Les Belles Lettres', Paris. Price: Fr. 30)

A thorough investigation of the dual in the Semitic languages. After an introduction, which goes into general notions such as the psychology of number, there are two main parts. The first assembles the facts about the forms and the use of the dual in the main branches of the language family, including Egyptian and Coptic. The second reviews in a historical fashion the theories which have been constructed to account for these facts. An appendix considers the comparison with Indo-European, and conclusions are briefly drawn. A further future treatment of the Hebrew dual is promised (p. xi).

J.B.

ISSERLIN, B. S. J.: *A Hebrew Work-book for Beginners*. First Edition 1971. Pp. vi, 148. (Printed in the Photography Department, University of Leeds. Price: £1.25)

In this refreshing accessory to the existing grammars, with which it is intended to be used, emphasis is on speaking the language (Hebrew script is not introduced until Lesson 3) and on acquiring a 'feeling for style'. Although vocabulary is biblical and many biblical 'tags' are quoted (with an infectious bias towards *Qohelet* and *Šir ha-širim*), examples and exercises are slanted towards spoken Modern Hebrew. This marriage between ancient and modern certainly helps to make biblical Hebrew live, but inevitably runs into difficulties on occasion (e.g. in a discussion of 'The Present Participle Active'). The arrangement of vocabulary into 'semantic fields' (i.e. scenery, society, food and drink, etc.) is immediately appealing, and the whole book bears the stamp of Dr. Isserlin's charm and originality (e.g. 'disgruntled' is his example of a derived stem for which there is no corresponding Qal). It is perhaps a pity that more innovations were not thought necessary to bring Hebrew language-teaching up to date with some of the presuppositions alluded to in the Preface. J.F.A.S.

ADDITIONAL NOTES ON SCHOOL TEXTBOOKS, ETC.

CAMPBELL, D. B. J.: *The Old Testament for Modern Readers*. 1972. Pp. viii, 136. (John Murray, London. Price: Library Edition £1.50; School Edition 70p)

This work is intended as an introduction for those who are beginning the study of the O.T. at the level of University qualifying examinations and the like. Though it is pleasantly written, and makes some useful points, it seems unlikely to achieve this aim satisfactorily. There are a number of errors and misleading inferences; it is difficult to see what principle has guided the arrangement of the material; and the lack of an index of references, and of any suggestions for further reading, seriously limits the book's usefulness. R.J.C.

*DICKSON, K.: *An Introduction to the History and Religion of Israel from Abraham to the Early Days of Israel in the Promised Land*. 1970. Pp. 160 (including 4 maps). (Darton, Longman and Todd, London. Price: 70p.)

*DICKSON, K.: *An Introduction to the History and Religion of Israel: From Hezekiah to the Return from Exile*. 1969. Pp. 144 (including 3 maps). (Darton, Longman and Todd, London. Price: 70p.)

These two textbooks present a simple but not simplified exposition of the O.T. texts (in the R.S.V.) prescribed for the O-level examination in Bible Knowledge of the West African Examinations Council, and should serve their purpose admirably. L.A.P.

*GAUBERT, H.: *The Bible in History. Volume 6. The Destruction of the Kingdom*. 1970. Pp. 212. (Darton, Longman and Todd, Ltd., London. Price: £1.40)

This volume is a lucidly written, well illustrated and generally reliable account of the period from the division of the kingdom until the end of the exile. L.A.P.

PATSON, A. G.: *A Visual Old Testament*. Book Two: *From Abraham to the Division of the Kingdom*. 1972. Pp. 47. (The Religious Education Press, Oxford. Price: 35p)

> The approach of this flexi-covered pictorial history is, like the style of the text, distinctly old-fashioned, and ignores recent educational developments.
>
> L.A.P.

*THOMAS, J.: *Crown and Testimony*, 1972. Pp. 122.

*HOOD, G.: *Festivals*, 1972. Pp. 148.
(Man and Religion Series Part 4: The Old Testament Scene). (R.E.P./ Pergamon Press, Oxford. Price: 60p each)

> With all too few new books encouraging the use of the O.T. in schools, these two volumes are particularly welcome. *Crown and Testimony* takes the theme of kingship and examines it with relation first to Ancient Israel and her neighbours, then to questions concerning monarchy and authority in the contemporary world. At times the links with today seem rather strained; perhaps there is over-anxiety to show the relevance of a subject which can be fascinating for its own sake and within its ancient setting. This book will probably be of most use as resource material upon which teachers may draw for ideas which can be adapted to their own situations.
> *Festivals* looks at the great festivals of the O.T. and the ancient Near East, examines some of their underlying assumptions, and sees how far these can be applied to festivals today. Perhaps this topic relates more easily to children's interests; certainly the author suggests a wide and attractive range of activities, making use of a variety of skills including dance and drama. There is also a useful bibliography. Both books are attractively produced and well written, with careful research underlying the necessarily simplified presentation of controversial material.
>
> E.B.M.

Index of Authors